REMEDIES IN INTERNATIONAL
HUMAN RIGHTS LAW

REMEDIES IN INTERNATIONAL HUMAN RIGHTS LAW

DINAH SHELTON
Notre Dame Law School

OXFORD
UNIVERSITY PRESS

OXFORD
UNIVERSITY PRESS

Great Clarendon Street, Oxford OX2 6DP

Oxford University Press is a department of the University of Oxford.
It furthers the University's objective of excellence in research, scholarship,
and education by publishing worldwide in

Oxford New York

Athens Auckland Bangkok Bogotá Buenos Aires Calcutta
Cape Town Chennai Dar es Salaam Delhi Florence Hong Kong Istanbul
Karachi Kuala Lumpur Madrid Melbourne Mexico City Mumbai
Nairobi Paris São Paulo Singapore Taipei Tokyo Toronto Warsaw

with associated companies in Berlin Ibadan

Published in the United States
by Oxford University Press Inc., New York

First published 1999
First published in paperback 2000

British Library Cataloguing in Publication Data

Data available

Library of Congress Cataloging in Publication Data

Shelton, Dinah.
Remedies in international human rights law / Dina Shelton.
p. cm.
Includes bibliographical references and index.
1. Human rights. 2. Remedies (Law) I. Title.
K3240.S53 1999
341.4′81—dc21 99–16150
ISBN 0-19-829859-5
ISBN 0-19-924302-6 (Pbk)

3 5 7 9 10 8 6 4 2

Typeset in Times by
Cambrian Typesetters, Frimley, Surrey

Printed in Great Britain
on acid-free paper by
Bookcraft Ltd., Midsomer Norton, Somerset

For Chris, Philip, and Elizabeth

Contents

PART II: THE INSTITUTIONAL FRAMEWORK

PART III: JURISPRUDENCE AND PRACTICE

Acknowledgements

This book emerged from discussions about human rights complaint procedures in courses and seminars over a number of years. Students often asked what redress applicants can expect to receive as a result of the international process. The question became a research project that turned into a law review article that evolved into the book. During the research and writing, many persons have assisted by providing materials, discussing issues and criticizing drafts. Without them the book could not have been completed. Barbara Fontana did the first seminar paper and law review comment on damages in the European Human Rights system in 1991. John Blakeley, Joseph Broussard, Willem Gravett and Paul Simo also provided valuable student assistance, while Tina Jankowski and Marilyn Imus spent many hours at word processors helping finalize the manuscript.

I am particularly grateful to those in the various international organizations who answered endless questions and were patient and unstinting with their time. At the Council of Europe, my thanks go to Hans Christian Kruger, Herbert Petzold, Michael O'Boyle, Caroline Ravaud, and the judges of the European Court who discussed the procedures and approaches to remedies in the European system. In the Inter-American system, Jorge Taiana, Robert Goldman, Domingo Azcevedo, David Padilla, Elizabeth Abi-Mershed, Pablo Savaadra, and Christina Cerna were extremely helpful. Manuel E. Ventura-Robles was always responsive to requests for documents from the Inter-American Court. Emmanuel Dankwa, Isaac Nguema, Germain Baricako and Julia Harrington at the African Commission assisted with information on developments in the African system. Viviana Krsticevic, John Finnis, Michael Anderson, Jay Tidmarsh, Garth Meintjes, and Burns Weston reviewed drafts, discussed theories and cases, and provided support. Finally, a special debt is owed to the late Richard Lillich who insisted that I write this book and to Alexandre Kiss who insisted that I finish it.

Table of Treaties and Other International Documents

Table of National Laws

Table of Cases

United Nations Human Rights Committee:

Introduction

The protection of human rights is generally recognized to be a fundamental aim of modern international law. In recent decades, almost every international organization, regional and global, has adopted human rights norms and responded to human rights violations by member states. Consideration of human rights issues has reached into all organs and bodies of the United Nations, including the Security Council, which has identified serious human rights violations as threats to the peace. With the opening of avenues of redress for individuals against oppressive action by government agents, international human rights law has reduced the content of the reserved domain of state sovereignty, with the consequence that at present no state can credibly claim that its treatment of those within its territory is a matter solely of domestic jurisdiction.

For all its revolutionary advances, however, human rights law has yet to develop a coherent theory or consistent practice of remedies for victims of human rights violations. While compensatory damages for both pecuniary and non-pecuniary injury are frequently afforded—they are, indeed, the rule in the Inter-American system—it is rare for non-monetary orders to be issued. Furthermore, human rights tribunals have been split on the awarding of attorneys fees and costs; the European Court of Human Rights almost routinely awards them, in whole or in part, to prevailing applicants while the Inter-American Court only recently has allowed victims to recover the costs of litigating their cases before the Court and the Inter-American Commission. The innovative nature of human rights litigation may account for the incoherence or inconsistency. Another factor may be the lack of national judicial experience of most members of international tribunals. In the case of the African Commission, its relative newness and limited experience also provides an explanation.

The most likely reasons, however, would appear to be the sudden development and unprecedented nature of international human rights law. Having emerged hesitatingly following the Second World War and then expanded rapidly in recent years, it displays an uneven proliferation of international complaints mechanisms and techniques that has created a mixture of remedies drawn from the traditional law of state responsibility for injury to aliens, from domestic legal systems, and from the different views of judges about the role of tribunals in affording relief to victims of state abuse. Remedies range from declaratory judgments to awards of widely differing amounts of compensatory damages to orders for specific state action. It is rare to find a reasoned decision articulating the principles on which a remedy is afforded. One former judge of the European Court of Human Rights privately states: 'We have no principles'. Another judge responds, 'We have principles, we just do not apply them'.

Analogous bodies of international and domestic law exist only approximately.

International law is weak or lacking in two of the most common procedures existing in domestic legal systems to remedy and deter wrongdoing: criminal sanctions[1] and civil remedies against the individual perpetrator. The international
community agreed to create a Permanent International Criminal Tribunal in 1998,
but the jurisdiction of the Tribunal is limited to a small list of international
crimes.[2] Only states have standing to bring cases to the International Court of
Justice. The international law of state responsibility is an inadequate model
because it derives from inter-state cases between juridically equal parties, where
diplomatic concerns and broader issues of cooperation or conflict affect the
results. International human rights law is the first area of international law where
individuals may bring actions against states in international tribunals,[3] but the
imbalance in respective power and juridical status between states and individuals
affects the procedures and the perceived role of the human rights institutions in
affording remedies. Further, unlike inter-state cases, most individual
complainants remain within the jurisdiction and subject to the power of the state
concerned, long after the proceedings are terminated.

Human rights cases differ from private actions in tort as well. Although international wrongs are committed by individuals and not by abstract entities (as was
pointed out at Nuremberg)[4] it is the state itself, not the person or persons who
inflicted the harm, that generally is held responsible. No international procedure
exists today for bringing an international civil action against an individual human
rights violator.[5] Rather than leave the victim without a remedy, the state is held

---

[1] Two ad hoc criminal tribunals exist. The United Nations created the International Criminal
Tribunal for the former Yugoslavia (ICTY) by Security Council Resolution 808 (1993) and adopted
the statute of the tribunal in S.C. Res. 827, U.N. SCOR, 48th Sess., 3217th mtg., U.N. Doc.
S/RES/827 (1993). It established the International Criminal Tribunal for Rwanda (ICTR) 16 months
later. The jurisdiction of both tribunals is limited. The ICTY was created 'for the prosecution of
persons responsible for serious violations of international humanitarian law committed in the territory
of the former Yugoslavia since 1991': Res. 808 (1993). The ICTR has concurrent jurisdiction with
national courts over crimes of genocide, war crimes and crimes against humanity. For the statute of
the ICTR, see S.C. Res. 955, U.N. SCOR, 3453d mtg., Annex, art. 6, U.N. Doc. S/RES 955 (1994).

[2] See the Rome Statute of the International Criminal Court, A/CONF.183/9, adopted 17 July
1998 by a vote of 120 in favour, 7 against and 20 abstaining.

[3] Other developments in international law are increasing the standing of non-state actors. For
example, the Convention on the Settlement of Investment Disputes between States and Nationals of
Other States, 17 U.S.T. 1270, T.I.A.S. No. 6090, 575 U.N.T.S. 159, the Seabed Dispute Chamber of
the Law of the Sea Tribunal (UNCLOS Art. 186–87), U.N. Doc. A/CONF.62/122, reprinted in (1982)
21 I.L.M. 1261, the North American Agreement on Environmental Cooperation, (1993) 32 I.L.M.
1480, and the Rotterdam Convention on Prior Informed Consent in regard to trade in hazardous chem-
icals, permit non-state actors to bring complaints against states in certain circumstances.

[4] 1 Trial of the Major War Criminals before the International Military Tribunal, Nuremberg
1946, 41 *Am.J. Int'l L.* 172, 223.

[5] The Rome Statute of the International Criminal Court, *supra* n. 2, foresees such a possibility
in Article 75, which mandates the Court to establish principles relating to reparations to or in respect
of victims of crimes within the jurisdiction of the Court. The Court may order reparations from the
person convicted or from an international Trust Fund for victims of crime, to be established pursuant
to Article 79.

responsible, a just and rational outcome in many instances even if individuals could be sued, given that many human rights violations result from the enactment of legislation or adoption of general policies by state organs. Where the violations derive from operation of the normal democratic process, it is appropriate to hold the state liable, despite the fact that any compensation awarded will come from the public treasury, the revenues of which may be derived at least in part from the victims of the violations.

The closest analogy to international human rights cases is found in domestic legal procedures against state officials who violate the constitutional or statutory rights of citizens. It is not a perfect analogy. In domestic legal systems, the individual victim bringing an action serves to assure the rule of law while obtaining redress for harm done. Further, in some jurisdictions, such actions can be brought only against named individuals or agencies within the government, not against the government or state as a whole.[6] In contrast, regional Commissions normally present and argue cases before the European[7] and Inter-American courts[8] and, in doing so, in the same proceedings where the individual victims seek redress, act as public advocates against allegedly delinquent states to uphold and further their regional treaty regime in the interest of the international community. The interests of the victims and the commissions do not always coincide.

In sum, precedents from international and domestic law can be used only with appropriate consideration given to the unique characteristics of international human rights cases. Many questions arise: Who is entitled to remedies? Should a distinction be made between individual cases and situations of gross violations of human rights? Should compensation be favoured as a remedy or are non-monetary remedies more important? What criteria should be applied to determine the amount of compensation and methods of payment? Does remedial justice demand the prosecution and punishment of those responsible for the violations? What part should the gravity of the offence play in the remedies afforded?

This book reviews the jurisprudence of international tribunals that have jurisdiction and competence to afford remedies to individuals whose human rights have been violated. It also looks at the comparative law of remedies, especially as reflected in national judicial decisions based on international human rights law. While the problems of systematic abuse and developing appropriate responses to it are discussed, with particular reference to the work of the United Nations, the focus is not on criminal prosecution and punishment. Nor does it consider responses to human rights violations that are intended to prevent further abuse rather than redress past injury, such as humanitarian intervention, sanctions and

---

[6] See Chapter 3 on Remedies in National Law.

[7] The European Commission on Human Rights merged with the Court upon entry into force of Protocol 11 to the European Convention on Human Rights. See *infra* Chapter 5.

[8] Administrative hearing bodies such as the National Labor Relations Board and the Equal Employment Opportunity Commission in the USA generally do not appear as parties in appeals by individuals from cases brought to the boards.

boycotts. The central concern is with the relationship between individual victims and the state causing injury, as well as with the powers and functions of the various international and national tribunals that have jurisdiction over human rights cases. The aim is to propose a theoretical foundation for human rights remedies, together with standards and principles on which future remedies may be based.

To place this theme in context, Chapter 1 discusses the development of human rights law and of the right to a remedy. Thereafter, Chapter 2 discusses theories of the nature and purpose of remedies and the unique nature of human rights cases. Chapter 3 presents an overview of remedies in national law and Chapter 4 considers the law of state responsibility for injury to aliens and the remedial decisions that provide the basis for much of the human rights jurisprudence. The remainder of the book is devoted to the remedial jurisdiction of international human rights tribunals, various types of remedies and the cases in which they have been awarded.

Human rights instruments refer to the obligation of states to provide effective remedies for human rights violations. In this book, the term 'remedies' and 'redress' are used interchangeably to refer to the range of measures that may be taken in response to an actual or threatened violation of human rights.[9] They thus embrace the substance of relief as well as the procedures through which relief may be obtained. Remedies may include an award of damages, declaratory relief, injunctions or orders, and attorneys fees and costs. The term 'reparations' is reserved for the law of state responsibility and, for clarity, will be used only in that context.

The variety of procedures that may be instituted to obtain redress for human rights violations gives rise to different terms for the person who files a claim: plaintiff, applicant, complainant, petitioner. To avoid confusion, the term 'victim' is used throughout to refer to one whose rights have been violated; the agent or agency perpetrating the violation is the 'wrongdoer'. The deprivation caused by human rights violations is referred to as the human rights 'harm' or 'injury', reserving 'damages' for the award of monetary compensation to redress the wrong.

---

[9]   There is considerable uncertainty even in the terminology used in this area. See S. Haasdijk, 'The Lack of Uniformity in the Terminology of the International Law of Remedies', (1992) 5 *Leiden J. Int'l L.* 245. Reparations can mean either the act or process of providing a remedy or the remedy itself. There is a tendency to use 'reparations' as the generic term for 'the various methods available to a State for discharging or releasing itself' from international responsibility: J. de Arechaga, 'International Responsibility' in M. Sørenson (ed.), *Manual of Public International Law* (1968), 564. See also I. Brownlie, *System of the Law of Nations, State Responsibility* (1983), Part I, 199. Similarly, remedies are 'the means by which a right is enforced or the violation of a right is prevented, redressed or compensated:' *Black's Law Dictionary*, 6th edn. (1990), 1294.

Part I

The Conceptual and Historical Framework

1

The Development of International Human Rights Law

A. THE EVOLUTION OF INTERNATIONAL HUMAN RIGHTS INSTITUTIONS

International concern for human rights is not entirely a new subject. The law of state responsibility has long held that when a citizen of one state is mistreated by an act or omission attributed to another state, the claim of the injured citizen who has exhausted local remedies in the mistreating state can be and often is espoused by the state of nationality, which itself is deemed to be injured under international law.[1] Such claims generally have been settled by negotiation or by submission of the matter to an international claims commission or arbitral tribunal. In contrast, a state's treatment of its own nationals escaped international scrutiny, with limited exceptions, until the latter half of this century.[2]

The atrocities perpetrated during the Second World War brought about a fundamental change in the law. Today, concern for the promotion and protection of human rights is woven throughout the United Nations Charter, beginning with the preamble which 'reaffirm[s] faith in fundamental human rights, in the dignity and worth of the human person, in the equal rights of men and women and of nations large and small'.[3] One of the basic purposes of the United Nations is to achieve international cooperation in promoting and encouraging respect for human rights and fundamental freedoms,[4] and to achieve these purposes, the Charter imposes obligations on the Organization and all member states. Article 55 calls on the United Nations to promote 'universal respect for, and observance of, human rights and fundamental freedoms for all without distinction as to race, sex, language, or religion'. In Article 56, 'all members pledge themselves to take joint and separate action in cooperation with the Organization for the achievement of the purposes set forth in Article 55'. The United Nations has determined that states that engage in a consistent pattern of violating internationally guaranteed human rights breach this Charter obligation.

The United Nations Charter does not define the term 'human rights', although it contains a clear prohibition of discrimination based on race, sex, language or religion. Indeed, the absence of a human rights catalogue in the Charter led to a

---

[1]   See Chapter 4 on Reparations in the Law of State Responsibility for Injury to Aliens.

[2]   For a discussion of the exceptions, see L. Sohn, 'The New International Law: Protection of the Rights of Individuals Rather than States', (1982) 32 *Am.U.L.Rev.* 1; L. Sohn and T. Buergenthal, *International Protection of Human Rights*, (1973), 1–337.

[3]   United Nations Charter, 26 June 1945, 59 Stat. 1031, T.S. 993, 3 Bevans 1153.

[4]   *Ibid.* Article 1(3).

continuing effort to define and codify human rights, beginning with the adoption, on 10 December 1948, of the Universal Declaration of Human Rights.[5] The Universal Declaration was followed, in 1965, by the United Nations Convention on the Elimination of All Forms of Racial Discrimination (CERD) [6] and, in 1966, by the International Covenant on Civil and Political Rights (CCPR)[7] and the International Covenant on Economic, Social and Cultural Rights (CESCR).[8] The codification effort in the United Nations and its specialized agencies, has resulted in a vast body of international human rights law.[9]

Many human rights instruments create international organs and procedures to monitor compliance by states with the norms prescribed. The CCPR, for example, establishes an 18-member Human Rights Committee consisting of independent experts nominated and elected by the states parties. The Committee supervises state compliance with the treaty by reviewing and commenting on periodic reports that must be filed by the states parties, by administering an optional inter-state complaint mechanism provided for in the CCPR, and by considering individual petitions submitted pursuant to the CCPR's First Optional Protocol.[10] The Protocol enables those claiming to be victims of a violation of the Covenant to file communications with the Human Rights Committee against a state party to the Covenant and the Protocol. The Convention against Torture and Other Cruel, Inhuman and Degrading Treatment (Convention against Torture) also provides for optional inter-state and individual complaints, patterned after the Civil and Political Covenant and Optional Protocol. The CERD provides for an optional individual complaint procedure, but a mandatory inter-state complaint process.

The CESCR, in contrast, contains progressive or programmatic obligations that are monitored via examination of periodic state reports.[11] There are no individual or inter-state complaint procedures, although efforts are underway to adopt an optional protocol containing a petition procedure. Even more restrained, the

---

[5] Universal Declaration of Human Rights, G.A. Res. 217A (III), UN Doc. A/810 (1948).

[6] Convention on the Elimination of All Forms of Racial Discrimination, 21 December, 1965, entered into force 4 January 1969, 660 U.N.T.S. 195.

[7] International Covenant on Civil and Political Rights, 16 December 1966, entered into force 23 March 1976, G.A. Res. 2200A (XXI), U.N. Doc. A/6316 (1966), 999 U.N.T.S. 171.

[8] International Covenant on Economic, Social and Cultural Rights, 16 December 1966, entered into force 3 January 1976, G.A. Res. 2200A (XXI) 993 U.N.T.S. 3.

[9] Other major United Nations human rights treaties include the Convention on the Prevention and Punishment of the Crime of Genocide, 9 December 1948, in force 12 January 1951, 78 U.N.T.S. 277; the Convention on the Elimination of All Forms of Discrimination against Women, 18 December 1979, in force 3 September 1981, G.A. Res. 34, 180, 34 U.N. GAOR, Supp. No. 46, U.N. Doc. A/34/46, at 193, 19 I.L.M. 33 (1980); the Convention against Torture and Other Cruel, Inhuman or Degrading Treatment, 10 December 1984, in force 26 June 1987, G.A. Res. 39/46, 39 U.N. GAOR, Supp. No. 51, U.N. Doc. A/39/51, at 197 (1984), 23 I.L.M. 1027 (1984); and the Convention on the Rights of the Child, 20 November 1989, in force 2 September 1990, G.A. Res. 44/25, Annex, 44 U.N. GAOR Supp. No. 49 at 167, U.N. Doc. A/44/49 (1989), (1989) 28 I.L.M. 1448.

[10] Optional Protocol to the International Covenant on Civil and Political Rights, 16 December 1966, in force 23 March 1976, 999 U.N.T.S. 171.

[11] The Convention on the Elimination of All Forms of Discrimination against Women and the Convention on the Rights of the Child contain comparable reporting mechanisms.

Genocide Convention creates no permanent institution to monitor compliance, but instead leaves the punishment of offenders to national courts and to the law of state responsibility.[12]

Virtually all United Nations organs and bodies deal with human rights matters, but the work of the Human Rights Commission is especially to be noted, including as it does special procedures to handle particularly serious violations. UN Economic and Social Council Resolutions 1235 (XLII) of 6 June 1967 and 1503 (XLVIII) of 27 May 1970, permit consideration by the Commission of information relevant to gross violations of human rights. According to Resolution 1235, the Commission may undertake a thorough study and report its findings to the Economic and Social Council where there is found to be a consistent pattern of such violations. Pursuant to this authority, the Commission has appointed working groups and special rapporteurs to report on large-scale violations in specific countries throughout the world. Resolution 1503 establishes a limited petition system for the Sub-Commission on Prevention of Discrimination and Protection of Minorities to consider non-state communications that 'appear to reveal a consistent pattern of gross and reliably attested violations of human rights and fundamental freedoms'. The Sub-Commission may forward the information to the Commission which may either undertake a thorough study according to the provisions of Resolution 1235, undertake an investigation by an ad hoc Committee with the consent of the state concerned, or take no action. The procedure is not designed to afford individualized remedies to the victims.

The United Nations Commission on Human Rights also has developed 'thematic' procedures to address specific human rights problems on a global basis. The first established thematic procedure was the Working Group on Enforced or Involuntary Disappearances, created in 1980 in response to the phenomenon of disappearances in Latin America.[13] The Working Group became a precedent for the creation in 1982 of the Special Rapporteur on Summary or Arbitrary Executions.[14] In 1985, the Commission appointed a Special Rapporteur

---

[12] The issue of state responsibility for the crime of genocide has come before the International Court of Justice in the *Case Concerning Application of the Convention on the Prevention and Punishment of the Crime of Genocide (Bosnia and Herzegovina v. Yugoslavia (Serbia and Montenegro))*, ICJ Reports 1993, pp. 3 and 325; 95 Int'l L. Rep. 1, 31. Bosnia alleges that Yugoslavia is responsible for breaches of the Genocide Convention. On 11 July 1996, the ICJ rejected the Preliminary Objections raised by Yugoslavia, emphasizing that the rights and obligations contained in the Genocide Convention are *erga omnes* and that each state is obligated to prevent and punish the crime of genocide regardless of the type of conflict or territorial limits. Article IX of the Convention does not exclude any form of state responsibility. ICJ Rep. 1996, paras. 31–32.

[13] 13 Reports of the Working Group are contained in: E/CN.4/1435 and Add. 1 (1981); E/CN.4/1492 and Add.1 (1982); E/CN.4/1984/21 and Add.1–2; E/CN.4/1985/15 and Add.1; E/CN.4/1986/18 and Add.1; E/CN.4/1987/15 and Add.1/ E/CN.4/1988/19 and Add.1; E/CN.4/1989/18 and Add.1; E/CN.4/1990/13; E/CN.4/1991/20 and Add.1; E/CN.4/1992/18; E/CN.4/1993/25; E/CN.4/1994/26; E/CN.4/1995/36; E/CN.4/1996/38; E/CN.4/1998/43.

[14] Now entitled the Special Rapporteur on Extrajudicial, Summary or Arbitrary Executions, reports of the Special Rapporteur are found in: E/CN.4/1983/16; E/CN.4/1984/29; E/CN.4/1985/17; E/CN.4/1986/21; E/CN.4/1987/20; E/CN.4/1988/22 and Add.1–2; E/CN.4/1989/25; E/CN.4/1990/22; E/CN.4/1991/36; E/CN.4/1993/46; E/CN.4/1994/7; E/CN.4/1996/60; E/CN.4/1997/60 and Add.1; E/CN.4/1998/68 and Add.1.

on Torture,[15] and in 1991 it created a Working Group on Arbitrary Detention.[16] Each Rapporteur or Working Group has its own mandate conferred by the Commission for a renewable term of three years. The approaches and working methods of the various individuals and groups have tended to expand and converge over time. Generally the working groups seek information from governments on cases, propose urgent action,[17] make country visits, and report to the Commission. In some instances, the thematic procedures can accept petitions and raise the issue of redress for victims of violations.

None of the permanent United Nations treaty or internal bodies has legal competence to order compensation or other remedies.[18] The Human Rights Committee, the Committee on the Elimination of Racial Discrimination, and other bodies that accept individual communications may make recommendations or express views to the state concerned. The recommendations sometimes call on the state to pay compensation or afford other remedies, but they do not specify amounts that may be due or other forms of redress.

Regional human rights bodies have the power to designate remedies that the state must afford to the victims of human rights violations.[19] The Statute of the Council of Europe, adopted by Western European nations in 1949, provides that every member must accept the principles of the rule of law and of the enjoyment by all persons within its jurisdiction of human rights and fundamental freedoms. Its system for the protection of human rights is based on the European Convention on Human Rights and Fundamental Freedoms and its protocols, plus the European Social Charter. Membership in the Council is *de facto* conditioned upon adherence to the European Convention.

The European Convention for the Protection of Human Rights and Fundamental Freedoms, signed 4 November 1950, entered into force on 3

---

[15] Reports of the Special Rapporteur are found in: E/CN.4/1986/15; E/CN.4/1987/13; E/CN.4/1988/17 and Add.1; E/CN.4/1989/10; E/CN.4/1990/17 and Add.1; E/CN.4/1991/17; E/CN.4/1993/26; E/CN.4/1994/31; E/CN.4/1995/34; E/CN.4/1996/35 and Add.1; E/CN.4/1998/38 and Add.1.

[16] Reports of the Working Group are found in: E/CN.4/1995/31 and Add.1–2; E/CN.4/1996/40 and Add.1; E/CN.4/1997/4; E/CN.4/1998/44 and Add.1.

[17] The urgent action procedure 'is basically humanitarian' and intended to prevent or halt violations rather than provide redress for prior victims. 'Hence the emphasis is laid on the element of "effectiveness" and on the adoption of preventive measures': *Torture and Other Cruel, Inhuman or Degrading Treatment or Punishment, Report of the Special Rapporteur, Mr. P. Kooijmans, pursuant to Commission on Human Rights Resolution 1992/32*, E/CN.4/1993/26 para. 15.

[18] The United Nations Compensation Commission was established to provide remedies to victims of the Iraqi invasion of Kuwait, but it is an ad hoc body and has jurisdiction over more than human rights violations. See U.N. Security Council Resolution 687 (1991) of 3 April 1991, U.N. Doc. S/RES/687 (1991), (1991) 30 I.L.M. 852 (1991) and Security Council Resolution 692 (1991) of 20 May 20 1991, (1991) 30 I.L.M. 864) (compensation is due for 'any direct loss, damage, including environmental damage and the depletion of natural resources, or injury to foreign Governments, nationals and corporations, as a result of Iraq's unlawful invasion and occupation of Kuwait': para. 16).

[19] On regional systems generally, see Dinah Shelton, 'The Promise of Regional Human Rights Systems' in B. Weston and S. Marks (eds.) *Fifty Years of Human Rights Law* (1999).

September 1953.[20] As originally adopted, it guaranteed a limited number of civil and political rights: right to life; freedom from torture, inhuman or degrading treatment and punishment; freedom from slavery; right to liberty, security of person, and due process of law; freedom from *ex post facto* laws and punishment; right to privacy and family life; freedom of thought, conscience and religion; freedom of expression and of peaceful assembly; and the right to marry and found a family. Non-discrimination in securing the enjoyment of these rights is required. Additional Protocols to the Convention have added rights to property, education, and free and secret elections (Protocol No. 1); freedom from imprisonment for breach of contractual obligations, from involuntary exile, from collective expulsion of aliens, and freedom of movement (Protocol No. 4); abolition of the death penalty (Protocol No. 6); rights of due process for aliens subject to deportation or expulsion, the right to appeal in criminal proceedings, freedom from double jeopardy, equality of rights between spouses, and the right to compensation in cases of miscarriage of justice (Protocol No. 7).

The European system was the first to create an international court for the protection of human rights and to create a procedure for individual denunciations of human rights violations. The European Court of Human Rights renders judgments in which it may afford 'just satisfaction' to the injured party, including compensation for both pecuniary and non-pecuniary damages.[21] The role of the victim initially was very limited and admissibility requirements were stringent. As the system has matured, however, the institutional structures have been considerably strengthened.

On 1 November 1998, a new full-time European Court of Human Rights was inaugurated. It has jurisdiction to decide all cases brought by victims against states parties to the Convention; the procedure is not optional for the states. The Convention originally created two institutions to ensure the observance of the obligations of states parties: the European Commission of Human Rights and the European Court of Human Rights.[22] In addition, a Committee of Ministers, the governing body of the Council, enforced decisions of the Court and decided cases not submitted to the Court, on the basis of the Commission's recommendation. The Committee of Ministers continues its enforcement role for the new Court, but the Commission has ceased to exist. The jurisprudence developed during the Commission's tenure, however, is likely to remain an important source of law for the new Court.

Until 1 November 1998, the Commission had jurisdiction to receive individual complaints if the state in question had declared that it accepted the right of

[20] European Convention for the Protection of Human Rights and Fundamental Freedoms, 4 November 1950, 213 U.N.T.S. 221 (hereinafter European Convention on Human Rights).

[21] *Ibid.* at Article 41.

[22] Protocol No. 11 merged the Commission and Court into the new European Court of Human Rights. Protocol No. 11 to the European Convention on Human Rights, E.T.S. No. 155, in force 1 November 1998, Article 19. The jurisdiction and powers of the Court are generally unchanged.

individual petition and conditions of admissibility were fulfilled.[23] Cases that were not settled were the subject of a report drawn up by the Commission. The report gave the facts and the Commission's opinion on whether the state had breached its obligations under the Convention. The report also could include any proposals the Commission wished to make. The report was not a judgment, because the Commission lacked the power to adjudicate a case. Damages or other remedies could be recommended, however, when a violation was found; either the Committee of Ministers or the European Court of Human Rights made the final decision. If the state concerned had accepted the jurisdiction of the Court, the Commission, the individual[24] or the state had three months to refer the case to the Court. Under the new procedures, individuals who claim to be victims have direct access to the Court which will decide the admissibility and merits of cases and award just satisfaction in appropriate instances.

The evolution of the European Community also has led its institutions, including the European Court of Justice, into the field of human rights. Individual claimants may plead for an award of damages or other remedies for violation of EC law, which, according to the European Court of Justice, includes respect for fundamental rights as an integral part of the general principles of law the Court is required to apply. For the nature of these rights, the Court looks to the European Convention on Human Rights.[25] The approach of the Court was confirmed in nearly identical language in Arts. F and K.2 of the 1992 Maastricht Treaty which transformed the European Community into the European Union.

Two other regional systems are modelled in part on the European Convention on Human Rights and on United Nations human rights law: the Inter-American and the African systems. In the Western hemisphere, the Organization of American States (OAS) adopted the American Declaration of the Rights and

---

[23] Admissibility requirements remain the same today. Petitions may be lodged only by those claiming to be victims of a violation of the rights set forth in the Convention. Other limits prohibit anonymous and duplicative petitions and petitions 'incompatible with the provisions of the . . . Convention, manifestly ill-founded, or an abuse of the right of petition': European Convention on Human Rights, *supra* n. 19, Article 26. Petitioners must demonstrate exhaustion of domestic remedies 'according to the generally recognized rules of international law' and petitions must be filed within six months from the date on which the final decision was taken. The domestic remedies requirement may be waived by the respondent state.

[24] Under Protocol 11, individuals, non-governmental organizations or groups of individuals who claim to be the victim of a violation of a right set forth in the Convention may lodge complaints at the court against any state party to the Convention. Prior to the entry into force of Protocol 11, individuals could only take a case to the Court if the state in question had ratified Protocol No. 9. Protocol No. 9, in force, 1 October 1994, E.T.S. 140, Article 3. Individual requests were reviewed by a three-judge panel to determine whether the case raised a serious question affecting the interpretation or application of the Convention or whether there was any other reason to warrant its consideration. The panel could unanimously reject the case and allow it to be decided by the Committee of Ministers.

[25] See e.g. *Hauer v. Land Rheinland-Pfalz* [1979] E.C.R. 3727, [1980] 3 C.M.L.R. 42, (1981) 3 E.H.R.R. 140. See generally, Nanette A. Neuwal and Allan Rosas (eds.), *The European Union and Human Rights* (1995); M.H. Mendelson, 'The European Court of Justice and Human Rights', (1982) 1981 *Y.B. Eur. Law* 125.

Duties of Man (American Declaration)[26] some months prior to adoption of the Universal Declaration of Human Rights in the United Nations General Assembly; and in 1969, it concluded the American Convention on Human Rights,[27] one of the longest human rights treaties. Two protocols have been adopted but were not in force as of 31 December 1998: the Additional Protocol on Economic, Social and Cultural Rights (1988) and the Protocol on Abolition of the Death Penalty (1990).

Two independent organs safeguard implementation of the American Convention: the Inter-American Commission on Human Rights and the Inter-American Court of Human Rights. In a reverse of the original European system, the OAS inter-state complaint mechanism is optional and the individual petition procedure is not. All states ratifying the Convention accept the right of 'any person or group of persons, or any non-governmental entity legally recognized in one or more member states of the Organization'[28] to present petitions to the Inter-American Commission. In addition, the Commission has jurisdiction over petitions filed by victims of human rights violations committed by OAS member states that have not ratified the Convention; the applicable human rights standards are those of the American Declaration.[29] Admissibility requirements for petitions are similar to those of the European Convention.

The Commission examines the petition and determines the facts. If a settlement is not reached, the Commission prepares a report and, if it finds a violation, makes recommendations to the state. The recommendations can specify remedies. Upon completion of procedures before the Commission, either the Commission or the state concerned can submit the case to the Court, if the state has accepted the Court's jurisdiction. The Court's judgment is binding, but there is no analogue to the European Committee of Ministers to oversee enforcement. The Court itself keeps the case open until full compliance with the judgment is achieved.

The African human rights system is the youngest regional system. The African Charter on Human and Peoples' Rights entered into force on 21 October, 1986[30] and it functions within the framework of the Organization of African Unity (OAU). The Charter emphasizes African traditions and values, guarantees peoples' rights as well as individual rights, particularly referring to the right to

[26] American Declaration of the Rights and Duties of Man, 2 May 1948, O.A.S. Res. XXX, adopted by the Ninth International Conference of American States (1948), reprinted in Basic Documents Pertaining to Human Rights in the Inter-American System, OEA/ser.L/V/II.92, doc.31 rev. 3 at 17 (1996) (hereinafter Basic Documents).

[27] American Convention on Human Rights, 22 November 1969, in force 18 July 1978, OEA/ser.L/V/II.23, doc. 21 rev. 6 (1979), O.A.S.T.S. No. 36 at 1, reprinted in Basic Documents, *supra* n. 26 at 25.

[28] American Convention on Human Rights, Article 44.

[29] The OAS created the Inter-American Commission in 1959, giving it a mandate to further respect for human rights among the OAS member states, hence its broad jurisdiction.

[30] African Charter on Human and Peoples' Rights, 27 June 1981, in force 21 October 1986, O.A.U. Doc. CAB/LEG/67/3 Rev. 5, (1982) 21 I.L.M. 58.

development, and proclaims economic, social and cultural rights as well as civil and political rights. The Charter allows the filing of inter-state and individual complaints. It also creates a mechanism similar to the United Nations procedure for responding to gross and systematic violations of human rights.

The Charter provides for an 11-member independent African Commission on Human and Peoples' Rights. The Charter confers four functions on the Commission: the promotion of human and peoples' rights in Africa; the protection of those rights; interpretation of the Charter; and the performance of other tasks that may be entrusted to it by the OAU Assembly of Heads of State and Government. A protocol adopted 8 June 1998, foresees an African Court of Human Rights.

Apart from tribunals established pursuant to human rights treaties, other international courts and decision-makers exercise jurisdiction over matters that may include human rights issues. As previously noted and as discussed in subsequent chapters, the European Court of Justice, global and regional administrative tribunals, and various ad hoc tribunals have contributed to the law of remedies for human rights violations.

B. THE RIGHT TO A REMEDY IN HUMAN RIGHTS INSTRUMENTS

There are close to one hundred human rights treaties adopted globally and regionally. Nearly all states are parties to some of them and several human rights norms have become part of customary international law. Yet, like all law, human rights law is violated. It has not ended governmental oppression and by itself cannot prevent or remedy all human rights abuses. Many violations are linked to long-standing political, economic, and social problems that require more than law alone can repair. Education and other broad social efforts are required to combat the causes of human rights abuse: prejudice, ignorance, disease, poverty, greed, corruption. Human rights law does have an impact, however, on the behaviour of persons inside and outside of government, having created an international climate less willing to tolerate abuses and more willing to support and use the institutions and organizations that have been designed to promote and protect human rights. The rising caseload of the European and Inter-American courts attests to the willingness and ability of victims to bring their own complaints against states that fail to comply with their international obligations. Appropriate remedies can have a dissuasive effect on those who would commit violations, as well as serving to redress the wrongs done to victims. Remedies are thus a significant aspect of ensuring the rule of law.

The right to a remedy when rights are violated is itself a right expressly guaranteed by global and regional human rights instruments. Most texts guarantee both the procedural right of effective access to a fair hearing and the substantive right to a remedy.[31] Some international agreements explicitly call for the development of judicial remedies for the rights they guarantee, although effective remedies could be supplied by non-judicial bodies.[32] The international guarantee of a remedy implies that a wrongdoing state has the primary duty to afford redress to the victim of a violation. The role of international tribunals is subsidiary and only becomes necessary and possible when the state has failed to afford the required relief. However, the role of the international tribunal is important to the integrity of the human rights system and victims of violations, particularly when the state deliberately and consistently denies remedies, creating a climate of impunity.

1. Global instruments

The Universal Declaration of Human Rights provides that '[e]veryone has the right to an effective remedy by the competent national tribunals for acts violating the fundamental rights granted him by the constitution or laws.[33] The International Covenant on Civil and Political Rights contains three separate articles on remedies. According to Article 2(3):

Each State Party to the . . . Covenant undertakes:

(a) To ensure that any person whose rights or freedoms as . . . recognized [in the Covenant] are violated shall have an effective remedy notwithstanding that the violation has been committed by persons acting in an official capacity;

(b) To ensure that any person claiming such a remedy shall have the right thereto determined by competent judicial, administrative or legislative authorities, or by any other competent authority provided for by the legal system of the State, and to develop the possibilities of judicial remedy;

(c) To ensure that the competent authorities shall enforce such remedies when granted.[34]

More specifically, Articles 9(5) and 14(6) provide that anyone unlawfully arrested, detained, or convicted shall have an enforceable right to compensation or be compensated according to law.[35] The Human Rights Committee has identified the kinds of remedies required, depending on the type of violation and the victim's condition. The Committee has indicated that a state that has engaged in human rights violations, in addition to treating and compensating the victim

---

[31] On access to justice, see Jeremy McBride, 'Access to Justice and Human Rights Treaties', (1998) 17 *Civil Justice Q.* 235.

[32] International Covenant on Civil and Political Rights, *supra* n. 7, Article 2(3)(b).

[33] Universal Declaration of Human Rights, *supra* n. 5, Article 8.

[34] International Covenant on Civil and Political Rights, *supra* n. 7, Article 2(3).

[35] *Ibid.*, Article 9(5): anyone who has been victim of unlawful arrest or detention shall have an enforceable right to compensation. Article 14(6): when a person has by a final decision been convicted of a criminal offence and when subsequently his conviction has been reversed or he has been pardoned on the ground that a new or newly discovered fact shows conclusively that there has been a miscarriage of justice, the person who has suffered punishment as a result of such conviction shall be compensated according to law.

financially, must undertake to investigate the facts, take appropriate action, and bring to justice those found responsible for the violations.

The Convention on the Elimination of Racial Discrimination, Article 6, also contains broad guarantees of an effective remedy:

States Parties shall assure to everyone within their jurisdiction effective protection and remedies, through the competent national tribunals and other State institutions, against any acts of racial discrimination which violate his human rights and fundamental freedoms contrary to this Convention, as well as the right to seek from such tribunals just and adequate reparation or satisfaction for any damage suffered as a result of such discrimination.[36]

Unlike some of the other provisions, this one anticipates the use of injunctive or other preventive measures against discrimination, as well as compensation or other remedies for consequential damages. A similar provision is found in the Convention on the Elimination of All Forms of Discrimination against Women, whereby the states parties undertake to establish 'legal protection of the rights of women on an equal basis with men' and to ensure through competent national tribunals and other public institutions 'the effective protection of women against any act of discrimination'.[37]

The United Nations Convention against Torture refers in Article 14 to redress and compensation for torture victims:

Each State Party shall ensure in its legal system that the victim of an act of torture obtains redress and has an enforceable right to fair and adequate compensation, including the means for as full rehabilitation as possible. In the event of the death of the victim as a result of an act of torture, his dependants shall be entitled to compensation.[38]

Several treaties refer to the right to legal protection for attacks on privacy, family, home or correspondence, or attacks on honour and reputation.[39] Among treaties adopted by the specialized agencies, the ILO Convention No. 169 Concerning Indigenous and Tribal Peoples in Independent Countries[40] refers to 'fair compensation for damages' (Art. 15(2)), 'compensation in money' (Art. 16(4)) and full compensation for 'any loss or injury' (Art. 16(5)).

Declarations, resolutions and other non-treaty texts also address the right to a remedy. In some instances, the issue is raised by human rights organs when issuing

---

[36] Convention on the Elimination of All Forms of Racial Discrimination, *supra* n. 6, Article 6.

[37] Convention on the Elimination of All Forms of Discrimination against Women, *supra* n. 9, Article 2(c).

[38] Convention against Torture and Other Cruel, Inhuman or Degrading Treatment, *supra* n. 9, Article 14.

[39] See Universal Declaration on Human Rights, *supra* n. 5, Article 12; International Covenant on Civil and Political Rights, *supra* n. 7, Article 17; Convention on the Rights of the Child, *supra* n. 9, Article 16; American Declaration of the Rights and Duties of Man, *supra* n. 26, Article v; American Convention on Human Rights, *supra* n. 27, Article 11(3); European Convention on Human Rights, *supra* n. 20, Article 8; African Charter on Human and Peoples Rights, *supra* n. 30, Article 5.

[40] Convention Concerning Indigenous and Tribal Peoples in Independent Countries, I.L.O. No. 169, 27 June 1989, in force 5 September 1991, (1989) 28 I.L.M. 1382.

'general comments'. The third General Comment of the Committee on Economic, Social and Cultural Rights, for example, concerning the nature of state obligations pursuant to Article 2(1) of the Covenant on Economic, Social and Cultural Rights, proclaims that appropriate measures to implement the Covenant might include judicial remedies with respect to rights that may be considered justiciable. It specifically points to the non-discrimination requirement of the treaty and cross-references to the right to a remedy in the Covenant on Civil and Political Rights. A number of other rights also are cited as 'capable of immediate application by judicial and other organs'.[41] In one of its general recommendations, the Committee on the Elimination of Discrimination against Women announced that states parties should make more use of temporary special remedial measures such as positive action, preferential treatment, or quota systems to advance women's integration into education, the economy, politics and employment.[42]

In 1998, the Working Group on Involuntary or Enforced Disappearances issued a General Comment to Article 19 of the 1992 Declaration on the Protection of All Persons from Enforced Disappearance.[43] Article 19 provides:

The victims of acts of enforced disappearance and their family shall obtain redress and shall have the right to adequate compensation, including the means for as complete a rehabilitation as possible. In the event of the death of the victim as a result of an act of enforced disappearance, their dependants shall also be entitled to compensation.

As noted by the Working Group, the Declaration imposes a primary duty to establish the fate and whereabouts of disappeared persons, itself an important remedy for victims, and Article 19 complements this duty. In cross-referencing the draft principles on the right to reparation for victims of violations of human rights, the Working Group stated that the right to redress referred to in Article 19 is broader than judicial remedies and depends for its exact content on the nature of the right violated. For disappearances the primary obligation is prosecution and punishment of perpetrators, which many victims and their families consider an important form of redress.

The Working Group elaborated on the Article 19 obligation to provide adequate compensation, announcing that it requires states to adopt legislative and other measures to enable victims and their families to claim compensation. Compensation is deemed 'adequate' if it is 'proportionate to the gravity of the human rights violation (e.g. the period of disappearance, the conditions of detention, etc.) and to the suffering of the victim and the family'.[44] Amounts shall be

---

[41] United Nations, *Compilation of General Comments and General Recommendations Adopted by Human Rights Treaty Bodies,* HRI/GEN/1/Rev.3, 63, para. 5.

[42] General Recommendation No. 5 (Seventh Session, 1988), A/43/38, reprinted in *ibid.* at 118. See also General Recommendation No. 23 (Sixteenth session, 1997), *ibid.* at 148.

[43] Report of the Working Group on Enforced or Involuntary Disappearances, E/CN.4/1998/43, 12 January 1998 at 16.

[44] *Ibid.* para. 73.

provided for any damage, including physical or mental harm, lost opportunities, material damages and loss of earnings, harm to reputation, and costs required for legal or expert assistance. In the event of the death of the victim, as a result of an act of enforced disappearance, the victims are entitled to additional compensation. Measures of rehabilitation should be provided, including medical and psychological care, rehabilitation for any form of physical or mental damage, legal and social rehabilitation, guarantees of non-repetition, restoration of personal liberty, family life, citizenship, employment or property, return to the place of residence, and similar forms of restitution, satisfaction and reparation that may remove the consequences of the enforced disappearance.[45]

Norms adopted in the area of crime prevention and criminal justice also mandate remedies. The United Nations Declaration of Basic Principles of Justice for Victims of Crime and Abuse of Power[46] contains broad guarantees for those who suffer pecuniary losses, physical or mental harm, and 'substantial impairment of their fundamental rights' through acts or omissions, including abuse of power. Victims are entitled to redress and to be informed of their right to seek redress. The Declaration specifically provides that victims of public officials or other agents who, acting in an official or quasi-official capacity, violate national criminal laws, should receive restitution from the state whose officials or agents are responsible for the harm inflicted. Abuse of power that is not criminal under national law but that violates internationally recognized norms relating to human rights should be sanctioned and remedies provided, including restitution and/or compensation, and all necessary material, medical, psychological, and social assistance and support.

The Declaration of Principles of Justice influenced the recent work of United Nations bodies considering the problem of remedies for gross and systematic violations of human rights, the 'mass torts' of human rights. In resolution 1988/11 of 1 September 1988, the Sub-Commission on Prevention of Discrimination and Protection of Minorities recognized that all victims of gross violations of human rights and fundamental freedoms should be entitled to restitution, fair and just compensation, and the means for as full a rehabilitation as possible for any

---

[45]   Report of the Working Group on Enforced or Involuntary Disappearances, para. 75.

[46]   U.N.G.A. Res. 40/34 of 29 November 1985. Paragraph 4 states that victims are entitled to access to the mechanisms of justice and prompt redress for the harm they have suffered. Procedures are to be expeditious, fair, inexpensive and accessible. Where appropriate, restitution should be made to victims, their families or dependants by offenders or third parties responsible for their behaviour: (para. 8). Victims of abuse of power are defined as those harmed by acts which do not yet constitute violations of national criminal laws. In 1990, the Eighth United Nations Congress on the Prevention of Crime and the Treatment of Offenders (Havana, Cuba, 27 August–7 September 1990), recommended that states base national legislation upon the Declaration and requested the United Nations Secretary-General to study the feasibility of establishing an international fund for victims of transnational crimes: Report of the Congress, A/CONF.144/28. The Council of Europe produced the European Convention on the Compensation of Victims of Violent Crimes (1983), a 1985 recommendation R(85) 11 on the position of the victim in the framework of criminal law and procedure, and a 1987 recommendation R(87)21 on assistance to victims and prevention of victimization.

damage suffered. The following year, the Sub-Commission appointed Theodoor van Boven to examine the possibility of developing basic principles and guidelines on remedies for gross violations.[47] The Sub-Commission discussions reflected a concern for ensuring that rights are coupled with effective remedies based on principles developed at the international level. In 1992, the Sub-Commission took up the related question of the impunity of perpetrators of violations of human rights.[48] The final report on impunity in regard to violations of civil and political rights speaks of three fundamental rights of victims: the right to know, the right to justice, and the right to reparation.[49]

Theo van Boven's work resulted in a preliminary report in 1990 on reparations for gross violations of human rights, followed by progress reports, and a 1993 final report to which he annexed draft principles on restitution, compensation, and rehabilitation.[50] In his final report, van Boven concluded that gross violations of

---

[47] United Nations Sub-Commission on the Prevention of Discrimination and Protection of Minorities, Resolution 1989/13 of 31 August 1989. The Human Rights Commission authorized the study by resolution 1990/35 of 2 March 1990, and the Economic and Social Council approved by resolution 1990/36 of 25 May 1990. In his reports, Mr. van Boven noted that there is no definition of 'gross violations of human right' but that the work of the International Law Commission regarding the draft Code of Crimes against the Peace and Security of Mankind as well as common Article 3 of the Geneva Conventions of 12 August 1949 provide guidance for both the serious character of the violations and also the type of human right that is being violated. He also cited section 702 of the Restatement (Third) of the Foreign Relations Law of the United States, concluding that 'while under international law the violation of any human right gives rise to a right to reparation for the victim, particular attention is paid to gross violations of human rights and fundamental freedoms which include at least the following: genocide; slavery and slavery-like practices; summary or arbitrary executions; torture and cruel, inhuman or degrading treatment or punishment; enforced disappearance; arbitrary and prolonged detention; deportation or forcible transfer of population; and systematic discrimination, in particular based on race or gender': E/CN.4/Sub.2/1993/8 at 7–8. After criticism of this approach, efforts were dropped to define gross violations in the draft principles.

[48] Sub-Commission Resolution 1992/23 of August 1992, approved by the Commission on Human Rights in resolution 1993/43 of 5 March 1993. The 1992 Vienna Conference on Human Rights supported the efforts of the Commission and Sub-Commission to intensify opposition to the impunity of perpetrators of serious violations of human rights. See the Vienna Declaration and Program of Action, A/CONF/157/3, para. II.91. The special rapporteurs, El Hadji Guisse and Louis Joinet, prepared an interim report for the 1993 session: E/CN.4/Sub.2/1993/6. In 1994, the Sub-Commission split the study into two parts, asking Mr. Guisse to complete the report in regard to economic, social and cultural rights, and Mr. Joinet to undertake to report on civil and political rights: Resolution 1994/34 of 26 August 1994, E/CN.4/Sub.2/1994/56, p. 81. Each rapporteur presented reports in 1995 and 1996. See: E/CN.4/Sub.2/1995/19; E/CN.4/Sub.2/1996/15; E/CN.4/Sub.2/1995/18.

[49] The right to know includes the right to the truth and the duty to remember. Two specific proposals call for the prompt establishment of extra-judicial commissions of inquiry as an initial phase in establishing the truth, and taking urgent measures to preserve access to archives of the period of violations. The right to justice implies the denial of impunity. The right to reparation refers to individual measures intended to implement the right to reparation (restitution, compensation and rehabilitation) as well as collective measures of satisfaction and guarantees of non-repetition.

[50] *Study concerning the right to restitution, compensation and rehabilitation for victims of gross violations of human rights and fundamental freedoms, Preliminary report submitted by Theo van Boven, Special Rapporteur*, E/CN.4/Sub.2/1990/10, 26 July 1990; *Progress reports*, E/CN.4/Sub.2/1991/7 and E/CN.4/Sub.2/1992/8; *Final report*, E/CN.4/Sub.2/1993/8. The final van Boven report was sent to the United Nations Commission on Human Rights for consideration at its 1994 session. The Sub-Commission also retained the item on its agenda for further examination of the

human rights are by their nature irreparable and any remedy or redress will fail to be proportional to the grave injury inflicted, particularly when the violations have been committed on a massive scale. The remedies thus must focus on the restoration of rights and the accountability of wrongdoers, calling it 'an imperative norm of justice that the responsibility of perpetrators be clearly established and that the rights of the victims be sustained to the fullest possible extent'.[51] The report also indicates that revelation of the truth is a fundamental requirement of justice.[52] Jose Zalaquett, former member of the Chilean National Commission on Truth and Conciliation, calls deterrence and redress the major reasons for requiring acknowledgment of the truth:

> To provide for measures of reparation and prevention, it must be clearly known what should be repaired and prevented. Further, society cannot simply block out a chapter of its history; it cannot deny the facts of its past, however differently these may be interpreted. Inevitably, the void would be filled with lies or with conflicting, confusing versions of the past. A nation's unity depends on a shared identity, which in turn depends largely on a shared memory. The truth also brings a measure of healthy social catharsis and helps to prevent the past from reoccurring.[53]

The member states of the Commission on Human Rights did not rush to embrace the van Boven principles. In 1994 and 1995, the Commission recommended the Sub-Commission continue its examination of them, declaring in rather weak terms that 'pursuant to internationally proclaimed human rights and humanitarian principles, victims of gross violations of human rights should receive, in appropriate cases, restitution, compensation and rehabilitation'.[54] The Commission also asked states to provide information to the Secretary-General about legislation already adopted and that being considered, related to restitution, compensation and rehabilitation of victims of grave violations of human rights and fundamental freedoms.

In 1996, at the request of the Sub-Commission, van Boven submitted a revised set of proposed basic principles and guidelines on remedies [55] which the

proposed basic principles and guidelines, creating a sessional working group for the purpose: Sub-Commission on Prevention of Discrimination and Protection of Minorities, Resolution 1993/29 of 25 August 1993, E/CN.4/Sub.2/1993/45, 69–70. Governments and non-governmental organizations were asked to comment.

[51]   *Final Report, ibid.,* at 53.

[52]   *Ibid.*

[53]   J. Zalaquett, 'The Matthew O. Tobriner Memorial Lecture. Balancing Ethical Imperatives and Political Constraints: The Dilemma of New Democracies Confronting Past Human Rights Violations', (1992) 43 *Hastings L.J.* 1425, 1433.

[54]   Commission on Human Rights, Resolution 1994/35 of 4 March 1994. During 1994, the secretariat prepared a report containing the comments of states, inter-governmental and non-governmental organizations. The principles were also considered by the sessional working group on the administration of justice and the question of compensation: Sub-Commission on Prevention of Discrimination and Protection of Minorities, E/CN.4/Sub.2/1994/22.

[55]   Sub-Commission on Prevention of Discrimination and Protection of Minorities, E/CN.4/Sub.2/1996/17.

Sub-Commission transmitted to the Commission for its consideration, together with its comments and those of the sessional working group on the administration of justice and the question of compensation.[56] The 1997 Session of the Commission on Human Rights took no action on the draft principles,[57] but, in 1998, it called for appointment of an expert to prepare a final draft for the 1999 session with a view to sending the principles to the General Assembly for adoption.[58]

The revised draft principles and guidelines reflect comments made by states and by inter-governmental and non-governmental organizations. The title of the document changed to place it more squarely in traditional international law and human rights law, from 'basic principles and guidelines on restitution, compensation and rehabilitation for victims of gross violations of human rights and fundamental freedoms' to 'basic principles and guidelines on the right to reparation for victims of [gross] violations of human rights and international humanitarian law'. In van Boven's view, reparation is the generic term that includes the various concepts used in the previous title. Two new elements have been added concerning applicable norms and the right to a remedy.

In the revised principles, unlike the earlier version, no effort is made to define 'gross violations of human rights'. The emphasis is on the scope of the obligation to respect and ensure respect for human rights, which, according to Principle 2, includes the duty:

to prevent violations, to investigate violations, to take appropriate action against the violators, and to afford remedies and reparation to victims. Particular attention must be paid to the prevention of gross violations of human rights and international humanitarian law and to the duty to prosecute and punish perpetrators of crimes under international law.

The right to a remedy is affirmed in Principle 4, which calls on every state to ensure that adequate legal or other appropriate remedies are available to any person claiming that his or her rights have been violated. Included is the right of access to international procedures for the protection of human rights.[59] The scope and nature of reparations to be afforded are broadly described in Principle 7, which asserts its basis in general international law:

---

[56] Sub-Commission on Prevention of Discrimination and Protection of Minorities, E/CN.4/Sub.2/1996/16, paras. 10–32.

[57] Commission on Human Rights Resolution 1997/29, *The right to restitution, compensation and rehabilitation for victims of grave violations of human rights and fundamental freedoms.*

[58] Commission on Human Rights Resolution 1998/43, E/CN.4/1998/L.76, adopted 17 April 1998.

[59] It is worth noting that the Constitution of Ukraine, adopted on 28 June 1996, affords such protection in article 55: 'The rights and freedoms of individuals and citizens shall be protected by the courts . . . Everyone shall have the right, after having exhausted all domestic remedies, to appeal for the protection of his rights and freedoms to the appropriate international legal bodies or to the appropriate organs of international organizations of which Ukraine is a member or in which it participates': Commission on Human Rights, *Right to restitution, compensation and rehabilitation for victims of grave violations of human rights and fundamental freedoms: Report of the Secretary-General,* E/CN.4/1997/29.

[In accordance with international law,] States have the duty to adopt special measures, where necessary, to permit expeditious and fully effective reparations. Reparation shall render justice by removing or redressing the consequences of the wrongful acts and by preventing and deterring violations. Reparations shall be proportionate to the gravity of the violations and the resulting damage and shall include restitution, compensation, rehabilitation, satisfaction and guarantees of non-repetition.[60]

Two goals are evident: first, to provide individual remedies for the victims; secondly, to uphold the public interest by deterring future violations. In this way, the principles take into account the object and purpose of human rights treaties and the concept of obligations *erga omnes*.

Humanitarian law also contains norms relating to remedies in case of a breach. Article 3 of the Hague Convention Regarding the Laws and Customs of Land Warfare obliges contracting parties to indemnify for a violation of the regulations. Similarly, Protocol I to the Geneva Conventions of 12 August 1949 and Relating to the Protection of Victims of International Armed Conflicts states that any party to a conflict who violates the provisions of the Geneva Conventions or the Protocol 'shall . . . be liable to pay compensation'.

2. Regional instruments

Regional instruments generally contain provisions requiring legal remedies for violations of human rights. The commissions and courts have interpreted and applied these guarantees in several cases.

(a) The European system

The European Convention on Human Rights modelled its general remedial provision—Article 13—on Article 8 of the Universal Declaration of Human Rights. Article 13 provides: 'Everyone whose rights and freedoms as set forth in this Convention are violated shall have an effective remedy before a national authority notwithstanding that the violation has been committed by persons acting in an official capacity'.[61] It has been referred to as 'the most obscure' provision in the Convention.[62] The Committee of Ministers reinforced Article 13 with a recommendation adopted in 1984 that calls on all Council of Europe member states to provide remedies for governmental wrongs.[63] Principle I of the recommendation says:

---

[60] *Revised Set of Basic Principles and Guidelines on the Right to Reparation for Victims of [Gross] Violations of Human Rights and International Humanitarian Law, prepared by Mr. Theo van Boven* E/CN.4/1997/104, Appendix.

[61] European Convention on Human Rights, *supra* n. 20, Article 13.

[62] *Malone v. United Kingdom* (1984) 82 Eur.Ct.H.R. (ser.A), partially dissenting opinion of Judges Matcher and Pinheiro Farinha.

[63] Recommendation No. R(84) 15 on Public Liability, adopted by the Committee of Ministers on 18 September 1984.

Reparation should be ensured for damage caused by an act due to a failure of a public authority to conduct itself in a way which can be expected from it in law in relation to the injured person. Such a failure is presumed in case of transgression of an established legal rule.

Principle V adds that reparation under Principle I should be made in full. The Commentary indicates that the victim must be compensated for all the damage resulting from the wrongful act which can be assessed in terms of money.

Article 13 establishes a minimum requirement linked to higher Convention protections such as the habeas corpus remedy of Article 5(4) and the requirement of compensation for unlawful arrest in Article 5(5),[64] as well as access to justice implied in Article 6(1). The attributes of an effective remedy include institutional independence of the remedial body from the authority responsible for the violation,[65] ability to invoke the Convention guarantee in question,[66] capability of the remedial body of affording redress,[67] and effectiveness in fact.[68] The general obligation to secure the rights and freedoms in the Convention allows the state to achieve this result by the means that it chooses within the Convention framework.[69] The remedy need not be judicial, but can include parliamentary and executive bodies,[70] so long as the remedy is effective. The Court's jurisprudence, however, suggests that a state that does not make the Convention directly enforceable in its national law risks breaching Article 13.

The right to a remedy is closely linked with the requirement that domestic remedies be exhausted before an individual has recourse to the European Court of Human Rights. The linkage emphasizes the primary role of national institutions and the subsidiary functions of the European Court.[71] In *Klass and others v. Germany*[72] the European Court of Human Rights noted that Article 13, read literally, seems to say that a person is entitled to a national remedy only if a 'violation'

---

[64] Article 5(5) requires compensation for breach of the right to be free from arrest in violation of the provisions of Article 5. When applicable, it requires a legally binding award of compensation. *Brogan v. United Kingdom* (1988) 145B Eur.Ct.H.R. (ser.A) and *Fox, Campbell and Hartley v. United Kingdom* (1990) 182 Eur.Ct.H.R. (ser. A). The state may require proof of damage resulting from the breach and probably has a wide margin of appreciation in regard to the quantum: *Wassink v. Netherlands* (1990) 185A Eur.Ct.H.R. (ser. A).

[65] *Silver v. UK*, (1983) 61 Eur.Ct.H.R. (ser. A), para. 116.

[66] *Soering v. United Kingdom*, (1989) 161 Eur.Ct.H.R. (ser.A), para. 121.

[67] *Ibid.*

[68] See *Airey v. Ireland* (1979) 32 Eur. Ct. H.R. (ser. A), and *Vilvarajah v. United Kingdom* (1991) 215 Eur.Ct.H.R. (ser. A), para. 125.

[69] *Swedish Engine Drivers' Union Case v. Sweden* (1976) 20 Eur.Ct.H.R. (ser. A).

[70] See e.g. *Klass v. Germany*, (1979) 28 Eur.Ct.H.R. (ser. A) and *Silver v. United Kingdom, supra* n. 65.

[71] In *Akdivar v. Turkey*, judgment of 16 September 1996, Reports of Judgments and Decisions 1996–IV, 1210 (hereinafter Reports) the Court refers to the requirement of exhaustion of local remedies as a reflection of the principle that the machinery of protection established by the Convention is subsidiary to the national systems safeguarding human rights: para. 65, citing *Handyside v. United Kingdom* (1976), 24 Eur.Ct.H.R. (ser. A), 22, para. 48.

[72] *Klass and others v. Germany, supra* n. 70 at 5, (1979–80), 2 E.H.R.R. 214.

has occurred; but a person cannot establish a violation before a national authority unless he or she is first able to lodge with such an authority a complaint to that effect. Thus, according to the Court, Article 13 guarantees an effective remedy 'to everyone who *claims* that his rights and freedoms under the Convention have been violated',[73] a ruling that the Court repeated in *Silver v. United Kingdom*, one of the few early cases where the Court found a violation of Article 13.[74] The Court said that '[a]n individual who has an arguable claim to be the victim of a violation of one of the rights in the Convention is entitled to a national remedy in order to have his claim decided and if appropriate to obtain redress'.[75] Although no single remedy may by itself entirely satisfy the requirements of Article 13, 'the aggregate of remedies provided for under domestic law may do so'.[76]

In the *Case of Boyle and Rice*, the European Commission on Human Rights[77] set forth its criteria for considering a claim 'arguable'. It said that such a claim should : (a) concern a right or freedom guaranteed by the Convention, (b) not be wholly unsubstantiated on the facts, and (c) give rise to a prima facie issue under the Convention. The Court, however, rejected any particular test for Article 13 saying that each case should be determined on its particular facts. At the same time, it indicated that it saw a link between having an arguable claim and the Convention's requirement that the Commission declare inadmissible any 'manifestly ill-founded' complaint.[78] For the Court, a Commission decision that a claim is inadmissible because it is manifestly ill-founded 'whilst not being decisive, provide[d] significant pointers as to the arguable character of the claims for the purpose of Article 13'.[79] In general, then, there is no right to a remedy for a manifestly ill-founded claim.

The Court has clarified if not modified some of its views on exhaustion of local remedies in recent cases against Turkey. It has emphasized that there is no obligation to have recourse to remedies that are inadequate or ineffective[80] and has applied a 'generally recognized rule of international law'[81] that absolves an

---

[73]   *Klass and others v. Germany* (emphasis added).

[74]   As of 1993, 46 cases reaching the Court claimed a violation of Article 13. See Gro Hillestad Thune, 'The Right to an Effective Remedy in Domestic Law: Article 13 of the European Convention on Human Rights', in Donna Gomien (ed.), *Broadening the Frontiers of Human Rights, Essays in Honour of Asbjorn Eide* (1993), 79–95. Since that time, some 60 cases against Turkey have been brought alleging a violation of Article 13.

[75]   *Silver v. United Kingdom, supra* n. 65, at para. 113.

[76]   *Ibid.*

[77]   *Case of Boyle and Rice*, (1986) Eur.Comm'n.H.R. Rep., para. 74.

[78]   Individual petitions are admissible if they are not manifestly ill-founded and meet other admissibility standards: European Convention, *supra* n. 20, Article 27(2), 213 U.N.T.S. 221.

[79]   *Boyle and Rice v. United Kingdom* (1988) 131 Eur.Ct.H.R. (ser. A) at para. 54.

[80]   *Akdivar and others v. Turkey, supra* n. 71, pp. 1210–13, paras. 65–76, citing *Ireland v. United Kingdom*, (1978) 25 Eur.Ct.H.R. (ser. A), p. 64, para. 159.; *Aksoy v. Turkey*, judgment of 18 December 1996, Reports 1996–VI, pp. 2275–76, para. 51–53; *Mentes and others v. Turkey*, judgment of 28 November 1997, para. 57, 59 Reports 1997–VIII 2693.

[81]   *Van Oosterwijck v. Belgium* (1980) 40 Eur.Ct.H.R. (ser. A), pp. 18–19, paras. 36–40.

applicant from the obligation to exhaust domestic remedies where there are 'special circumstances'.[82] Such circumstances may include the passivity of national authorities in the face of serious allegations of misconduct or infliction of harm by state agents, for example, where they have failed to undertake investigations or offer assistance.[83] In *Akdivar v. Turkey*,[84] the Court found that the remedies cited by the government were inadequate because the administrative courts that could award compensation could not determine in the course of such proceedings that the property had been destroyed by members of the gendarmerie. Without the attribution of responsibility or any meaningful investigation, the prospects of success in civil actions were negligible.

The European Court also indicated a new flexibility in application of the rule of exhaustion of remedies, referring to the 'due allowance' that must be made for the fact that the rule is applied in the context of human rights proceedings. According to the Court, the rule must be applied 'with some degree of flexibility and without excessive formalism'[85] with a realistic assessment of the general legal and political context in which the remedies operate and the personal circumstances of the applicant. In the Turkish cases, the general situation of violence in the regions in question was seen to create obstacles to the proper functioning of the system of the administration of justice, including the securing of probative evidence, and making the pursuit of judicial remedies futile.

In addition to requiring that remedies be afforded for arguable claims, the Convention requires that national remedies comply with the fair hearing guarantees of Article 6.[86] The European Court interpreted the right to a fair hearing to include the right of access to justice in the case of *Golder v. United Kingdom*,[87] where the government's refusal to allow a prisoner to communicate with a lawyer in order to institute proceedings was found to violate an implicit Article 6 right of

[82] Both the European and the Inter-American Courts apply a shifting burden of proof in regard to the exhaustion of local remedies. The applicant first must indicate what efforts were made to exhaust local remedies. It is then incumbent on the government claiming non-exhaustion to demonstrate the existence of a remedy that was an effective one available in theory and in practice at the relevant time, one that was accessible, was capable of providing redress in respect of the applicant's complaints and offered reasonable prospects of success. Once this burden has been satisfied, it falls to the applicant to establish that the remedy was in fact exhausted or was for some reason inadequate or ineffective in the particular circumstances of the case or that there existed 'special circumstances' absolving him or her from the requirement: *Akdivar v. Turkey*, *supra* n. 71, para. 68; *Mentes v. Turkey*, *supra* n. 80, para. 57. *Austria v. Italy (Admissibility)*, 11 January 1961, 4 Y.B. 166. The Court in *Akdivar* cites the *Velasquez Rodriguez Case (Preliminary Objections)* (1987) 1 Inter-Am.Ct.H.R. (ser. C) and the Inter-American Court's Advisory Opinion on exceptions to the exhaustion of local remedies, (1990) 11 Inter-Am.Ct.H.R. (ser. A).

[83] *Selçuk and Asker v. Turkey*, 24 April 1998 71 Reports 1998–II 891; *Akdivar and others*, 16 September 1996, Reports 1996–IV, pp. 1210–11, paras. 65–69 and *Mentes*, *supra* n. 80, p. 2706, para. 57.

[84] *Akdivar v. Turkey*, *supra* n. 71.

[85] *Ibid.*, p. 1211, para. 69; see also *Aksoy*, *supra* n. 80, p. 2276, para. 53.

[86] The guarantee in the American Convention is broader, applying to 'rights and obligations of a civil, labor, fiscal or any other nature', while the African Charter mandates a fair hearing in regard to 'fundamental rights'.

[87] *Golder v. United Kingdom*, (1975) 18 Eur. Ct. H.R. (ser. A).

access to justice. According to the Court, there should be no hindrance in law or fact to the ability to institute proceedings, unless the action is justified by and proportionate to a legitimate aim.[88] In general, an individual applicant 'must have a *bona fide* opportunity to have his case tested on its merits and, if appropriate, to obtain redress'.[89]

On the modalities of judicial procedure, states may impose reasonable restrictions, including statutes of limitations or a requirement of legal representation, to ensure the proper administration of justice.[90] The right of access thus may be subject to limitations, particularly regarding the conditions of admissibility of an appeal; however, limitations must not restrict exercise of the right in such a way or to such an extent that the very essence of the right is impaired.[91] They must pursue a legitimate aim and there must be a reasonable proportionality between the means employed and the aim sought to be achieved.[92] Where representation by a lawyer is necessary in law or in fact, the state may be obliged to provide legal aid for indigent litigants to ensure their effective access to justice. In *Airey v. Ireland*, the Court held that a lawyer must be provided where legal representation is compulsory or where the law and procedure involved are of a complexity to make legal advice indispensable.[93] No cases thus far have discussed the adequacy of state-provided representation.

The European Court tests whether a tribunal is 'independent' for the purposes of Article 6(1), by examining, *inter alia*, the manner of appointment of its members and their term of office, the existence of safeguards against outside pressures and the question whether it presents an appearance of independence.[94] As to the condition of 'impartiality' within the meaning of that provision, there are two tests applied: the first seeks to determine the personal conviction of a particular judge in a given case and the second to ascertain whether the judge offered guarantees sufficient to exclude any legitimate doubt in this respect.

[88] On the permissibility of immunities to limit litigation see *Fayed v. United Kingdom*, (1994) 294B Eur.Ct.H.R. (ser. A) where the principle of proportionality was applied to uphold an immunity conferred on those investigating the affairs of a company.

[89] *Leander v. Sweden*, (1987) 116 Eur.Ct.H.R. (ser. A).

[90] Cf. *Stubbings v. United Kingdom*, (1997) 23 E.H.R.R. 213, *Hennings v. Germany*, (1992) 251A Eur. Ct.H.R. (ser. A).

[91] *Ashingdane v. United Kingdom*, (1985) 93 Eur.Ct.Hum.Rts. (ser. A), pp. 24–25, para. 57.

[92] *F.E. v. France*, judgment of 30 October 1998; *Fayed v. United Kingdom*, (1994) 294–B Eur.Ct.Hum.Rts. (ser. A), pp. 49–50, para. 65; *Bellet v. France*, (1995) 333–B Eur.Ct.Hum.Rts. (ser. A), p. 41, para. 31; and *Levages Prestations Services v. France*, 1996–V Reports of Judgments and Decisions, p. 1543, para.40. In the *F.E.* case, the applicant who had contracted AIDS due to tainted blood, had not had effective access to a civil court, because the French Court of Cassation had quashed the Court of Appeal's judgment without remanding the case, thus precluding any possibility of reconsideration of the merits of his claim for additional compensation in respect of the damage caused by his infection. The same Court had also refused to apply the *Bellet* judgment, delivered on 4 December 1995 by the European Court, which held that France had breached the European Convention in a similar case.

[93] *Airey v. Ireland*, (1979) 32 Eur.Ct.H.R. (ser. A).

[94] See *Findlay v. United Kingdom*, judgment of 25 February 1997, Reports 1997–I, p. 281; *Cirklar v. Turkey*, judgment of 28 October 1998.

When applied to a body sitting as a bench, it means determining whether, quite apart from the personal conduct of any of the members of that body, there are ascertainable facts which may raise doubts as to its impartiality. Appearances may be of some importance and in deciding whether there is a legitimate reason to fear that a particular body lacks impartiality, the standpoint of those claiming that it is not impartial is important. It is not, however, decisive; what is decisive is whether the fear can be held to be objectively justified.[95]

The distinction between denial of a remedy and denial of access to justice are important. It may be legitimate for a state to deny access to courts under Article 6 for claims that have no substantive basis in its national legal order, but if the lack of substantive protection arguably concerns a right guaranteed by the Convention and no other remedial process is established, the state may be in breach of Article 13.[96] In a series of cases involving Turkey, the Commission and the Court addressed the relationship between the right of access to court, the fair hearing requirements of Article 6, and the right to an effective remedy in Article 13. Although a majority of the Commission found a breach of Article 6 in some of the Turkish cases, dissenting opinions affirmed, instead, that Article 13 was violated because of a general failure in the remedial system. In their views, the applicants thus were not denied access to available remedies, because there were no remedies to which they *could* have access.[97] The Court generally has found a violation of Article 13, rather than Article 6.[98]

Until recently, the European Court rarely looked at the adequacy of the remedies under Article 13, unless the facts indicated potential violations of the fair trial provisions of Articles 5[99] and 6.[100] In the 1990s, however, the European system

---

[95] See *Gautrin and others v. France*, judgment of 20 May 1998, Reports 1998–III, para. 58.

[96] See *Powell and Rayner v. United Kingdom*, (1990) 106 Eur.Ct.H.R. (ser. A).

[97] See the partly dissenting opinion of Mrs. G.H. Thune in *Aydin v. Turkey*, Application No. 23178/94, Report of the Commission adopted 7 March 1996. She asserted that the systematic failure to provide effective redress should be regarded as more fundamental than a failure to provide access to court to obtain damages.

[98] See *Kurt v. Turkey*, judgment of 25 May 1998. In this disappearance case, the Court found there was no concrete evidence proving beyond reasonable doubt the individual was killed by authorities. The Court did find, however, a violation of Article 5 because of an unacknowledged detention. Further, the failure to account for her son was a violation of the applicant mother's Article 3 rights (6–3) and Article 13, which imposes an obligation to conduct for the benefit of relatives a thorough investigation. Article 13 was seen as broader than the substantive right in requiring an effective investigation into the disappearance of a person in government custody, entailing a thorough and effective investigation capable of leading to the identification and punishment of those responsible with effective access for the relatives: para. 140.

[99] European Convention on Human Rights, *supra* n. 20, Article 5 guarantees the right to liberty and security of person. A person arrested is entitled to be informed promptly, in a language which he understands, of the reasons for the arrest and the charges; to be brought promptly before a judge or other officer authorized by law to exercise judicial power; to trial within a reasonable time or to release pending trial; and to take proceedings by which the lawfulness of the detention shall be decided speedily by a court: Article 5(2–4). Those unlawfully arrested or detained in violation of Article 5 'shall have an enforceable right to compensation': Art. 5(5).

[100] *Ibid.* Article 6 (in the determination of civil rights and obligations or of any criminal charge against an individual, the person is entitled to 'a fair and public hearing within a reasonable time by

began receiving numerous cases against Turkey alleging torture, unlawful killings, arbitrary detention, disappearances, the destruction of homes, property and villages, and the forced eviction of populations.[101] The pattern asserted is one of deliberate suppression of the Kurdish ethnic minority without sanction for the perpetrators or remedies for the victims. The Court has recognized the concept of a practice of violations, something the Court calls 'an aggravated violation'.[102] In such cases, the right to a remedy does not function or the practice would not exist, as the Commission has recognized.[103] The unavailability of remedies itself evidences official tolerance for the practice.

The applicants in the Turkish cases consistently have alleged the absence of an effective remedy and Commission sustained their claims in more than 60 cases, although the Court has not found a practice of violations in the cases submitted thus far. In a 1994 case, *Akdivar v. Turkey,* the Commission observed that the government had failed to provide a single example of compensation being awarded to villagers for the destruction of homes or villages and the forced eviction of inhabitants by Turkish military forces.[104] In addition, the government failed to show that there had been any significant examples of successful prosecutions against members of the security forces for the destructions and expulsions. The Court's judgment in the same case referred to the absence of compensation or prosecution, although it indicated that its judgment should not be interpreted as a conclusion that all remedies in Turkey were ineffective.[105]

---

an independent and impartial tribunal established by law'). Elements of what constitutes a fair hearing are specified: judgment shall be pronounced publicly by the court but the court may exclude the press and public from all or part of the trial in specified circumstances. For criminal proceedings, Article 6 also includes the presumption of innocence, the right to be informed of the charges, the right to defence and defence counsel, the right to cross-examination, and the right to an interpreter.

[101] See Aisling Reidy, Francoise Hampson and Kevin Boyle, 'Gross Violations of Human Rights: Invoking the European Convention on Human Rights in the Case of Turkey', (1997) 15 *Neth.Q.H.R.* 161.

[102] Such a practice consists of 'repetition of acts and official tolerance'. See *Denmark, Norway, Sweden and the Netherlands v. Greece*, Application Nos. 3321–23/67, XI Yearbook, and 3344/67, XII Yearbook at 195.

[103] 'When there is a practice of non-observance of certain Convention provisions the remedies will of necessity be side-stepped or rendered inadequate . . . Judicial remedies prescribed would be rendered ineffective by the difficulty of securing probative evidence, and administrative inquiries would either not be instituted or if they were, would likely be half-hearted and incomplete': Greek Case, *ibid.* 35 D&R 143, 164–65.

[104] *Akdivar and others v. Turkey*, Application No. 21893/93, Decision of 19 October 1994. See also *Mentes and others v. Turkey*, Application No. 23186/94, Decision of 9 January 1995; *Cetin v. Turkey*, Application No. 22677/93, Decision of 9 January 1995; *Isiyok v. Turkey*, Application No. 22309/93, Decision of 3 April 1995; *Yilmaz v. Turkey*, Application No. 23179/94, Decision of 15 May 1995; *Ovat v. Turkey*, Application No. 23180/94, Decision of 3 April 1995; *Sahin v. Turkey*, Application No. 23181/94, Decision of 15 May 1995; *Asker v. Turkey*, Application No. 23184/94, Decision of 28 November 1994; and *Selcuk v. Turkey*, Application No. 23185/94, Decision of 3 April 1995.

[105] *Akdivar and others v. Turkey*, supra n. 71, judgment of 16 September 1996. The Court also noted the threat of reprisals and intimidation of applicants and their lawyers.

In *Mentes and others v. Turkey*,[106] one of the cases where the government was accused of destroying the applicants' homes, the government argued that compensation could be awarded for the destruction and thus an effective domestic remedy existed. The applicants contended that the administrative proceedings in question were based on a theory of social risk and would 'necessarily mask the truth of the circumstances of the burning of their houses and possessions'.[107] According to them, any remedy that consisted of compensation and that ignored the responsibility of the government security forces was 'wholly unacceptable'. Further, any civil claim for damages would be doomed to failure in the absence of criminal proceedings against those responsible. The Court characterized the case as one of lack of a proper investigation into the allegations that the security forces were responsible. It reiterated that the right of access to a court in civil matters constitutes one aspect of the 'right to a court' embodied in Article 6(1). The Court nonetheless found that the issue was more properly considered in relation to the general obligation of the state to provide an effective remedy.

In other cases, as well, the Commission and the Court have focused in some detail on the failure to investigate complaints against the security forces and failure to prosecute; in a series of decisions it has linked such a failure to violation of the underlying right, as well as or instead of a violation of the right to a remedy. In *McCann and others v. United Kingdom*,[108] the Court held that the effective protection of the right to life has a procedural component and entails a requirement that the taking of life by state officials be investigated. The Court expanded on this obligation in *Kaya v. Turkey*, [109] where the applicant alleged a deliberate killing by the government and a failure to investigate. The Court held that there was insufficient factual basis for concluding that government intentionally killed the deceased, but held that Article 2 was nonetheless violated due to the absence of an investigation. The Court noted that protection of the right to life would be ineffective in practice, if there existed no procedure for reviewing the lawfulness of the use of lethal force by state authorities.

The obligation to protect the right to life under Article 2, read in conjunction with the State's general duty under Article 1 of the Convention to 'secure to everyone within their jurisdiction the rights and freedoms in [the] Convention', requires by implication that there should be some form of effective official investigation when individuals have been killed as a result of the use of force by, *inter alios*, agents of the State.[110]

This procedural protection of the right to life 'secures the accountability of agents of the State for their use of lethal force by subjecting their actions to some form

---

[106] *Mentes and others v. Turkey*, judgment of 28 November 1997, *supra* n. 80.

[107] *Ibid.*, para. 84.

[108] *McCann and others v. United Kingdom*, (1995) 324 Eur.Ct.H.R. (ser. A).

[109] Judgment 10 February 1998. The applicant alleged his brother had been wrongfully killed by authorities, leaving a widow and seven children. The government claimed the deceased was a rebel killed in a military operation.

[110] Para. 86, citing *McCann and others*, *supra* n. 108, p. 47 para. 161.

of independent and public scrutiny capable of leading to a determination of whether the force used was or was not justified in a particular set of circumstances'.[111] The Court added that, for the purposes of Article 13, violations of the right to life 'cannot be remedied exclusively through an award of compensation to the relatives of the victim'.[112] Respecting the denial of the right to life, 'one of the most fundamental in the scheme of the Convention', the remedies must be guaranteed for the benefit of the relatives of the victim. Where those relatives have an arguable claim that the victim has been unlawfully killed by agents of the State, the notion of an effective remedy for the purposes of Article 13 entails, in addition to the payment of compensation where appropriate, a thorough and effective investigation capable of leading to the identification and punishment of those responsible and including effective access for the relatives to the investigatory procedure. The requirements of Article 13 are broader than the procedural obligation under Article 2 to conduct an effective investigation. Because of the high standard of proof at the European Court, the conclusion on the merits does not dispense with the requirement that the government conduct an effective investigation into the substance of the allegation.

In *Ergi v. Turkey*,[113] the Court similarly distinguished the 'procedural requirement' implicit in Article 2, taken in conjunction with Article 1 of the Convention, from the right to a remedy in Article 13. As before, the Court held that by implication there must be some form of effective official investigation when individuals have been killed as a result of the use of force. [114] Even the mere knowledge of a killing on the part of the authorities gives rise to such an obligation. Independently, the failure to investigate could be a breach of Article 13. The applicants asserted that the scope was not the same because the Article 2 obligation was limited to what had occurred, whereas under Article 13, the investigation was part of the system of securing an effective remedy. The Court agreed that the nature of the right must have implications for the nature of the remedies which must be guaranteed and entails a thorough and effective investigation. 'Seen in these terms the requirements of Article 13 are broader than a Contracting State's procedural obligation under Article 2 to conduct an effective investigation'.[115]

As the right to life cases indicate, the 'nature and gravity' of arguable claims have implications for Article 13. According to the European Court, where there are allegations of serious violations, including deliberate destruction of homes and possessions in violation of Article 8, the right to a remedy imposes, without prejudice to any other remedy, an obligation on the respondent state to carry out

---

[111]   Para. 88.

[112]   Citing *Aksoy*, *supra* n. 80, pp. 2285–86, paras. 93–94, and *Aydin*, *supra* n. 97, pp. 1894–96 and paras. 100–03.

[113]   *Ergi v. Turkey*, judgment of 28 July 1998.

[114]   *Ibid.*, para. 82, citing *McCann*, *supra* n. 108, p. 49, para. 161 and *Kaya v. Turkey*, Judgment of 19 February 1998, 65 Reports of Judgments and Decisions 1998-I 297, paras. 78, 86.

[115]   *Ibid.*, para. 98.

a thorough and effective investigation of allegations brought to its attention, an investigation capable of leading to the identification and punishment of those responsible and including effective access for the complainant to the investigative procedure. In *Aksoy v. Turkey*[116] the Court similarly established the link between the prohibition of torture in Article 3 and the Article 13 requirement of a remedy. According to the Court, the fundamental importance of the ban on torture means that Article 13 imposes, without prejudice to any other domestic remedy, 'an obligation on states to carry out a thorough and effective investigation of incidents of torture'.[117] This duty arises whenever an individual has an 'arguable claim' of torture committed by state agents. It entails 'in addition to the payment of compensation where appropriate, a thorough and effective investigation capable of leading to the identification and punishment of those responsible and including effective access for the individual to the investigatory procedure'.[118] According to the reasoning in the *McCann* judgment, the failure to investigate could be a violation of Article 3 as well as Article 13.[119]

The scope of authority to afford remedies where the state has failed to is one of the most important questions faced by international human rights tribunals. The European Court has regularly declared that it is limited to ordering financial compensation and is not empowered to order other remedial measures because 'it is for the State to choose the means to be used in its domestic legal system to redress the situation that has given rise to the violation of the Convention'.[120] While true, the Court's approach conflates means and result. The Court could decide that release of a prisoner wrongfully held is the appropriate remedy, in order to ensure that the applicant receives just satisfaction and leave the means by which that result is achieved to the state (e.g. judicial review, executive order, legislative action).

While a domestic court is not obliged to give the judgments direct effect[121] the state is obliged by international law, however, to change a law or practice found

---

[116] *Aksoy supra* n. 80.

[117] *Ibid.*, at para. 98.

[118] *Ibid.*

[119] See also *Aydin v. Turkey*, judgment of 27 September 1997. The Court held that the applicant had been subjected to torture by being raped and subjected to other ill-treatment in violation of Article 3. The vote was 14 to 7, the dissenters objecting that the evidence did not prove the allegations beyond a reasonable doubt. A divided vote also resulted from the second violation asserted, a denial of a remedy contrary to Article 13 (16–5). The applicant contended that the failure of the authorities to carry out an effective investigation into her treatment constituted a separate breach of Article 3. The Court assimilated this to her complaints under Articles 6 and 13. The Court recalled that Article 6(1) 'embodies the right to a court, of which the right of access, that is, the right to institute proceedings before a court in civil matters, constitutes one aspect'. The Court found that in this case the essence of the complaint was a failure to conduct an effective investigation, which placed the claim under Article 13.

[120] *Zanghi v. Italy*, (1991) 194 C Eur. Ct.H.R. (ser. A) at 48.

[121] *Vermeire v. Belgium*, (1991) 214C Eur.Ct.H.R. (ser. A). Some national courts can enforce judgments of the European Court (e.g. Malta, Spain) and others cannot (e.g. Germany). See 'The European Convention on Human Rights: Institution of Relevant Proceedings at the National Level to Facilitate Compliance with Strasbourg Decisions', Council of Europe Committee of Experts Study, (1992) 13 *H.R.L.J.* 71.

incompatible with the Convention to comply with its Article 1 obligation to secure the rights and freedoms guaranteed. The European Court adopted a narrow interpretation of its remedial powers probably because the individual was not the focus of the system at its inception.[122] It has held to this view because in large part states have complied with the Court's judgments by changing laws and practices, although the changes have not always had retrospective effect to remedy the consequences of the violation to the applicant. Other states have not complied or have done so only after great delay and the risks are greater with the new member states of the system. The European Court's present approach has led to successive cases against the same state for the same breach, because the Court failed to direct the state to remedy the wrong in the first instance. It also has left several applicants without a remedy to repair the consequences of the violation.[123]

(b) The Inter-American system

In the Inter-American system, Article XVII of the American Declaration of the Rights and Duties of Man[124] guarantees every person the right to resort to the courts to ensure respect for legal rights and to obtain protection from acts of authority that violate any fundamental constitutional rights. The American Convention on Human Rights goes further, entitling everyone to effective recourse for protection against acts that violate the fundamental rights recognized by the constitution 'or laws of the state or by the Convention', even where the act is committed by persons acting in the course of their official duties (Article 25).[125] The states parties are to ensure that the competent authorities enforce the remedies granted and, indeed, are obliged to respect and ensure the free and full exercise of all rights guaranteed by the Convention (Article 1(1)). These obligations are linked to the fair trial provisions of Article 8, which requires the state to provide a fair hearing before a competent, independent and impartial tribunal. Article 10 of the Convention further provides that every person has the right to be compensated in accordance with the law in the event he has been sentenced by a final judgment

---

[122] 'The original purpose of the Convention was not primarily to offer a remedy for particular individuals who had suffered violations of the Convention but to provide a collective inter-state guarantee that would benefit individuals generally by requiring the national law of the contracting parties to be kept within certain bounds. An Article 25 application was envisaged as a mechanism for bringing to light a breach of an obligation owed by one state to others, not to provide a remedy for an individual victim': David Harris, Michael O'Boyle, and Colin Warbrick, *Law of the European Convention on Human Rights* (1995) 33.

[123] See, e.g. *Incal v. Turkey*, a Grand Chamber decision of 9 June 1998. By a 12–8 vote, the Court decided that Turkey had violated the freedom of expression and right to a fair trial of the applicant. The consequence of the conviction included a substantial loss of civil rights. The applicant could not found an association or trade union, or become a member of trade union executive committee. He was also barred from founding or joining a political party and could not stand for election and was debarred from entering civil service. The applicant sought a restoration of his civil rights. The Court said it had no jurisdiction to order such measures.

[124] American Declaration of the Rights and Duties of Man, *supra* n. 26.

[125] American Convention on Human Rights, *supra* n. 27, Article 25.

through a miscarriage of justice.[126]

The Inter-American Court has commented on the obligation of states to make effective internal remedies available, stating that:

Under the Convention, States Parties have an obligation to provide effective judicial remedies to victims of human rights violations (Art. 25), remedies that must be substantiated in accordance with the rules of due process of law (Art. 8(1)), all in keeping with the general obligation of such States to guarantee the free and full exercise of the rights recognized by the Convention to all persons subject to their jurisdiction (Art. 1).[127]

The Court has concluded that the obligation of Convention parties to ensure rights generally requires that remedies include due diligence on the part of the state to prevent, investigate, and punish any violation of the rights recognized by the Convention.[128] The Commission has added that, in the case of disappearances, the obligation to investigate continues as long as the uncertainty over the final fate of the disappeared person persists.[129]

The case of *Gustavo Carranza*, decided 30 September 1997,[130] discussed the requirements of a full and fair remedy as guaranteed by Article 25 of the American Convention, holding that Argentina violated the Convention when its courts applied the political question doctrine and refused to decide a case on the merits. The petitioner was a judge removed from office in 1976 by the military government of Argentina.[131] He sought a judicial remedy and was denied access to the courts on the grounds that his dismissal constituted a political question. The petitioner sought and received a Commission determination that he had been wrongfully denied a remedy in the courts of Argentina, successfully arguing that the political question doctrine does not apply to a law or action of the executive in violation of the rights and guarantees of the Constitution, including the unconstitutional removal of judges from office.

The Commission first reviewed the political question doctrine, finding it grounded in the democratic system of separation of powers, by virtue of which the judiciary abstains from reviewing acts that presuppose a political or discretionary

---

[126] *Ibid.*, Article 10. Article 3 of Protocol 7 to the European Convention on Human Rights similarly provides for compensation when a criminal conviction is reversed or the accused is pardoned 'on the ground that a new or newly discovered fact shows conclusively that there has been a miscarriage of justice . . . unless it is proved that the non-disclosure of the unknown fact in time is wholly or partly attributable to him': Protocol 7 to the European Convention on Human Rights, E.T.S. 117.

[127] *Velasquez Rodriguez Case* (Preliminary Exceptions), (1987) 1 Inter-Am.Ct.H.R.(ser. C) para. 91.

[128] *Velasquez Rodriguez Case* (Merits), (1988) 4 Inter-Am. Ct.H.R. (ser .C), para. 166.

[129] Report No. 25/98, Chile, IACHR, Annual Report of the Inter-American Commission on Human Rights 1997, OEA/Ser.L/V/II.98 doc. 7 rev. (1998) at 535.

[130] Report No. 30/97, Case, 10.087, *Gustavo Carranza v. Argentina*, Annual Report of the Inter-American Commission on Human Rights 1997, OEA/Ser.L/V/II.98, Doc. 7 rev. (1998) at 254.

[131] Although the dismissal was nearly 20 years prior to the filing of the petition, and before Argentina ratified the American Convention, the case was deemed admissible because the petitioner began domestic litigation in 1984, after the date of ratification, and filed his petition on 31 August 1987, within six months of the 24 February 1987 final judgment of the Argentine Supreme Court.

judgment reserved exclusively for another branch of government. The Commission stated it would not pass judgment on the wisdom or efficacy of a judicial doctrine 'unless its application results in a violation of any of the rights protected by the American Convention'.[132] The Government of Argentina having relied on the United States Supreme Court decision in *Baker v. Carr*,[133] the Commission analysed the case and noted that judges 'have frequently redefined the scope of political questions'.[134] It also referred to the fact that the courts of Argentina used the political question doctrine to justify the actions of a *de facto* military government that took power by unconstitutional means and found this fact determinative:

> removal of magistrates by order of the competent body and in accordance with established constitutional procedure is one thing, but the 'dismissal of a magistrate' by an illegitimate authority without competence, with utter disregard for the procedure prescribed by the Constitution, is quite another. The first [act] under internal legislation might well be non-justiciable, but the second would be unconstitutional and unlawful, and it is up to the courts to review it and declare so.[135]

The Commission then elaborated on the requirements of Convention Articles 8 and 25. It interpreted Article 8 as requiring procedural due process to determine rights. It set forth the conditions that must be met to ensure the suitable defence of persons whose rights or obligations are under judicial consideration, including determination of the issue by a competent, independent and impartial judicial body. The Commission interpreted Article 25 to encompass the right to 'effective' judicial protection, not mere access to a judicial body. According to the Commission, this means that the tribunal 'must reach a reasoned conclusion on the claim's merits, establishing the appropriateness or inappropriateness of the legal claim that, precisely, gives rise to the judicial recourse'.[136] The Commission held that there was no effective legal remedy in this case and recommended that the petitioner be compensated for the violation.

The Inter-American Court addressed procedural aspects of the right to a remedy in *Genie Lacayo v. Nicaragua*.[137] The petitioner and the Commission alleged a violation of the right to a fair trial (Article 8), the right to judicial protection (Article 25), and the right to equal treatment (Article 24), stemming from

---

[132] *Carranza v. Argentina, supra* n. 130 at 261.

[133] *Baker v. Carr*, 369 U.S. 186 (1962).

[134] *Carranza v. Argentina, supra* n. 130 at 261.

[135] *Ibid.,* at 263.

[136] *Ibid.,* at 266–67. The Commission cites Report 5/96 wherein it held that 'the right to a recourse set forth in Article 25, interpreted in conjunction with the obligation in Article 1(1) and the provisions of Article 8(1), must be understood as the right of every individual to go to a tribunal when any of his rights have been violated (whether a right protected by the Convention, the constitution, or the domestic laws of the state concerned), to obtain a judicial investigation conducted by a competent, impartial, and independent tribunal that will establish whether or not a violation has taken place and will set, when appropriate, adequate compensation'.

[137] *Genie Lacayo Case*, (1998) 30 Inter-Am.Ct.H.R (ser. C).

judicial procedures following the death of a 16-year-old youth allegedly killed by the Nicaraguan military. Judicial action commenced approximately nine months after the event; after a further year of investigation, the civilian criminal court transferred jurisdiction to the military courts. The father of the deceased appealed the decision but the decision to transfer was upheld on appeal. During the subsequent military proceedings, according to the Commission, evidence disappeared, witnesses refused to appear, and pressure was placed on the prosecutor.

The Commission asserted that for any crime in which there was evidence of involvement of a member of the military, the jurisdiction of military tribunals violates equal protection. In addition, it asserted that the military courts of Nicaragua, as constituted by the national decrees, 'created conditions conducive to the violation of the right to a fair trial, to due process and to equal treatment by granting broad margins of discretion and leaving it to the Army's High commanders to sanction those "involved" or to let them go unpunished'.[138] The Commission questioned the impartiality of the military courts and the willingness of the government to investigate the killing.[139] It also complained of the length of proceedings, in particular the failure of the Supreme Court of Nicaragua to render judgment on appeal from the military court for over two years.

The Court found 'abundant evidence' that the Nicaraguan military authorities obstructed justice and failed to cooperate with the investigations conducted by the Attorney General's office and the civilian court of first jurisdiction over the case. It also found that there was an unreasonable delay in rendering judgment on appeal to the Supreme Court, in violation of Article 8(1) of the Convention.[140] On the other hand, it found that the decrees concerning military trials in Nicaragua did not violate the principle of equality nor diminish the independence or impartiality of the military tribunals. It made clear that in its view the fact that a case was heard in military courts 'does not *per se* signify that the human rights guaranteed the accusing party by the Convention are being violated'.[141] On the facts of this case, the Court found that the deceased's father had been able to participate in the proceedings, submit evidence, and apply to the Supreme Court for judicial review of the decision of the military courts. Consequently, he could not claim that the application of the decrees on military trials restricted his procedural rights protected by the Convention.

The decision on impartiality and independence seems clearly wrong. The Court accepted that the second instance military court was made up of senior

---

[138] *Ibid.,* at para. 15.

[139] The Commission questioned the impartiality based on Article 52 of Decree 591 which required military courts to assess evidence in accordance with the 'Sandinista juridical conscience': *ibid.,* para. 38(c).

[140] In establishing the parameters of reasonableness, the Court considered the factors utilized by the European Court of Human Rights: (a) the complexity of the case; (b) the judicial activity of the interested party; and (c) the behaviour of the judicial authorities. See *ibid.,* para. 77, citing the *Motta* case, (1991) 195A Eur.Ct.Hum.Rts. (ser. A) and *Ruiz-Mateos*, (1993) 262 Eur.Ct.Hum.Rts. (ser. A).

[141] *Ibid.,* para. 84.

army officers called upon to decide the case on the basis of 'Sandinista juridical conscience' and that one of the decrees in question replaced criminal responsibility with disciplinary responsibility. Nonetheless, the Court said it 'feels' that these provisions, which could impair the independence and impartiality of the military tribunals, were not applied in this specific case.[142]

The 1998 decision in the disappearance case of *Blake v. Guatemala*[143] reinforced the links between Article 8(1), Article 25 and Article 1(1), emphasizing the need to combat impunity. The Court held that Article 8(1), which affirms the right of each person to a hearing by a competent, independent and impartial tribunal for a determination of rights, extends to the family of a victim. Together with Article 25 and Article 1(1), it ensures to each person that those responsible for violations of human rights will be judged and that the victims can obtain a remedy for damage suffered. The Court refers to the right to a remedy as one of the basic pillars not only of the American Convention, but of the rule of law and a democratic society.[144] The state must use all the legal means at its disposal to combat the chronic repetition of violations and impunity, defined by the Court as the failure to investigate, prosecute, capture, adjudge, and condemn those responsible for the violation of rights protected by the American Convention.[145] The Court held that Guatemala had the obligation to investigate the facts that led to the violations, identify and sanction those responsible, and adopt the measures in internal law necessary to assure compliance with its obligations.

(c) The African system

The African Charter has several provisions on remedies. Article 7 guarantees every individual the right to have his cause heard, including 'the right to an appeal to competent national organs against acts violating his fundamental rights as recognized and guaranteed by conventions, laws, regulations and customs in force'. In addition, Article 21 refers to 'the right to adequate compensation' in regard to 'the spoliation of resources of a dispossessed people'.[146] Article 26 imposes a duty on states parties to the Charter to guarantee the independence of the courts and allow the establishment and improvement of appropriate national institutions entrusted with the promotion and protection of rights and freedoms guaranteed by the Charter. The African Commission emphasizes the need for independence of the judiciary and the guarantees of a fair trial, calling attacks on

---

[142] *Ruiz-Mateos*, (1993) 262 Eur.Ct.Hum.Rts. (ser. A), para. 85.

[143] *Blake v. Guatemala, (Merits)* judgment of 24 January 1998; *(Reparations)* judgment of 22 January 1999.

[144] *Blake v. Guatemala (Reparations)*, para. 63; *Castillo Paez v. Peru*, (1997) 34 Inter-Am. Ct. H.R. (ser. C), paras. 82, 83; *Suarez Rosero v. Ecuador*, (1998) 35 Inter-Am.Ct.H.R. (ser. C), para. 65; *Paniagua Morales and others v. Guatemala*, (1998) 37 Inter-Am.Ct.H.R. (ser. C); *Loayza Tamayo v. Peru (Reparations)*, judgment of 27 November 1998, para. 169; *Castillo Paez v. Peru (Reparations)*, judgment of 27 November 1998, para. 106.

[145] *Blake v. Guatemala (Reparations)*, supra n. 143, para. 64.

[146] African Charter on Human and Peoples Rights, *supra* n. 30, Article 21(2).

the judiciary 'especially invidious, because while it is a violation of human rights in itself, it permits other violations of rights to go unredressed'.[147]

C. CONCLUSIONS

It is clear that the existence of effective remedies is an essential component of international human rights law. A state that fails to protect fully individuals against human rights violations or that otherwise violates remedial rights commits an independent, further violation of internationally-recognized human rights. International instruments do not clarify, however, what are considered to be 'effective' remedies. Nor do they indicate what remedies should be made available through international procedures in the event a state fails to afford the necessary redress. It is thus necessary to look at the theory and practice of international and domestic courts to determine what constitutes an effective remedy.

As will be shown in the chapters that follow, international remedies that have been afforded thus far are often partial and unimaginative, and typically fail to resolve the human rights problem that led the victim to bring the case. International tribunals seem unwilling to recognize the importance of their decisions, not only in providing a remedy for past abuse, but in persuading those in power to comply with human rights norms in the future. Effective enforcement of norms can influence the incidence of violations. Although international law, drawing upon municipal legal concepts,[148] governs remedies for international law violations, no coherent approach to the issue has developed. Consistency and principled decision-making can help avoid forum shopping, provide remedies for victims and bring wrongdoers to justice, and enhance the legitimacy of international tribunals. To these goals we now turn, beginning with an analysis of the theoretical foundations of a law of remedies.

---

[147] African Commission on Human Rights, Communication No. 129/94, *Civil Liberties Organization v. Nigeria*, AGH/207(XXXII) Annex VIII 17, at 19. The Commission deemed the ousting of jurisdiction of the Nigerian courts 'an attack of incalculable proportions on Article 7': *ibid*. The Commission also referred to Article 26, stating that it 'clearly envisions the protection of the courts which have traditionally been the bastion of protection of the individual's rights against the abuses of State power': *ibid.*

[148] References to municipal law principles are particularly prevalent on payment and rate of interest and lost profits. Specific references are few and there is no systematic borrowing from municipal law.

2

Theories of Remedies

Rarely are the theoretical foundations of remedies discussed in international human rights law and practice. Yet the aim of remedies, to vindicate interests that have been injured, requires that human rights law, representing fundamental interests, develop not only a primary theory of what duties are owed, but a secondary theory of what duties exist when a primary duty is violated. In most legal systems, including the international legal system, the philosophy of remedial justice provides the foundation for the law of remedies. More recently, economic analysis has provided a different theoretical model to understand issues of compensation and deterrence. This chapter discusses theoretical approaches to remedies in national and international law and the differences between private law and public law cases.

A. REMEDIAL JUSTICE

The primary function of corrective or remedial justice is to rectify the wrong done to a victim, that is, to correct injustice.[1] Aristotle described the conceptual framework for compensatory justice on which much of the modern law of remedies is based:

What the judge aims at doing is to make the parties equal by the penalty he imposes, whereby he takes from the aggressor any gain he may have secured. The equal, then, is a mean between the more and the less. But gain and loss are each of them more or less in opposite ways, more good and less evil being gain, the more evil and the less good being loss. The equal, which we hold to be just, is now seen to be intermediate between them. Hence we conclude that corrective justice must be the mean between loss and gain. This explains why the disputants have recourse to a judge; for to go to a judge is to do justice ... What the judge does is to restore equality.[2]

Thus, the essential features of compensatory justice are: (1) the parties are treated as equal; (2) there is damage inflicted by one party on another; (3) the remedy seeks to restore the victim to the condition he or she was in before the unjust activity occurred.

Remedies thus are designed to place an aggrieved party in the same position as he or she would have been had no injury occurred. To achieve this end by holding

---

[1] On corrective justice as the basis for tort litigation, see E. Weinrib, 'Understanding Tort Law', (1989) 23 *Val.U.L.Rev.* 485.

[2] Aristotle, *The Ethics* (J.A.K. Thompson trans., 1955), 148–49.

the wrongdoer responsible for providing the remedy serves a moral need; on a practical level collective insurance can as easily make the victim whole. The wrong is an essential element; it is the rights-infringing wrongful conduct that is the source of a claim. Otherwise a person's losses due to a falling tree would be legally equivalent to injury resulting from torture. Even rights-violating conduct that causes no compensable harm or that brings an economic benefit to the victim is cause for complaint because it creates a moral imbalance between the victim and the wrongdoer and a moral claim concerning a wrong done.[3]

Aristotle's compensatory justice ideal pertains to acts between individuals, not to unjust acts committed by 'society' against a group or a government against an individual. Nevertheless, the approach provides a basis also for public law remedies. Violations of human rights are wrongs committed against the individual victim *and* against the social order, and may be considered particularly serious wrongs because human rights are 'maximally weighty moral claims',[4] powerful enough to block utility-maximizing actions by others. Individuals, being committed to maximizing their own values, have projects that give directive force—i.e. meaning—to their lives, and with each individual having distinct projects and goals, the potential for conflict is clear, creating the need for an ordering principle that maximizes opportunities for all individuals. As one astute observer has commented, '[a]lthough neither you nor I has reason to be impartial between advancement of his own ends and advancement of the other person's ends, we each have reason to acknowledge the rationality from the perspective of each person of lending special weight to the values constituted by that individual's personal projects'.[5] Everyone therefore shares a reciprocal reason to value non-interference, and, consequently, a moral order that is characterized by mutual restraint. Non-interference with rights is valuable instrumentally to promote individual aims on the basis of personality, but it also is a basic demand of a self-directing person and indicative of respect for the inherent dignity of all persons.[6]

Human rights law thus establishes a minimal order of forbearance or moral baseline to allow personal development through pursuance of individual goals and projects. When rights are violated, the ability of the victim to pursue self-determination is impaired because of an unwarranted act of interference. As the Inter-American Court indicated in the *Loayza Tamayo (Reparations)* decision, individuals lack true freedom if they cannot design life according to their own

---

[3] Of course, some actions have broader import and may be punished as a crime against the general order.

[4] L. Lomasky, 'Compensation and the Bounds of Rights', in J. Chapman (ed.), *Compensatory Justice* (1991), 13, 24.

[5] *Ibid.*, at 25.

[6] As St. Peter expresses it: 'Of a truth I perceive that God is no respecter of persons': Acts 10:34. St. Paul agrees, telling the Romans 'there is no respect of persons with God': Rom. 2:11. Paul also writes to the churches of Galatia of the equality of all persons: 'There is neither Jew nor Greek, there is neither bond nor free, there is neither male nor female: for you are all one in Christ Jesus': Gal. 3:29.

goals and strive to achieve their desires.[7] These options have a very high existential value. This gives rise to injustice and a justifiable claim to be restored to the prior position, resulting in demands for rectification or compensation, either restoring precisely what was lost or something equivalent in value. A morally adequate response addresses itself in the first instance to restoring the position of the victim. The moral adequacy of a substitute remedy, usually money, will vary considerably but may allow the victim to further his or her legitimate projects or goals. In sum, rectification and compensation in the framework of basic rights serve to restore to individuals to the extent possible their capacity to achieve the ends that they personally value.

B. ECONOMIC ANALYSIS OF REMEDIES

The impact of 'law and economics' theories has been considerable in Western legal systems, from the common law systems of the USA, England, and Canada to civil law jurisdictions including Germany, the Netherlands, and Italy.[8] The creation of a Latin American Association of Law and Economics indicates the spread of the approach,[9] which uses economic models as theoretical constructs for analysing the laws and legal doctrines of a given society.[10] Although not universally accepted in all areas of the law, neoclassical economic theories provide a widely-used alternative approach to assessing the nature and purpose of remedies.

Law and economics theory holds that the law should always be efficient. An activity that is profitable even after payment of all the costs it imposes on others is said to be efficient or economical. Therefore, unlike the corrective justice model, which primarily determines the consequences of a wrongful act, economic theory is said to help to define the substance of what constitutes the wrong.[11] The

---

[7] *Loayza Tamayo (Reparations)*, (1998) 42 Inter-Am.Ct.H.R. (ser. C), para.147. See also the separate opinions of Judges Cancado Trindade and Abreu Burelli, who emphasize the human needs and aspirations that go beyond economic worth. They point to affirmation in the Preamble of the American Declaration of the Rights and Duties of Man that 'the spiritual development is the supreme end of human existence and the highest expression thereof'. In their view, the determination of reparations in human rights law should take into account the totality of the human person and the impact of human rights violation on this life.

[8] Although traditionally distinct, the common law and civil law have seen convergence and transplants. The growth of European law may hasten this phenomenon. Thus, 'western legal system' is more recently used by comparative law scholars. B.S. Markensinis, *A Comparative Introduction to the German Law of Torts* 3rd edn., (1994), 1.1.

[9] In Mexico and some other Latin American countries, the legal tradition is civil law in the private sphere, while public law doctrines have been influenced by United States common law.

[10] Robin Paul Malloy, Law and Economics: *A Comparative Approach to Theory and Practice* (1990), 3.

[11] See R. Posner, 'The Concept of Corrective Justice in Recent Theories of Tort Law', (1981) 10 *J. Leg.Studies* 187, 193 ('the Aristotelian concept of corrective justice does not tell us who is a wrongdoer or who has vested rights; all it tells us is that a wrongful injury is not excused by the moral superiority of the injurer to the victim').

economic reasoning behind the theory is based on at least three fundamental assumptions: (1) that conditions of scarcity preclude the fulfilment of every human desire; (2) that in a condition of scarcity most individuals behave rationally most of the time to maximize the achievement of their various goals and desires; (3) that individuals are the best, even the only, judges of their own preferences, and therefore act in their own self interest. These assumptions, together with an assumption of negligible transaction costs, lead economic analysts to conclude that individuals tend to bargain efficient results between themselves. As a result, a cost-benefit analysis can be used to predict whether a change in the law will lead to the desired response in those subject to it. An increase in costs will discourage behaviour that is undesirable.

The deterrence rationale seems inherent in the market model and its cost-benefit analysis: damages are warranted as long as the cost to society of paying them will deter possible wrongdoers from imposing greater costs in the future. In this framework, compensatory damages, like criminal penalties, compel law violators to take account of the harm they inflict.[12] The amount of damages need not be compensatory in fact, if that term denotes some direct relationship between the damages paid and the victim's loss and its magnitude. Instead, damages are set at the appropriate level to deter the misconduct, a level that may be higher or lower than the actual losses of the victim. In most cases, however, economic analysis equates the value of damages with the value of harm.

If deterrence is the basis of an award of damages, an accurate assessment of the amounts due is important in inducing wrongdoers to exercise levels of precaution that reflect the magnitude of the harm they may generate. Damage liability that is less than the harm inflicted will encourage potential defendants to violate the law when it is inefficient to do so. On the other hand, damage liability in excess of the harm inflicted will cause potential defendants to obey the law when it is inefficient to do so. A further factor also must be considered: not every wrongdoer expects to be caught and held liable for every incident. According to economic analysis, to make liability an effective market deterrent, it is necessary to inflate compensatory damages to correct the expectation of wrongdoers that they might escape from paying the full costs in every case. The proper deterrence measure thus may exceed the compensatory measure. In any event, a proper measure of one is not necessarily a proper measure for the other. Accuracy in damage awards alters the level of precautions based on the amount of the potential damage award.[13]

In neoclassical economic analysis, deterrence—which seeks to influence the behaviour of all potential actors, not just the future conduct of a particular defendant—is assumed to work because rational actors weigh the anticipated costs of

---

[12] *Ibid.,* at 194.
[13] See L. Kaplow and S. Shavell, 'Accuracy in the Assessment of Damages', (1996) 39 *J.Law & Econ.* 191.

transgressions against the anticipated benefits. Guido Calebresi distinguishes between general and specific deterrence.[14] The former seeks to measure the costs imposed by an activity without evaluating the moral value of the activity or the generator of it. It assumes that individuals decide how to behave by calculating the personal benefits of engaging in activities and balancing them against the costs that liability (general deterrence) will impose. It contemplates that different actors will respond to a liability rule in different ways. Specific deterrence, in contrast, evaluates particular activities, deciding which are wrongful or undesirable. These it prohibits *ex ante* and punishes *ex post*. As the prospect of punishment may affect future conduct, the question becomes one of how much deterrence is desired. If the 'price' of violations is set high enough, if anticipated damages accurately reflect the true cost of the violations and the sanction is certain, the 'product' will be priced off the market. This requires full and accurate compensation for each victim of each incident. The rational actor generates the cost-justified number of incidents when faced with the prospect of 'perfect' liability.

Although Calebresi discusses wrongfulness in his concept of specific deterrence, economic analysis in general is open to criticism for its lack of a moral dimension, treating human rights as merely another form of social bargaining and trade. Social utility, its sole normative foundation, is insufficiently justificatory and thus open to serious question. As Robin Malloy observes:

[b]y use of neoclassical economics, the conservatives reduce rights and obligations to numerical calculations and then proceed to balance countervailing claims by means of scientific equations. It is argued that an efficient result will maximize wealth and that wealth maximization produces the best attainable social arrangement. With the conservative vision of law and economics there is, therefore, no concept of inherent rights of the individual merely as a result of being a human being.[15]

Thus, slavery could be deemed permissible if efficient[16] and racial minorities treated as a neighbourhood 'nuisance' because of their depressive effect on land values. Judge Posner writes: 'In these circumstances some form of segregation would be wealth maximizing'.[17]

In other words, in neoclassical economic analysis, injuries to life and health are 'costs', as are sums expended to prevent wrongdoing, against which they are balanced, and its reasoning seeks to maximize the value of conflicting activities, calling on society to choose or allow the most 'efficient' behaviour. Critics point out that, in legal traditions where the notion of obligation is stronger than the notion of right (e.g., China), bargaining in self-interest may not be a correct assumption, undermining the economic construct.

---

[14] G. Calebresi and D. Melamed, 'Property Rules, Liability Rules, Inalienability: One View of the Cathedral', (1972) 85 *Harv. L.Rev.* 1089.

[15] Malloy, *supra* n. 10, at 60–61.

[16] R. Posner, *The Economics of Justice* (1983), 86, 102.

[17] *Ibid.*, at 84–85.

The neoclassical economic approach seems destined to allow wrongdoers to continue their harmful acts as long as they pay for the damage they cause; injuries are commensurable with money, a cost to the victim. Such a 'commodification' seems inappropriate for human rights discourse and practice because rights violations are often incommensurable. Compensation can only provide something equivalent in value to that which is lost; rectification or restitution restores precisely that which is taken. If what is taken from the victim is a chosen, specific pursuit, then having money to pursue another aim is not the same. Where the choices and values are incommensurable, a loss is sustained for which full compensation is impossible. Money does not replace a lost loved one and 'most people would not exchange their lives for anything less than an infinite sum of money if the exchange were to take place immediately'.[18] Posner's answer is that courts cannot pay infinite awards and must award 'reasonable' compensation, ignoring the value of the deceased's life to herself or himself. This exchange, of rights violation for money, may be seen as conflicting with the notion of 'inalienable' rights, but cannot be avoided when the loss has occurred and is irreparable. Yet, as Mark Yudoff has observed, 'society's interest in human dignity is so great that the recovery may exceed any plausible estimate of economic injury'.[19] Non-monetary remedies thus should be devised that encourage persons to bring suit to deter violations. This requires restitution where possible and defraying the costs of litigation, in addition to compensating for actual harm.

Economic analysis need not be viewed as inescapably in conflict with remedial justice and the moral basis for remedies. Indeed, Posner argues that the Aristotelian concept of corrective justice is compatible with, even required by, economic theory.[20] Both approaches provide a theoretical foundation for *why* damages must be afforded the individual victim. Compensatory justice further indicates the minimum that must be done to restore the moral order, while economic analysis provides a basis for evaluating the upper range of remedies, *how* remedies should be determined in order to protect the societal as well as the individual interest. The economic approach considers the impact of violations on society as a whole, aiming to deter violations through the adjustment of damage awards. In the human rights context, such an approach can help in calculating the amounts needed to uphold a treaty regime by adequately deterring state misconduct. It suggests that international tribunals may need to consider awarding far higher amounts of damages than have heretofore been adjudged.

---

[18] R. Posner, *Economic Analysis of Law*, 2nd edn. (1977), s. 6.12 at 197.

[19] M. Yudof, 'Liability for Constitutional Torts and the Risk-Averse Public School Official', (1976) 49 *S.Cal.L. Rev.* 1322, 1379–80.

[20] Posner, *supra* n. 11, at 188.

C. INTERNATIONAL LAW THEORIES

Reparation is the generic term that describes various methods available to a state to discharge or release itself from state responsibility for a breach of international law, i.e. to remedy an international wrong. The duty to provide reparation is itself an international obligation that arises upon the commission of an internationally wrongful act, because any breach of international law causes moral injury to the state whose interests have been infringed.[21] As Anzilotti put it:

A violation of a rule always constitutes trespass upon the interest which the rule protects and, consequently, upon the subjective right of the person whose interest is affected; in international relations, the injury caused is generally moral (failure to respect the honor and dignity of the state as a juridical person) rather than material (financial or patrimonial injury in the true sense of the term).[22]

In its judgment concerning the *Chorzow Factory (Indemnity) Case*, the Permanent Court of International Justice called the obligation to make reparation for breach of an engagement 'a general principle of international law' and 'a general conception of law'.[23]

1. The purposes and kinds of reparations

A basic purpose of international reparations essentially mirrors that of the law of remedies generally: to make good the injury caused to persons or property by a wrongful act. Grotius described the Aristotelian theory by which damage should be made good in private injuries, defining damage as having less than belongs to a person. 'By nature a man's life is his own, not indeed to destroy, but to safeguard; also his own are his body, limbs, reputation, honor and acts of his will'.[24] When any of these is wronged, the law gives particular rights which both the state and individual citizens can demand. In inter-state relations, according to Vattel, every state has the right to obtain complete reparation when an injury is done.[25] Thus, reparations must seek to place the injured state where it would have been at the moment of judgment if the injury had not occurred. Eagleton similarly asserts that the ideal form of reparation is the restoration of the situation exactly as it was before the injury.[26] Where restitution or rectification is not possible, substitute remedies, including damages, are required. In fact, monetary compensation is the most common form of reparation because, as Grotius says, 'money

---

[21] F.V. Garcia-Amador, *The Changing Law of International Claims* (1984), vol. 2, 567.

[22] D. Anzilotti, *Teoria Generale Della Responsabilita Dello Stato Nel Diritto Internazionale* (1902), 13–14.

[23] *Factory at Chorzów (Germany v. Poland)* 1928 P.C.I.J. (ser. A) No. 17 at 29 (September 13).

[24] H. Grotius, *De Jure Belli Ac Pacis Libri Tres*, (Kelsey trans., 1925), vol. II, ch. XVII, 430–31.

[25] Vattel, *The Law of Nations*, 7th edn. (1849), bk II, s. 51.

[26] C. Eagleton, 'Measure of Damages in International Law', (1929) 39 *Yale L.J.* 52, 53.

is the common measure of valuable things'.[27] The amount of compensation must correspond to the value of restitution in kind.

Arbitral tribunals frequently restate the theory that reparation 'must wipe out all the consequences' of the illegal act. In the *Lusitania* cases, the arbiter Parker stated that the 'remedy must be commensurate with the injury received . . . The compensation must be adequate and balance as near as may be the injury suffered'.[28] These cases also noted the imprecision and difficulty of measuring damages. Personnaz argues that this difficulty means that reparations should not be understood as demanding restoration of the *status quo ante*, which is impossible, but should afford an equivalent to that which has been lost.[29] In most cases this will require both partial restitution and pecuniary damages.

International remedies serve an additional purpose. In the absence of a collective sanctioning or enforcement authority, the injured party claiming reparations acts to uphold the public interest or legal order by punishing and deterring wrongdoing. Vattel asserts that 'the offended party have [*sic*] a right to provide for their future security, and to chastise the offender, by inflicting upon him a punishment capable of deterring him thenceforward from similar aggressions, and of intimidating those who might be tempted to imitate him'.[30] Garcia-Amador similarly claims that the concept of reparation in international law traditionally has included both a compensatory element (restitution or damages) and a punitive one (satisfaction). He views satisfaction as punitive because the scope of this form of reparation is determined more by the nature of the wrongful act than by the injury actually caused.[31] Indeed, he asserts that satisfaction 'is essentially and invariably penal in character'.[32] Thus, an injured state may ask for punishment of the wrongdoer[33] and 'all other suitable redress' to ensure deterrence, as well as an apol-

---

[27] H. Grotius, *supra* n. 24, at 437.   [28] *Lusitania Cases*, 7 R.I.A.A. 35, 36.

[29] J. Personnaz, *La Reparation Du Prejudice En Droit International* (1938), 197–98.

[30] Vattel, *supra* n. 25, at bk. II, s. 52.

[31] Garcia-Amador, *supra* n. 21, at 559.

[32] Garcia-Amador, *supra* n. 21, at 575. Nonetheless, the notion of strictly punitive damages is controversial. Jimenez de Arechega disapproves, finding them 'incompatible with the basic idea of reparation. Imposition of such damages goes beyond the jurisdiction conferred on the International Court of Justice by its Statute and that normally attributed to arbitral tribunals, which are not invested "with a repressive power" ': Eduardo Jimenez de Arechega and Attila Tanzi, *International State Responsibility'* in M. Bedjaoui (ed.), *International Law: Achievements and Prospects* (1991), 347, 369, citing Jimenez de Arechaga, 'International Responsibility' in M. Søerensen (ed.), *Manual of Public International Law* (1968), 549, 571.

[33] Punishment of individual perpetrators was given formal recognition in the work of the Preparatory Committee of the Hague Conference of 1930. The Basis of Discussion Draft 29 says: 'Responsibility involves for the State concerned an obligation to make good the damage suffered in so far as it results from failure to comply with the international obligation. It may also, according to the circumstances, and when this consequence follows from the general principles of international law, involve the obligation to afford satisfaction to the State which has been injured . . . , in the shape of an apology (given with the appropriate solemnity) and (in proper cases) the punishment of the guilty persons': League of Nations Publ. (1929) at 151. The Basis of Discussion draft substantially reproduced the text of Article 10 of a prior draft produced by the Institut de Droit Internationale at its 1927 session. See II Y.B. Int'l L. Comm'n 228 (1956).

ogy.[34] In cases of egregious harm, the principle of proportionality[35] may permit an increase in the award of damages in satisfaction (punitive damages) due to the degree of misconduct by the defendant state.[36]

Satisfaction is used not only to punish; it functions to redress moral, immaterial, or non-pecuniary damage caused by a state, including disrespect and impairing a state's dignity and honour. Measures of satisfaction operate to acknowledge the wrong and express regret, similar to the purpose served by nominal or moral damages in national legal systems. Anzilotti posits, however, that in every case 'there is invariably an element of satisfaction and an element of reparation, the idea of punishing the wrongful act and that of making good the damage sustained; what varies is, rather, the relative proportion of the two elements'.[37] Brigitte Stern argues against monetary compensation as satisfaction for a legal wrong. In her view, a legal remedy is required and pecuniary measures should be reserved for pecuniary losses, i.e. the nature of the remedy should conform to the nature of the harm.[38] In practice, the logical distinction has not been followed; in the absence of legal restitution, money frequently is paid as satisfaction to deter future misconduct and sanction the wrong. Satisfaction also can consist of apologies, missions of expiation, the construction of monuments,[39] or a judicial declaration of the unlawful character of an act, if the nature of the harm does not demand more.[40]

The International Law Commission has completed the first reading of its draft articles on the obligations of a state whose responsibility has been engaged because of injury to another state. The provisions on reparations include requirements of cessation of wrongful conduct (Article 6), reparation (Article 6bis), restitution in kind (Article 7), compensation (Article 8), satisfaction (Article 10), and assurances and guarantees of non-repetition (Article 10bis).[41] Taken together these forms of action can provide full reparation. Restitution in kind is defined as

---

[34] J. B. Moore, (1916) 5 *Digest of International Law* 41; see also (1916) 6 *Digest of International Law* 857; Garcia-Amador *supra* n. 21, at 569–70; P. A. Bissonnette, *La Satisfaction Comme Mode de Reparation en Droit International* (1952), 55–61.

[35] See R. Wolfrum, 'Reparation for Internationally Wrongful Acts', (1987) 10 *Encyclopedia of Public International Law* 351 (hereinafter EPIL); Art. 2, International Law Commission's Third Report on State Responsibility, UN Doc. A/CN.4/354, Adds 1, 2.

[36] E. Riedel, 'Damages', (1987)10 EPIL 70.

[37] Anzilotti, *supra* n. 22 at 425.

[38] 'Théoriquement la "relaxation" du préjudice juridique devrait consister soit dans le rétablissement de l'ordre juridique violé, par l'annulation de l'acte juridique non conforme au droit international—soit de restitutio in integrum—, soit si ce rétablissement du statu quo n'est pas ou n'est plus possible, dans la declaration du caractère illicite de l'acte matériel ou juridique incriminé, par un jugement déclaratif qui constitue une sorte de reparation par équivalent . . . De toutes faces, la relaxation pécuniaire devrait entre reservé au dommage matériel': B. Bolecker-Stern, *La Préjudice dans la Théorie de la Responsibilité Internationale* (1973), 34.

[39] E. Riedel, 'Satisfaction', in (1987)10 EPIL 383.

[40] *Corfu Channel Case (Merits)*, [1949] I.C.J. Rep.1, at 35.

[41] Report of the International Law Commission on the Work of Its Forty-Fourth Session, A/47/10, para. 12; A/CN.4/L/472.

the re-establishment of the situation that existed before the wrongful act was committed. Compensation is to be provided, where restitution is impossible or inadequate, for any economically assessable damage sustained by the injured party. Importantly, satisfaction, in particular moral damage, is to be obtained if and to the extent necessary to provide full reparation and may take the form of (a) an apology, (b) nominal damages, (c) in case of gross infringement of rights, damages reflecting the gravity of the infringement, (d) in cases of serious misconduct or criminal conduct, disciplinary action or punishment of those responsible (Article 10).

2. The uniqueness of human rights cases

The legal basis for state responsibility for violations of human rights derives from breach of a human rights treaty or a human rights norm of customary international law.[42] Most human rights treaties impose a duty on states parties to respect and ensure the rights recognized, a formulation that imposes a due diligence obligation to respond to violations committed by private persons as well as to abstain from state-authored violations.[43]

The nature of human rights obligations is different from that of most other rights and duties in international law. Treaty and customary obligations generally are reciprocal or contractual in nature. Treaty partners confer equal benefits on each other and accept equal duties in return. In consequence, most acts in breach of a treaty cause direct and usually immediate injury to the interests of another state. The state committing the wrongful act incurs state responsibility and the duty to make reparations for the harm caused. In contrast, human rights obligations have 'the purpose of guaranteeing the enjoyment of individual human beings of those rights and freedoms rather than to establish reciprocal relations between States'.[44] As the Inter-American Court has emphasized:

modern human rights treaties in general . . . are not multilateral treaties of the traditional type concluded to accomplish the reciprocal exchange of rights for the mutual benefit of the contracting States. Their object and purpose is the protection of the basic rights of individual human beings, irrespective of their nationality, both against the State of their nationality and all other contracting States. In concluding these human rights treaties, the States can be deemed to submit themselves to a legal order within which they, for the common

---

[42] The Restatement (Third) of the Foreign Relations Law of the United States, s. 702 says that a state violates customary international law if, as a matter of state policy, it practises, encourages, or condones (a) genocide, (b) slavery or slave trading, (c) the murder or disappearance of individuals, (d) torture or other cruel, inhuman, or degrading treatment or punishment, (e) prolonged arbitrary detention, (f) systematic racial discrimination, or (g) a consistent pattern of violations of internationally recognized human rights.

[43] See D. Shelton, 'Private Violence, Public Wrongs, and the Responsibility of States', (1989–90) 13 *Fordham Int'l L.J.* 1.

[44] *Other Treaties Subject to the Advisory Jurisdiction of the Court* (Article 64 ACHR), (1982) 1 Inter-Am.Ct Hum.Rts, (ser. A), (1982) 3 H.R.L.J. 140.

good, assume various obligations, not in relation to other States, but towards all individuals within their jurisdiction.[45]

Traditional inter-state responsibility for breaches of international law, designed for reciprocal obligations, thus does not correspond exactly to the needs of the objective human rights regime. For example, when the state committing the breach does not directly injure another state, an issue arises of standing to make a claim.

The International Law Commission has responded to this problem by expanding the concept of 'injured state' when the breach concerns a multilateral treaty or rule of customary international law created or established for the protection of human rights and fundamental freedoms.[46] Every other state party to the convention or bound by the relevant rule is deemed affected by the interests protected by human rights provisions; hence all must be considered injured states in case of a breach of obligation.[47]

The approach of the ILC is based upon international law doctrine that distinguishes inter-state obligations from those due to the international community as a whole. Human rights obligations are among the latter as declared by the International Court of Justice in the *Case Concerning the Barcelona Traction, Light and Power Company, Ltd.*:

[A]n essential distinction should be drawn between obligations of a State towards the international community as a whole, and those arising vis a vis another State in the field of diplomatic protection. By their very nature the former concern all States. In view of the importance of the rights involved, all States can be held to have a legal interest in their protection; they are obligations *erga omnes*. Such obligations derive, for example, in contemporary international law, from the outlawing of acts of aggression and of genocide, and also from the principles and rules concerning the basic rights of the human person, including protection from slavery and racial discrimination. Some of the corresponding rights of protection have entered into the body of general international law; others are conferred by international instruments of a universal or quasi-universal character.[48]

Thus, human rights obligations are obligations *erga omnes*, and all states have the right to vindicate them.

State responsibility for breaches of human rights obligations particularly concerns states participating in the legal order created by a multilateral human rights treaty. Within the European system, the European Commission has stated that a party claiming a violation of the European Convention by another state party is not enforcing its own rights, or the rights of its nationals, but vindicating

---

[45] *The Effect of Reservations on the Entry into Force of the ACHR* (Articles 74 and 75), (1982) 2 Inter-Am. Ct Hum.Rts. (ser. A) (1982) 3 H.R.L.J. 153.

[46] Draft Articles on State Responsibility, Pt.2, article 5, para. 2(e)(iii), 1985 Y.B. Int'l L. Comm'n, vol. II (Part II), at 24–25.

[47] Commentary on Draft Articles on State Responsibility, pt. 2, article 5, para. 2(f), Yearbook of the International Law Commission 1985, vol. II (Part II), para. 20, p. 27.

[48] *Barcelona Traction, Light and Power Company, Ltd. (Belgium v. Spain)* 1970 I.C.J. 4, at 32.

the public order of Europe.[49] Similarly, the Inter-American Court has referred to the obligations owed by all contracting states which have submitted themselves 'to a legal order' for the protection of human rights. Despite this public policy, it is rare to find inter-state human rights complaints invoking the law of state responsibility[50] because states often view the political and economic costs of complaints as too high in the absence of a specific injury. In addition, accusations of human rights violations may be deemed unfriendly acts.

A second problem in the law of state responsibility lies in the traditional right of the injured state to take proportionate counter-measures in retaliation for the breach. It is impossible to accept the system of counter-measures in regard to human rights obligations, however; one state's commission of torture never can justify similar brutality on the part of another state. Accordingly, international human rights law has created innovative compliance mechanisms that respect the unique character of human rights treaties. Supervisory organs oversee the implementation of human rights obligations by states parties and act to uphold the international community interest in ensuring the effectiveness of the treaty regime. The most appropriate procedure is that which allows victims to seek remedies for injuries resulting from human rights violations. Although these procedures generally are created by human rights treaties, the international institutions applying them often return to the law of state responsibility to assess the nature and extent of the remedies available to the victims.

The collective or *erga omnes* nature of human rights obligations has implications in the area of remedies. It requires that the supervisory organs in human rights systems ensure that the remedies afforded not only protect the individual litigant but serve to deter violations and uphold the legal order that the treaties create. Concern for victims not part of the litigation, as well as for potential victims, must be among the factors taken into account in affording remedies. The traditional concept of satisfaction can be useful in this regard with its focus on deterrence and guarantees of non-repetition.

In redressing human rights violations it must be recognized as well that actions against the state, whether undertaken in a national or international forum, differ from private proceedings, and for a number of reasons.[51] First, there is the added importance of ensuring the rule of law by institutions created in large part for that purpose.

In a government of laws, the existence of the government will be imperilled if it fails to observe the law scrupulously . . . For good or ill, it teaches the whole people by its example. Crime is contagious. If the government becomes a lawbreaker, it breeds contempt for law; it invites every man to become a law unto himself; it invites anarchy.[52]

---

[49] *Austria v. Italy*, Application No. 788/60, 1961 Y.B. Eur. Conv. on H.R. 116 (Eur. Comm'n on H.R.). See also *Ireland v. United Kingdom*, (1978) 25 Eur.Ct.H.R. (ser. A), 91.

[50] In the European human rights system only 12 inter-state cases have been brought since the treaty entered into force. No inter-state cases have been submitted to the Inter-American or African Commissions on Human Rights or at the United Nations treaty bodies.

[51] Peter Schuck, *Suing Government: Citizen Remedies for Official Wrongs* (1983).

[52] *Olmstead v. United States*, 277 U.S. 438, 485 (Brandeis, J., dissenting).

Thus, society as well as the individual victim is injured when human rights are violated.

The denial of a remedy in human rights cases can have a particularly negative impact on the judiciary. Continued respect for and acceptance of the exercise of judicial power depends on preserving the perceived and actual fairness and integrity of the system.[53] 'The absence of an affirmative vision of the judicial role that responds to concerns about fairness and proper allocation of governmental power fuels the political and theoretical attack on legitimacy, which in turn contributes to a public perception of judicial illegitimacy'.[54] To develop and enhance institutional competence and legitimacy, remedies against the state are thus not only necessary but necessarily different from, and greater than, those appropriate in private law tort actions. In this regard, '[t]he remedies that individuals may invoke against governmental wrongdoing inevitably reflect some normative conception of the relationship between citizen and state, some notion of the legal and political obligations that they owe one another'.[55]

Human rights violations committed by the state are qualitatively different from private injury because of the motives and nature of the conduct as well as the identity of the wrongdoer. Individuals expect protection from the state; indeed, one of its fundamental purposes is to provide the institutional and other means to ensure the safety and well-being of those within its power.[56] For the government itself to cause harm adds an element of outrage generally not present in purely private wrongdoing. The Inter American Court of Human Rights recognized the profound impact that such violations can have. In the *Loayza Tomayo v. Peru (Reparations)*[57] decision, it pointed out that the very existence and conditions of life of a person are altered by unfairly and arbitrarily imposed government actions taken in violation of existing norms and the trust that is placed in the hands of public power, whose duty is to protect and provide security in order for individuals to exercise their rights and satisfy their legitimate personal interests. The remedies afforded should reflect the breach of trust involved, because, in general, the more outrageous the wrongdoer's conduct, the more outraged and distressed the victim will be and the more the harm that will be suffered.[58]

When the state has committed human rights violations, remedies can provide the important psychological and social functions of reintegration and rehabilitation of

---

[53] S. Sturm, 'A Normative Theory of Public Law Remedies', (1991) 79 *Geo.L.J.* 1357.

[54] *Ibid.,* at 1403.

[55] Schuck, *supra* n. 51 at 29.

[56] J. Locke, *Two Treatises of Government* (G. Rutledge (ed.), 1857), vol. II, s. 127–31. R. Pound, *Social Control Through Law* (1942), 25.

[57] *Loayza Tomayo v. Peru*, judgment of 27 November 1998, (1998) 43 Inter-Am.Ct.H.R. (ser. C).

[58] D. Dobbs, *Handbook on the Law of Remedies* (1986), s. 7.3(2) at 310.

the victimized.[59] Victims of governmental abuse often are blamed for their victimization or avoided because of the horrific nature of the stories they have to tell. Bystanders' guilt may also lead to rejecting the victims. Not infrequently, the social reaction is indifference or avoidance leading to a silence that is detrimental to the victims, producing isolation and mistrust. Children of victims may adopt these reactions and themselves become victims over time. The need to readapt to normal society and return to pre-victim ways of being and functioning is crucial, even if not entirely realizable. Cognitive recovery involves the ability to develop a realistic perspective of what happened, by whom, and to whom, and to accept the reality that events happened the way they did, in an impersonal unfolding. The Latin American Institute of Mental Health and Human Rights in Santiago, Chile, emphasizes that individual therapy is not enough, that victims 'need to know that their society as a whole acknowledges what has happened to them . . . Social reparation is thus . . . simultaneously a socio-political and a psychological process. It aims to establish the truth of political repression and demands justice for the victims . . . both through the judicial process and through the availability of health and mental health services'.[60] In this context, compensation can become a symbolic act, signifying vindication and a government's admission of wrong-doing or apology. Money is the tangible confirmation of responsibility. Of course, other forms of remedy are also important to this goal, including, in particular, rituals and commemorations of those injured.

Like remedies in private law cases, human rights remedies also must aim to deter behaviour that presents a danger that exceeds its social value.[61] In this regard, it may be necessary to augment the level of the remedy when there is corporate or institutional rather than individual responsibility in order to deter unlawful conduct. The level of award that would serve to deter an individual is likely to be inadequate when the state is the defendant, because any compensation awarded will be paid from the public treasury which has resources far beyond those of individual wrongdoers. The level of the award or the nature of the remedy must be such that the state is deterred and not permitted to purchase an option to continue violating human rights.

Remedies also express opprobrium to the wrongdoer. This is usually incorporated in the application of punishment, sometimes as a vindication of society's

---

[59] On the psychological impact of human rights violations, see Y. Danieli in *Seminar on the Right to Restitution, Compensation and Rehabilitation for Victims of Gross Violations of Human Rights and Fundamental Freedoms* (SIM Special No. 12), at 196; Y. Danieli, 'On the Achievement of Integration in Aging Survivors of the Nazi Holocaust', (1981) 14 *Journal of Geriatric Psychiatry* 191; R.K. Kordon, L.I. Edelman, D.M. Lagos, E. Nicoletti and R.C. Bozzolo, *Psychological Effects of Political Repression* (1988).

[60] D. Becker, E. Lira, M.I. Castillo, E. Gomez, and J. Kovalskys, 'Therapy with Victims of Political Repression in Chile: The Challenge of Social Reparation', (1990) 40 *Journal of Social Issues* 133, 147–48.

[61] C. Gregory, H. Kalven and R. Epstein, *Cases and Materials on Torts,* 3rd edn. (1977), xxii–xxiii; R. Posner, *Economic Analysis of Law,* 2nd. edn., (1977), s.6.16, 154–57.

interest in retribution, or it can take the form of fines or exemplary or punitive damages.[62] Sanctions express the social conviction that disrespect for the rights of others impairs the wrongdoer's status as a moral claimant.[63] Remedies and sanctions thus affirm, reinforce, and reify the fundamental values of society.

Impunity, particularly governmental immunity that leaves human rights victims without a remedy, calls into serious question the integrity of human rights norms and the rule of law.[64] If the primary purpose of rights is to affect the distribution of power between individual and state—specifically, to protect individuals from the abuse of state power—then rights without remedies are ineffectual for this purpose. The government's duty to respect such rights then would be illusory. Even the symbolic value of rights could disappear once it became obvious that rights could be violated with impunity. The structural limits on the powers of government would exist only in the unlikely event that those with governmental power did not seek to aggrandize it.

If society as a whole is injured by human rights violations, so also may society as a whole benefit from public remedies. Any action the state is required to take to remedy human rights violations will likely have effects beyond the individual plaintiff. Remedies for public wrongs must be seen, then, as serving not only private redress but public policy, as an important means of promoting compliance with the human rights norm.[65] In a broad sense, actions against the state test the reasonableness of the state's activity in its context, the need to protect society, and the fairness of allowing the victim's damage to go unredressed; and in so doing they give rise to several critical, even competing, considerations: how serious is the injury to the particular person; how should others similarly situated be treated; can workable standards of conduct be formulated; is there a social interest in permitting the conduct; what burdens would be imposed by judicial intervention; does the remedy interfere with other values; is such a remedy necessary to protect the interests in question; and, finally, is the remedy too effective in that it acts to dissuade permitted behaviour?

The problems of potentially conflicting interests can be seen in human rights cases that concern widespread and long-standing violations. Constructing a remedy is often more difficult than determining the liability. For example, human rights norms establish that prisons must meet minimum standards, but they do not indicate the appropriate remedy when there has been a failure of compliance by

---

[62] W. Prosser, *Handbook of the Law of Torts*, 4th edn. (1971), s. 2, 9–10.

[63] See generally L. Lomasky, *Persons, Rights and the Moral Community* (1967), 141–47; J, Chapman (ed.), *Compensatory Justice* (1991).

[64] See H. Packer, *The Limits of the Criminal Sanction* (1968), 287 ('respect for law generally is likely to suffer if it is widely known that certain kinds of conduct, although nominally criminal, can be practised with relative impunity').

[65] S. Sturm, *supra* n. 53.

the state. In the face of possibly irreparable injuries, the courts may be unwilling to allow monetary compensation to justify continued toleration of the wrong.[66] Negative injunctions also cannot be used in some cases for other reasons; release of prisoners due to poor prison conditions is generally not an acceptable remedy, nor is paying the prisoners compensation and allowing the violation to continue.

More comprehensive and long-term approaches may be needed. Owen Fiss introduced the term 'structural injunction' into United States civil rights litigation to indicate the broad reforms ordered in cases of this type.[67] When such measures and other alternatives fail to improve prison conditions, courts may order the release of inmates.[68] The choice of remedy may be driven by conceptions of good management, financial resources, control, and the proper goals of punishment, as much as by the liability norm.

It has been suggested that, because they serve to 'realize' legal norms, remedies in human rights actions against the state constitute 'the area of judicial activity that most clearly embodies the tension between the ideal and the real'.[69] From this perspective, the question of possible non-compliance becomes important, including whether the ideal should adjust to the reality of popular opposition to a legal rule.[70] The response by a tribunal may depend on whether it adopts a rights-maximizing approach or one of interest-balancing.

Interest-balancing considers the efficiency in achieving a remedy as one of several social interests that must be considered. Others interests taken into account include the effects on persons who bear the costs of the remedy. In the USA, the Supreme Court sometimes has called for remedying rights violations 'to the greatest possible degree ... taking into account the practicalities of the situation',[71] and it has spoken of reconciling public and private needs.[72] In *Milliken v. Bradley* (Milliken II)[73] the Court stated that remedies 'must be designed as nearly as possible to restore the victims of discriminatory conduct to the position they would have occupied in the absence of such conduct,' but also must 'take into account the interests of state and local authorities in managing

---

[66]   See *Zepeda v. United States Immigration & Naturalization Serv.*, 703 F.2d 719, 727 (8th Cir. 1985) (injury resulting from INS violations of fourth amendment rights 'could not be compensated adequately by money damages').

[67]   O. Fiss, *The Civil Rights Injunction* (1978) at 7.

[68]   See *Inmates of Allegheny County Jail v. Wecht*, 573 F. Supp. 454, 457–58 (W.D. Penn. 1983).

[69]   P. Gewirtz, 'Remedies and Resistance', (1983) 92 *Yale L.J.* 585.

[70]   In *Worcester v. Georgia*, 31 U.S. (6 Pet.) 515 (1832) the United States Supreme Court found the State of Georgia's conviction and sentence of four year's confinement of Samuel Worcester to be unconstitutional. The State of Georgia never did carry out the Supreme Court's decision and the plaintiff remained in a Georgia prison under a law which the Supreme Court had declared to be unconstitutional: F. Cohen, *Handbook of Federal Indian Law* (1942), 123. See also *Martin v. Hunter's Lessee*, 13 U.S. (1 Wheat.) 304 (1816).

[71]   *Davis v. Board of School Comm'rs*, 402 U.S. 33, 37 (1971).

[72]   *Brown v. Board of Educ.* 349 U.S. 294, 300 (1955).

[73]   *Milliken v. Bradley*, 433 U.S. 267, 280–81 (1977).

their own affairs'. Thus, remedies may be limited to avoid compelling action unnecessary to cure the violation.[74]

It may be asked whether costs ever should play a limiting role in affording remedies. Alan Gewirtz[75] suggests that it is appropriate to consider conflicting interests that are not taken into account at the rights stage (interests that are not relevant to the question of whether a right has been violated) but ones that are relevant at the remedy stage and may even, on occasion, override the value of remedying violations of the right.[76] When the violation was long-lasting and broad in scope, and therefore had widespread effects, the potential scope of a remedy creates pressure to accept constraints on relief.[77] An effective remedy is often not possible without imposing significant and direct costs on selected third parties who are non-violators. All enterprise liability, however, imposes costs that are shared among the members of the group who are neither wrongdoers nor distinctive beneficiaries of prior wrongs.

Balancing may lead to undervaluing individual rights if the 'costs' being evaluated include the risk of non-compliance. It has been suggested that, in the landmark desegregation case of *Brown v. Board of Education*,[78] the United States Supreme Court allowed delay in affording the remedy in part to accommodate opposition to the decision, deferring to those violating the very right it had proclaimed.[79] Immediate enforcement might have exacerbated opposition; on the other hand a strong Court opinion might also have inspired greater public co-operation and accommodation to remedy clearly imposed dignitary harms.

In theory, damage awards can play an important role in reducing rights violations by forcing officials to internalize the costs of their wrongful conduct and deterring illegal conduct when the expected costs exceed the expected benefits.[80] The injuries caused by public law violations frequently are intangible, symbolic, and difficult to measure, however; damages often undervalue the rights, and paying to violate is cheaper than compliance. If tribunals seek to maximize the value of the rights being protected, they should afford a remedy that will be the most effective in redressing harm to the victims as well as successfully eliminating the adverse consequences of the violations.

D. CONCLUSIONS

The remedial task is to convert law into results, to deter violations and restore the moral balance when wrongs are committed. The human rights litigant typically

---

[74] A. Katz, 'The Jurisprudence of Remedies: Constitutional Legality and the Law of Torts in Bell v. Hood', (1968) 117 *U. Penn. L.Rev.* 1.
[75] Gewirtz, *supra* n. 69.
[76] *Ibid.,* at 604.
[77] See Chapter 12 on Gross and Systematic Violations.
[78] *Brown v. Board of Educ., supra* n. 72.
[79] Gewirtz, *supra* n. 69.
[80] R. Posner, *Economic Analysis of the Law supra* n. 18 at 147–97.

seeks to have government conduct declared wrongful and to have a remedy imposed against the state, even where the act or omission is based on the will of the majority expressed in legislation. In the range of remedies, relatively non-intrusive remedies, such as declaratory judgments and damages, may give way to injunctions, prohibitions and affirmative orders. The declaratory judgment merely pronounces a particular practice or condition to be illegal, leaving officials free to choose if and how to remedy the situation. The damage award assesses the harm that the misconduct has caused and imposes the cost upon wrongdoer. All relief seeks to create a hypothetical: the situation 'as if' the wrongdoer had not violated the rights of the victim.

As compensation is the most common remedy, every legal system should strive for certainty in calculating damages to avoid under- or over-compensating a victim. Uncertainty and arbitrariness in awards undermines respect for the law; legal certainty represents one of modern jurisprudence's central concerns as the law searches for order and predictability. The rule of law implies that society administers justice by fixing standards that individuals may determine prior to controversy and that reasonably guarantee all individuals like treatment. Accurate assessment also is necessary because inadequate or excessive awards frustrate the compensatory, retributive and deterrent functions of the law.

The prevalence of compensation as a remedy should not diminish consideration of the need for other kinds of redress. When rights are infringed, someone has been victimized because of an unwarranted act of interference and can therefore justifiably reclaim his or her prior position. This focus on the victim demands provision of something equivalent in value to that which was lost, or restoring precisely that which was removed. The primary goal of human rights remedies should be rectification or restitution rather than compensation. When rights are violated, the ability of the victim to pursue self-determination is impaired and it is not justifiable generally to assume that compensation restores the moral balance *ex ante*. A morally adequate response addresses itself in the first instance to restoring what was taken.

The Latin maxim *ubi jus ibi remedium* (for the violation of every right, there must be a remedy) is not, and perhaps cannot be, strictly observed in practice. Rights have gone unremedied in the past, and likely as not some will go unremedied in the future. Yet, many remedies that national judicial bodies were once reluctant to impose, because they were perceived to exceed the judicial power or believed to be simply unenforceable, are now taken for granted, such as injunctions. The question is not, however, whether every right has a remedy, but whether every right should have one. Many writers include the element of enforceability in their definition of legal rights,[81] because rights entails a correlative duty to act

---

[81] See M. Ginsberg, *On Justice in Society* (1965), 74; I. Jenkins, *Social Order and the Limits of Law* (1980), 247.

or refrain from acting for the benefit of another person.[82] Unless a duty is some-how enforced, it is only a voluntary obligation that can be fulfilled or ignored at will.

The theories of remedies just discussed have been applied by national and international courts throughout the world. The range of remedies the courts afford indicates a general concern for compensation, rehabilitation, deterrence and punishment. The surveys of national and international decisions that follow show how these theories are put into practice.

---

[82]   W. Hohfeld, *Fundamental Legal Conceptions* (W. Cook (ed.), 1919), 38.

3

Remedies in National Law

Remedies for international human rights violations serve purposes similar to those of remedies in national law.[1] It is thus appropriate and probably inevitable that international tribunals draw upon national law, as well as international law, to develop remedies. In turn, as national tribunals hear and decide more cases alleging violations of international human rights norms, they look to international law, including the object and purpose of human rights agreements and the jurisprudence of international tribunals. The result is a complex interplay and mutual influence of national and international law, both public and private.

Remedial rules on the national level are intertwined with legal procedure and the social, historical, economical, and technological environment of the legal system. State liability in most legal systems has been built on the framework of tort law which everywhere addresses the same set of problems: the foundation of liability, causation, justifications or excuses, and remoteness of damage. The relatively homogeneous framework of remedies, including declaratory relief, damages, restitution, specific performance and injunction, is founded on considerations of compensatory justice, deterrence, punishment, and the relationship with other systems of compensation, such as insurance and welfare.

The compensatory goal may differ from the aim of deterrence and lead to different forms of relief. Remedies may compensate without deterring (insurance) or deter without compensating (fines). Generally, 'there is probably widespread agreement that loss-spreading through compensation is singularly justified when citizens are injured through no fault of their own by officials whose capacity (and perhaps even motivation) to injure has been created by the public for public ends'.[2] In public law, however, private law notions such as enterprise liability, contractual risk-shifting, strict liability, punitive damages, and efficiency have been slow to take root and compensation of victims often has been subordinated to other goals. Still, there is a growing view that damages against large entities must be correlated to the magnitude and capacity for harm of the entity to have a deterrent effect.[3]

---

[1] Burlington N., Inc. v. Boxberger, 29 F.2d 284, 291 (9th Cir. 1975) (compensatory damages should restore injured persons to the status they would have had in the absence of injury). See generally, D. Laycock, *Modern American Remedies: Cases and Materials*, 2nd edn. (1994). The primary purpose of remedies, as discussed *supra* in Chapter 2, is to provide redress to an injured party for the wrong done. Giving victims redress restores their rightful position by enabling them to replace the thing they lost, with damages serving as a substitution for restitution. Where market value exists (e.g. for injury to property) there is little problem with a money substitute. Where the loss is of something unique, however, valuation may be difficult and even the concept of value may be dubious.

[2] Peter Schuck, *Suing Government: Citizen Remedies for Official Wrongs* (1983), 23.

[3] See the *M.C. Mehta* case, 1987 AIR (SC) 1086.

The current chapter provides an overview of national remedies against the state for wrongs done by it or its agents, providing examples from different regions and different legal traditions. The first section gives a brief description of the evolution of legal remedies. The main objective of the chapter is to identify the general principles of the law of remedies on which international and national judges draw in deciding human rights cases. The specific content and scope of the various remedies are discussed in more detail in later chapters.

A. THE EVOLUTION OF THE LAW OF REMEDIES

Early legal systems unified the goals of redress, deterrence, and punishment, failing to distinguish between public and private law when an individual committed a wrong; punishment of the perpetrator and justice for the victim usually were merged through victim self-help encouraged or regulated by law. Retaliation, a form of negative restitution by equivalence, was permitted by several ancient codes, including the Code of Hammurabi,[4] Mosaic,[5] and Roman law.[6]

It has been suggested that the law of remedies developed in legal systems to replace private revenge.[7] Roman law came to permit wrongdoers in certain cases to

---

[4] The Code of Hammurabi proclaimed: 'If you cause the loss of an eye, your eye shall be taken. If you shatter a limb, your limb shall be shattered, but if it is a poor man's eye or limb you may pay money. If you cause loss of a tooth, your tooth comes out': Code of Laws promulgated by Hammurabi, King of Babylon B.C. 2285–2242 in C.H.W. Johns, *The Oldest Code of Laws in the World* (1903), 43.

[5] In Mosaic law the penalties for wrongs under the *lex talonis* are based on return for what has been done: death for death, eye for eye, tooth for tooth, hand for hand: Exodus 21: 23–25.

[6] The Roman Twelve Tables provided compensation for unintentional killing, but for homicide 'the killer, once the fact of killing had been determined by a court, was left to the revenge of the victim's kinsmen'. The penalty of retaliation (*talio*) was exacted for serious physical injury while a fixed financial penalty was imposed for less serious harm; the amount depended on the nature of the injury: G. MacCormack, 'Revenge and Compensation in Early Law', (1973) 21 *Am.J.Comp.L.* 69, 72. In cases not covered by a statutory amount, compensation was provided with the amount depending on the nature of the injury, the character of the injured, and the general surrounding circumstances: see R.W. Leage, *Roman Private Law* (1937), 377. Medical expenses and loss of employment also were considered in cases not involving death: *ibid.* at 381. Vicarious liability of employers for acts of their employees also existed.

[7] For a study of this thesis, see G. MacCormack, *supra* n. 6 The author uses two approaches to early law, evaluation of archaic society from recorded history and study of contemporary primitive societies. *Contra* D. Daube, *Studies in Biblical Law* (1948), 102 *et seq*, 116 *et seq*, 128, who argues that revenge and compensation are equal in age and that the principle of revenge is itself incorporated as an element of compensation. It has been suggested that Islamic decision-makers in Africa turned to compensation because of difficulty in determining the exact retribution due in applying the law of retaliation: J.N.D. Andersen, *Islamic Law in Africa* (1970), 201. The concept of restitution by equivalent can be seen in such early local customs as the Nigerian requirement that a deliberate killer had to supply a boy to serve as son to the parents of the deceased. The accidental killer need only supply a goat for sacrifice: *ibid.* at 203. Maliki law had a tariff for wounds, determined by asking how the injury would affect the market value of a slave with like damage. Tables were used in some cases, with values for damage to different parts of the body. Certain grave losses of faculties were valued as equivalent to death: F.H. Ruxton, *Maliki Law* (1916), 312. According to Ruxton, at least one Islamic school

pay compensation in money or in kind. The offer of the appropriate amount excluded the right to take revenge.[8] Similarly, traditional Islamic law established alternative remedies for causing grievous bodily harm: *diya* (monetary compensation) or *qisas* (retaliation by inflicting the exact harm on the offender).[9] Other legal systems merged punishment of wrongdoers and compensation of victims in penal law.[10] The Chinese Tang Code (619–906 A.D.)[11] allowed 'redemption' of a wrongdoer through the payment of compensation.[12] Some African Bantu societies redressed by compensation instead of retaliation because 'all blood belongs to the chief'.[13]

As legal systems developed, they came to separate the private action for redress and the public criminal prosecution on behalf of society as a whole, which claimed the right to punish wrongdoers.[14] Modern societies thus distinguish those acts that necessitate redress between individuals from those that are prohibited

---

of jurisprudence holds that the state entered the picture to ensure that the injury to the wrongdoer did not exceed that inflicted by him: *ibid.*

[8] G. MacCormack, *supra* n. 6, at 74. Money as a remedy was established by the end of the twelfth century in English law, derived from German customary law.

[9] The basis can be found in the Koran: 'O ye who believe! The law of equality is prescribed to you in cases of murder: the free for the free, the slave for the slave, the woman for the woman. But if any remission is made by the brother of the slain, then grant any reasonable demand, and compensate him with handsome gratitude. This is a concession and mercy from your Lord. After this whoever exceeds the limits shall be in grave penalty': Koran 2:178 quoted in M. Lippman, S. Mcconville and M. Yerushalmi, *Islamic Criminal Law and Procedure* (1988), 87. See also A. A. An-Na'im, 'The Right to Reparation for Human Rights Violations and Islamic Culture(s)', in *Seminar on the Right to Restitution, Compensation and Rehabilitation for Victims of Gross Violations of Human Rights and Fundamental Freedoms* (SIM Special Pub. No. 12), 174, 180.

[10] P. Catala and J.A. Weir, 'Delict and Torts: A Study in Parallel', (1963) 37 *Tul. L. Rev.* 573, 582. In Indonesia, Adat legal institutions included compensation of victims as part of the punishment: C. Fasseur, 'Colonial Dilemma: Van Vollenhoven and the Struggle Between Adat Law and Western Law in Indonesia' in W.J. Mommsen and J.A. DeMoor (eds.), *European Expansion and the Law* (1992), 245.

[11] The Tang Code (W.C. Johnson, trans., 1979).

[12] If the person was killed, the redemption money generally went to the government, but an injured party received the redemption money personally: *ibid.* at 55, 60. During the Qing dynasty (1644–1911 A.D.), the Great Qing Code added other remedies. A serious disability inflicted on another led to the wrongdoer's property being confiscated and given to the victim's family: *The Great Qing Code* (W.C. Jones trans., 1994), 224. Redemption money also became designed to cover burial and medical expenses: *ibid.* at 279.

[13] Compensation for the murder went to the chief, who could compensate the victim's family as he saw fit: T. O. Elias, 'The Nature of African Customary Law' in E. Cotran and N.N. Rubin (eds.), *Readings in African Law* (1969), 106. Among the Tswana also, certain crimes against bodily security are crimes that also provide civil remedies. For assault the chief levied a fine, which belonged to the chief—part if not all was awarded to the victim. The aspect which wronged the individual was seen to merit restitution/redress; the aspect which wronged the society to merit punishment: I. Schapera, 'A Handbook of Tswana Law and Custom' in *Readings in African Law, ibid.* at 112. The Basuto assessed damages for assault based on whether or not blood was shed, the gravity of the injury, the nature of the assault, the degree of provocation, the relative status of the parties, the wilfulness of the offender and the nature of the weapon used. Amounts assessed could aim both to compensate the victim and punish the wrongdoer: H. Ashton, 'The Basuto' in *Readings in African Law, ibid.* at 141.

[14] According to MacCormack, the place of retaliation remains in a few societies today and serves the same purpose as other remedies, it 'imports an element of compensation . . . it is not positive compensation. But it may be described as negative compensation in the sense that the loss is made good through the infliction of a similar loss on the killer's group': G. MacCormack, *supra* n. 6, at 81.

and punished if committed. In general, national legal systems redress individual wrongs through judicially-awarded and enforceable remedies to provide compensatory justice, deterrence, and, to some extent, punishment.[15] As is shown in Chapter 8, the distinction that punishment pertains to crime and that compensation pertains to tort/obligation is not uniformly applied in legal systems today. Many national systems permit the award of punitive or exemplary damages in civil actions to punish and deter. The desire to punish the wrongdoer as part of redress may express a popular view of justice or fairness. Penalties are seen as deserved, whether or not they act to deter others from similar misconduct, because other remedies do not sufficiently illuminate the blameworthiness of the act that caused the injury.

The specific elements of redress are often set forth by statute.[16] The most common principle in all legal systems is that a wrongdoer has an obligation to make good the injury caused, reflecting the aim of compensatory justice.[17] Nearly all legal systems call for restitution of property wrongfully taken and full compensation for the material and non-material harm resulting from physical or emotional

---

[15] These purposes are specified in the United States Restatement (Second) of Torts, s. 901, which states that the rules for determining the measure of damages are based upon the purposes for which actions of tort are maintainable:

(a) to give compensation, indemnity, or restitution for harms;

(b) to determine rights;

(c) to punish wrongdoers and deter wrongful conduct;

(d) to vindicate parties and deter retaliation or violent and unlawful self-help.

A leading authority on tort law in Portugal, points out that 'the obligation to pay compensation in Portuguese law is not only reparative in character, but also punitive': Ricardo Ben-Oliel, 'New Guidelines in Tort Law in the Portuguese Civil Code' in J. Spier (ed.), *Limits of Liability: Keeping the Floodgates Shut* (1996), 343.

[16] Article 134 of the Chinese Civil Code, for example, lists the forms of remedies available separately or in combination when civil liability is established: cessation of infringement; elimination of obstructions; elimination of danger; return of property; restoration of original condition; repair, reconstruction, or replacement; payment of compensation; payment of [agreed] contract breach money; elimination of effects and restoration of reputation; apology. The People's Court in civil cases may, in addition to using the above provisions, issue admonitions, order repentance, or confiscate property used for illegal activities or things obtained illegally, and may also in accordance with law impose fines or detention: Chinese Civil Code, Article 134 (H.R. Zheng trans.), (1986) 34 *Am.J.Comp.L.* 669.

[17] Morocco's Code of Obligations is typical. It sets forth the principle of compensation for victims of wrongdoing in Article 77 which provides: 'Any act whatsoever perpetrated by a person who, without being authorized by law, knowingly and intentionally causes material or moral injury to another person obliges its perpetrator to redress that injury, once it has been established that the act is the direct cause of the injury. Any stipulation to the contrary is void': Morocco, in *Right to restitution, compensation and rehabilitation for victims of grave violations of human rights, Report of the Secretary-General prepared pursuant to Commission resolution 1995/34*, at 5, E/CN.4/1996/29/Add.1 (1996). Article 78 specifies that every individual is responsible for any moral or material injury he may have caused. The Penal Code, Article 105 provides that during criminal proceedings a decision imposing a penalty or measure may rule on restitution and the award of damages to the victim. The award of damages 'shall ensure that the victim obtains full redress for the personal, current and established injury he has been directly caused by the offence'.

injury.[18] The advent of modern social security legislation has shifted some of the emphasis in remedies from compensation to risk allocation and deterrence. Many states today provide a public system of compensation to victims.[19] If social security or insurance pays the victim's losses, the state or insurance company may be able to claim from the wrongdoer the amount paid to the victim.[20]

B. The Right to a Remedy in National Laws

National guarantees of a right to a remedy are long-standing, if originally aimed at redressing private wrongs. The English Magna Carta states: '*Nulli vendemus, nulli negabimum, aut differemus, rectum aut justicam*' (no one will be sold, no one will be refused or deferred, right or justice). Coke in his Second Institute asserted that 'every Subject . . . for injury done to him in *bonis, terris, vel persona* . . . may take his remedy by the course of the Law, and have justice and right for the injury done to him, freely without sale, fully without any denial, and speedily without delay'.[21]

The right to a remedy for injury done by the state or state agents emerged recently in many states. Until the nineteenth century, most European civil law countries denied state responsibility for injury to individuals in part because Roman law had no concept of protecting the individual against the group.[22] Fault, the basis of responsibility for damages in Roman law, could be ascribed only to individuals. The development of rules of personal liability of state agents gradually led to acceptance of public law actions for damages based on injuries caused

---

[18] In Israel, the aim of compensation is *restituto in integrum* or 'putting the injured party back in the position he was in, or would have been in, had the tort not been committed': Israel Gilead, 'Tort Law' in I. Xamir and S. Colombo (eds.), *The Law of Israel: General Surveys* 475 (1995). Similarly, in Portugal, a new civil code adopted in 1966 and drawing on the German and Italian codes, includes the principle of restitution.

[19] All Scandinavian penal codes contain provisions governing indemnification for criminal acts, e.g., Finland, Law on compensation out of public funds for damages caused by crime of 21 December 1973; Norway, Regulations on compensation by the State for personal injuries caused by punishable 'acts' of 11 March 1976; Sweden, Law on damage caused by crime of 18 May 1978. France adopted the Law of 3 January 1977 providing compensation to certain victims of bodily injury resulting from criminal acts. Austria similarly has enacted the Act for payment of assistance to victims of crime of 9 July 1972. Germany provides public indemnification for victims of violent crime through the Law on compensation of victims of crime of 11 May 1976 as does the Netherlands. The Council of Europe European Convention on the Compensation of Victims of Violent Crime, 23 November 1983, Eur.T.S. No. 116, discussed *infra* in Chapter 5, establishes regional norms on this issue.

[20] In Europe the liable party generally must reimburse the welfare service for welfare or social security payments made to the injured. Denmark is an exception, where the state pays for all medical expenses and does not claim recoupment from awards. Perhaps because of this, damages awards are very low in Denmark. See D. Mcintosh and M. Holmes, *Personal Injury Awards in EU and EFTA Countries: An Industry Report*, 2nd edn. (1994). For German law, see generally, B.S. Markensinis, *A Comparative Introduction to the German Law of Torts*, 3rd edn. (1994).

[21] Coke, *Second Institute*, 4th edn. (1671), 55–56.

[22] H. Street, *Governmental Liability: A Comparative Study* (1953), 13.

by administrative acts.[23] By the nineteenth century European states generally accepted the liability of the state for *actes de gestion privée* (private acts). *Actes de puissance publique* (public acts) have incurred state responsibility in most states only this century.[24]

1. Express and implied remedial rights

Today, most written constitutions explicitly secure remedial rights. The Constitution of Trinidad and Tobago, for example, guarantees to any citizen who alleges that a provision of the Constitution is being or is likely to be contravened in relation to her or him leave to apply to the High Court for redress, and China similarly provides for remedies for governmental misconduct per Article 41 of its Constitution.[25] Many provisions refer explicitly to injury caused by the state. The Constitution of Paraguay accords everyone 'fair and proper compensation for harm or injury caused by the State', as regulated by law.[26] The Constitution of Ukraine grants individuals and citizens the right to compensation from the government in respect of any material and moral injury caused by the unlawful decisions, acts or omissions of state government bodies, local government bodies, civil servants or officials in the performance of their duties.[27] The Portuguese Constitution, Article 22, contains a similar guarantee.[28] The Zimbabwe

[23] L. Trotabas, 'Liability in Damages under French Administrative Law', (1930) 12 *J.Comp.L.* 44, 49.

[24] The French Conseil d'Etat has developed a jurisprudence of administrative liability applying special rules that take account of the need to balance the rights of the state and the citizens. These rules appear to have influenced the European Court of Human Rights. For example, moral injury caused by a wrongful act is held to be repaired by the formal declaration on the part of the Conseil d'Etat that there has been an administrative fault: 'To award money damages in such a case would not, as in private law, restore the balance between the estate of the wrongdoer and the estate of the victim: it would lay upon the public funds, that is to say, the funds of the taxpayers in general, who are not to blame for the fault and take no benefit by it, the burden of paying a sum arbitrarily fixed as equivalent to the moral damage sustained': *ibid.* at 63.

[25] 'Citizens who have suffered losses through infringement of their civic rights by any State organ or functionary have the right to compensation in accordance with the law': quoted in *Report to the United Nations on Human Rights in China*, HRI/CORE/1/Add.21 (1993).

[26] Constitution of Paraguay, Article 34.

[27] A citizen has the right to complain to a court if she or he considers that a right guaranteed by law has been infringed by the actions of an official: Code of Civil Procedure, Article 248–1. See the *Report to the United Nations on Human Rights in the Ukraine*, HRI/CORE/1/Add.63. Article 17 of the Japanese Constitution of 1946 laid down the principle that state and public institutions are to be held liable. Statute no.125 of 1947 established that claims against the government are private causes of action, governed by the Civil Code except where otherwise stated.

[28] Article 22 provides for the liability of the state, public bodies, and state agents for acts or omissions in the exercise of their functions which result in violations of the rights, freedoms or safeguards of persons. Other provisions establish the potential civil, criminal or disciplinary liability of civil servants and officials of the state and of other public authorities in respect of acts or omissions in the exercise of their functions or caused by such exercise which result in infringement of those rights or interests of the individual that are protected by law. The Constitution also states that 'citizens who have been unjustly convicted shall have the right, in the conditions to be determined by law, to have their sentences reviewed and to be compensated for any injury suffered': Constitution of Portugal,

Constitution, Section 24, gives the Supreme Court original jurisdiction to enforce the provisions of the Declaration of Rights against government action, including the power to make orders, issue writs and give directions as it may consider appropriate. Thirty-five states of the USA[29] have constitutional provisions guaranteeing remedies, following the example of Maryland, the first state in the USA to adopt a constitution, in 1776.[30] In sum, the right to a remedy for governmental misconduct is so widely accepted that the Namibian Supreme Court suggests 'it is arguable that the recognition of a right to an effective remedy for violations of human rights . . . forms part of customary international law'.[31]

Often judicial bodies infer a remedy in the absence of a written constitutional or statutory provision. In the English case of *Ashby v. White*,[32] Chief Justice Holt proclaimed: 'If the plaintiff has a right, he must of necessity have a means to vindicate and maintain it, and a remedy if he is injured in the exercise or enjoyment of it; and indeed it is a vain thing to imagine a right without a remedy; for . . . want of a right and want of remedy are reciprocal'.[33] Chief Justice Marshall of the United States Supreme Court similarly affirmed the power of the judiciary to fashion a remedy in *Marbury v. Madison*:[34] 'The very essence of civil liberty certainly consists in the right of every individual to claim the protection of the laws, whenever he receives an injury. One of the first duties of government is to afford that protection'.[35] Marshall also declared that 'the

---

Article 29, para. 6. The constitutional provisions were followed by Decree-Law 48051, of 30 November 1967, which addresses the matter of the State's extra-contractual liability for acts of public administration and provides: 'The State and other public legal persons shall bear civil liability towards third parties for violations of their rights and of the legal provisions intended to protect their interests, if the injury is the result of wilful unlawful acts committed by their agencies or officials in the performance of their duties'. Finally, legislation supplementing the constitutional provisions regarding states of emergency provides that compensation shall be awarded to citizens whose rights, freedoms and guarantees have been violated as a result of the declaration of a state of siege or a state of emergency, or by an unconstitutional or unlawful measure adopted in the course of implementation of such a declaration, particularly because of unlawful or unjustified deprivation of liberty: Act No. 44/86, Art. 2, para. 3, of 30 September 1986. See *Report to the United Nations on Human Rights in Portugal* HRI/CORE/1/Add.20.

[29] Common Law Remedies in 'Note, Constitutional Guarantees of a Certain Remedy', (1964) 49 *Iowa L. Rev.* 1202.

[30] Md. Code Ann., Declaration of Rights, Art. 17. Maryland's provision echoed the language of the Magna Carta, in providing '[t]hat every freeman, for any injury done him in his person or property, ought to have remedy, by the course of the law of the land, and ought to have justice and right freely without sale, fully without denial, and speedily without delay, according to the law of the land'.

[31] *Mwandingi v. Minister of Defence* [1991] 1 S.A. 851 (Namib.)

[32] *Ashby v. White*, 92 Eng. Rep. 126 (K.B. 1703). The plaintiff claimed he was deprived of a right to vote and brought an action for damages. The majority on the King's Bench held for the defendant, indicating that the interest in voting was protected only by the criminal law and not by civil law in the absence of a clear statement by Parliament. The Chief Justice disagreed in an opinion that was accepted by the House of Lords, which reversed the King's Bench and entered judgment for the plaintiff.

[33] *Ashby v. White*, *supra* n. 32 at 136.

[34] *Marbury v. Madison*, 5 U.S. (1 Cranch) 137 (1803).

[35] *Ibid.* at 163.

right of coercion is necessarily surrendered to government, and this surrender imposes on government the correlative duty of furnishing a remedy'.[36] Indeed, judicial tribunals 'are established . . . to decide on human rights'.[37]

These and more recent cases, such as the Indian court opinion in *People's Union for Democratic Rights v. State of Bihar* [38]are fundamentally about the judicial power to infer a cause of action and a remedy from the existence of substantive rights.[39] The Indian court observed that public interest litigation which is intended to bring justice within the reach of all is different from traditional litigation involving a dispute between two parties. The former is intended to vindicate the public interest, which demands that violations of constitutional or legal rights of large numbers of people who are poor, ignorant, or in a socially or economically disadvantaged position, should not go unredressed. Subsequently, the Indian court in *Rudul Shah v. State of Bihar*,[40] a case of unlawful detention, proclaimed its inherent power not only to order the victim's release but to award compensation, stating:

the refusal of this Court to pass an order of compensation in favor of the petitioner will be doing mere lip-service to his fundamental right to liberty which the State Government has so grossly violated. Article 21 [of the Constitution] which guarantees the right to life and liberty will be denuded of its significant content if the power of this court were limited to passing orders of release from illegal detention. One of the telling ways in which the violation of that right can reasonably be prevented and due compliance with the mandate of Article 21 secured, is to mulct its violators in the payment of monetary compensation. The right to compensation is some palliative for the unlawful acts of instrumentalities which act in the name of public interest and which present for their protection the powers of the state as a shield.[41]

2. Immunity of the state and its agents

Governmental immunity, which once erected an almost impenetrable barrier against any recovery for state misconduct, has been substantially reduced, even if it has not entirely disappeared: French *actes de gouvernement*, the English 'acts of state' and the American 'political questions' remain immune from court review.[42] All Latin American states today can be sued without their consent, but

---

[36] *Ogden v. Saunders*, 25 U.S. (Wheat.) 213, 346–47 (1827).

[37] *Fletcher v. Peck*, 10 U.S. (6 Cranch) 87, 133 (1810).

[38] *People's Union of Democratic Rights v. State of Bihar*, A.I.R. (S.C.) 355 (1978) involved the police shooting into a peaceful procession, killing 21 persons. The court found the government's *ex gratia* payment of 10,000 rupees inadequate, stating that 'it is a normal feature of which judicial notice can be taken' that the state comes forward to compensate for human rights violations. The court ordered an additional 20,000 rupees as death compensation and 5,000 rupees for injury 'without prejudice to any just claim for compensation that may be advanced by the victims'.

[39] S. Bandes, 'Reinventing Bivens: The Self-executing Constitution' (1995) 68 *S. Cal.L.Rev.* 289 (1995).

[40] *Rudul Shah v. State of Bihar*, 1983–4 S.C.C.141, A.I.R. (S.C.)1086 (1983).

[41] *Ibid.*

[42] H. Street, *supra* n. 22 at 16.

the causes of action may be limited.[43] In Europe, the Austrian Federal Act of 1958 imposes state liability for injurious actions that are unlawful and that have occurred in the performance of official duties. In Denmark, an individual is entitled to compensation for any loss or damage incurred as the result of a human rights violation for which Danish authorities are responsible.[44]

In the United Kingdom, little immunity remains for the state.[45] The Crown may be subject to liability (1) where torts are committed by servants/agents of the government; (2) for breach of an employer's duty of care to an employee; and (3) for breach of duties with respect to ownership, occupation, possession or control of property.[46] In addition, misfeasance in public office, i.e., an *ultra vires* act in which an official knowingly acts in excess of his powers or acts with malice toward the plaintiff, is actionable.[47] Countries formerly part of the British Empire inherited England's common law rules on Crown proceedings, although many have made radical statutory changes. Canada, Australia, New Zealand, and South Africa permit suits against the state. In many other countries there is a trend toward increased liability for public authorities and public servants. In Israel, courts have large potential to remedy violations of statutory duty based on new human rights legislation.[48] The Israeli Knesset abolished most of the privileges and immunities of the state in tort. In China, the Administrative Suits Act states that anyone whose rights and interests have been infringed through the specific actions of an administrative organ or an employee may bring an action for compensation.[49]

---

[43] Argentine government liability 'covers all damage caused by the state, the provinces, and the municipalities, if there is a relationship of subordination between the tortfeasor and the state, or the respective state authority'. A Federal Court of Appeal awarded compensation to the victim's father for moral damage caused by his daughter's abduction and disappearance: *Report of the Working Group on Enforced or Involuntary Disappearances to the Commission on Human Rights at its Forty-ninth Session*, E/CN.4/1995/25, para. 77.

[44] *Report to the United Nations on Human Rights in Denmark*, HRI/CORE/1/Add.58. The Swedish Tort Liability Act similarly establishes the liability of the state or a municipality to pay compensation for any loss of life, personal injury, or damage to property and financial loss which has been caused by a wrongful act or omission in the course of, or in connection with, the exercise of public authority.

[45] B.S. Markensinis, *supra* n. 20, at 327.

[46] Crown Proceedings Act 1947, s. 2(1).

[47] See the Crown Proceedings Act 1947 and the Law Reform (Personal Injuries) Act 1948.

[48] I. Gilead, 'The Evolvement of Israeli Tort Law from its Common Law Origins' in A.M. Rabello (ed.), *European Legal Traditions and Israel* (1994), 528.

[49] *Right to restitution, compensation and rehabilitation for victims of grave violations of human rights and fundamental freedoms*, Report of the Secretary-General prepared pursuant to Commission Resolution 1995/34, E/Cn.4/1996/29 (1996). On 12 May 1994, China promulgated the State Compensation Act that calls for administrative compensation for losses resulting from a violation of personal or property rights by an administrative body or employee during the exercise of administrative functions. It includes compensation for illegal detention or illegal restrictions on personal freedom; unlawful arrest; personal injury from beating or other violence, including the illegal use of weapons; other illegal behaviour causing bodily injury or death of a citizen; illegal fines or confiscation of property, and other illegal injury to property. Another category of 'criminal compensation' refers to losses resulting from abuses in the criminal justice system, such as extraction of a confession by torture.

Not all states have eliminated state immunity. In the USA, sovereign immunity remains a major hurdle to accountability for certain types of cases and remedies. The United States Supreme Court has affirmed that the right of access to the courts 'assures that no person will be denied the opportunity to present to the judiciary allegations concerning violations of fundamental constitutional rights', such as those recognized in the Civil Rights Act of 1871,[50] but United States courts traditionally have presumed that damage actions against the federal government—although not injunctive relief—must be authorized by Congress through explicit waiver of sovereign immunity.[51] At present, the Federal Tort Claims Act makes the USA liable for 'money damages . . . for injury or loss of property, or personal injury or death' caused by federal government agents.[52] In addition, the United States Congress no longer exempts itself from major civil rights legislation, including the Privacy Act, Title VII, Title IX, the Freedom of Information Act, the Americans with Disabilities Act, the Age Discrimination Act, the Family and Medical Leave Act, the Ethics in Government Act, and the Occupational Safety and Health Act.[53]

The United States Supreme Court has held that, even without statutory authorization, damages may be assessed against the particular government agents that committed a constitutional wrong,[54] but it has failed to extend the doctrine to suits against a federal agency.[55] In addition, no monetary damage suits may be filed against a state and no state can be sued in its own name.[56] The decision of the United States Supreme Court in the case of *Monell v. Department of Social Services* allows an action against local governments, but only when 'the action that is alleged to be unconstitutional implements or

[50] *Wolff v. McDonnell*, 418 U.S. 539, 577–80 (1974).

[51] For example, both the Federal Tort Claims Act, 28 U.S.C. 1346(b), 2671–2680 (1988 and Supp. IV 1992), and the Tucker Act, 28 U.S.C. 1346(a), 1491 (1988 and Supp. IV 1992), authorize damage actions against the federal government. See Jeremy Travis, 'Note, Rethinking Sovereign Immunity after Bivens', (1982) 57 *N.Y.U.L. Rev.* 597, 642–52.

[52] Act of 20 April 1871, s. 1, 17 Stat. 13. The 1871 statute was derived from s. 2 of the Civil Rights Act of 1866, 14 Stat. 27. Today, the section is codified at 42 U.S.C.A. s. 1983, along with a jurisdictional counterpart, 28 U.S.C.A. 1343(a), and the Civil Rights Attorney's Fees Awards Act of 1976, Pub. L. No. 94–559, 90 Stat. 2641, codified at 42 U.S.C.A. s. 1988 (1982).

[53] See, e.g., Freedom of Information Act, 5 U.S.C. 551 (1988); Privacy Act of 1974, 5 U.S.C. 552(a) (1988); Educational Amendments of 1972 902, 20 U.S.C. 1682 (1988); Ethics in Government Act of 1978 3601(a), 28 U.S.C. 591 (1988); Age Discrimination in Employment Act of 1967 11, 29 U.S.C. 630 (1988); Occupational Safety and Health Act of 1970 3, 29 U.S.C. 652 (1988); Family and Medical Leave Act of 1993 101, 29 U.S.C. 2611(2)(b) (Supp. 1993); Americans with Disabilities Act of 1990 101, 42 U.S.C. 1201 (Supp. 1990); Title VII of the Civil Rights Act of 1964 701, 42 U.S.C. 2000(e) (1988).

[54] *Bivens v. Six Unknown Named Agents of the Federal Bureau of Narcotics*, 403 U.S. 388 (1971).

[55] See *F.D.I.C. v. Meyer*, 510 U.S. 471, 114 S.Ct. 996, 127 L.Ed.2d 308 (1994).

[56] The Eleventh Amendment to the United States Constitution has been held to prohibit money damage suits against state governments: *Edelman v. Jordan*, 415 U.S. 651, 663 (1974) holding that 'a suit by private parties seeking to impose a liability which must be paid from public funds' was barred by the Eleventh Amendment. *Hans v. Louisiana*, 134 U.S. 1 (1890) does allow injunctive relief.

executes a policy statement, ordinance, regulation or decision officially adopted and promulgated by that body's officers'.[57] No punitive damages can be awarded against a public entity.[58]

Individual government agents are no longer immune from liability in most legal systems. In the USA, a wrongful act in violation of the constitution by a federal agent acting under colour of law gives rise to a cause of action for damages against the agents, according to the United States Supreme Court opinion *Bivens v. Six Unknown Named Agents of the Federal Bureau of Narcotics*.[59] As the Court correctly observed, '[a]n agent acting—albeit unconstitutionally—in the name of the United States possesses a far greater capacity for harm than an individual trespasser exercising no authority other than his own'.[60] The Court subsequently explained that a 'damages remedy against the offending party is a vital component of any scheme for vindicating cherished constitutional guarantees'.[61] Actions against officials of other levels of government are permitted by statute,[62] although state and local officials are immune from money damages so long as they act in good faith and some local officials remain absolutely immune.

Where both the state and the agent are liable, the question of whether the state should be primarily or secondarily liable receives different answers. Most states

---

[57] *Monnell v. Department of Social Services*, 436 U.S. 658 (1978).

[58] *City of Newport v. Fact Concerts, Inc.* 453 U.S. 247 (1981) (no punitive damages may be awarded against a public entity).

[59] *Bivens v. Six Unknown Named Agents of the Federal Bureau of Narcotics, supra* n. 54. Although the Federal Tort Claims Act, 28 U.S.C. s. 1346, provides a possible basis for suit, the limited scope of the law was one reason for the *Bivens* decision implying a remedy for constitutional wrongs. See *Kosak v. U.S.*, 46 U.S. 848, 862 (Congress must be addressed to extend remedies under the Federal Tort Claims Act). *Bivens* has been extended in *Carson v. Green,* 446 U.S. 14, 100 S.Ct. 1468, 64 L.Ed.2d 15 (1980) (*Bivens* action permitted to remedy cruel and unusual punishment) and in *Davis v. Passman*, 442 U.S. 228, 99 S.Ct. 2264, 60 L.Ed.2d 846 (1980) (*Bivens* action permitted for violations of due process). Although the courts will supply a remedy where none exists, they will not create additional *Bivens* remedies '[w]hen the design of a government program suggests that Congress has provided what it considers adequate remedial mechanisms for constitutional violations that may occur in the course of its administration': *Bush v. Lucas*, 462 U.S. 367, 103 S.Ct. 2404, 76 L.Ed. 648 (1983). G.R. Nichol counters that '[i]f . . . the Constitution by its own force truly demands the recognition of causes of action for the violation of rights . . . it would seem to be of little consequence what Congress thinks of the matter': G.R. Nichol, 'Bivens, Chilicky, and Constitutional Damage Claims', (1989) 75 *VA.L.Rev.* 1117.

[60] *Bivens, supra* n. 54, at 392.

[61] *Gomez v. Toledo*, 446 U.S. 635, 639 (1980).

[62] The United States Civil Rights Act of 1871, also known as the Ku Klux Klan Act, 42 U.S. C. s. 1983 reads: 'Every person who, under color of any statute, ordinance, regulation, custom, or usage, of any State or Territory, subjects or causes to be subjected, any citizen of the United States or any other person within the jurisdiction thereof to the deprivation of any rights, privileges, or immunities secured by the Constitution and laws, shall be liable to the party injured in an action at law, suit in equity, or other proper proceeding for redress'. It was enacted to include a damages remedy 'to aid in the preservation of human liberty and human rights': *Owen v. City of Independence*, 445 U.S. 622, 636 (1980) (quoting Cong. Globe, 42nd Cong., 1st Sess., App. 68 (1871)). Employers or superior officers are not liable for the acts of their employees or subordinates unless there is some degree of fault on the part of the supervisor. See, e.g. *Arroyo v. Schaefer*, 548 F.2d 47, 51 (2d Cir. 1977).

accept joint responsibility for damages caused by the fault or negligence of a public official,[63] but in a few states, the agent is primarily liable.[64] In Japan and Austria, the state is primarily liable and the agent is not liable to the victim, but must reimburse the damages paid by the state if the actions were wilfully or grossly negligent. In Norway, the state and employee are jointly and severally liable[65] while in Poland the state is liable only where damage is caused by a decision or decree and if fault is established in criminal proceedings.

C. REMEDIES AGAINST THE STATE

Where the state is liable for the violation of human rights, remedies range from the relatively non-instrusive declaratory judgment to damages to injunctions and affirmative orders. Many courts have fashioned innovative remedies in order to ensure that the public interest in the rule of law is fulfilled, as well as to provide redress to the individual whose rights were violated.

1. Declaratory judgments

Courts generally have the power to declare rights, status and other legal relations whether or not further relief is or could be claimed. A declaratory judgment is the broadest form of non-coercive remedy for resolving uncertainty in legal relations. It merely pronounces particular practices or conditions to be illegal, leaving officials free to choose whether and how to remedy the situation. As such, it normally is used as an anticipatory device to obtain a judgment *before* harm has occurred, when it is imminently threatened. In *Steffel v. Thompson*,[66] for example, declaratory relief was used to protect free speech against threatened arrest. In an important citizenship case in Botswana, the applicant sought and received a declaration

---

[63] In Morocco, 'the State and the municipalities are responsible for any injury caused directly by the functioning of their departments and by errors committed by their employees in the course of the duties': Moroccan Code of Obligations and Contracts, Article 79, quoted in *Right to restitution, compensation and rehabilitation for victims of grave violations of human rights*, Report of the Secretary-General prepared pursuant to Commission resolution 1995/34, E/CN.4/1996/29/Add.1 at 4 91996. Belgian public administrative agencies are obliged in civil law to repair harm caused by the illegal acts of their agents: *Report to the United Nations on Human Rights in Belgium*, HRI/CORE/1/Add.1/Rev.1. In Greece, also, if the law is violated by a public official acting in the exercise of his authority, the victim has a right to compensation and the wrongdoer is equally responsible with the state or municipalities and other entities: Article 105, Civil Code of Greece.

[64] In Ethiopia the state is not liable for employees that have transgressed their function in bad faith and in Finland, the state is liable only if a claim against the employee cannot be enforced: State Liability Act of 1927. In Italy, express prohibition of an act severs any causal link for government liability, but some courts hold the state liable as long as the injurious act occurs in the performance of the wrongdoer's duty. See generally G. Eorsi, 'Private and Governmental Liability for the Torts of Employees and Organs', *International Encyclopedia of Comparative Law,* vol. XI, 4–167.

[65] Tort Liability Act of 13 June 1969, ch. 2.

[66] *Steffel v. Thompson*, 415 U.S. 451 (1974).

that a section of the Botswana Citizenship Act of 1984 improperly discrimi-
nated on the basis of sex and thereby was *ultra vires*. [67] In most states, a
declaratory judgment is not considered an adequate remedy after the injury has
taken place.

2. Compensation

States uniformly use money to reimburse out-of-pocket expenses and to
compensate for provable future direct and indirect[68] losses resulting from the
injury. Many states compensate also for pain and suffering resulting from physical injury, under the heading 'pecuniary harm'. Other states consider pain and
suffering as part of intangible losses, compensated by moral damages.
Compensable injury includes the same basic elements in virtually all legal
systems:[69]

(1)   Medical and other expenses;[70]
(2)   Loss of past and future earnings;[71]
(3)   Loss of or injury to property, including lost profits;[72]
(4)   Pain and suffering and injury to health;[73]

---

[67]   *In re Dow v. Attorney Gen. of Bots.*, Case No. Misc. A.124/90 (High Ct. 1991) (Bots.). The
Court of Appeal affirmed the judgment: *Attorney Gen. v. Dow*, Court of Appeal No. 4/91 (Ct. App.
1992) (Bots.).

[68]   In property cases, a direct loss is a reduction in the value of property presently owned by the
injured party, the amount of which is determined by the cost of replacement or repair. An indirect loss
is a loss of benefits that might be obtained, such as loss of the use of property.

[69]   Article 199 of the Chinese Civil Code exemplifies a general compensation provision: '1.
Where personal injury is caused to a citizen, compensation must be paid for medical expenses, loss
of income from work, expense of living as a disabled person, and similar expenses; when death is
caused, there must also be payment for funeral expenses as well as expenses such as necessary maintenance for the deceased's dependents'.

[70]   Medical expenses are expressly referred to in e.g. the Greek Civil Code, Article 929; German
Civil Code; Argentine Civil Code, Article 1086; Austrian Civil Code, Article 1325; Czech Civil Code,
s. 449; Polish Civil Code, Article 444, para.1.

[71]   e.g. Austria, Germany; Czech Civil Code, s. 445–447. Hungary allows the claims for future
salary increases, provided these are established with some certainty. In contrast, in Italy the courts
have regard not only to the earning capacity the claimant has already demonstrated but also to the
possibilities indicated by his technical and professional training. The Norwegian Penal Code provides
that in personal injury and false imprisonment cases compensation for future loss is paid only as
seems equitable considering the fault of the acting party and all other circumstances of the case. The
Swiss federal Code des Obligations, Article 45(2), Article 46(1) specifies 'that damages can be given
for loss or detriment to one's future'. The German Civil Code, s. 842, specifies that damages can be
given for loss or detriment to one's future. In contrast, in China, lost wages are fully recoverable, but
no damages are awarded for loss of earning capacity. If a person is injured but able to resume work,
he or she cannot recover damages on the theory that the injury will prevent him or her from receiving
promotions or otherwise advancing his or her career: Robert Force and Xia Chen, 'An Introduction to
Personal Injury and Death Claims in the People's Republic of China', (1991) 15 *Maritime Lawyer*
245.

[72]   e.g. Czech Civil Code, ss. 442–443. In Germany restitution is required.

[73]   e.g. Austria.

(5)   Funeral expenses in wrongful death cases;[74]
(6)   Loss of the services of a deceased.[75]

Some states recognize additional losses, reflecting cultural differences.[76] Adjustments to awards also vary, with most states adjusting awards to take into account inflation or devaluation of currency.[77]

National legal systems vary in the methods used to assess the recoverable elements and in the amounts awarded. This is not surprising given the differing economic conditions around the world[78] and the differing weight given to the compensatory and deterrent functions of damages. The level of wrongdoing is particularly important where deterrence plays a large role in redress.[79] In other states, wrongdoing is less relevant because '[t]he purpose of compensation is to facilitate the injured person's ability to get well soon and to restore his ability to manage his own affairs and to work, by means of medical treatment and nourishment'.[80] Compensation is thus awarded to victims on the principle of full and fair redress, without regard to the conduct of the injuring party.

The categorization and measurement of pain and suffering is one of the most difficult issues in damages, with large differences from one state to another.[81] The underlying theories vary. Some courts take a functional approach and seek to assess the amount that will enable the injured party to acquire benefits to substitute for those lost. Others take a personal approach based on injury to the subjective feelings of happiness or unhappiness of the victim. A third approach considers that the victim has been deprived of an asset which has objective value in case of loss or damage. Even within states, courts disagree at times on the valuation of subjective elements such as compensation for back pain or for bereavement in case of death. In some instances, pain and suffering awards are designed

---

[74]   *Contra* the Netherlands, based on the rationale that the family would eventually have to pay the expenses. A draft amendment would change this (draft CC Article 6.1.2.12.1).

[75]   e.g. Germany.

[76]   The Austrian Civil Code also provides that, where the victim of an injury is of female sex, any disfigurement thereby caused to her must be taken into account to the extent that her future advancement may be hindered (s. 1326). The Greek and Belgian Civil Codes contain similar provisions to compensate women for economic losses due to reduced marriage prospects in disfigurement cases. France awards damages for the victim's lost opportunity of obtaining a promotion in his or her career. It also compensates for loss of leisure and the ability to enjoy sex: D. Mcintosh and M. Holmes, *supra* n. 20, at 6.

[77]   In Ireland, the award for future loss of earnings incorporates an allowance for inflation and an allowance for the risk that the injured party might not be employed for all of her or his full working life; however, it is rare for interest on pre-trial losses to be awarded. In Italy, claims to cover compensation for monetary devaluation are allowed.

[78]   Within Europe, Greek awards are the lowest because the level of earnings are the lowest: D. Mcintosh and M. Holmes, *supra* n. 20, at 6.

[79]   East African cases have considered embarrassment of the plaintiff; the motive or state of mind of the defendant; aggravation by the defendant's post-injury conduct, and consequential losses as relevant factors in awarding damages: E. Veitch, *East African Cases on the Law of Tort* (1972), 178.

[80]   W.C. Jones, *Basic Principles of Civil Law in China* (1989), 188.

[81]   Traditional Islamic law is one of the few legal systems that allows no compensation for pain and suffering, but modern codes do include them as recoverable damages.

not only to ensure adequate compensation for damage but 'to make a statement to tortfeasors that they owe the victim satisfaction',[82] making them closer to a form of moral damage.

Moral damages are widely recognized. Nearly all legal systems accept claims for non-pecuniary injury such as harm to reputation, dignity, and other wrongs for which monetary value must be presumed as it cannot be assessed. Compensation for such non-pecuniary harm is sometimes assessed as a separate claim independent of pecuniary losses[83] while in other states, the amount of moral damages is directly linked to the amount of pecuniary injury or otherwise limited to a maximum amount.[84] In some states, a statutory scale of damages may be introduced for certain types of harm[85] and states often specify the types of actions or injuries for which moral damages are recoverable or they define the term moral injury.[86]

Many states take into account the fault of the defendant in making awards of moral damages.[87] Austria, Germany, Greece, Italy, Portugal, Switzerland,[88] the Netherlands,[89] and Norway take fault into account. French cases involving

---

[82] B.S. Markensinis *supra* n. 20, at 921.

[83] e.g. Austria, Belgium, Germany, South Africa, Switzerland.

[84] Under the Prussian Code, Part I, Title 6, s. 113, judges were not permitted to grant pain and suffering awards smaller than one half the medical expenses, nor greater than twice the medical expenses. The Colombian Penal Code of 1936, Article 35, placed a limit on monetary reparation for non-pecuniary harm.

[85] e.g. a 1971 German statute (BGBl. I 157, s. 7) introduced standardized non-pecuniary compensation for false imprisonment. The Ethiopian Civil Code, Article 2116 places a general limit on monetary reparation for non-pecuniary harm. In China, compensation for wrongful detention is calculated on the basis of average daily earnings by state workers over the preceding year.

[86] Chinese law provides remedies for non-pecuniary harm in Civil Code, Article 120: 'Where the right of a citizen to his name, likeness, reputation or honor is infringed, he has a right to demand that the infringement cease, the reputation be restored, and the effects [of the infringement] be eliminated, and to demand an apology; he may also demand compensation for loss. Where the right of a legal person to its name, reputation or honor is infringed, the above provisions apply': *General Principles of Civil Law of the People's Republic of China* (H.R. Zheng and W.H. Gray trans., 1986), reprinted in (1986) 34 *Am.J.Comp.L.* 715. Similarly, the 1951 Civil Code of Iraq provides that every interference with freedom, honour, dignity, reputation or public esteem establishes a claim to the reparation of the non-pecuniary harm. A 1997 modification to Hungarian law now allows 'compensation for non-pecuniary detriment insofar as the injurious event impaired the aggrieved individual's participation in community activities or otherwise resulted in a continuing or onerous impediment to the conduct of his life or interfered with a legal entity's participation in commercial activity'. The Polish Civil Code allows non-pecuniary damages in cases of personal injury, wrongful death, false imprisonment, sexual assault and the intentional interference with personal rights. Mexico's law refers to *el dano moral*, 'moral damages', which cover damage to the feelings, affections, beliefs, appearance, honour, reputation, private life, physical aspects or the reactions of others to him or her. The code recognizes that the impact of the injury will differ depending on the injured person's profession and income. There is no longer a limit on the amount of 'moral damages'. The Mexican Civil Code of 1928, Article 1916, placed a limit on monetary reparation for non-pecuniary harm to one-third of the pecuniary harm: *The Mexican Civil Code* (Michael W. Gordon trans., 1995).

[87] e.g. the Austrian Supreme Court takes the view that the wrongdoer pays non-pecuniary damage only if he acted with intent or gross negligence unless the law specifies otherwise.

[88] *Report of Switzerland to the United Nations on Human Rights*, HRI/CORE/1/Add.29.

[89] J. Spier, 'How to Keep Liability Within Reasonable Limits? A Brief Outline of Dutch Law', in *Limits of Liability supra* n. 15, at 97–110.

transmission of HIV by transfusion of tainted blood seem based on fault, awarding higher amounts because some defendants knew the blood was contaminated.
Similarly, in the Danish case of the Scandinavian Star Ferry, the awards were 'at
least 50% above' the legal compensation levels required by law, probably because
of outrage over the conduct of the defendants.[90] States that take fault into account
in assessing moral damages inject a punitive element into the civil remedy.

The subjective nature of valuation for moral injury means that even where the
same factors are considered, their evaluation differs from one state to another and
even from one case to another in the same state. Judges usually have discretion to
assess non-pecuniary compensation on an equitable basis.[91] On the one hand,
nominal damages can be used where a party seeks to vindicate a right and/or
obtain moral satisfaction without obtaining a higher award.[92] At the other end of
the spectrum, high awards can compensate, punish and deter.

States generally do not tax the damages received because of another's wrongdoing because they are compensatory in nature, restoring the victim to the pre-
injury position. Thus, they do not represent a gain. If they include lost wages,
however, that would have been taxable, the part attributable to the wages usually
will be taxed. Recoveries for pain and suffering, bodily injury and dignitary harm
generally are excluded from taxation. Some states do not tax any part of an award,
on the basis of compassion for the victim.

In actions for human rights violations by the state, monetary damages are
frequently awarded with deterrence as well as compensation in mind.[93] The Indian
Supreme Court has awarded compensation for illegal detention,[94] police beatings,[95] and wrongful deaths from police shootings.[96] In one case, the court
declared that cases of misconduct by state officials should be governed by
common law tort principles of recovery for battery, assault, false imprisonment,
physical injuries and death. As such, victims could recover damages for mental
pain, distress, indignity, loss of liberty, and death. In Romania, case law establishes
that compensation for human rights violations includes costs of medical treatment
and recovery and compensation for loss of possession during imprisonment or
infirmity, and moral damages, including rehabilitation and social reintegration.[97]

---

[90] D. Mcintosh and B. Holmes, *supra* n. 20, at 6.
[91] The Bulgarian Act on Obligations and Contracts of 1950, Article 52, provides that courts
should apply principles of equity when assessing damages for non-pecuniary harm.
[92] Sometimes, as noted in a British case, nominal damages constitute 'a peg to hang costs on':
Beaumont v. Greathand 2 CB 494, 499 (1846) quoted in B.S. Markensinis, *supra* n. 20, at 686.
[93] *Carey v. Piphus*, 435 U.S. 247 (1978).
[94] *People's Union for Democratic Rights v. Police Commissioner Delhi Police* 1983–4 S.C.C.
730. In *State of Maharashtra v. Ravikant S. Patil*, A.I.R. (S.C.) 871 (1991), the court awarded 10,000
rupees for violation of the fundamental rights of a detainee who was handcuffed and taken through
the streets in a procession by the police during an investigation.
[95] *Saheli v. Commissioner of Police Delhi* 1990–1 S.C.C. 422, A.I.R. (S.C.) 513 (1990).
[96] *People's Union for Democratic Rights v. State of Bihar*, *supra* n. 38.
[97] *Right to restitution, compensation, and rehabilitation for victims of grave violations of human
rights and fundamental freedoms, Report of the Secretary-General prepared pursuant to Commission
resolution 1995/34*, E/CN.4/1996/29/Add.3 at 4 (1996).

The emphasis on dignitary harm caused by deprivation of rights is important because in many cases the victim's pecuniary losses are minimal. The harm caused by a violation of free speech or the right to a fair hearing is difficult to measure in practice. Ordinary approaches to compensation can result in under-valuing the right. The Sri Lankan Supreme Court has recognized that economic loss is inadequate to compensate for a politically-motivated deprivation of free speech, stating that the deprivation of a fundamental right 'was to be measured against the yardstick of liberty, and not weighed simply on the scales of commerce'.[98]

Similarly, in *Yoko Safati Skaggo v. Lango District Administration*,[99] an East African court found that the plaintiff, who had been wrongfully imprisoned for two weeks, was 'entitled to substantial damages for the loss of his liberty and dignity as a man; though no injury to his health or his pocket is involved'.[100] In contrast, a divided United States Supreme Court has held that the abstract value of a constitutional right cannot form the basis for an award of damages, suggest-ing instead the use of nominal damages where there is no actual injury.[101] The concurring opinion in the case emphasized that the violation of a constitutional right, in a proper case, could itself constitute a compensable injury, including emotional distress, humiliation and personal indignity, embarrassment, fear, anxi-ety, feelings of unjust treatment, and reputational harm.[102] Other decisions support the approach of presuming damage for a human rights violation where the quantum of harm suffered would be impossible to prove.[103]

---

[98] *Deshapriya and another v. Municipal Council, Nuwara Eliye and other*, judgment of 10 March 1995, reported in [1996] 1 CHRD 115. The mayor of an area seized 450 copies of an anti-government newspaper from a sales agent and coerced him into ceasing to carry the paper. The owner and editor of the seized newspaper sued. The Supreme Court held that the action was a governmental act of the mayor that deprived the plaintiffs of freedom of speech and expression. The newspaper was sold for seven rupees a copy, but the Court awarded 100,000 rupees and 10,000 rupees costs, holding that the action of the mayor was grave, deliberate and unprovoked.

[99] Civil Case No. 462 of 1965, cited in Veitch, *supra* n. 79 at 205.

[100] *Ibid*. In another case, the court awarded exemplary damages paid out of public funds for the humiliation and wrong done a man arrested, tied to a pole and left for two hours by local officers: *A.B. Sindano v. Ankolo District Administration*, cited in Veitch, *ibid*. at 207. Ugandan courts award general damages in recognition that a right has been violated and special damages to compensate the victim for expenses or costs arising directly out of the violation, including medical expenses, transport expenses and loss of income. See E. Khiddu-Makubuya, 'Uganda', in *Seminar on the Right to Restitution, Compensation and Rehabilitation for Victims of Gross Violations of Human Rights and Fundamental Freedoms* (SIM Special No. 12), 86, at 90.

[101] *Memphis Community School District v. Stachura*, 477 U.S. 299, 106 S.Ct. 2537, 91 L.Ed.2d 249 (1986). The Supreme Court reversed the trial court's decision because of jury instructions that called for an assessment of the 'value or importance of the constitutional rights that were violated'. The Supreme Court commented that '[h]istory and tradition do not afford any sound guidance concerning the precise value that juries should place on constitutional protections'.

[102] The concurrence relied on *Hobson v. Wilson*, 737 F.2d 1, 62 (D.C. Cir. 1984), cert. denied, 105 S.Ct. 2547 (1985) (lost opportunity to express free speech rights is compensable, proportional to the actual loss sustained).

[103] See *Nixon v. Herndon*, 273 U.S. 536 (1927) (presumed damages appropriate in a voting rights case because the harm that plaintiff suffered would be impossible to prove) and *Hessel v. O'Hearn*,

In English law, particularly malicious, insulting or oppressive behaviour can result in aggravated damages, applied where losses cannot be calculated precisely. Typically this includes malicious prosecution, false imprisonment and racial discrimination. The factors considered in making an award for aggravated damages include: defendant's behaviour, defendant's intentions or motives, high-handedness and the effect on the plaintiff. Aggravated damages are still compensatory in nature, addressing hurt feelings and dignity, but at times the line between aggravated and punitive damages is hard to discern.[104] The law of damages in South Africa, which was heavily influenced by the Roman-Dutch law[105] also allows for vindictive damages, nominal damages, and special or sentimental damages.[106] High damage awards are justified because they can force the state to internalize the costs of its wrongful conduct and deter such behaviour when the expected costs would exceed the expected benefits.

3. Punitive or exemplary damages

Punitive or exemplary damages are neither new[107] nor limited to a few countries, but instead are found in legal systems throughout the world.[108] According to some, the very antiquity of such a remedy 'is something of a prima facie case for its usefulness'.[109] In most common law countries, punitive or exemplary damages may be awarded in cases of egregious wrongdoing. They are, as their names imply, damages by way of punishment or deterrence, given entirely without reference to any proved actual loss suffered by the plaintiff. In a Ugandan case of military authorities abusing civil rights, the court found that the plaintiff was entitled

---

977 F.2d 299, 301–02 (7th Cir. 1992) (presumed damages 'may be recoverable when substantive constitutional rights, such as the right to freedom of speech, or the right to be free from unreasonable searches and seizures, are infringed').

[104] B.S. Markensinis, *supra* n. 20. In *Tynes v. Barr*, Supreme Court (Bahamas) 28/3/94, [1996] 1 CHRD 116, the Supreme Court awarded aggravated damages because the police delayed in producing documents, failed to apologize to the victim, and unnecessarily delayed the trial.

[105] After 1879, significant weight was given to English authority on personal injury damages. This has evolved to where liability is determined under Roman-Dutch principles and damages calculated under the English rules of assessment. See generally H.J. Erasmus, 'The Interaction of Substantive Law and Procedure' in R. Zimmerman and D. Visser (eds.), *Southern Cross: Civil Law and Common Law in South Africa* (1996), 156.

[106] *Ibid.* at 155.

[107] The Code of Hammurabi imposed a 30-fold-the-value payment for theft of an ox, sheep, ass, pig or goat from a temple or palace. Babylonian laws of restitution in theft cases ranged from two to 30 times the value of the stolen property. The Twelve Tables in Roman law similarly called for multiple damages and the Hindu Code of Manu contained a reference to enhanced awards: A Kocourek and J. Wigmore, *Sources of Ancient and Primitive Law* (1915), 391, 469. Plato's writings also include discussion of increased monetary damages: Plato, *Protagoras*, 324b; Plato Laws 9.85b and 9.93a.

[108] See Melvin M. Belli, Sr, 'Punitive Damages: Their History, Their Use and Their Worth in Present-Day Society', (1980) 49 *UMKC L.Rev* 1 (1980).

[109] Clarence Morris, 'Punitive Damages in Tort Cases', (1931) 44 *Harv. L. Rev.* 1173, 1206.

to both punitive and exemplary damages,[110] using the civil law of trespass to the person. The Indian Supreme Court awarded exemplary costs in the disappearance of two persons[111] and in custodial death cases.[112] It has emphasized that courts must take into account not only the interest of the applicant and the respondent but also the interests of the public as a whole with a view to ensuring that public bodies and officials do not act unlawfully and perform their duties properly, especially where the fundamental rights of a citizen are concerned.[113]

Punitive or exemplary[114] damages are found outside common law countries, as well, including Brazil,[115] Ethiopia,[116] and South Africa.[117] The Chinese Civil Code does not provide punitive damages in name, but it allows the court in a civil case to impose a fine or warning.[118] Norway, Switzerland, and Morocco allow

---

[110] *Kanike v. Att. General of Uganda* Civ. Case No. 196 (1967). See also *Kiwanuka v. Att. General of Uganda* Civil Case No. 159 (1964). Ugandan courts may award exemplary or punitive damages to victims in cases where the agents of the state have conducted themselves in an oppressive, arbitrary or unconstitutional manner. Decisions of the High Court show that it considers a number of factors in determining the nature and amount of compensation payable: actual physical or mental injury; prospective injury based on the prediction of future aggravation of damage; consequential injury or damage to third parties, and, in particular, loss of financial and emotional support; and the conduct of the defendant or agents: Khiddu-Makubuya, *supra* n. 100 at 91.

[111] *Sebastian M. Hongray v. Union of India*, A.I.R. (S.C.) 1026 (1984), 1 S.C.C. 339 (1984); 3 S.C.C. 81. The Supreme Court also awarded exemplary damages in *Saheli, A Women's Resource Centre v. Comm'r of Police, Delhi*, A.I.R. (S.C.) 513 (1990) on behalf of a woman whose child was beaten to death.

[112] *Nilabati Behera v. State of Orissa and others*, 2 L.R.C. 99 (1994). The family of a young man found dead on train tracks after being in police custody established police liability for the death. See also *Rudul Sah v. State of Bihar*, A.I.R. (S.C.) 1086 (1983); *Bhim Singh v. State of Jammu and Kashmir* (1984) Supp. S.C.C. 504 and 4 S.C.C. 677 (1985).

[113] *Nilabati Behera*, *supra* n. 112 at 114.

[114] The Philippines courts may award exemplary damages. Article 2229 of the 1949 Philippine Civil Code says that 'exemplary or corrective damages are imposed by way of example or correction for the public good, in addition to the moral, temperate, liquidated or compensatory damages'. Exemplary damages may also be imposed, separate and apart from penal fines, as a consequence of civil liability for all criminal offences whenever the misdeed was committed under 'one or more aggravating circumstances'. Philippine Civil Code, s. 2230. Under Article 2231 exemplary damages may also be awarded for gross negligence when the misdeed is not criminal.

[115] The Brazilian Civil Code requires the wrongdoer who injures another's person or health to pay the injured party, in addition to his medical costs and loss of earnings, a sum in atonement (*multa*) equal to one half the corresponding penal fine for the particular misdeed. This sum is doubled if the personal injury results in a mutilation or disfigurement: Brazilian Civil Code, Article 1538(1). Civil Code, Article 1538(2) adds that if the disfigured or paralyzed victim of an injury is a spinster or a widow of a marriageable age, her compensation shall consist of a dowry.

[116] The Ethiopian Civil Code, for example, allows the court to order the defendant to make a payment in excess of actual damages to either the plaintiff or charity. South Africa also awards exemplary damages as an accepted principle of Roman-Dutch law: H. Stoll, 'Consequences of Liability: Remedies', in *International Encyclopedia of Comparative Law* (1983), vol. XI, 8–114. East African systems award punitive damages as well as aggravated damages for injury to pride or dignity.

[117] In Roman/Dutch law, the basic purpose of a civil action is to compensate the victim for actual harm done; however, in the case of an injury to personality or honour, the court may increase the pain and suffering award 'in order to punish a defendant for particularly insolent, vindictive or malicious conduct': J.C. Van Der Walt, *Delict in the Law of South Africa*, ss. 18, 54 (1979).

[118] Civil Code of China, Article 134, *supra* n. 86, at 669.

'private' penalties in some cases, either in a civil action or as an award to the victim in a criminal proceeding. Norway revised its Law of Damages in 1973 to provide for a private penalty, known as *oppreisning*, as a remedy for non-pecuniary harm. 'Particularly in cases of intentional or grossly negligent infliction of personal injury, wrongful death, or other interference with personal rights as well as in connection with certain criminal acts, the wrongdoer can be adjudicated liable for payment of a private penalty in an amount deemed reasonable by the court'.[119] The Swiss Penal Code, Article 60, similarly authorizes the judge to rule that a fine be paid directly to the victim, wholly or in part.[120]

Although some jurisdictions use the terms interchangeably, punitive damage awards generally are based on the punishment rationale,[121] while exemplary damages focus on deterrence. Some states reverse the usage, while others use the terms interchangeably. The punishment rationale supports a requirement that the wrongdoer's misconduct be exceptional. Such a requirement does not fit with the deterrence model that would allow additional damages even for negligent conduct because it encourages potential defendants to act more carefully. Similarly, the requirement that the punitive damages award relate to the particular wrong done to the particular victim is consistent with notions of corrective justice[122] but that requirement is not part of the deterrence rationale where the particular parties are used as a means to achieve some greater social goal. A third term used is aggravated damages. As previously discussed, aggravated damages, a version of moral damages, serve a compensatory function in recognizing that the defendant's misconduct aggravated the plaintiff's injuries, especially injury to his or her security, self-esteem or reputation.

The courts of various countries enhance damages for egregious government misconduct. In some legal systems, punitive damages can be awarded against individual officials for flagrantly wrongful acts,[123] but government entities cannot be subject to such awards on the grounds that punitive damages would punish tax-

---

[119]   Stoll, *supra* n. 116, Supp. 8–20.

[120]   *Ibid.* at 8–60.

[121]   In England, punitive damages are exceptional but 'are properly awarded whenever "it is necessary to teach a wrongdoer that tort does not pay." ' *Rookes v. Barnard* [1964] AC 1129, 1227. In Canada, also, the punishment rationale governs, based on retribution for a debt to society. The imposition and measurement of punitive damages are based on the wrongful conduct and are proportionate to the gravity of the act. Conduct that warrants punitive damages is generally described as 'vindictive', 'reprehensible and malicious', or 'extreme', that is, conduct that 'offends the ordinary standards of morality or decent conduct in the community in such marked degree that censure by way of damages is . . . warranted': *Vorvis v. I.C.B.D.*, 58 D.L.R.4th 193, 208 (1989) (Can.S.C.).

[122]   Dobbs, in fact, argues that the function of punitive damages as retribution should be dropped because there is no agreed method of measurement; because intangible injury is really pain and suffering under a different label; and the most effective goal for civil litigation is deterrence not punishment. Therefore, courts should reflect the deterrence objective in assessing damages: D. Dobbs, *Handbook on the Law of Remedies* (1986).

[123]   In the USA, the Supreme Court has stated that punitive damages are available against individual officials for civil rights violations based on 42 U.S.C. 1983, even though the legislation makes no reference to the nature and extent of the damages that can be awarded: *Carlson v. Green*, 446 U.S. 14, 21–22, 100 S.Ct. 1468, 1472–73, 64 L.Ed.2d 15 (1980); *Smith v. Wate*, 75 L.Ed.2d 632 (1983), *Carey v. Piphus*, 435 U.S. 247, 257 n. 11 (1978).

payers who took no part in the misconduct. It is also posited that the deterrent function served by punitive damages is less necessary in the case of a government entity, because the government is likely to sanction an offending official even without the award.[124] Other legal systems award punitive damages on the basis that the damages benefit the community and restrain the transgressor.[125]

4. Non-monetary remedies

A nineteenth century Russian legal scholar said that 'only one seized by a profound disrespect for the human personality would attempt to persuade another human being that money makes good moral afflictions of every sort'. Money as a substitute for the exercise of guaranteed human rights is particularly problematic, leading many victims and their representatives to seek other remedies. Many legal systems allow courts to issue specific orders of restitution or other acts by the wrongdoer to repair the harm caused.[126] In some Asian countries, acknowledgment of wrongdoing, coupled with an apology, is particularly important in eliminating the wrong and guaranteeing non-repetition.[127] Other forms of non-monetary remedies include acts of rehabilitation,[128] punishment of the wrongdoers,[129] and restitution of rights or property.[130]

Courts in common law countries may order non-monetary remedies with or without statutory authority. In the United States case of *Bell v. Southwell*,[131] after almost all African-American voters were excluded from an election, the court ordered a new election because it said it could not be presumed that the African American candidate who lost would have lost an election untainted by racial

---

[124]   L. Lurwitz, *The State as Defendant: Governmental Accountability and Redress of Individual Grievances* (1982), 453.

[125]   See *Rashid bin Abdulla v. Major Cartwright*, 1 Z.L.R. 407 reprinted in E. Veitch, *East African Cases on the Law of Torts* (1972), 204. The court identified the standard as one of cruelty or great negligence, or an offence of a grossly unconstitutional nature. See also *Minister of Home Affairs v. Allen* [1986] 1 Z.L.R. 263 (SC); *Makomboredze v. Minister of State (Security)* [1986] 1 Z.L.R. 73 (HC); *Granger v. Minister of State (Security)* [1985] 1 Z.L.R. 153 (HC). In general, the courts of Zimbabwe award higher damages in cases of wrongful arrest and detention, expulsion and other serious violations of human rights. In the *Makomboredze* case, in which the plaintiff was wrongfully deported to Mozambique where he was kept in a detention camp for 20 months, lost his wife, children, home and job, the court awarded $50,000, the equivalent of 30 years of income for the victim.

[126]   e.g. in Israel, the Civil Wrongs Ordinance, s. 76(1) provides that '[c]ompensation may be awarded either alone, or in addition to, or in substitution for, an injunction': quoted in I. Gilead, 'Tort Law', in I. Zamir and S. Colombo (eds.), *The Law of Israel: General Surveys* (1995).

[127]   See E/CN.4/Sub.2/1997 at 5.

[128]   The Romanian Constitution establishes the right to compensation in case of judicial errors in criminal cases. The Code of Penal Procedure adds that anyone who at the time of a wrongful arrest was employed is entitled to have the period of the arrest counted as part of the period of employment, an extremely important provision for the calculation of salary entitlements, sickness benefits and pensions: Code of Penal Procedure, Article 504(4).

[129]   e.g. Ukrainian law.

[130]   e.g. the Expropriated Properties Act of Uganda, Act No. 9 of 1982.

[131]   *Bell v. Southwell*, 376 F.2d 659 (5th Cir. 1967).

discrimination. Additionally, 'state-imposed racial discrimination cannot be tolerated and to eliminate the practice or the temptation toward it, the law must extinguish the judgment wrought by such a procedure'.[132] In *Rizzo v. Goode*[133] the United States Supreme Court directed the drafting of a comprehensive programme for dealing with complaints about illegal and unconstitutional mistreatment by police officers and in *Newman v. Alabama*,[134] the court held that an order to ensure reasonably adequate food, clothing, shelter, sanitation, necessary medical addition, and personal safety of prisoners is within the sound discretion of the judiciary.

Other states also award non-monetary remedies. In *Sebastian M. Hongray v. Union of India*[135] the Indian Supreme Court issued a mandamus to the Superintendent of Police directing him to take the judgment of the court 'as information of cognizable offense and to commence investigation as prescribed by the relevant provisions of the Code of Criminal Procedure'.[136] The Supreme Court has insisted in several cases that provision be made for training and education, medical care, employment programmes and other related measures of assistance to victims of official misconduct.[137]

In a seminal article on public law adjudication,[138] Professor Chayes observed that many remedies for rights violations are necessarily equitable and prospective because they do not involve a closed set of events. Specific decrees are particularly important where the harm may continue or be repeated. In the USA, courts have become 'creator and manager of complex forms of on-going relief' due to repetitive violations.[139] An order for specific conduct does more than eliminate the present unlawful conditions. It denies to the wrongdoer the possibility of

---

[132] *Bell v. Southwell*, at 663.

[133] *Rizzo v. Goode*, 423 U.S. 362, 96 S.Ct. 598, 46 L.Ed.2d 561 (1976).

[134] *Newman v. Alabama*, 559 F.2d 283, rev'd in part on other grounds, 438 U.S. 781 (1978).

[135] *Sebastian M. Hongray v. Union of India*, supra n. 111.

[136] See, generally, U. Baxi, 'Taking Suffering Seriously: Social Action Litigation in the Supreme Court of India' (1988), *Law and Poverty* 387–415.

[137] In *Basu v. State of West Bengal* [1997] 2 LRC 1, the finding that the government was liable for two custodial deaths was accompanied by orders directing that police badges with names be worn by all arresting and interrogating police officers; that a memorandum of arrest should be served on the family member of the person arrested; that a member of the family or friend should be informed of the venue of custody; and that the detainee should be medically examined every 48 hours during detention. *See* also U. Baxi, in *Seminar on the Right to Restitution*, supra n. 9.

[138] A. Chayes, 'The Role of the Judge in Public Law Litigation' (1976), 89 *Harv.L.Rev.* 1281, 1292.

[139] Chayes, *ibid.* at 1284. In 1984, 600 school districts, prisons in 30 states and some 270 local jails were under federal judicial orders. Robert F. Nagel, 'Controlling the Structural Injunction', (1974) 7 *Harv. J. L & Pub.Pol'y* 395, 396. Frank M. Coffin also contrasts conventional adjudication and institutional remedial litigation. The predominant areas into which courts have been thrust are public education, jails, mental institutions and police departments. The issues involve substantive rights and the means of compelling a public body to effectuate those rights. Remedies sought may be more intended to affect the future than the past and their impact is much more widespread: Frank M. Coffin, 'The Frontier of Remedies: A Call for Exploration', (1979) 67 *Cal.L.Rev.* 983. See also Dan Braveman, *Protecting Constitutional Freedoms: A Role for Federal Courts* (1989).

paying damages and continuing to do harm. It also obviates the need for victims to have the will and financial ability to initiate repeated litigation for declaratory judgments or damages. They reduce the plaintiffs' risk that the remedy will turn out to be ineffective.[140] In general, it may be argued that remedial orders are a better approach than compensation to individuals. Rather than place money in individual hands, they redress the harm and implement broad social benefits by injunction or order that can effectuate a comprehensive remedy.[141] Injunctions are not less intrusive than ordering governments to pay money and probably are more effective. Finally, deterrence is an important factor favouring non-monetary remedies. As one court noted, '[t]he Constitution promises that government will not inflict certain injuries, not that it must purchase the right to inflict them'.[142]

5. Habeas corpus and *amparo*

The writ of habeas corpus has its origins in English law, being mentioned in the Magna Carta.[143] The writ of habeas corpus protects individuals against arbitrary and wrongful imprisonment or confinement. It has been viewed as the 'great writ of liberty'.[144] A common law right to habeas corpus exists in many states; in others it is provided by statute or constitutional provision.

Many Latin American countries recognize *amparo*, a broader remedy than habeas corpus. It is a procedure whereby individuals who are deprived of or threatened with deprivation of constitutional rights may seek redress from the judiciary. The Constitution of Paraguay, for example, provides that any person harmed or threatened with immediate harm as a result of a manifestly unlawful act or omission by an authority or private individual in regard to constitutional or other legal rights and guarantees may submit an application for *amparo* to a judge. The judge is entitled to safeguard the right or guarantee or immediately rectify the situation in law.[145]

Habeas corpus and *amparo* are particularly important remedies when evidence

---

[140] P. Gewirtz, 'Remedies and Resistance', (1983) 92 *Yale L.J.* 585, 597–98. In *Hutto v. Finney*, 437 U.S. 678 (1978), the court issued a comprehensive order to insure against the risk of inadequate compliance, based on a 'long and unhappy history' of non-compliance with prior orders to meet constitutional standards in the Arkansas prison system. On 1 January 1990, eight states and Puerto Rico were operating prison systems under court order or consent decree resulting from litigation over unconstitutional conditions: National Prison Project, *Status Report: The Courts and Prisons* (1990). See also Susan P. Sturm, 'A Normative Theory of Public Law Remedies', (1991) 79 Geo.L.J. 1357.

[141] Christina Whitman argues that preference should be given to equitable remedies because 'money judgments often disrupt local government to a greater degree than the returns in the vindication of constitutional rights can justify': Christina Whitman, 'Constitutional Torts', (1980) 79 *Mich. L.Rev.* 5, 42.

[142] *Owen v. City of Independence*, 445 U.S. 622, 650–51 (1980).

[143] See W. Duker, *A Constitutional History of Habeas Corpus* (1980).

[144] *Ibid.* at 3.

[145] Constitution of Paraguay, Article 133, quoted in *Report to the United Nations on Human Rights in Paraguay*, HRI/CORE/1/Add.24.

is in the hands of the state. In some cases the court may shift the burden of proof to the government on a writ of habeas corpus.[146]

6. Attorneys' fees and costs

There is considerable difference in the treatment of fees and costs from one state to another. The English rule is that prevailing parties recover fees as a matter of course from the losing party. This is followed in most common law countries and in Western Europe. The rule in the USA is that each side pays its own costs and fees unless a court is authorized by statute or recognized equitable exception to shift payment of the fees to the opposing party.[147] Japan follows the same rule as the USA.

Two reasons are given for not awarding fees and costs to the prevailing party. First, fee-shifting could discourage the poor from bringing lawsuits out of fear of having to pay the other side's fees. Secondly, and probably more important, fee-shifting would impose too great a burden on judicial administration due to the inherent difficulty in computing fees.[148] Unfortunately, the vast majority of human rights cases are brought by the poor, who cannot afford legal counsel to challenge wrongdoing. As a result, even where attorneys' fees and costs normally are not awarded for private litigation, domestic law often allows their recovery in public interest cases such as human rights. In federal civil rights litigation in the USA, the Civil Rights Attorney's Fees Awards Act[149] allows reasonable attorney's fees to ensure 'effective access to the judicial process' for those seeking vindication of civil rights.

D. INTERNATIONAL HUMAN RIGHTS CASES IN NATIONAL COURTS

Customary international human rights law and human rights treaties have had an impact on the development of remedies in national legal systems. International treaties may be used directly, if the state automatically incorporates international treaty norms or has enacted the norms into domestic law,[150] or indirectly, to

---

[146] See *Sebastian M. Hongray v. Union of India, supra* n. 111.

[147] *Arcambel v. Wiseman*, 3 U.S. (3 Dall.) 306, 1 L.Ed. 613 (1796). More than 100 American federal statutes now authorize courts to award attorneys' fees: 'Federal Statutes Authorizing the Award of Attorney's Fees', (1986), 9 Attorney Fee Award Rep. 5. Equitable exceptions exist to award fees to the prevailing party in bad faith lawsuits and vexatious or oppressive litigation. See *Kansas City Southern R. Co. v. Guardian Trust Co.*, 281 U.S. 11, 50 S.Ct. 194, 74 L.Ed. 659 (1930). Fees are also awarded plaintiffs in class actions where the plaintiff has preserved or generated a common fund for the benefit of the class and in shareholders' derivative suits where the defendant is perceived to benefit from the suit.

[148] See e.g., *Fleischmann Distilling Corp. v. Maier Brewing Co.*, 386 U.S. 714, 87 S.Ct. 1404, 18 L.Ed.2d 475 (1967).

[149] 42 U.S.C. s. 1988 (1988).

[150] e.g., The United Kingdom introduced Article 14(6) of the International Covenant on Civil and

resolve ambiguity or uncertainty in national constitutions and legislation and to fill gaps in the law. Several common law countries apply international standards in domestic cases.[151] Statutes and courts do not always cite international instruments, even when they are the source of the right and/or remedy, but the inspiration may be evident. The Honduran Constitution of 1982, Article 15, makes binding international judicial and arbitral decisions. Colombia adopted legislation to enforce decisions of the Inter-American Commission on Human Rights and the Human Rights Committee, requiring the government to pay compensation for injuries caused by human rights violations in respect of which express decisions are taken by one of the two bodies.[152] A similar Bill has been introduced in Argentina, while Peru makes decisions of all human rights monitoring bodies capable of enforcement in domestic courts.[153] Costa Rica enforces decisions of the Inter-American Court of Human Rights pursuant to the Headquarters Agreement between the state and the Organization of American States. Mexico's law implementing the United Nations Convention against Torture establishes the liability of persons who commit any of the designated offences for the legal, medical, funeral, rehabilitation and other expenses incurred by the victim or relatives of the victim.[154]

European states provide compensation as a result of unjustified imprisonment according to the requirements of the European Convention on Human Rights. Compensation is provided for economic losses, but not always for non-material injury.[155] Under Danish law the accused can opt instead of receiving compensation to have a statement of non-culpability issued by the chief of police, indicating that the arrest or imprisonment 'lacked any basis and was not deserved'.

Political Rights through the provisions of s. 133 of the Criminal Justice Act 1988. It permits a person convicted of a criminal offence which has been quashed by the Court of Appeal to apply for payment of compensation under specified circumstances: *Report to the United Nations on Human Rights in the United Kingdom of Great Britain and Northern Ireland*, HRI/CORE/1/Add.5/Rev.1.

[151] Senior Commonwealth judges addressed the subject of domestic application of international human rights norms at two colloquia held for them. See *Judicial Colloquium in Bangalore, Developing Human Rights Jurisprudence: The Domestic Application of Human Rights Norms (1988); Judicial Colloquium in Harare, Developing Human Rights Jurisprudence: A Second Judicial Colloquium on the Domestic Application of International Human Rights Norms* (1989). In *Nilabati v. State of Orissa*, the Supreme Court of India referred to the International Covenant on Civil and Political Rights in granting compensation for an unlawful arrest: *Nilabati v. State of Orissa*, 1993 A.I.R. (S.C.) 1960.

[152] Law No. 00288 of 18 July 1996, cited in *Right to restitution, compensation and rehabilitation for victims of grave violations of human rights and fundamental freedoms, Report of the Secretary-General*, E/CN.4/197/29 at 2 (1997).

[153] Law 23406, Article 40.

[154] Federal Act for the Prevention and Punishment of Torture, Article 10. The law also calls for the offender to make good the damage for loss of life, impairment of health, loss of freedom, loss of income, incapacity for work, loss of or damage to property, and defamation of character. See *Report to the United Nations on Human Rights in Mexico*, HRI/CORE/1/Add.12/Rev.1.

[155] e.g. Norway, Sweden, Denmark, Germany, France and England. See Stoll, *supra* n. 116 at ch. 8; H. McGregor, 'Personal Injury and Death', *International Encyclopedia of Comparative Law* (1983) ch. 9. In Switzerland, a person who has been victim of a rights violation may take legal action to obtain compensation for loss or injury or seek a declaratory judgment that the rights in question have been violated.

In the USA, cases involving international human rights issues have been litigated with increasing frequency since the 1970s.[156] The statutory basis for bringing actions lies in 28 U.S.C. sec. 1350 (The Alien Tort Claim Statute), a grant of jurisdiction to federal district courts over suits brought by aliens for a tort committed in violation of a treaty or 'the law of nations'.[157] The United States Supreme Court has held that the Foreign Sovereign Immunities Act governs all suits against states, including those within the terms of section 1350, with the result that human rights victims generally may bring actions only against individuals or legal persons who are present within the USA.

In *Filartiga v. Pena-Irala*,[158] the first of the modern section 1350 cases, the Federal Court of Appeals for the Second Circuit determined that because international law forms an integral part of the common law of the USA 'federal jurisdiction over cases involving international law is clear'.[159] In such cases, international law 'does not require any particular reaction to violations of law . . . Whether and how the United States wishes to react to such violations are domestic questions'.[160]

The *Filartiga* court held that acts of torture committed under state authority violate international law[161] and then sought to ascertain the applicable law on

---

[156] See generally B. Stephens and M. Ratner, *International Human Rights Litigation in U.S. Courts* (1996).

[157] The Alien Tort Claim Act was adopted by the first Congress of the United States in 1789. The Congressional motivation in enacting the law has been subject to considerable debate.

[158] *Filartiga v. Pena-Irala*, 630 F.2d 876 (2d Cir. 1980).

[159] *Ibid.* at 887.

[160] *Ibid.* at 777–78 (quoting L. Henkin, *Foreign Affairs and the Constitution*, (1972), 224. 'Nothing more than a violation of the law of nations is required to invoke section 1350': *ibid.* at 779.

[161] *Ibid.* at 880–84 (discussing declarations of the United Nations General Assembly, human rights conventions prohibiting torture, modern municipal law, and the works of jurists). The Court in the Marcos case agreed: '[t]he right to be free from official torture is fundamental and universal, a right deserving of the highest stature under international law, a norm of jus cogens. The crack of the whip, the clamp of the thumb screw, the crush of the iron maiden, and, in these more efficient modern times, the shock of the electric cattle prod are forms of torture that the international order will not tolerate. To subject a person to such horrors is to commit one of the most egregious violations of the personal security and dignity of a human being'. See also *Hanoch v. Tel-Oren*, 726 F.2d at 781 (Edwards, J., concurring) (torture is violation of customary international law); *Tel-Oren*, 726 F.2d at 819–20 (Bork, J., concurring) ('the proscription of official torture [is] a principle that is embodied in numerous international conventions and declarations, that is "clear and unambiguous" . . . and about which there is universal agreement "in the modern usage and practice of nations" '); *Forti v. Suarez-Mason*, 672 F. Supp. 1531 at 1541 (prohibition against official torture is 'universal, obligatory, and definable'). The USA signed the Convention Against Torture and Other Cruel, Inhuman or Degrading Treatment or Punishment, 39 U.N. GAOR Supp. (No. 51), (1987) 23 I.L.M. 1027, to which the United States Senate gave its advice and consent. The prohibition against summary execution or causing 'disappearance' is similarly universal, definable, and obligatory: *Forti*, 672 F. Supp. at 1542, amended, 694 F. Supp. at 710–11. The *Filartiga* court warned that courts 'are not to prejudge the scope of the issues that the nations of the world may deem important to their interrelationships', the court stated that it is only where the nations of the world have demonstrated that the wrong is of mutual, not merely several, concern, by means of express international accords, that a wrong becomes an international violation within the meaning of the statute: *ibid.* at 888. Actionable violations of international law must be of a norm that is specific, universal, and obligatory. See *Filartiga*, 630 F.2d at 881; cf.

remedies, referring the matter to a magistrate. Plaintiffs argued that the magistrate should 'look to the practice under international law', meaning that domestic remedies should be taken into account except when they frustrate rather than fulfil the goals of the international community.[162] An *amicus curiae* brief urged the district court to award sizeable punitive damages, although they are not recognized in Paraguay. Supporting the plaintiffs' position, the brief acknowledged that damages should be assessed under Paraguayan law in the first instance, but said Paraguayan law should not be determinative 'when the application of such law is inconsistent with the public policy of the forum'.[163] The international character of the tort of torture provided the evidence that withholding punitive damages would violate the public policy of the forum.[164]

The magistrate looked exclusively to Paraguayan law and recommended that the plaintiffs receive $150,000 each as compensation for emotional pain and suffering, loss of companionship and disruption of family life; that the father receive $50,000 for past expenses related to funeral and medical expenses and lost income and that the sister receive $25,000 for future medical expenses for treatment for psychiatric impairment. No expenses of litigation or punitive damages were included.

The district court disagreed with the magistrate in regard to the applicable law. It found that if the tort constituted a violation of international law, then the court must look to international law to determine what principles to apply; the remedy 'must satisfy international standards'. The district court considered the interests of Paraguay 'to the extent they do not inhibit the appropriate enforcement of the applicable international law or conflict with the public policy of the United States'.[165] Balancing the contacts of the litigants with the USA and Paraguay, the court concluded that it should look first to Paraguayan law to determine the remedy for the violation of international law. The court recognized that international law does not ordain detailed remedies but sets forth norms, and thus the court must 'choose and develop federal remedies to effectuate the purpose of the international law incorporated into United States common law'.[166] It agreed with

Guinto v. Marcos, 654 F. Supp. 276, 280 (S.D. Cal. 1986) ('violation of the First Amendment right of free speech does not rise to the level of such universally recognized rights and so does not constitute a "law of nations" '); see also *Forti v. Suarez-Mason*, 672 F. Supp. 1531, 1539–40 (N.D. Cal. 1987) ('This "international tort" must be one which is definable, obligatory (rather than hortatory), and universally condemned'), amended in part, 694 F. Supp. 707 (N.D. Cal. 1989).

[162] Plaintiffs' Post-Trial Memorandum of Facts and Law 44, *Filartiga v. Pena-Irala*, 577 F. Supp. 860 (E.D.N.Y. 1984). A footnote to the text adds: 'Since this Court sits as an enforcer of the law of nations as part of federal common law, the rules applied by the federal courts in deciding whether to incorporate state law or fashion a wholly independent federal common law also guide this court in applying international principles here': *ibid.* at 44.

[163] Brief of the International Human Rights Law Group as Amicus Curiae in Support of Plaintiffs' Objections to the Magistrate's Report at 4, *Filartiga v. Pena-Irala*, 577 F.Supp. 860 (E.D.N.Y. 1984).

[164] *Ibid.* at 7–9.

[165] *Filartiga*, 577 F.Supp. at 863–64.

[166] *Ibid.* 577 F. Supp. at 862.

the plaintiffs that national law should be used only if it does not inhibit the appropriate enforcement of the applicable international law.

The district court thus reversed the magistrate's decision denying litigation expenses, finding they were compensable under Paraguayan law. In respect to punitive damages, admittedly not recoverable under the Paraguayan Civil Code, the court found that the objectives behind the international prohibition of torture 'can only be vindicated by imposing punitive damages'.[167] It justified punitive damages by looking directly to international law. It accepted—as plaintiffs had conceded—that damages 'designated punitive have rarely been awarded by international tribunals'.[168] It noted, however, that the case was not an inter-state one, but against an individual defendant, so that diplomatic concerns and issues of sovereignty were not involved. It concluded that it was 'essential and proper to grant the remedy of punitive damages in order to give effect to the manifest objectives of the international prohibition against torture'.[169]

In determining the amount of punitive damages, the court considered a variety of factors including the nature of the acts for which damages were being assessed:

Chief among the considerations the court must weigh is the fact that this case concerns not a local tort but a wrong as to which the world has seen fit to speak. Punitive damages are designed not merely to teach a defendant not to repeat his conduct but to deter others from following his example . . . To accomplish that purpose this court must make clear the depth of the international revulsion against torture and measure the award in accordance with the enormity of the offense. Thereby the judgment may perhaps have some deterrent effect.[170]

Looking to the precedent of *Letelier v. Republic of Chile*,[171] where a punitive award of $2,000,000 was awarded, the court found that an award of damages of no less than $5,000,000 to each plaintiff was appropriate to reflect adherence to the world community's proscription of torture and to attempt to deter its practice. Thus, in 1980, *Filartiga* produced a judgment of $10,385,364 against the defendant.[172]

Judgments in subsequent cases have ranged up to billions of dollars, although courts are split on the issue of the applicable law of damages in Alien Tort Claim cases. In *Trajano v. Marcos,* where the torture, death and execution of the deceased were held to be a gross violation of the law of nations, the district court explicitly grounded its award of damages upon various articles of the Philippine

[167]   *Filartiga*, 577 F.Supp, at 864.
[168]   As precedent, it referred to *The I'm Alone (Canada v. United States)*, (1941) 2 G. Hackworth, Digest of International Law 703, 708.
[169]   *Filartiga*, 577 F.Supp. at. 865.
[170]   *Ibid.* at 866.
[171]   *Letelier v. Republic of Chile*, 502 F.Supp. 259 (D.D.C. 1980). After the United States court decision, the *Letelier* case was considered by a Commission established under the 1914 Treaty for the Settlement of Disputes that May Occur Between the United States and Chile. See *infra* Chapter 4 for a discussion of the award.
[172]   577 F.Supp. at 860 (E.D.N.Y. 1984).

Civil Code.[173] *In Martinez-Baca v. Suarez-Mason*,[174] the district court seemed to follow *Filartiga* and to base damages on international law:

International law principles, as incorporated in United States common law, provide the proper rules for calculating the damages . . . International law requires that an injured plaintiff must be compensated for all actual losses. Federal common law remedies likewise provide compensation for losses resulting from a defendant's wrongdoing. Accordingly, plaintiff should be awarded all pecuniary and non-pecuniary damages, including pain and suffering and loss of employment, resulting from his torture and prolonged arbitrary detention. An award of punitive damages is also proper in order to punish and deter such acts and thereby further international human rights. Humans must be deterred from inflicting such cruel punishment on fellow humans.[175]

In its conclusions of law the court found that both compensatory and punitive damages were 'proper under the law of nations, the statutory and common law of the United States and the common law of California'.[176]

Nearly all Alien Tort Claim actions decided to date have involved issues of torture, summary execution, disappearance, or genocide. Perhaps not surprisingly, the damage awards have been high and all have included punitive damages. The following describes in chronological order the cases brought and the awards made.

Filartiga v. Pena-Irala[177] (Torture to death): $175,000 to sister, $200,000 to father in compensation, $ 5,000,000 to each as punitive damages.

Martinez-Baca v. Suarez-Mason[178] (Systematic arbitrary detention and torture): $11,170,699 in compensation (including lost earnings), $10,000,000 in punitive damages to victim.

Forti v. Suarez-Mason[179] For first plaintiff, for arbitrary detention, torture, and witnessed abuse and execution of brother: $3,000,000 compensatory, $3,000,000 in punitive; for second plaintiff, for arbitrary detention, abuse and 'disappeared' mother: $2,000,000 in compensation, $1,000,000 punitive.

Trajano v. Marcos[180] (Torture and summary execution): $236,000 in lost earnings, $175,000 moral damages, $1,250,000 exemplary damages to victim's estate; $ 1,250,000 in compensation, $1,250,000 exemplary to victim's mother.

Siderman v. Argentina[181] (Torture): compensatory damages totaling $2,607,575.63 to victim, a decision reversed on jurisdictional grounds.

173　*Trajano v. Marcos*, No. 86–0207, slip op. at 3 (D. Haw. March 25, 1991).
174　No. C–87–2057–SC, slip op. at 1 (N.D. Cal. Apr. 22, 1988).
175　*Ibid.* at 4.
176　*Ibid.* at 8.
177　*Filartiga*, 577 F. Supp. at 860 (E.D.N.Y. 1984).
178　*Martinez-Baca v. Suarez Mason*, No. 87–2057 SC (N.D. Cal., Apr. 22,1988).
179　*Forti v. Suarez Mason*, No. 87–2058–DLJ (N.D. Cal. Apr. 25, 1990).
180　*Trajano v. Marcos*, No. 86–0207, (D. Haw., May 19, 1991).
181　*Siderman v. Argentina*, No. CV–82–1772–RMT (MCX) (C.D. Cal. Sep. 28, 1984) vacated on other grounds; No. CV–82–1772–RMT (MCx) (C.D. Cal. Mar. 7 1985), rev'd and remanded, 965 F.2d 699 (9th Cir. 1992).

Quiros de Rapaport, et al. v. Suarez-Mason[182] (Torture and murder of one victim, disappearance of another): $10,000,000 in compensation, $10,000,000 punitive damages to victims' widows, $5,000,000 in compensation, $5,000,000 punitive damages to victims' mother and sister, respectively.

Todd v. Panjaitan[183] $2,000,000 in compensation to mother as administratrix of son's estate, $2,000,000 in compensation to mother, and $10,000,000 in punitive damages.

Paul v. Avril[184] (Torture and arbitrary detention): six victims each awarded between $2,500,000 and $3,500,000 in compensatory damages, together with $4,000,000 each in punitive damages.

In re Estate of Marcos A very important set of cases followed Ferdinand Marcos, former President of the Philippines, to the USA. Some half a dozen civil lawsuits were filed in federal courts for human rights violations. The suits alleged that Marcos was personally responsible for summary executions; disappearances; torture; cruel, inhuman and degrading treatment and punishment; and prolonged arbitrary detention in the Philippines between 1971 and 1986. Two types of lawsuits were filed: actions on behalf of approximately 30 named individuals, and a class action on behalf of an estimated 10,000 victims of torture, disappearance, and summary execution from Marcos' declaration of martial law in September 1972 until his departure from the Philippines.

The court separated the consolidated cases into three phases.[185] First in 1992 a jury trial was held on liability. While the case was pending, on 1 November 1991, the plaintiffs moved for a preliminary injunction to prevent the Estate from transferring or secreting any assets in order to preserve the possibility of collecting a judgment. The Estate had earlier been enjoined from transferring or secreting assets in an action brought by the Republic of the Philippines against Ferdinand Marcos. That preliminary injunction had been appealed, and was affirmed.[186]

On 24 September 1992, the jury rendered a verdict in favour of the class and the individually-named plaintiffs with one exception. Judgment was entered in favour of the prevailing plaintiffs. The preliminary injunction was modified on 16 November 1993, to set forth the jury verdict on liability, to compel the legal representatives of the Estate to fully and completely answer plaintiffs' interrogatories regarding the assets of the estate, to name the Swiss banks at which the Marcos's had deposited monies as representatives of the Estate, and to permit the plaintiffs to take discovery regarding these assets.

---

[182] *Quiros de Rapaport v. Suarez Mason*, No. C87–2266 JPV (N.D. Cal. Apr. 11, 1989).

[183] *Todd v. Panjaitan*, No. CV–92–12255–PBS (D. Mass. Oct. 26, 1994).

[184] *Paul v. Avril*, No. 91–399–CIV (S.D. Fla. July 1, 1994).

[185] See *Trajano v. Marcos (In re: Estate of Ferdinand E. Marcos Litigation)*, 978 F.2d 493 (9th Cir. 1992) ('Estate I'), cert. denied, 113 S.Ct. 2960 (1993), 125 L. Ed. 2d 661 (1993).

[186] See *Republic of Philippines v. Marcos*, 862 F.2d 1355 (9th Cir. 1988) (en banc), cert. denied, 490 U.S. 1035, 109 S.Ct. 1933 (1989), 104 L. Ed. 2d 404.

The district court then ordered the damage trial split into two phases, one on exemplary damages and one on compensatory damages. On 23 February 1994, the jury awarded the plaintiffs $1.2 billion in exemplary damages. The injunction against transferring assets was maintained.[187]

The court appointed a special master to supervise proceedings related to the compensatory damages phase. The jury reconvened to consider damages on the basis of the report and awarded $766 million to the class. The estate appealed on several grounds including the question of whether exemplary damages could be available against the estate. Plaintiffs argued for the application of Philippine law which does allow such damages against an estate. The appellate court agreed that the district court followed Philippine law on the issue of damages, citing Philippine Civil Code, Articles 2229 and 2231. The former provides that 'exemplary or corrective damages are imposed, by way of example or correction for the public good, in addition to the moral, temperate, liquidated or compensatory damages'. Section 2231 allows exemplary damages if the defendant 'acted with gross negligence'. The Estate did not challenge that Philippine law allows exemplary damages. The court of appeals upheld the decision.[188]

Xuncax et al v. Hector Gramajo; Ortiz v. Gramajo[189] Nine expatriate citizens of Guatemala and Dianna Ortiz, a citizen of the USA, brought separate actions against Hector Gramajo, formerly Guatemala's Minister of Defense, seeking compensatory and punitive damages for injuries they suffered from conduct of Guatemalan military forces. The Guatemalan military forces ransacked their villages and some of the plaintiffs were subjected to torture and arbitrary detention; others were forced to watch as their family members were tortured to death or summarily executed; one plaintiff's father was caused to 'disappear'. All of the plaintiffs, in exile, demonstrated severe psychological disorders and disturbances due to the nature of the traumas inflicted upon them. Dianna Ortiz, an Ursuline nun and a citizen of the USA, was kidnapped, tortured and subjected to sexual abuse in Guatemala by personnel under Gramajo's command. When word of her treatment became public, Gramajo defamed her by falsely asserting her injuries were inflicted by an angry lover. Gramajo was found liable for most of the alleged wrongs on the basis of his command responsibility.[190]

The damages sought by the plaintiffs and awarded by the court were as follows:

---

[187] *Hilao et al. v. Estate of Ferdinand Marcos*, 25 F.3d 1467; 1994 U.S. App. LEXIS 14796. *Hilao v. Marcos*, 103 F.3d 767 (1996).

[188] The issue of how compensatory damages were calculated is discussed in Chapter 12.

[189] *Xuncax et al. v. Hector Gramajo; Ortiz v. Gramajo*, 886 F. Supp. 162 (D. Ct Mass 1995).

[190] In *In re Yamashita*, the Supreme Court held a general of the Imperial Japanese Army responsible for a pervasive pattern of war crimes committed by his officers when he knew or should have known that they were going on but failed to prevent or punish them. Such 'command responsibility' is shown by evidence of a pervasive pattern and practice of torture, summary execution or disappearances.

(1) Summary execution: plaintiffs Xuncax, Doe and Pedro-Pascual, 'on their own behalf and on behalf of their next-of-kin', (Complaint 59), sought compensatory damages 'in excess of $2,000,000' each and punitive damages 'of at least $5,000,000' each (Complaint 62 and 63.) The court awarded the full amounts.

(2) Disappearance: plaintiff Callejas, 'on his own behalf and on behalf of his father sought compensatory damages' 'in excess of $2,000,000' and punitive damages 'of at least $5,000,000' (Complaint 67 and 68.) The court awarded the full amount.

(3) Torture: plaintiffs Xuncax, Doe and Diego-Francisco, 'on their own behalf and on behalf of their next-of-kin', (Complaint 69), sought compensatory damages 'in excess of $2,000,000' each and punitive damages 'of at least $5,000,000' each (Complaint 73 and 74.) The court awarded $1,000,000 in compensatory damages and $2,000,000 in punitive damages for plaintiff Diego-Francisco on his own behalf.

(4) Arbitrary detention: plaintiffs Xuncax, Doe and Diego-Francisco, 'on their own behalf and on behalf of their next-of-kin', (Complaint 79), sought compensatory damages 'in excess of $1,000,000' each and punitive damages 'of at least $1,000,000' each (Complaint 82 and 83). The court awarded $500,000 in compensatory damages and $500,000 in punitive damages for plaintiff Diego-Francisco on his own behalf.

(5) Cruel, inhuman, or degrading treatment: each Xuncax plaintiff sought compensatory damages 'in excess of $1,000,000' and punitive damages 'of at least $1,000,000' on this count (Complaint 77 and 78). The court awarded $1,000,000 in compensatory damages and $1,000,000 in punitive damages each for plaintiffs Xuncax, Diego-Francisco, Doe; $500,000 in compensatory damages and $500,000 in punitive damages each for Francisco-Marcos, Juan Ruiz-Gomez, Miguel Ruiz-Gomez; and $750,000 in compensatory damages and $750,000 in punitive damages for Callejas, each on his own behalf.

(6) Dianna Ortiz sought compensatory recovery 'in excess of $1,000,000' for the harm she suffered as a result of the acts of torture inflicted upon her by the defendant (Complaint 42) and $1,000,000 in punitive damages (Complaint 43).[191] The court found that an award of compensatory damages

---

[191] Her case differed from the others; not being an alien, she could not sue under the Alien Tort Claim Statute. Instead, she brought her action under the Torture Victim Protection Act, passed after American ratification of the United Nations Convention against Torture. On the issue of punitive damages, the court noted that the TVPA by its terms neither explicitly permits nor prohibits the federal district court from granting awards of punitive damages. Section 2(a) of the statute in relevant part provides simply that the tortfeasor 'shall be liable for damages in a civil action'. It cited the precedents of other human rights cases where all the courts issued sizable punitive awards, often in excess of the corresponding compensatory recovery. Further, the court pointed out that the *Filartiga* decision was quoted with approval in the Senate Report accompanying the TVPA bill. See S. Rep. No. 249, 102d Cong., 1st Sess. 4 (1991) at 4 ('Senate Report'). The court presumed that Congress was aware

in the amount of $3,000,000 would be both proper and reasonable, particularly when it compared the torture inflicted on Ortiz with that inflicted on Diego-Francisco. It also awarded the punitive damages claimed.

In arriving at the amounts awarded, the court had regard to 'the developing body of federal common law precedent which has allowed both compensatory and punitive damages for such harms, along with consideration of both the grievous nature of the instant harms as well as the clear aspiration of the community of nations to put an end to such offenses'. The Guatemalan plaintiffs also sought compensatory damages for violations of Guatemalan law. The court rejected these claims as duplicative of the international human rights they had asserted.

Mushikiwzabo v. Barayagwiza[192] (incitement to genocide) Five plaintiffs documented the massacre of a number of relatives during the genocide in Rwanda. Three plaintiffs sued under the ATCA and two pursuant to the TVPA. The court held that the defendant, described as one of the political leaders in Rwanda, was liable for inciting the massacres. The court had some difficulty placing a monetary value on the damages, although it found that the counsel had carefully documented the lost earnings and pain and suffering damages of each of the plaintiffs' relatives and the emotional damages of each of the plaintiffs. The problem came in the magnitude of the suffering: 'This Judge has seen no other case in which monetary damages were so inadequate to compensate the plaintiffs for the injuries caused by a defendant. One cannot place a dollar value on the lives lost as the result of the defendant's actions and the suffering inflicted on the innocent victims of his cruel campaign. Unfortunately, however, a monetary judgment is all the court can award these plaintiffs'.[193] Each plaintiff claimed $1.5 million for each relative killed, but the court found this excessive under 'traditional principles for an award of pain and suffering' because in almost all cases the actual killing took place in a brief period of time. Therefore, the pain and suffering award was calculated at $500,000 per relative. In addition, the court added an award of punitive damages in the amount of $1,000,000 per relative victim. In total, the court awarded Louise Mushikiwabo $35,204,577; Louis Rutare $10,736,227; Rangira Beatrice Gallimore $16,746,291; Julie Mukandinda Mugemanshuro $20,215,869; and Faustin Semuhungu $22,364,970.

Parallels to the United States Alien Tort Claim Act seem to be developing in other countries. In March 1996 several Spanish legal associations filed a complaint against Argentine security forces. The court opened a criminal investigation that led to an international arrest warrant for General Leopoldo Galtieri, a

that the district court awarded the plaintiffs $5,000,000 in punitive damages each, in addition to a combined compensatory award of $375,000 and that Congress might therefore have contemplated the award of punitive damages when it enacted the TVPA. See Senate Report at 4 (stating that the TVPA 'would establish an unambiguous cause of action that has been successfully maintained under . . . @ 1350').

[192] *Mushikiwabo v. Barayagwiza*, 1996 U.S. Dist. LEXIS 4409 (S.D.N.Y. 1996).
[193] *Ibid.*

former Argentine president. The indictment said Galtieri was responsible for killing four members of a Spanish family in 1976 in Argentina. In July 1997, Switzerland froze the assets of four Argentine military officers that Spain has accused of torturing, kidnapping and killing 320 Spanish citizens during the 1970s repression in Argentina. Spain requested the action as part of its criminal investigation that has led to charging 110 former and active military and police officers. Argentina has refused to cooperate.[194] In the United Kingdom, the non-governmental organization Redress has prepared a Bill to be introduced in Parliament that if passed would allow torture victims to sue for torture committed anywhere in the world if the torturer is found within the United Kingdom.

Finally, it is worth noting that the large damage awards in the Alien Tort Claim cases have served primarily to vindicate morally the victims and to deter violators from coming to or remaining in the USA. Few, if any, victims have been able to execute the judgments rendered.[195] Many of the defendants either have had no assets in the USA or were able to transfer them out of the country during the pendency of the litigation. Assets in foreign countries have been difficult to locate. Nonetheless, the Alien Tort Claim cases have had enormous impact. First, there is no doubt that they have vindicated the individual plaintiffs, allowing them to confront their tormentors and have the truth told. The suits have also provided accountability in regard to violators who escaped any responsibility in their own states and served notice that the USA cannot be considered a safe haven for human rights violators. The cases also served to document abuses for possible further action, from deportation to criminal prosecution in the state where the events occurred. Finally, on a global basis, these decisions helped to move the issue of redress for victims of human rights to the forefront of international attention and stimulated the United Nations to begin its study of the issue.

E. CONCLUSIONS

A credible and fair legal system should remedy every significant invasion of rights but usually does not. The development of legal remedies should be governed by the desire for consistent redress, but more often is determined by administrative feasibility, institutional functions and relationships, and, too often, by government's desire not to be held accountable. As United States President James Madison recognized '[i]n framing a government which is to be administered by men over men, the great difficulty lies in this: you must first enable the government to control the governed; and in the next place oblige it to control itself. A

---

[194] Marlise Simons, 'Swiss Freeze Assets of 4 Argentines Accused in Spain', *New York Times*, 4 July 1997.

[195] Thus far, only $400 has been collected, from Argentine General Suarez-Mason: B. Stephens and M. Ratner, *supra* n. 156 at 218.

dependence on the people is, no doubt, the primary control on the government; but experience has taught mankind the necessity of auxiliary precautions'.[196]

The forms and sources of official misconduct are many: lack of understanding, lack of capacity or capability, lack of resources, negligence, or intent to violate the law. Each source may require a discrete response targeting the origin of the problem. Society seeks to discourage official wrongdoing, in order to reduce the probability that it will occur. Holding the government responsible may have such broad impact because the government can employ the incentives, education, constraints and other conditions that influence officials' behaviour.

As this chapter has demonstrated, national law generally allows courts to award nominal or compensatory damages and often permits imposition of exemplary, aggravated or punitive damages. Nominal damages are awarded when the court finds no harm done but legal rights have been violated. Compensatory damages are awarded to make good or replace the direct and consequential losses caused by the wrong or injury. Exemplary damages are awarded when the defendant's conduct has aggravated the situation after the wrong or when the defendant has demonstrated a wanton disregard for the plaintiff's legal rights. Punitive damages punish particularly egregious misconduct.

Reference to national law can be helpful if the differences in public and private law cases are recognized. In some instances, the interests protected by a particular constitutional (or human) right may not also be protected by an analogous tort or private obligation. The difficult task is one of adapting rules of damages to provide fair compensation for injuries caused by the deprivation of a right. The purpose of human and civil rights litigation would be defeated if injuries caused by the deprivation of constitutional rights went uncompensated simply because the law does not recognize an analogous cause of action in tort. The rules governing compensation for injuries caused by the deprivation of rights should be tailored to the interests protected by the particular right in question. This raises a problem with procedural violations in particular: if the result would have been the same in the matter, even with no violation, what is the wrong and what is the remedy? It can be argued that all procedural violations should be compensated because the purpose of the procedural right is to ensure feelings of just treatment as well as to minimize the risk of mistake in the outcome. In a proper case, persons might recover damages for mental and emotional distress caused by the denial of procedural due process. Similarly, damages should be awarded for humiliation and distress caused by unlawful arrests, searches and seizures, and the wrongful deprivation of the right to vote.[197]

---

[196] A. Hamilton, J. Jay, J. Madison, *The Federalist*, No. 51.

[197] *Wayne v. Venable*, 260 F.63 (8th Cir. 1919) cited in *Hostrop v. Board of Junior College* Dist. No. 515, 523 F.2d 569 (7th Cir. 1975) cert. denied, 425 U.S. 963, 96 S.Ct. 1748, 48 L.Ed.2d 208 (1976) and *Ashby v. White*, 1 Eng.Rep. 417, 8 St.Tr. 89, 1 Bro.Parl.Cas. 62 (H.L.1703), rev'g 2 Ld.Raym, 938, 92 Eng.Rep 126 (K.B.1703); *Nixon v. Herndon*, 273 U.S. 536, 47 S.Ct. 446, 71 L.Ed. 759 (1927); *Carey v. Piphus*, 98 S.Ct. 1042, 55 L.Ed.2d 252 (1978).

Remedies available reflect some normative conception of the relationship between the citizen and the state. The development of international human rights law has led to important developments in national legal systems, as states have increasingly limited their governmental immunities and developed innovative responses to human rights violations. As the next chapter will show, the traditional law of state responsibility drew upon national remedies as it attempted to provide redress, particularly in cases of injury to aliens. Modern human rights tribunals could similarly develop human rights remedies by application of some common principles of national law.

4

Reparations in the Law of State Responsibility for Injury to Aliens

International human rights law has developed innovative procedures to allow victims of human rights violations to bring complaints directly against the offending state. Prior to the development of these procedures, violations of international law—including those involving the mistreatment of individuals—were met with responses under the law of state responsibility. This traditional body of law, particularly the part of it that concerns the mistreatment of aliens, contains useful precedents for evaluating the nature and scope of remedies afforded in state practice. Clearly, the law of state responsibility remains applicable to the violation by a state of internationally-recognized human rights, because such an act constitutes a breach of an international obligation. The present chapter therefore reviews the law of state responsibility, in particular the redress afforded for injury to aliens, attempting to discern general principles and precedents that may be applicable or useful in addressing human rights violations.

The law of state responsibility requires a state to make reparations when it fails to comply, through an act or omission attributable to it, with an obligation under international law.[1] Encompassed in this straightforward statement are many unsettled issues, including the nature and range of attributable acts giving rise to responsibility, the standard of care owed, and the nature and scope of reparations.[2] Sometimes the term 'reparations' is used narrowly in the sense of money damages; more generally, it refers to the entire range of remedies available for a breach of an international obligation.[3] Although the losses of injured individuals may form one measure of damages, the injuries for which reparations are due are those suffered by the state itself.[4] The claim may be based on presumed injury

---

[1]   Cheng relies on legal reasoning in claiming that reparation is due for any legal wrong: 'It is a logical consequence flowing from the very nature of law and is an integral part of every legal order': B. Cheng, *General Principles of Law as Applied by International Courts and Tribunals* (1953), 170.

[2]   The first rapporteur for the International Law Commission posited that the lack of uniformity on issues of state responsibility 'is quite often attributable to differences of opinion concerning substance' which leads to 'individual, and at times capricious' interpretation of the issues: F.V. Garcia-Amador, *Responsibility of the State for injuries caused in its territory to the person or property of aliens—reparation of the injury*, U.N. Doc. A/CN.4/134 & Add 1, 1961–II Y.B.Int'l.L.Comm'n. 7.

[3]   Graefrath speaks of reparation for material damages and satisfaction which covers moral or political damages: B. Graefrath, 'Responsibility and Damages Caused: Relationships between Responsibility and Damages', (1984) 185 *Receuil des Cours* 69. See also E. Riedel, 'Satisfaction', in 10 *Encyclopedia of Public International Law* 383 (R. Bernhardt ed., 1987) (hereinafter EPIL); R. Wolfrum, 'Reparation for Internationally Wrongful Acts' in 10 EPIL at 353.

[4]   *Factory at Chorzow Case (Germany v. Poland) (Merits)* 1928 P.C.I.J. (Ser. A.) No. 21 at 28. Also, in the *Corfu Channel Case*, 1949 I.C.J. 4, the International Court of Justice recognized that

deriving, e.g. from a failure to permit the exercise of a right, without resulting material or pecuniary loss.[5] Where material damages are claimed, they must not be too remote from the wrongful conduct. Civil law jurisdictions tend to treat this problem in terms of equivalent or adequate causal connections, while common law jurisdictions look to the proximate or natural consequences of acts. Tribunals also look to intervening acts: contemporaneous or subsequent intervening acts will negate or reduce damages.[6]

While they are often stated as cumulative or alternative, an award of damages generally presupposes that restitution and satisfaction are not adequate to remedy the harm done.[7] The well-known ICJ formulation of the obligation to redress harm is stated in the *Chorzow Factory* case:

reparation must, as far as possible, wipe out all consequences of the illegal act and re-establish the situation which would, in all probability have existed if that act had not been committed. Restitution in kind, or, if this is not possible, payment of a sum corresponding to the value which a restitution would bear; the award, if need be, of damages for loss sustained which would not be covered by restitution in kind or payment in place of it—such are the principles which should serve to determine the amount of compensation due for an act contrary to international law.[8]

In theory, therefore, restitution should be afforded when possible, and should be the preferred or normal remedy. Decisions of international tribunals, however, are not consistent on this point, nor are commentators.[9] In the *Temple of Preah Vihear* case,[10] the International Court of Justice ruled that Cambodia had to leave the unlawfully occupied temple circle in Thailand and restore all religious objects it might have removed. Similarly, restitution was granted as the primary remedy in the *Libya Oil Companies Arbitration,* [11] while in *British Petroleum v. Libya*[12] no restitution was ordered.

Reparations act or at least aim to restore the prior juridical situation.[13]

---

damage to two British warships and the cost of pensions and medical treatment as a result of the killing and injuring of crew members were cognizable claims, but that the injury was to the state.

[5]   A.S. De Bustamante, (1986) III *Derecho International Publico* 481.

[6]   See the Naulilaa Arbitration, 2 R.I.A.A. 1013 (1928) (rejecting a claim for damages as too remote where a native uprising followed upon wrongful German reprisals on a Portuguese colonial territory).

[7]   Another formulation of the duty calls on states to: (1) cease the violation; (2) release and return anything wrongfully taken; (3) prevent and remedy effects of the breach; and (4) re-establish the situation as it existed before. See Article 6 of Part II of the International Law Commission's Draft Articles on State Responsibility, 1985 Y.B. Int'l L.Comm'n, vol. II (Part II) at 25.

[8]   *Factory at Chorzow Case, supra* n. 4, at 47.

[9]   See T. van Boven, *Study concerning the right to restitution, compensation and rehabilitation for victims of gross violations of human rights and fundamental freedoms, Preliminary report submitted by Theodoor van Boven, Special Rapporteur,* E/CN.4/Sub.2/1990/10, 26 July 1990, 5.

[10]   *Temple of Preah Vihear (Cambodia v. Thailand),* 1962 I.C.J. 6.

[11]   *Topco v. Libya,* 53 Int'l L.Rep. 389.

[12]   *British Petroleum v. Libya,* 53 Int'l L.Rep. 297.

[13]   'La réparation est une tentative de rétablissement de l'équilibre juridique prévu et voulu par le droit international. Plus précisement, la réparation est constituée par l'ensemble des mesures tendant

Reparations may envisage restitution (i.e. the re-establishment of the right injured or the state of legality), compensation for damages suffered in the past, and assurances against future breaches of the same obligation, an approach that aims simultaneously at remedial justice and deterrence. In all cases, '[a] correlation exists between the significance of the international obligation breached and the reparations owed [and this] correlation is governed by the principle of proportionality'.[14]

A. REPARATIONS IN THE LAW OF STATE RESPONSIBILITY

1. International judicial decisions

In international judicial practice, states have requested awards under all the headings mentioned: restitution, damages, specific performance satisfaction, and injunctive relief. Damages have been pleaded in about one-third of the cases submitted to the Permanent Court of International Justice and the International Court of Justice, but only two awards have been made[15] and even they are of limited precedential value. In the *Wimbledon* case,[16] Germany did not contest the amount claimed, and in the *Corfu Channel* case,[17] wide discretion was left to court-appointed experts to assess the damages.

Judgments of reparations other than damages usually have been in the context of express agreement, e.g. a provision in the Special Agreement submitting to the court's jurisdiction in the *Free Zones of Upper Savoy and the District of Gex* case, allowing for the possibility of an order to France.[18] In the *Iranian Hostages* case,[19] the court issued an order, without discussing its jurisdiction to do so, after finding that Iran had violated its international obligations to the USA. In its decision, the Court:

Decide[d] that the Government of the Islamic Republic of Iran must immediately take all steps to redress the situation . . . and to that end:

a rétablir, soit en nature, soit par équivalent, la situation qui existerait si certains événments dommageables ne s'étaient pas produits': B. Bollecker-Stern, *Le Prejudice Dans la Théorie de la Responsabilité Internationale* (1973), 10. See also L. Sohn and R. Baxter, 'Responsbility of States for Injuries to the Economic Interests of Aliens', (1961) 55 *Am.J. Int'l L.* 545, 580 (reparations consist of all the measures necessary to re-establish the situation of legality). See also Graefrath, *supra* n. 3.

[14] R. Wolfrum, 'Reparation for Internationally Wrongful Acts', in 10 EPIL, *supra* n. 3, at 352–353.
[15] C. Gray, 'Is there an International Law of Remedies', (1985) 65 *Brit. YB Int'l L.* 25, 36.
[16] *The S.S. Wimbledon Case (Great Britain, France, Italy, Japan and Poland, intervening, v. Germany)*, 1923 P.C.I.J. (ser. A/B) No.5.
[17] *Corfu Channel Case (U.K. v. Albania)* 1949 I.C.J. 4.
[18] *Free Zones of Upper Savoy and the District of Gex (France v. Switzerland)*, 1932 P.C.I.J. (ser. A/B) No. 46.
[19] *Case Concerning United States Diplomatic and Consular Staff in Teheran (U.S. v. Iran)* 1980 I.C.J. 3.

(a) must immediately terminate the unlawful detention of the United States Charge d'Affaires and other diplomatic and consular staff and other United States nationals now held hostage in Iran, and must immediately release each and every one and entrust them to the protecting Power . . .

(b) must ensure that all the said persons have the necessary means of leaving Iranian territory, including means of transport;

(c) must immediately place in the hands of the protecting Power the premises, property, archives and documents of the United States Embassy in Tehran and of its Consulates in Iran.[20]

The limited number and nature of precedents in judicial practice are far exceeded by arbitral decisions on the specific topic of state responsibility for injury to aliens. Although such claims have been widely superseded by international human rights procedures, the remedies afforded may suggest the scope of remedial powers of international human rights tribunals; in particular, they may provide additional insight into the intent of the drafters of Article 50 of the European Convention on Human Rights in using the term 'just satisfaction'.

2. International arbitral claims

International claims commissions have been in existence at least since the Jay Treaty of 1794 to adjudicate large numbers of international claims, especially those concerning injury to aliens.[21] Article 7 of the Jay Treaty created a mixed commission to settle claims arising from violations of the laws of neutrality.[22] The tribunal assumed that international law was the source of the rules to be applied on the assessment of damages. Later tribunals rarely referred back to these decisions, or to other international decisions on remedies, however, and state practice has not assisted, as most *compromis* omit provisions on remedies and assessment of damages. As a result, international arbitrators generally have wide discretionary powers to assess damages. It has been argued in fact that, because of the discretion afforded and the range of possible reparations, customary international law cannot provide 'any principles, criteria or methods for determining *a priori* how reparation is to be made for the injury caused by a wrongful act or omission'.[23] This is perhaps overstated, because arbitral decisions often contain articulated principles and some consistency.

---

[20] *(U.S. v. Iran)* 1980 I.C.J. 3, at 44–45.

[21] According to Gray, damage claims for injury to aliens forms the largest class of claims presented over the past 200 years. Some 261 of 435 tribunals formed between 1794 and 1972 dealt with such claims: *supra* n. 15, at 35, citing A.M. Stuyt, *A Survey of International Arbitrations* (1972), 1794–1970 .

[22] See 3,4 Moore, *International Arbitrations* and 4 *International Adjudications*; C. Gray, *supra* n. 15, at 33.

[23] See F.V. Garcia-Amador *et al*, *Recent Codification of the Law of State Responsibility for Injury to Aliens* (1974), 89 ; L. Reitzer, *Comme Consequence de L'Acte Illicite en Droit International* (1938), 111.

In the 1960s and 1970s, claims practice shifted as economic injury due to nationalizations and other deprivations of wealth became more prevalent than traditional claims for personal injury. Lump sum settlement agreements creating national commissions began to substitute for international adjudication.[24] In some instances, large businesses negotiated their own settlements.[25] Today, aliens have recourse to international human rights procedures for many traditional claims, while claims commissions and lump sum agreements take care of other types of cases. Most lump sum agreements serve to settle property claims, most frequently in reference to nationalization and expropriation. Personal injury or death, which was at the origin of most pre-Second World War state responsibility claims and is perhaps most analogous to a serious human rights claim, is not commonly covered by the post-war settlement agreements.[26] Of the 155 agreements studied by Lillich and Weston, only eight expressly authorized personal injury and death claims and one did so by implication. Five of these concerned injuries or deaths caused by Nazi actions. Article 1(1) of the Norwegian–German Agreement[27] is typical. It compensated: 'Norwegian nationals who were victimized by National Socialist persecution because of their race, beliefs or opinions and whose freedom or health was in consequence impaired, and also on behalf of the survivors of persons who died as a result of such persecution'.[28] Two settlement agreements included remedies for private violence: the United States-Panama Agreement, Article 1(b) of which terminated 'claims ... for personal injuries sustained by six soldiers of the United States Army during disturbances which occurred in the city of Panama in the year 1915';[29] and the British-Indonesian Agreement, which in Paragraph 1(c) settled claims of the British Government and of British nationals 'in respect of loss or damage suffered,

---

[24] See R. Lillich and B. Weston, *International Claims: Their Settlement by Lump Sum Agreements* (1975) (hereinafter Lillich and Weston).

[25] See B. Weston, 'International Law and the Deprivation of Foreign Wealth: A Framework for Future Inquiry', in R. Falk and C. Black (eds.) *The Future of the International Legal Order* (1970), vol. 2, 36, 154–55.

[26] Lillich and Weston, *supra* n. 24, at 175.

[27] Norway-Federal Republic of Germany, signed 7 August 1959, entered into force 23 April 1960, 358 U.N.T.S. 185.

[28] The total amount foreseen by the agreement was 60 million Deutsche Mark: *ibid.*, Article 1(1). The distribution of the sum is left to the discretion of the Norwegian government. Similar provisions: Article 1(1) of the French–German Agreement, signed 15 July 1960, entered into force 4 August 1961, (1961) 88 *J. Du Droit Int'l* 1200; [1961] R.G.D.I.P 914 (400,000,000 DM to be paid those who were the object of persecution and who sustained injury to the liberty and integrity of their person or to the successors of those who died); the British German Agreement, signed 9 June 1964, entered into force 9 June 1964, G.B.T.S. No. 42 (Cmnd. 2445), 539 U.N.T.S. 187 (payment of one million pounds sterling) ; the Swedish German Agreement, signed 3 August 1964, entered into force, 3 August 1964 [1964] S.O. No. 58 (payment of 1 million DM for 'Swedish nationals affected by Nazi measures of persecution'; and the Belgian German Agreement, signed 28 September 1960 [1961] Monit. 6856 (September 2) (80 million DM). For further information on German reparations see *infra* Chapter 12.

[29] United States-Panama, signed 26 January 1950, entered into force 11 October 1950, 1 U.S.T. 685, T.I.A.S. No. 2129, 132 U.N.T.S. 233; Lillich and Weston, *supra* n. 24 at 35.

directly or indirectly, during or as a consequence of the riots and public disorder in Indonesia between 10 and 30 September 1963'.[30]

In sum, the procedures for obtaining reparations for injury to aliens traditionally rested upon the terms of arbitration agreements or treaties setting up mixed-claims commissions. In most cases, the states involved did not dictate the scope or nature of the remedies to be afforded, leaving it to the judgment of the arbitrator or commissioner to draw upon relevant domestic and international legal principles. In recent cases, arbitral tribunals or commissions have exercised inherent judicial power to fashion remedies.[31]

In all instances, however, it must be recalled that the state making the claim is in theory asserting its own injury and not necessarily representing the individual by presenting all the damages a person may have suffered. The decisions on reparations can be seen as somewhat analogous to remedies for human rights violations, but the inter-state element is important, especially the role played by the respective power of the two states and their views in each case.

3. Codification of the general principles of state responsibility

Various unsuccessful efforts to codify the law of state responsibility have taken place during the past century, uncertainty about reparations proving to be one of the problems. In 1930, the Hague Codification Conference Subcommittee on Damages concluded that it was best to leave the issue of reparations for future development as there had not yet been sufficient crystallization of the principles in state practice to warrant codification.[32]

The United Nations International Law Commission (ILC) has struggled with the issue of state responsibility since its creation in 1949,[33] most of the time based

---

[30]   Great Britain-Indonesia, 1 December 1966, G.B.T.S. No. 34 (Cmnd. 3277) 606 U.N.T.S. 125, Lillich and Weston, *supra* n. 24 at 336.

[31]   In the *Rainbow Warrior* case, the arbitral tribunal claimed such power: The authority to issue an order for the cessation or discontinuance of a wrongful act or omission results from the inherent powers of a competent tribunal which is confronted with the continuous breach of an international obligation which is in force and continues to be in force. The delivery of such an order requires, therefore, two essential conditions intimately linked, namely that the wrongful act has a continuing character and that the violated rule is still in force at the time in which the order is issued: Decision of 30 April 1990 by the France-New Zealand Arbitration Tribunal, (1990) 82 *Int'l L. Rep.* 573.

[32]   League of Nations Publication 1930, xvii at 234. Article 3 of the draft articles adopted by the Third Committee of the Conference stated, somewhat unhelpfully: 'The international responsibility of a State imports the duty to make reparation for the damage sustained in so far as it results from failure to comply with its international obligation': see, F.V. Garcia-Amador, *The Changing Law of International Claims* (1984), vol. 2, 559–617.

[33]   At its first session, the ILC provisionally listed the law of state responsibility as one of 14 topics suitable for study. See *Report of the International Law Commission to the General Assembly*, 4 U.N. GAOR Supp. No. 10 at 3, U.N. Doc. A/925 (1949), reprinted in [1949] Y.B. Int'l L.Comm'n 278, 281, U.N. Doc. A/CN.4/SER.A/1949.

on a mandate of the United Nations General Assembly to undertake a codification of the principles of international law governing the topic.[34] In 1980, the ILC provisionally adopted 35 draft articles,[35] Articles 4 and 5 of which concern reparations. Article 4 called on the state committing an internationally wrongful act to discontinue the act, apply internal remedies, and re-establish the situation as it existed before the breach. When materially impossible to provide the restitution required, the draft insisted on payment of a sum of money corresponding to the value which a fulfilment of those obligations would bear and also on provision of satisfaction in the form of an apology and of appropriate guarantees against repetition of the breach.[36] Article 5 concerned the specific issue of injury to aliens and gave the wrongdoing state the option of applying Article 4(1) or (2).

In 1993, the ILC provisionally adopted new draft articles on reparations, Articles 6 to 10*bis*, which substantially expand on and improve the 1980 draft.[37] The primary exigency is expressed in Article 6, which requires a state committing an internationally wrongful act to cease that conduct. Technically, cessation is not part of reparation, although in some cases its consequences may be indistinguishable from restitution in kind.[38] The function of cessation is to put an end to a violation of international law and to safeguard the continued validity and effectiveness of the infringed norm. According to the ILC commentary, '[t]he rule on cessation thus protects not only the interest of the injured state or states but also

---

[34] G. A. Res. 799, 8 GAOR Supp. No. 17, 52 U.N. Doc. A/2630 (1953). In 1955, the ILC appointed Prof. F.V. Garcia-Amador as Special Rapporteur. From 1956 to 1961 he submitted six annual reports focused exclusively on state responsibility for injuries to aliens: F.V.Garcia-Amador, *First Report on State Responsibility*, U.N. Doc. A/CN.4/96 (1956), reprinted in [1956] 2 *Y.B.Int'l L. Comm'n* 173–231, U.N. Doc. A/CN.4/SER.A/1956/Add.1; Garcia-Amador, *Second Report on State Responsibility*, U.N. Doc.A/CN.4/106 (1957) reprinted in [1957] 2 *Y.B. Int'l L. Comm'n* 104–30, U.N. Doc. A/CN.4/SER.A/1957/Add.1; Garcia-Amador, *Third Report on State Responsibility*, reprinted in [1958] 2 Y.B. *Int'l L. Comm'n* 47–73, U.N. Doc. A/CN.4/SER.A/1958/Add.1; Garcia-Amador, *Fourth Report on State Responsibility*, U.N. Doc. A/CN.4/119 (1959), reprinted in [1959] 2 Y.B. *Int'l L. Comm'n* 1–36, U.N. Doc. A/CN.4/SER.A/1959/Add.1; Garcia-Amador, *Fifth Report on State Responsibility*, U.N. Doc. A/CN.4/125 (1960), reprinted in [1960] *Y.B. Int'l L. Comm'n* 41–68, U.N. Doc. A/CN.4/SER.A/1960/Add.1; and Garcia-Amador, *Sixth Report on State Responsibility*, U.N. Doc. A/CN.4/134 and Add.1 (1961), reprinted in [1961] 2 *Y.B. Int'l L. Comm'n* 1–54, U.N. Doc. A/CN.4/SER.A/1961/Add.1. Opposition to the limited focus on injury to aliens led the ILC to appoint a Sub-Committee on State Responsibility to study the approach it should take to the topic. After considerable debate, the Sub-Committee recommended that the ILC study 'the general rules governing the international responsibility of the State': *Report of the Sub-Committee on State Responsibility to the International Law Commission*, U.N. Doc. A/CN.4/152 (1963) at 11, 12, reprinted in [1963] 2 *Y.B. Int'l L. Comm'n* 227, U.N. Doc A/CN.4/SER.A/1963/Add.1 at 231, 228. The ILC then named Judge Ago as the new Special Rapporteur with a mandate to separate general principles of state responsibility from particular rules applicable to wrongful acts.

[35] *Report of the International Law Commission to the General Assembly*, 35 U.N. GAOR Supp. No. 10 at 59–68, U.N. Doc. A/35/10 (1980), reprinted in 2 *Y.B.Int'l L. Comm'n* 1, 30– 63, U.N. Doc./CN.4/SER.A/1980/Add.1 (Pt.2).

[36] [1981] 1 *Y.B. Int'l L. Comm'n* 126.

[37] [1993] 2 *Y.B. Int'l L. Comm'n* 54.

[38] e.g. liberation of persons or the restitution of objects or premises involves both restitution and cessation of the wrong.

the interests of the international community in the preservation of, and reliance on, the rule of law'.[39]

The general provision on reparations, Article 6*bis*, provides that an injured state is entitled to full reparation in the form of restitution in kind, compensation, satisfaction, and assurances and guarantees of non-repetition. Fault is now expressly added as an element in determining the scope of reparations due.[40] The article thus lays down the general rule that full reparation should seek to wipe out the consequences of the internationally wrongful act, adding that states cannot invoke domestic law as justification for failure to provide reparation.

Articles 7 to 10*bis* detail the various forms of reparation. In Article 7, restitution in kind, that is, the re-establishment of the situation that existed before the wrongful act was committed, is set forth as a requirement provided that it is not materially impossible, would not involve breach of a peremptory norm of international law, would not involve a disproportionate burden, and would not seriously jeopardize the political independence or economic stability of the state committing the wrongful act. The concept of restitution does not include compensation due for the loss suffered between the wrongful act and the remedial action. This is left to compensation. In other words, restitution in kind is limited to what *was* and not what *would have been*, avoiding the construction of a hypothetical present. It may include handing over persons or property, or modification of a legal situation such as the revocation, annulment, or amendment of the law enacted in violation of international law, rescinding of an administrative or judicial measure unlawfully adopted, or the nullification of a treaty.

The injured state is entitled also to compensation for the damage caused by an internationally wrongful act if and to the extent that the damage is not made good by restitution in kind (Article 8). Article 8(2) concerns the scope of compensation and includes all economically assessable damage, such as damage to the state's territory, military installations, diplomatic premises, ships, aircraft, spacecraft, and injury to persons. The latter includes moral damage to injured nationals or agents caused by mental suffering, injury to feelings, humiliation, shame, degradation, loss of social position or injury to credit and reputation. Compensation may include interest and lost profits. The commentary notes that the ILC decided to keep the rules on compensation relatively general and flexible in light of the diverse practice of arbitral tribunals and commissions.[41]

The requirement of a causal link between the wrongful act and the harm is discussed at length in the commentary to draft Article 8. The ILC rejects the traditional distinction between 'direct' and 'indirect' harm, as well as use of 'proximate cause', calling both ambiguous and of scant utility. Instead, the criterion is

---

[39]   [1993] 2 *Y.B. Int'l L. Comm'n* 54, at 55.

[40]   'In the determination of reparation, account shall be taken of the negligence or the wilful act or omission of: (a) the injured State; or (b) a national of that state on whose behalf the claim is brought; which contributed to the damage': Article 6bis(2).

[41]   *Ibid.* at 68.

'the presence of a clear and unbroken causal link between the unlawful act and the injury for which damages are being claimed', a relationship of cause and effect. According to the ILC, 'an injury is so linked to an unlawful act whenever the normal and natural course of events would indicate that the injury is a logical consequence of the act or whenever the author of the unlawful act could have foreseen the damage it caused'.[42] Thus, injury that a reasonable person would view as normal and foreseeable will be presumed as causally related and therefore compensable. The injury may be relatively remote in time, as long as it is caused exclusively by the wrongful act and linked to the wrongful act by a chain of events which, however long, is uninterrupted. The ILC also calls for proportional damages when there are multiple causes.

Satisfaction is covered by Article 10 which entitles the injured state to obtain relief for other damage, in particular moral damage, to the extent necessary to provide full reparation. Satisfaction can take the form of an apology, nominal damages, or, in case of gross infringement of the rights of the injured state, 'damages reflecting the gravity of the infringement'. The last remedy is said to be appropriate when the wrong done 'was aggravated by circumstances of violence, oppression, malice, fraud or wicked conduct on the part of the wrongdoing party'.[43] In the view of the ILC, satisfaction generally is a matter of atonement and reflects the necessity of having a preventive as well as punitive function for the moral, political, and juridical wrong suffered, which will vary according to the gravity of the wrongful act. Satisfaction also may include disciplinary action or punishment of officials guilty of serious misconduct or private individuals guilty of criminal conduct. In assessing a claim for satisfaction, the principle of full reparation applies.

The present ILC rapporteur on state responsibility has paid attention to the role of fault, in particular in connection with satisfaction. He concludes that satisfaction is a form of reparation different from compensatory forms of reparation, and that fault is particularly significant in regard to satisfaction as a complement to pecuniary compensation, as well as to the kinds and number of forms of satisfaction claimed or obtained.[44] According to him 'one must also recall the frequent inclusion, in satisfaction, of "exemplary", "vindictive" or "punitive" damages'.[45] The broad meaning of this term is important in analysing the powers of the European Court of Human Rights to afford 'just satisfaction' pursuant to Article 50 of the European Convention on Human Rights,[46] as it suggests the Court has too narrowly interpreted its powers to afford redress.

---

[42] *Ibid.* at 69.

[43] *Ibid.* at 79. A footnote to this comment explicitly cross-references to the common law award of exemplary damages.

[44] Eighth Report on State Responsibility, A/CN.r/476/Add.1 para. 50 (1996).

[45] Preliminary Report on State Responsibility, U.N. Doc. A/CN.4/416 and Corr. 1 and 2, para. 4 (1988).

[46] For the drafting history of Article 50 and the Court's interpretation of its powers, see *infra* Chapter 5.

The final aspect of reparations is assurances or guarantees of non-repetition, contained in Article 10*bis*. Where there is a risk of repetition of the wrongful act and re-establishment of the prior legal situation is considered insufficient, guarantees of non-repetition may be sought. The measures envisaged may involve formal assurances from the wrongdoing state, instructions to government agents, or adoption of certain conduct considered preventive in nature.

All of the ILC rapporteurs have agreed that the aim behind the various reparations for internationally wrongful acts is to make good the injury caused to persons or property.[47] The 'injury' need not be material injury; indeed, material damage is no longer considered a constituent element of an internationally wrongful act entailing state responsibility. The violation of an international obligation as such is what gives rise to the international responsibility of the state.[48]

The conceptual evolution away from material injury demonstrates a shift in the underlying rationale of state responsibility. If the existence of distinct and measurable damage is required to engage responsibility, that is, if the obligation to repair requires a demonstrated loss caused to one state by another, then international responsibility serves to uphold the sovereignty and equality of states. In contrast, if the violation of law itself is an injury—'legal damage' (*prejudice juridique*) giving rise to an obligation to make reparation—then the role of responsibility becomes one to uphold the rule of law (*garantie de l'ordre juridique international*).[49] In the former theory, state claims depend upon a state's interests being harmed; under the latter, reparation serves broadly to conform state action to international law. Each state has a right to see that international law is respected, acting as a representative of the international community in assuring respect for law.

In support of the latter theory, Anzilotti claimed that harm is implicitly contained in the illegal character of the act,[50] asserting that the violation of a norm always disturbs the interest it protects as well as the right(s) of the person(s) having the interest.[51] He added that, because much of international law concerns non-economic matters, the element of moral damage is much more important in international law than it is in national legal systems. This is clearly the case with most human rights violations. When a violation of international law in and of itself causes harm to another state, the obligation to make reparation is inherent.

[47] E. Riedel, 'Damages', in 10 EPIL, *supra* n. 3, 68.

[48] Graefrath, 'Responsibility and Damages Caused', *supra* n. 3 at 73; A. Tanzi, 'Is Damage a Distinct Condition for the Existence of an Internationally Wrongful Act?' in M. Spinedi and B. Simma (eds.), *UN Codification of State Responsibility* (1987), 1–33.

[49] B. Bollecker-Stern, *supra* n. 13, at 20.

[50] D. Anzilotti, 'La Responsabilité internationale des Etats á raison des dommages soufferts par des étrangers', (1906) 13 RGDIP 5.

[51] 'La violation de la regle est éffectivement toujours un dérangement de l'interêt qu'elle protege et, par voie de conséquence, aussi du droit subjectif de la personne à laquelle l'interêt appartient; il en est d'autant plus ainsi que dans les rapports internationaux, le dommage est, en principe, plutot un dommage moral . . . qu'un dommage materiél': *ibid*.

When the damage results from the very violation of the law, the remedy is the re-establishment of the legal order. Cheng goes further, stating that this inherent obligation to redress and re-establish the status quo 'is an indispensable element of any legal system. The legal order thus provides for its own protection and its theoretical inviolability'.[52]

Applied to human rights law, the concept of legal harm means that any violation of a human rights obligation gives rise to state responsibility, engaging the duty to cease the wrong and make reparations, even if the victim or state bringing the action can demonstrate no pecuniary loss. Multilateral human rights agreements give each state party a right to complain that another state party has not lived up to the obligations of the agreement, the compromissory clause contained in human rights instruments recognizing this in advance. Even if the complaining state has no concrete material interest, there is a common interest in accomplishing the objectives of the treaty,[53] a collective interest in the integrity of the commitments involved.[54] If violations of international law affect the juridical order and may be complained of by all states,[55] the result is a public action in favour of the treaty system. This approach has implications for the nature and scope of remedies that may be afforded because of the focus on compliance and deterrence. While the ICJ in the *South-West Africa* cases rejected the notion of an *actio popularis*,[56] later, in *dictum* in the *Barcelona Traction* decision, it recognized the existence of obligations *erga omnes*.[57]

B. REPARATIONS IN THE LAW OF STATE RESPONSIBILITY FOR INJURY TO ALIENS

Of all the breaches of international law that give rise to state responsibility, those involving injury to aliens are the closest to modern international human rights violations. The considerable jurisprudence developed by claims commissions and other tribunals thus provides instructive precedent on the theory and practice of

---

[52] Cheng, *supra* n. 1, at 170.

[53] S. Rosenne, *The Law and Practice of the International Court* (1985), 520.

[54] See [1967] 1 *Y.B.Int'l L. Comm'n* at 225 (Comments of delegate M. Tammes).

[55] Jenks felt all violations of international law harm all other states. See C.W. Jenks, *The Prospects of International Adjudication* (1964), 524 .

[56] *South-West Africa Case (Ethiopia v. South Africa; Liberia v. South Africa (Second Phase)* 1966 I.C.J. 6 at 47.

[57] *Barcelona Traction, Light and Power Company, Limited (Belgium v. Spain)*, 1970 I.C.J. 3. Criticism of the earlier decision may have induced the Court to make its statement that 'an essential distinction should be drawn between the obligations of a state toward the international community as a whole, and those arising vis-a-vis another state . . . By their very nature the former are the concern of all states. In view of the importance of the rights involved, all states can be held to have a legal interest in their protection: they are obligations erga omnes'. The Court identified some of these obligations as deriving from the principles and rules concerning the basic rights of the human person. Others, it said, 'are conferred by international instruments of universal or quasi-universal character': *ibid.*

remedies for violations of individual rights, keeping in mind that the analogy is not perfect because of distortions imported due to disparity of state power and interest in presenting claims.

1. Legal basis of claims for injury to aliens

In some regards, the law on state responsibility for injury to aliens can be viewed as a precursor to international human rights law, in spite of long-standing debate over whether the required standard of treatment was an 'international minimum'[58] or 'national treatment'[59] standard. For at least the past 200 years, in arbitral and judicial decisions as well as settlements and other agreements, states have asserted and responded to claims of wrongdoing causing harm to individuals, in the process developing extensive practice on the issue of remedies.[60]

According to traditional doctrine, when a state injures an individual it indirectly injures the state of nationality.[61] The government may adopt the grievance and espouse it as an international claim against the offending foreign state. The claimant state is deemed to be asserting its own rights,[62] with the injuries to the individual becoming essentially a convenient basis for calculating the reparation due the state.

The normative basis of state responsibility for injury to aliens is the wrongful act of the state. The breach may come from the injurious actions of state officials directly or from the failure of the state to perform its international duty to take all reasonable and adequate measures to prevent private wrongs, including the duty to arrest and bring an offender to justice. The state is not held directly and primarily responsible for the private wrongs because such an approach would have the effect of making the state an insurer of the safety and well-being of aliens. Lack of due diligence of state organs nevertheless renders the state responsible for private wrongs, that is, when the state 'has failed to take such measures as in the circumstances should normally have been taken to prevent, redress or inflict punishment for the acts causing the damage'.[63]

---

[58] Borchard is among those who argued for minimum international standards of fundamental human rights applicable to the treatment of aliens: E.M. Borchard, *The Diplomatic Protection of Citizens Abroad* (1915), 13–15.

[59] The Montevideo Convention on Rights and Duties of States (26 December 1933) formulated the principle that 'Nationals and foreigners are under the same protection of the law and national authorities, and foreigners may not claim other or more extensive rights than those of the nationals': Article 9, reprinted in *Septima Conferencia International Americana* (1933), 192, 197.

[60] Compilations and discussions of decisions can be found in J. Ralston, *International Arbitral Law*, ch. IX; J. B. Moore, *International Adjudications Ancient and Modern* (1929–33) (hereinafter Moore, *International Adjudications*); J.B. Moore, *History and Digest of the International Arbitrations to which the United States Has Been a Party* (1898) (hereinafter Moore, *International Arbitrations*); and M. Whiteman, *Damages in International Law* (1937), vol. I.

[61] E. de Vattel, *Law of Nations*, (1758), vol. 2, s. 71.

[62] *Mavrommatis Palestine Concessions Case*, 1924 P.C.I.J., (ser. A) No. 2 at 12. See also D. Anzilotti, *Corso de Diritto Internazionale* 4th edn. (1935), vol. I, 423.

[63] Text approved at the 1930 Hague Conference, p. 560.

There are various theories to explain state responsibility for injury to aliens caused by private actors. One is that the state is acting in complicity with the actual wrongdoer. According to Vattel, '[t]he sovereign who refuses to cause reparation to be made for the damage done by his subject, or to punish the offender, or, finally, to deliver him up, renders himself in some measure an accomplice in the injury, and becomes responsible for it'.[64] Where there is actual complicity on the part of the government, this approach makes sense, but in many cases there is no knowledge or other participation in the wrong. Thus an alternative theory posits that state failure to prevent or remedy the harm amounts to condoning the injury. It imposes responsibility if the state grants amnesty or otherwise shows some approval or acquiescence in the wrong. The arbitrator in the *Janes (U.S.) v. Mexico* case appears to have adopted this approach: '[C]ertainly there is no violence to logic and no distortion of the proper meaning of the word "condone" in saying that a nation condones a wrong committed by individuals when it fails to take action to punish the wrongdoing'.[65]

The illegal act giving rise to state responsibility often has been denominated 'denial of justice'.[66] The concept of denial of justice is linked closely with what today would be called the right to a remedy, including the elements of fair trial associated with it. Denial of justice often has been defined as the refusal of access to the tribunals of a country.[67] Mostly it dealt with procedural irregularity irrespective of

---

[64] Vattel, *supra* n. 61, at s. 77.

[65] *Janes Case (U.S. v. Mexico, 1926)* 4 U.N.R.I.A.A. 82, at 123.

[66] The concept of denial of justice has a long history. From an early period, law regarded it as an iniquity to deny justice to an alien. The law of the Visigoths sanctioned reprisals against a judge who denied justice to individuals not domiciled within the jurisdiction. Roman law was similar. See the *Codex Theodosianus*, II, 1, 6. In English law, liability for denial of justice was recognized as early as the twelfth century. In an early case concerning an English plaintiff and defendants from Groningen, denial of justice by the lord who possessed jurisdiction was the basis of liability not the default of the individuals who repudiated the debt: *Wynand Morant v. Andrew Papyng and Partners*, H. Hall, *Select Cases Concerning the Law of Merchant* (1930), vol. 12, 81–83. Failure of the magistrates to afford justice was looked at as a community responsibility. In 1353 a statute passed during the reign of King Edward III restricted international reprisals to the case of denial of justice: 27 Edw. III, stat. 2, c. 17. In Italy and Germany the rule was adopted by treaties so that by the end of the thirteenth century nearly all treaties of friendship contained restrictions on reprisals, generally conditioning it on 'justitiam facere denegare'. By the time of the Spanish School, Vittoria could write that a precondition to reprisals is a 'breach of duty' on the part of the state, i.e. a breach which constitutes neglect to vindicate the right against the wrongdoer, a denial of justice: James Brown Scott, *The Spanish Origin of International Law* (1933), vol. 1, cxxiii. Covarruvias (1512–1577) also stressed that the state must suffer if it fails to punish wrongs committed by its nationals: Covarruvias, *Opera Omnia*, 1638, I, 492; II, 148. Gentili and Grotius both distinguish *deni* and *defi* de justice, the latter concerning wrongs originally committed by the state, the former being a denial of justice for an individual wrong: Gentili, *De Juri Belli Libri* (1598) (James Brown Scott (ed.), 1933) vol. III, Bk. I, chap. XXI (Rolfe's translation); Grotius, *De Jure Belli Ac Pacis*, Bk. III, ch. 2.

[67] In 1758 Vattel wrote that justice may be refused in several ways: (1) by denial of justice or by refusal to hear the complaints of a state or its subjects or to allow the subjects to assert their rights before ordinary tribunals; (2) by pretended delays; (3) by a decision manifestly unjust and one-sided. Similar formulations followed from the Institut de Droit International and the 1930 Hague codification conference.

the substantive law. The 1902 Convention Concerning the Rights of Aliens[68] provides that no diplomatic claims shall be made 'except in the cases where there shall have been, on the part of the tribunal, manifest denial of justice, or abnormal delay, or evident violation of the principles of international law'. According to Latin American legal doctrine, the limited circumstances where the state is responsible for denial of justice include cases where:

(1)   the courts decline, without legal justification, to entertain an action brought by an alien;

(2)   the court refuses to render a formal decision after it has entertained the action;

(3)   there is a voluntary, abnormal or culpable delay in administering justice; and

(4)   there is disregard or notorious misapplication of the law in violation of the law, a treaty, or the principles of international law.

A wrong decision is not enough; there must be fraud, corruption, or denial of legal opportunity to present a case.[69] Failure to execute the judgment of a relevant court is also a denial of justice.

No treaty defined the term 'denial of justice', but it was used frequently in diplomatic correspondence during the first half of this century.[70] The requirement of exhaustion of local remedies often makes it hard to know if claims were grounded in the original wrong or the failure to provide a remedy, but it seems that denial of justice was used mostly when the alien was unable to obtain redress before local tribunals. It appears to have encompassed both the denial of and inadequacy of local remedies, including the failure to grant access to courts or to hear interested parties, as well as other instances of manifest injustice.

Scholars disagree about the scope of the term denial of justice. The narrowest view is that the term applies only to the refusal to grant access to or hearing in a court, or the refusal of a court to pronounce a definite, just sentence. Others extend the term to most acts of the judiciary, including delays of justice and manifest injustice, but not the acts of other departments of government. Broader still is the view that it applies to any failure of local remedies or that it applies to all internationally illegal acts by any branch of government connected with the administration of justice.[71] Fitzmaurice, for example, argues that the term means a wrong connected with the process of administering justice, committed by any organ of the government in its official capacity.[72] Other definitions include any

---

[68]   Article 3, Convencion relativa a los derechos de extrajeria, Actas y documentos de la Segunda Conferencia Pan-Americana 825, 826 (Mexico City, 29 January 1902), reprinted in Consol. T.S. 445.

[69]   Borchard, *supra* n. 58 at 332. See also Moore, *International Arbitrations, supra* n. 60 at 2134, 3497.

[70]   See the cases in J.B. Moore, *supra* n. 60 at 262, 268, 270, 272, 270, 661, 699.

[71]   G. Fitzmaurice, 'The Meaning of the Term Denial of Justice', (1932) 13 *Brit.Y.B.Int'l L.* 93, 108 *et seq.*

[72]   *Ibid.* at 98, 108.

violation of any legal right, privilege or immunity of any person[73] or any illegal treatment of aliens, irrespective of the means of redress afforded the individual.[74]

The term as used in international tribunals shows a variety of meanings as well. In the *Janes* case, denial of justice was said to apply to all acts of the executive and the legislature, as well as the judiciary.[75] In contrast, in the *Chattin* case, denial of justice was restricted to the failure of the authorities to give reparation for a wrong suffered by the claimant.[76] The Commission in the *Chattin* case pointed out the ambiguous usage:

> How confusing it must be to use the term 'denial of justice' for both categories of governmental acts is shown by a simple deduction. If 'denial of justice' covers not only governmental acts implying indirect liability [ie. failure to provide redress] but also acts of direct liability [original injury], and if, on the other hand, denial of justice is applied to acts of executive and legislative authorities as well as to acts of judicial authorities—as is often being done—there would exist no international wrong [involving injury to aliens] that would not be covered by the phrase 'denial of justice' and the expression would lose its value as a technical distinction.[77]

The question of remedies is linked to the issue of when state responsibility arises: at the moment of injury; at the moment of injury by a state agent, but not a private party; or at the failure of local remedies. The second is widely accepted, but the third has been applied most often in practice.[78] The first approach implies that a state is responsible for the injurious act of any person that does harm to an alien, but that the proper operation of local remedies discharges that responsibility. In contrast, the third theory suggests that no responsibility appears until local remedies have failed and that the only form of reparation possible is that made state to state. It is difficult to reconcile the theories that the state is responsible only for its own acts with state practice that measures reparations by the harm done to aliens by non-state actors. It is much more logical to say that the state is responsible in all cases, but discharges its responsibility through effective local remedies.

Inconsistent theories are only part of the problem. The jurisprudence regarding state responsibility for injury to aliens and reparations itself often fails to discuss the bases for reparations, and many of the decisions appear *ad hoc* or arbitrary. International arbitral tribunals have sometimes borrowed from municipal

[73] O. Lissistyn, 'The Meaning of Denial of Justice in International Law', (1936) 30 *Am. J. Int'l L.* 632.

[74] Hyde, *International Law Chiefly as Interpreted and Applied by the United States* (1951), vol. I, 491–2; Moore, *Digest of International Law* (1906) 651 (hereinafter Moore, *Digest*); A.G. Lapradelle and N.S. Politis, *Recueil Des Arbitrages Internationaux* (1924), vol. 2, 31, 'Affaire Croft' note doctrinale.

[75] *Janes case, supra* n. 65 at 117.

[76] *Chattin Case*, United States–Mexican Claims Commission, Opinions (1927) 426–29. See also *Stephens Case, ibid.* 397, 400–01.

[77] *Ibid.* at 427.

[78] C. Eagleton, 'Measure of Damages in International Law', (1929–30) 34 *Yale L.J.* 52, 59.

law and sometimes created their own theories of international law on damages or other remedies, and as a consequences their jurisprudence has been widely criticized as inconsistent, even incoherent.[79] In a study of the Mexican Claims Commission, 1923–1934, A.H. Feller notes that '[n]o part of the law of international claims is more fragmentary or confused than that relating to the measure of damages'.[80] Similarly, Briggs comments that '[n]o one who reads through the printed decisions of the various Mexican claims tribunals set up in the last decade can fail to notice their helpless flounderings in the seas of inconsistency when dealing with the measure of damages'.[81] Others voice a suspicion that such arbitral decisions have more to do with imposition of the power of large states over smaller ones than with the rule of law.[82] Yet it is worth studying the decisions to identify principles that are articulated and to observe how they are applied, as most of these cases concern what today would constitute violations of international human rights law.

2. Reparations for injury to aliens

In the *Chorzow Factory* case, it will be recalled, the Permanent Court of International Justice articulated a general principle of reparations: 'The essential principle contained in the actual notion of an illegal act . . . is that reparations must, as far as possible, wipe out all the consequences of the illegal act and re-establish the situation which would, in all probability, have existed if that act had not been committed'.[83] In the earlier *Lusitania* arbitration, arbitrator Parker expressed his view that the concept contemplates that the remedy be 'commensurate with the injury', and that compensation be 'adequate and balance as near as may be the injury suffered'.[84] Although both of these decisions were concerned with compensation only, it is clear that in traditional international law the 'duty to make reparation' comprises restitution and/or damages, as well as measures of 'satisfaction' which frequently have accompanied those of reparation *stricto sensu*. The latter are determined much more by the nature of the imputable

---

[79]   C. Gray, *Judicial Remedies in International Law* (1987), 10–11.

[80]   A.H. Feller, *The Mexican Claims Commissions 1923–1934: A Study in the Law and Procedure of International Tribunals* (1935), 290.

[81]   H. Briggs, 'The Punitive Nature of Damage in International Law and Failure to Apprehend, Prosecute or Punish', in *Essays in Political Science in Honor of W.W. Willoughby*, (1937) 348.

[82]   The Supreme Court of Brazil referred in one case to foreign claims as the 'terrorism of the indemnities': *Araujo Goes v. Uniao Federal*, 87 Rev. Dir.Civ.Com.Crim. 51 at 54. The Supreme Court of Peru complained they showed 'naught but the constant display of might over weakness': *Herrera v. Saco y Flores*, 23 C.S., An Jud. 493 at 495. See, further, Gray, *supra* n. 79 at 6.

[83]   *Factory at Chorzow Case, supra* n. 4 at 47. It has been noted that in this case measures of satisfaction were not included and the articulated principles discuss only how to measure compensation. Arechaga posits that the Court was dealing only with material damage, while Graefrath says the Court was narrowing the concept of reparations wrongly: J. de Arechaga cited in L. Sohn and R. Baxter, *supra* n. 13 at 565; Graefrath, *supra* n. 3 at 46. None of the authors indicate if measures of satisfaction were requested in the case.

[84]   *Opinion in the Lusitania Cases* (1923) 7 R.I.A.A. 35, 35–36.

act than by the injury actually caused and in some cases may be considered 'punitive' in character and purpose.[85]

Arbitral agreements generally say little about proof of loss other than requiring the claimant state to furnish all information necessary to enable the respondent state to examine the requests for compensation.[86] Damages also may be limited by political agreement or considerations, as in the *Alabama Claims* arbitration.[87] In general, however, claimants must prove they have suffered actual losses attributable to acts by the breaching state to qualify for relief. The same considerations of certitude and public policy limiting recovery for remote injury govern international tribunals as govern municipal courts. Lack of certainty or evidence has led to claims being rejected, and tribunals generally reject those they call 'speculative'.[88] Causality is a major consideration and damages caused by intervening acts are excluded.[89]

International tribunals have met with the same problem as municipal ones in attempting to draw a line between injuries and losses that are sufficiently proximate and those that are too remote to be the subject of recovery. Cases reveal a wide range of factors and considerable discretion on the part of arbitrators. Remote damages have been uniformly disallowed by claims commissions,[90] but

[85] F.V. Garcia-Amador, *supra* n. 32, vol. 2 at 559.

[86] G. Yates III, 'Postwar Belgian International Claims: Their Settlement by Lump Sum Agreements', (1973) 13 *VA.J. Int'l L.* 554, 596. See also Lillich and Weston, *supra* n. 24 at 174.

[87] See the discussion in Eagleton, *supra* n. 78 at 67.

[88] See e.g. the War-Risk Insurance Premium Claims, United States-Germany Mixed Claims Commission, Decisions and Opinions at 134; *Pelletier Case*, Moore, *International Arbitrations*, *supra* n. 60, vol. 4 at 1779; *Brig William*, Moore, *ibid.* at 4226; *Di Caro Case*, J. Ralston, *Venezuelan Arbitrations of 1903* at 817. Yntema claims that tribunals use the term speculative to deny the claims they do not wish to accept: H. Yntema, 'The Treaties with Germany and Compensation for War Damages', (1024) 24 *Colum. L. Rev.* 135, 139 (1924).

[89] See the *Lusitania Cases*, *supra* n. 84; *Yuille, Shortridge and Co.*, A. Lapradelle and N.S. Politis, *supra* n. 74, vol. 2 at 109; and *Wielemans Case*, Tribunaux Arbitraux Mixtes, vol. 2, 230.

[90] See, e.g. *Grant (Gt. Brit) v. U.S.*, 8 May 1871, Hale's Rep. 162 (destruction of business); *Pelletier (U.S.) v. Haiti*, 24 May 1884, Moore, *International Arbitrations*, *supra* n. 60, vol. 4 at 1779 (alleged loss of investments of real estate, and claims in consequence of his imprisonment); *Dix (U.S.) v. Venezuela*, 17 February 1903, Ralston, *supra* n. 88, 7 (sale of cattle at inadequate price, owing to revolution); *Oliva (Italy) v. Venezuela*, 13 February 1903, Ralston, *supra* n. 88, 782 (sale of business at reduced price to enable claimant to enter on a concession contract with the government; too many elements may have contributed to reduce price); *Valentiner (Germany) v. Venezuela*, 13 February 1903, Ralston, *supra* n. 88, 564 and *Plantagen Gesellschaft*, *ibid.*, 631 (loss of crop owing to draft of claimant's labourers); *Monnot (U.S.) v. Venezuela*, 17 February 1903, Ralston, *supra* n. 88, 171 (loss of business prospects); *Bischoff (Germany) v. Venezuela*, 13 February 1903, *ibid.* 81 (injury to business resulting from unreasonable detention of property lawfully seized); *Brig William (U.S.) v. Mexico*, 11 April 1839, *ibid.* 4226 (prospective profits when vessel wrongfully detained disallowed); *Hammaken (U.S.) v. Mexico*, 4 July 1868, *ibid.* 3471 (consequential damages considered of an uncertain and imaginative nature); *Salvador Commercial Co. (U.S.) v. Salvador*, 19 December 1901, For. Rel. 1902, 857, 872 ('probable future profits of the undertaking' disallowed); *Rudloff (U.S.) v. Venezuela*, 17 February 1903, Ralston, *supra* n. 88, 182, 198 (average profits of a business venture disallowed, because unable to show that profits would have been made); *De Caro (U.S.) v. Venezuela*, 13 Febuary 1903, Ralston, *supra* n. 88, 810 (average profits disallowed, when other causes, such as warfare, might have prevented them); *Poggioli (Italy) v. Venezuela*, 17 February 1903, *ibid.* 847 (claim

indirect losses that are considered as reasonably certain may be recovered. It seems that, in general, a state is not charged with responsibility for indirect damages to the same extent as are private individuals in municipal tort litigation. Instead, the criteria of proximity, certainty and consequence are more stringently applied. In some instances, the test of foreseeability is applied.[91]

There are difficulties in assessing indirect damages in property claims, particularly lost profits. Some early cases referred to Grotius, Pufendorf, and Vattel to justify the award of lost profits.[92] In the *Alabama* arbitration,[93] the arbitrators expressed the opinion that based upon general principles of international law, certain indirect claims arising out of the loss resulting from the transfer of the American merchant marine to the British flag did not constitute good foundation for an award of damages between nations: the enhanced payments of insurance, the prolongation of the war, and the addition to the cost of the war and the suppression of the rebellion. The arbitral decision also refused to award future earnings 'inasmuch as they depend in their nature upon future and uncertain contingencies'. Other tribunals also refused anticipated profits, loss of credit, and other consequential losses.[94] More recently, in the *Norwegian Shipowners*[95] and *Lighthouses*[96] cases, consideration of lost future profits has been accepted. The primary question seems to be whether there is a reasonable prospect of future profitability.

Other forms of indirect damage may also be claimed. Lump sum agreements sometimes refer to waivers of taxes and other charges or debts owed.[97] In general, however, such agreements involve only partial compensation for property taken.[98]

---

for threats against claimants' debtors disallowed, as indirect and uncertain). Such a result was often compelled by the arbitration agreement. See, e.g. Article 3 of the Protocol of Arbitration between France and Haiti, which said the Commission 'shall throw out claims concerning indirect losses or damages': Protocol of Arbitration, 10 September 1913; Suppl. to (1914) 8 *Am.J.Int'l L.* 125.

[91] In the Samoan claims the commissioners held that 'the damages for which a wrongdoer is liable are the damages which are both, in fact, caused by his action, and cannot be attributed to any other causes, and which a reasonable man in the position of the wrongdoer at the time would have foreseen as likely to ensue from his action': 1902 Germany–Great Britain, United States, 9 U.N.R.I.A.A. 15.

[92] See *The Betsy*, in Moore, *International Adjudications, supra* n. 60, vol. 4 at 194; and *The Neptune*, Moore, *ibid.* at 372.

[93] *Alabama Arbitration*, Moore, *International Arbitrations, supra* n. 60, vol. 1, 623, 646, 658; Moore, *Digest, supra* n. 74, vol. 6 at 999.

[94] United States Acts of Congress authorizing domestic commissions to distribute international awards have excluded anticipated profits and indirect losses from consideration as elements of damage. See Act of 23 June 1874, s. 11, 18 Stat. L. 247 on Alabama Claims held to exclude a claim for loss of catch in consequence of a vessel being driven away from whaling grounds: *Gannett v. U.S.*, Moore, *International Arbitrations, supra* n. 60, at 4295. Similarly, the Spanish Treaty Claims Commission, created by Act of 2 March 1901, s. 11, 31 Stat. L. 879 stated that 'Awards shall be only for the . . . actual and direct damage. . . . Remote and prospective damages shall not be awarded'.

[95] *Norwegian Shipowners Claims* (Nor. V. U.S.) (Perm.Ct.Arb.), 1 U.N.R.I.A.A. 307 (1922).

[96] *Lighthouses Arbitration Between (France v. Greece)* (Perm.Ct.Arb.) (1956), 23 I.L.R. 299 (1956).

[97] Lillich and Weston, *supra* n. 24, at 220 *et seq.*

[98] *Ibid.* at 239.

In claims for injury to aliens, as with human rights claims, problems of proof arise due to actions by the defendant state. If the state refuses to permit physical investigations by experts or will not otherwise help claimants to obtain evidence in support of their claims, a tribunal has several options. It may reject the claims for failure to meet the burden of proof, liberalize its demands of proof and accept uncorroborated evidence, or even recognize a presumption or inference sufficient to meet the burden of proof and support an award. The balance is difficult because, while compensation cannot be computed with absolute certainty, it should not be fixed on the basis of conjecture.

(a) Restitutio in integrum

A form of redress in Roman law, *restituere in integram* calls for re-establishment of the situation *ex ante*. In the narrow sense, it calls for the return of a thing taken or the exact re-establishment of what has been lost. It is not damages but rather restoration *in natura*. It can be the restoration of objects unlawfully seized or the release of persons unlawfully arrested or detained. It also can involve the repeal or amendment of laws, administrative acts or decisions that are internationally wrongful. In the *Martini* case, regarding reparation for an unlawful demand of payment, the tribunal held that the obligations should be annulled ('doivent être annulées') applying the principle that the consequences of the illegal act should be wiped out ('les conséquences de l'acte illicite doivent être effacées').[99] In the *Mavrommatis* case, the PCIJ annulled the offensive clause that violated international law even though it found no pecuniary harm to the individual.[100]

Where domestic law is incompatible with international obligations, 'legal restitution' is thought to pose particular problems. Adoption of a legislative measure or recission of an executive or administrative decision may be possible, but repealing a law in force or revoking a judicial decision is said to be more difficult. In the past, some governments have argued that even where a decision is manifestly inconsistent with a state's international obligations, the decision must be enforced.[101] Perhaps for this reason, restitution sometimes is limited to material restitution, although nothing precludes an international tribunal from declaring the incompatibility and calling upon the state to bring its law or practice into conformity with its international obligations.

(b) Compensation

Payment of compensation constitutes the most usual form of reparation. Monetary awards are intended, in lieu of restitution, to indemnify fully all pecuniary and non-pecuniary losses, with the latter often being assessed equitably on

---

[99] *Martini Case (Italy v. Venezuela)* 1930 2 U.N.R.I.A.A. 977, 1002.

[100] 'La clause de l'article 29 de la concession Rutenberg . . . doit etre considereé comme effaceé': *The Mavrommatis Palestine Concessions Case, supra* n. 62, at 51.

[101] F.V. Garcia-Amador, *supra* n. 32, vol. 2 at 597; see Istvan Vasarhelyi, *Restitution in International Law* (1964).

the basis of the injury presumed to result from the breach. The degree of governmental misconduct can be an important factor in the assessment. The injury itself
may include both material and moral losses, although more strictly and more
rarely injury refers only to material losses. For each type of alien injury, issues of
causality, proximate harm, interest, and costs and fees are important in assessing
damages.

In the early 1970s, Garcia-Amador, Sohn, and Baxter attempted to codify
compensable claims for personal injury, including physical and psychological
injury or wrongful deprivation of liberty.[102] According to them, the elements of
harm include: harm to the body or mind; pain, suffering, and emotional distress;
loss of earnings and of earning capacity; reasonable medical and other expenses;
harm to property or business resulting directly from the physical or psychological injury or deprivation of liberty; and harm to reputation.[103] In nearly all legal
systems, as seen *supra* in Chapter 3, damages for these injuries would be recoverable from the actor causing the harm. In inter-state claims, less consistency is
found due to the fact that the state is pursuing the claim for its own injury and
only indirectly for that of the individual or individuals involved. Still, it is still
possible to group together and analyse the most common types of claims for
injury to aliens and the relief afforded.

(i) Wrongful death Many human rights violations involve the death of individuals at the hands of government agents in circumstances similar to those found
in cases of injury to aliens. Damages in the latter cases generally have been based
on evaluation of the losses of the surviving heirs or successors. Factors used in
making the assessment generally have included:

(1)   the age and station in life of the deceased;
(2)   the life expectancy of the deceased and surviving beneficiaries;
(3)   the deprivation of comforts and companionship to the survivors;
(4)   the degree of relationship to the deceased;
(5)   the shock to the surviving members of the family; and
(6)   the degree of government misconduct.

The *Lusitania* arbitrator Parker set out the formula most often cited to assess
damages in cases of death, based on factors he found to be so 'firmly established
by both the civil and common law authorities as to make further elaboration
wholly unnecessary'.[104] He stated that a calculation of compensation should:

Estimate the amounts (a) which the decedent, had he not been killed, would probably have
contributed to the claimant, add thereto (b) the pecuniary value to such claimant of the
deceased's personal services in claimant's care, education, or supervision, and also add (c)
reasonable compensation for such mental suffering or shock, if any, caused by the violent

---

[102]   F.V. Garcia-Amador *et. al.*, *supra* n. 23.
[103]   *Ibid.*, Article 28, at 321.
[104]   *Lusitania Cases* (1923), *supra* n. 84, at 364.

severing of family ties, as claimant may actually have sustained by reason of such death. The sum of these estimates, reduced to its present cash value will generally represent the loss sustained by claimant.[105]

Parker added that other factors also were to be taken into account in making the calculation:

(a) the age, sex, health, condition and station in life, occupation, habits of industry and sobriety, mental and physical capacity, frugality, earning capacity and customary earnings of the deceased and the uses made of such earnings by him;

(b) the probable duration of the life of deceased but for the fatal injury, in arriving at which standard life-expectancy tables and all other pertinent evidence offered should be considered;

(c) the reasonable probability that the earning capacity of the deceased, had he or she lived, would either have increased or decreased;

(d) the age, sex, health, condition and station in life, and probable life expectancy of each of the claimants;

(e) the extent to which the deceased, had he or she lived, would have applied income from earnings or otherwise to personal expenditures from which claimants would have derived no benefits.

According to Parker, interest rate and present-value tables should be used in reducing the amount to present value. The deceased's pain and suffering would not be considered nor would life insurance proceeds. Punitive damages would not be included, but moral damage would. 'That one injured is, under the rules of international law, entitled to be compensated for an injury inflicted resulting in mental suffering, injury to his feelings, humiliation, shame, degradation, loss of social position or injury to his credit or to his reputation, there can be no doubt, and such compensation should be commensurate to the injury'.[106]

The Arbitrator assisted claimants by indicating the evidence that would be deemed to prove each element of the claim. The amount of financial support that a deceased would have contributed to a claimant could be established by evidence of the relationship of the two, the age of the deceased at the time of death, the deceased's life expectancy according to actuarial tables, and expected income. The last could be shown by statements of employers, income patterns, rank and position, and statements of business or professional associates regarding future potential together with an estimate of the percentage of the income that would have gone to the claimant had the death not occurred. Damages for the loss of the deceased's personal services could be established by affidavits of the claimant, others with personal knowledge of the extent and value of deceased's services, and estimates by qualified persons of personal care and similar items of expense. Reasonable compensation for mental suffering, shock, or loss of companionship

---

[105] *Ibid.* at 363.   [106] *Ibid.* at 40.

could be estimated by medical opinion. Expenses of the estate could be claimed by the administrator or by the heirs if paid by them.[107] Medical, hospital, and perhaps funeral expenses could be included and established by receipts, bills, statements, or correspondence. Where an executor or administrator is not one of the survivors of the deceased, a separate claim brought on behalf of an estate could be joined with the claim of the deceased's survivors.

In another wrongful death case, the *Di Caro* case in the Venezuelan Arbitrations of 1903, the arbitrator evaluated 'the extent of comforts and amenities of which the wife has been the loser, . . . the deprivation of personal companionship and cherished associations consequent upon the loss of a husband or a wife unexpectedly taken away. Nor can we overlook the strain and shock incident to such violent severing of old relations'.[108] The United States–Mexican General Claims Commission in the *Janes* case also allowed compensation beyond material losses, for damages in respect of indignity, grief, and similar consequences of the wrongs done.[109]

The *Janes* case also established that damages are to be assessed on the basis only of the injury actually caused by the respondent government.[110] The USA, espousing the claim of a widow and four children of an American engineer murdered in Mexico, argued that the measure of damages for Mexico's failure to apprehend and punish the murderer should be $25,000 because the omissions had condoned and ratified the wrongful act. The Mexican agent rejoined that such damages could be awarded only if it could be shown that the negligence of the government and not the crime itself had directly caused the damage.

The General Claims Commission rejected the theory of complicity or condoning as argued by the USA, pointing out the problems with the 'old theory', to wit, that the widow and children would be better off financially if the state failed to apprehend and punish because they would get reparations for the killing, whereas no reparations would be due for the killing itself if the state lived up to its obligations. The Commission found however 'claimants always have been given substantial satisfaction for serious dereliction of duty on the part of a Government, and this world-wide international practice was before the Governments of the United States and Mexico when they framed the Convention'[111] providing for the Commission. The failure to apprehend and prosecute was deemed a separate injury from the damage caused by the killing, and the claimants were entitled to be compensated not for the damage caused by the murder, but for the damage caused to them by the government's failure to prosecute. While the Commission conceded the difficulty of measuring damage that 'cannot be computed by merely stating the damages caused by the private delin-

---

[107] Whiteman, *Digest of International Law* (1963), vol. I. 789.
[108] *Di Caro (U.S.) v. Venezuela*, J. Ralston, *Venezuelan Arbitrations of 1903* (1904), 769, 770.
[109] *Janes Case, supra* n. 65, at 118.
[110] *Ibid.* at 108.   [111] *Ibid.* at 117–118.

quency', it found that a computation of this character is not more difficult than computations in other cases of denial of justice such as illegal encroachments on one's liberty, harsh treatment in jail, insults and menaces of prisoners, or even non-punishment of the perpetrator of a crime that is not an attack on one's property or one's earning capacity—for instance, a dangerous assault or attack on one's reputation and honour. The Commission found that 'a reasonable and substantial redress should be made for the mistrust and lack of safety, resulting from the Government's attitude'.[112]

In the *Janes* case, the United States–Mexican General Claims Commission accepted that regular non-prosecution and non-punishment could assume the character of non-prevention, making the government primarily liable for the killing. In general, however, the government's liability would be premised on its failure to act, not on the private crime. In this regard the various degrees of a government's improper conduct would be taken into account in determining the amount of damages to be awarded—indeed, it is virtually the only articulated criterion for setting the amount of reparations. 'One among the advantages of severing the Government's dereliction of duty from the individual's crime', the Commission reasoned, 'is that it grants an opportunity to take into account several shades of denial of justice, more serious ones and lighter ones'.[113] In this case, '[g]iving careful consideration to all elements involved, the Commission holds that an amount of $12,000, without interest, is not excessive as satisfaction for the personal damage caused the claimants by the non-apprehension and non-punishment of the murderer of Janes'.[114] Thus, the losses due to the killing itself—lost earnings and other contributions to the family—were not the measure. The measure was the grief and indignity caused relative to the extent of government dereliction. No breakdown was given of the total award; the Commission noted only that it was based on 'all elements involved'.

Following *Janes*, two General Claims Commission decisions in cases of wrongful death resulted in somewhat higher awards of $15,000. One involved a consul to whom special duties of protection were owed, [115] the other involved negligence of a jailer in allowing a murderer to escape from jail.[116] Two other Commission judgments awarded $10,000 for failure to prosecute a murder. In one of the cases the murderer was rendered immune because of a general amnesty;[117] in the other case the murderer was indicted but never brought to trial.[118] Other claims resulted in awards of between $5,000 and $8,000 for dereliction of the

---

[112] *Ibid.* at 118–119.   [113] *Ibid.*   [114] *Ibid.*

[115] *U.S.A. (William E. Chapman) v. United Mexican States*, Opinions of Commissioners, 1927, 228.

[116] *U.S.A. (Gertrude Parker Massey) v. United Mexican States*, Opinions of Commissioners, 1927, 228.

[117] *U.S.A. (F.R. West) v. United Mexican States*, Opinions of Commissioners, 1927, 408.

[118] *United Mexican States (Salome Lerma de Galvan) v. U.S.A.*, Opinions of Commissioners, 1927, 412.

duty to prosecute.[119] However, where adequate punishment was carried out and no denial of justice was shown, the awards were considerably less.[120] Complementarily, where the government was responsible both for the death and for failure to punish, the awards were substantial. In such cases, while the Commission awarded no separate damages for each violation,[121] direct pecuniary losses were taken into account,[122] and the Commission awarded damages for grief and indignity where pecuniary losses were not shown.[123] In the *Youmans* case, both direct pecuniary damages and damages for grief and indignity were awarded.[124]

The decision in the 1992 *Letelier* arbitration provides a modern example of assessment of damages for wrongful death. The case between the USA and Chile arose from a 1976 car bombing in Washington D.C. that killed former Chilean ambassador Orlando Letelier and Ronni Moffitt, another passenger in the car. On

---

[119] Eight thousand dollars were awarded in *U.S.A. (Ethel Morton) v. United Mexican States*, Opinions of Commissioners, 1929, 151 (inadequate sentence) and *U.S.A. (Helen O. Mead) v. United Mexican States*, Opinions of Commissioners, 1931, 150 (failure to prosecute). Seven thousand dollars was awarded in five cases: *U.S.A. (Richard A. Newman) v. United Mexican States*, Opinions of Commissioners, 1929, 284; *U.S.A. (Sarah Ann Gorham) v. United Mexican States*, Opinions of Commissioners, 1931, 132 (failure to apprehend); *U.S.A. (Elvira Almaguer) v. United Mexican States*, Opinion of Commissioners, 1929, 291; *U.S.A. (Lillian Greenlaw Sewell) v. United Mexican States*, Opinion of Commissioners, 1931, 112; *U.S.A. (Minnie East) v. United Mexican States*, Opinion of Commissioners, 1931, 140 (improper trial procedures). The most common award was $5,000. It was given in *U.S.A. (Hazel M. Corcoran) v. United Mexican States*, Opinions of Commissioners, 1929, 211; *U.S.A. (Martha Ann Austin) v. United Mexican States*, Opinions of Commissioners, 1931, 108 (failure to apprehend); *U.S.A. (George Adams Kennedy) v. United Mexican States*, Opinions of Commissioners, 1927, 289 (inadequate sentence); *U.S.A. (Ida R.S. Putnam) v. United Mexican States*, Opinions of Commissioners, 1927, 222 (prisoners allowed to escape); *U.S.A. (Louise O. Canahl) v. United Mexican States*, Opinions of Commissioners, 1929, 90 (failure to apprehend); *U.S.A. (John D. Chase) v. United Mexican States*, Opinions of Commissioners, 1929, 17; *U.S.A. (J.J. Boyd) v. United Mexican States*, Opinions of Commissioners, 1929, 78 (undue delays in prosecution). In two cases where the assailants were prosecuted for homicide, but not for theft, the claimants received $2,500: *U.S.A. (George M. Waterhouse) v. United Mexican States*, Opinions of Commissioners, 1929, 221; *U.S.A. (Norman T. Connolly) v. United Mexican States*, Opinions of Commissioners, 1929, 87.

[120] See *United Mexican States (Thodoro Garcia) v. U.S.A.*, Opinions of Commissioners, 1927, 163 ($2,000 for the wrongful death of a child shot by American soldiers).

[121] See *U.S.A. (J.W. and N.L. Swinney) v. United Mexican States*, Opinion of Commissioners, 1927, 131 (killing by Mexican border guards and failure to punish resulting in an award of $7,000).

[122] See *U.S.A. (Lillie S. Kling) v. United Mexican States*, Opinions of Commissioners, 1931, 36 ($9,000 for shooting by Mexican soldiers who were not punished); *U.S.A. (Margaret Roper) v. United Mexican States, Opinions of Commissioners*, 1927, 205 ($6,000 for drowning of Americans fleeing Mexican police shots); *U.S.A. (Mamie Brown) v. United Mexican States*, Opinions of Commissioners, 1927, 211 ($8,000 on same facts); *U.S.A. (Rosetta Small) v. United Mexican States*, Opinions of Commissioners, 1927, 212 ($5,000 on same facts).

[123] *U.S.A. (Charles S. Stephens) v. United Mexican States*, Opinions of Commissioners, 1927, 397 (disallowing pecuniary damages as too speculative while awarding $7,000 for grief and indignity). See also *U.S.A. (Agnes Connelly) v. United Mexican States*, Opinions of Commissioners, 1927, 159 ($18,000 for grief and indignity where no evidence of material support); *U.S.A. (Mary E.A. Munroe) v. United Mexican States*, Opinions of Commissioners, 1929, 314 ($11,000, apparently for grief and indignity).

[124] *U.S.A. (Thomas A. Youmans) v. United Mexican States*, Opinions of Commissioners, 1927, 150 ($20,000).

11 January 1992, the Commission with jurisdiction to rule on the matter[125] issued its decision regarding the deaths of Letelier and Moffitt and injuries sustained by Moffitt's husband, Michael Moffitt. The sole issue before the Commission was compensation. Chile, without admitting liability, was required to pay the compensation determined by the Commission totalling $2,611,892 for all claimants, which included allocation for loss of support, moral damages, health expenses, and other expenses incurred. The Commission noted that, though there was no admission of liability, it was to determine the amount of the payment 'as though liability were established'.[126]

The United States–Chilean Commission relied upon the *Chorzow Factory* case, cited by Chile and the USA, because it saw it 'as enunciating a general rule' on reparations.[127] In assessing damages, the Commission examined the loss of financial support and services and the material and moral damages suffered by each of the claimant family members.

For Letelier, the Commission made 'the most likely assumption' about the remainder of his working life as if he had not been killed, taking into account salary and fringe benefits from 1976 to at least 1990. It also took into account 'the amount which would have been paid to him as salary and retirement pension for the remainder of his expectation of life (until 2007) had he returned to Chile in 1990 and worked in public service' in some capacity such as Minister of State, Ambassador, or Senator.[128] The Commission did not include income from conferences, lectures or publications:

because it considered that there were insufficient bases on which to establish such income in this case. Nor did the Commission include an award for the provision by Mr. Letelier of household services, such as carpentry, because it considered such activities on his part to be more in the nature of an occasional pastime to which it was not in a position to attribute a pecuniary value.[129]

In total, the Commission awarded $1.2 million to Letelier's widow and sons in pecuniary damages, $160,000 in moral damages to the widow, and $80,000 to each of the four children. In assessing the amount, 'the Commission took into account, by way of comparison, the amounts granted for moral damages by jurisdictional

---

[125] The Commission was established after the USA made an international claim against Chile in respect of the deaths and injuries, invoking the provisions of the Bryan-Suarez Mujica Treaty of 1914 between the two states: Treaty for the Settlement of Disputes that May Occur Between the United States and Chile, 1914, U.S T.S. 621, 39 Stat. 1645, T.S. No. 621. Chile denied responsibility, but indicated that it was prepared to make an *ex gratia* payment to the USA on behalf of the families of the victims. The two states concluded an Agreement in 1990 under which Chile agreed to make payment as if liability had been established: Chile-United States: Agreement to Settle Dispute Concerning Compensation for the Deaths of Letelier and Moffit, 1990, (1991) 30 I.L.M. 422. Commission reviewed numerous legal and factual issues pertaining to the question of compensation and unanimously awarded sums totalling just over 2.5 million dollars. See 88 I.L.R. 727 and (1992) 31 I.L.M. 1. See also Marian Nash (Leich), 'Claims for Wrongful Death', (1992) 86 *Am.J.Int'l L.* 347; J.G. Merrills, *International Dispute Settlement*, 3rd edn. (1998), at 55–58.

[126] Award, reprinted in Nash, *supra* n. 125, at 348, para. 20.

[127] *Ibid.* at para. 21.   [128] *Ibid.* at 349, para. 29.   [129] *Ibid.*

organs of the inter-American system and those ordered, also in recent years, by arbitration or judicial tribunals',[130] factual differences being borne in mind. The Commission also granted $16,400 to Letelier's widow for medical expenses.

For the death of Ronni Moffit, the Commission found her husband's, Michael Moffit's, losses to have included contribution for services in the home plus loss of financial support, and awarded $233,000 under these headings. For moral damages, the Commission said that it was 'virtually impossible' to assign a separate value for Michael Moffit's own injuries in the bombing and that caused by the loss of his wife[131] and therefore considered the two together as amounting to $250,000. Costs of $12,000 were also awarded.

Further, in a claim filed by Ronni Moffit's father, the Commission found no causal link between her death and her father's health problems; however, in respect of this claim, it awarded moral damages of $300,000, costs of $20,000, and $100,492 for the 'special expenses which the families have jointly incurred as a consequence' of the bombing.

Developments in Chile played an important role in the assessment of moral damages: 'In considering the compensation for moral damages, the Commission has taken into account the significant steps undertaken by the Chilean Government and Congress to remedy human rights problems as well as the efforts undertaken towards financial reparation at the domestic level for families of victims'.[132] In addressing moral compensation in his concurring opinion, Professor Orrego Vicuna noted that Chile had already tried to satisfy some of the moral injury through the Head of State's apology to the families of the victims and through the establishment of the National Commission on Truth and Reconciliation. The government also asked Congress to enact legislation on compensation, and sought to prosecute those involved in the Letelier case. 'This positive attitude has certainly a bearing on the determination of compensation for moral damages', Professor Orrego Vicuna observed.[133]

(ii) Deprivations of liberty   Arbitral decisions in cases of false arrest or imprisonment vary in their valuation of the damage caused by deprivation of individual liberty due to the wrongful detention. The different amounts seemed to depend upon several factors:

(1)   the arbitrariness of the arrest (i.e. the degree of wrongdoing by the government);
(2)   any physical or moral suffering connected with the imprisonment;
(3)   the duration of the imprisonment;
(4)   the character or station in life of the person arrested or detained;
(5)   the proximate consequences of the deprivation of liberty; and
(6)   other special circumstances.

---

[130] Nash, *supra* n. 125, at para. 31.   [131] *Ibid.* at 349–350, para. 35.
[132] *Ibid.* at para. 41.   [133] *Ibid.* at 351.

Among these factors, the most troublesome is consideration of the social status or character of the victim. In the *Oliva* case in the Venzuelan Arbitrations of 1903, the Italian commissioner distinguished an earlier case as follows: 'In the *Boffolo* case, the umpire, in granting 2000 bolivars, was influenced by what seemed to be the unworthy character of the man. In the present case, the claimant appears to have been a man of standing and character and recognized by a branch of the Venezuelan government, as a worthy concessionary'.[134] Accordingly, the commissioner proposed to calculate the indemnity 'considering the good reputation always enjoyed by the claimant, his industrious character, and the high social class in which he moves'.

In general, the character of the victim should not be considered because it is irrelevant to the wrong and to the remedy, and implies a value judgment on the worth of an individual that has nothing to do with the injury suffered.[135] Of course, if the victim caused the damage through his or her actions, the denial of a remedy would be justified. Similarly, when the victim is seeking damages for injury to reputation, it is appropriate to consider the nature of the victim's reputation both before and after the state action, to measure the harm done.

Valuation of dignitary harm, like loss of liberty, has given arbitrators considerable difficulty. In some instances, a set amount has been presumed to reflect the injury and been applied in the absence of circumstances dictating an adjustment. Decisions of the United States–Mexican Claims Commission during the 1920s first announced a principle of $100 per day for unlawful arrest and imprisonment,[136] but did not always apply the standard consistently because in two cases identical awards were given for five days detention and for unlawful arrest for 28 hours.[137] Higher amounts were given for worse conditions of confinement, but *per diem* amounts seem to have decreased with longer periods of detention, though it is not clear why.[138] In many cases, convincing proof of pecuniary

---

[134] *Oliva (Italy) v. Venezuela*, 10 U.N.R.I.A.A. 600.

[135] As Brigitte Stern says: 'Dans certain hypothèses, semble avoir été prise en considération 'la valeur' d'une personne pour l'évaluation de la réparation qui lui était due. Cette attitude est absolument inadmissible, car elle implique un jugement de valeur sur un individu, jugement qui n'a aucun rapport avec le dommage qu'il a subi, celui-ci devant être évalué de façon aussi objective que possible': Bollecker-Stern, *supra* n. 13, at 314.

[136] Ralston was the first to calculate damages for false imprisonment at $100 a day, a figure accepted by the Mexican Claims Commission, with 50 per cent added because of the changed value of money: J. Ralston, *The Law and Procedure of International Tribunals* (1926) at 262 *et seq*; *U.S.A. (Walter H. Faulkner) v. United Mexican States*, Opinions of Commissioners, 1927, 86, relying on the *Topaze Case*, British-Venezuelan Commission, J. Ralston, *Venezuelan Arbitrations of 1903*, 329.

[137] Compare *U.S.A. (Louis Chazen) v. United Mexican States*, Opinions of Commissioners, 1931, 20 and *U.S.A. (Fannie P. Dujay) v. United Mexican States*, Opinions of Commissioners, 1929, 180. $500 was awarded in both cases.

[138] *U.S.A. (Daniel Dillon) v. United Mexican States*, Opinions of Commissioners, 1929, 61 ($2,500 for 12 days' detention and being held incommunicado); *U.S.A. (Harry Roberts) v. United Mexican States*, Opinions of Commissioners, 1927, 100 ($8,000 for 19 months); *U.S.A. (Russell Strother) v. United Mexican States*, Opinions of Commissioners 1927, 392 (same); *U.S.A. (Mary Ann*

loss was lacking and equity or justice became the basis for the award.[139] The French–Mexican Commission, the German–Mexican Commission, and the Italian–Mexican Commission reduced the amount of damages or awarded on an equitable basis if no exact proof was produced.[140]

The British–Mexican Claims Commission also awarded damages for pecuniary losses suffered in cases of personal injury resulting from incarceration, but rarely for pain or suffering.[141] One case where it did make an assessment was the *William McNeil* case[142] where the victim suffered a serious and long-lasting nervous break-down following his incarceration and mistreatment in a Mexican prison. The Commission compensated him on the basis of his lost earnings from a lucrative profession and for the heavy expenses he incurred to overcome his breakdown. The Commission said that the compensation must be 'in just proportion to the extent and to the serious nature of the personal injury which he sustained'.[143]

In sum, arbitral decisions demonstrate a concern for liberty and recognition of the pecuniary and non-pecuniary harm suffered by wrongful detention and imprisonment. They were often generous in their awards, particularly when abusive conditions of confinement accompanied the violation of personal liberty.

(iii) Injury to property   Human rights violations affect property as well as personal security. From destruction of homes as part of ethnic cleansing to unjustified takings, human rights tribunals must consider the value of the victim's losses. Considerable international jurisprudence on state responsibility contains guidelines for property valuations.

Computation of damages for property losses, unless otherwise provided by agreement or statute, has generally been based upon the value of the property at the time of taking or destruction, or upon the difference in the value of the property before and after the damage occurred.[144] Some orders or agreements allow assessment of losses 'as seems just and equitable to the Commission having regard to all the circumstances',[145] others specify a date of valuation, while still others address the problem of property valuation itself. In the treaties between Mexico and various European states, specific choice of law was made, as in Article VI of the British-Mexican Convention:

Turner) v. United Mexican States, Opinions of Commissioners, 1927, 416 ($4,000 for five months' detention); *U.S.A. (Clyde Dyches) v. United Mexican States*, Opinions of Commissioners, 1929, 193 ($8,000 for 18 months' detention).

[139] *Ibid.* at 303–04. See *Mexico City Bombardment Cases*, Decisions and Opinions of Commissioners, 100, 105.

[140] See e.g. *Rep. française (Georges Pinson) v. Etats-unis mexicains*, Jurisprudence de la commission franco-mexicaine des reclamations, 132; A.H. Feller, *supra* n. 80, at 306–07.

[141] See A.H. Feller, *supra* n. 80, at 302–3.

[142] Decision of 19 May 1931 of the British–Mexican Claims Commission, 5 U.N.R.I.A.A. 164 (1952).   [143] *Ibid.* at 168.

[144] R. Lillich and G. Christenson, *International Claims: Their Preparation and Presentation* (1962), 74. See also Whiteman, *supra* n. 60, vol. 2 at 1085.

[145] R. Lillich, *International Claims: Post-War British Practice* (1967), 113.

In order to determine the amount of compensation to be granted for damage to property, account shall be taken of the value declared by the interested parties for fiscal purposes, except in cases which in the opinion of the Commission are really exceptional. The amount of the compensation for personal injuries shall not exceed that of the most ample compensation granted by Great Britain in similar cases.

Evidence of the value of the loss may include purchase price, age and condition of the property, appraisals by experts and by individuals having personal knowledge of the facts, as well as rental income and values determined for similar types of property in the same or adjacent areas. Total loss value is generally the reasonable or fair market value of the property.[146] Many factors can be included in computing market value: tax value, the last sale value, mortgage value, sales value of other similar realty, condition at the time of sale, condition of the industry in which the property was to be used, adaptability for use, etc. [147] '[E]ven if all available methods are used in documentation of a claim for damages, no single criterion exists for deciding what weight should be given to each.'[148]

Settlement agreements are not a source of precise normative guidelines on compensation.[149] They represent a compromise between the state seeking full compensation and the other state and may reflect considerable conflict over the concept of property and value, centering on the manner in which the value of property is determined. The problem is not the principle of compensation, but the method of calculating value that is the problem.[150] In an economic analysis of lump sum agreements, Norman Mintz explains the problem.[151] There are three different methods for valuing property: fair market value; application of a discount rate to the expected flow of earnings; and replacement cost. All are subject to considerable uncertainty when dealing with a forced sale. Moreover, replacement cost and the economic worth of an asset may diverge considerably. Thus, 'a single and unquestionable value for a given asset cannot be determined'.

---

[146] G.H. Hackworth, *Digest of International Law* (1943), vol. 5, 758–60.

[147] Also includable are contracts, deeds, tax roles, documentation of the nature and cost of subsequent improvements, amount of mortgages or encumbrances on the property, amount of depreciation, appraisals by qualified experts, book value of business or corporate property, studies and reports by industrial engineers, and affidavits of persons with special knowledge of the reasonable value of the property at the time of loss. Photographs, extracts from corporate books, accountant's reports, measurements and statistics of industrial capacity and physical plant, income derived from the property for several years previous, etc. will corroborate an expert's estimate of the fair market value. Add evidence of inventories, accounts, and other supplies on hand. Insurance appraisals can also be useful.

[148] R. Lillich and G. Christenson, *supra* n. 144, at 77.

[149] According to one scholar, such settlements 'do not employ the terminology beloved of international lawyers—"full compensation", "fair compensation", "prompt, adequate and effective compensation"—nor is there any discernible line of principle whereby one might determine the proper quantum of compensation': Q. Baxter, Treaties and Custom, (1970–I) 129 *Recueil des Cours* (Hague Academy of International Law) 25 at 87–88.

[150] R. Lillich and B. Weston, *supra* n. 24, at 254.

[151] N. Mintz, 'Economic Observations on Lump Sum Agreements', in R. Lillich and B. Weston, *supra* n. 24, at Appendix A, 264.

The owner and government are likely to differ substantially on value and to have the issue resolved in negotiations or adjudication.

The Iran Claims Tribunal has the most extensive recent practice on compensation and valuation of property loss.[152] While a few cases have awarded restitution and specific performance, the Tribunal generally has awarded compensatory damages for takings of property and, in most cases, its Chambers have utilized a 'full compensation' standard based on the fair market value at the time of taking, including the present value of goodwill and likely future profits for going concerns.[153] The Chambers have almost unanimously found that this standard reflects customary international law.[154]

Members of the Tribunal began in disagreement over the issue of whether there is a single standard that applies to both lawful and unlawful seizures. In *INC Corporation and the Islamic Republic of Iran*, Judge Langergren argued for two standards, stating that full compensation, a monetary version of *restitutio in integrum*, is required where there is a prior unlawful act, but that contemporary international law suggests that 'appropriate compensation' is the more flexible criterion to be applied in certain cases of lawful large-scale nationalizations.[155] Judge Holtzmann expressed his strong disagreement, arguing for full compensation in all cases.[156] In the *Phelps Dodge* case,[157] the Chamber held that it was irrelevant whether or not the taking had been lawful, while Judge Brower's

---

[152]   See, generally, Aldrich, *The Jurisprudence of the Iran-United States Claims Tribunal: An Analysis of the Decisions of the Tribunal* (1996); Amerasinghe, 'Issues of Compensation for the Taking of Alien Property in the Light of Recent Cases and Practice', (1992) 41 I.C.L.Q. 22; Clagett, 'The Expropriation Issue Before the Iran–United States Claims Tribunal: Is 'Just Compensation' Required by International Law or Not?' (1984) 16 Law & Pol'y Int'l Bus 813; Mouri, *The International Law of Expropriation as Reflected in the Work of the Iran–U.S. Claims Tribunal* (1994); Seidl-Hohenveldern, 'Evaluation of Damages in Transnational Arbitrations', (1987) 33 *Annuaire Francais de Droit International* 7.

[153]   The standard is based on the 1955 U.S.–Iran Treaty of Amity, Economic Relations and Consular Rights which requires 'prompt payment of just compensation' in the event of one party taking property belonging to a national of the other state: Treaty of Amity, Economic Relations, and Consular Rights (U.S–Iran) signed 15 August 1955, entered into force 16 June 1957, 8 U.S.T. 899, T.I.A.S. No. 3853, 284 U.S.T.S. 93. According to Article IV(2), '[s]uch compensation shall be in an effectively realizable form and shall represent the full equivalent of the property taken'.

[154]   See e.g. *American International Group, Inc. and Islamic Republic of Iran*, (1983–III) 4 C.T.R. 96 (customary international law requires full compensation even in the case of a lawful nationalization). Beginning with *Phelps Dodge Corporation & Overseas Private Investment Corp. and Islamic Republic of Iran*, (1986–I) 10 C.T.R. 121 reprinted in (1986) 25 I.L.M. 619, the Tribunal has consistently applied the bilateral Treaty as a source of obligation governing compensation, finding it equivalent to the standards previously applied. See *Sedco, Inc. and National Iranian Oil Company and The Islamic Republic of Iran (Interlocutory Award)*, (1986–I) 10 C.T.R. 180, reprinted in (1986) 25 I.L.M. 629 and annotated at (1986) 80 *Am.J. Int'l L.* 969 (the Treaty is a relevant source of law and customary international law requires full compensation).

[155]   *INA Corporation and Islamic Republic of Iran*, (1985–I) 8 C.T.R. 373, annotated at (1986) 80 *Am.J. Int'l L.* 181 at 385–86 (separate opinion of Langergren, J.).

[156]   (1985–I) 8 C.T.R. at 391, 399 (Holtzmann, J., concurring). Judge Ameli dissented from the award stating that the principle of *restitutio in integrum* has no place in discussions of lawful expropriation: *ibid.* at 403 (Ameli, J., dissenting).

[157]   *Phelps Dodge, supra* n. 154, (1986–I) 10 C.T.R. at 130.

concurrence in the *SEDCO* case found the difference between lawful and unlawful takings in the requirement of restitution as a remedy for an unlawful taking; in the event that restitution is impossible, then the remedy becomes the same as that of a lawful taking: full compensation.[158] In the *Amoco* case, Chamber Three became the only one to hold that the legal consequences are different according to the characterization of the taking and that lost profits can only be recovered as an element of restitution in cases of wrongful expropriations.[159] In subsequent cases, however, the Chambers have clearly and consistently applied the standard of full compensation regardless of the lawfulness of the taking.

The early decision in the *American International Group* case[160] rejected the Iranian argument for book value as the proper standard, holding instead that 'the appropriate method is to value the company as a going concern, taking into account not only the net book value of its assets, but also such elements as good will and likely future profitability'.[161] In *INA Corp.*, Chamber One defined fair market value as:

the amount which a willing buyer would have paid a willing seller for the shares of a going concern, disregarding any diminution of value due to the nationalization itself or the anticipation thereof, and excluding consideration of events thereafter that might have increased or decreased the value of the shares.[162]

The Tribunal has consistently required payment that reflects the genuine economic worth of the enterprise, taking into account relevant economic prospects of going concerns,[163] which requires valuing both tangible and intangible assets, including goodwill and commercial prospects.

Generally, the Tribunal has applied the 'discounted cash flow' method of valuation, but not without controversy.[164] This approach values an income-producing asset on the basis of its future rather than its past worth (cost, past profits, etc.). The analysis requires a projection of the net cash flow over its useful life

---

[158] *Sedco, Inc, supra* n. 154, (1986–I) 10 C.T.R. at 105, 203 (Brower, J., concurring).

[159] *Amoco International Finance Corp. and Islamic Republic of Iran (Partial Award)*, (1987–II) 15 C.T.R. 189 at 244–7, reprinted in (1987) 27 I.L.M. 1314 and (1990) 83 I.L.R. 502, annotated at (1988) 82 A.J.I.L. 358.

[160] *American Int'l Group, supra* n. 154, (1983–III) 4 C.T.R. at 109.

[161] *Ibid.* at 109. Taking 'all relevant circumstances' into account, including reports by independent experts, the Chamber fixed the value of the claim at $10 million (about 25 per cent of the amount claimed) plus 8.5 per cent interest from the date of the taking.

[162] *INA Corp., supra* n. 155, (1985–I) 8 C.T.R. at 380. The Chamber awarded INA $250,000, the full amount it had claimed. The amount was what INA had paid for its investment in the company one year prior to nationalization. Judge Lagergran did suggest that the standard for compensation might be different in large-scale and lawful nationalizations: *INA Corp.*, (1985–I) 8 C.T.R. at 378.

[163] *Starrett Housing (Final Award)*, (1987–III) 16 C.T.R. 112 at 122. See *INA Corp., supra* n. 156, (1985–I) 8 C.T.R 373.; *Saghi and Islamic Republic of Iran*, Award No. 544–298–2 (22 January 1993); *Amoco, supra* n. 159, (1987–II) 15 C.T.R. at 270; *American Int'l Group*, (1983–III) 4 C.T.R. at 109.

[164] See *Starrett Housing, supra* n. 163, (1987–III) 4 C.T.R. at 157; *Phillips Petroleum and Islamic Republic of Iran and National Iranian Oil Co.*, (1989–I) 21 C.T.R. 79; *contra Amoco (Partial Award)*, (1987–II) 15 C.T.R. 189.

discounted to present value and may take into account risk, inflation, and interest that might affect an investor's decision. Evidence of an asset's worth can be supplied through expert testimony, evidence of transactions in comparable property, or past transactions involving the same property. In *Khosrowshahi and Islamic Republic of Iran*[165] the Chamber referred to nearly contemporaneous market prices for the shares in question as 'the best available evidence'. Where there is no market, the Tribunal must make an approximation or best estimate of the future life and profitability of the company 'in view of the relevant conditions'.[166]

For land and other tangible property, fair market value represents the standard, but the methods differ from those used to value going concerns. In *SEDCO*, the Chamber stated that '[i]n determining the full value of tangible assets . . . our task is substantially to determine the fair market value of the property, i.e., what a willing buyer and a willing seller would reasonably have agreed on as a fair price at the time of the taking in the absence of coercion on either party'.[167]

Finally, it should be noted that the expenses incurred in the presentation and prosecution of a claim have been allowed as recoverable damages in many, although not all, cases, the exceptions being mostly expropriation cases. In the latter, a justified item is the cost of exhausting local remedies, including court costs, translations, attorneys' fees, and necessary travel costs.[168] These expenses can be established by affidavits, receipts, and certified court records. In some cases opponents have noted that such expenses were not recoverable under municipal law and the claim was disallowed.

(c) Interest

The principle that interest is due on losses is generally accepted and was established in large part through reliance on domestic law. In the *Russian Indemnity* case, the Permanent Court of Arbitration found that the law of European states and earlier Roman law recognized the obligation to pay interest for delay in settling a legal obligation for the payment of money.[169] References to domestic law are most common in regard to awards of interest, where the rates of interest in particular states, most often the wrongdoing state, are those used in the award.[170] In theory, using the wrongdoing state's interest rate is correct, based on the expectations of both the state and the injured party. In the *Georges Pinson*

---

[165] *Khosrowshahi and Islamic Republic of Iran*, Award No. 558–178–2 (30 June 1994) para. 47.
[166] *American Int'l Group*, *supra* n. 154, (1983–III) 4 C.T. R. 107.
[167] *Sedco III*, (1987–II) 15 C.T.R. 23 at 35. Decisions have allowed claims based on 'net book value' (*Computer Sciences Corporation and Islamic Republic of Iran*, (1986–I) 10 C.T.R. 269) and 'replacement value' (*Petrolane, Inc. and Islamic Republic of Iran*, (1991–II) 27 C.T.R. 64, 101).
[168] Whiteman, *supra* n. 60, vol. 3 at 2020–28.
[169] *Russia–Turkey* (1912), 11 U.N.R.I.A.A. 421, at 442.
[170] *Delagoa Bay Railway Company Case*, Moore, *Digest, supra* n. 74, vol. 6 at 1865; *Orinoco Steamship Company Case, United States–Venezuela* (1909), 9 U.N.R.I.A.A. 421 at 442; *Religious Properties Case, France, U.K. and Spain–Portugal* (1920), 1 U.N.R.I.A.A. 7.

case,[171] however, the panel held that private law had no direct relevance to the question of interest under the independent and entirely different sphere of international law.

The ability of arbitral tribunals to expand awards is seen in the decisions concerning interest. None of the Mexican Claims Conventions made any provision for the calculation of interest on awards. The French–Mexican Commission looked to prior international practice, deciding that interest at the rate of 6 per cent per annum would be added to any claim where liability was based on principles of international law rather than on a promise *ex gratia*.[172] The United States–Mexican Claims Commission began by awarding interest in three contract cases, without discussion,[173] and, in the *Illinois Central* case[174] the Commission's award of interest was deemed 'a proper element of compensation' because, it said, the purpose of the Convention was to afford nationals of both parties 'just and adequate compensation for their losses or damages'.[175] Just compensatory damages meant not only the sum due under a contract but compensation for the loss of the use of that sum during the relevant period of time. Interest was not allowed on claims for personal injuries or wrongful death.

(d) Satisfaction

In a broad sense, satisfaction applies to every form of redress repairing non-pecuniary wrong.[176] Satisfaction may be any measure that the author of a breach is bound to take including (a) apologies or other acknowledgment of wrongdoing, (b) prosecution and punishment of the individuals concerned, (c) taking measures to prevent a recurrence of the harm, and (d) performing symbolic acts of atonement. It is not an alternative to compensation. Satisfaction thus may include injunctive relief to preclude continuation or repetition of the breach or to establish accountability. Disclosure of the truth following an official and thorough factual investigation also is important. The most common types of satisfaction are apologies, punishment of the guilty,[177] assurances as to the future, and pecuniary satisfaction. Some say that satisfaction should be limited to the presentation of official regrets and apologies, the punishment of guilty 'minor' officials, and the formal acknowledgment or judicial declaration of the unlawful character of the

---

[171] *Pinson Case, France–Mexico* (1928) 5 U.N.R.I.A.A. 327 at 448.

[172] *Ibid.*

[173] *U.S.A. (John B. Okie) v. United Mexican States*, Opinions of Commissioners, 1927, 61; *U.S.A. (William A. Parker) v. United Mexican States*, Opinions of Commissioners, 1927, 82; *U.S.A. (J. Parker Kirlin) v. United Mexican States*, Opinions of Commissioners, 1927, 162.

[174] *U.S.A. (Illinois Central R.R. Co.) v. United Mexican States*, Opinions of Commissioners 1927, 187.

[175] *Ibid.* at 189.

[176] Tanzi asserts that forms of reparation for non-material injuries are within the sphere of satisfaction: A. Tanzi, *supra* n. 48. See also E. Riedel, *supra* n. 3, at 383.

[177] In the case of Dr. Shipley, the USA stated that an apology was the minimum to be afforded where an American national was assaulted and robbed by a Turkish policeman. The USA said it might also demand the dismissal of the policeman: Moore, *Digest, supra* n. 74, vol. 6 at 746– 47.

act, excluding the payment of money.[178] In practice, however, money has been paid as part of an apology.[179]

There is no agreement on the rationale for measures of satisfaction. Some focus on prevention or deterrence. Graefrath calls satisfaction '[a]ll measures taken by the author State of an internationally wrongful act to affirm the existence of the affected obligation and to prevent continuation or repetition of the wrongful act'.[180] Borchard similarly says: 'the inarticulate purpose of such damages, which may or may not be actually compensatory, must involve the theory that by such penalty the delinquent government will be induced to improve the administration of justice and the claimant government given some assurance that such delinquencies, to the injury of its citizens, will, if possible, be prevented in the future'.[181] Most view satisfaction as compensatory, serving to repair non-pecuniary injury to the state's honour and dignity, i.e. moral injury. As such it does not remedy harm to individuals.[182]

With less agreement, some argue that satisfaction is essentially punitive in nature. Vattel was perhaps the first to speak of punitive damages in international law: 'Finally, the offended party have [sic] a right to provide for their future security and to chastise the offender, by inflicting upon him a punishment capable of deterring him thenceforward from similar aggressions, and of intimidating those who might be tempted to imitate him'.[183] This form of punishment, through proportionate reprisals involving the use of force, is now illegal because the dangers inherent in a unilateral determination of punishment are widely recognized. Nonetheless the retributive interest in some form of punitive measure remains and suggests the possibility of an award of punitive or exemplary damages in appropriate cases.

Modern scholarly opinion is divided over the acceptability of, and state practice regarding, punitive and exemplary damage awards. Personnaz notes the conflicting doctrine and state practice,[184] but accepts that punitive measures do exist. Garcia-Amador, on the other hand, notes that 'international tribunals and claims commissions have at times expressly and categorically denied that reparations for injuries caused to aliens can be punitive in character', citing the

---

[178] Jimenez de Arechega, 'State Responsibility' in M. Søerensen, *Manual of Public International Law*, (1968) 572 .

[179] See Bollecker-Stern, *supra* n. 13, at 185–223. In the *Corfu Channel Case (United Kingdom v. Albania) (Assessment of Compensation)* 1949 I.C.J. Rep. 244 the measure was the actual losses. Contrast *I'm Alone (Canada v. United States)* 1935 3 U.N.R.I.A.A., 1609, *infra*.

[180] Graefrath, *supra* n. 3, at 86.

[181] E.M. Borchard, 'Important Decisions of the Mixed Claims Commission, United States and Mexico', (1927) 21 *Am.J Int'l L.* 518.

[182] See C. Gray, *supra* n. 79, at 41. If Gray is correct, then the incorporation of the term just satisfaction in Article 50 of the European Convention on Human Rights is particularly anomalous because the very purpose of the treaty is to protect the rights of individuals and afford them an effective remedy when a state party violates those rights.

[183] Vattel, *Law of Nations* (1758).

[184] J. Personnaz, *La Reparation du Prejudice en Droit International Public* (1938), 303–5.

Lusitania cases. Commissioner Parker explicitly stated that 'the fundamental concept of damages is satisfaction, reparation for a loss suffered'. Eagleton responds that refusals to award punitive damages usually have been based on the jurisdictional limits of the tribunal contained in the *compromis*, not on theoretical objections.[185] Whiteman indicates that punitive damages based upon aggravated assaults or grave injustices are sometimes allowed[186] and posits that where they are denied in injury to aliens cases it stems from the fact that in many of those cases the wrong was committed by someone other than an official of the state. The failure to investigate, try, and punish usually is deemed free of the malice or serious intentional wrong which justifies an award of punitive damages.[187] In this regard, many human rights cases can be distinguished because of the deliberate governmental policy involved in the violations.

Most authors are cautious. 'In some cases', writes Ralston, 'the umpires have refused in terms the granting of punitive awards, indicating by suggestion at least that they would, the circumstances permitting, entertain the idea, although, as we have said, the power to inflict such damages has never been expressly claimed'.[188] Some argue that all remedies are repressive.[189] Judge Ammoun, in his separate opinion in the *Barcelona Traction* case, was less categorical, referring to the repressive nature of certain reparations, which lead them to have a punitive character. [190] Even if the accepted rationale for measures of satisfaction is compensatory, to repair moral injury, the measure of the damages most likely will involve an element of condemnation that will vary according to the nature of the wrong. The greater the wrong, the greater the moral outrage and the greater the indemnity awarded to express disapproval of the act.[191]

According to Borchard, '[p]unitive or exemplary damages have been demanded by the United States and Great Britain in numerous cases where the injury to its citizens consisted in a violent and inexcusable attack on their lives or property, where the defendant government seemed criminally delinquent or where the citizen occupied a position carrying national dignity, such as a consul'.[192] Van Boven, on the other hand, asserts that 'the possibility of punitive or exemplary damages is a matter of some debate in international law. It is generally believed, however, that

---

[185] C. Eagleton, *supra* n. 78. Parker explicitly based his refusal to consider punitive damages in the *Lusitania Cases* on the terms of the Charter and the Treaty of Berlin: *Lusitania Cases*, 7 U.N. R.I.A.A. at 41.

[186] M. Whiteman, *Damages in International Law* (1939), 722.

[187] M. Whiteman, *Damages in International Law* (1937), 716.

[188] J. Ralston, *The Law and Procedures of International Tribunals, supra* n. 137, at s. 174.

[189] Georges Berlia, 'De la responsabilite internationale de l'Etat' in *Etudes en L'Honneur de Georges Scelle* (1950), 875.

[190] *Barcelona Traction Case, supra* n. 57, Separate opinion of Judge Ammoun, 292.

[191] G. Cohn, 'La theorie de la responsabilite internationale', (1939) 68–II, *Receuil des Cours*, 321.

[192] Borchard, *supra* n. 58, at 419. For examples where punitive or exemplary damages have been claimed and awarded, see e.g. *Boxer Indemnity of 1900*, For. Rel. 1901, Appendix; *Murder of French and German Consuls in Salonica*, 1876, 65 ST. PAP. 949; *Lienchou Rios*, 1904, For. Rel. 1906, 308, 319.

the imposition of such damages go beyond the jurisdiction conferred on the International Court of Justice and beyond the jurisdiction normally attributed to arbitral tribunals'.[193]

In state practice, measures of satisfaction frequently have been demanded by the state of nationality in cases involving injury to the person of aliens.[194] In the majority of cases, punishment of the guilty persons has been requested, either alone or in conjunction with other measures of satisfaction. Most of the cases relate to arbitrary expulsion, unlawful arrest or imprisonment, bodily injury, loss of life, or exceptionally serious denials of justice. States most often demand the punishment of the perpetrator in cases of death.[195] In an even greater number of cases, satisfaction is afforded in the form of assurances or guarantees against repetition of the wrongful acts. Sometimes this takes the form of guarantees or assurances of the enactment of legislation, as with the amendment of the United States Habeas Corpus Act adopted in 1842 to prevent recurrence of the problem involved in the *Caroline* claim (1840).[196]

Some international tribunals consider a declaratory judgment—stating the violation of a right and breach of a duty—as an act of satisfaction where this is requested by the parties. Declaratory judgments may be useful where the act or omission imputed to the state is unlawful but where there is no material or objective injury suffered or it is not possible to prove the injury. In general, however, a declaration of wrongdoing is rarely sufficient to remedy the harm done to an individual, national or alien. This is perhaps why recourse to declarations has been late in coming to international adjudication and particularly limited in cases involving state responsibility for injury to aliens.[197] In the *Carthage* and *Manouba* cases,[198] the tribunal considered that a declaration constituted satisfaction for breach of an obligation, in the context refusing to award the damages sought by France as reparation for the moral and political injury it suffered due to 'the failure to observe general international law and conventions binding on both Italy and France'. The tribunal stated that the 'establishment of this fact,

---

[193] T. van Boven, *Study on Restitution, Rehabilitation and Compensation for Gross and Systematic Violations of Human Rights*, U.N. Commission on Human Rights, U.N. Doc. E/CN.4/1990/10 at 6.

[194] For a case of property damage see the *Natalia Sugar Plantation* (1897). Spanish forces occupied, looted and destroyed the property of three United States citizens in Cuba. In a note to the Spanish Minister at Washington, the United States Secretary of State asserted that the acts in question violated treaty rights of the United States citizens and the ordinary rules of war. The USA requested not only that full compensation should be made to the individuals concerned, but that the matter should be investigated, the guilty persons punished and strict orders given to prevent the recurrence of such acts: *Natalia Sugar Plantation* (1897), Moore, *Digest, supra* n. 74, vol. 6 at 970.

[195] See *Frank Pears* (1900), Moore, *Digest, supra* n. 74, vol. 6 at 762; *Webber* (1895), *ibid.* at 746 and *W. Wilson* (1894), *ibid.* at 745–46. In the *Webber* case, the USA also demanded that Turkey remove the governor of the prison where the United States national died as a result of ill-treatment.

[196] Moore, *Digest, supra* n. at 74, vol. 6 at 30.

[197] See Gray, *supra* n. 79, at 17. As the author notes, declaratory judgments are not discussed by early writers on reparations in international law.

[198] *(France v. Italy)* 1913 11 U.N.R.I.A.A. at 460, 475.

especially in an arbitral award, constitutes in itself a serious penalty and this penalty is made heavier in such case by the payment of damages for material losses'.[199] The International Court of Justice issued a declaration in the *Corfu Channel* case, but noted that it was 'in accordance with the request made by Albania through her Counsel'.[200] Similarly, in the *Nuclear Test* cases,[201] the ICJ asserted that 'a declaration is a form of "satisfaction" *which the Applicant might have legitimately demanded* when it presented its final submissions in the present proceedings, independently of any claim to compensation'.[202] It is not clear whether, at present, a declaratory judgment would be considered an adequate remedy without any other relief if other forms of satisfaction were demanded by the applicant state. It might depend on what the court views as the rationale for measures of satisfaction; declaratory relief is less likely to be viewed as adequate satisfaction under a deterrence rationale. It should be noted also that the line between a declaratory judgment and an order to take action is sometimes blurred. The ICJ, for example, has 'declared' in one case that a state was 'under a duty immediately to cease and refrain from all such acts as may constitute breaches of the foregoing legal obligations'.[203]

Pecuniary satisfaction has been claimed and awarded often. In connection with the murder of a missionary in Persia, the USA asserted a claim for 'the remedial reparation due to the widow' and 'the exemplary redress due to the Government of the United States'. Other cases awarded a sum specified to include compensation plus satisfaction.[204] Some agreements establishing Mixed Commissions have empowered the commissions to settle pending claims with pecuniary satisfaction.[205] In the *Stephens* case, the General Claims Commission contrasted the role of satisfaction and that of compensatory damages, noting that if the plaintiffs proved the injustice for which Mexico is liable, 'the claimants shall be entitled to an award in the character of satisfaction, even when the direct pecuniary damages suffered by them are not proved or are too remote to form a basis for allowing damages in the character of reparation (compensation)'.[206] Excessive demands may be refused.[207]

Sometimes pecuniary reparations of a punitive or exemplary character are awarded, accepted and defined in unequivocal terms.[208] One claim against

---

[199] J. B. Scott, *La Travaux de la Cour Permanete D'Arbitrage de la Haye* (1921), 356–57.

[200] *Corfu Channel Case, supra* n. 4, at 36.

[201] *Australia v. France; New Zealand v. France*, 1974 I.C.J. 253.

[202] *Ibid.* at para. 18.

[203] *Case Concerning Military and Paramilitary Activities against Nicaragua (Merits)* 1986 I.C.J. at 149, para. 12.

[204] See e.g. *Maninat Case* (1903) in J. Ralston, *French-Venezuelan Arbitrations* (1906), 78.

[205] See J. Ralston, *Venezuelan Arbitrations of 1903, supra* n. 88, at 643.

[206] *Stephens Case*, 4 U.N.R.I.A.A. at 266.

[207] See Eagleton, *supra* n. 78, at 304 for a case in which the measures demanded included an investigation conducted according to stringent conditions; imposition of the death penalty on the perpetrators; and payment of a large indemnity within five days of the demand.

[208] *Ibid.* at 721–33.

Panama sought 'such measure or redress as will be amply compensatory to the persons aggrieved or to their dependents, sufficiently exemplary for the grave offence, and strongly deterrent against similar occurrences in the future'.[209] The United States–Mexican Claims Commission sometimes said its award was based on a desire to condemn.[210] Other tribunals have accepted the award of punitive damages in theory, but found that the facts of the cases did not indicate such an award to be warranted.[211] In one domestic case involving an international dispute, *The Mariana Flora*,[212] the court said 'an attack from revenge and malignity, from gross abuse of power, and a settled purpose of mischief . . . may be punished by all the penalties which the law of nations can properly administer'.

In some cases where moral damages were assessed, it in fact appears that the amounts were indicated as a penalty. In the *Maal* case, the Netherlands was awarded damages for the indignity suffered by one of its nationals stripped in public by Venezuelan police officials. In the *Roberts* claim, Mexico paid the USA $8,000 for seven months of illegal imprisonment of the claimant, a substantial portion of the damages relating to Robert's having been subjected to cruel and degrading treatment during the period of imprisonment. In other cases, the USA expressly renounced the claim of punitive damages.[213] This prior practice suggests that in theory a penalty may be assessed against a delinquent state for particularly serious breaches of human rights, although it might be based on the measure of the wrong to the international community, not the individual.

In *Moke's* case, punitive damages were clearly assessed:

The forced loans were illegal; the imprisonment was only for one day, and resulted in no actual damage to claimant or his property; but we wish to condemn the practice of forcing loans by the military, and think an award of $500 for 24 hours' imprisonment will be sufficient . . . If larger sums in damages, in such cases, were needed to vindicate the right of individuals to be exempt from such abuses, we would undoubtedly feel required to give them.[214]

Given that the standard of the day was $100 for 24 hours' imprisonment, it seems clear that there were elements of sanction or punishment in the case.

In the *I'm Alone* case (1935),[215] the Joint Final Report of the Commissioners found that the sinking of a Canadian ship by a United States coast guard vessel was an unlawful act and called on the USA formally to acknowledge its illegality and

---

[209] *Foreign Relations of the United States* (1909), at 476.

[210] *Moke Case*, in Moore, *International Arbitrations*, *supra* n. 60, vol. 4 at 3411.

[211] See e.g. the *Delagoa Bay Railway Company Case* in Moore, Digest, *supra* n. 74, at 1865; *Cheek's Case, United States v. Siam*, 1898 in Moore at 1899 and 5068; *Metzger and Torrey, United States v. Venezuela*, 1903, 9 U.N.R.I.A.A. 225.

[212] 24 U.S. (11 Wheat.) 1, 6 L.Ed. 405 (1826).

[213] Moore, *International Arbitrations*, *supra* n. 60, vol. 4 at 3411.

[214] 3 U.N.R.I.A.A. at 1609, 1618.

[215] See For. Rel. (1906), ss. 808–10; for the Salonica matter, (1991) 65 *British and Foreign State Papers* 949.

to apologize to the Canadian Government. Further, 'as a material amend in respect of the wrong', the Commission recommended payment of the sum of $25,000. Britain demanded penalties after the Lienchou riots and the murder of its consuls at Salonica.[216] The USA claimed them in the *Labaree* case and France did so in the *Mannheim* case, where it received one million francs in *amende* in addition to 100,000 francs for the victim's family. In the case of the *Aerial Incident of 2 July 1955*, before the International Court of Justice, the United States Government argued for a broad view of reparations in the context of the shooting down of a civilian aircraft:

If we were to follow only the compensatory theory of civil damages in general, we might conceivably reach a point where no damages would be payable, though treacherous murders were committed internationally by one government on the nationals of another government. Additional amends to the injured government are therefore desirable and even necessary . . . The whole problem of the freedom of the air and the safety of the nationals of all governments from murderous attack by the government of overflown terrain is involved.[217]

The USA asked for an additional $100,000 for the principle of the freedom of the air. No judgment issued.

Recent jurisprudence also provides an example of apparent exemplary damages in the *Rainbow Warrior* case.[218] The matter involved the sinking of a ship in Auckland harbour in 1985 by agents of the French security services who used false Swiss passports to enter New Zealand. New Zealand demanded a formal apology from France and payment of US$10 million, a sum that far exceeded the value of material losses sustained. The case was ultimately submitted to the Secretary-General of the United Nations, who decided, *inter alia*, that France should pay US$7 million.[219]

Thus, in those cases where the issue of awarding punitive or exemplary damages has arisen explicitly, most tribunals admit to the theoretical possibility of awarding them, but in practice often refuse to do so, either because they view their specific powers as limited to compensatory awards or because the facts are deemed not to warrant them.[220] In sum, states in diplomatic claims often have

---

[216] I. Fauchille, *Traite de Droit International Public* (1922), 528 .

[217] 1958 I.C.J. Memorials, Memorial of the United States, 246–48.

[218] *Rainbow Warrior Case*, Decision of 30 April 1990 by the France–New Zealand Arbitration Tribunal, (1990) 82 Int'l L. Rep. 573. [219] *Ibid.*

[220] In the *Lusitania Cases*, the tribunal refused because of the specific agreement, although the arbitrator opposed punitive damages in general in international law. Parker expressed his belief that the 'fundamental concept of damages is satisfaction, reparation for a loss suffered, a judicially ascertained compensation for wrong: *Lusitania Arbitration, supra* n. 84, at 39. In the case concerning German responsibility for acts committed after 31 July 1914 and before Portugal participated in the war, Portugal claimed an indemnity of 2 million marks because of all the offences against its sovereignty and for attacks on international law: 2 U.N.R.I.A.A. 1076. The arbitrators rejected this as being neither a claim for material nor moral damage, but a sanction, a penalty inflicted on the guilty state and inspired by ideas of retribution, warning and intimidation.

demanded punitive or exemplary damages.[221] While some of the cases have involved a strong state making demands of a weaker one, the fact is that many states consider it appropriate to demand an award in the nature of a sanction for the commission of outrageous illegal acts. Tribunals adjudicating claims of state responsibility have awarded damages in response to these claims, although some reject the practice in general or in light of the specific limits of their jurisdiction.

C. CONCLUSIONS

It appears from the law of state responsibility for injury to aliens that restitution is often impossible due to the nature of the injury and that compensation for material and moral harm therefore constitutes the general form of reparation. The aim is to wipe out the consequences of the harm. In addition, a strong deterrent element can be seen in many of the awards of satisfaction, where the state claim and resulting award seem to make use of measures intended to ensure non-repetition of the violation and to deter other potential wrongdoers.

There are significant differences in the circumstances surrounding the law of reparations for injury to aliens and remedies for violations of human rights. In the former context, the state is in theory asserting that its own right has been violated and, thus, issues of state power and the threat of reprisals have been important in claims practice relative to injury to aliens. There may be bias in the amounts of the awards as a result, and this may limit the utility of using them as a measure of appropriate compensatory damages in human rights cases. Nonetheless, the wide range of measures of satisfaction that generally have been granted lend meaning to the term 'satisfaction' in the European Convention on Human Rights and suggest that the European Court of Human Rights has broader powers than it has used so far to ensure respect for the Convention.

A second difference between state responsibility for injury to aliens and human rights law is in regard to domestic remedies. The decision to afford a domestic remedy formerly was left to the discretion of the wrongdoing state, subject to the vague and uncertain doctrine of denial of justice. Today, human rights law requires states to afford an effective remedy for any violation of rights.

Finally, the primary role of restitution in international law generally has not been mirrored in human rights law specifically because, like injury to aliens, many of the violations are irreparable. Where life has been lost or other personal injury done, the individual cannot be placed back in the situation that existed before the violation. For this reason, too, the declaratory judgment, which is used in the European human rights system,[222] is not viewed as adequate in most

---

[221] See Eagleton, *supra* n. 78, at 62–63; I.C. Hyde, *supra* n. 74, at 515; Borchard, *supra* n. 58, at s. 174.

[222] See *infra* Chapter 7.

circumstances to repair injury that has been done. Violations of property rights seem increasingly common, however, and may lead to more frequent demands for restitution in the future.

The powers of international tribunals to afford remedies for injuries to aliens are rarely specified in detail. The general jurisdictional provisions of treaties and dispute settlement agreements allow many tribunals to develop remedies through the exercise of inherent judicial powers. In this regard, it should be noted that a proposal to include in the statute of the PCIJ a provision permitting the court to 'define the nature of the crime, to fix the penalty, and to decide the appropriate means of carrying out the sentence'[223] was rejected in part because of a belief that the Permanent Court itself could decide upon such matters. [224] The same is true of existing tribunals whose jurisdictional mandate often is broad and undefined. This presents a challenge and an opportunity for judges to draw upon principles and practices that allow development of full and effective remedies that further the purposes of human rights law.

---

[223] Records of the First Assembly of the League of Nations, 1 Committees 494.

[224] According to Eagleton, the court, as finally established, had only 'the power to assess penal damages'. Eagleton, *supra* n. 78, at 64.

Part II

The Institutional Framework

5

International Institutions and Tribunals

A. INTRODUCTION

Close to a dozen international procedures allow victims to denounce violations of their human rights by a state party to the relevant treaty. To enhance compliance with the human rights obligations contained in the United Nations Charter, public and private procedures address gross and systematic violations of internationally-recognized human rights[1] and thematic rapporteurs or working groups appointed by the United Nations Commission on Human Rights accept complaints or information about violations of specific human rights. Within the larger United Nations system, the International Labor Organization[2] and UNESCO[3] have developed human rights complaint procedures for violations of rights within their mandates. Human rights treaty bodies established pursuant to the International Covenant on Civil and Political Rights, the Convention on the Elimination of All Forms of Racial Discrimination, and the Convention Against Torture may receive petitions within their specific jurisdictional limits. Regional systems in Europe, the Americas, and Africa parallel and extend the global efforts.

Petitions may be filed only after all local remedies have been exhausted and within a limited period following a final judgment of the competent local tribunal. The state thereby is given an opportunity to redress its own violations. International supervisory organs generally 'have competence with respect to matters relating to the fulfillment of the commitments made by the States Parties to th[e] Convention'.[4] An independent committee or commission usually undertakes fact-finding and attempts to achieve a friendly settlement of admissible complaints, following which it prepares a report. The report may declare that a violation has occurred and recommend an appropriate course of action, including remedies such as compensation to the victim. At present only the European and Inter-American systems allow cases to be heard by a permanent international court, although the African system approved the creation of an African human rights court in June 1998. The European and Inter-American courts can issue

---

[1] United Nations Economic and Social Council Resolutions 1235 (XLII) (1967) and 1503 (XLVIII) (1970).

[2] See Nicolas Valticos, 'The International Labor Organization', in S. Schwebel (ed.), *The Effectiveness of International Decisions* (1971), 134; V.-Y. Ghebali, *The International Labor Organization: A Case Study on the Evolution of U.N. Specialized Agencies* (1989).

[3] See Philip Alston, 'UNESCO Procedure for Dealing with Human Rights Violations', (1980) 20 *Santa Clara L.Rev.* 665; S. Marks, 'The Complaint Procedure of the United Nations Educational, Scientific and Cultural Organization', in H. Hannum (ed.), *Guide to International Human Rights Practice* (1992), 92.

[4] American Convention on Human Rights, 22 November 1969, Article 33, 36 O.A.S.T.S. 1.

binding judgments on remedies, as can the European Court of Justice of the European Union (EU), whose jurisdiction includes some human rights issues.

In addition to institutions with general human rights jurisdiction, other permanent international tribunals are competent to adjudicate specific human rights matters. The Administrative Tribunals of international organizations hear cases involving workers' rights, discrimination and sexual harassment. These tribunals have considerable remedial competence. The permanent international criminal court, once established, will allow victims of international crimes to file claims for redress following prosecution of the accused and the court may order remedies directly against the person convicted or compensation to be paid from an international Trust Fund.[5]

Other international tribunals either limit standing to states only, e.g. the International Court of Justice, or are not established as permanent courts. Two ad hoc United Nations tribunals, established for the former Yugoslavia and for Rwanda, are criminal courts where individuals may be prosecuted for violating specific international crimes, including war crimes and crimes against humanity such as genocide. The tribunals do not have competence to afford redress to victims other than prosecuting and convicting the perpetrator of the harm. Two other ad hoc tribunals, the Iran–United States Claims Commission and the United Nations Gulf War Claims Commission, have jurisdiction over disputes that can involve human rights issues.

The jurisdiction and competence of the various institutions and tribunals to afford redress are considered in this chapter.

B. THE UNITED NATIONS SYSTEM

No global human rights treaty makes specific reference to the competence of an international supervisory body to afford remedies for human rights violations. International petition procedures were late in coming to the United Nations—first included as a optional clause in the 1965 Convention on the Elimination of All Forms of Racial Discrimination—and they remain weaker than the regional mechanisms. Constitution-based procedures developed by the ILO, UNESCO, and the United Nations Human Rights Commission are based usually on vaguely worded mandates that similarly omit discussion of remedies. Human rights institutions that recommend remedies thus have done so largely on the basis of implied powers.

---

[5]   Statute of the Permanent International Criminal Court, Article 75(4). Article 75 also requires the ICC to establish principles relating to reparations for victims, including restitution, compensation and rehabilitation. The ICC may, on request or on its own motion in exceptional circumstances, determine the scope and extent of any damage, loss or injury to victims and must state the principles on which it is acting. Before any order is made, the ICC may invite and shall take account of representation from or on behalf of the convicted person, victims, and other interested persons or states. Article 79 calls for establishment of a Trust Fund for the victims of crimes within the jurisdiction of the ICC. Any money or other property collected through fines or forfeiture can be transferred to the fund.

1. United Nations organs

In furtherance of the human rights provisions of the United Nations Charter, the Commission on Human Rights (Commission) has created various working groups and appointed special rapporteurs to monitor specific human rights issues. Many of these groups and individuals discuss the issue of remedies in the context of their mandates.

The Commission created the Working Group on Disappearances to 'examine questions' concerning enforced or involuntary disappearances. Its primary role is 'as a channel of communication between families of the missing persons and the governments concerned, with a view to ensuring that sufficiently documented and clearly identified individual cases are investigated and the whereabouts of the missing persons clarified'.[6] It works on individual cases, country reports, and the general phenomenon of disappearances, including the question of impunity. It has emphasized the importance of habeas corpus as 'one of the most powerful legal tools for discovering the fate or whereabouts of a disappeared person; its rapid implementation could help to prevent grave violations of human rights from occurring and enhance the accountability of those responsible for disappearances and arbitrary detention'.[7] The Working Group also has called for investigation, prosecution and punishment of those responsible for disappearances. The Declaration on the Protection of All Persons from Enforced Disappearance expanded the Working Group's mandate to monitor compliance with duties under the Declaration, including the obligation to establish civil liability as well as criminal responsibility for disappearances.[8]

In June 1997, the Working Group wrote to all countries with more than 20 pending cases of alleged disappearance, asking information about their practices regarding financial compensation for victims of enforced disappearance. Twelve countries responded with information about domestic laws on redress.[9] After reviewing these provisions and other procedures, the Working Group concluded that 'the aspect of compensation is extremely important' and it would continue to exchange views with governments, non-governmental organizations and families of victims.

Other thematic procedures accept complaints or petitions. The Working Group on Arbitrary Detention, which may investigate cases of arbitrary deprivation of liberty,[10] accepts communications from detained individuals or their families as

---

[6] E/CN.4/1994/26, para. 2. As of its 1998 report, the Working Group had transmitted to governments a total of 47,758 cases of disappearances of which 44,940 were still active cases: E/CN.4/1998/43, para. 4.

[7] *Ibid.*, para. 45(a).

[8] E/CN.4/1996/38, para. 3. The Declaration refers to the right to a prompt and effective judicial remedy, as well as unhampered access of national authorities to all places of detention, the right to habeas corpus, the duty to investigate, prosecute, and punish perpetrators.

[9] E/CN.4/1998/43, paras. 24–25.

[10] See United Nations Commission on Human Rights, Res. 1991/42, 1992/28, 1993/36, 1994/32, 1995/59, 1996/28 and 1997/50.

well as governments and inter-governmental and non-governmental organizations. If the Working Group decides after investigation that the arbitrary nature of the detention is established, it makes recommendations to the government concerned and transmits these to the complainant three weeks after sending them to the government. The language of the recommendation is identical in every case:

Consequent upon the decision of the Working Group declaring the detention of . . . to be arbitrary, the Working Group requests the government of . . . to take the necessary steps to remedy the situation in order to bring it into conformity with the provisions and principles incorporated in the Universal Declaration of Human Rights and the International Covenant on Civil and Political Rights.[11]

Giving greater precision to the generality of this recommendation, the Working Group has cited the right to a remedy contained in the Universal Declaration of Human Rights and the guarantee contained in the Covenant on Civil and Political Rights that anyone deprived of liberty is entitled to test the lawfulness of the detention before a court. The Working Group identifies the latter remedy as habeas corpus, calling it 'the best remedy' against unlawful or unjust imprisonment.[12] In the same report the Working Group calls for preparation of an international document on this remedy, 'particularly regarding the non-derogable nature of habeas corpus as an inherent human right'.[13] The Working Group also has recommended to all states that they legislate the remedy of habeas corpus as an individual right.[14]

The Special Rapporteur on Extrajudicial, Summary or Arbitrary Executions also bases his work on the receipt of communications that provide him with information about violations of the right to life.[15] The primary function of the Special Rapporteur is to ascertain whether the state has complied with its obligations under international law to prevent violations of the right to life, or, if the executions have already occurred, to investigate the cause and circumstances of the death, identify the perpetrators, and impose appropriate sanctions. The Rapporteur also considers the rights of victims, based on the Declaration of Basic Principles of Justice for Victims of Crime and Abuse of Power, in particular Principle 11, which calls on the state to redress harm caused by official conduct.[16] States are expected to provide indemnification 'on a systematic basis' in compliance with the norms and principles contained in the pertinent international instruments.[17]

In a 1994 report to the United Nations Human Rights Commission, the Special

[11] See e.g. Decision 43/1993 (People's Republic of China) in E/CN.4/1995/31/Add.1 at 3.
[12] E/CN.4/1995/31, para. 45.   [13] *Ibid.*
[14] E/CN.4/1996/40, para. 124(4).   [15] E/CN.4/1993/46, para. 12.
[16] *Ibid.* at para. 68.   [17] E/CN.4/1993/46, para. 688.

Rapporteur called the duty to provide compensation to victims of violations of the right to life an international obligation[18] linked to other international legal duties:

Governments are obliged under international law to carry out exhaustive and impartial investigations into allegations of violations of the right to life, to identify, bring to justice and punish their perpetrators, to grant compensation to the victims or their families, and to take effective measures to avoid future recurrence of such violations. The recognition of the duty to compensate victims of human rights violations, and the actual granting of compensation to them, presupposes the recognition by the Government of its obligation to ensure effective protection against human rights abuses on the basis of the respect for the fundamental rights and freedoms of every person.[19]

The Special Rapporteur consistently requests information from a government to clarify allegations regarding an execution, including 'the nature and amount of any compensation made to the family of the victim'[20] and has complained repeatedly that states fail to provide this information.[21]

The Special Rapporteur on Torture and other Cruel, Inhuman or Degrading Treatment or Punishment has focused primarily on the prevention of torture and rarely has discussed remedies for past victims, although the Rapporteur receives information, most often provided by non-governmental organizations, on specific cases of alleged torture. This information can be brought to the attention of the government concerned, which is asked for comments. The Rapporteur 'does not take a stand on whether such allegations are well-founded. He merely requests the Government to look into the matter and to see to it that, if the outcome of the inquiry confirms the allegation is true, the perpetrators will be punished and the victims will be compensated'.[22] The information received from governments is the basis of an annual report to the Commission on the extent of the practice of torture. In the annual reports, the Rapporteur recommends an end to torture and sometimes calls for specific remedial measures, including habeas corpus or *amparo* to allow all detained persons to challenge the lawfulness of detention.[23] In addition, the Rapporteur has recommended that an inquiry always be undertaken when there is a complaint of torture. If the complaint is well-founded, it should result in compensation to the victim or relatives. Anyone suspected of committing torture or severe maltreatment should be tried and, if found guilty, punished.

---

[18] E/CN.4/1994/7, para. 11.   [19] *Ibid.*, para. 688.

[20] E/CN.4/1993/46, para. 79(g).

[21] See *ibid.* at para. 688 (only the government of Tunisia responded, informing that a monthly allowance had been granted the families of two men killed); and E/CN.4/1994/7, para. 711 ('The Special Rapporteur notes with concern that, with the exception of Nepal, no Government provided him with information about any such compensation provided to victims or their dependents').

[22] E/CN.4/1993/26, para. 15.

[23] E/CN.4/1995/34, para. 926(f), (g).

2. United Nations treaty bodies

The Human Rights Committee, created pursuant to the International Covenant on Civil and Political Rights, reviews state reports on implementation of and compliance with the Covenant, issues interpretive 'General Comments' on rights and duties established by the treaty, and considers individual petitions submitted against states party to the Covenant's First Optional Protocol. Decisions of the Committee that a state has violated the Covenant are expressed in 'views' which may include recommended appropriate steps to remedy the violation. Although the Committee has never discussed in general the nature or scope of remedies, to date the recommended actions have included:

(a) public investigation to establish the facts;[24]
(b) bringing to justice the perpetrators;[25]
(c) paying compensation;[26]
(d) ensuring non-repetition of the violation;[27]
(e) amending the law;[28]

---

[24] Comm. No. 30/1978 (*Irene Bleier Lewenhoff and Rosa Valino de Bleier v. Uruguay*) U.N. UAOR, 37th Sess. Supp., No. 40, at 130, U.N. Doc. A/37/40 (1982) (deprivation of the right to life); Comm. No. 84/1981 (*Guillermo Ignacio Dermit Barbato and Hugo Harold Dermit Barbato v. Uruguay*) U.N. GAOR , 38th Sess., Supp. No. 40 at 124, U.N. Doc. A/38/40 (1983) (deprivation of the right to life); Comm. No. 107/1981 (*Elena Quinteros Almeida and Maria del Carmen Almeida de Quinteros v. Uruguay*) (disappearance) U.N. GAOR, Hum.Rts. Comm., 38th Sess., Supp. No. 40 at 216, U.N. Doc. A/38/40 (1983); Comm. No. 146/1983 and 148–154/1983 (*John Khemraadi Baboeram et al. v. Suriname*) U.N. GAOR, 40th Sess., Supp. No. 40 at 187 U.N. Doc. A/40/40 (1985) (deprivation of the right to life); Comm No. 161/1983 (*Joaquin David Herrera Rubio v. Columbia*) (disappearance and death) U.N. GAOR, Hum. Rts. Comm., 43rd Sess., Supp. No. 40, at 190, U.N. Doc. A/43/40 (1988); Comm. No. 194/1985 (*Jean Miango Muigo v. Zaire*) U.N. GAOR, Hum. Rts. Comm., 43rd Sess., Supp. No. 40, at 218, U.N. Doc. A/43/40 (1988) (right to life); Comm. No. 181/1984 (*A. and H. Sanjuan Arevalo v. Columbia*) (disappearances) U.N. GAOR, Hum. Rts. Comm., 45th Sess., Supp. No. 40, at 31 (Vol. 1), U.N. Doc A/45/40 (1990); Comm. No. 25/1978 (*Carmen Amendola and Graciela Baritussio v. Uruguay*) U.N. GAOR, Hum. Rts. Comm., 37th Sess., Supp. No. 40 at 187, U.N. Doc A/37/40 (1982) (torture); Comm. No. 124/1982 (*Tshitenge Muteba v. Zaire*) U.N. GAOR, Hum. Rts. Comm., 39th Sess., Supp. No. 40 at 182, U.N. Doc A/39/40 (1984) (torture); Comm No. 176/1984 (*Walter Lafuente Penarrieta et al. v. Bolivia*) U.N. GAOR, Hum. Rts. Comm., 43rd Sess., Supp. No. 40, at 199, U.N. Doc A/43/40 (1988).

[25] Cases *Bleier, Barbato, Quintero, Baboeram, Miango, Muteba, supra* n. 24.

[26] Cases *Bleier, Barbato, Muteba, Quinteros, Baboeram, Miango and Penarrieta, supra* n. 24; Case 45/1979 (*Suarez de Guerrero v. Colombia*) (killing by deliberate police action) U.N. GAOR, Hum. Rts. Comm., 37th Sess., Supp. No. 40, at 137, U.N. Doc A/37/40 (1982); Case No. 25/1978 (*Carmen Amendola and Graciela Baritoussio v. Uruguay*) (torture and detention); Case No. 110/1981 (*Antonio Viana Acosta v. Uruguay*) U.N. GAOR, Hum. Rts. Comm., 39th Sess., Supp. No. 40, at 169, U.N. Doc A/39/40 (1984) (torture).

[27] Cases *Bleier, Barbato, Quintero, Baboeram, Herrera supra* n. 24; Case No. 80/1980 (*Elena Beatriz Vasilskis v. Uruguay*) U.N. GAOR, Hum. Rts. Comm., 38th Sess., Supp. No. 40 at 173, U.N. Doc A/38/40 (1983) (torture); Case No. 88/1981 (*Gustavo Raul Larrosa Bequio v. Uruguay*) U.N., GAOR, Hum. Rts. Comm., 38th Sess., Supp. No. 40 at 173, U.N. Doc A/38/40 (1983) (torture), *Muteba, Penarrieta, supra* n. 24.

[28] Case of *Suarez de Guerrero, supra* n. 26.

(f) providing restitution;[29]

(g) providing medical care and treatment.[30]

Guarantees of non-repetition are an important aspect of the Committee's approach to remedies. It frequently calls upon states parties to take steps to ensure that similar violations do not occur in the future. It also has stressed repeatedly that states parties are under an obligation to take immediate steps to ensure strict observance of the provisions of the Covenant.[31] In the *J.D. Herrera Rubio* case, the Committee concluded that Colombia had not taken the measures needed to prevent the disappearance and death of the parents of the author of the communication, had failed to adequately investigate, and that accordingly it had the duty to adopt effective measures of reparations, proceed with the investigations, and take measures to ensure that similar violations did not occur in the future.[32]

In a series of prisoner cases involving Jamaica and Trinidad and Tobago, the Committee has called on each state to take specific remedial action in response to its findings. The Committee also has elaborated on the right to a remedy, finding that the failure to provide legal aid interferes with the right to pursue legal remedies in violation of Article 14(3)(d) in conjunction with Article 2(3).[33] Most of these cases involve prisoners who were condemned to death, but whose sentences were commuted. The violations alleged include denial of the right to appeal; cruel, inhuman and degrading treatment; and procedural delay. The Committee has insisted that the applicants be afforded an effective remedy and has suggested appropriate remedies, including release,[34] 'further measures of clemency',[35] payment of compensation,[36] improved conditions of confinement,[37] release from

---

[29] Comm. No. 63/1979 (*Raul Sendic Antonaccio v. Uruguay*) (cruel, inhuman or degrading treatment or punishment).   [30] *Ibid.*

[31] In 1990, the Committee decided to appoint a Special Rapporteur to recommend to the Committee action on all letters of complaint from individuals found to have been victims of a violation who claim that no remedy has been provided: Report of the Human Rights Committee to the 45th Session of the General Assembly, A/45/40, vol. II, Annex XI.

[32] CCPR, views of 2 November 1987, ICCPR, Selected Decisions of the Human Rights Committee under the Optional Protocol, vol. II, 1990, 194–95.

[33] *Thomas v. Jamaica*, Communication No. 532/1993, Views of 3 November 1997, II Rep. of the Human Rights Committee, GAOR, 53rd Sess, Supp. No. 40, U.N. Doc. A/53/40, 1 (1998) (hereinafter, II Reports.)   [34] *Ibid.* at 5, para. 7;

[35] *R. LaVenda v. Trinidad and Tobago*, Communication No. 554/1993, Views of 29 October 1997, II Reports, *supra* n. 33, at 8, 13; *R. Morrison v. Jamaica*, Communication No. 635/1995, Views of 27 July 1998, II Reports at 113, 125; *C. Smart v. Trinidad and Tobago*, Communication No. 672/1995, Views of 29 July 1998, II Reports at 142, 149.

[36] *J. Leslie v. Jamaica*, Communication No. 564/1993, Views of 31 July 1998, II Reports, *supra* n. 33, at 21, 29; *T. Jones v. Jamaica*, Communication No. 585/1994, Views of 6 April 1998, II Reports at 45, 54; *I. Chung v. Jamaica*, Communication No. 591/1994, Views of 9 April 1998, II Reports at 55, 61; *B. Young v. Jamaica*, Communication No. 615/1995, Views of 4 November 1997, II Reports at 69, 75; *A. Finn v. Jamaica*, Communication No. 617/1995, Views of 31 July 1998, II Reports at 78, 86; *Deidrick v. Jamaica*, Communication No. 619/1995, Views of 9 April 1998, II Reports at 87, 93; *R. Morrison*, *supra* n. 35; *C. Smart*, *supra* n. 35;

[37] *P. Matthews v. Trinidad and Tobago*, Communication No. 569/1993, Views of 31 March 1998, II Reports *supra* n. 33, at 30, 34.

prison,[38] medical treatment,[39] and for those still subject to the death penalty, commutation of the sentence.[40] In cases of mistreatment it has urged the state to carry out an official investigation into the allegations and where appropriate identify the perpetrators and punish them.[41] In all the cases where it found a violation the Committee affirmed that the state is under an obligation to ensure that similar violations do not occur in the future.

The Committee has asserted its implied powers to ensure compliance with its decisions, relying on Article 5(1) of the First Optional Protocol, which calls on it to 'consider' cases. According to the Committee 'the word "consider" in Article 5, paragraph 1 of the Optional Protocol need not be taken as meaning consideration of a case only until the adoption of a final decision, but consideration in the sense of engaging in those tasks deemed necessary to ensure implementation of the provisions of the Covenant'.[42] It thus instituted a follow-up procedure to ensure that its recommendations are followed, calling on states to provide information within 90 days about the measures taken in connection with the Committee's views.

The Committee on the Elimination of Racial Discrimination recommended that compensation be paid in a case brought under Article 14 of the Convention on the Elimination of All Forms of Racial Discrimination.[43] It called on the Netherlands to compensate for moral damages after it found that state officials had failed to respond adequately to racial incidents directed at the applicant and that the police and judicial proceedings did not afford the victim effective protection and remedies as required by Article 6 of the Convention.

Finally, in the case of *O.R., M.M. and M.S. v. Argentina*, the United Nations

---

[38] *T. Jones v. Jamaica, supra* n. 36. See also *V. P. Domukovsky, Z. Tsiklauri, P. Gelbakhiani and I. Dokvadze v. Georgia*, Communications No. 623–624–626–627/1995, Views of 6 April 1998, II Reports, *supra* n. 33, at 95, 112; *A.S. Yasseen and N. Thomas v. Guyana*, Communication No. 676/1996, Views of 30 March 1998, II Reports at 151, 162; *R. Espinoza de Polay v. Peru*, Communication No. 577/1994, Views of 6 November 1997, II Reports, *supra* n. 33, at 36, 43. In the Peruvian case, the Committee found that the victim had been sentenced on the basis of a trial that failed to provide the basic guarantees of a fair trial. It considered that he should be released unless Peruvian law provided the possibility of a new trial that conformed to the requirements of the Covenant. In its suggested remedy, the Committee's decision is similar to that of the Inter-American Court of Human Rights in the case of *Loayza Tamayo v. Peru*, 34 Inter-Am.Ct.Hum.Rts. (ser. C) (1997).

[39] *Williams v. Jamaica*, Communication No. 609/1995, Views of 4 November 1997, II Reports, *supra* n. 33, at 63, 68.

[40] *S. Shaw v. Jamaica*, Communication No. 704/1996, Views of 2 April 1998, II Reports, at *supra* n. 33, at 164, 171; *D. Taylor v. Jamaica*, Communication No. 705/1996, Views of 2 April 1998, II Reports at 174, 180; *B. Whyte v. Jamaica*, Communication No. 732/1997, Views of 27 July 1998, II Reports at 195, 202; *A Perkins v. Jamaica*, Communication No. 733/1997, Views of 19 March 1998, II Reports at 205, 211.

[41] *D. McTaggart v. Jamaica*, Communication No. 749/1997, Views of 31 March 1998, II Reports, *supra* n. 33, at 221, 228.

[42] *Recommendations for Enhancing the Effectiveness of the United Nations Activities and Mechanisms: Follow-up On Views Adopted Under the Optional Protocol to the International Covenant on Civil and Political Rights*, A/CONF.157/TBB/3 (1993).

[43] *LO. Karim v. the Netherlands*, Communication No. 4/1991.

Committee against Torture, found the cases inadmissible because they related to events prior to the entry into force of the Convention for the state. The Committee nonetheless expressed its view that the national 'Full Stop Law' and 'Law of Due Obedience' (the second adopted after ratification of the Convention) were 'incompatible with the spirit and purpose' of the Convention against Torture. The Committee observed that it could not fail to indicate that 'even before the entry into force of the Convention against Torture, there was a general rule of international law that obliged all States to take effective measures to prevent torture and to punish acts of torture'. The state was encouraged to adopt 'appropriate measures' of reparation.[44]

3. UNESCO

The Executive Board of the United Nations Educational, Scientific and Cultural Organization created a complaint procedure in 1978 to permit human rights advocates to submit individual cases and general questions of human rights violations to UNESCO.[45] A communication may originate 'from a person or group of persons who, it can be reasonably presumed, are victims of alleged violations' or 'from any person, group of persons or non-governmental organization having reliable knowledge of these violations'. The issues must be within the educational, scientific and cultural mandate of UNESCO.

Upon receipt of a communication, the organization sends a questionnaire that includes a question about the object of the complaint. The communications are transmitted to the government, then brought to the Committee on Conventions and Recommendations during its semi-annual meetings. The Committee gathers information and attempts to achieve a friendly settlement, sometimes with the Director-General, who has a specific role in helping to reach solutions to particular human rights problems. The preamble of the Executive Decision creating the procedure refers to 'moral considerations' and 'international cooperation' and explicitly states that 'UNESCO should not play the role of an international judicial body'. Thus, the Committee works to settle matters but does reach some decisions on the merits and recommends measures to redress the situation.

Once the Committee deems a communication to be admissible, it may request further information from the government concerned and/or the author of the communication or recommend some other action. It can, for example, request the Executive Board to invite the Director-General to address an appeal to a government for clemency or the release of a detainee. The Committee prepares

[44] Communications 1/1988, 2/1988, and 3/1988, decision of 23 December 1989, U.N. Report of the Committee against Torture, G.A.O.R. XLV Sess. 1990 at 111–112.

[45] Decision 104 EX/3.3 of the Executive Board of UNESCO, reprinted at <http://www.unesco.org/general/eng/legal/hrights/text.htm>. See Stephen P. Marks, 'The Complaint Procedure of the United Nations Educational, Scientific and Cultural Organization', in H. Hannum (ed.), *Guide to International Human Rights Practice* 86 (1992).

confidential reports to the Executive Board containing information about the communications that it has examined as well as recommendations. The Executive Board examines them in closed meetings and may endorse the Committee's views. According to UNESCO's statistics, 460 communications were considered by the Committee from 1978 to October 1997, of which 274 were deemed to have been settled. Most of these settlements involved release of detained persons before completion of their sentence or authorization to return to their country from exile.[46]

4. The International Labor Organization

The mandate of the International Labor Organization includes many human rights issues, including the rights to form trade unions and collectively bargain, the right to freedom of association, rights of indigenous peoples and migrant workers, and the rights to be free from child labour, discrimination in employment, and forced labour. The ILO monitors state compliance with its norms and standards, contained in conventions and recommendations, through various procedures, including international complaint mechanisms.

Three ILO complaint procedures have been utilized to raise human rights issues: (1) representations made pursuant to ILO Constitution, Article 24; (2) complaints under Constitution Article 26; and (3) complaints on freedom of association. Representations that a state has failed to observe any ILO Convention to which it is a party may be submitted by a trade union or an employer organization. The Governing Body appoints a special committee to examine the substance of the representation and reviews the report of the committee, including its recommendations. The Governing Body may publish the representation, the government's reply and its analysis of the case.

Article 26 complaints may be filed by governments, delegates to the ILO Conference, or the Governing Body on its own motion, and are considered by a quasi-judicial Commission of Inquiry. The Commission makes conclusions and recommendations, following which a report of the case is communicated to the Governing Body and published. A recommendation may suggest changes in law or practice to conform to ILO Conventions. If the government does not implement the recommendations within a specified time, the Governing Body may recommend to the Conference such action as it may deem wise and expedient to secure compliance.[47]

---

[46] The figures given on settled cases relate to: release from prison (150); return from exile (34); return to employment or activity (29); emigration (20); resumption of a banned publication or broadcast (14); granting of passports, grants or diplomas (11); elimination of a discriminatory measure in education (7); release after completion of a sentence (6); and return to 'normal life following a cessation of threats' (3): UNESCO document 154 EX/16, Annex II, Summary of the Results of the Application of the Procedures Laid Down by 104 EX/Decision 3.3. For a critical analysis of 64 cases concerning 190 individuals considered between 1980 and 1991, see David Weissbrodt and Rose Farley, 'The UNESCO Human Rights Procedure: An Evaluation', (1994) 16 *Human Rights Quarterly* 391–414.

[47] ILO Constitution, Article 33.

Most ILO complaints are brought under the procedure on freedom of association, established by agreement between the ILO and the UN Economic and Social Council (ECOSOC) in 1950. A Committee on Freedom of Association (CFA) hears complaints filed by trade unions, employer organizations, governments, the United Nations General Assembly, or ECOSOC and may refer the case to a Fact-Finding and Conciliation Commission on Freedom of Association. If the CFA finds that a violation has occurred, it makes recommendations to the parties to remedy the situation, including changes in law or practice.

In 1991, the ILO created a Commission of Inquiry in accordance with Article 26(4) of the ILO Constitution to report to the Governing Body on a complaint concerning Romania's observance of Convention No. 111 on discrimination in employment.[48] The report included a chapter on reparations that described measures taken to remedy the consequences of human rights violations committed by the former regime in Romania.[49] The Report reviewed measures by the new government that included amnesties, establishment of ad hoc committees to settle cases of persons claiming to have been wronged, adoption of regulations designed to remove discriminatory measures, re-examination of certain verdicts, and compensation granted by tribunals.

C. REGIONAL HUMAN RIGHTS SYSTEMS

1. The European human rights system

The European Convention on Human Rights (ECHR) created the first regional human rights system in 1950.[50] The Convention permits both states and individuals to bring communications against states parties to the Convention.[51] Until 1998, the obligations of states parties were overseen by two organs, the European Commission on Human Rights and the European Court of Human Rights.[52] A reform of the system, enacted by Convention Protocol 11, created a new Court of Human Rights to 'ensure the observance of the engagements undertaken by the

---

[48] Commission of Inquiry to Examine the Observance by Romania of the Discrimination (Employment and Occupation) Convention 1958 (No. 111), *Report of the Commission of Inquiry* 74 ILO OFF.BULL. (ser. B) (1991), supp. 3.

[49] *Report of the Commission of Inquiry, ibid.* at paras. 471–506.

[50] On remedies in the European system, see J.L. Sharpe, 'Article 50' in L.-E. Pettiti, E. Decaux, P.-H. Imbert (eds.), *La Convention Europeene des Droits de L'Homme: Commentaire Article par Article* (1995), 809–42; Alastair Mobray, 'The European Court of Human Rights' Approach to Just Satisfaction' [1997] *Public Law* 647.

[51] Although the Convention makes the right of individual petition optional for the states parties, all 40 states parties to the Convention have accepted the petition process. With the entry into force of Protocol 11, individual petition is a matter of right.

[52] The Commission was created out of fears that a Court alone would be inundated with frivolous complaints and exploited for political ends. States were unwilling to allow individuals immediate and direct access to an international court.

High Contracting parties in the Convention and Protocols thereto'.[53] The new Court replaces the former European Commission on Human Rights and the European Court of Human Rights. The Court functions on a permanent basis with full-time judges resident in Strasbourg.[54]

(a) Jurisdiction to afford remedies

The European Convention on Human Rights gives the Court competence to afford remedies when it determines that a breach of the Convention has occurred. Former Article 50, now slightly amended as Article 41, provides:

> If the Court finds that a decision or a measure taken by a legal authority or any other authority of a High Contracting Party is completely or partially in conflict with the obligations arising from [the] Convention, and if the internal law of the said party allows only partial reparation to be made for the consequences of this decision or measure, the decision of the Court shall, if necessary, afford just satisfaction to the injured party.

According to some commentators, 'this provision shows the Court's lack of competence to annul or nullify acts of member states which are in conflict with the Convention'.[55] As discussed further below, the inability to nullify legislative or other acts does not limit the Court's power to rule that amendment or nullification of measures that violate the Convention is an appropriate remedy.

Under prior procedures, when a case was not submitted to the Court, the Committee of Ministers, pursuant to Article 32, decided whether or not a breach of the Convention had occurred, based on a report of the European Commission on Human Rights. The Committee could require that specific remedial measures be taken by the state, including an award of just satisfaction, although the latter is not explicitly mentioned in Article 32.[56] The Committee of Ministers now supervises the execution of the legally-binding judgments of the Court.

The drafters of the European Convention made clear their concern with affording adequate remedies to victims of human rights violations. The idea of a European human rights system emerged at the 1948 Congress of Europe, convened by the International Committee of Movements for European Unity. In the 'Message to Europeans' adopted at the final plenary session, the Congress delegates expressed the following: 'We desire a Charter of Human Rights guaranteeing liberty of thought, assembly and expression as well as the right to form

---

[53] European Convention for the Protection of Human Rights and Fundamental Freedoms, 4 November 1950, Article 10, 213 U.N.T.S. 221 as amended by Protocol No. 11, 11 May 1994, Europ. T.S. 155 (1994).

[54] On the new Court, see Hans Christian Kruger, 'Selecting Judges for the New European Court of Human Rights', (1996)17 *Hum.Rts.L.J.* 401.

[55] S. Thomsen, 'Restitution', in (1987) 10 *Encyclopedia of Public International Law* 378.

[56] From 1987 until December 1991, Committee Rule 5 specified the authority of the Committee to recommend the payment of just satisfaction on the basis of proposals made to it by the Commission under Article 31(3) of the Convention. The Committee's authority today rests exclusively on Article 32.

a political opposition; We desire a Court of Justice *with adequate sanctions* for the implementation of this Charter'.[57]

The Congress adopted a resolution in which it stated that it:

6. Is convinced that in the interest of human values and human liberty, the (proposed) Assembly should make proposals for the establishment of a Court of Justice with adequate sanctions for the implementation of this Charter (of Human Rights), and to this end any citizen of the associated countries shall have redress before the Court, at any time and with the least possible delay, of any violation of his rights as formulated in the Charter.[58]

The draft Convention presented by the Congress to the Committee of Ministers in 1949 envisaged a Court able to prescribe both monetary compensation and to require that the state concerned take penal or administrative action against the person responsible for infringing human rights. The Court also could require the 'repeal, cancellation or amendment' of the act complained of.[59] At the first session of the Consultative Assembly of the Council of Europe in 1949, it became clear that the proposal for a Court with sanctioning power was not universally accepted,[60] although the draft report of the Legal and Administrative Commission of the Assembly contained a proposal very similar to that of the Congress.[61] The final report submitted by the Commission to the Assembly omitted the proposal.[62]

The Committee of Experts on Human Rights which first met in February 1950 worked on a list of unresolved questions including 'the competence of the Court to pronounce judgments according damages, reparations (*restitutio in integrum*) or moral damages'.[63] In the end the Committee recommended the adoption of a provision substantially like Article 50. The Committee noted in its report to the

---

[57] See Council of Europe, *Report of the Control System of the European Convention on Human Rights*, H (92) 14, (December 1992), 4.

[58] *Ibid.*

[59] Council of Europe, *Collected Edition of the 'Travaux Preparatoires' of the European Convention on Human Rights* (1975), vol. I, 301–3 (hereinafter I *Trauvaux Preparatoires*).

[60] See e.g. the remarks of Churchill during the first session: 'we hope that a European Court might be set up, before which cases of the violation of these rights in our own body of twelve nations might be brought to the judgment of the civilized world. Such a Court, of course, would have no sanctions and would depend for the enforcement of their judgment on the individual decisions of the States now banded together in this Council of Europe': Council of Europe, I *Travaux Preparatoires, supra* n. 59, at 34. See also I *Trauvaux Preparatoires* at 156, 213, 217–35 and II T*ravaux Preparatoires* at 275–83.

[61] The proposal stated: 'Art. 24. The verdict of the Court shall order the State concerned: (1) to annul, suspend or amend the incriminating decision; (2) to make reparation for damage caused; (3) to require the appropriate penal, administrative or civil sanctions to be applied to the person or persons responsible': I *Travaux Preparatoires, supra* n. 59, at 212.

[62] *Ibid.* at 217–35.

[63] III *Travaux Preparatoires, supra* n. 59, at 36. M. Perassi proposed the current text of Article 50: II *Travaux Preparatoires* at 231; IV *Travaux Preparatoires* at 75. An earlier version perhaps more clearly called for just satisfaction 'if the constitutional law of the said party only allows the consequences of th[e impugned] decision or measure to be imperfectly repaired': III *Travaux Preparatoires* at 230.

Committee of Ministers that 'the Court will not in any way operate as a Court of Appeal, having power to revise internal orders and verdicts'.[64]

In a Report to the Committee of Ministers,[65] Article 50 as adopted was said to be:

in accordance with the actual international law relating to the violation of an obligation by a State. In this respect, jurisprudence of a European Court will never, therefore, introduce any new element or one contrary to existing international law. In particular, the Court will not have the power to declare null and void or amend Acts emanating from the public bodies of the signatory States.[66]

At the Second Session of the Consultative Assembly a proposal again was made to enlarge the powers of the Court to give it 'appellate jurisdiction', so that 'the Court may declare the impugned judicial laws to be null and void'.[67] The Committee rejected the proposal by majority vote, retaining the present version of Article 50.[68]

The language of Article 50 was derived from treaty provisions on the enforcement of arbitral awards in inter-state proceedings, notably Article 32 of the 1928 General Act on Arbitration, which provides:

If, in a judicial sentence or arbitral award it is declared that a judgment, or a measure enjoined by a court of law or other authority of one of the parties to the dispute, is wholly or in part contrary to international law, and if the constitutional law of that party does not permit or only partially permits the consequences of the judgment or measure in question to be annulled, the parties agree that the judicial sentence or arbitral award shall grant the injured party equitable satisfaction.[69]

The reliance on precedents from arbitration agreements may have been based on an expectation that adjudication before the Court would be primarily inter-state in nature, rather than based on individual communications, and that earlier arbitral practice would therefore be particularly relevant.[70] Clearly, the primary concern was to avoid the Court becoming an appellate tribunal.

The European Court recognized early that Article 50 was modelled after the provisions of dispute settlement treaties, including the General Act quoted above

---

[64]   I *Travaux Preparatoires*, *supra* n. 59, at 204.

[65]   Doc. CM/WP I (50) I; A 847 of 24 February 1950, III *Travaux Preparatoires*, *supra* n. 59, at 246–47.

[66]   *Ibid.* at 276; IV *Travaux Preparatoires* at 44.

[67]   IV *Travaux Preparatoires* at 10.

[68]   *Ibid.* at 64.

[69]   Manley O. Hudson, *International Adjudication* (1931), 2529.

[70]   It should be recalled that former Article 25 allowing individual communications was optional with states parties to the European Convention while inter-state jurisdiction was compulsory. The entry into force of Protocol 11 eliminated the optional acceptance of the right of individual petition; Article 34 of the amended Convention extends the jurisdiction of the Court to applications from any person, non-governmental organization or group of individuals claiming to be the victim of a violation by one of the states parties of the rights set forth in the Convention and protocols.

and Article 10 of the German-Swiss Treaty on Arbitration and Conciliation.[71] The relevant provisions clearly contemplated cessation of the breach, and *restitutio in integrum,* based on principles of state responsibility. At the same time, the agreements acknowledged, in effect, the problem of enforcing an international arbitral judgment. Where strict compliance could not be obtained, the treaties allowed compensation and other forms of satisfaction in lieu of restitution, where the constitutional law of the wrongdoing state made it difficult or impossible to annul or amend offending legislation or other measures. Their intent was to ensure that the complex and varied relations between international and municipal law in different countries should not prevent redress for the injured alien and state of nationality. The approach is of dubious merit when applied to modern human rights cases. Injured aliens could accept compensation and leave the state that committed the injury, escaping further violation of their rights. Human rights victims, in contrast, normally are harmed by their state of nationality and remain subject to its laws and practices. Compensation may remedy a violation that has already occurred, but does not reduce the threat of future violations if the law or practice is not changed.

The term 'satisfaction' as used in arbitral treaties and in the European Convention draws upon international practice in regard to state responsibility for injury to aliens. As discussed *supra* in Chapter 4, injuries to aliens ranged from wrongful death to property losses, while the indirect harm to the state of nationality generally affected its honour and dignity. The state usually claimed pecuniary and non-pecuniary reparations for the injury to the alien, and non-monetary satisfaction to remedy its own moral injury. Satisfaction could require punishment of the guilty and assurances as to future conduct, monetary awards, or declaration of the wrong, especially when coupled with an apology from the offending state. Many such non-monetary remedies afforded under the heading of satisfaction in inter-state proceedings could be appropriately applied in the human rights context, especially apologies, guarantees of non-repetition and/or punishment of wrongdoers.

(b) The former European Commission on Human Rights

The Commission, until November 1998, determined the admissibility of petitions, undertook fact-finding, and reported on whether the facts alleged in admissible petitions indicated the state had breached one or more of the rights guaranteed in the Convention or a Protocol. The Commission also was obliged to seek a friendly settlement between the government and the applicant 'on the basis of respect for human rights as defined in [the] Convention'.[72] The Commission thus served not only to mediate between the victim and the state, but to uphold

---

[71] *De Wilde, Ooms and Versyp* cases (*Vagrancy* cases) (Article 50), 14 Eur. Ct. H.R. (ser. A) (1972).
[72] The discussion of Commission procedures in friendly settlements is based on interviews with members of the Commission and its legal staff.

the principles of the Convention and the public interest. In quite a few cases governments paid compensation as part of a friendly settlement reached in accordance with Article 28(b) of the European Convention. Such compensation, and measures to prevent the re-occurrence of the violations, served the system as a whole in addition to providing redress to the individual victim.

In the processing of a case, the initial burden was on the applicant to present a claim for 'just satisfaction'. The Commission did not recommend compensation if it was not requested by the applicant and normally would not recommend more than the applicant requested, even if the applicant claimed only a nominal amount. In some cases a government offer of compensation was received before the applicant's monetary claim. In such instances, if the government offered more than the applicant requested, the Commission recommended the higher amount. Applicants and, on occasion, governments sometimes asked the Commission to suggest an amount it viewed as equitable to settle the matter. If the Commission then suggested a fair settlement that the government accepted, but the applicant declined, the Commission made a 10 per cent deduction from that amount in its recommendations to the Committee of Ministers, to discourage what it viewed as an unreasonable attitude precluding resolution of the case and slowing down the system as a whole.

Once the Commission finished its report, the case proceeded to the Committee of Ministers, unless either the Commission, the state concerned, or, in some instances, the individual[73] submitted the matter to the Court within three months of the Commission's report. In cases before the Court, the Commission appointed one of its members to appear as its Delegate. The Commission's role, defined by the Rules of Court, was limited. It was not a party to the proceedings, but rather an advisor to the Court. It could be consulted on requests for the taking of evidence (Rule 48(1)) or for interim measures (Rule 36(2)), and it could submit comments on the merits of the case and the question of just satisfaction. The Commission appeared at Court hearings to explain the Commission's report and opinion and offer views on issues of fact and law.

The Commission's role was thus akin to that of the Advocate General before the European Court of Justice; it acted in the public interest rather than as the representative of the applicant. In the first case before the Court, Sir Humphrey Waldock described the specific role of the Commission:

The Commission . . . does not understand its function before the Court to be to defend the interests of the individual as such. The Commission's function is that stated in Article 19, namely to ensure the observance of the engagements undertaken by the Contracting Parties in the Convention; when it refers a case to the Court, it does so in order that the Court may give a decision as to whether or not the Convention has been violated. The Commission,

---

[73] Article 5 of Protocol No. 9, amended Article 48 of the European Convention, enabling individuals to submit their cases to the Court. Protocol No. 9 to the Convention for the Protection of Human Rights and Fundamental Freedoms, 6 November 1950, Europ. T.S. No. 40.

will, it is true, have expressed an opinion on that point, in the Report transmitted to the Minsters. But that opinion has the character not of a legal decision, but of an expert opinion to provide the basis for a legally binding decision either by the Ministers or by the Court. The function of the Commission before the Court, as we understand it, is not litigious; it is ministerial. It is not our function to defend before the Court, either the case of the individual as such, or our own opinion simply as such. Our function, we believe, is to place before you all the elements of the case relevant for the determination of the case by the Court.[74]

The Court concurred, describing the main function of the Commission as one 'to assist the Court'. The drafting history of the Convention contradicts this narrow aproach. The Committee of Experts drafting the Convention insisted that it was never proper for an individual to appear before the Court because '[t]he interests of individuals would always be defended either by the Commission, in cases where the latter decided to seek a decision of the Court, or by a State'.[75]

The Commission's restrictive view of its role led it to take a somewhat passive role on the issue of remedies. When the issue was first presented in the *Vagrancy* cases,[76] the Commission initially had no comment and, in most subsequent cases, it did not discuss the Article 50 claims of the applicant. The Commission never provided to the Court a legal analysis of Article 50 principles on which the Court could base decisions about remedies. Unfortunately, applicants themselves and their attorneys were similarly unhelpful, asking for a variety of remedies without briefing the powers of the Court or providing a rationale or principles on which damages should be calculated or other relief awarded.[77] The Court thus has operated without much assistance from those appearing before it.

When the issue of remedies first arose, the Commission limited itself to quoting the decision of the Permanent Court of International Justice in the *Chorzow Factory* case, and providing some drafting history concerning the origins of Article 50. Submissions to the Court contained no discussion of the object and purpose of the system nor of whether the differences between inter-state and individual remedies should lead to the development of new principles in regard to the latter. No distinction was made between the public or community interest in remedies and individual redress. In later years, the Commission's increasing workload led it to be less rather than more involved in Court proceedings. As commentators noted, '[d]elegates rarely file written comments on the memorials submitted by the "parties" and their oral pleadings tend to be limited to a bare restatement of the Commission's opinion carefully tailored to avoid expressing

---

[74] *Lawless v. Ireland*, 1 Eur. Ct. H.R. (ser. B) (1961) at 261–62.

[75] IV *Travaux Preparatoires*, *supra* n. 59, at 44.

[76] *Vagrancy* cases (Article 50) 14 Eur. Ct. H.R. (ser. A) (1972).

[77] For example, in *Kjeldsen, Busk Madsen and Pedersen v. Denmark*, (1976) 23 Eur. Ct. H.R. (ser. A), (1979–80) 1 E.H.R.R. 711 (1979–80) the applicants simply stated 'we want the law about the obligation of integral sexual education changed so that the lessons either are to be given as special sexual lessons and so that the children's participation is voluntary or in relation to knowledge of life or family': 149.

any view on issues which the Commission as a whole has not had an opportunity to consider'.[78]

(c) Interpretation of Article 50 by the Court

By 1 November 1998, when the new European Court of Human Rights was inaugurated, the former Court had considered nearly 900 cases, representing about 10 per cent of the cases found admissible by the Commission. The Court found at least one violation in approximately 70 per cent of its judgments. During 1997 and 1998, nearly 200 cases were decided under an expedited screening procedure, as not raising issues requiring full consideration by the Court.

During its first decade the Court did not have to address the issue of remedies. It found no violation in the *Lawless* case,[79] its first judgment, while the second case, *De Becker*, was settled.[80] In the *Belgian Linguistics* case,[81] the Constitution and institutions of Belgium were revised and reformed to comply with the Court's decision without the issue of remedies being decided. No violation was found in *Wemhoff*.[82] Not until 1968, in the *Neumeister*[83] case, did the issue of remedies require adjudication by the Court. The Court separated its consideration of just satisfaction from the proceedings on the merits and, ultimately, decided the Article 50 claim after its 1972 judgments on just satisfaction in the *Vagrancy* cases and *Ringeisen*.[84]

Between 1972 and 1998, the former Court awarded one or more of the following remedies in application of Article 50:

(a)   a declaration that the state had violated the applicant's rights;
(b)   pecuniary damages;
(c)   non-pecuniary damages;
(d)   costs and expenses.

The Court held on various occasions that it has no jurisdiction to make 'consequential orders' in the form of directions or recommendations to the state to remedy violations. It rejected requests, for example, that the state be required to refrain from corporal punishment of children or to take steps to prevent similar breaches in the future.[85] It also refused to insist that a state judged to have wrong-

---

[78]   D. Harris, M. O'Boyle and A. Warbrick, *Law of the European Convention on Human Rights* (1995) at 667.

[79]   *Lawless v. Ireland*, (1961) 3 Eur. Ct.H.R. (ser. A), (1979–80) 1 E.H.R.R. 15.

[80]   Belgium revised its law to relax the restrictions applicable to de Becker because of collaboration with the enemy during the Second World War: *De Becker v. Belgium*, (1962) 4 Eur.Ct.H.R. (ser. A).

[81]   Case 'relating to certain aspects of the laws on the use of languages in education in Belgium', (1968) 6 Eur.Ct.H.R. (ser. A).

[82]   *Wemhoff v. Germany*, (1968) 7 Eur.Ct.H.R. (ser. A).

[83]   *Neumeister v. Austria*, (1968) 8 Eur.Ct.H.R. (ser. A).

[84]   *Ringeisen v. Austria*, (1971) 13 Eur.Ct.H.R. (ser. A).

[85]   See *Campbell and Cosans v. United Kingdom*, (1982) 48 Eur.Ct.H.R. (ser. A) at para. 16; *McGoff v. Sweden*, (1984) 83 Eur.Ct.H.R. (ser. A) at para. 31; *Dudgeon v. United Kingdom*, (1981) 45 Eur.Ct.H.R (ser. A) at para. 15; *Gillow v. United Kingdom*, 109 Eur.Ct.H.R. (ser. A) at para. 9.

fully expelled an alien allow the victim to rejoin his family.[86] Recently, however, it indicated that such steps implicitly may be required of each state. In *Papamichalopoulos and others v. Greece*,[87] the Court expressed its opinion that Convention Article 53 imposes a duty on each state to do more than compensate the victim. 'It follows that a judgment in which the Court finds a breach imposes on the respondent State a legal obligation to put an end to the breach and make reparation for its consequences in such a way as to restore as far as possible the situation existing before the breach'.[88] Each state can choose the manner of execution of the judgment, but '[I]f the nature of the breach allows of *restiutio in integrum*, it is for the respondent State to effect it, the Court having neither the power nor the practical possibility of doing so itself'.[89]

In general, the former Court did not demonstrate much enthusiasm for Article 50, reflected in its rules and its decisions. The narrow interpretation of Article 50, given by the Court in its first case,[90] hampered the evolution of remedies in the European system. The approach developed in that case was followed consistently, though often criticized. It left the Court with little flexibility. The Court gave unnecessarily important weight to the words 'if necessary', setting stringent requirements of a causal link between the violation and the injury and rarely affording relief that corresponded to the harm done. In numerous cases it found that the judgment alone afforded just satisfaction for the moral injury.[91] There was no indication of concern for deterrence, although that was traditionally a focus of 'satisfaction' in the law of state responsibility for injury to aliens.

In early cases, governments argued that applicants must undertake a second domestic proceeding to seek remedies before the Court could apply Article 50. In the *Ringeisen* case, the first in which compensation was awarded, the government of Austria argued that a judgment on the merits closed the proceedings, necessitating a new claim for compensation following exhaustion of local remedies. The Court rejected the argument as 'formalistic' and 'alien to international law', and stating that 'in the proper administration of justice' consideration of the repara-

---

[86] *Mehemi v. France*, Eur.Ct.H.R., judgment of 26 September 1997, (1997-VI) 51 Reports of Judgments and Decisions at 1959 (holding that the judgment of violation constituted just satisfaction with regard to the non-pecuniary damage and that the Court did not have jurisdiction to order the respondent state to permit the applicant to return to French territory and issue him a residence permit).

[87] *Papamichalopoulos and others v. Greece*, (1995) 330–B Eur.Ct.H.R.(ser. A) (Article 50).

[88] *Papmichalopoulos, ibid.* at para. 34.

[89] *Ibid.* at para. 34.

[90] *Lawless v. Ireland*, (1960) 1 Eur.Ct.H.R. (ser. A) at para. 20.

[91] Rosalyn Higgins justifiably criticized this practice: '[t]he phrase "the decision of the Court shall if necessary afford just satisfaction to the party" does *not* refer to the Court decision (judgment) as to whether there has been a breach of the Convention. In other words, the intention is not that a party has to rest content, in the last analysis, with the judgment as his satisfaction. In spite of the unclear terminology, the intention is exactly the opposite—that the Court shall itself be able to assist by providing, if necessary, for "just satisfaction" '. Rosalyn Higgins, 'Damages for Violation of One's Human Rights', in Nicolas A. Sims (ed.), *Explorations in Ethics and International Relations* (1981), 45, 47.

tion of damage flowing from violation of the Convention should be entrusted to the judicial body which found the violation. The Court's progressive decision on this point is at odds with its conservative interpretation and application of Article 50 in other respects, but is supported by considering the purpose of Article 50, which is to enable the Court to afford without delay just satisfaction to the person who is a victim of a violation. In the *Vagrancy* cases, the Belgian government argued also that the phrase 'if the internal law of the country allows only partial reparation' meant that the victims must take the judgment to the domestic courts for enforcement before obtaining relief under Article 50. The government added that the internal law of Belgium enabled the national courts to order the state to make reparation for damage caused by an illegal situation for which it was responsible, whether derived from a breach of internal law or of international law. The Court rejected this argument stating:

if the victim, after exhausting in vain the domestic remedies before complaining at Strasbourg of a violation of his rights, were obliged to do so a second time before being able to obtain from the Court just satisfaction, the total length of the procedure instituted by the Convention would scarcely be in keeping with the idea of the effective protection of human rights. Such a requirement would lead to a situation incompatible with the aim and object of the Convention.[92]

The Court also noted that the treaties from which Article 50 was developed had in view cases where total reparation was possible through giving effect to the arbitral award, but where the internal law of the state precluded that being done.

More generally, Belgium argued in the *Vagrancy* cases that litigants should never receive compensation if challenging a law applicable to a broad segment of the population.[93] The state appeared to have assumed that successful litigants would receive a windfall, while others would remain uncompensated. The Court rightly rejected this argument. The fact that some injured parties choose not to enforce their rights has never been deemed a justification for refusing to redress the wrongs done to those who do seek their vindication. Indeed, the failure to compensate them would deter anyone from challenging government wrongdoing.

In the same case, the Court outlined the requirements for affording just satisfaction:

(i)   the Court must find a decision or measure taken by an authority of a Contracting State to be in conflict with the obligations arising from the Convention;

(ii)   there is an injured party; i.e. material or moral damage; and

(iii)   the Court considers it necessary to afford just compensation.[94]

---

[92] *Vagrancy* cases, (Article 50) (1972) 14 Eur. Ct. H.R. (ser. A) at para. 16.
[93] *Ibid.*
[94] *Ibid.* para. 21.

The Court may decide no compensation is due: 'as is borne out by the adjective "just" and the phrase "if necessary" the Court enjoys a certain discretion in the exercise of the power conferred by Article 50'.[95] The Court repeatedly stated that applicants are not entitled to an award of just satisfaction, rather the Court has discretion to grant a remedy based on equitable considerations and the facts of each case.[96] This narrow view seems to undermine the remedial purpose of Article 50; there is moral damage, at least, in every case where a state violates the fundamental rights of an individual. The Court's application of Article 50 seemingly has ignored the principle it applies in interpreting substantive rights:

As has been noted on previous occasions the Convention must be interpreted in the light of its special character as a treaty for the protection of individual human beings and its safeguards must be construed in a manner which makes them practical and effective.[97]

As will be seen in subsequent chapters, the character of an applicant, including any criminal offences committed, and the nature of a breach, especially the attitude of the government concerned, both towards the violation and towards the request for a remedy, are factors that have been particularly important in decisions to award compensation. Violations of procedural rights, such as failure to provide a speedy trial, rarely have resulted in relief beyond a declaration of the violation. No compensation has been given most prisoners, except where physical mistreatment is proven.[98] Homosexuals, vagrants, and aliens also generally have been denied compensation.

Where applicants alleged violations of the fair trial provisions of Article 5[99] states sometimes argued that Article 5(5) provides *lex specialis* requiring the Court to consider the possibility of domestic remedies. In the Court's view, however, the Article 5(5) right of compensation for wrongful detention corresponds to a substantive duty imposed on states party, while Article 50 is a jurisdictional norm applicable to the Court. In *Barbera, Messegue, and Jabardo v. Spain*[100] the government asserted that the applicants should be required to undertake domestic compensation procedures after their first conviction was overturned in a second trial. The Court rejected the argument, finding that a third proceeding in domestic courts would be inconsistent with the effective protection of human rights. If *restitutio in integrum* is impossible, no domestic proceeding is

---

[95] *Guzzardi v. Italy*, (1980) 39 Eur. Ct. H. R. (ser. A) at para. 114.

[96] See *Delcourt v. Belgium*, (1970) 11 Eur.Ct.H.R. (ser. A) at para. 114; *Handyside v. United Kingdom*, (1976) 24 Eur.Ct.H.R.(ser. A) at para. 9.

[97] *Cruz Varas and others v. Sweden*, (1991) 201 Eur.Ct.H.R. (ser. A) at para. 94.

[98] *Contrast Campbell v. United Kingdom*, (1991) 223 Eur.Ct.H.R. (ser. A) at paras. 68–70 with *Tomasi v. France*, (1992) 241–A Eur.Ct.H.R. (ser. A) at paras. 127–130.

[99] See *supra* Chapter 1.

[100] *Barbera, Messegue and Jabardo v. Spain*, (1994) 285C Eur.Ct. H.R. (ser. A) para. 17 (Article 50).

required;[101] however, the possibility of domestic relief could cause the issue to be reserved.[102]

The former Court's decisions on Article 50 vary considerably and lack a coherent approach. The Court sometimes seemed to apply a notion of presumed damages while, in other proceedings, it refused to make an award based on the lack of proof of a causal link between the violation and the injury. The Court enunciated clear standards only in regard to awarding costs and fees; they must have been actually incurred, necessarily incurred and reasonable in amount.[103] Even so, the Court viewed the award as discretionary and often did not award the full amount.[104]

(d) Role of the Committee of Ministers

Until establishment of the restructured Court, if the case was not settled or submitted to the Court, the Commission's report was sent to the Committee of Ministers, a political body comprised of the Foreign Ministers of the Member States of the Council of Europe. The Committee nearly always adopted the recommendations of the Commission, including the payment of compensation. The decisions of the Committee of Ministers, including those concerning just satisfaction, are binding under Article 32(4).

The Convention contains no express provision on the competence of the Committee of Ministers to award just satisfaction. Such power is implicit, however, in Article 32, para. 1 according to which the Committee may 'prescribe a period during which the High Contracting Party concerned must take the 'measures required by the decision of the Committee of Ministers'. The first published decision of the Committee of Ministers referring to compensation dates only from 1986. Until then the Committee either found no violation or confined itself to taking note of the measures proposed by the state to carry out the judgment. The first case in which the government reported offering the applicant compensation as an implementing measure was *Andorfer Tonwerke v. Austria*.[105]

It is worth noting that the Committee of Ministers has never ruled that the finding of a violation constitutes in itself sufficient just satisfaction. The Commission never proposed this solution because it contrasted the open, fully

---

[101] See *Ringeisen v. Austria* (1972) 15 Eur.Ct.H.R. (ser. A) at paras. 15–16 (Article 50); *Neumeister v. Austria* (1974) 17 Eur.Ct.H.R. (ser. A) at para. 30; *Vagrancy* cases, (Article 50) paras. 15–16 (1972); *Guzzardi v. Italy,* (1980) 39 Eur.Ct.H.R. (ser. A) at para. 113; *Sunday Times v. United Kingdom,* (1980) 30 Eur.Ct.H.R. (ser. A) at para. 13 (Article 50); *Konig v. FRG,* (1980) 36 Eur.Ct.H.R. (ser. A) at para. 15 (Article 50).
[102] See *Unterpertinger v. Austria,* (1986) 110 Eur.Ct.H.R. (ser. A.) at para. 35.
[103] *Sunday Times* v. *United Kingdom,* (1979) 30 Eur.Ct.H.R. (ser. A).
[104] See *Matznetter v. Austria,* (1969) 10 Eur. Ct. H.R. (ser. A); *Engel and others v. The Netherlands,* (1976) 22 Eur.Ct.H.R. (ser. A); *National Union of Belgian Police v. Belgium,* (1975) 19 Eur.Ct.H.R. (ser. A); *Johnston and others v. Ireland,* (1986) 112 Eur.Ct.H.R. (ser. A).
[105] Committee of Ministers, Resolution (83)9 of 23 June 1986 (violation of Article 6(1) due to lengthy compensation proceedings after expropriation).

litigated hearings of the Court with the closed proceedings before the Commission and Committee of Ministers, finding that the absence of a full hearing with the applicant present necessarily undermined the adequacy of a declaratory remedy. Thus the Committee of Ministers, unlike the Court, awarded nominal damages when they were requested by the applicant.[106] It also almost always followed the recommendation of the Commission in awarding just satisfaction.[107]

Finally, the Committee's review often extended to noting measures taken by the respondent state to change the law or practice in question.[108] Christian Kruger asserts that the state 'may be required to remove such deficiencies by general measures such as changes of practice or legislative amendments', although the states have a wide margin of appreciation in this respect.[109] Nonetheless, the Court has consistently refused demands for changes in law or practice and the Committee of Ministers generally has limited itself to noting the measures taken. With the restructured Court in place, the major role of the Committee of Ministers in the human rights system now is to supervise the execution of the Court's judgments.

It is relatively easy to demonstrate the effect of the European Convention and Court judgments: Austria, for example, has modified its Code of Criminal Procedure;[110] Belgium has amended its Penal Code, its laws on vagrancy and its Civil Code;[111] Germany has modified its Code of Criminal Procedure regarding pre-trial detention, given legal recognition to transsexuals, and taken action to expedite criminal and civil proceedings;[112] The Netherlands has modified its

---

[106] For a survey of earlier practice of the Committee of Ministers, see A. Tomkins, 'Civil Liberties in the Council of Europe: A Critical Survey' in C. A. Gearty (ed.), *European Civil Liberties and the European Convention on Human Rights: A Comparative Study* (1997), 37.

[107] Although the Committee resolutions never state the Commission's recommendations, those closely involved in the work of the European system indicate that the Committee has only twice reduced the amount of just satisfaction recommended by the Commission. In both those cases, the governments involved objected strongly to the amounts recommended by the Commission.

[108] See e.g. *X v. United Kingdom*, (1981) 46 Eur.Ct.H.R. (ser. A) in which the Court found a violation of Article 5(4) in regard to the involuntary psychiatric hospitalization of the applicant. Just satisfaction was awarded in (1982) 55 Eur.Ct.H.R. (ser. A) (Article 50). In Resolution DH (83)2 of 23 March 1983, the Committee of Ministers noted the changes of legislation introduced by the United Kingdom, as well as the payment of the sum awarded in just satisfaction. Other changes in the law were reported following *Dudgeon v. United Kingdom*, (1981) 45 Eur.Ct.H.R. (ser. A) para. 10, Committee of Ministers Resolution DH (83)13 of 27 October 1983; *Frau v. Italy*, (1991) 195–E Eur.Ct.H.R. (ser. A), Committee of Ministers Resolution DH (9254 of 17 September 1992; and *Vallee and Karakaya v. France*, (1995) 289A and B Eur.Ct.H.R. (ser. A), Committee of Ministers Resolutions DH (95)7 and 6 of 26 April and 26 August 1995.

[109] H.C. Kruger, 'Reflections on Some Aspects of Just Satisfaction under the European Convention on Human Rights' in *Liber Amicorum Marc-André Eissen* (1995).

[110] See *Neumeister*, (1968) 8 Eur.Ct.H.R. (ser. A); *Stogmuller*, (1969) 9 Eur.Ct.H.R. (ser. A); *Matznetter*, (1969) 10 Eur.Ct.H.R. (ser. A); *Ringeisen*, (1971) 13 Eur.Ct.H.R. (ser. A); and *Bonisch*, (1985) 92 Eur.Ct.H.R. (ser. A).

[111] *De Wilde, Ooms and Versyp* (*Vagrancy* cases), (1971) 12 Eur.Ct.H.R. (ser. A) and *Marckx*, (1979) 31 Eur.Ct.H.R. (ser. A) (discrimination between legitimate and illegitimate children).

[112] See e.g. *Luedicke, Belkacem and Koc*, (1978) 29 Eur.Ct.H.R. (ser. A) (interpreters' fees).

Code of Military Justice and the law on detention of mental patients;[113] Ireland created a system of legal aid;[114] Sweden introduced rules on expropriation and legislation on building permits;[115] Switzerland amended its Military Penal Code and completely reviewed its judicial organization and criminal procedure applicable to the army;[116] France has strengthened the protection for privacy of telephone communications.[117] According to Thomas Buergenthal, 'the decisions of the European Court are routinely complied with by European governments. As a matter of fact, the system has been so effective in the last decade that the Court has for all practical purposes become Western Europe's constitutional court. Its case law and practice resembles that of the United States Supreme Court'.[118]

2. The European Social Charter[119]

The European Social Charter has evolved and gained strength over time,[120] adding to its list of rights by an Additional Protocol adopted in 1988 and a Revised Charter in 1996 and reforming its system of supervision in a 1991 Protocol.[121] In 1995, a further Additional Protocol[122] created a mechanism for the consideration of collective complaints from trade unions and employers' organizations and from non-governmental organizations, along the lines of procedures established at the International Labor Organization. After a complaint has been filed, a Committee of Independent Experts (CIE) prepares a report that it transmits to the Committee of Ministers. On the basis of the report, the Committee of Ministers adopts a resolution or, if the CIE finds that the Charter has not been applied in a satisfactory manner, the Committee of Ministers can adopt by a two-thirds majority, a recommendation addressed to the state concerned. The state must provide information on the measures taken to comply with the recommendation of the Committee of

---

[113] *Engel v. The Netherlands*, (1976) 22 Eur.Ct. H.R. (ser. A) (military penal code) and *Winterwerp v. The Netherlands*, (1979) 33 Eur.Ct.H.R. (ser. A) (mentally ill).

[114] *Airey v. Ireland*, (1979) 32 Eur.Ct.H.R. (ser. A).

[115] *Sporrong and Lonnroth v. Sweden*, (1985) 88 Eur.Ct.H.R. (ser. A).

[116] *Eggs v. Switerland*, Committee of Ministers, Res. DH (79) 7 of 19 October 1979.

[117] *Kruslin v. France*, (1990) 176–A Eur. Ct. H.R. (ser. A); *Huvig v. France*, (1990) 176–B Eur. Ct. H.R. (ser. A).

[118] T. Buergenthal and D. Shelton, *Protecting Human Rights in the Americas* (1996) at 34.

[119] European Social Charter of 18 October 1961, E. T.S. No. 35.

[120] For a general review of the evolution of the European Social Charter, see David Harris, 'The Council of Europe (II): The European Social Charter' in R. Hanski and M. Suksi (eds.), *An Introduction to the International Protection of Human Rights*, (1997), 243.

[121] Although the latter Protocol is not yet in force, most of its provisions have been implemented by the Charter's supervisory organs. The Committee of Ministers agreed to expand the Committee of Independent Experts that reviews state reports from seven to nine members. The Amending Protocol also codifies the practice of the CIE in assessing the compliance of national law and practice with the obligations imposed on states parties by the Charter: Article 24(2) Amending Protocol. Finally, there has already been implementation of the provisions of the Amending Protocol that provide for meetings between the CIE and representatives of a state party at the request of either.

[122] Additional Protocol to the European Social Charter Providing for a System of Collective Complaints, E.T.S. No. 158, entry into force 1 July 1998.

Ministers in its next report to the Secretary General under Article 21 of the Charter. The first complaint under the procedure was filed in December 1998.

3. The European Court of Justice

Although not a human rights court *per se*, the European Court of Justice considers issues of human rights in the European Community (EC). The Court has stated that 'international treaties for the protection of human rights on which the Member States have collaborated or of which they are signatories, can supply guidelines which should be followed within the framework of Community law'.[123] The EC Treaty itself contains no enumeration of fundamental rights and freedoms, but the Single European Act, signed on 17 February 1986, refers in the preamble to respect for the fundamental rights recognized in the constitutions and the laws of the member states, in the European Convention on Human Rights and Fundamental Freedoms and in the European Social Charter. The Treaty on European Union states in Article F(2) that the Union 'shall respect fundamental rights, as guaranteed by the European Convention for the Protection of Human Rights and Fundamental Freedoms . . . and as they result from the constitutional traditions common to the Member States, as general principles of Community law'.[124] Article J.1(2) of the Treaty defines the development of the respect for human rights and fundamental freedoms as one of the objectives of the common foreign and security policy. Article K.2(1) refers to compliance with the Convention in the field of justice and home affairs. In this framework, the European Court of Justice has developed a law of remedies that provides a useful contrast to the jurisprudence of the European Court of Human Rights.[125]

The European Community itself is potentially liable for injury, pursuant to Article 215(2) EC, for non-contractual liability in actions where there is an illegal act of an EC institution; the existence of quantifiable damage, either actual or imminent; and proof of a direct causal link between the contested illegal act and the damage allegedly sustained.[126] The first two requirements are the 'indispensable minimum which must be shown to exist in every action brought'.[127] The

---

[123] Case 4/73, *Nold v. Commission* (*Nold II*), [1974] E.C.R. 491 at 507, para. 13.

[124] This provision confirms jurisprudence of the ECJ which classified fundamental rights as 'general principles of Community law'. See Case 29/69, *Stauder v. Ulm* [1969] E.C.R. 419; Case 11/70, *Internationale Handelsgesellschaft* [1970] E.C.R. 1125; Case 4/73, *Nold v. Commission, supra* n. 123.

[125] See, generally, T. Heukels and A. McDonnel (eds), *The Action for Damages in Community Law* (1997).

[126] Case 4/69, *Lutticke v. Commission* [1971] E.C.R. 325 at 337: 'By virtue of the second paragraph of Article 215 and the general principles to which this provision refers, the liability of the Community presupposes the existence of a set of circumstances comprising actual damage, a causal link between the damage claimed and the conduct alleged against the institution, and the illegality of such conduct'.

[127] A. Toth, 'The Concepts of Damage and Causality as Elements of Non-Contractual Liability', in *The Action for Damages in Community Law, supra* n. 125, at 179, 180.

European Court of Justice has exclusive and unlimited jurisdiction.[128] In a proceeding for compensation seeking to repair damage caused by the Community, the governing treaty provisions call for application of 'general principles common to the laws of the Member States'. The most obvious parallels are with provisions of national laws concerning state liability.

Actions based on normative or legislative acts that involve choices of economic policy require additional proof of a 'sufficiently flagrant violation of a superior rule of law for the protection of the individual'. Such 'superior rules of law' are found in the constituent treaties and general principles of Community law developed by the Court, such as protection of legitimate expectations, vested rights, equal treatment and fundamental rights. The Court requires that the norm allegedly violated has as its aim, at least indirectly, to protect the interests of the applicant.[129] In practice, however, the EC has rarely been held liable for damages.

On the other hand, the Court has developed extensive criteria for member state liability and remedies.[130] As early as 1960 the ECJ declared that if it ruled in a given case that a legislative or administrative measure is contrary to Community law, 'the Member State is obliged . . . to rescind the measure in question and make reparation for any unlawful consequences which may have ensued'.[131] In addition, directives that are addressed to member states must be implemented by them in their national law within the prescribed period of time. In *Dillenkofer v. Federal Republic of Germany,*[132] the Court held that when a member state fails to take adequate measures to implement a directive in the prescribed period, this constitutes *per se* a serious, or manifest and grave, breach of Community law.

In *Francovich and Bonifaci v. Italian Republic,*[133] the Court held that a member state may be liable in damages for failure to implement a directive because 'the full effectiveness of Community rules would be weakened if individuals were unable to obtain compensation when their rights are infringed by a breach of Community law for which a Member State can be liable'.[134] The Court's stated requirements for liability are:

(1) the directive must confer rights on individuals;
(2) the content of the rights should be identifiable, and
(3) there should be a causal link between the damage suffered and the member state's failure to implement the directive.

---

[128] The provisions governing Community liability are Articles 34 and 40 ECSC, 188 EAEC and 215 EC. The Court's jurisdiction is conferred by Articles 40 ECSC, 151 EAEC, and 178 EC.

[129] See Joined Cases C–46/93 and C–48/93, *Brasserie du Pecheur v. Germany* and *R. v. Secretary of State for Transport, ex parte Factortame* [1996] ECR I–1029, para. 74.

[130] *Ibid.*

[131] Case 6/60, *Humblet v. Belgium* [1960] E.C.R. 559.

[132] Joined Cases C–178/94, C–179/94, C–188/94, C–189/94 and C–190/94, *Erich Dillenkofer v. Federal Republic of Germany* [1996] E.C.R. I–4867.

[133] C–6/90 and C–9/90, *Francovich and Bonifaci v. Italian Republic* [1990] 1 E.C.R. I–5357.

[134] *Ibid.*, para. 33.

R. v. Secretary of State for Transport, ex parte Factortame (Factortame III) and *Brasserie du Pecheur v. Germany*[135] concern member states' obligations to repair damage caused to individuals by national legislation adopted in breach of directly effective provisions of the EC Treaty. The Court found that a member state is liable for damages that it has caused by infringing a rule of law intended to confer rights on individuals, if there is a causal connection between the breach of the Community obligation and the damage suffered by the individual, and if the breach is sufficiently serious. The breach is deemed sufficiently serious if the member state in question gravely and manifestly disregards the limits of its discretion.

In *Brasserie du Pecheur*, several governments intervened, arguing that the Community law had not established a general system of member state liability for infringements of Community law. The Court disagreed, taking the view that the right of individuals to rely on the directly effective provisions of the Treaty before national courts in a private action is not in itself sufficient to ensure the full and complete implementation of the Treaty. In its view, the right to a remedy for state action or inaction is a necessary corollary of the direct effect of the Community provision. Breach of such a provision may give rise to an action for damages.

In *Brasserie du Pecheur*, the Court indicated its approach to remedies due to applicants for violation of Community law.[136] The Court relied on its case law on non-contractual liability of the Community because it found that the liability of member states should not differ from that of the Community in like circumstances.[137] The Court applied the principle that the state must make good the damage in accordance with its national law on liability, stating that:

reparation for loss or damage caused to individuals as a result of breaches of Community law must be commensurate with the loss or damage sustained so as to ensure the effective protection for their rights. In the absence of relevant Community provisions, it is for the domestic legal system of each Member State to set the criteria for determining the extent of reparation. However, those criteria must not be less favorable than those applying to similar claims based on domestic law and must not be such as in practice to make it impossible or excessively difficult to obtain reparation.[138]

More specifically, in answer to a question raised by the German national court in which the Brasserie du Pecheur had sued for damages, the Court made clear that 'national legislation which generally limits the damage for which reparation may be granted to damage done to certain, specifically protected individual interests not including loss of profit by individuals is not compatible with Community law'.[139] In response to a British question about exemplary damages, the Court replied that if such damages may be awarded on similar claims or actions founded

---

[135] *Brassrie du Pecheur* [1996] E.C.R. I–1029.
[136] *Ibid.* at para. 82.
[137] *Ibid.* citing *Francovich* [1990] E.C.R. I–5357, para. 45.
[138] *Ibid.* at paras. 82–83.
[139] *Ibid.* at para. 90.

on domestic law, it must be possible to award them pursuant to actions founded on Community law.

The Court has exercised a degree of supervisory power over the remedies provided by member states. On the basis of the principle of subsidiarity it has declared itself competent to decide whether or not national courts provide an adequate remedy. In the *von Colson* judgment, the Court discussed the duty on national courts to construe national law in conformity with Community law. The case related to Article 6 of Council Directive 76/207 of 9 February 1976, pursuant to which member states must provide an effective judicial remedy and impose sanctions in respect of prohibited discrimination between men and women. The Court noted that actions for damages are not only intended to repair existing damages, but also to prevent future harm; thus, compensation must be 'effective' and 'have a deterrent effect'. '[C]ompensation must in any event be adequate in relation to the damage sustained and must therefore amount to more than purely nominal compensation'.[140] The Court held that the prohibition of discrimination must be enforced by sanctions that have a real deterring effect and that national law must be interpreted to achieve the result envisaged by Article 6.

In *Dekker*[141] and *Marshall v. Southampton and South West Hampshire Area Health Authority,*[142] the Court expanded on the duty to provide effective remedies. In *Dekker*, the Court held that the duty to provide effective judicial protection set forth in Article 6 of the directive implies that unlawful discrimination constitutes an objective breach of the principle of equal treatment and entails liability on the part of the employer without need for further proof of fault or the absence of any ground discharging such liability.

Marshall, a case from the United Kingdom, concerned gender discrimination in respect of the age of retirement. *Marshall I* resulted in a finding in the individual's favour[143] and the case was remanded by the English Court of Appeal to the Industrial Tribunal on the question of a remedy. The national Sex Discrimination Act prohibited sex discrimination, but treated it differently from other types of employment discrimination, including placing a limit on compensation for breaches (at the time it was UK£6,250). After the statutory maximum was paid by the health authority, the Industrial Tribunal found that Marshall's financial loss was actually UK£18,405, including interest on the loss. The Tribunal awarded that amount plus UK£1,000 for moral injury. The Tribunal specifically found that the statutory limit made the compensatory remedy inadequate and this inadequacy constituted a further breach of the EC directive. On appeal, the House of Lords referred the question to the ECJ for a preliminary ruling on the compatibility of the statutory remedy with Article 6 of Council Directive 76/207.

---

[140] *Von Colson and Kammann v. Lord Nordrhein-Westfalen* [1994] E.C.R. 1891, at 1909, para. 28.
[141] Case C–177/88, [1990] E.C.R. I–3941.
[142] Case C–271/91, [1993] E.C.R. I–4400, [1993] 3 C.M.L.R. 293.
[143] *Marshall v. Southampton and Southwest Hampshire Area Health Authority* [1986] E.C.R. 723, [1986] 1 C.M.L.R. 688.

During the ECJ proceedings, Advocate General van Gerven referred to the Court's earlier decision in *Johnston v. Chief Constable of the Royal Ulster Constabulary*[144] where it held:

The requirement of judicial control stipulated by [article 6 of the directive] reflects a general principle of law which underlies the constitutional traditions common to the Member States. That principle is also laid down in Articles 6 and 13 of the European Convention for the Protection of Human Rights and Fundamental Freedoms . . .

By virtue of Article 6 of [the directive], interpreted in the light of the general principle stated above, all persons have the right to obtain an effective remedy in a competent court against measures which they consider to be contrary to the principle of equal treatment for men and women laid down in the directive. It is for the Member States to ensure effective judicial control as regards compliance with the applicable provisions of Community law and of national legislation intended to give effect to the rights for which the directive provides . . .

In so far as it follows from that article, construed in the light of a general principle which it expresses, that all persons who consider themselves wronged by sex discrimination must have an effective judicial remedy, the provision is sufficiently precise and unconditional to be capable of being relied upon as against a Member State which has not ensured that it is fully implemented in its internal legal order.

The Advocate General added that member states are obliged to secure the full effectiveness of Community law by imposing sanctions under civil, administrative or criminal law, depending on the case. The duty derives from the obligation to guarantee the application and effectiveness of community law imposed on member states by Article 5 EEC.

The Advocate General argued that limiting damages to a nominal amount 'would not satisfy the requirements of an effective transposition of the directive'. Similarly, criminal penalties must be 'effective, proportionate and dissuasive'. Sanctions for violating community law should be comparable to those applicable to corresponding infringements of national law, with analogous procedural and substantive conditions. The criterion of comparability applies to both civil and criminal sanctions.

The Advocate General also observed that the Court's criterion of 'adequate' compensation does not equal 'full' compensation. National divergences are still permitted, including recovery limits, provided they are high enough not to deprive the sanction of its 'effective, uniform and deterrent' nature and are adequate in relation to the damage. More specifically, the Advocate General argued that a remedy should compensate adequately for the harm, 'having regard to the most important components of damage which are traditionally taken into account in rules governing liability'. These include: loss of physical assets (*damnum emergens*), loss of income (*lucrum cessans*), moral damage and damage on account of the passage of time. National courts must take account of each of the four

[144] Case 222/84, [1986] E.C.R. 1651, [1986] 1 C.M.L.R. 240.

elements cited. If no award is made for one of those four types of damage, or if the award is purely nominal, 'it cannot be said that the compensation, taken as a whole, is adequate in relation to the damage sustained'. The award of interest must also be regarded as 'an essential component of compensation for purposes of restoring real equality of treatment' given the loss in value of money over time. In sum, the right to full compensation for violation, i.e. the right to a remedy is an essential factor for attaining 'the fundamental objective of equal treatment for men and women'.

The Court adopted much of the Advocate General's opinion. It decided that it is impossible to establish real equality without an appropriate system of sanctions that the state is free to choose within limits. The system of sanctions must be appropriate: i.e. 'such as to guarantee real and effective judicial protection. Moreover it must also have a real deterrent effect on the employer'. Therefore, if the state chooses to sanction through the award of compensation to victims of a breach, that compensation must be adequate in relation to the damage sustained.

In *Heylens*,[145] the Court cited to *Johnston*, reiterating that effective remedies must be provided for all breaches of fundamental rights in the Community:

Since free access to employment is a fundamental right which the Treaty confers individually on each worker in the Community, the existence of a remedy of a judicial nature against any decision of a national authority . . . is essential in order to secure for the individual effective protection for his right. As the Court held in its judgment of 15 May 1986 in Case 222/84 Johnston v. Chief Constable of the Royal Ulster Constabulary [1986] ECR 1651, at p. 1663, that requirement reflects a general principle of Community law which underlies the constitutional traditions common to the Member States and has been enshrined in Articles 6 and 13 of the European Convention for the Protection of Human Rights and Fundamental Freedoms.[146]

The developing jurisprudence of the ECJ is helpful in emphasizing the underlying purpose of affording a remedy to those who are injured by breaches of the law. Its concern with both the compensatory and deterrent effects of remedies offers a useful approach that could be applied by other international tribunals seeking to uphold the rule of law as well as provide justice to victims.

4. The Organization for Security and Cooperation in Europe (OSCE)

The Helsinki Final Act (1975) which is at the origin of the OSCE brought human rights into the context of European peace and security. The various follow-up meetings to the Helsinki Conference strengthened human rights protections, sometimes adding details not found in other regional or global instruments,[147]

---

[145]   Case 222/86, [1987] E.C.R. 4097.
[146]   *Ibid.*, at para. 14.
[147]   See Arie Bloed, 'The Human Dimension of the OSCE: Past, Present and Prospects', in OSCE *Office for Democratic Institutions and Human Rights Bulletin*, vol. 3, 15 at 16.

although the OSCE has tended to focus on human rights issues primarily through diplomatic intervention for conflict-prevention and mediation. An Office for Democratic Institutions and Human Rights, established in Warsaw, assists the democratization process in OSCE states and monitors the implementation of OSCE commitments regarding the human dimension.

A 'Human Dimension Mechanism', created in 1989 and subsequently modified, establishes a procedure for the consideration of human rights cases or situations, initiated by inter-state representations. In 1991, the participants at the Moscow Conference decided to establish a list of experts from whom a group could be appointed to undertake a mission 'to facilitate resolution of a particular question or problem relating to the human dimension'[148] at the invitation of a state.

5. The Inter-American system

The Inter-American system for the protection of human rights has a dual institutional structure, one having evolved from the Charter of the Organization of American States (1948) and the other created by the entry into force of the American Convention on Human Rights (1969). In both instances, the Inter-American Commission on Human Rights is vested with authority to receive communications from individuals and groups alleging a violation of human rights contained in either the American Declaration of the Rights and Duties of Man or the American Convention. All complaints are considered by the seven member Commission which first determines whether the complaint meets admissibility requirements. The Commission then may hold hearings on the complaint, and, if appropriate, try to effectuate a friendly settlement.

The Commission began to emphasize friendly settlement in recent years. In 1998, in Cases Nos. 11.478 and 11.868 against Ecuador, the Commission negotiated settlements that included wide-ranging remedies and large compensatory damages. In Case No. 11.868, the settlement agreement was signed on 20 May 1998 between the government and the petitioner, father of two young men who disappeared in Ecuador on 8 January 1988. Efforts to pursue domestic remedies had been unavailing, as the government asserted that the youths had died in a traffic accident. In the settlement, the government accepted responsibility for the disappearances and denial of justice and agreed that possibly the bodies had been

---

[148]   Follow-up conferences have been held in Madrid (1983), Vienna (1989), Copenhagen (1990) and Budapest (1994). The Madrid meeting focused on the issue of trade union freedoms in light of the advent of the Solidarity movement in Poland. Specific and detailed guarantees regarding freedom of religion, non-discrimination, minority rights, freedom of movement, conditions of detention and capital punishment were added at the Vienna meeting. See Concluding Document of Vienna (1989). Copenhagen also resulted in considerable standard-setting in several areas of human rights protections, especially concerning national minorities. Document of the Moscow Meeting of the Conference on the Human Dimension of the CSCE, October 1991, at para. 5.

thrown into a specific lagoon. It agreed to pay the father of the boys US$2,000,000 as a lump sum settlement without prejudice to civil remedies against the perpetrators and to conduct a new 'complete, total and definitive' search for the bodies of the brothers in the Yambo lagoon and to recover their bodies. The government agreed to make available specially-trained military divers joined by one or more international teams under the supervision of the government and international or national human rights institutions. Further, the government promised not to interfere with any ceremonies commemorating the youths organized by the victims' family, friends and human rights organizations. The government agreed to rehabilitate the reputation of the family by affirming that there was no indication that any of them had been involved in activities against Ecuadoran law or morality. It agreed to reject any speculation, rumour or suspicion against the honour and name of the petitioner and his family and affirmed, instead, that they had performed legitimate and honourable work contributing to the progress of Ecuador. Finally, the government agreed to investigate, prosecute and punish those responsible for the disappearances and presumed deaths of the two sons of the petitioner and to keep the Inter-American Commission informed of its compliance with the agreed remedies.

The petitioners in the second case, *campesinos* living in Putumayo near the Colombian border, were represented by the Catholic Bishop of Sucumbios. They alleged that after an ambush of a military patrol by unknown persons they had been illegally detained, held *incommunicado* and subjected to physical, sexual, and psychological torture. Efforts to achieve a domestic remedy were unavailing, although evidence was available both of their innocence and of the injury they had suffered. The negotiated settlement, signed on 25 June 1998, was also significant for the scope of remedies afforded the victims. The government accepted its responsibility for the violations and agreed to pay each of the 11 petitioners US$100,000 without prejudice to remedies against the individuals responsible for the illegal and arbitrary detention and torture. As satisfaction, the government recognized that the individuals had been victims of the alleged violations and instructed the armed forces and national police to observe due process in regard to all accused of penal offences. It further agreed to investigate the violations and prosecute and punish those responsible. In both settlements, the government agreed to report periodically to the Inter-American Commission on its compliance with the obligations it assumed in the agreements.

In cases where no settlement is reached, the Commission proceeds to consider the merits of the case. The American Convention creates a two-stage process at the conclusion of a case before the Commission. First, reports are approved in accordance with Article 50 and transmitted to the state, which is not authorized to publicize the report. The report contains findings of facts and conclusions. If a violation has been found, the report will also include the Commission's proposals and recommendations. Article 51 provides that if the case is not settled or submitted to the Court within three months of the date of transmittal of the report, the Commission may set forth its opinion and conclusions on the case. This second report also may include recommendations to remedy the situation examined and a time period for compliance. After the stated time period has elapsed, the Commission decides whether to publish its report.

The Commission has begun to make more detailed comments on reparations and to report on the measures states have taken in response to the recommendations in the Article 50 report.[149] The Commission normally recommends that a state found to have violated human rights pay monetary compensation to the victim or, in the case of death or disappearance, to the family members of the victims. The Commission has stated that when such a recommendation is made, the duty to provide compensation becomes an international legal obligation that may not be limited by national law.[150] In addition to or as an alternative to compensation, the Commission has recommended reform of a military court system,[151] investigation, prosecution and punishment of violators,[152] adoption or modification of legislation,[153] and guarantees for the safety of witnesses.[154] The Court has said that 'the Commission may recommend to a state the derogation or amendment of a conflicting norm that has come to its attention by any means whatsoever, whether or not that norm has been applied to a concrete case'.[155]

In providing detail concerning the nature and scope of required remedies, the Commission has applied the law of other human rights bodies. In death cases, the Commission has adopted the criteria established in the 'principles governing the effective prevention and investigation of extralegal, arbitrary or summary executions'. The principles were adopted by the United Nations Economic and Social Council in resolution 1989/65, in order to determine whether or not a state has fulfilled its obligation to investigate immediately, exhaustively, and impartially the summary executions of persons under its exclusive control.[156] The principles provide that the investigation of cases of this nature must aim to determine the

---

[149] See e.g. Report No. 4/98, Case 9853, *Ceferino ul Musicue and Leonel Coicue v. Colombia*, IACHR, Annual Report 1998, OAS/Ser.L/V/II.91 Doc. 7, rev.3 (1996), paras. 68–70: 'The state has notified the Commission that the government and the petitioners are collaborating to develop an educational project to benefit the Paez indigenous community. The plan would include several educational workshops on human rights. The Commission recognizes the importance of this project. If the project is carried out in a serious manner, it will constitute a valuable means of providing reparation to the community for the human rights violations committed against two of its members'. The state also informed the Commission that it would seek to execute internally the Commission's recommendation that monetary compensation be provided to the victims.

[150] Report No. 26/97, Case 11.142, Colombia, IACHR, Annual Report 1997, 478, OEA/Ser.L/V/II.98, Doc. 7 rev. (1998). [151] *Ibid.*

[152] *Ibid.* See also Report 3/98, Case 11.221 *Tarcisio Medina Charry v. Colombia, ibid.* at 482, 508.

[153] Report 3/98, *ibid.* at 509.

[154] Report 26/97, *supra* n. 150.

[155] Inter-Am.Ct.H.R., Advisory Opinion OC–14/94 (9 December 1994), 1994 II Inter-Am Y.B.H.R. 1510 at para. 39.

[156] See Report No. 10/95, Case 10.580, Ecuador, IACHR, Annual Report 1995, OAS/Ser.L/V/II.91 Doc. 7, rev.3 (1996), paras. 32–34; Report 55/97, Case 11.137, *Juan Carlos Abella v. Argentina*, IACHR, Annual Report 1998, OEA/Ser.L/V/II.98 Doc. 7 rev. (1998), para. 413; Report No. 48/97, Case 11.411, Mexico, IACHR, Annual Report 1998 at 637, 659.

cause, manner and time of death, the person responsible and the procedure or practice which might have led to the events.

As noted by the Inter-American Commission, the United Nations principles have been complemented by a *Manual on the effective prevention and investigation of extralegal, arbitrary or summary executions'*,[157] that gives guidelines on how to ascertain the truth about events leading to the suspicious death of a person. The *Manual* suggests that investigators:

(a) identify the victim;
(b) recover and preserve probative elements related to the death in order to assist in any future trial of the persons responsible;
(c) identify any possible witnesses and obtain statements from them concerning the death;
(d) determine the cause, manner, place and time of death, as well as any modality or practice that might have led to the death;
(e) distinguish between natural death, accidental death, suicide and homicide;
(f) identify and apprehend the person or persons who might have participated in the execution, and
(g) bring the perpetrator or perpetrators suspected of having committed a crime to a competent court established by the law.

The Manual also establishes procedures for gathering evidence.[158] The Commission applies the principles and the procedures to test whether or not the government has fulfilled its duty to investigate suspicious deaths. Failure to comply with these requirements seems to establish a prima facie case that the state has violated its obligations under the Convention, exacerbated when the state's own criminal procedures are not followed.[159]

---

[157] U.N. Doc. ST/CSDHA/12.

[158] The standards require that:

(A) the area surrounding the corpse must be secured. Access to the area must be permitted only to investigators and their staff;

(B) colour photographs of the victim must be taken, since, in comparison with black and white photos, colour photographs may reveal in greater detail the nature and circumstances of the death of the victim;

(C) both the interior and exterior of the place must be photographed, as well as any physical evidence;

(D) a record must be made of the position of the corpse and of the condition of the clothing;

(E) a note should be taken of the following factors which serve to determine the time of death:

(i)   temperature of the body (warm, cool, cold);

(ii) position of corpse and degree of discolouration;

(iii) rigidity of corpse; and

(iv) state of decomposition.

(J) All evidence of the existence of weapons, such as firearms, projectiles, bullets and shells or cartridges, must be collected and preserved. Where appropriate, efforts must be made to find the residue from shots fired and/or to detect metal fragments.

[159] In the *Abella* case, *supra* n. 156, at 373–74, the Commission found that the minimum requirements for conducting investigations were expressly provided for in the Argentinean Code of Criminal Procedure and were not followed in the case.

The Inter-American Commission has been particularly concerned with the issue of impunity as it relates to prior violations and the prospect of future ones. In the report on the Uruguayan *Ley de Caducidad*, the Commission concluded that the impunity granted to officials who had violated human rights during the period of military rule was in breach of Articles 1, 8 and 25 of the American Convention on Human Rights.[160] The Commission noted that Uruguay had not undertaken any official investigation to establish the truth about past events and that this constituted a violation of the state's undertaking to ensure the full and free exercise of the affected rights. The Commission recommended that the government pay the petitioners just compensation for their violated rights. With similar reasoning, the Commission also found that Argentina's 'Due Obedience' and 'Punto Final' laws, and Presidential Pardon No. 1002, violated the American Convention.[161]

After the Commission procedures have been completed, either the state or the Commission can refer the case to the Inter-American Court of Human Rights, if the state involved is a party to the Convention and has expressly recognized the Court's jurisdiction.[162] The Commission appears in all cases that it sends to the Court.[163] The American Convention does not give individuals standing to bring a case before the Court or to appear separately, although Article 23 of the new Rules of Court provides that the victims may be represented directly during the reparations phase of the proceedings.

The Commission's role has been likened by the Court to that of a 'Ministerio Publico', akin to a public prosecutor.[164] While the individual petitioner may name an attorney for proceedings before the Commission, this does not extend to the Court except during the reparations phase.[165] The absence of direct victim

---

[160] IACHR, Report 29/92, Cases 10.029, 10.036, 10.145, 10.305, 10.372, 10.373, 10.374, 10.375, Uruguay, Annual Report of the Inter-American Commission on Human Rights 1992–1993, OEA/Ser.L/II.83, doc. 14, corr. 1, 12 March 1993, pp 154–165. Article 1 of the Convention contains the generic obligation to protect rights and freedoms; Article 8 concerns the right to a fair trial; and Article 25 contains the right to a remedy.

[161] IACHR, Report 28/92, Cases 10.147, 10.181, 10.240, 10.262, 10.309 and 10.311, Argentina, Annual Report of the Inter-American Commission on Human Rights, 1992–1993, OEA/Ser.L/II.83, doc. 14, corr.1, 12 March 1993, pp. 41–51.

[162] Seventeen of the 25 states parties to the American Convention have accepted the compulsory jurisdiction of the Court: Argentina, Bolivia, Chile, Colombia, Costa Rica, Ecuador, El Salvador, Guatemala, Honduras, Nicaragua, Panama, Paraguay, Peru, Suriname, Trinidad and Tobago, Uruguay, and Venezuela: Annual Report of the Inter-American Court of Human Rights 1996, 273, OAS/Ser.L/V/III.35, Doc. 4 (1997).

[163] The decision to send a case to the Court is based on the Commission's resources and the possible impact of the case on the system. See C. Grossman, 'Disappearances in Honduras: The Need for Direct Victim Representation in Human Rights Litigation', (1992) 15 *Hastings Int'l & Comp. L. Rev.* 363.

[164] *Matter of Viviana Gallardo*, Decision of 13 November 1981, Inter-Am.C.H.R. No. G 101/81, para. 22, reprinted in (1981) 20 I.L.M. 1424, 1428. See D. Shelton, 'The Participation of Nongovernmental Organizations in International Judicial Proceedings', (1994) 88 *Am. J. Int'l L.* 622, 625.

[165] Jo Pasqualucci, 'The Inter-American Human Rights System: Establishing Precedents and Procedure in Human Rights Law', (1994–1995) 26 *Inter-Am.L.Rev.* 297) at 320.

representation at the Court imposes an extra responsibility on the Commission to advocate for the victim.[166] However, Judge Antonio Cancado-Trindade distinguishes the role of the petitioners as the real party in interest from that of the Commission. In his view, the Commission 'is reserved the role of defender of the "public interests" of the system, as the guardian of the correct application of the American convention'. As he correctly notes, 'an undesirable ambiguity' is created if the Commission has the additional function of defending the interests of the alleged victims, mediating between them and the Court. The latter 'paternalistic and anachronistic' function lacks support or meaning, in his view, in a modern human rights tribunal.[167]

The American Convention on Human Rights gives the Inter-American Court broad remedial jurisdiction:

If the Court finds that there has been a violation of a right or freedom protected by this Convention, the Court shall rule that the injured party be ensured the enjoyment of his right or freedom that was violated. It shall also rule, if appropriate, that the consequences of the measure or situation that constituted the breach of such right or freedom be remedied and that fair compensation be paid to the injured party.[168]

The plain language indicates the Court's power to order remedies measures other than compensation. The drafting history of Article 63(1) of the American Convention reveals no debate about conferring broad remedial competence on the Court. The first draft of the Convention was prepared by the Inter-American Commission on Human Rights and was the basic working document at the Conference of San Jose. It gave the Court the power to award compensation in Article 52(1).[169] The Commission itself had worked from three drafts prepared by the Inter-American Council of Jurists (ICJ), the Government of Chile and the Government of Uruguay. All of these earlier drafts generally replicated the language of Article 50 of the European Convention on Human Rights and thus were more restrictive than the draft finally produced by the Commission.[170]

---

[166] Convention Article 61 says that the Commission has standing to bring a case. Article 57 requires the Commission to appear. Regulation 75 provides that when the Commission decides to refer a case to the Court, the Executive Secretary shall immediately notify the petitioner and the alleged victim of the Commission's decision and offer them the opportunity of making observations in writing on the request submitted to the Court, 'The Commission shall decide on the action to be taken with respect to these observations'.

[167] *Castillo Paez Case*, (1998) 34 Inter-Am.Ct.Hum.Rts. (ser. C), Separate Opinion of Judge A.A. Cancado Trindade, paras. 16–17. See also *Loayza Tamayo Case*, (1998) 25 Inter-Am. Ct. Hum.Rts. (ser. C), paras. 16–17.

[168] Article 63(1), American Convention on Human Rights, 22 November 1969, entered into force 18 July 1978, 36 O.A.S. T.S. 1, reprinted in *Basic Documents Pertaining to Human Rights in the Inter-American System* (1996), 47.

[169] Draft Article 52(1) contained the language of the last part of present Article 63(1), allowing the Court to order that fair compensation be paid: Buergenthal and Norris, *Human Rights: The Inter-American System*, vol. 2, Bk. 13, p. 20.

[170] OAS, Inter-American Council of Jurists, Fourth Meeting, Santiago, Chile, August–September 1959, OAS Doc. 128, Rev. (1959), reprinted in Buergenthal and Norris, *Human Rights: The Inter-American System*, vol. 3, Bk. 16(1) at 26, 57, 86.

The Commission did not indicate the reasons for or origin of the changes it made.

Guatemala's written comments on the Commission's draft sought to strengthen the article further, to add that the Court might order remedies for the consequences produced by the act or measure that impaired the injured rights and that the injured party be guaranteed the enjoyment of the violated right or freedom.[171] The drafting Committee, Committee II, largely accepted these proposals. The Rapporteur stated that Committee II had 'approved a text which is broader and more categorically in defense of the injured party than the Draft'.[172] The Plenary adopted the Committee version of Article 63(1) without discussion, giving the Court the three powers it currently enjoys to order measures that: (1) ensure that the victim enjoys future respect for the right or freedom that was violated, (2) remedy the consequences of the violation, and (3) compensate for the harm.

Like the early practice of the European Court, the Inter-American Court generally reserves the issue of reparations for a second phase after its judgment on the merits of a case.[173] In general the parties are given six months to settle the issue of reparations. The Court will 'verify the fairness' of any agreement reached. When there is no agreement, as has generally been the case, the Court will decide the issue. Memorials are sought from the Commission, the state, and the victims and public hearings usually are held. The judgment is final, but may be subject to a request for interpretation. The Inter-American system has no organ equivalent to the European Committee of Ministers to oversee compliance with the judgment, and thus the Court holds cases open until the state complies with all the remedial measures directed by the Court.

The Court has made broad use of its jurisdiction. It has awarded pecuniary and non-pecuniary damages, granting both monetary and non-monetary remedies. Unlike the European Court, the Inter-American Court has ordered a state to take specific action to remedy a breach of the Convention. Where legislation is incompatible with the Convention, the Court has held it need not make a specific order; it may declare that the law is incompatible with the Convention and the state is obliged then to bring the law into conformity with the Convention. The Court has been innovative in controlling all aspects of the awards, including setting up trust funds, and maintaining cases open until the awarded remedies have been fully carried out. In contrast, the Court until recently consistently denied costs and attorney's fees for proceedings before the Inter-American institutions. With direct representation of victims during the reparations phase of cases, the Court's practice changed and attorneys fees and costs are now awarded, at least in part.

The Court's jurisdiction to afford remedies is dependent upon the findings on

---

[171] *Ibid.* at 132.   [172] *Ibid.* at 232.

[173] The exceptions are *Gangarem Panday v. Suriname*, (1994) 16 Inter-Am.Ct.H.R. (ser. C) and Inter-Am.Ct.H.R. (ser. C), and *Genie Lacayo v. Nicaragua*, (1997) 30—Inter-Am.Ct.H.R.(ser. C).

the merits, which in turn are affected by the temporal limits of the Court's jurisdiction. In *Blake v. Guatemala (Reparations)*, a judgment of 22 January 1999, the
amount of damages were limited because the deprivation of liberty and death of
Blake were determined to be outside the Court's jurisdiction *ratione temporis*,
occurring before Guatemala accepted the Court's jurisdiction. The Court found
that it could only determine reparations based on Guatemala's failure to provide
a remedy in contravention of Articles 8(1) and 1(1), a continuing violation, and a
breach of Article 5, the right to physical and moral integrity, due to the on-going
lack of knowledge about the disappeared. As a consequence, the Court denied
pecuniary damages based on the loss of life and awarded only costs and expenses
incurred in attempting to discover what had happened to Blake. It also awarded
moral damages to the family.

In contrast to the temporal limitation, the Court has been receptive to innovative theories and claims concerning reparations. In *Suarez Rosero v. Ecuador
(Reparations)*,[174] the petitioner expressed concern over a fine that had been
imposed upon him in the domestic proceedings. The Court agreed that because
the process against the applicant was itself a violation of the Convention, the state
must not execute the judgment imposing the fine and should expunge the record.
In *Loayza Tamayo v. Peru (Reparations)*, the Court accepted the applicant's argument for a third category of damages, in addition to *dano emergente* and *lucrum
cessans*. The judgment recognized that human rights victims suffer interference
with their '*proyecto de vida*', a concept similar to but broader than enjoyment of
life. Linked to the notion of individual self-determination, it allows a damage claim
for interference with the victim's fulfilment founded upon personal capabilities and
goals.[175] Judge Jackman's concurrence expressed hesitation about the new
approach. In his view Article 63 gives the Court the power to base a reparations
decision on whatever identifiable damage is suffered as a result of the violations,

---

[174]   *Suarez Rosero v. Ecuador* was the first contentious case against Ecuador and the first in which
the victim appeared to give testimony in the Court. The case concerned prolonged preventive detention and the right to a speedy and fair trial. *Suarez Rosero* was arrested on 23 June 1992, during an
investigation into drug-trafficking although no drugs were found around him. He was held *incommunicado* without charges or presentation to a judge for more than a month. When he finally appeared
before a judge, the judge ordered him held in preventive detention. He remained incarcerated and
without trial for nearly four years after his arrest, until several months after the case was submitted to
the Inter-American Court. On 9 September 1996, he was convicted in the trial court and sentenced for
covering up the crime of drug-trafficking, for which the maximum sentence is two years in prison. He
was also fined, although the law does not provide a fine for the crime of which he was convicted. The
Court found that the government had illegally arrested the individual, because there was no judicial
order, which was necessary under domestic law. It also held that he had been held for an unreasonable time period, that he had been denied access to the courts, and that his rights to the presumption
of innocence and to prepare a defence were violated. It additionally found that he had been subjected
to cruel, inhuman and degrading treatment by reason of being held *incommunicado* and because of
the conditions in the jail: *Suarez Rosero v. Ecuador (Reparations)*, Judgment of 20 January 1999,
(1999) 44 Inter-Am.Ct.H.R. (ser. C).

[175]   As discussed *infra* in Chapter 8, the Court placed no monetary value on the claim in the
Loayza case.

including lost opportunities, if the Court determines that they can be quantified. A new heading is therefore an unnecessary invitation to expanded litigation and argumentation. Other judges expressed their view that human rights law requires reparations that take into account the totality of the human person and the impact of a human rights violation on this life, departing from a material perspective and looking at all potentialities and capacities. In their view, non-monetary reparations are therefore much more important than compensation.[176]

6. The African human rights system

The African Charter on Human and Peoples' Rights, which entered into force on 21 October 1986,[177] obliges states parties to recognize the rights, duties, and freedoms contained in the Charter and to adopt legislative or other measures to give effect to them. States are to report biennially on these measures. In addition, states parties have a duty to promote and ensure respect for the rights, through teaching, education and publication. The Charter provides for an African Commission on Human and Peoples' Rights whose functions are 'to promote human and peoples' rights and ensure their protection in Africa'[178] as well as monitor state compliance with the provisions of the Charter. The Commission is composed of 11 members, elected in their individual capacities by the OAU's Assembly of Heads of States and Governments. The Commission may receive communications from individuals, non-governmental organizations or other entities who have exhausted local remedies. It may investigate the merits of admissible claims and make recommendations to the states concerned. In formulating and laying down principles and rules aimed at solving legal problems relating to human rights,[179] the Commission is to draw inspiration from other international human rights instruments, customary international law, and general principles of law recognized by African states.[180]

As an organ of the youngest human rights system, the African Commission is still exploring the scope of its powers.[181] By the end of its first decade, the

---

[176] *Loayza Tamayo v. Peru (Reparations)*, (1998) 43 Inter-Am.Ct.H.R. (ser. C), Separate opinion of Judges Antonio Cancado Trindade and Y.A. Abreu Burelli, paras. 10–11.

[177] African Charter on Human and Peoples' Rights, adopted 27 June 1981, entered into force 21 October 1986, O.A.U. Doc. CAB/LEG/67/3 Rev. 5, reprinted in (1982) 21 I.L.M. 59.

[178] Article 30.

[179] African Charter, Article 45(1)(b).

[180] Articles 60, 61.

[181] The former Secretary-General of the OAU claims that 'it was left to the Commission to affirm its role without complex or hesitation and to elaborate its jurisprudence and pronounce the law in the absence of something better': Edem Kodjo, 'The African Charter on Human and Peoples' Rights' (1990) 11 *Hum.RtsL.J.* 271, 289. Others have argued that the Commission lacks a mandate to address individual communications. See Rachel Murray, 'Decisions by the African Commission on Individual Communications Under the African Charter on Human and Peoples' Rights', (1998) 46 *Int'L & Comp.L.Q.* 412, 413; Wolfgang Benedek, 'The African Charter and Commission on Human and Peoples' Rights: How to Make it More Effective', (1993) *Neth.Q.Hum.Rts.* 25 at 31.

Commission had decided over 100 cases, recognizing that the objective of the process is to remedy the prejudice complained of.[182] It has made specific recommendations on remedies in several cases, including demanding the release of persons wrongfully imprisoned[183] and repeal of laws found to be in violation of the Charter.[184] Only one applicant among the cases decided on the merits to date has submitted a request for damages. That case was returned to the domestic legal system for an assessment of the quantum.[185]

The Commission has not discussed the scope of its remedial powers, but in a case against Nigeria, it indicated it would follow up to ensure state compliance with its recommendations. Communication 87/93[186] was brought on behalf of seven men sentenced to death under the Nigerian Civil Disturbances (Special Tribunal) Decree No. 2 of 1987. This decree provided no judicial appeal against decisions of the special tribunals and prohibited Nigerian courts from reviewing any aspect of the operation of the special tribunals, in violation of the right to appeal to competent national organs against acts violating fundamental rights (Article 7(1)(a) of the African Charter). The communication also complained that the conduct of the trials before the special tribunals, including harassment and deprivation of defence counsel, violated the right to be defended by counsel of one's choice (Article 7(1)(c)). More generally, applicants complained that the special tribunals, composed of members of the armed forces and police in addition to judges, violated the right to be tried by an impartial tribunal (Article 7(1)(d)). The Commission found for the applicants in regard to all the allegations and recommended that the Government of Nigeria free the complainants. The

[182] See Communications 25/89, 47/90, 56/91, 100/93, *World Organization Against Torture, Lawyers Committee for Human Rights, Union Interafricaine des Droits de l'Homme, Les Temoins de Jehovah v. Zaire (Merits)*, adopted at the 19th Ordinary Session of the Commission, Ouagadougou, Burkina Faso, March 1996, at para. 39.

[183] In Communication 60/91, *Constitutional Rights Project v. Nigeria (in respect of Wahab Akamu, G. Adega and others)*, the Commission found that a Nigerian Decree creating special tribunals which imposed the death penalty without the possibility of appeal violated the right to an appeal to competent national organs against acts violating fundamental rights, guaranteed by Article 7, paragraph 1(a) of the African Charter. The Commission recommended that the Government of Nigeria free the complainants: 8th Annual Report of the ACHPR 1994–1995, ACHPR/8TH/ACT/RPT/XVII, Annex IX.

[184] Communication 101/93, *Civil Liberties Organization in re the Nigerian Bar Association v. Nigeria*, protested against the Legal Practitioners' Decree which decree established a new governing body of the Nigerian Bar Association, namely the Body of Benchers. Of the 128 members of this body, only 31 were nominees of the Bar Association. The rest were nominees of the government. The decree excluded recourse to the Courts and made it an offence 'to commence or maintain an action or any legal proceeding whatever relating to or connected with or arising from the exercise of any of the powers of the Body of Benchers'. The decree was given retroactive effect. The applicants argued that the prohibition on litigation violated Article 7 of the African Charter and that the new governing body violated Nigerian lawyers' freedom of association guaranteed by Article 10 of the African Charter. Finally, they argued that the decree violated the Charter protection against *ex post facto* laws. The Commission agreed and stated that the decree should therefore be annulled 8th Annual Report, *ibid.*

[185] Communication 59/91, *Embga Mekongo Louis v. Cameroon*, 8th Annual Report, *ibid.*

[186] Communication 87/93, *The Constitutional Rights Project (in respect of Zamani Lakwot and 6 Others) v. Nigeria*, 8th Annual report, *supra* n. 183.

Commission decided to bring the file to Nigeria during a planned mission in order to ensure that the violations had been repaired.[187]

The Commission's decisions thus far give little indication of how broadly or narrowly it views its powers. On the one hand, it has issued recommendations of specific conduct which appear close to injunctive orders. On the other hand, the Commission unfortunately declined to address the first request for damages submitted to it. The latter result is anomalous among international human rights tribunals and perhaps was due to the specific facts of the case. In another case, it appeared to presume that the applicant was satisfied with measures taken by a new government to remedy violations by the previous regime.[188]

In June 1998, the Organization of African Unity adopted a draft Protocol to the African Charter on Human and Peoples' Rights on the Establishment of an African Court on Human and Peoples' Rights.[189] The Protocol provides that the Commission, a complainant state or a respondent state may submit cases to the Court concerning the interpretation and the application of the African Charter, the Protocol or 'any other applicable African Human Rights instrument'.[190] States may declare that they accept the competence of the Court to receive from individuals and non-governmental organizations with observer status, cases that are urgent and those alleging serious, systematic or massive violations of human rights.[191] Article 26(1), the remedies provision in the draft, states that '[i]f the Court finds that there has been a violation of a human or people's right, it shall make appropriate orders to remedy the violation, including the payment of fair compensation or reparation'. This provision is broader than all the current mandates to afford remedies to victims of human rights abuse.

D. INTERNATIONAL ADMINISTRATIVE TRIBUNALS

The idea of administrative tribunals dates to the League of Nations which proposed a Tribunal 'to be exclusively a judicial body set up to determine the legal rights of officials on strictly legal grounds'.[192] The first international administrative judicial organ actually created was the Administrative Tribunal of the

---

[187] Contrast Communication 11/88, *Henry Kalenga v. Zambia* (*Amicable Resolution*), adopted at the 7th Ordinary Session of the Commission, Banjul, The Gambia, April 1990. On the basis of a letter from the Zambian Ministry of Legal Affairs indicating that the applicant had been released from prison, the Commission concluded that the case had been amicably resolved. It did not investigate whether the detention itself was incompatible with the Charter nor whether the applicant sought other remedies, including compensation for the detention.

[188] See *Comite Cultural Pour la Democratie au Benin, Hilaire Badjougoume, El Hadj Boubacar Diawara v. Benin (Merits)*, adopted at the 16th Ordinary Session of the Commission, October 1994, para. 38.

[189] The Draft Nouakchott Protocol is OAU/LEG/EXP/AFCHPRPROT(2), April 1997.

[190] *Ibid.*, Article 3.

[191] *Ibid.*, Article 6.

[192] League of Nations, 8th Ass., 4th Comm., 58 Official J. 250–51 (Spec. Supp.).

International Labor Organization (ILOAT). Its competence extends to several specialized agencies, including United Nations Educational, Scientific, and Cultural Organization (UNESCO), World Health Organization (WHO), Food and Agriculture Organization (FAO), World Meteorological Organization (WMO), International Telecommunications Union (ITU), and the International Atomic Energy Agency (IAEA). The United Nations General Assembly subsequently established the United Nations Administrative Tribunal (UNAT) by resolution of 24 November 1949.[193] The World Bank and the International Monetary Fund have had their own procedure since 1980 and, in 1981, the Inter-American Development Bank created its Administrative Tribunal (IADBAT).

Although their competence varies, international administrative tribunals generally deal with appeals by international civil servants against measures taken by an organization in breach of conditions of appointment and benefits, including violations of workers' rights, discrimination, and sexual harassment. The tribunals may revoke the decisions of employers in some cases and may grant financial compensation. UNAT, for example, if it finds an application well-founded, 'shall' order the rescinding of the decision contested or the specific performance of the obligation invoked. It also fixes the amount of compensation to be paid to the applicant for the injury sustained if the Secretary-General chooses to deny restitution or specific performance. The compensation normally will not exceed the equivalent of two years' net base salary of the applicant, but the Tribunal can, in exceptional cases when it considers it justified, order the payment of a higher indemnity.[194] The Tribunal also has decided that compensation may be afforded where specific performance or recission would be an inadequate remedy.[195] Moral damages sometimes have been awarded for distress and prejudice.

The ILOAT statute confers unlimited authority on the Tribunal to award 'compensation for the injury' in cases where recission or specific performance is not possible or advisable.[196] Like other international tribunals with discretion to award compensation, ILOAT does so on an equitable basis in light of all the circumstances.[197] To assess damages for lost earnings, it has referred to a principle that requires calculating the amount of pay due minus actual or probable

[193] The Statute of the UNAT was adopted by the General Assembly by Resolution 351A(IV) on 24 November 1949 and amended by Resolution 782B(VIII) on 9 December 1953 and by Resolution 957(X) on 8 November 1955.

[194] Article 9, Statute of the UNAT, *supra* n. 193. Article IX of the Statute of the Inter-American Development Bank is virtually identical, although it states more clearly that compensation is to be awarded if the President of the Bank or the General Manager of the Corporation decides 'not to comply' with the terms of the judgment ordering recission of the decision or specific performance of the obligation.

[195] *Bulsara v. Secretary General of the United Nations*, 24 I.L.R. 728 (Admin. Trib. of U.N. 1957).

[196] Article VIII, Statute of the International Labor Organization Administrative Tribunal. See B.M. de Vuyst, *Statutes and Rules of Procedure of International Administratve Tribunals* (1981).

[197] See *Goyal v. UNESCO*, 43 I.L.R. 396 (Int'l Lab. Org. Admin. Trib. 1969).

outside earnings, but generally the Tribunal does not explain its awards for either pecuniary or non-pecuniary harm. The ICJ has approved the ILOAT practice of affording compensation on an equitable basis saying that when the precise amount of compensation could not be based on a specific rule of law, equity can provide the 'true' and 'reasonable' measure of compensation.[198]

In *Franks and Vollering v. EPO*, the ILOAT stated that 'the law that the Tribunal applies in entertaining claims that are put to it includes not just the written Rules of the defendant organization but the general principles of law and basic human rights'.[199] In exercising its discretion to afford equitable relief, the ILOAT has ordered the payment of lost wages, moral damages,[200] interest,[201] and costs.[202] It also has imposed a penalty on occasion for failure to comply with a decision.[203]

Petitioners before the IADBAT similarly and successfully have challenged acts violating their employment rights.[204] The IADBAT's first judgment for an applicant awarded a 2 per cent salary increase it found had been wrongfully denied by the Bank. The increase was from the date of the denial to the date of the decision.[205] The Tribunal also has ordered a transfer quashed,[206] nullified a flawed performance evaluation, awarded salary,[207] ordered either reinstatement or compensation,[208] and awarded retroactive merit increases.[209]

The issue of costs came up in two cases. In the first, the petitioner sought reimbursement for the travel expenses of his lawyer, who received notice too late of a change in the date of a hearing. The Tribunal granted reimbursement even though no other remedy was awarded, the Tribunal finding that the administrative irregularities

[198] Administrative Tribunal of the International Labor Organizations (Advisory Opinion) 1956 I.J.C. 77.

[199] *Franks and Vollering* v. EPO, ILOAT Judgment No. 1333 of 31 January 1994, Consideration 5.

[200] *Unninayar v. WMO*, ILOAT Judgment No. 972 of 27 June 1989 (awarding 25,000 Swiss francs for moral injury).

[201] *Manaktala v. WHO*, ILOAT Judgment No. 1338 of 13 July 1994. See *De Alarcon v. WHO*, ILOAT Judgment No. 479 of 28 January 1982, Consideration 14: 'Interest at the market rate is composed in part of a sum considered to be sufficient to protect the lender against inflation and in part interest in the old sense, that is the payment made for the use of stable money'.

[202] See e.g., *Labben v. WHO*, ILOAT Judgment No. 1026 of 26 June 1990, *Leprince v. UNESCO*, ILOAT Judgment No. 942 of 8 December 1988. In *Ghaffar v. WHO*, ILOAT Judgment No. 320 of 21 November 1977, the Tribunal stated that in principle a complainant whose complaint is allowed in whole or in part is entitled to costs paid by the defendant organization.

[203] *Bluske v. WIPO*, ILOAT Judgment No. 1362 of 13 July 1994. WIPO was ordered to pay the applicant 10,000 Swiss francs 'by way of penalty' for each month of delay in failing to discharge its obligation of reinstatement.

[204] Applicants succeeded on the merits in 14 of the first 40 cases submitted to the Tribunal. Six cases were discontinued before a decision was taken. The Bank prevailed in the remaining 20 cases.

[205] *Benjamin Castro v. IDB*, Judgment Case No. 7, 11 October 1985.

[206] *Tula Amas v. IDB*, Judgment Case No. 9, 4 April 1986.

[207] *Benjamin Castro v. IDB*, Judgment Case No. 11, 3 April 1987.

[208] *Alfredo del Rio v. IDB*, Judgment Case No. 13, 2 April 1987.

[209] *Marcelo Nunez Ribeiro v. IDB*, Judgment Case No. 14, 3 April 1987.

the petitioner challenged were harmless errors.[210] In *Case 16*, one of four filed by the same applicant, the Bank requested costs be assessed against the applicant. The Tribunal refused, finding no provision authorizing assessment of costs in its Rules and stating that as a policy matter such a rule would serve to discourage the Bank's employees from asserting their rights before the Tribunal.[211]

The IADBAT's approach to remedies has become more innovative in recent years, perhaps in response to more egregious cases of misconduct. In *Arminda Buria-Hellbeck v. IDB*[212] the applicant complained of a decision not to confirm her appointment to the professional staff of the Bank. She asked for an appointment; expunging of her performance evaluation; back pay; $50,000 for 'damages to her professional reputation, anguish, and humiliation', and attorneys' fees. Her complaint alleged due process violations during her consideration for appointment. The Tribunal found that at various stages of the appointment process, officials showed bias or prejudice in regard to charges she raised of sexual harassment and improperly treated her complaint. The Tribunal found her complaint of sexual harassment 'colored the Bank's perception' of her suitability for confirmation. The Tribunal concluded that the incidents of sexual harassment 'were not frivolous' and that they were not investigated in a timely and serious manner by the Bank:

Indeed, Bank officials seem to have been so preoccupied with what they perceived

to be Complainant's personality as reflected in the fact of her grievance or the nature of the various facts being alleged by and against Complainant, that they lost sight of the chilling effect their treatment of the Complaint would have on future grievances that might be filed against the Bank.[213]

The Tribunal also noted that the petitioner's file was 'amplified' after the fact in order to strengthen the position of the Bank in the case. In conclusion, the Tribunal strongly cautioned the Bank that '[a]llegations of sexual harassment may not and should not have been dealt with as they were, in a superficial manner, without adequate investigation, written conclusions or even oral conclusions made available for judicial review at the appropriate time'. The Tribunal found lack of due process and, although it did not order a new procedure for confirmation in an appointment, it ordered applicant's file expunged of all documents irregularly added to it and the addition of the judgment, if the applicant so desired. No back pay or attorneys' fees were explicitly awarded, but the Tribunal found the applicant 'entitled to fifty thousand dollars as compensation for material and moral injury' resulting from the lack of due process. The award seems to be based on the fact that neither restitution nor specific performance was capable

[210] *Juan Ramon Duval v. IDB*, Judgment Case No. 12, 2 October 1986.
[211] *Julio C. Cabo v. IDB*, Judgment Case No. 16, 13 November 1987.
[212] Case No. 23, 18 November 1989.
[213] *Ibid.*

of remedying the violation; compensation was thus awarded based on the Tribunal's inherent powers. The amount is sufficiently high that an award of attorneys' fees probably was included *sub rosa*.[214]

Similar awards of compensation have followed in cases concerning forced retirement,[215] inadequate housing allowance,[216] breach of personnel policies regarding the confidentiality of medical records,[217] a punitive transfer,[218] and denial of merit pay increases.[219]

E. CONCLUSIONS

The authority of human rights tribunals to afford remedies is uncontested. Judicial bodies have inherent power to remedy breaches of law in cases within their jurisdiction. In addition, some human rights treaties confer explicit competence to afford redress on the organs they create to hear cases. The language conferring this authority differs in the European and American Conventions but the linguistic distinctions alone cannot explain the different views of the courts on the scope of their powers. Instead, the initial conservatism of the European Court, understandable in the context of its ground-breaking role, has solidified into an unsatisfactory jurisprudence. The court's explicitly conferred powers are broader than it assumes them to be, as shown by the law of state responsibility, to which may be added the inherent remedial powers enjoyed by all courts. The drafting reference to and reliance on arbitral treaties was primarily designed to prevent the court from becoming a tribunal of 'fourth instance' or an appellate court that could itself annul a wrongful conviction or strike down legislation incompatible with treaty obligations. Nothing precludes the court from ruling that such a

---

[214] The IADBAT's Statute provides that 'each party shall bear its own costs in presenting a case to the Tribunal'.

[215] *Osvaldo S. Rossello v. IDB*, Case No. 25, 12 July 1991. Complainant was awarded US$53,720 in compensation.

[216] *Francois de Backer v. IDB*, Case No. 27, 13 November 1992. Notably, the Tribunal acknowledged in this case that housing costs were not formally part of the employment contract, but saw them as an inducement to sign and one based on misrepresentation by the Bank. The Tribunal unanimously awarded US$13,000.

[217] *Noel X. Belt v. IDB*, Judgment Case No. 29, 13 November 1992. The case centered on a denial of merit increases, which the Tribunal ordered. The damages for breach of confidentiality, in the amount of US$10,000, were in addition to the retroactive merit increases and benefits. One judge dissented, finding the relief awarded outside the powers conferred on the Tribunal by the statute.

[218] *Mariana C. Renart v. IDB*, Judgment Case No. 32, 13 November 1992. In this case, the Tribunal was able to award restitution of the position which the applicant had been denied. It awarded, in addition, the equivalent of one year of her salary, US$55,596, for damages sustained. The Tribunal specifically denied the request for attorneys's fees, although they may be seen as included in the amount of damages awarded.

[219] *Rolando H. Castaneda v. IDB*, Judgment Case No. 34, 19 October 1993. The Tribunal ordered restitution, a retroactive increase in merit pay of 11.15 per cent from 1 August 1991. It added an award of US$30,000 'for damages sustained'.

remedy would be the appropriate one in a given case and calling on the state to implement the decision in its domestic law.

The Inter-American Court, while more generous to litigants, has suffered from inconsistency and some poorly reasoned opinions. It has not welcomed victim representation, as will be seen below in the discussion of attorneys' fees and costs. In both the Inter-American and the European courts, litigants bear considerable responsibility for the state of the law. In most cases, the memorials and briefs filed show a lack of attention to the issue of remedies. With the entry into force of Protocol 11 and the election of a new European Court, there is an opportunity for victims and their representatives to develop new jurisprudence on remedies. The effort should be made not only there, but in the Inter-American and African systems as well.

Finally, other human rights bodies, including the United Nations Human Rights Committee, the Committee on the Elimination of All Forms of Racial Discrimination and the Special Rapporteurs of the Human Rights Commission, need to pay greater attention to remedies. In most cases, it is not enough to declare that a right has been violated. States need guidance and direction on the measures necessary to afford redress to those whose rights have been violated and who have sought relief, often at considerable risk to themselves and their families. The right to a remedy is well-established, even a norm of customary international law. Where states fail to provide the necessary remedies for human rights violations, international institutions are the forum of last resort. Affording redress to victims not only serves the interests of remedial justice, it can help reduce the climate of impunity that exists in many regions and, thereby, induce greater compliance with human rights norms.

6

Procedural Issues

International tribunals have adopted rules and decided cases setting forth the procedural requirements to claim remedies, including standing to file claims, presentation of claims, and the power of the tribunals to oversee the execution of judgments. This chapter reviews the rules and case law on these issues, leaving problems of proof and causality for discussion in the following chapter.

A. WHO MAY CLAIM REDRESS

When human rights violations occur, the victim of the violation has the right to seek redress. The designation of a 'victim' is an international question and at a minimum includes the individual whose right or freedom has been violated. It generally is not necessary that the victim be a national or resident of the defendant state.[1] When the victim is deceased or the injury has consequences for other persons, third parties also may be characterized as victims of the violation.

The European Court may afford just satisfaction to the 'injured party' if it finds a violation. In several cases the Court has indicated that it views the term 'injured party' as synonymous with the term 'victim'as used in Article 34 to establish standing to file a case.[2] The former European Commission defined the term 'victim' as including 'not only the direct victim or victims of the alleged violation, but also any person who would indirectly suffer prejudice as a result of such violation or who would have a valid personal interest in securing the cessation of such violation'.[3] Similarly, in *Colozza and Rubinat v. Italy,*[4] the Court awarded non-pecuniary damages to the victim's widow for her own moral injury, when the violation involved the denial of the deceased's right to a fair

---

[1] Case 186/87, *Cowan v. Tresor Public* [1989] E.C.R. 195 (Community law prevents a member state from making the award of state compensation for harm suffered in that state subject to the condition that the victim hold a residence permit or be a national of a country with which that state has a reciprocal agreement).

[2] See *De Wilde, Ooms* and *Versyp (Vagrancy* cases) (1972) 14 Eur.Ct. H.R. (ser. A) (Article 50); *Airey v. Ireland* (Article 50), (1981) 41 Eur.Ct.H.R. (ser. A), 3 E.H.R.Rep. 592; and *Le Compte, Van Leuven and De Meyere v. Belgium* (Article 50), (1983) 54 Eur.Ct.H.R. (ser. A), 5 E.H.R.Rep. 183.

[3] *X v. Federal Republic of Germany*, App.4185/69, (1970) 35 Eur.Comm'n H.R. Dec.& Rep. 140, 142. See also *Koolen v. Belgium*, 1478/62 13 Eur. Comm'n H.R. Dec. & Rep. 89; *X v. Germany*, 282/57, I Y.B. Eur. Conv. On H.R.166; *Andronicou and Constantinou v. Cyprus* (Admissibility), (1995) 82B Eur.Comm'n H.R. Dec. & Rep. 112.

[4] *Colozza and Rubinat v. Italy*, (1985) 89 Eur.Ct.H.R. (ser. A).

trial, but in *Leudicke, Belkacem and Koç v. Germany*[5] the Court held that the applicant's lawyer could not be considered an injured party. The Court has held that an award of pecuniary damages to the direct victim can be recovered by heirs and successors if the applicant dies during the proceedings, while non-pecuniary or moral damages do not survive unless the court deems it necessary to advance the cause of justice.[6] The Court awarded FF50,000 moral damages in *Gulec v. Turkey*, after it found that the government violated Article 2 by opening fire on unarmed demonstrators, causing the death of the applicant's son and failing to conduct a proper investigation after the death. Two judges dissented, asserting that in principle they disapprove of an award of moral damages for relatives of a victim, 'finding it rather unseemly to derive financial gain from the death of a relative'. This unusual approach is hard to understand; it ignores the very real suffering attendant on the loss of a child or other close family member due to government misconduct and offers no alternative to financial compensation to remedy that loss.[7]

Among the cases decided by the Inter-American Court of Human Rights to the end of 1998, few direct victims have survived the breaches to bring an international complaint. In all remaining cases, various family members and other dependants of the deceased have been the claimants. In such cases they have sought remedies for (1) injuries to the deceased prior to death; (2) wrongful death; and (3) consequential damages they have suffered in their own right. The first category should survive, to avoid making it 'cheaper' for the state to kill the victim than to ensure his or her survival.

International tribunals have long made awards in response to claims brought by individuals for wrongful death, although the jurisprudence of international human rights tribunals varies on the issue of survivability of such claims. The Inter-American Court has held that both pecuniary and non-pecuniary claims survive and automatically pass to the victim's heirs or successors. There is nonetheless a distinction made between those who are entitled to damages for injury inflicted prior to death and those due for the loss of life. Parents, for example, may recover the former because they are presumed to suffer moral injury for harm inflicted on their children, but must prove economic losses to recover the latter.

In general, the Court requires the state to remedy the harm caused to those who

---

[5] *Leudicke, Belkacem and Koc v. Germany* (Article 50), (1980) 36 Eur.Ct.H.R. (ser. A), 2 E.H.R.Rep. 433.

[6] *X v. United Kingdom*, (1982) 55 Eur.Ct.H.R. (ser. A) at paras. 18–19 (Article 50); *Colozza and Rubinat v. Italy*, (1985) 89 Eur.Ct.H.R. (ser. A) at para. 38; *Deumeland v. Germany*, (1986) 100 Eur.Ct.H.R. (ser. A) at para. 97; *Gillow v. United Kingdom*, (1986) 109 Eur.Ct.H.R. (ser. A) at para. 23.

[7] The judges also argued that no damages should be awarded because the victim had died while participating in a violent demonstration. The reduction or denial of moral damages because of the Court's assessment of the victim's conduct is a pattern in decisions of the European Court. See *infra* Chapters 7 and 8.

suffer the 'immediate effects' of its breaches of human rights guarantees, when those effects are sufficiently direct and proximate.[8] The Inter-American Court has held as well that this is only to the extent 'legally recognized' because 'to compel the perpetrator of an illicit act to erase all the consequences produced by his action is completely impossible'. This unhelpful test does not make clear if the legal recognition is a question of domestic or international law and if it applies to the identification of those entitled to redress (i.e. who is a victim) as well as to the extent of harm entitled to be repaired.

In several recent cases, questions again arose about the range of beneficiaries entitled to remedies. In *Loayza Tamayo v. Peru*, the Court held that the victim's family members were also 'injured parties' within the meaning of Article 63(1) and could present their own claims during the reparations phase of the case. Noting earlier cases, the victim and the Commission asserted that the Court has interpreted the concept of family in a flexible and broad manner. They argued for recognition of the victim's extended family, which they said was established by its permanence and the frequency of its close contacts. Although the state opposed this argument, the Court considered that the term 'family members' should be understood in a broad sense to include all those persons linked by a close relationship, including the children, the parents and the siblings. The Court awarded the compensation of US$176,190.30 divided between the victim and her family. Her children received US$15,000 each; her parents US$10,000 each and her siblings US$3,000 each. In *Blake v. Guatemala*, the parents and siblings of the disappeared all claimed to be directly injured by Blake's disappearance and death. The Commission agreed, while the government argued that the claimants were not entitled to damages because they had not demonstrated a dependent relationship with the actual victim. The Court recalled that its judgment on the merits had determined that the violations had caused prejudice to Blake's family and that the members of it thereby constituted 'injured parties' within the meaning of Article 63(1). The Court referred to the especially grave context of forced disappearance that caused the family anguish and suffering, together with insecurity, frustration and impotence in the face of the government's failure to investigate. Finding that the family had experienced grave moral damage and suffering as a result of the violations, it awarded each member of the family US$30,000 each.

Finally, in *Suarez Rosero v. Ecuador*,[9] the Inter-American Court awarded damages for the illegal detention of the petitioner, as well as for denial of his rights of access to court and to an effective remedy. The applicant had been detained in prison under suspicion of drug-trafficking although there was no evidence on which to base the accusation. In additional to pecuniary damages, the applicant sought US$20,000 in moral damages for himself, and US$20,000 for

---

[8] *Aloeboetoe v. Suriname*, (1994) 15 Inter-Am.Ct.H.R. (ser. C) para. 49.
[9] *Suarez Rosero v. Ecuador (Reparations)*, Inter-Am.Ct.H.R., Judgment of 20 January 1999.

his wife and daughter. The Court awarded US$20,000 each to him and his wife, and US$10,000 to the daughter, holding that it is human nature to suffer in the circumstances he had been through and that no proof was required. Further, there must be presumed repercussions on his wife and daughter. The Court based its award on the totality of the circumstances and awards made in similar cases.

The Human Rights Committee has indicated that family members may be considered victims of violations perpetrated on one of their relatives. In the case of a disappearance, the Committee found that the mother of the disappeared was a victim:

The Committee understands the anguish and stress caused to the mother by the disappearance of her daughter and by the continuing uncertainty concerning her fate and whereabouts. The mother has a right to know what has happened to her daughter. In these respects, she too is a victim of the violations of the Covenant suffered by her daughter, in particular Article 7.[10]

The Committee has on several occasions demanded that compensation be paid to the families of deceased victims of torture or disappearance for mistreatment of the victim prior to death.[11]

Survivability of claims as well as direct harm to third party victims has involved human rights tribunals in questions of choice of law regarding inheritance and succession. The Inter-American Court has tended to develop its own law rather than deferring to the national law of the state concerned. According to the Court, in the case of international human rights violations, beneficiaries need not be heirs under the law of the state where the violation occurred to be considered such by the Court.[12]

In *Velasquez Rodriguez v. Honduras*[13] and *Godinez Cruz v. Honduras*[14] the Commission and the state agreed on a designation of beneficiaries that was limited to the wife and children of the disappeared, 'once they had fulfilled the requirements of Honduran law to be recognized as heirs of the victims'. The

---

[10] Comm. No. 107/1981, *Quinteros v. Uruguay*, U.N. GAOR, Hum. Rts. Comm., 38th Sess., Supp. No. 40, at 216, U.N. Doc. A/38/40 (1983) para. 14.

[11] See *ibid. Bleier v. Uruguay*, Comm. No. 30/1978, Hum.Rts. Comm., 37th Sess., UN GAOR Supp. No. 40 at 130, UN Doc. A/37/40, Annex X (1982). The Committee has formulated the obligation to pay compensation in various ways:

(a) compensation to the victim (the disappeared person) and family for 'any injury which he has suffered' (Comm. No. 30/1978, *Bleier v. Uruguay*);

(b) compensation to the husband for the death of his wife (No. 45/1979, *Suarez de Guerrero v. Colombia*);

(c) 'appropriate' compensation to the family of a person killed (No. 84/1981, *Dermit Barbato v. Uruguay*) or to the 'surviving family' (No. 146/1983 and 148–154/1983 *Baboeram et al. v. Suriname*);

(d) compensation 'for the wrongs suffered' (No. 107/1981, *Quinteros v. Uruguay*);

(e) compensation for physical and mental injury and suffering caused to the victim by the inhuman treatment to which he was subjected (No. 110/1981, *Antonio Viana Acosta v. Uruguay*).

[12] *Velasquez Rodriguez v. Honduras* (Compensatory Damages), (1990) 7 Inter-Am.Ct.H.R. (ser. C) para. 54.

[13] *Ibid.*

[14] *Godinez Cruz v. Honduras* (Compensatory Damages), (1989) 8 Inter-Am.Ct.H.R. (ser. A).

Court rejected this limited agreement, holding that 'the family members . . . need only show their family relationship. They are not required to follow the procedure of Honduran inheritance law'. In fact, the secretariat of the Court, under instructions from the President, requested information from Honduran officials, including 'the names and status of their wives; and those of any concubines recognized in any official document, and names and civil status of their children, those of the marriage and any outside the marriage'.[15]

The Court has held that it applies 'general principles of law' on succession in the absence of treaty or custom on point.[16] In *Aloeboetoe v. Suriname*,[17] the Inter-American Court faced the difficult problem of identifying those among the family members of the deceased who would be entitled to compensation once the violation was found. The case was brought by members of the Saramacas, or Maroons, descendants of African slaves who maintain a traditional culture, including a matriarchal social structure and polygamy.

The Court, applying what it called a generally recognized choice of law principle, determined that local law should apply to determine next of kin and beneficiaries of the victims. Surinamese law holds that a victim's next of kin includes the legally recognized spouse, the children, and perhaps dependent parents of the victims. The law does not recognize polygamy. In contrast, Saramaca tribal customary law accepts multiple marriages and the duty of adult children to care for their parents. The Court found that Surinamese family law was not effective in the region and was therefore not the local law for purposes of the case.[18] As a result, the multiple wives and children of the victims were recognized by the Court.[19]

The Commission also argued that the Saramaca tribe suffered direct moral damage and was entitled to compensation. According to the Commission:

[i]n the traditional Maroon society, a person is not only a member of his own family group, but also a member of the village community and of the tribal group. In this case, the damages suffered by the villagers due to the loss of certain members of its group must be redressed. Since the villagers, in practice, constitute a family in the broad sense of the term . . . they have suffered direct emotional damages as a result of the violations of the Convention.[20]

It was asserted that in the Saramaca culture, a communal matrilineal group takes responsibility for the welfare of its members and for such matters as determining

---

[15] *Ibid.* para. 13(4), (5).

[16] Aloeboetoe, *supra* n. 8, at para. 61.

[17] *Ibid.*

[18] Marriages were not registered with the government, partly due to lack of knowledge among the Saramaca about civil law and partly because the government failed to provide accessible facilities to register births, deaths and marriages.

[19] The Court found no issue under the Convention with recognition of polygamy. In contrast, the Court refused to place the monetary compensation under the control of the female head of the family because this would involve gender discrimination.

[20] *Aloeboetoe case*, *supra* n. 8, para. 19. See also *ibid.* paras. 81–84.

which family members are to share in compensation rendered. The attorneys relied on the decisions of earlier tribunals that found the right to recover rests on the direct personal loss, if any, suffered by each of the claimants.[21] '[T]he direct personal loss referred to is pecuniary in nature and is measured principally by the degree of financial dependence which existed between the claimant and the deceased.' The Court rejected this part of the claim, apparently—and wrongly—believing that it was based on racial motivation for the killings or violation of the 1762 treaty establishing Saramaca autonomy.

In the *Aloeboetoe* case, the Court established new law regarding entitlement to damages. It held that successors to wrongfully killed victims may be presumed to suffer injury and the burden of proof is on the government to show that such injury does not exist.[22] Non-successor third parties also may suffer injury, but they bear the burden of proof. Three conditions must be satisfied before non-successors may be awarded damages:

(1)   The damages sought must be based on payments actually made by the victim to the claimant, whether or not they constituted a legal obligation to pay support. These must be regular, periodic payments either in cash, in kind or in services. The test is the effectiveness and regularity of the contributions.

(2)   The nature of the relationship between the victim and the claimant should be such that it provides some basis for the assumption that the payments would have continued had the victim not been killed.

(3)   The claimant must have experienced a financial need that was periodically met by the contributions made by the victim. This requires that the person received a benefit that he or she could not have obtained on his or her own.

Governments push for application of national laws of succession to decide on those entitled to compensation, while the families of victims continue to seek broader redress. In the case of *Neira Alegria v. Peru*,[23] the Commission sought compensation for the wife, three minor children, and sister of one victim. For another, it presented claims for the victim's companion and his daughters by two women, while for the third victim, a bachelor, the claimants were his father, mother and two brothers. The government argued that Peruvian law establishes who a person's successors are and the sister of Neira Alegria should not be included. The Court agreed in part, recalling that all aspects of reparations including the designation of beneficiaries, are governed by international, not domestic, law. It recalled its previous finding that most legal systems designate a person's children and surviving spouse as successors. Thus, the sister was not included in the list of beneficiaries entitled to compensation. Unlike the *Blake* and *Loayza*

---

[21]   Arbitral Decision No. II, in 7 U.N.RIAA 27.

[22]   *Aloeboetoe* case, *supra* n. 8, para. 54.

[23]   *Neira Alegria v. Peru*, (1995) 20 Inter-Am. Ct. H.R. (ser. A).

Tamayo casees, the sister did not claim to be an injured party herself, and would only have shared in an award as a successor to the victim.

It should be noted, finally, that in cases of death or disappearance the Court's succession law has resulted in a division of awards between spouse and children that provides less to the surviving spouse than would be the case in many national legal systems. In the *Velasquez Rodriguez* and *Godinez Cruz* cases, the Court, without indicating the basis of its judgment, divided all amounts awarded between the surviving spouse and the children, giving one-quarter to the surviving spouse and three-quarters to the children, even when there was only one child, as in *Godinez Cruz*.[24] In *El Amparo v. Venezuela* [25] the Court altered the proportions for dividing pecuniary damages, awarding one-third to the spouse and two-thirds to the children. If the victim had no spouse, but had a companion, the spouse's portion would go to the companion. Where there was both a wife and a companion, with children fathered by both, the two families would equally divide the indemnity. In the event there was neither spouse nor companion, the damages would be paid to the victim's surviving parent or parents and if none to the victim's siblings. Moral damages were divided with one-quarter going to the spouse, one-quarter to the parents, and one-half to the children. If the parents are deceased, their share goes to the children. All the deceased thus far have been male and many have had double families recognized by the Court.

B. PRESENTATION OF CLAIMS

The European Court of Human Rights does not award compensation without a claim from the applicant.[26] The plea for damages must be specific. Similarly, if the applicant fails to include a request for fees, the lawyer for the applicant cannot later file a request.[27] In *Sunday Times v. United Kingdom*,[28] the Court refused to award damages because the applicant's submissions 'contained some references to material and moral damage allegedly suffered' but the actual claim was confined to costs and expenses.[29] The European Commission, representing the interests of the system, suggested that because the intrinsic nature of the violation (infringement of freedom of expression) prevented restitution, the Court should award moral damages even though they were not claimed. The Court disagreed, holding that 'no question of public policy' required it to consider on its own motion whether the applicant had been harmed.[30] The Court was mistaken. The

---

[24] The *Gangaram Panday* case is an exception. The Court divided the US$10,000 damage award equally between the widow and the children: *Gangaram Panday Case* (Merits), (1994) 16 Inter-Am. Ct. H.R. (ser. C) para. 70.

[25] *El Amparo Case*, (1996) 28 Inter-Am. Ct. H.R. (ser. C) (Reparations).

[26] *Sunday Times v. United Kingdom*, (1980) 38 Eur.Ct.H.R. (ser. A) (Article 50) 14.

[27] *Delta v. France*, (1990) 191–A Eur.Ct.H.R. (ser. A) at 47.

[28] *Sunday Times v. United Kingdom*, (1980) 38 Eur.Ct.H.R. (ser. A) (Article 50) at 9.

[29] *Ibid.* at 9.   [30] *Ibid.*

public interest is involved each time there is a violation of the European Convention and a necessary component of upholding the treaty regime is the Court's role in affording relief that will deter future violations and indicate the inherent moral injury caused to the victim of the violation. The Commission's views on the need for a remedy beyond what the applicant seeks should have been given greater consideration by the Court. The Court may have felt that moral damages are uniquely within the comprehension of the victim and that an award when it is not claimed would over-compensate. Yet, the Commission was well placed to judge the seriousness of the violation in the larger context of all claims filed. With the Commission no longer extant, the present Court itself may consider whether 'just satisfaction' in the public interest is warranted even when not pleaded.

The European Court has referred to a 'general interest' which could allow it to award presumed damages 'if necessary' from the Court's perspective to afford just satisfaction. The Court also has recognized both an individual and a general interest when cases are resolved by friendly settlement. In *Skoogstrom v. Sweden*,[31] the Court approved a friendly settlement in a case involving the right of a person held in detention on remand to be brought promptly before a judge or other officer authorized by law to exercise judicial power. The settlement included payment to Mr. Skoogstrom of his legal costs (expenses and loss of time) in the sum of SEK5,000. In addition, the government created a Commission for Revision of Certain Parts of the Code of Judicial Procedure to which the applicant's lawyer was named. The Delegate of the Commission commented that the settlement 'satisfied the individual interests of the case' but that the general interest ought to include review of the nature of the amendments and time for them to be adopted into Swedish law. The Delegate proposed that the Court should not strike the case, but should adjourn its examination until it could determine that the legislation was being adopted. The Court declined to do so, seeing no reason of public policy 'sufficiently compelling' to warrant retaining the case. The decision was four to three with the dissenting judges stating that the decision 'does not seem ... to be consonant with the general interest attaching to observance of human rights, which interest the Court is responsible for safeguarding'.[32] The dissent believed that the Court should have ruled on the merits of the case to guide the Commission and Swedish legislature.

The Rules of Procedure of the European Court require that any claim for just satisfaction be set out in the applicant's memorial on the merits or, if there is none filed, in a special document filed at least two months before the hearing.[33] In addition, a claimant must supply itemized particulars of all claims made, together with relevant supporting documents or vouchers. In its early years, the Court

---

[31] *Skoogstrom v. Sweden*, (1984) 83 Eur.Ct.H.R. (ser. A).
[32] *Ibid.* Joint dissenting opinion of Judges Wiarda, Ryssdal and Ganshof van der Meersch.
[33] Rule 60(1), Rules of Court of the European Court of Human Rights, 4 November 1998.

issued decisions on just satisfaction in a separate phase of each case, which increased the length of the proceedings. The Court retains this practice today only for complex cases, such as expropriation claims under Protocol I, Article 1 (right to property), where valuation is difficult,[34] but may invite any party to submit comments on the claim for just satisfaction at any time during the proceedings.

The Inter-American Commission on Human Rights has no provision in its regulations concerning presentation of a request for relief by the applicant, probably because the American Convention makes no reference to a Commission role in this regard. The Rules of Procedure of the Inter-American Court however, Article 33, indicate that the written brief containing the application to the Court shall indicate, *inter alia*, 'the purpose of the application'. The 1996 revisions that adopted this rule also deleted the former Article 44 that allowed a claim for relief to be invoked 'at any stage of the proceedings, even when reference thereto was not made in the application', further indicating that the claim must be submitted with the application to the Court.

In the *Velasquez Rodriguez* case, the Commission requested the Inter-American Court to award compensation to the victims of the violation, but offered no evidence regarding the amount of damages or the manner of payment. It also failed to plead costs. The Court held that it would not be 'proper' for the Court to rule on them in the absence of a pleading. The issue was raised again during the compensatory damages phase of the case. The Court again rejected the award of attorneys' fees and costs because they were not pleaded or proven opportunely. The present rules allow representatives of the victims or of their next of kin to submit their own arguments or evidence at the reparations stage of a case.[35]

The Rules of Procedure of the African Commission on Human and Peoples' Rights ask that applicants submit a statement of the purpose of a communication filed with the Commission. To date, there is no jurisprudence on the timing and mode of presenting such information.

C. SUPERVISING EXECUTION OF THE JUDGMENT

International tribunals have jurisdiction to protect the awards made to victims. The Inter-American Court has exercised extensive powers in this regard, establishing trust funds and overseeing payments. Indeed, it does not close a case until there has been full compliance with all remedial orders and awards. In the

---

[34] See *Sporrong and Lonnroth v. Sweden*, (1982) 52 Eur.Ct. H.R. (ser. A) (Article 50); *Pine Valley Developments Ltd v. Ireland*, (1991) 222 Eur.Ct.H.R. (ser. A) (Article 50); *Papamichalopoulos v. Greece*, (1993) 260–B Eur.Ct.H.R. (ser. A).

[35] Rules of Procedure of the Inter-American Court of Human Rights, Article 23, in Inter-Am. Ct.H.R., Annual Report of the Inter-American Court of Human Rights 1996, 229, OAS/Ser.L/V/III.35 Doc. 4 (1997).

Velasquez Rodriguez and *Godinez Cruz* cases, the Court began a consistent practice of governing the mode of payment. The Court ordered a lump sum payment within 90 days, free of taxes, or payment in six equal monthly instalments, beginning within 90 days. In the latter case, the amount remaining due was subject to interest at current rates in Honduras. The Court ordered the establishment of a trust fund for the children, created in the Central Bank of Honduras 'under the most favorable conditions permitted by Honduran banking practice'. The children received monthly payments from the fund until the age of 25 years, when it was distributed. On 6 September 1996, the Court ordered the *Velasquez Rodriguez* and *Godinez Cruz* cases closed after it found that the government had complied with the reparations orders.[36]

The reparations awarded in the *Aloeboetoe* case totalled US$453,102. As in the Honduran cases, the Court ordered the establishment of a trust fund, only this time the Court ordered it to be established in United States dollars and administered by a Foundation. The Court appointed the members of the Foundation, whose duty was to obtain the best returns for the sums received in reparation and to act as trustee of the funds. The government was ordered to make a one-time contribution of $4,000 or its equivalent in local currency to the operating expenses of the Foundation. Suriname was ordered not to restrict or tax the activities of the Foundation or the operation of the trust fund. Each adult beneficiary could withdraw up to 25 per cent of the sum due to them at the time the government made the deposit. The duration of the trust fund was between three and 17 years, with semi-annual withdrawals permitted. The Foundation could set up a different system in undescribed special circumstances. In 1998, the Court found that the judgment had been complied with and closed the case.

In the European system, a few creditors of applicants have attempted to seize the sums awarded by the European Court of Human Rights. In several instances, the applicant asked the Commission to request the Court for an interpretation of the award in order to protect it from such seizure. The Commission agreed to do so in two cases, including *Ringeisen v. Austria*,[37] the first case in which the Court awarded monetary compensation. After the Court held that Austria had violated Article 5(3) of the Convention due to the excessive length of Ringeisen's detention on remand, it awarded 20,000 German marks for the damage he suffered as a result of the detention.[38]

Ringeisen's receiver in bankruptcy sought the sum on behalf of creditors. Austria deposited the money in an account where the receiver could claim it, arguing that the Austrian courts could fix the priority of payment in accordance

---

[36] *Velasquez Rodriguez Case*, Inter-Am.Ct.H.R. Order of 10 September 1996, reprinted in Annual Report of the Inter-American Court of Human Rights 1996, OAS/Ser.L/V/III.35, Doc.4 (1997) at 209: *Godinez Cruz Case, ibid.* at 213.

[37] *Ringeisen v. Austria*, (1971) 13 Eur.Ct.H.R. (ser. A).

[38] *Ringeisen v. Austria*, (1972) 15 Eur.Ct.H.R. (ser. A) (Article 50). The award was largely for moral damage.

with Austrian law, because the European Court had not made any indications in this regard. Ringeisen addressed a request to the Commission seeking clarification of the Court's judgment. The Commission in turn addressed two questions to the Court. First, because Ringeisen was living in Germany, 'what was the intended effect of the order for payment of compensation in Deutsch marks, particularly in respect of the actual currency and place of payment?' Second, was the term 'compensation' 'to be understood as payment of a sum free of any lawful claims made against it under Austrian law or subject to such claims?'[39]

The Court answered both questions in favour of Ringeisen.[40] It indicated that the award was in German Marks because Ringeisen was living in Germany and should receive the award speedily in light of his health and needs.[41] In response to the second question the Court held that '[b]y the term "compensation" the Court meant an award of a sum to be paid to Michael Ringeisen personally as compensation for non-material damage'[42] and the amount was intended to be free from attachment.

More recently, the Commission asked the Court to apply the Ringeisen ruling in the case of *Allenet de Ribemont v. France*.[43] On the merits, the Court found violations of Article 6 because of public accusations that the applicant had been involved in the murder of a member of Parliament, accusations which were not pursued for lack of evidence. The government statements were found to violate the presumption of innocence. In addition, in regard to a civil action brought by the applicant for damage to reputation and loss of business, France was found to have violated the requirements of Article 6(1) (right to trial within a reasonable time) because the proceedings lasted over 11 years. Pursuant to Article 50, the Court awarded FF2,000,000[44] in pecuniary and non-pecuniary damages, as well as FF100,000 for costs and expenses.[45]

The applicant did not receive the funds because the heirs of the murdered parliamentarian seized them in execution of a civil judgment they had obtained in 1979. Through the Commission, the applicant sought a clarification of the Article 50 award, asking the Court to indicate what part of the award constituted non-pecuniary damages exempt from seizure. The Commission asked the Court three questions: (1) whether Article 50 in general meant any sum awarded must be paid to the injured party personally and be exempt from attachment; (2) where legal claims were made under French law, whether there was a distinction between pecuniary damage awards and non-pecuniary damages; and (3), what part of the

---

[39] *Ringeisen v. Austria*, 14 Eur.Ct.H.R. (ser. B) (interpretation of the judgment of 22 June 1972) at 6–7.
[40] *Ringeisen v. Austria*, 16 Eur.Ct.H.R. (ser. A) (interpretation of the judgment of 22 June 1972) (1973).
[41] Ringeisen suffered from severe heart problems and required constant medical attention.
[42] *Ringeisen v. Austria*, (1973) 16 Eur.Ct.H.R. (ser. A) at para. 15.
[43] *Allenet de Ribemont v. France*, (1995) 308 Eur.Ct.H.R. (ser. A).
[44] Approximately US$400,000.
[45] Approximately US$20,000.

award in the *Allenent* case was for pecuniary damage and what part for non-pecuniary damage?

In a judgment of 7 August 1996, the Court avoided explicitly overruling its decision in *Ringeisen* on exemption of damages from seizure, but left the law very murky. The Court declined to answer the first question, finding it so general as to be an 'invitation to interpret Article 50 in a general, abstract way' beyond the contentious jurisdiction of the Court or the scope of an interpretation governed by Rule 57. In *Ringeisen* the Court was asked—and it answered—the question 'whether the term "compensation" in the judgment was to be understood as payment of a sum free of any lawful claims made against it under Austrian law, or subject to such claims'. There seems to be little difference in the formulation of the questions in the two cases. As the dissenting opinion of Judge de Meyer notes, the abstraction of the first question was a matter of appearance only. In fact, the issue related to whether this particular applicant should receive his award personally and exempt from attachment.

Despite the *Ringeisen* precedent, the French government argued that the Court lacks power to declare exempt from attachment the sums it awards in compensation. In the alternative, the government pleaded French law, perhaps because the Court in *Ringeisen* noted that the principle of awards free of attachment 'applied also in Austrian law in analogous cases'.

The applicant referred to the purpose of just satisfaction, autonomous from domestic law, to compensate for specific damage arising from a breach of the Convention and to penalize the state. The applicant did not explain why the latter purpose would be defeated if the state pays a third party, other than to refer to the 'indissoluble bond between the award and the recipient', which he argued, makes the award exempt from attachment whatever the domestic rules on the subject.

Unlike Ringeisen, Allenet had asked during the merits phase that any award given be free from attachment, and specifically referred to the 1979 civil judgment. The Court declined to so hold, deciding that 'it does not have jurisdiction to issue such an order to a Contracting State'. The Court's decision on this point also seems inconsistent with *Ringeisen* where the Court held 'that the . . . compensation is to be paid to Michael Ringeisen personally and free from attachment' in spite of the existence of pre-existing creditors.

In response to the third question, the Court referred to the fact that it had already declined to identify the proportions corresponding to pecuniary and non-pecuniary damage, adding that it 'is not bound to do so when affording "just satisfaction" under Article 50 of the Convention'. The Court noted its difficulty in making such a distinction, citing earlier judgments. In fact, the Court seems to make an aggregate award most often when the applicant fails to prove specific pecuniary loss and the Court wants to award some compensation. Rather than denying relief, the Court disguises the lack of evidence with a lump sum award. The Court declined to revisit the earlier *Allenet* opinion, finding 'nothing' left to interpret. The result is that an applicant who receives a lump sum settlement cannot protect any of the award against domestic creditors if local law allows attachment, a result that implicitly overrules the judgment in *Ringeisen*.

In two other cases, the Commission refused requests to ask the Court to interpret judgments, where the governments involved set off their claims for amounts still owing for costs and expenses in domestic proceedings against the Court's awards of costs and expenses.[46] The Commission accepted that this set-off should be permitted.

D. CONCLUSIONS

The development of remedies for human rights violation has led to the expansion of international law and procedures into new areas of concern. International tribunals have used their implied powers to ensure that the term 'victim' or 'injured party' is interpreted to achieve the goal of wiping out the consequences of the harm, even where the consequences are collateral to the immediate injury. In so doing, the Inter-American Court has developed a practice of dividing awards among survivors according to its own view of appropriate succession. While the issue should not be subject entirely to national law, it might be better considered as a matter of future treaty negotiation rather than the Court's developing and inconsistent jurisprudence.

All international tribunals have expressed concern over ensuring that their views, decisions, and judgments are made effective and that remedies are afforded to the victims of human rights violations. Some of the most innovative developments in the law of remedies can be seen in this regard, including the establishment of trust funds by the Inter-American Court. The issue is likely to arise in the European and African systems in the future as they have to confront states unable or unwilling to comply with remedial decisions.

[46] See *Eckle v. Germany*, (1983) 65 Eur.Ct.H.R. (ser. A) (Article 50), *Hauschildt v. Denmark*, (1989) 154 Eur.Ct.H.R. (ser. A).

Part III

Jurisprudence and Practice

7

Declaratory Judgments

From the perspective of a defendant state, a declaratory judgment is the least intrusive remedy that a tribunal can afford the victim of a human rights violation. If the state concerned is committed to the rule of law, a declaratory judgment still should be effective to end the violation and prevent similar breaches in the future. In fact, for states committed to upholding a treaty and fulfilling in good faith their obligations, the adjudication itself may be of greatest significance, as Borchard noted:

The adjudication, not the command, is the essence of judicial power, and in our civilized communities, it is the adjudication, and not the command, which evokes respect and official sanction, because it is a determination by the societal agent appointed to perform that function, and thus irrevocably fix legal relations.[1]

A binding judgment that the state is in breach of its obligations could even be viewed as morally equivalent to an injunction, requiring a change in law or practice.

Declaratory judgments are the remedy most often sought and granted in inter-state litigation. States parties to cases before international courts and arbitral tribunals often request a declaration of the applicable law and of their rights and duties, on the basis of which they may negotiate a resolution of their dispute. Frequently, the conflict has caused no measurable economic injury to either party and there may be no sense of wrongdoing or injustice in the behaviour of the parties, such as in many cases involving the delineation of a land or maritime boundary. In other cases, the facts indicate that restitution remains possible once the rights and duties are proclaimed, so the parties do not press for measures of compensation or satisfaction.

When an inter-state dispute concerns an asserted norm of customary international law, the authoritative declaration of the tribunal is particularly important in determining the existence and application of the rule. In the absence of negotiation or codification, a declaratory judgment is the primary means of resolving questions about the existence or content of customary international law; it is preferable to the use of coercive measures by one or more states to impose a particular assertion of the disputed norm. Legal uncertainty thus can be resolved by declaratory judgments and they may be useful in some human rights cases.

In national law, declaratory judgments are prevalent in both civil law and common law legal systems. Equitable declaratory relief has been available in

---

[1] E. Borchard, *Declaratory Judgments* (1934), 10.

England since 1688 and in the USA such actions are permitted under the Federal Declaratory Judgment Act, first passed by Congress in 1934.[2] In France, the Conseil d'Etat and Conseils d'Administration have the right to declare an administrative act void for *exces de pouvoir*.[3] Declaratory judgments are particularly important in relations between the individual and the government, where the judgment may avoid irreparable harm by establishing the scope of state duties and the right of the individual not to be subjected to the threatened injury, such as a planned extradition in violation of human rights guarantees or prior censorship of a publication or broadcast. As Borchard asserts:

With the growing complexity of government and the constantly increasing invasions of private liberty, with ever widening powers vested in administrative boards and officials, the occasions for conflict and dispute are rapidly augmenting in frequency and importance. Yet the very fact that such disputes turn mainly upon questions of law, involving the line marking the boundary between private liberty and public restraint, between private privilege and immunity, on the one hand, and public right and power, on the other, makes this field of controversy particularly susceptible to the expeditious and pacifying ministrations of the declaratory judgment.[4]

There are clear advantages to an individual in being able to adjudicate the lawfulness of a statute carrying criminal penalties, e.g. statutes criminalizing homosexuality, without the necessity of violating the statute and risking the sanction. In addition, a statute that is discriminatory or otherwise facially violates human rights injures those within its purview as soon as it is enacted.[5] To require a member of the affected group to await enforcement of the statute or regulation before challenging its legality, ignores the fact that, as soon as the statute is in force, unlawful limitations are placed upon individual freedom of action. The declaratory judgment also can be useful when the violation is one that is likely to be repeated or the situation is on-going, e.g. deprivation of the right to vote or exclusion of disabled students from schools.

The importance of a determination that the state has violated internationally-guaranteed human rights should not be underestimated. Governments violate human rights and do not like to be called to account when they do so. Having a

---

[2] Federal Declaratory Judgment Act, 28 U.S.C.A. 2201 (West 1988).

[3] See L. Fanichi, *La Justice Administrative* (1980).

[4] E. Borchard, 'Challenging "Penal" Statutes by Declaratory Action', (1942) 52 *Yale L.J.* 445. In politically sensitive cases, the United States Supreme Court has recognized that 'a Court may grant declaratory relief even though it chooses not to issue an injunction': *Powell v. McCormack*, 395 U.S. 486 at 499 (1969) (reversing and remanding a dismissal on the ground of political question in a case challenging whether the United States House of Representatives could exclude a duly elected person). In various cases where state criminal prosecution is threatened, but has not commenced, a declaratory judgment is permissible, even though constitutional principles might preclude an injunction or render it impolitic: *Steffel v. Thompson*, 415 U.S. 452, 475 (1974). See D. Rendleman, 'Prospective Remedies in Constitutional Adjudication', (1976) 78 *W. Va. L.Rev.* 155; D. Rendlman, 'The Inadequate Remedy at Law Prerequisite for an Injunction', (1981) 33 *U.Fla.L.Rev.* 346.

[5] *Dudgeon v. United Kingdom*, (1981) 45 Eur.Ct.H.R. (ser. A), (1982) 4 E.H.R.Rep. 149.

credible and authoritative finding of the facts and a legal determination that the state violated the applicant's human rights establishes the truth of the allegations and vindicates the victim. It also should lead the state to alter its behaviour.

Unfortunately, a declaratory judgment generally has prospective effect only and as such it will rarely serve to redress the consequences of the harm already suffered. In the example of exclusion of disabled students from school, it is highly unlikely that a declaration will suffice to remedy all the harm caused by the violation. International human rights tribunals may choose to leave the applicant with a declaration, assuming that further domestic proceedings for damages or other reparations are possible, or they may proceed to determine the nature and scope of redress due when restitution of the violated right is impossible. The latter is preferable, to avoid the possibility that the victim will be without adequate remedies and thus deprived of compensatory justice.

A declaration that the responding state has or has not violated a guaranteed right or rights of the victim forms the heart of the judgment in all international human rights complaint procedures. United Nations organs and the regional Commissions issue such a declaration as the basis for recommending measures that the state should take to remedy the wrong. The recommendations can be very general recommendations, such as providing reparations, or may be more detailed as to the nature and scope of redress that should be afforded.

Regional human rights courts judge the merits of a case by declaring that the applicant's rights have or have not been violated. The European Court often denies moral damages by finding that the judgment of state wrongdoing is adequate to afford just satisfaction, even where the violation has already occurred and is on-going. The European Court has never stated any basis other than 'equity' for distinguishing cases where moral damages are necessary from those where they are not. The declaratory judgment is thus used as a retrospective remedial measure, not only to prevent harm. When this approach is combined with a strict causality test for awards of pecuniary damages, the result is a large number of European cases where the applicant wins on the merits but obtains no redress other than some or all litigation expenses.

Some individual applicants seek only a statement of right, a clarification of the legality of state action, and make no claim for monetary compensation or other redress. Another reason why the European Court may limit itself to declaratory judgments is that they have been effective. In the overwhelming majority of cases, the states concerned have reported to the Committee of Ministers changes in domestic law or practice to remedy the violation found. The Court may feel that the public purpose of upholding the treaty is thereby served. The Court also may feel that many of the matters they deal with do not involve government misconduct serious enough to warrant an award of damages. Until recently, the cases brought to the Court generally have not involved loss of life, torture or other gross abuses and the countries involved have relatively good human rights records. Despite this context, the denial of damages or other remedies should be exceptional because a violation of human rights is *ipso facto* an infringement of the individual's moral dignity and demands a personal remedy, not simply a prospective change in law or practice.

A study prepared by a Committee of Experts on improving the European Convention's procedures noted that it is generally accepted that judgments of the European Court are binding, but merely establish that a violation of the Convention has taken place. They leave it to the discretion of states to take the appropriate measures to comply with the judgment rather than obliging states to give the judgment the binding force of a domestic court decision. Where the violation was one that impugned a domestic judicial decision, this poses problems unless national law allows the reopening of the proceeding. If the individual is in prison the ability to enforce the Strasbourg judgment is crucial; compensation will not redress the unlawful deprivation of liberty. Other violations similarly require compensation or non-monetary relief to afford redress.

Unlike many international agreements, the Convention is a 'living instrument' whose primary purpose is to ensure that the states parties comply with their obligation to European human rights standards. The obligations are owed to individuals and not only to other states parties. National law could provide for the reopening of national judicial proceedings where the declared violation occurred in the context of a specific case. For some states this would avoid constitutional problems that could arise if the European Court judgments were deemed self-executing, although some might view the process as undermining respect for the principle of *res judicata*. Other alternatives exist to give effect to the European Court's judgment that a violation has taken place.[6] In this framework, it could assist the national authorities to be given indications by the Court about what constitutes adequate redress where restitution is impossible. Many elements of this are being developed in regard to Article 13's right to a remedy, but other aspects particular to an individual case may require attention.

Some applicants unsuccessfully have sought to obtain specific relief in the form of a declaration. In response, the Court has emphasized the obligations of states parties attendant upon a finding that they have breached the Convention. In *Selçuk v. Turkey*, the applicants asked for a declaration that they should be re-established in their village, which the Court found had been burned by Turkish authorities.[7] The Court refused, recalling 'that a judgment in which it finds a

---

[6] In Austria, the General Public Prosecutor has the power to file before the Supreme Court a plea of nullity in criminal cases in the interests of the proper application of the law when there has been a violation or incorrect application of the law. This procedure was followed in the *Unterpertinger v. Austria* case after a judgment of the European Court of Human Rights.

[7] See also *Mentes and others v. Turkey*, where applicants asked the Court 'to confirm' that just satisfaction must include the state bearing the costs of infrastructural repairs to the village. They sought assurances that they could return to their village. The government said restitution of this nature was not possible due to the emergency situation in the village and that resettlement must await the end of 'terrorist atrocities'. As in *Selçuk and Asker v. Turkey*, the Court held that supervision of compliance with the Court's judgment is a matter for the Committee of Ministers: *Mentes and others v. Turkey*, judgment of 28 November 1997, Reports of Judgments and Decisions 1997–VIII 2693, para. 24.

breach imposes on the respondent state a legal obligation to put an end to the breach and make reparation for its consequences in such a way as to restore as far as possible the situation existing before the breach (*resititutio in integrum*)'. If *restitutio in integrum* is in practice impossible, 'the respondent states are free to choose the means whereby they comply with a judgment in which the court has found a breach, and the Court will not make consequential orders or declaratory statements in this regard. It falls to the Committee of Ministers of the Council of Europe, acting under Article 54 of the Convention, to supervise compliance in this respect'.

Arguably, the Court has abdicated part of its judicial function by leaving to the Committee of Ministers the decision about whether specific remedies are necessary or appropriate to end the breach of the Convention. The role of the Committee is to supervise compliance, not to design the measures to be complied with. The Court's general declaration of a violation may make it difficult for the Committee to determine whether or not the state has complied, especially where the violation is based on actions or practices and not on an incompatible law or regulation. The Court's approach is also incompatible with the practice of other human rights tribunals, even those whose mandate arguably is narrower than that of the European Court. All human rights tribunals except the European Court will declare, for example, that release is the appropriate remedy for an individual found to be illegally detained. While the European Court's reference to *restitutio in integrum* implies that release is necessary, the Court could and should make specific this obligation, which then may be supervised by the Committee of Ministers. In addition, the Court is inconsistent in its judgments. While refusing to declare that one type of remedy is required in the Turkish cases, it has declared that others are required, in particular investigation, prosecution and punishment of the perpetrators.

Applicants to the European system are concerned to know if there is a pattern to the Court's decisions limiting just satisfaction to a declaration that the state has violated the rights of an individual. According to one former judge, the Court's view of the merits of the case is a key factor in its decision on any remedy to be afforded.[8] The closer the decision on the merits and the more divided the Court on whether or not a violation of the Convention has taken place—which often occurs in the most innovative and ground-breaking cases— the less likely the Court is to give damages, the judges feeling that they have already strained to give a judgment favourable to the applicant.[9] There is clear concern for the reaction of governments: although the Court is described by the judge as 'parsimonious', its caution is deemed warranted because 'one mistake and the whole system collapses'. As a result of this hesitant approach, the Court

---

[8] Personal interview with a judge of the European Court, July 1997.

[9] A little known part of the European practice is the marking of files of controversial or politically sensitive cases with the letters 'H.P.' ('hot potato').

closely scrutinizes each claim for just satisfaction, even when there is no opposition from the government.

Several judges of the European Court have questioned its approach to using the judgment as just satisfaction. In *Engel and others v. The Netherlands*,[10] the separate opinion of Judges Ganshof van der Meersch and Evrigenis contested the use of the judgment as just satisfaction. As they viewed it:

according to Article 50 of the Convention, the Court shall afford, on the conditions laid down in that provision, 'just satisfaction' to the injured party if it finds a breach of the Convention. It seems difficult to accept the proposition that the finding by the Court of a breach of the substantive provisions of the Convention, whilst constituting a condition for the application of Article 50, can at the same time be the consequence in law following from that same provision.

In their view it was not necessary that the individual be afforded just satisfaction in that case. Judge Bindschedler-Robert, in contrast, thought an indemnity was due for the moral damage suffered.

The jurisprudence of the European Court of Human Rights indicates the circumstances in which the Court is likely to limit 'just satisfaction' to its judgment finding a violation. In the first decade in which the issue arose, from 1972 to 1981, the Court awarded monetary damages in seven Article 50 decisions (*Ringeisen v. Austria*,[11] *Engel and others v. Netherlands*,[12] *Deweer v. Belgium*,[13] *Konig v. Germany*,[14] *Artico v. Italy*,[15] *Guzzardi v. Italy*,[16] and *Airey v Ireland*[17]). In two other cases (*Sunday Times v. United Kingdom*[18] and *Tyrer v. United Kingdom*)[19] rights violations were found, but no timely Article 50 claims were made.[20] Three claims for damages were rejected (*Neumeister v.*

---

[10] *Engel and others v. The Netherlands*, (1976) 22 Eur.Ct.H.R. (ser. A), (1976) 1 E.H.R.Rep. 706.

[11] *Ringeisen v. Austria*, (1971) 13 Eur.Ct.H.R. (ser. A), (1971) 1 E.H.R.Rep. 455 (violation of Article 5(3) for wrongful and excessive detention).

[12] *Engel and others v. The Netherlands*, *supra* n. 10 (unlawful arrest and excessive detention, as well as in camera proceedings for military discipline).

[13] *Deweer v. Belgium*, (1980) 35 Eur.Ct.H.R. (ser. A), (1980) 2 E.H.R.Rep. 439 (coercion of the applicant to waive his right to a fair hearing).

[14] *Konig v. Republic of Germany*, (1979) 27 Eur.Ct.H.R. (ser. A) (unreasonable proceedings to revoke a medical doctor's licence to practise).

[15] *Artico v. Italy*, (1981) 37 Eur.Ct.H.R. (ser. A), (1980) 3 E.H.R.Rep. 1 (3,000,000 lira moral damages awarded for 'a distressing sensation of isolation, confusion and neglect' after applicant was denied effective legal assistance in a fraud case).

[16] *Guzzardi v. Italy*, (1980) 39 Eur.Ct.H.R. (ser. A), (1980) 3 E.H.R.Rep. 557 (suspected mafiosi detained in strict supervision on an island pending trial).

[17] *Airey v. Ireland*, (1979) 32 Eur.Ct.H.R. (ser. A), (1981) 3 E.H.R.Rep. 592 (denial of legal aid to indigent applicants for legal separation violates the right of access to court).

[18] *Sunday Times v. United Kingdom* (Merits), (1979) 30 Eur.Ct.H.R. (ser. A), (1979) 2 E.H.R.Rep. 245.

[19] *Tyrer v. United Kingdom*, (1978) 26 Eur.Ct.H.R. (ser. A), (1978) 2 E.H.R.Rep. 1.

[20] In the *Sunday Times* case, the applicants, without quantifying their claims, requested the Court to declare that the United Kingdom government should pay the costs and expenses of the litigation. No Article 50 claim was made for material or moral damage: *Sunday Times v. United Kingdom*, (1980) 38 Eur.Ct.H.R. (ser. A), (1981) 3 E.H.R.Rep. 317. For a discussion of costs and fees in the case, see

Austria,[21] *Golder v. United Kingdom,*[22] and *Marckx v. Belgium)*[23], with the Court finding that the judgment constituted an adequate remedy. *Neumeister* and *Golder* were cases concerning prisoners while in *Marckx*, the applicant had asked only for one Belgian franc in symbolic damages. The cases in which damages were awarded involved denial of access to justice, unlawful detention, and violations of fair trial procedures.

During its second decade, from 1982 to the end of 1991, applicants claimed moral damages in 51 cases where the Court found that the judgment alone was 'just satisfaction' for the moral damage caused by the violation. The cases where moral damages were denied share certain general characteristics. First, the Court was often highly divided on the merits. In almost one-third of the 51 cases, judges filed dissenting opinions, a proportion that is significantly higher than the overall frequency of dissents. Two of the cases were won by only one vote[24] and votes of 6–3 or 5–2 are common among these decisions; one plenary decision was decided by a vote of 11–6,[25] others by 10–6,[26] 8–6[27] and 12–5.[28] Secondly, the large majority of the cases denying compensation—40 of the 51—concern persons accused or convicted of criminal conduct. Two other applicants were mental hospital inmates and two were homosexuals. Two cases concerned professional disciplinary proceedings (medical and legal). In nearly all the cases, the applicants were asserting procedural errors in actions against them, in violation of Article 5 or 6 of the Convention. The most common provision invoked was Article 6(1).

The relatively few non-prisoner cases in which moral damages were denied also concerned procedural errors in civil or administrative hearings. In fact, only four cases of the 51 cases denying moral damages involved challenges to substantive law: two of the four concerned restrictions on divorce[29] and two challenged the criminalization of homosexuality.[30] In three of these cases, the Court was divided on the merits (15–4 in *Dudgeon v. United Kingdom*, 9–8 in *F v. Switzerland*; and 8–6 in *Norris v. Ireland*). Only *Johnston and others v. Ireland*,

infra Chapter 11. In *Tyrer v. United Kingdom*, (1978) 26 Eur.Ct.H.R. (ser. A), a case of corporal punishment, the applicant made a claim, but subsequently withdrew from the proceedings. The Court unanimously found it unnecessary to apply Article 50.

[21] *Neumeister v. Austria*, (1974) 17 Eur.Ct.H.R. (ser. A).

[22] *Golder v. United Kingdom*, (1975) 18 Eur.Ct.H.R. (ser. A), (1975) 1 E.H.R.Rep. 524.

[23] *Marckx v. Belgium*, (1979) 31 Eur.Ct.H.R. (ser. A), (1979) 2 E.H.R.Rep. 330.

[24] *F. v. Switzerland*, (1987) 128 Eur.Ct.H.R. (ser. A); *Fox, Campbell and Hartley v. United Kingdom*, (1990) 182 Eur.Ct.H.R. (ser. A).

[25] *Benthem v. The Netherlands*, (1985) 97 Eur.Ct.H.R. (ser. A).

[26] *Ekbatani v. Sweden*, (1988) 134 Eur.Ct.H.R. (ser. A).

[27] *Norris v. Ireland*, (1988) 142 Eur.Ct.H.R. (ser. A), (1988) 13 E.H.R.R. 186.

[28] *Hauschildt v. Denmark*, (1989) 154 Eur.Ct.H.R. (ser. A).

[29] *Johnston and others v. Ireland*, (1987) 112 Eur.Ct.H.R. (ser. A), (1986) 9 E.H.R.R. 203; *F. v. Switzerland*, (1987) 128 Eur.Ct.H.R. (ser. A), (1987) 10 E.H.R.R. 411.

[30] *Dudgeon v. United Kingdom*, (1982) 45 Eur.Ct.H.R. (ser. A), (1981) 4 E.H.R.R. 149; *Norris v. Ireland*, (1988) 142 Eur.Ct.H.R. (ser. A), (1988) 13 E.H.R.R. 186.

involving restrictions on divorce and remarriage in Ireland, was a unanimous chamber judgment.

Silver v. United Kingdom[31] is typical of cases where the Court deemed the finding of a violation just satisfaction for the moral damage caused by the state's actions. The case concerned interference with a prisoner's correspondence with his lawyer. In a supplementary memorial regarding the application of Article 50, the applicants asserted the absence of any local remedy. They claimed that the finding of a violation could not 'in principle' be considered as just satisfaction, but must depend upon the particular facts and circumstances of each case. The applicants recommended the approach of the European Court of Justice in deciding whether to award damages for non-contractual liability of the institutions of the EEC in accordance with Article 215 of the Treaty of Rome. On the facts of this case, they asserted that although the level of the applicants' damage could not be precisely calculated, 'it should be substantial if it is adequately to represent the extent to which their rights have been violated'.[32] In focusing on the government's breach, the applicants called on the court 'to have regard to aggravating factors . . . in assessing the sum to be awarded to each applicant by way of general damages'.[33] The government responded that it was neither necessary nor appropriate to award damages because many prisoners' letters did get through and 'as the Court is aware, in the light of the Commission's report in this case, the Government made significant changes in the arrangements governing correspondence to and from prisoners'.[34]

In reply, the applicants again focused on the fault of the state, pointing out that interference with prison correspondence is particularly serious because it is the 'principal means of developing and maintaining contact with the outside world, which is an important part of the process of rehabilitation'. As for the changes in practice that the state had made, the applicants correctly distinguished the interests of the applicants from the treaty regime and the inadequacy of a declaratory judgment from their perspective: according to them, the measures already taken by the government:

related to the 'general interest' element in the case and not to the applicants' claim under Article 50 . . . They cannot compensate the applicants for past interference with their correspondence. Some of the applicants are no longer detained and will, accordingly, derive no benefit from these changes for the future.[35]

The applicants asked for UK£4,500 per year of incarceration in general damages and for their distress. The Court awarded no damages, deeming the

---

[31] *Silver v. United Kingdom*, (1983) 61 Eur.Ct. H.R. (ser. A), (1983) 5 E.H.R.R. 347 (Article 6(1) and 8 violations for stopping mail between solicitor and prisoner).
[32] Applicant's Memorial, (1981–1983) 51 Eur.Ct.H.R. (ser. B) at 338.
[33] *Ibid.*
[34] *Ibid.* at 352.
[35] *Ibid.* at 367.

judgment just satisfaction for their moral injury.[36] The Court said the prisoners 'may have experienced some annoyance and sense of frustration as a result of the restrictions that were imposed on particular letters' but it was not of 'such intensity' that it would justify an award. Moreover, significant improvement in government behaviour had occurred.

In this case, as in other prison cases, the Court appeared to undervalue the impact of the violation by the state on those subject to its power. The result could send a negative message to those in prison and supposedly undergoing rehabilitation that those in power 'get away with' violations of the law. The *Silver* decision has further significance because one applicant had died and the Court held the moral damage claim was not survivable: 'The injury under this head was of a purely personal nature' because it was not claimed that it affected his estate or involved material damage nor were his next of kin claiming to be injured parties in their own right. So 'the cause of justice' did not require money in compensation for his mental distress.

Dudgeon v. the United Kingdom, like the prisoner cases, is an instance where the Court seems to have overlooked the impact of the violation on the victim. The applicant was challenging the existence of Northern Irish laws that criminalized certain homosexual acts between consenting adult males. The applicant had been campaigning for repeal of the laws for some time. At one point, the police questioned him for some four and a half hours about his sexual life, although eventually the prosecutor decided not to institute proceedings against him. He claimed an interference with his private life in violation of Convention Article 8 and discrimination in violation of Article 14 in conjunction with Article 8. The Court held that his rights had been violated, but agreed with the government's view that its judgment reflected a conclusion that the law on homosexuality 'became' unjustified as standards changed regarding respect for private life under Article 8. The Court denied Dudgeon's request for UK£5,000 for the police action taken and another UK£10,000 for general fear and distress. He asked the latter amount 'to signify the seriousness of the breach' and 'the exceptional nature of the denial of the right to respect for his private life'.[37] The Court found that the change in law which occurred in the United Kingdom fulfilled Dudgeon's aim in bringing the complaint and that it was not necessary to afford any monetary compensation in redress for the law criminalizing homosexuality.

In regard to the police investigation, Dudgeon, like other applicants, unsuccessfully sought damages by using domestic analogies, such as false imprisonment, and cited domestic damages awarded in such cases. The Court denied moral damages, noting that the police were merely applying the law as it then existed. The holding seems clearly erroneous; to *enact* a law in violation of a right

---

[36] *Silver and others v. United Kingdom*, (1991) 67 Eur.Ct.H.R. (Article 50) (ser. A), (1988) 13 E.H.R.R. 582. The applicants did receive a large part of their legal fees.

[37] Applicant's Memorial, (1980–1982) 40 Eur.Ct.H.R. (ser. B) at 226.

guaranteed by the Convention causes generalized harm to all those within the affected or target group, creating apprehension and fear of prosecution; to *apply* such a law against a particular person causes individualized and more serious harm that should be redressed. The Court has created a dangerous precedent by suggesting that a state will be excused from redressing individual harm on a 'good faith' defence if the police enforce a law that violates the Convention.

In *Dudgeon* and the subsequent *Norris* decision concerning the same topic, the Court indicated it was denying damages for non-pecuniary harm at least in part in view of the states' duty to change the law—although the Court will not issue an order to that effect. Yet, the Court has awarded non-pecuniary damages in other cases where the same duty arises (*X and Y v. Netherlands*,[38] *Bonisch v. Austria*,[39] *Feldbrugge v. Netherlands*)[40].

Soering v. United Kingdom[41] was the first case where the European Court used the declaratory judgment to prevent an imminent violation. The applicant, a German national, was detained in England pending extradition to the USA to face murder charges in the state of Virginia. The offences charged could have subjected the applicant to the death penalty if he were convicted. Soering alleged that the decision to send him to the United States would give rise to a breach by the United Kingdom of Article 3 of the Convention due to his exposure to the 'death row' phenomenon. The Court held in favour of the applicant and declared that the decision to extradite, if implemented, would give rise to a breach of Article 3. He was extradited only after ensuring that he would not be sentenced to death.

The pattern established in the former Court's Article 50 decisions continued throughout its tenure. From the beginning of 1992 until the inauguration of the new Court on 1 November 1998, the Court found that the judgment is adequate to repair the moral injury in 79 cases, 50 of which concerned prisoners or detained aliens. The non-prisoner cases where damages were denied involve homosexuals, aliens not in detention, religious minorities and legal persons[42] and the Court was divided on the merits of many of these cases. Another important factor is whether the challenge is to a procedural or substantive right. Those who contest the lawfulness of detention or procedural violations in criminal prosecutions usually have been awarded moral damages only when there are aggravating factors in the government conduct, such as clearly abusive search and seizure, ill-treatment during custody, extremely lengthy proceedings (18 years) or when the individuals have later been acquitted or successfully challenged the substantive law.[43]

---

[38] *X and Y v. The Netherlands*, (1986) 91 Eur.Ct.H.R. (ser. A).

[39] *Bonisch v. Austria*, (1986) 103 Eur.Ct.H.R. (ser. A) (Article 50).

[40] *Feldbrugge v. The Netherlands*, (1986) 99 Eur.Ct.H.R. (ser. A).

[41] *Soering v. United Kingdom*, (1989) 161 Eur.Ct.H.R. (ser. A), (1989) 11 E.H.R.Rep. 439.

[42] The Court has expressed some doubt about whether companies are capable of suffering moral damage.

[43] See e.g. *Allenet de Ribemont v. France*, (1995) 308 Eur.Ct.H.R. (ser. A).

It thus seems that the most significant factors in determining whether or not damages will be awarded are the character of the applicant, the unanimity of the Court, and the procedural or substantive nature of the right violated. The Court seems close to the view that those accused or convicted of crimes should receive no damages for procedural violations unless they can demonstrate actual innocence. The conduct of the government appears to be much less significant, although severe government misconduct sometimes can overcome the bias against prisoners.

The Court seems to imply that the government may violate the rights of those who have themselves committed a wrong subject only to the payment of some or all of the legal costs if the prisoner files a case in the European system. The approach of the Court, seen in *Silver and others* above, is also clear in the early judgment in *Golder v. United Kingdom*.[44] Golder was denied access to a lawyer and a court, contrary to Articles 6(1) and 8 of the Convention. The Court was nonetheless unanimous in holding that the findings 'amount in themselves to adequate just satisfaction under Article 50' and that it was not necessary to afford further relief. A similar result obtained in *Engel and others v. the Netherlands*,[45] where the applicants complained that their case had been heard *in camera* by the Supreme Military Court. The Court found a violation of Article 6(1) but did not grant further relief, despite the applicants' plea that their status as conscientious objectors meant they had suffered considerable anguish and anxiety over the proceedings.

In *Eckle v. Germany*,[46] the applicants successfully complained of the unreasonable length of proceedings against them, but according to the Court, they did not allege that the situation provoked in them feelings of anxiety and distress, nor did they evidence particular concern to have the proceedings conducted as speedily as possible. The Commission claimed the prosecutions must have constituted a source of some anxiety and caused them non-pecuniary damage, but viewed the applicants' damages claim as too high and out of proportion to the violation. The Court presumed harm, saying that the fact of exceeding the 'reasonable time' limits of the Convention must have exposed the applicants to some disadvantages and inconvenience, but some of the domestic procedures mitigated the harm. 'In addition, as was rightly observed by the Delegate of the Commission, it cannot be overlooked that they were charged with serious acts of fraud committed to the detriment of, amongst others, persons lacking substantial financial resources and that the Trier Regional Court imposed heavy prison sentences on them'.[47] Thus, the character of the applicants became a factor in the decision to deny damages.

A similar result is seen in wire-tapping cases, which seem particularly affected

---

[44] *Golder v. United Kingdom*, (1975) 18 Eur.Ct.H.R. (ser. A), (1979–1980) 1 E.H.R.Rep. 524.

[45] *Engel and others v. The Netherlands* (Article 50), (1976) 22 Eur.Ct.H.R. (ser. A), (1979–1980) 1 E.H.R.Rep. 706.

[46] *Eckle v. Germany*, (1983) 65 Eur.Ct.H.R. (ser. A) (Article 50).

[47] *Ibid.* at para. 24.

by what is heard on the wire-tap and why it was done. In *Kruslin v. France*,[48] the applicant was convicted of armed robbery and attempted armed robbery and sentenced to 15 years' imprisonment. The recording of the telephone conversation 'was a decisive piece of evidence in the proceedings' against him. He continued to protest his innocence and sought FF1,000,000 compensation for the imprisonment, which he alleged to be the direct result of the breach. The Court accepted that the conviction rested on the wire-tapping, but seems to have been influenced by the fact that in another case, which it discusses although not part of this application, he was convicted and sentenced to life imprisonment for premeditated murder. The applicant received no damages and only a part of the costs.

The decision in *McCann v. United Kingdom*[49] was the first where the European Court condemned a country for violating Article 2 and where the character of the victims led the Court to deny damages for deprivations of the right to life. The applicants denounced the killing by members of the British security forces of three members of the IRA suspected of involvement in a bombing mission in Gibraltar. It was claimed that two of the three were shot in the back by soldiers attempting to arrest them. One soldier testified that his intent had been to shoot to kill in order to stop the suspect from becoming a threat and detonating a bomb. Several witnesses testified that two of the suspects had been shot while lying on the ground, although others disagreed. The circumstances of the third shooting were also in dispute, in particular concerning whether the suspect was shot in the back or on the ground. The Commission found no convincing support for the allegation that the soldiers shot any of the suspects in the back. All, however, were shot in close range. The Commission by vote of 11–6 found no violation of Article 2 of the Convention. The Court, sitting in a Grand Chamber, found a violation of the right to life by a vote of 10–9. It was not persuaded 'that the killing of the three terrorists constituted the use of force which was no more than absolutely necessary in defense of persons from unlawful violence'. The applicant family members of the deceased requested an award of damages at the same level as would be awarded for wrongful death under English law, as well as exemplary damages if the killings were found to be deliberate or the result of gross negligence. The Court dismissed the claim for pecuniary and non-pecuniary damage, finding it not 'appropriate' to make an award *because* 'the three terrorist suspects who were killed had been intending to plant a bomb in Gibraltar'.[50]

The 'bad man' basis for denying compensation is seen also in *Welch v. United Kingdom*,[51] concerning the confiscation of assets of a drug-trafficker. The Court found that the confiscation order amounted to *ex post facto* imposition of a penalty in breach of Article 7(1) of the Convention. Welch sought pecuniary and non-pecuniary damages and reimbursement of costs and expenses. The Court

---

[48] *Kruslin v. France*, (1990) 176–A Eur.Ct.H.R. (ser. A).
[49] *McCann v. United Kingdom*, (1995) 324 Eur.Ct.H.R. (ser. A), (1996) 21 E.H.R.Rep. 97.
[50] *Ibid.* at para. 219.
[51] *Welch v. United Kingdom*, (1995) 307 Eur.Ct.H.R. (ser. A), (1995) 20 E.H.R.Rep. 247.

denied damages and, in an unprecedented decision, decided that because the applicant's claims for compensation failed, it saw no reason why an award in respect of costs and expenses for the Article 50 phase of the proceedings should be made.

The European Convention on the Compensation of Victims of Violent Crimes partly supports the European Court's approach, calling for the denial of compensation to a victim who engages in misconduct or is involved in organized crime.[52] Article 8 states:

(1) Compensation may be reduced or refused on account of the victim's or the applicant's conduct before, during or after the crime, or in relation to the injury or death.

(2) Compensation may also be reduced or refused on account of the victim's or the applicant's involvement in organized crime or his membership in an organization which engages in crimes of violence.

(3) Compensation may also be reduced or refused if an award or a full award would be contrary to a sense of justice or to public policy ('ordre public').[53]

Other international tribunals acknowledge that declaratory judgments can be appropriate but rarely limit the victims to declaratory relief alone. The European Court of Justice, in the *Kampffmeyer* case, held that Article 215[54] did not prevent the Court from declaring the Community liable for 'imminent damage foreseeable with sufficient certainty even if the damage cannot yet be precisely assessed. To prevent even greater damage it may prove necessary to bring the matter before the Court as soon as the cause of damage is certain'.[55] To award damages, the Court insists that the injury must be 'actual, significant and definite',[56] 'direct',[57] 'real',[58] or 'actual and certain'[59] and that pecuniary damage must be (1) certain and specific, (2) proved and (3) quantifiable. Pain and suffering is included as an element in awards, but never articulated as a basis for non-pecuniary damages.

Defendant states have asked the Inter-American Court of Human Rights to limit remedies to declaratory judgments, but thus far the Court has refused. In *El Amparo v. Venezuela*,[60] the Court noted Venezuela's reference to the practice of the European Court of Human Rights. Although accepting in theory that it could

---

[52] Council of Europe: European Convention on the Compensation of Victims of Violent Crimes opened for signature by Member States of the Council of Europe on 24 November 1983, Articles 7–8, Eur. T.S. No. 116, at 3; (1983) 22 I.L.M. 1021.

[53] *Ibid.*, at Article 8, Eur. T.S. No. 116, at 3.

[54] The provision states that the Community shall 'in accordance with the general principles common to the laws of Member States make good any damage caused by its institutions or by its servants in the performance of their duties'.

[55] Joined Cases 56–60/74, *Kurt Kampffmeyer Muhlenvereinigung KG and others v. Commission* [1976] E.C.R. 711, 741.

[56] Case 23/59, *Acciaieria Ferrieradi Roma v. High Authority* [1959] E.C.R. 245, 250.

[57] Case 18/60, *Louis Worms v. High Authority* [1962] E.C.R. 195, 206.

[58] Case 4/65, *S.A. Metallurgique Hainaut-Sambre v. High Authority* [1965] E.C.R. 1099, 1112.

[59] Joined Cases 67–85/75, *Lesieur, Cotelle et Associés, S.A. v. Commission* [1976] E.C.R. 391, 408.

[60] *El Amparo v. Venezuela (Reparations)*, (1996) 22 Inter-Am.Ct.H.R. (ser. C).

similarly limit relief, the Court found that a declaratory judgment would not be adequate to remedy the moral injury in *El Amparo* given the gravity of the violations.

The views of other human rights bodies, as noted earlier, generally contain findings of fact and decisions on the law, together with recommendations for remedies. Most of them go beyond a declaration that a violation has been found, although often the recommendations are quite general in nature.

Advisory opinions are another way to obtain a declaration about the specific content of international obligations, and is the only means when the tribunal lacks contentious jurisdiction over those who seek an answer to the specific question. The advisory jurisdiction of the International Court of Justice, for example, often has been used to declare the legal obligations of international organizations, which have no standing to bring cases before the court. The advisory jurisdiction of the European Court is so limited that it is unlikely it ever will be used.[61] In contrast, the advisory jurisdiction of the Inter-American Court of Human Rights is extremely broad; indeed, it is more extensive than that accorded any other international tribunal. All OAS member states may consult the Court regarding the interpretation of the Convention or other treaties concerning the protection of human rights in the Americas.[62] They also may request an opinion on the compatibility of any existing or proposed domestic laws with such instruments.[63] Various OAS organs, including the Inter-American Commission on Human Rights, also may seek advisory opinions on matters falling 'within their spheres of competence'.[64]

There are several distinctions between requests for advisory opinions and declaratory judgments. First, advisory jurisdiction, unlike jurisdiction over contentious cases, is permissive. The Inter-American Court generally exercises its discretion, however, stating that it 'must have compelling reasons founded in the belief that the request exceeds the limits of its advisory jurisdiction under the Convention before it may refrain from complying with a request for an opinion'.[65] The Court has pointed out other major differences between advisory and contentious jurisdiction calling the former 'a parallel system . . . an alternate judi-

---

[61] Protocol 2 to the European Convention on Human Rights, E.T.S. 44, confers on the Court competence to give advisory opinion at the request of the Committee of Ministers. The opinions cannot deal with any question relating to the content or scope of the rights or freedoms guaranteed in the Convention and Protocols or with any other question which the Commission, the Court or the Committee of Ministers might have to consider in consequence of any inter-state or individual communication. A decision of the Committee of Ministers to request an advisory opinion requires a two-thirds majority vote.

[62] Convention, Article 64(1); see T. Buergenthal, 'The Advisory Practice of the Inter-American Court', (1985) 79 *Am.J.Int'l L.* 1; D. Shelton, 'The Jurisprudence of the Inter-American Court of Human Rights', (1994) 10 *Am.U.J. Int'l L. & Pol'y* 333.

[63] Convention, Article 64(2). See Proposed Amendments to the Naturalization Provisions of the Constitution of Costa Rica, Advisory Opinion No. OC–4/84, (1984) 4 Inter-Am.Ct.H.R. (ser. A).

[64] Convention, Article 64(1).

[65] Enforceability of the Right to Reply or Correction (Articles 14(1), 1(1) and 2, American Convention on Human Rights), Advisory Opinion No. OC–7/86, (1986) 7 Inter-Am.Ct.H.R. (ser. A), para. 12.

cial method of a consultative nature, which is designed to assist states and organs to comply with and to apply human rights treaties without subjecting them to the formalism and the sanctions associated with the contentious judicial process'.[66] The Court has noted that there are no parties (complainants and respondents) to advisory proceedings; no state is required to defend itself against formal charges; no judicial sanctions are envisaged and none can be decreed. 'All the proceeding is designed to do is to enable OAS Member States and OAS organs to obtain a judicial interpretation of a provision embodied in the Convention or other human rights treaties in the American states.'[67] In contrast, in a contentious proceeding, the Court 'must not only interpret the applicable norms, determine the truth of the acts denounced and decide whether they are a violation of the Convention imputable to a State party: it may also rule "that the injured party be ensured the enjoyment of his right or freedom that was violated"'.[68] Most significantly, the parties to contentious proceedings are legally bound to comply with the decisions of the Court, although in practice the advisory opinions of international tribunals carry considerable weight in the development and application of the law.

The decisions and recommendations of commission, committees and special rapporteurs can be considered as falling between an advisory opinion and binding judgments of courts, but closer in nature to the latter. They constitute authoritative findings on the facts and the law which states parties to the treaties should comply with in good faith.

Finally, it should be recalled that in the law of state responsibility, the declaration that a state has breached an international obligation automatically imposes a duty to cease the wrongful conduct. In this respect, it is a necessary component of any international judgment, including those concerning human rights violations. It is also important, however, that the consequences of the breach be remedied, including indemnification of losses suffered by the victims. This aspect of the matter generally will require the tribunal to determine what were the consequences of the breach, who suffered them, and how they should be redressed. International tribunals abdicate their responsibility to the victims of human rights violations and to the system when they fail to make the findings and indicate the reparations that should be afforded.

Declaratory relief still has an important role in human rights litigation, in particular, in preventing a violation that is threatened but has not yet caused measurable harm. Generally, however, a declaratory judgment will not in and of itself be an adequate remedy. Nor should it be used to deter unsympathetic victims from seeking a remedy by denying them redress. It is the beginning of remedies, not the end.

---

[66] Restrictions to the Death Penalty (Articles 4(2) and 4(4) American Convention on Human Rights), Advisory Opinion OC–3/83, (1983) 3 Inter-Am.Ct. H.R. (ser. A) para. 43.
[67] *Ibid.*, para. 22.
[68] *Ibid.*, Para. 32.

8

Compensation

The primary function of corrective justice is to rectify the harm done a victim of wrongdoing.[1] Corrective justice generally aims at restitution or compensation for loss, assuming that when victims are made whole, wrongdoers are sanctioned and deterred from engaging in future misconduct.[2] For many victims of human rights abuses, damages are important because prospective changes in law or practice resulting from a declaratory judgment usually will fail to redress the injuries they suffered due to the violation. In a case of discrimination in education, for example, a judgment that discrimination has taken place and must end will not repair the harm done to the student who challenged the discrimination but will graduate before reforms take effect. The length of time between a violation and the decision of an international human rights tribunal also militates in favour of an award of compensation for justice delayed, especially in response to knowing and deliberate breaches of guaranteed rights.[3]

The sum of money awarded as damages is designed to compensate plaintiffs for harm they have suffered, intended to make the victim as well off as he or she would have been if the injury had never occurred. Both corrective justice (focusing on fairness to the victim) and the economic model (focusing on incentives to the wrongdoer) call for damages that equal the full value of the injury to the victim. They are inevitably retrospective; an *ex post* remedy that is granted after harm has occurred, incapable of restoring or replacing the rights that have been violated and, as a substitute remedy, is sometimes inadequate to redress fully the harm. One who is physically or emotionally disabled as a result of torture cannot, by the payment of money, have the means restored that were there originally. Damage awards, however, supply the means for whatever part of the former life and projects remain possible and may allow for new ones. It must be recognized that large amounts of money may be necessary to place the victim in the same position of relative satisfaction that he or she occupied before the event. The economic approach to law holds that the wrongdoer should be made to internalize the costs of causing harm in order to have the optimum incentive to avoid injuring others.[4]

---

[1] Kenneth York and John Bauman, *Remedies: Cases and Materials*, 3rd edn. (1979).

[2] See J. Love, 'Presumed General Compensatory Damages in Constitutional Tort Litigation: A Corrective Justice Perspective', (1992) 49 *Wash. & Lee L.Rev.* 69, 79.

[3] The average case in the European system takes five and one-half years from filing to judgment. It should be recalled that the requirement of exhaustion of domestic remedies means often lengthy national procedures must be undertaken first.

[4] D. Friedman, 'What is "Fair Compensation" for Death or Injury', (1982) 2 *Int'l Rev. L. & Econ.* 81.

It should be recognized that wrongdoing harms not only the victim, it undermines the rule of law and societal norms.[5] For this reason, 'compensation is inevitably a second-best response that comes into play when full rectification is impossible'.[6] Valuation of loss is nearly always imperfect and may omit significant wrongs that deserve legal protection: interests in sentiment, autonomy, and individuality which lack economic expression. If substantive law protects more than remedial law recompenses, then the resulting imbalance should be resolved either by inflating the remedial measure or by abandoning monetary damages in favour of enjoining the wrongdoer's conduct.

The assessment or calculation of damages is complex. Physical injury, for example, can cause harm in two ways: (1) it lowers the level of income received and (2) it usually lowers the value of any income that is received, because of the loss of possibilities to enjoy it. In the economic model, if only the first is considered, compensation may be viewed as 'inefficient' because it transfers income from the uninjured who receive large benefits from it, to injured persons who receive very small benefits. The more serious the harm, the more adequacy of damages becomes a problem:

Damage awards for pain and suffering, even when apparently generous, may well under-compensate victims seriously crippled . . . Since the loss of vision or limbs reduces the amount of pleasure that can be purchased with a dollar, a very large amount of money will frequently be necessary to place the victim in the same position of relative satisfaction that he occupied before the accident. The problem is most acute in a death case. Most people would not exchange their lives for anything less than an infinite sum of money if the exchange were to take place immediately.[7]

Compensation as a remedy can be seen to imply that money can replace the thing lost, or at least that money is the best alternative when no restitution is possible. From this perspective, monetary awards to some extent inevitably commodify human rights, with the purpose of restoring the status quo ante. On the other hand, even if human rights violations and money are not commensurable, damages are still justified because an award of damages serves to affirm public respect for the victim and give public recognition of the wrongdoer's fault in failing to respect basic rights.

The theoretical approach to this issue has a practical impact because it may determine whether or not damages are awarded and the amount of compensation given. Viewing compensation as a matter of public policy may lead to more frequent awards of damages. Indeed, 'presumed damages', as discussed below, may be given for the value of the right violated, even though there is no provable loss. Although such awards are fundamentally compensatory because

[5] See G. Calabresi and A. D. Melamed, 'Property Rules, Liability Rules and Inalienability: One View of the Cathedral', (1972) 85 *Harv. L. Rev.* 1089–1128.

[6] L. Lomasky, *Persons, Rights and the Moral Community* (1967), 143.

[7] Richard Posner, *Economic Analysis of Law* (1992), s. 6.12 at 197.

they look at the degree of harm caused, with the aim of making the injured whole, they are nonetheless influenced by the level of wrongfulness of the conduct.

There are three kinds of compensatory damages: nominal (a small sum of money awarded to symbolize the vindication of rights and make the judgment a matter of record); pecuniary damages (intended to represent the closest possible financial equivalent of the monetary loss or harm suffered); and moral damages (compensation for dignitary violations, including fear, humiliation, mental distress). Compensatory damages generally provide for:

(1)   past physical and mental suffering;
(2)   future physical and mental suffering;
(3)   medical expenses;
(4)   loss of earnings and earning capacity;
(5)   incidental out of pocket expenses, including e.g. travel, nursing care;
(6)   property injury or loss; and
(7)   permanent disability and disfigurement.[8]

In national law, some states use charts or statutory wage grids to assess pecuniary damages.[9] Other states limit judicial discretion for non-pecuniary damages, binding judges to use a statutory 'Table of Damages for Pain and Suffering'.[10] In other states, schedules have received no support as a general solution for limiting damages because they often result in giving too much or too little.[11] These states allow the decision-maker to assess damages independently on the basis of numerous factors: the extent and duration of pain, disfigurement, suffering and intrusion, finances of the wrongdoer and blameworthiness of both parties.[12] In the absence of statutory guidelines, judges usually assess pain and suffering taking

---

[8]   *Berry v. City of Muskogee*, 900 F.2d 1989 (10th Cir. 1990): 'In an action involving death, appropriate compensatory damages would include medical and burial expenses, pain and suffering before death, loss of earnings based upon the probable duration of the victim's life had the injury not occurred, the victim's loss of consortium, and other damages recognized in common law tort actions'.

[9]   In Mexico, the Civil Code specifically refers the judge to the Federal Labor Code: 'When damage is caused to persons and results in death, total or permanent incapacity, partial permanent, total temporary or partial temporary incapacity, the amount of damages shall be determined according to the provisions established by the Federal Labor Law'. To calculate the appropriate indemnity one should take as a base four times the 'highest minimum daily salary'. In death cases, that sum is multiplied by the maximum time period for which the law recognizes total permanent incapacity: Mexican Civil Code, s. 1915(2) (M. Gordon trans., 1980).

[10]   In Denmark, for example, pain and suffering is compensated according to set numbers for in- and out-of-hospital recovery; the standardization rules were set to promote predictability and settlement. In cases of permanent injury, normative tables set percentages for losses of various limbs or capacities. This is reduced proportionately for the elderly: D. Mcintosh and M. Holmes, *Personal Injury Awards in EU and EFTA Countries: An Industry Report*, 2nd edn. (1994), 282, 923.

[11]   *Ibid.* at 33.

[12]   Case 110–Bundesgerichstof (Great Civil Division) 6 July 1955, BGHZ 18, 149. Norway and Greece also consider the degree of fault and the financial status of both parties in awarding damages for pain and suffering.

into account the same factors, and amounts of pain and suffering damages range widely.[13]

Most human rights instruments, like national laws, give only general, qualitative guidelines for awards of damages. They provide almost no meaningful quantitative guidelines for how to compute them. Studies indicate that in many instances this lack of direction leads to under-compensation of victims.[14]

The present chapter discusses monetary awards given by international tribunals in human rights cases. It begins with an overview of compensatory awards, then continues with discussion of pecuniary damages, moral damages, causation and presumed harm, issues of valuation and calculation, and, finally, modes of payment, inflation, interest and taxation. Procedural delay cases decided by the European Court of Human Rights are analysed together at the end of the chapter.

A. OVERVIEW

The practice of international tribunals in awarding compensatory damages varies considerably. The African Commission has decided only one case, brought against the Cameroons, involving a claim for compensation.[15] Without any specific treaty provision on the subject, the Commission accepted in principle the need for an award of compensation, but sent the matter back to the domestic system to set the quantum. The European and Inter-American Courts, in contrast, have both decided that all issues concerning an award of compensatory damages are governed by international law.

---

[13] English compensation for pain and suffering, for example, is viewed as high by European standards: W.H.V. Roger, J. Spier and G. Viney, 'Preliminary Observations' in J. Spier (ed.) *Limits of Liability: Keeping the Floodgates Shut* (1996), 7. In Greece, in contrast, damages for non-pecuniary loss must be reasonable—which in Greek law means lower than full damages: K.D. Kerameus and K. Rousses, 'Confines and Limitation of Damages Under the Greek Law of Tort' in *Limits of Liability* at 51. In Germany, damages for non-physical injuries of the body or the health or a deprivation of freedom, i.e. pain and suffering, are assessed in accordance with severity, magnitude and duration of the pain, the circumstances of the wrongdoer's action and its culpability, and the economic situation of the parties: BGB, s. 847, para. 1.

[14] Even in the USA, where tort litigation is most common, the findings of several studies suggest that the legal system usually fails to compensate adequately. 'So little compensation is achieved through the tort system that only as an act of hyperbole can it be said to be part of an injury compensation system': S.S. Huebner and K. Black, JR., *Life Insurance*, 7th edn. (1969), 186. However, it may be doing better as a deterrent because many people overestimate the vigilance of the system and magnitude of its sanctions.

[15] Case 59/91, *Embga Mekongo Louis v. Cameroon*, 8th Annual Report of the ACHPR 1994–1995, ACHPR/8TH/ACT/RPT/XVII, Annex IX. Embga Mekongo, a Cameroonian citizen, alleged false imprisonment, miscarriage of justice and damages for which he claimed the sum of US$105 million. The Commission found that the author had been denied due process, contrary to Article 7 of African Charter and had suffered damages. 'Being unable to determine the amount of damages, the Commission recommends that the quantum should be determined under the law of Cameroon': *ibid.*

1. The European Court of Human Rights

The European Court awards monetary compensation 'if necessary' for (a) pecuniary losses; (b) non-pecuniary damage, and (c) costs and expenses. The amounts of all but proven pecuniary losses are assessed on an 'equitable' basis because 'the Court enjoys a certain discretion in the exercise of the power conferred by Article 50'.[16] Any award depends upon a finding that a violation occurred[17] and that the violation caused the harm.[18] Applicants do not always claim compensation, although the practice was established in the first case (*Lawless*), where the applicant claimed an unspecified amount. It is more common now to quantify damages, especially pecuniary damages, although applicants have been known to request 'compensation for prejudice suffered' 'of an amount to be determined equitably'.

Claims for nominal or symbolic sums have been rejected in most cases, but in *Engel and others v. The Netherlands*,[19] 'a token indemnity' of 100 Dutch guilders (approximately US$50) was awarded for an unlawful detention in 'strict arrest' that lasted between 22 and 26 hours. The detention had already been largely remedied because the applicant did not have to serve a two-day sentence for the offence of which he was convicted; the earlier detention was set off against the penalty. The Court emphasized that the set-off did not constitute *restitutio in integrum* (as one freedom can never substitute for another deprivation of freedom), but found 'it is nevertheless relevant in the context of Article 50'. The other defendants in the case, who complained of a hearing *in camera*, were found not to have suffered any damage, 'indeed the said [national] Court improved the lot of two of their number'.[20] No causal link was found between the fact that the hearings were not public and the severity of the punishment inflicted. Therefore, the judgment was held to be adequate satisfaction.

During its first decade of deciding cases, 1971 to 1981, the European Court found violations in 21 of the cases submitted to it. The applicants claimed pecuniary or non-pecuniary damages, not including attorneys' fees and costs,[21] in 16 of the cases where a violation was found. Two of the 16 claims were settled

---

[16] *Handyside v. United Kingdom*, (1976) 24 Eur.Ct.H.R. (ser. A).

[17] *Lawless* case, (1961) 3 Eur.Ct.H.R. (ser. A), (1979–80) 1 E.H.R.Rep. 15; *National Union of Belgian Police v. Belgium*, (1975) 19 Eur.Ct.H.R. (ser. A) at 22, para. 50, 1 E.H.R.Rep. 578; *Swedish Engine Drivers' Union v. Sweden*, (1976) 20 Eur.Ct.H.R. (ser. A), at 18, para. 51, 1 E.H.R.R. 617; *Schmidt and Dahlstrom v. Sweden*, (1976) 21 Eur.Ct.H.R. (ser. A) at 18, para. 43, 1 E.H.R.R. 637; *Kjeldsen, Busk Madsen and Pedersen v. Denmark*, (1976) 23 Eur.Ct.H.R. (ser. A) at 29, para. 58, 1 E.H.R.Rep. 711; *Handyside v. United Kingdom*, (1976) 24 Eur.Ct.H.R. (ser. A) at 31, para. 67, 1 E.H.R.Rep. 737.

[18] *Airey v. Ireland*, (1981) 41 Eur.Ct.H.R. (ser. A) (Article 50) at 8–9, para. 12, 2 E.H.R.Rep. 305.

[19] *Engel and others v. The Netherlands*, (1976) 22 Eur.Ct.H.R. (ser. A).

[20] *Ibid.* at para. 11.

[21] For a discussion of awards of attorneys' fees and costs, see *infra* Chapter 11.

before the Court could render a decision[22] and four matters remained pending at the end of time period. The Court thus decided 10 Article 50 claims, awarding pecuniary and/or non-pecuniary damages in seven of the 10.[23] From 1982 to 1991, the Court continued to award damages in the majority of cases where they were claimed and a violation of the Convention was found. Claims were made in all but 11 of the 152 cases decided during this period where at least one violation was found. In 15 cases, the parties settled the claim. Among the remaining 126 cases of violations, the Court awarded compensation for pecuniary or non-pecuniary damages in approximately two-thirds of them; thus, the impression that the Court normally awards no compensation is wrong. In the overwhelming number of instances the award was for non-pecuniary or moral damages. Thirty-six claims of pecuniary damage were rejected because the Court found no causal link between the violation and the claim; three other claims were found to be 'speculative'.

The large majority of cases where moral damages were awarded concerned civil proceedings and substantive violations. Most cases involving accused or convicted criminals in which moral damages were awarded were cases against Italy for the excessive length of proceedings. Only one judgment of the court awarding compensation before the beginning of 1992 was taken by the Court sitting in plenary session and only two cases involved a decision that was not unanimous. It appears, then, that damages are more likely to be awarded for routine and non-controversial substantive violations or procedural violations where there is a pattern of non-compliance. Damages are more likely to be denied when the court is split on the merits or where the violations are in criminal proceedings and deemed not to have affected the ultimate findings of guilt or innocence of the applicant.

The same pattern has continued in the judgments issued since the beginning of 1992. Those cases where applicants requested and were awarded moral damages involve civil proceedings approximately three times more frequently than criminal ones, although cases originating with detainees are filed more frequently.

---

[22] In *Luedicke, Belkacem and Koç v. Germany*, (1980) 36 Eur.Ct.H.R. (ser. A) (Article 50), the claims were settled through the provision of legal aid at the Commission level. *Winterwerp v. The Netherlands*, (1981) 47 Eur.Ct.H.R. (ser. A) (Article 50) was settled with the payment of 10,000 florins.

[23] The Court awarded compensation in *Ringeisen v. Austria*, (1972) 15 Eur.Ct.H.R. (ser. A); *Engel and others v. The Netherlands*, (1976) 22 Eur.Ct.H.R. (ser. A) (Article 50); *Deweer v. Belgium*, (1980) 35 Eur.Ct.H.R. (ser. A); *Konig v. Germany*, (1980) 36 Eur.Ct.H.R. (ser. A) (Article 50); *Artico v. Italy*, (1980) 37 Eur. Ct.H.R. (ser. A); *Guzzardi v. Italy*, (1980) 39 Eur.Ct.H.R. (ser. A) and *Airey v. Ireland*, (1981) 41 Eur.Ct.H.R. (ser. A) (Article 50). The judgment was found to be sufficient to afford just satisfaction for non-pecuniary harm in *De Wilde Ooms and Versyp v. Belgium* (the '*Vagrancy*' cases), (1972) 14 Eur.Ct.H.R. (ser. A) (Article 50); *Neumeister v. Austria*, (1974) 17 Eur.Ct.H.R. (ser. A) (Article 50) and *Marckx v. Belgium*, (1979) 31 Eur.Ct.H.R. (ser. A). In *Sunday Times v. United Kingdom*, (1980) 38 Eur.Ct.H.R. (ser. A) (Article 50) and *Tyrer v. United Kingdom*, (1978) 26 Eur.Ct.H.R. (ser. A) no claim was made for pecuniary or non-pecuniary damages, although costs and fees were requested and granted.

Claims of pecuniary loss continue to be almost routinely rejected for lack of adequate proof: only 19 such claims were accepted between 1991 and 1997 out of several hundred cases. In general, stringent requirements of proof and causality have made it nearly impossible for applicants to demonstrate a connection between the loss and the violation.

The former European Court awarded all the damages and costs claimed by the applicant in just over half a dozen judgments.[24] The conduct of the government seems to have been an important factor in all the decisions. *X v. France* was the first case to reach the Court concerning French haemophiliacs who contracted AIDS through contaminated blood transfusions knowingly made by the government. The applicant died at the age of 29 years and his parents continued the proceedings. The applicant, who was disabled due to haemophilia and received transfusions in late 1984, was one of some 400 persons who were found to have contracted HIV from the blood. The scandal was widely reported in the French media during many months and the judges sitting in Strasbourg can hardly have been unaware of the events. The Court found a violation of Article 6(1) in the delay of proceedings regarding state responsibility for the contamination. The applicant claimed FF150,000 (approximately US$25,000) for non-pecuniary damage resulting from the delay which prevented him from obtaining compensation and thus being able to live independently and in better psychological conditions for the remaining period of his life. The Court awarded the entire amount as well as all the costs claimed.

Aksoy v. Turkey was the European Court's first decision involving official torture. In addition, there were claims that the applicant was killed in reprisal for bringing his human rights case to the European system. Although the latter claim could not be proven, the alleged torture, which resulted in paralysis of the applicant's arms, was found to be substantiated. He also was (posthumously) awarded the total amount he had requested.

Five of the cases where the applicants received all the compensation they claimed are among the multitude of applications against Italy because of failures in its judicial system. Over 150 judgments have been rendered against Italy since 1982 when applicants began alleging excessive delays in civil and criminal proceedings, in some cases lasting nearly two decades. It is unclear why these five cases among the many decisions resulted in full awards, while others received only a portion of their claim or a decision that the judgment constituted just satisfaction for moral damages. It does seem clear that the Italian government thus far has chosen to pay damages rather than repair its legal system; perhaps larger awards are deemed necessary to exert pressure for change.

---

[24] *Triggiani v. Italy*, (1991) 197 Eur.Ct.H.R. (ser. A); *Caleffi v. Italy*, (1991) 206 Eur.Ct.H.R. (ser. A); (1991) *Vocaturo v. Italy*, 206 Eur. Ct.H.R. (ser. A); *X v. France*, (1992) 236 Eur.Ct.H.R. (ser. A); *Salese v. Italy*, (1993) 257 Eur.Ct.H.R. (ser. A); *Scollo v. Italy*, (1995) 315 Eur.Ct.H.R. (ser. A) and *Aksoy v. Turkey*, Judgment of 18 December 1996, Eur.Ct.H.R. 26, Reports of Judgments and Decisions 1996–VI, at 2263, (1997) 23 E.H.R.Rep. 553.

2. The European Court of Justice

The European Court of Justice has never articulated general principles respecting the kinds of loss for which compensation may be claimed or the methods to calculate loss.[25] The Court generally measures damages by comparing the claimant's financial situation at the time of litigation with what it would have been if the illegal or wrongful act or omission had not been committed:

It is well known that the legal concept of 'damage' covers both a material loss *stricto senso*, that is to say, a reduction in a person's assets, and also the loss of an increase in those assets which would have occurred if the harmful act had not taken place (these two alternatives are known respectively as *damnum emergens* and *lucrum cessans*) ... The object of compensation is to restore the assets of the victim to the condition in which they would have been apart from the unlawful act, or at least to the condition closest to that which would have been produced if the unlawful act had not taken place: the hypothetical nature of that restoration often entails a certain degree of approximation ... [T]hese general remarks are not only limited to the field of private law, but apply also to the liability of public authorities, and more especially to the non-contractual liability of the Community.[26]

Damnum emergens includes not only the direct loss brought about by a wrongful act or omission, but also any expenses necessarily and reasonably incurred as a consequence.[27] Compensation for lost profits (*lucrum cessans*) is acceptable in principle, but the Court is conservative in estimating these due to the speculative nature of commercial transactions. In some cases, the Court of First Instance determines whether the evidence establishes the existence of damage and assesses the most appropriate compensation and the Court of Justice has no jurisdiction on appeal to revise the award.[28]

3. The Inter-American Court of Human Rights

In its first 20 years, between 1978 and 1998, the Inter-American Court issued 11 judgments on remedies.[29] One proceeding was dismissed after the parties reached

---

[25] See, generally, A.G. Toth, *Legal Protection of Individuals in the European Communities* (1978), 84, n. 22.

[26] Comments of Advocate General Capotorti, in Case 238/78, *Ireks-Arkady v. Council and Commission* [1979] E.C.R. 2955 at 2998–99.

[27] See Cases 5,7, 13–224/66, *Kampffmeyer v. Commission* [1967] E.C.R. 245.

[28] Case C–136/92, *Commission v. Brazzelli Lualdi and others* [1994] E.C.R. I–1981 at 2033.

[29] *Velasquez Rodriguez Case (Compensatory Damages)*, (1989) 7 Inter-Am.Ct.H.R. (ser. C); *Godinez Cruz Case (Compensatory Damages)*, (1989) 8 Inter-Am.Ct.H.R. (ser. C); *Velasquez Rodriguez (Interpretation of the Judgment of Compensatory Damages)*, (1990) 9 Inter-Am.Ct.H.R. (ser. C); *Godinez Cruz Case (Interpretation of the Judgment of Compensatory Damages)* (1990) 10 Inter-Am.Ct.H.R. (ser. C); *Aloeboetoe et al. Case (Reparations)*, (1993) 15 Inter-Am.Ct.H.R. (ser. C); *Gangaram Panday Case*, (1994) 16 Inter-Am.Ct.H.R. (ser. C); *El Amparo Case (Reparations)* (1996) 28 Inter-Am.Ct.H.R. (ser. C); and *Neira Alegria et al Case (Reparations)* (1996) 29 Inter-Am.Ct.H.R. (ser. C); *Caballero Delgado and Santana Case*, (1996) 31 Inter-Am.Ct. H.R. (ser. C) and *Garrido and*

a settlement approved by the Court.[30] In all but one case, the Court issued its judgment on reparations after the issue was briefed by the parties following the Court's decision on the merits. In *Gangaram Panday v. Suriname*,[31] the Court did not follow this procedure, but awarded a 'nominal' sum in its judgment on the merits. In *Loayza Tamayo v. Peru*,[32] the Court ordered Peru to release the victim from prison in the proceedings on the merits, but held the issue of damages for a later phase in the case. Its subsequent reparations opinion made significant changes in the law of remedies.

The Court's jurisprudence on damages reveals less generosity towards victims than might be expected on the basis of the text of Article 63(1) and its drafting history. The opinions are not consistent and indicate a fundamental misunderstanding of the sometimes different interests and roles of the victims and the Commission. Nonetheless, the Court's judgments provide the most wide-reaching remedies afforded in international human rights law to date.

Velasquez Rodriguez v. Honduras and *Godinez Cruz v. Honduras* were the first contentious cases decided by the Court.[33] The Inter-American Commission on Human Rights brought the cases, alleging state responsibility for the disappearance of the two named individuals. The Court found the government responsible and asked the parties to negotiate an agreement on the amount of damages.[34] The Court kept the cases open, reserving the right to approve the agreements or, if no agreements were reached, to set the amount and order the manner of payment.[35] The Court noted that in the circumstances of a disappearance it could not order that the victim be guaranteed the enjoyment of the rights and freedoms violated.[36]

The Court clearly recognized the importance of the precedent that these cases would set on the subject of remedies. By resolution, it authorized the President to initiate whatever studies and name whatever experts might be convenient so that the Court would have the elements necessary to set the form and amount of compensation.[37] When the parties failed to reach agreement, the cases returned to the Court for judgment. Honduras argued that the applicants should receive 'the

---

Baigorria Case, 39 Inter-Am. Ct.H.R. (ser. C) (2 February 1996), 1996 Y.B. Inter-Am. Conv. H.R. 1714 (Inter-Am.Ct.H.R.); *Loayza Tamayo v. Peru (Reparations)*, (1998) 43 Inter-Am.Ct.H.R. (ser. C); *Blake v. Guatemala* (Reparations), Judgment of 22 January 1999 (1999) 48 Inter-Am.Ct.H.R. (ser. C) (Reparations); *Suarez Rosero v. Ecuador (Reparations)*, Judgment of 22 January 1999 (1999) 44 Inter-Am.Ct.H.R. (ser. C) (Reparations).

[30]　*Maqueda Case*, (1995) 18 Inter-Am.Ct.H.R. (ser. C).

[31]　*Gangaram Panay v. Suriname*, (1994) 16 Inter-Am.Ct.H.R. (ser. C).

[32]　*Loyaza Tamayo v. Peru (Reparations)*, (1998) 43 Inter-Am.Ct.H.R. (ser. C).

[33]　*Velasquez Rodriguez Case (Merits)*, (1988) 4 Inter-Am.Ct.H.R. (ser. C); *Godinez Cruz Case (Merits)*, (1989) 5 Inter-Am.Ct.H.R. (ser. C).

[34]　*Velasquez Rodriguez Case (Merits)* at 191–92. In the *Godinez Cruz Case*, the Court held it would fix the amount of the compensation in execution of the judgment, after hearing the interested parties, unless they reached an agreement in the interim. As in the *Velasquez Rodriguez Case*, the Court reserved the right to approve any such agreement.

[35]　*Ibid.*　　　　　　　　　　　　　　　　　　　　　　　　　　　[36]　*Ibid.* at 189.

[37]　*Velasquez Rodriguez Case (Compensatory Damages)*, *supra* n. 29, at para. 4.

most favorable benefits' that Honduran legislation provided for Hondurans in the case of accidental death. The Commission countered that the amount and form of payment constituting just compensation should be determined by the requirements of international law.

The Court considered at length the basis for an award of damages, noting that international law requires restitution of the *status quo ante* where possible and compensation where it is not possible, citing the judgment of the International Court of Justice in the *Chorzow Factory Case* and its advisory opinion *Reparation for Injuries Suffered in the Service of the United Nations*.[38] It added:

> Reparation of harm brought about by the violation of an international obligation consists in full restitution (*restitutio in integrum*), which includes the restoration of the prior situation, the reparation of the consequences of the violation, and indemnification for patrimonial and non-patrimonial damages, including emotional harm.[39]

The Court emphasized that the law on damages, including scope, characteristics, beneficiaries, etc. is governed by international law. Compliance with a judgment on reparations is not subject to modification or suspension by the respondent state through invocation of provisions of its own domestic law.[40] In this regard, the Court distinguished between future action by the state, which must conform to the Convention and ensure the enjoyment of the right or freedom that was violated, and reparations for past actions. Where, as in the case under consideration, the violation involves a loss of life or other right that cannot be restored, compensation must be in an amount sufficient to remedy all the consequences of the violations that took place. The Court established that there are no rigid criteria, but that compensation should be based upon a prudent estimate of damages and, as discussed in the next section, that assessment of moral damages requires application of principles of equity. Finally, the Court stated that *restitutio in integrum* is 'one way in which the effect of an international unlawful act *may* be redressed, but it is not the only way in which it *must* be redressed, for in certain cases such reparation may not be possible, sufficient or appropriate'.[41]

B. PECUNIARY DAMAGES

Pecuniary losses include the value of the very thing to which the plaintiff was entitled and any special/consequential harms or losses, such as lost profits, resulting from harm to the thing to which the plaintiff was entitled. Damages are thus

---

[38] According to the Inter-American Court, '[i]t is a principle of international law, which jurisprudence has considered "even a general concept of law", that every violation of an international obligation which results in harm creates a duty to make adequate reparation. Compensation, on the other hand, is the most usual way of doing so (Factory at Chorzow, Jurisdiction, Judgment No. 8, 1937, P.C.I.J., Series A, No. 17, p. 29; Reparation for Injuries Suffered in the Service of the United Nations, Advisory Opinion, I.C.J. Reports 1949, p. 184).'

[39] *Velasquez Rodriguez Case (Compensatory Damages)*, *supra* n. 29, at paras. 6, 25–26.

[40] *Ibid.*, para. 44.   [41] *Ibid.*, para. 49 (emphasis in original).

an award of the reasonable costs of procuring a substitute for the things lost.[42] In the European Court of Human Rights, compensatory damages have been awarded for lost earnings, pensions,[43] fines and interpreter's costs wrongly paid[44] and reduction in the value of property.[45] Lost opportunity costs are sometimes awarded as well, particularly where pecuniary damage is clear, but the amount is often difficult to quantify or assess.[46] In very few cases has the European Court assessed pecuniary damage with precision. In most cases, a lump sum is awarded, sometimes including moral damages and costs and expenses, making it impossible to determine the basis for the award. While lump sum awards are easy for the Court, they can present practical problems for the applicant and government. As noted below, some countries exempt only moral damages from taxation or attachment. Given such difficulties, the Court should always distinguish pecuniary and non-pecuniary awards.

The European Convention on the Compensation of Victims of Violent Crimes,[47] which encompasses human rights violations and could provide guidance to litigants and the European Court, provides that compensation shall cover *at least the following*: loss of earnings; medical, hospitalization, and funeral expenses; and, for dependents, loss of maintenance.[48] National compensation schemes may set upper limits of compensation and a *de minimis* standard. Article 7 allows compensation to be reduced or refused on account of the applicant's financial situation.

The few discussions of pecuniary damages in the European Court have taken place almost entirely in property cases. The Court has held that the payment of compensation is a necessary condition for the taking of property of anyone within the jurisdiction of a contracting state.[49] In *Sporrong and Lonnroth v. Sweden*,[50] the European Court first considered how it should approach the issue of material damage in a case where the right to property was infringed because of long-term prohibitions on construction. The applicants proposed an economic analysis and deterrent principal for assessing their claim:

---

[42] D. Dobbs, *The Law of Remedies* (1993), 220.

[43] *Young, James and Webster v. United Kingdom,* (1981) 44 Eur.Ct.H.R. (ser. A), 4 E.H.R.Rep. 38. All three applicants had been dismissed from their employment for failure to join a trade union. The Court found a violation of the right to freedom of association (Article 11) and awarded past earnings with interest, pension rights and travel privileges in monetary amounts. Young received US$27,900.20; James, US$71,570.82 and Webster, US$12,783.50.

[44] *Pine Valley Developments et al. v. Ireland,* (1993) 246–B, Eur.Ct.H.R. (ser. A).

[45] *Ibid.; E. v. Norway,* (1990) 181–A Eur.Ct.H.R. (ser. A) at para. 70.

[46] *Allenet de Ribemont v. France,* (1995) 308 Eur.Ct.H.R. (ser. A), (1995) 20 E.H.R.Rep. 557.

[47] Council of Europe, European Convention on the Compensation of Victims of Violent Crime, 23 November 1983, Eur.T.S. No. 116, 22 I.L.M. 1021.

[48] See Nicholas Katsoris, 'The European Convention on the Compensation of Victims of Violent Crimes: A Decade of Frustration', (1990/1991) 14 *Fordham Int'l L.J.* 186, 196. He states that pain and suffering damages are also included, but no reference to them appears in the text.

[49] *James v. United Kingdom,* (1986) 98 Eur.Ct.H.R. (ser. A).

[50] *Sporrong and Lonnroth v. Sweden,* (1982) 52 Eur.Ct.H.R. (ser. A).

[T]he applicants wish to point out the risk of a gradual deterioration of the legal rights of the individual if the balance of interest is not effectively restored. In these cases this can only be done by awarding the individual such compensation that the responsible authorities are obliged to weigh the costs inflicted upon the individual on the one hand against the public benefit which it is trying to achieve on the other.[51]

To the applicants it seemed clear that reparation should take the form of *restitutio in integrum*, but since it was impossible, a pecuniary assessment of the loss became necessary, including past development losses. A lifting of restrictions on the property development could not be considered an adequate remedy because of the economic losses that occurred during the years when use was restricted. The applicants maintained that they should have been entitled either to make use of their properties in a normal fashion within a reasonable time or have been given the option of selling them at a normal price, as if the restrictions had not been in place. They noted that the economy was much better at the time the restrictions were in place than at the time of the litigation. Sporrong claimed damages of SEK13,284,540 (US$1,621,846) and Lonnroth SEK10,912,303 (US$1,332,231). The Court agreed that compensation was necessary for the taking; however, although there was no objection from the government to the amounts claimed, the Court awarded only SEK1 million (US$122,085), without discussing its basis for assessing the damages.

In the Inter-American Court, all the decisions in the first 20 years involved human rights violations causing death or other physical harm. The Court thus faced the difficult challenge of constructing a measure for the value of a lost life and pain and suffering. The compensation sought by the victims in the *Velasquez Rodriguez* and *Godinez Cruz* cases included a fund for the primary, secondary, and university education of the children of the disappeared; guaranteed employment of working-age children; and establishment of a retirement fund for the parents of the disappeared. For its part, the Commission requested compensatory damages including payment to the spouse of 'the highest pension recognized by Honduran law' and payments to the children through completion of their university education; title to an adequate house; general damages for the wife and children (200,000 lempiras)[52], damages for lost earnings (2,422,420 lempiras) and emotional harm (4,845,000 lempiras), based upon an expert opinion offered by the victim's family. The Court accepted that lost earnings and similar losses formed part of recoverable pecuniary harm. Emotional harm was considered under the heading of moral damages.

In *Aloeboetoe*[53] the Court dealt only with the issue of reparations, after Suriname accepted responsibility for the kidnapping and deaths on 31 December

---

[51] *Sporrong and Lonroth v. Sweden*, (1980–1981) 46 Eur.Ct.H.R. (ser. B) at 215.

[52] Two lempiras equal approximately one US dollar.

[53] *Aloeboetoe Case, supra* n. 29. See also David J. Padilla, 'Reparations in Aloeboetoe v. Suriname', (1995) 17 *Hum.Rts.Q.* 541.

1987 of six young men and a 15-year old boy of the Saramaca tribe. The victims were forced to dig their own graves before six of them were killed. The seventh was shot and seriously wounded while trying to escape. He later died of his wounds after testifying about the massacre. On behalf of the victims' families, the Commission sought indemnification for material and moral damages, based on *restitutio in integrum*, other non-monetary reparations,[54] and reimbursement of expenses and costs incurred by the victims' next of kin. The Commission used questionnaires-affidavits, administered with the permission of the Saramaca, to determine appropriate remedies. These were reviewed by an actuary from the accounting firm of Coopers and Lybrand to apply the 'present value added' method to determine projected earnings of the victims. The Commission identified 37 beneficiaries and submitted a total demand for pecuniary damages comprising a lump sum of US$2,557,242 ($557,000 for material damages to the children, and an annual payment of $42,000 adjusted, for actual damages to the adult dependants).[55] The Court followed the same approach it had used in the earlier cases to divide pecuniary and non-pecuniary damages.

In the 1999 judgment in *Suarez Rosero v. Ecuador*, the applicant sought damages due to unlawful detention. The applicant's wife suffered from cancer due to which a leg had been amputated and she was dependent upon her husband for personal services in the home. In addition, both husband and wife suffered medical and psychological harm as a result of the detention. The applicant asked for lost wages and moral harm, as well as the cost of a housekeeper for the period of incarceration, the costs and fees of the attorneys, rehabilitation, medical and psychological treatment. The government did not contest most of the evidence on damages. The court agreed that he was entitled to indemnification for the lost wages, plus the cost of the domestic help, and expenses for past and future medical treatment.

C. NON-PECUNIARY DAMAGES

Intangible injuries such as physical pain and suffering have long been recognized as legitimate elements of damages.[56] Mental anguish independent of physical

---

[54] In its earlier report on the case, the Commission had recommended that Suriname investigate the violations and try and punish those responsible, as well as take necessary measures to avoid a recurrence of the incident. In its memorial to the Court of 1 April 1991, the Commission added requests for measures to be taken to restore the good name of the victims, a public apology and the return of the remains of the seven victims to their families: *Aloeboetoe Case, supra* n. 29, at paras. 9, 20.

[55] In its brief, the Commission asked for a lump sum of 5,114,484 Surinamese florins broken down into SF1,114,484 for material damages to the children; SF660,000 for moral damages to the children; SF1,340,000 for moral damages to the adult dependants; and SF2 million for moral damages to the tribe. It also asked for an annual sum of SF84.040 for actual damages payable to the adult dependants and various sums for legal costs and expenses.

[56] The first award in the USA is dated to 1763: James F. Blumstein, *et al., Beyond Tort Reform: Developing Better Tools for Assessing Damages for Personal Injuries* (1990).

injury is also now recognized as an element of recovery,[57] including humiliation, loss of enjoyment of life and other non-pecuniary losses.[58] Loss of consortium when one is deprived of a spouse may include loss of love and companionship as well as services in the home, society, and sexual relations. The impairment of any of these gives a right to damages. Interference with parent/child relations may lead to damages for loss of companionship, comfort, guidance, affection and aid. All these factors represent the irreplaceable intangibles of family life. In civil law systems, '*préjudice moral*' includes pain and suffering, sadness and humiliation caused by disfigurement, loss of amenities, loss of recreational ability, loss of any of the five senses, enjoyment of sexual relations, harm to marriage possibilities, and generally damage to the enjoyment of life. Overall, where there has been an injury, the focus is at least in part on diminution of the injured person's expectations of life, sometimes called hedonic damages.[59]

In the European system, moral damages have been awarded for anxiety,[60] distress, 'isolation, confusion and neglect',[61] abandonment, feelings of injustice, impaired way of life, 'harassment and humiliation'[62] and other suffering. General feelings of sadness may be insufficient.[63] In some cases, due to the nature of the violation, the Court has presumed moral injury.[64] In other cases, as already discussed, the Court has found that the judgment in itself constitutes just satisfaction. In *Ribitsch v. Austria*,[65] the applicant complained of mistreatment in custody, allegations that were denied by the government. The Court found that the government had an obligation to provide a plausible explanation of how the applicant's injuries were caused. When no convincing explanation was forthcoming, the Court found a violation of Article 3. The applicant claimed ATS250,000 (US$19,805). The government made no comment on the claimed amount, while the Delegate of the Commission argued that a relatively high sum should be awarded in order to encourage people in the same position as Mr. Ribitsch to bring court proceedings. In spite of this, the Court awarded only ATS100,000 (US$7,922), possibly influenced more by the applicant's conduct (he was accused of selling heroin responsible for the death of two persons) than that of the government.

---

[57] See *supra*, text to nn. 8–13.

[58] C.R. Cramer, 'Loss of Enjoyment of Life as a Separate Element of Damages', (1981) 12 *Pac.L.J.* 965.

[59] Laycock, *Modern American Remedies* (1996), at 175.

[60] *Konig Case*, (1980) 36 Eur.Ct.H.R. (ser. A) at 16–17, para. 19.

[61] *Artico Case*, (1980) 37 Eur.Ct.H.R. (ser. A) at 21–22, paras 46–48.

[62] *Case of Young, James and Webster*, (1981) 44 Eur.Ct.H.R. (ser. A) at 7, paras 12–13.

[63] See *Sidiropoulos and others v. Greece*, Judgment of 10 July 1998. The Court found a violation of Article 11 due to the government's politically-motivated refusal to register a Macedonian group as a cultural organization. The applicants asked for but were refused moral damages based on alleged reputational harm and sadness.

[64] *Abdulaziz, Cabales and Balkandali v. United Kingdom* (1985) 94 Eur.Ct.H.R. (ser. A), para. 96.

[65] *Ribitsch v. Austria*, (1995) 21 E.H.H.Rep. 573.

The award of moral damages is influenced by the government's conduct, but excessive amounts will not be awarded in the nature of aggravated or punitive damages. In *Loizidou v. Turkey*, the applicant sought CYP621,900 (US$1,171,473) in non-pecuniary damages for her distress, frustration, and feelings of helplessness as well as for 'factors related to considerations of the public interest and public order of Europe'. The applicant said that a high award should be made to act as an inducement to the government to observe the legal standards set out in the Convention and should take into account the dilatory attitude of the government and its unfounded objections. The Commission objected to some of the claimed aggravating circumstances and especially objected to bringing in a punitive element 'since the "public policy" considerations adduced by the applicant concerned the global situation of displaced Greek Cypriots and thus went far beyond the perimeters of the individual case'.[66] The Court awarded CYP20,000 (US$37,674) for the applicant's anguish and feelings of helplessness and frustration, but expressly rejected consideration of the general situation.

The Inter-American Court has characterized moral damages as 'the result of the psychological impact suffered by the family . . . because of the violation of rights and freedoms guaranteed by the American Convention', and, in the Honduran cases, '*especially* by the dramatic characteristics of the involuntary disappearance of persons'.[67] The Court seems to be rightly suggesting that one factor in assessing moral damages is the egregiousness of the conduct of governmental authorities.

In the *Velasquez Rodriguez* and *Godinez Cruz* cases, the attorneys for the victims, designated as 'counselors or advisers to the Commission' in order to permit them a role before the Court,[68] asked for and were granted a public hearing to present a psychiatric report on the moral damages suffered by the victims' families.[69] At the hearing, the families demonstrated the existence of moral damages through expert psychiatric testimony which the government did not refute. The government offered 150,000 lempiras; the Court awarded 250,000. In its decision, the Court seemed to suggest that awards for emotional harm are particularly appropriate in cases of human rights violations[70] based upon the principles of equity. It also reiterated that reparations generally are to be effective and independent of the limitations of national law.

---

[66] *Loizidou v. Turkey*, (1995) 310 Eur.Ct.H.R. (ser. A), para. 38.

[67] *Velasquez Rodriguez Case*, (1990) 7 Inter-Am.Ct.H.R. (ser. C), para. 50 (emphasis added).

[68] Only the states parties and the Commission have the right to submit a case to the Court: American Convention on Human Rights, 22 November 1969, Article 61, O.A.S.T.S. 36, O.A.S. Off.Rec. OEA/Ser.L/V/II.23, doc. 21, rev. 6 (1979). The Commission is represented by Delegates, who may be assisted by any person of their choice, including attorneys for the victims: Article 22, Rules of Procedure of the Court. This is the only means by which the victims may directly participate in arguing the merits of their case before the Court.

[69] The Commission supported the claim for moral damages, including some of the families' requests for non-monetary measures under the heading of moral damages: e.g. public homage through naming a street, thoroughfare, school or other public place and a public condemnation of disappearances.

[70] *Velasquez Rodriguez Case*, *supra* n. 67, para. 27.

In the *Aloeboetoe* case, the Court awarded moral damages for pain and suffering to the parents of the victims, presuming emotional injury from the violation: 'it is essentially human for all persons to feel pain at the torment of their child'.[71] In *El Amparo v. Peru,* the Court awarded moral damages for wrongful death, but it did not say whether they were for the deceased's injuries or those of the successors. The Court stated, however, that when the violation is sufficiently serious, moral suffering of the victims 'and their families' must be compensated.[72] Families of those who survived the attack did not receive moral damages. Either the Court felt that they had not suffered an independent injury, or it assumed they would benefit from what the actual victim was awarded.

In several cases, including *Suarez Rosero v. Ecuador,* the Court has stated that its precedents can serve to orient it in regard to the amount of moral damages to award, to demonstrate principles to apply, although prior jurisprudence is not the only factor it will consider. In theory, the judgment itself can serve as satisfaction, but a finding of serious or grave violations will preclude this being the only award.[73]

D. PROYECTO DE VIDA

The Inter-American Court of Human Rights took a major step in the evolution of the law of remedies in its reparations judgment in *Loayza Tamayo v. Peru*[74] when it recognized and accepted the concept of *proyecto de vida*, lost opportunities and enjoyment of life, as an element of damages independent of lost future earnings. The Court described *proyecto de vida* as the applicant's reasonable expectations for the future.[75] While accepting the claim in principle and finding that the applicant had suffered harm to her *proyecto de vida*, the Court failed to make an award under this heading; instead, it appeared to invite future victims and their representatives to present a methodology for calculating such damages.

The government of Peru objected to the admissibility of the claim, arguing that the injury was contained in other headings, such as *dano emergente* and *lucum cessante,* for which the applicant was being compensated through reinstatement in her previous position and other awards. The Court agreed with the applicant, however, that the concept of *proyecto de vida* is different from other headings of damage and has been recognized in recent jurisprudence and doctrine, none of which are cited in the judgment. Unlike pecuniary damage for provable past losses and *lucro cessante* for quantifiable lost future earnings, *proyecto de vida* alludes to the 'personal fulfilment' of the affected person, taking into account the vocation,

---

71 *Aloeboetoe Case, supra* n. 29.
72 *El Amparo Case, supra* n. 29.
73 See also *Blake v. Guatemala,* Judgment of 22 January 1999, *supra* n. 29.
74 *Loayza Tamayo v. Peru (Reparations), supra* n. 29.
75 *Ibid.,* para. 144.

skills, circumstances, potentialities, and aspirations that reasonably could be determined and expected. The concept is thus linked to self-actualization of the person, grounded in individuality. If the *proyecto de vida* are cancelled or subject to interference, the loss cannot be ignored by the Court.

The Court held that Loayza Tamayo's natural and foreseeable development, and not just her existing situation, had been interrupted and denied by the acts violating her human rights. The violations drastically changed the course of her life, imposing new and adverse conditions and modifying the plans and projects that she had formulated in light of the normal conditions of her existence and the aptitudes and skills that she possessed to achieve these aims.[76] The violations prevented her from the realization of her personal and professional goals by obliging her to interrupt her studies and move abroad, away from her normal environment, to live in isolation and in economic hardship, under severe physical and psychological stress. The Court found it obvious that these circumstances taken together and directly attributable to the violations had altered her life in a serious and probably irreparable way, preventing her from achieving her reasonable personal, familial, and professional goals. The Court, therefore, found it reasonable to conclude that the human rights violations injured her *proyecto de vida*.

The Court appeared to limit the claim of injury to *proyecto de vida* to cases demonstrating irreparable loss or severe impairment of the opportunities for personal development. Where such injury has occurred, the 'exigencies of justice' and the aim of reparations, which is to restore the individual to a situation as close as possible to the position he or she would have occupied had the violation not occurred, justify an award. In other words, it may approximate *restitutio in integrum*. Nonetheless, in this case the Court found it could not translate the injury into economic terms and therefore it abstained from awarding compensation for the loss, noting also that the access of the victim to the international tribunal and the decision itself could be seen as a form of satisfaction. Judge Carlos Vicente de Roux Rengifo dissented on the last point, finding that the Court's compensatory award of US$25,000 was inadequate. He recognized that the Court had taken a progressive step in recognizing the concept of *proyecto de vida* injury, but criticized its failure to actually award damages for the harm caused. He would limit such awards to cases of death, disability, or serious interruption of career, modifications to the status of the victim that might continue long after the specific violation had ceased and that deprive the applicant of affection, pleasures, and satisfaction in life. In his view, not every modification deserves to be compensated, but only those changes of such a magnitude that they alter the foundations of life, such as the spiritual and emotional setting in which life goes on or the impairment of the professional evolution in which the person has placed great effort. Given the specific harm in this case, he would have granted an additional US$124,190.30 to her.

---

[76] *Loayza Tamayo v. Peru (Reparations)*, (1997) 43 Inter-Am.Ct.H.R. (ser. C)., para. 150.

Judges Cançado Trindade and Abreu Burelli added a separate opinion to rein-force their view that reparations should consider the individual as more than *homo economicus*, 'a mere agent of economic production', but rather should accept that humans have needs and aspirations that go beyond economic worth. They pointed to the preamble of the American Declaration of the Rights and Duties of Man with its affirmation that 'spiritual development is the supreme end of human existence and the highest expression thereof'. In their view, the Court should reorient and enrich the international jurisprudence regarding reparations in light of this approach that comes from international human rights law. The recognition of *proyecto de vida* injury is a first step in this direction that could lead to true restitution. The concept is strongly and indivisibly linked to the notion of freedom as the right that every person has to choose his or her own destiny. Such freedom has high existential value and is lacking when real options are absent to develop and actualize individual projects. The cancellation or impairment of options implies an objective reduction of freedom and a loss of value that cannot be ignored by the Court. The damage to *proyecto de vida* threatens the ultimate goal of and value of life itself to the person, harming the core of the human being and affecting the spiritual sense of life. They invite a rethinking of all reparations in light of the integrity of the victim and the restora-tion of human dignity.

E. CAUSATION AND PRESUMED HARM

Wrongdoing leads to immediate and more long-range harm. Like a stone thrown into a lake, the consequences of the wrong ripple outward in ever-widening circles. Legal concepts of foreseeability and consequential loss affect who may claim injury and for what losses. In most legal systems, doctrines similar to 'prox-imate cause' are used to define the extent of liability by excluding more remote consequences where there is an uncertain critical link, or cumulative uncertain-ties about causation, making it impossible to say according to the accepted stan-dard of proof that the wrong caused the harm. The burden of proof is generally on the claimant who is assumed to be in the best position to know and marshal evidence of the consequences of the wrong. However, where deterrence is espe-cially important, as in human rights cases, the risk of uncertainty or lack of proof may be shifted to the wrongdoer.

In general, all damages directly attributed to the wrong done are compensable and causation is a crucial question. If the victim has suffered no loss, or would have suffered the same loss without the wrongdoer's conduct, then compensation is not due. Damages must have been caused in fact by the wrongdoer and the wrong must be the proximate cause of the damage suffered. Once causation is established, the wrongdoer is charged with all harm that naturally flows from the wrongful act even though it was not foreseen at the time of the misconduct.

Most courts allow claims for future consequences that are reasonably certain. Damages cannot be awarded when they are too conjectural and speculative to form a sound basis for measurement, but absolute certainty is not required in establishing damages.[77] Compensatory damages are often at best approximate; they have to be proved with whatever definiteness and accuracy the facts permit. In injury to property cases, provable injury caused by the wrong may include damage to business reputation and goodwill, using methods of calculation accepted by economists and accountants.[78] Loss may be determined in any manner which is reasonable under the circumstances, such as a diminution in the value of the business when it was sold. For intangible injury, proof of causation can be a problem for the victim, in contrast to items of economic expense, like prior medical bills or lost earnings.

In actions against the state, corrective justice theory may lead to presuming compensable harm when rights are violated, since the harm is inherently intangible and therefore impossible of proof.[79] The presumption of harm may be particularly important in human rights cases where the victims are complaining of violations such as deprivation of the right to vote or invasion of privacy. It is difficult to demonstrate the monetary value of such intangible, irreparable losses. Yet, if the victim is not awarded damages for the harm, the judgment may have neither compensatory nor deterrent effect.[80] Many courts thus value the intangible interests by determining what amount of damages would reasonably suffice for someone in the place of the victim and presuming the victim suffered to that extent, often inferring both the fact of the harm and the extent of the harm from the circumstances surrounding the wrongdoer's conduct.[81] Some injury clearly flows

---

[77] *Johnson v. Baker*, 11 Kan.App. 2d, 719 P.2d 752 (1986).

[78] *Lewis River Golf, Inc. v. O.M.Scott & Sons*, 120 Wash.2d 712, 845 P.2d 987 (1993).

[79] J. Love, *supra* n. 2; M. Wells, 'The Past and the Future of Constitutional Torts: From Statutory Interpretation to Common Law Rules', (1986) 19 *Conn.L.Rev.* 53; D. Dobbs, *The Law of Remedies* (1994) at 528.

[80] As in private tort law, damages for constitutional violations serve both to compensate and to deter: *Carey v. Piphus*, 435 U.S. 247, 254–57 (1978). On the deterrent function of compensatory damages in constitutional tort litigation see J. Newman, 'Suing the Lawbreakers: Proposals to Strengthen the Section 1983 Damage Remedy for Law Enforcers' Misconduct', (1978) 87 *Yale L.J.* 447, 464–67; D. Rendleman, 'The New Due Process: Rights and Remedies', (1975) 63 *Ky.L.J.* 531, 566–67; M. Yudof, 'Liability for Constitutional Torts and the Risk-Averse Public School Official', (1976) 49 *S.Cal.L.Rev.* 1322, 1366–83; J. Niles, 'Comment, Civil Actions for Damages under the Federal Civil Rights Statutes', (1967) 45 *Tex.L.Rev.* 1015; J. Love, 'Damages: A Remedy for the Violation of Constitutional Rights', (1979) 67 *Cal.L.Rev.* 1242; M. Pilkington, 'Damages as a Remedy for Infringement of the Canadian Charter of Rights and Freedoms', (1984) 62 Can.B.Rev. 517; J. Jeffries, Jr., 'Damages for Constitutional Violations: The Relation of Risk to Injury in Constitutional Torts', (1989) 75 *Va.L.Rev.* 1461; S. Nahmod, 'Constitutional Damages and Corrective Justice: A Different View', (1990) 76 *Va.L.Rev.* 997; D. Rotenberg, 'Private Remedies for Constitutional Wrongs—A Matter of Perspective, Priority and Process', (1986) 14 *Hastings Const.L.Q.* 77.

[81] Restatement (Second) of Torts, s. 904, cmt. A (1979): 'there need be no proof of the extent of harm, since the existence of the harm may be assumed and its extent is inferred as a matter of common knowledge from the existence of the injury'.

from the mere fact of the wrongful act and compensation for such dignitary harms redresses the outrage felt by an individual whose fundamental rights have been violated.

National courts long have used presumed general damages for loss of the right to vote, because the loss constitutes non-monetary harm that cannot easily be quantified, but is likely to have occurred.[82] In one United States case,[83] African–American and Hispanic registered voters brought a class action for interference with their voting rights during a local election. They sought compensatory damages for being prevented or discouraged from voting. The court ruled that the plaintiffs were entitled to recover presumed general damages.[84] The class of approximately 1,000 plaintiffs entered into a settlement agreement with the defendants whereby each plaintiff was entitled to 'nominal damages' of US$50. Additional damages were awarded based upon 'damage points' that were given according to the degree of interference with the right: one point for being 'subjected to obstacles in voting'; two points for harassment, intimidation or abuse; three points for actual prevention from voting. After payment of the nominal damages, the settlement fund was distributed in accordance with the damage points.[85] The distinctions made indicate that the award was for actual damages, not the inherent value of the constitutional right, which would have resulted in identical damages for each plaintiff. Instead, those who suffered more harm by being actually prevented from voting received more than those who were merely harassed or mildly obstructed.

Courts also may vindicate deprivations of fundamental rights that are not shown to have caused actual injury through the award of a nominal sum of money. By making the deprivation of such rights actionable for nominal damages, the law recognizes the importance to organized society that those rights be observed. At the same time, this approach upholds the principle that substantial damages should be awarded only to compensate actual injury or to deter or punish egregious violations.

The former European Court of Human Rights was strict in requiring allegations and proof of pecuniary harm and moral injury,[86] but sometimes presumed moral and even pecuniary injury from the nature of the violation. As noted by the Commission and the Court in *Konig v. Germany*,[87] it is in fact an extremely difficult matter to identify with precision the prejudice suffered as a result of certain types of violations, such as those involving the undue length of domestic proceed-

---

[82] A common law precedent more than 200 years old allows presumed general damages for deprivation of the right to vote. See *Ashby v. White*, 2 Ld.Raym. 938, 92 Eng.Rep. 126 (K.B. 1703).

[83] *Vargas v. Calabrese*, 634 F.Supp. 910, 913 (D.N.J. 1986).

[84] Love, *supra* n. 2 at note 122.

[85] *Ibid.*

[86] See *Konig v. Germany*, (1980) 36 Eur.Ct.H.R. (ser. A) (Article 50) at 14, para. 19 ('Dr Konig alleges . . . injury but he does not prove their existence or specify their extent; neither does he indicate the sums to which he considers himself entitled by way of just satisfaction').

[87] *Ibid.*

ings. Dr. Konig asked for moral damages in an amount to be set by the Court. 'Although applicants should as a rule quantify their claims, the Court would be failing to pay proper regard to the principle of equity imposed by Article 50 were it not to take into consideration the problems confronting Dr. Konig in this respect.' Accordingly, the Court did not deem it 'appropriate' to have him called on to plead the exact amount of compensation he was claiming. The Court noted that Dr. Konig was kept in a state of 'prolonged uncertainty' during the more than 10 years of proceedings, which led him 'to defer unduly, in view of his age, the search for an alternative career'. This fact had to be taken into account as well as the impact the delay had in his postponing the sale or lease of his medical clinic. Considering the lost opportunities and the deep anxiety he felt, the Court awarded DM30,000 (US$16,720). Other judgments similarly have awarded presumed moral damages, where the Court has admitted that distress or anxiety cannot be concretely proven.[88]

The Court may make a lump sum award where it finds evidence of injury, but the valuation cannot be determined with adequate proof. In *Hornsby v. Greece*[89] two British nationals proved a violation of Article 6(1) because of delay by the government in complying with a final judgment of the Supreme Administrative Court of Greece that they were entitled to a licence to open a foreign language school in Rhodes. The applicants admitted their inability to furnish conclusive proof of pecuniary damage, which was in the form of lost profits, but asserted there were objective indications of its scale such as a fall in the number of existing pupils when it became known that the school was unlicensed. The Court found the applicants' lost fee estimates to be speculative, but agreed that the inability to advertise properly and the pupils' uncertainty about the legal status of the school 'may have caused the applicants over a number of years a loss of income which it is not, however, possible to assess precisely'. To this must be added the applicants' own uncertainty and anxiety and 'deep feeling' of injustice due to government non-compliance with the judgments of its courts. The Court awarded a lump sum of 25 million drachmas (US$84,840) plus costs.

In general, European Court awards for pecuniary losses are far less common than non-pecuniary because of the Court's strict requirements of causality and proof. The burden of proof is on the applicant to prove harm was suffered and that

---

[88]   See *Airey v. Ireland*, (1981) 41 Eur.Ct.H.R. (ser. A) (Article 50); *Lawless v. Ireland*, (1961) 2 Eur.Ct.H.R. (ser. A); *Stögmüller v. Austria*, (1969) 9 Eur.Ct.H.R. (ser. A); *Swedish Engine Drivers' Union v. Sweden*, (1976) 20 Eur.Ct.H.R. (ser. A); *König v. Germany*, (1978) 27 Eur.Ct.H.R. (ser. A); *Klass and others v. Germany*, (1978) 28 Eur.Ct.H.R. (ser. A); *Eckle v. Germany*, (1982) 51 Eur. Ct.H.R. (ser. A); *Piersack v. Belgium*, (1982) 53 Eur.Ct.H.R. (ser. A); *Le Compte, van Leuven and De Meyere*, (1982) 54 Eur.Ct.H.R. (ser. A) (Article 50); *De Jong, Baljet and Van den Brink*, (1984) 77 Eur.Ct.H.R. (ser. A).

[89]   *Hornsby v. Greece*, Judgment of 1 April 1998, 69 Reports of Judgments and Decisions 1998–II 727.

the harm was caused by the violation.[90] The Court nonetheless has recognized that circumstances within a country may make it difficult if not impossible to adduce the evidence necessary to prove specific values for pecuniary harm.[91] In most cases involving procedural violations, Article 50 awards are refused because the applicant understandably fails in the burden of proof, there being no way to demonstrate what result the domestic court would have reached in the absence of the violation.[92] In *Ruiz-Mateos v. Spain*[93] for example, the Court found a violation of Article 6(1) because the applicant could not participate in proceedings concerning the expropriation of assets and the proceedings were not conducted within a reasonable time. The Court rejected the family's claim for 2,000 million pesetas (US$13,814,265) for damage, holding that:

There is nothing to suggest that, in the absence of these violations, the Constitutional Court would have declared the infringed law void and the European Court cannot speculate as to the conclusion which the national court would have reached.[94]

In *Eckle v. Germany,*[95] the Court indicated that it will not presume damages in procedural cases. Like Dr. Konig and Ruiz-Mateos, the Eckles complained of the unreasonable length of domestic proceedings. They pleaded both pecuniary (DM5,049,284 = US$2,814,265) and non-pecuniary (DM703,124,150 = US$391,892,788) injury. The Court held that 'the alleged financial losses of Mr. and Mrs. Eckle result from the very existence and outcome of the prosecutions brought against them. There is nothing in the evidence submitted to support the view that the asserted damage was attributable to the failure to comply with the requirements of Article 6'.[96] The Court denied both claims, awarding only a portion of the claimed fees and costs.

The Court is not consistent in regard to its requirements of proof, especially in procedural cases. It seems more influenced by its own view of the unfairness of

---

[90] *Lawless v. Ireland*, (Merits) (1961) 3 Eur.Ct.H.R. (ser. A); *Neumeister v. Austria*, (1968) 8 Eur.Ct.H.R. (ser. A).

[91] See, in particular *Akdivar and others v. Turkey*, Judgment of 1 April 1998 (Article 50), 69 Reports of Judgments and Decisions 1998–II 711; *Mentes and others v. Turkey, Selçuk and Asker v. Turkey*, Judgment of 24 April 1998, 71 Reports of Judgments and Decisions 1998–II 891.

[92] See e.g., *Neumeister v. Austria*, (1974) 17 Eur.Ct.H.R. (ser. A) (Article 50); *Leudicke, Belkacem and Koç v. Germany*, (1980) 36 Eur.Ct.H.R. (ser. A) (Article 50).

[93] *Ruiz Mateos v. Spain*, (1993) 262 Eur.Ct.H.R. (ser. A).

[94] *Ibid.* at paras. 69–70. See also the following cases where the Court has emphasized 'that it cannot speculate as to what the outcome of the proceedings might have been had there been no breach of the Convention. Since no causal connection between the violation and the alleged damage has been established, the claim must be dismissed': *Bricmont v. Belgium*, (1989) 158 Eur.Ct.H.R. (ser. A) at 33, para. 97; *Skarby v. Sweden*, (1990) 180B Eur.Ct.H.R. (ser. A) at para. 35; *Hakkansson and Sturesson v. Sweden*, (1990) 171A Eur.Ct.H.R. (ser. A) at para. 72; *Philis v. Greece*, (1991) 209 Eur.Ct.H.R. (ser. A) at 25, para. 71.

[95] *Eckle v. Germany*, (1982) 51 Eur.Ct.H.R. (ser. A); *Eckle v. Germany*, (1983) 65 Eur.Ct.H.R. (ser. A) (Article 50).

[96] 65 Eur.Ct.H.R. at para. 20. Note that the Eckles were complaining regarding a criminal prosecution where they were found guilty. Dr. Konig's case was a civil one.

the proceedings and the character of the applicant than by available proof of harm. In *Vidal v. Belgium*,[97] for example, in contrast to the *Ruiz-Mateos* and *Eckle* cases, the Court awarded a lump sum of BF250,000 (US$6,757) in pecuniary and non-pecuniary damages and BF300,000 (US$8,108) for costs and expenses for a criminal appeal in which the applicant's sentence was enhanced. The defence counsel had attempted to call four witnesses but the court had refused without giving reasons. The European Court of Human Rights found this a violation of Article 6. The applicant claimed BF2 million (US$54,045) in non-pecuniary damage and BF548,242 (US$14,815) in pecuniary damage. The Court, while saying it could not speculate on the outcome of the proceedings had the witnesses been called, nonetheless said that there was non-pecuniary damage and 'it appears not unreasonable to regard him as also having suffered a loss of real opportunities'.

Delta v. France[98] is another case where witnesses were not examined in open court. The European Court seemed concerned that the procedural irregularity might have affected the outcome of the case. In the *Delta* case, two girls who accused the applicant never appeared in Court, without explanation, and the immigrant defendant was convicted solely on the basis of the girls' police statements. On appeal, the defendant expressly sought to have witnesses called on his behalf but the Court refused, upholding his conviction. The applicant was released after two years and five months in prison. The Court unanimously found a violation of the right to a fair trial. The applicant claimed FF156,698.49 (US$26,040) in pecuniary damage for lost earnings quantified on the basis of the national guaranteed minimum wage, and FF600,000 (US$99,7100) in non-pecuniary damage for his feelings of distress and deprivation of liberty. While the Court repeated that it could not speculate on the outcome of the trial, it added that 'it does not find it unreasonable to regard Mr. Delta as having suffered a loss of real opportunities'[99] and awarded him FF100,000 (US$16,618) for both pecuniary and non-pecuniary harm. The amount is significant, given that the applicant was unemployed and was receiving no benefits at the time he was arrested. It may be noted that in an earlier case concerning the length of criminal proceedings followed by acquittal, the French government settled the claim for the same amount of damages.[100]

Moreira de Azevedo,[101] an Article 6(1) case where the reasonable time in a

---

[97] *Vidal v. Belgium*, (1992) 235–B Eur.Ct.H.R. (ser. A).

[98] *Delta v. France*, (1990) 191–A Eur.Ct.H.R. (ser. A).

[99] *Ibid.* at para. 43.

[100] See *Clerc v. France*, (1990) 176–C Eur.Ct.H.R. (ser. A). The government subsequently reported that a domestic court judgment in another case would preclude repetition of the violation and that the judgment would be taken into account in the event of a revision of the Code of Criminal Procedure. In other cases where the applicants could prove that the outcome of the trial was affected, the Court also awarded substantial damages. See also *Bonisch v. Austria*, (1985) 92 Eur.Ct.H.R. (ser. A); (1986) 103 Eur.Ct.H.R. (ser. A) (Article 50) (ATS700,000 damages plus costs).

[101] *Moreira de Azevedo v. Portugal*, (1991) 189–A Eur.Ct.H.R. (ser. A); (1991) 208–C Eur.Ct.H.R. (ser. A) (Article 50).

domestic proceeding was exceeded, included a claim of 8 million escudos (US$43,500) in pecuniary damages and 2 million escudos (US$10,875) in non-pecuniary damages, as well as reimbursement for costs and expenses. The domestic proceeding was a *partie civile* case in which the applicant sought to hold a criminal defendant liable in damages for assault. The proceedings began in 1988 and were not completed by the date of the European Court's judgment in 1991. The government noted that the damages he sought were more than double his claim in the domestic court proceedings. The Court, finding that there still might be damages awarded in the domestic proceedings, awarded him 4 million escudos (US$21,750) undifferentiated pecuniary and non-pecuniary damages, holding that 'the excessive length of the criminal proceedings must have caused the applicant pecuniary damage, and definitely caused him non-pecuniary damage'.[102] He was also awarded all his costs.

Finally, in *Weeks v. United Kingdom*, where the Court found a breach of Article 5(4) due to the applicant's inability to challenge the lawfulness of his detention, the Court, in contrast to the *Ruiz* case, engaged in speculation:

It cannot be entirely excluded that he might have been released earlier and, in view of his age, might have obtained some practical benefit. Consequently, Mr. Weeks may be said to have suffered a loss of opportunities by reason of the absence of such proceedings, even if in the light of the recurrence of his behavioral problems the prospect of his realizing them fully was questionable.[103]

In cases where the applicant can demonstrate that the arrest and prosecution were unlawful, and not simply that there were procedural violations during a lawful proceeding, the Court appears more willing to recognize the causal link between the violation and the claim of damages. *Teixeira de Castro v. Portugal*,[104] involved police entrapment in a drug offence in violation of Article 6(1). The applicant claimed 2,052,000 escudos (US$11,157) for loss of earnings for the three years he spent in prison based on his monthly salary before the arrest. He also asked 15,000,000 escudos (US$81,561) for lost future earnings because of his inability to find a job due to his prosecution. The government argued there was no causal link between the violation and the injury while the Commission supported his claim on the basis that his detention derived from unlawful police conduct. The Court agreed with the Commission and the applicant:

The documents in the case file suggest that the term of imprisonment complained of would not have been imposed if the two police officers had not intervened. The loss by

---

[102] 208–C Eur.Ct.H.R. at para. 12.
[103] *Weeks v. United Kingdom*, (1988) 145–A Eur.Ct.H.R. (ser. A) para 13 (Article 50). See also *Goddi v. Italy*, (1984) 76 Eur.Ct.H.R. (ser. A) para. 35; *Bonisch v. Austria*, (1986) 103 Eur.Ct.H.R. (ser. A); para. 11 (Article 50); and *Barbera, Messegue and Jabardo v. Spain*, (1994) 285–C Eur.Ct.H.R. (ser. A) paras 15–20.
[104] *Teixeira de Castro v. Portugal*, Judgment of 9 June 1998.

[the applicant] of his earnings while he was deprived of his liberty and of opportunities when he came out of prison were actual—and indeed are not disputed by the Government—and entitle him to an award of just satisfaction. Likewise, the applicant has indisputably sustained non-pecuniary damage, which cannot be compensated for merely by finding that there has been a violation.

Some judges have objected to the difference in approach between unfair proceedings *ab initio* and unfairness in the proceedings, finding that a causal link between the violation and damages should be presumed in both cases. In *Van Mechelen and others v. The Netherlands*[105] the Court found violations of Article 6(1) and 6(3) after four applicants were convicted based on the evidence of police officers whose identities were unknown to the defence and whose demeanour could not be observed. The applicants were sentenced to 14 years in prison, but after the judgment of the European Court on the merits of the case, the Minister of Justice suspended the execution of the prison sentences for three months and later released the applicants and told them there was no need to serve the remainder of their sentences. One of the applicants required psychiatric treatment for depression and suicidal tendencies resulting from the length of his detention and prolonged uncertainty as to the outcome of the proceedings. Under the law of the Netherlands, the criminal proceedings could not be re-opened, so restitution was impossible. During the subsequent Article 50 proceedings, the applicants said that they would have had a realistic chance of being acquitted if the proceedings were according to Convention standards, therefore, their convictions were unsafe and their detentions illegal. They sought NLG250 (US$125) for each day of detention, a sum they viewed as justified by the extreme length of the detention, approximately half of which they had spent in detention on remand under a regime more restrictive than that applicable to convicted prisoners serving their sentence. They said they had suffered psychological harm and their sense of justice had been outraged. Due to widespread press coverage they were still viewed as guilty, their honour and reputation remained tarnished and their criminal records remained.

The Court said that it could not speculate as to the outcome of the proceeding, but noted that there was a breach and as both sides agreed, no retrial was possible, thus damages were appropriate. The dissent of Judge Foighel is convincing. In his view, the trial was not fair and as a result of it the applicants were convicted and spent several years in prison after being denied a real opportunity to secure for themselves a more favourable outcome of their trial. 'Admittedly it is not for our Court to speculate as to what the outcome of the proceedings might have been had it been otherwise. But that is not the point.' Article 6 enshrines the presumption of innocence and provides the accused with procedural guarantees for a fair trial, which were not afforded. 'Accordingly, it is by no means established ("until

---

[105] *Van Mechelen and others v. The Netherlands* (Article 50), 56 Reports of Judgments and Decisions 1997–VII 2426.

proved guilty according to law") that the applicants would have received such heavy sentences, or even been convicted, had the proceedings against them met the standards of the Convention. It is up to the Government to challenge this presumption, if possible.' The applicants must continue to benefit from the presumption of innocence and on this basis he would have awarded NLG150,000 (US$75,000).

The standard of proof required to demonstrate a causal link between the loss and the violation is high and lack of such proof is the most important factor in rejecting claims for pecuniary damages,[106] even where common sense suggests the causal link is there. In the *Airey* case the Court found that Mrs. Airey's move from one home to another, causing her a loss of IR£1500, was not due to her inability to obtain access to a Court where she could petition for judicial separation, but rather 'by her general situation underlying her wish to have such access and, in particular, by her fear of molestation by her husband'.[107] The Court thus rejected her claim, although *but for* the violation, Mrs. Airey likely would have had judicial protection against her husband and would not have needed to move to escape him. Similarly, in *Doustaly v. France*,[108] the applicant was an architect in Nimes who spent nine years trying to collect on a contract to build a school for the city. He asserted that he sustained a considerable loss resulting from the prolonged failure to determine his rights, which damaged his reputation and had a negative effect on his ability to carry on his profession. In fact he had closed his practice after he was excluded from the public, semi-public and quasi-public projects of the city once the dispute arose and lost private clients. He noted that the amount due him amounted to more than 30 per cent of his practice for the year 1984 when it should have been paid by the city government. The Court found that the applicant 'was to a certain extent professionally dependent as an architect on

---

[106] See, e.g., *Lawless v. Ireland*, (1961) 1 Eur.Ct.H.R. (ser. A); *Neumeister v. Austria*, (1968) 8 Eur.Ct.H.R. (ser. A); *Stögmüller v. Austria*, (1969) 9 Eur.Ct.H.R. (ser. A); *De Wilde, Ooms and Versyp v. Belgium* ('Vagrancy' cases), (1971) 12 Eur.Ct.H.R. (ser. A); *Ringeisen v. Austria*, (1971) 13 Eur.Ct.H.R. (ser. A); *Swedish Engine Drivers' Union v. Sweden*, (1976) 20 Eur.Ct.H.R.(ser. A); *Engel and others v. The Netherlands*, (1976) 22 Eur.Ct.H.R. (ser. A) at 68–9; *Handyside v. United Kingdom*, (1976) 24 Eur.Ct.H.R. (ser. A); *König v. Germany*, (1978) 27 Eur.Ct.H.R. (ser. A); *Airey v. Ireland*, (1979) 32 Eur.Ct.H.R. (ser. A); *Deweer v. Belgium*, (1980) 35 Eur.Ct.H.R. (ser.A); *Buchholz v. Germany*, (1981) 42 Eur.Ct.H.R. (ser. A); *Dudgeon v. United Kingdom*, (1981) 45 Eur.Ct.H.R. (ser. A); *Van Droogenbroeck v. Belgium*, (1982) 50 Eur.Ct.H.R. (ser. A); *Adolf v. Austria*, (1982) 49 Eur.Ct.H.R. (ser. A); *Le Compte, Van Leuven and De Meyere v. Belgium*, (1982) 54 Eur.Ct.H.R. (ser. A) 7–8; *X. v. United Kingdom*, (1982) 55 Eur.Ct.H.R. (ser. A) 15–16; *Albert and le Compte v. Belgium*, (1983) 58 Eur.Ct.H.R. (ser. A); *Dudgeon v. United Kingdom*, 59 Eur.Ct.H.R. (ser. A) (Article 50); *Silver and Others v. United Kingdom*, (1983) 61 Eur.Ct.H.R. (ser. A); *Pakelli v. Germany*, (1983) 64 Eur.Ct.H.R. (ser. A); *Silver and others v. United Kingdom*, (1983) 67 Eur.Ct. H.R. (ser. A) (Article 50); *Albert and Le Compte v. Belgium*, (1983) 68 Eur.Ct. H.R. (ser. A) (Article 50); *Van der Mussele v. Belgium*, (1983) 70 Eur.Ct.H.R. (ser. A); *Sutter v. Switzerland*, (1984) 74 Eur.Ct.H.R.; *Corigliano v. Italy*, (1982) 57 Eur.Ct.H.R. (ser. A).
[107] *Airey v. Ireland*, (1981) 41 Eur.Ct.H.R. (ser. A), at 8–9.
[108] *Doustaly v. France*, Judgment of 23 April 1998, 70 Reports of Judgments and Decisions 1998–II 850.

Nîmes City Council'[109] and therefore it was necessary to bring to a close as quickly as possible the dispute that affected his profession. The Court thus considered that 'special diligence' was required in this case, regard being had to the fact that 'the amount the applicant claimed was of vital significant to him and was connected with his professional activity'.[110] Yet, although the applicant submitted evidence by an independent auditor of pecuniary losses of FF8,956,468 (US$1,488,428) plus FF170,000 on miscalculation of interest and the Commission found that the deliberate delay of the city supported by the courts led 'to the complete and permanent ruin of his architect's practice', the Court said a causal connection between the closure of his practice and the city's failure to pay was not established. It did find that he had a loss of reputation leading to a fall-off in private clients, resulting in 'considerable loss caused by the climate of distrust' brought about by the litigation. It awarded FF500,000 (US$80,092) and the full amount of FF100,000 (US$16,618) claimed for moral damages, plus FF40,000 of FF50,502 claimed in costs and expenses. The amount seems extremely low in light of the facts.

In other judgments, the Court has presumed lost opportunities and awarded compensation for them without proof of loss.[111] In *Campbell and Cosans v. United Kingdom*,[112] the Court presumed compensable injury in holding that the use of corporal punishment in Scottish schools breached objecting parents' right to ensure their children's education was in conformity with their own religious and philosophical convictions and that the suspension of a student who refused to accept such punishment violated the student's right to education. The Court awarded pecuniary damages to the student, in spite of a lack of quantifiable loss, finding that his educational level and opportunities would have been different in the absence of the violation.[113] It denied damages to the student's mother, who claimed the cost of obtaining private education for her children because of the public school corporal punishment. The Court noted that she furnished no supporting evidence and that a newspaper reported that her son Gordon was attending an independent school which used corporal punishment. The Commission Delegate had asked Mrs. Campbell to provide the name of the

---

[109] *Doustaly v. France*, para. 48.

[110] *Ibid.*, citing *Ruotolo v. Italy*, (1992), 230D Eur.Ct.H.R. (ser. A) para. 17.

[111] See *Colozza and Rubinat v. Italy*, (1985) 89 Eur.Ct.H.R. (ser. A) at 17, para. 38; *Delta v. France*, (1990) 191–A Eur.Ct.H.R. (ser. A); *De Geouffre de la Pradelle v. France*, (1992) 253–B Eur.Ct.H.R. (ser. A) at para. 39; *H v. United Kingdom*, (1988) 136–B Eur.Ct.H.R. (ser. A) at 17, para. 13 (Article 50); *O v. United Kingdom*, (1988) 136–A Eur.Ct.H.R. (ser. A) at 9, para. 12 (Article 50); *W v. United Kingdom*, (1988) 136–C Eur.Ct.H.R. (ser. A) at 25, para. 12; *B v. United Kingdom*, (1988) 136–D Eur.Ct.H.R. (ser. A) at 33, para. 10 (Article 50); *R v. United Kingdom*, (1988) 136–E Eur.Ct.H.R. (ser. A) at 42, para. 12 (Article 50); *Bonisch* case, *supra* n. 100, at 8, para 11 (Article 50).

[112] *Campbell and Cosans v. United Kingdom*, (1983) 60 Eur.Ct.H.R. (ser. A), (Article 50).

[113] According to the Court, 'It is true that, in the normal course of events, an individual who has not had the full benefit of educational opportunities will be likely to encounter greater difficulties in his future career than one who has; *ibid.* at 13, para. 26. The Court set an award of US$4,748.70 for both pecuniary and non-pecuniary damage.

school, which she declined to provide and, indeed, she had 'not denied the truth of the newspaper report'.[114]

In two cases, married couples were unable to occupy their homes. One couple alleged a violation of Article 8 (privacy and family life) and the other applicants asserted procedural violations of Article 6. The results suggest that the facts were more significant than the specific Convention articles invoked, but in neither case was the Court generous. In *Gillow v. United Kingdom*,[115] the applicants sought an order directing the government to restore their residence qualifications to live on the island of Guernsey and also requested pecuniary damages because the government refused them permanent and temporary residence licences. They alleged that the denial was a violation of Article 8 and caused them to sell their home at a price less than the true market value. They sought the difference between the selling price and the market price. They also sought the difference between the proceeds of the sale and what they would have to pay for a replacement property in Guernsey. They asked UK£50,000 (US$80,905) plus the estate agent's fees on the sale and a house survey fee in pecuniary damages. The government objected to the demands. The Court found that the couple could have retained and rented the house, but did not act unreasonably in deciding to dispose of it, so they should be reimbursed the fees involved in the sale. The Court found that the sales price could not be considered as less than market value because it was within the estimates of real estate agents. The claim for the costs of a replacement property was held unsubstantiated by evidence and thus denied. The couple also claimed moral damage of UK£100,000 (US$161,810) for severe stress and anxiety. The government argued for a rejection of the claim or a maximum award of UK£1,000 (US$1,618). The Court called the moral damage 'significant', due to the couple's feelings of insecurity about whether they could live in their home or not, and awarded UK£10,000 ($16,181).

Lechner and Hess v. Austria[116] similarly involved a government's refusal to let owners occupy a house. The applicants did not allege a violation of Article 8, but rather of Article 6(1) because of the length of proceedings concerning occupation of their house in Vienna. The applicants, a married couple and the mother of the wife, purchased the house in 1970, moving in one month after the purchase. A few weeks later the sellers informed the buyers that the planning department had not given permission for the house to be occupied. On 20 March 1972 the buyers received a permit to occupy part of the house only. They appealed this decision, at the same time pointing out a number of structural defects in the dwelling. Six months later, the city authorities withdrew the permit, but the applicants continued to live in the house until October 1978. In the meantime, they commenced legal action against the sellers in 1972—a case

[114] *Ibid.* at 7–8, para. 11.
[115] *Gillow v. United Kingdom*, (1986) 109 Eur.Ct.H.R. (ser. A), 11 E.H.R.Rep. 335.
[116] *Lechner and Hess v. Austria*, (1987) 118 Eur.Ct.H.R. (ser. A).

that continued until 1980—while the sellers filed criminal actions for defamation against them. The wife was acquitted in the defamation action, but the husband was convicted. In 1973, the buyers filed a criminal complaint against the sellers but the Public Prosecutors refused to take the case forward. The buyers continued to press this matter until 1976 without success. On 6 August 1975 the buyers asked for ATS2.5 million (US$198,052) in compensation from the city of Vienna because, due to the unlawful conduct of the planning department, the sellers had lived in the building for 15 years without a permit and the building was then sold with its structural defects. The damages action was unsuccessful and the house was sold at auction to pay a fine imposed for unlawful occupancy of the house as well as creditors' claims. Reviewing this nightmare, the European Court concluded that the Austrian authorities were at least partly responsible for the excessive time of the proceedings, a violation of Article 6(1). In response to the applicants claim of equivalent property to that which they had lost or a lump sum compensation of ATS3 million (US$237,662) plus non-pecuniary damages, the Court presumed lost opportunities, as well as prolonged uncertainty and anxiety. In the absence of detailed proof of pecuniary losses, however, the applicants were awarded ATS200,000 (US$15,844) plus ATS150,000 (US$19,805) in costs, out of the ATS3 million claimed.

The Court seems unduly stringent in its causality requirement, particularly in regard to procedural violations. Most award requests fail in these cases because of the burden to demonstrate the hypothetical results were it not for the violation in the underlying proceedings, something that probably never can be proved. One alternative would be to shift the burden of proof. The Court could require no more than evidence of the violation. If it is shown, then the burden should shift to the state to show that the error was harmless, i.e. that the outcome would have been the same absent the violation.

Another reasonable method for determining lost opportunities resulting from procedural violations would be, first, to establish how much better off the victim would have been had the outcome of the proceedings been favourable: secondly, estimate the probability of a favourable outcome if the violated rule had been observed, assuming there is no clear proof of either harmless error or the certainty of a different verdict. The applicant should receive the proportion of the amount equal to the probability of success. In cases of high probability the entire amount may be awarded. Conversely, no amount of pecuniary compensation may be given where there is extremely low probability of success in the absence of procedural violation, although moral damages will be warranted in most cases because of the inherent harm to the rule of law and frustration to litigants produced by violations of fair trial procedures.

Like the European Court of Human Rights, the European Court of Justice has a high standard of proof for allegations that the Community caused damage to the applicant, requiring 'conclusive evidence as to the actual occurrence and exact amount of the damage'.[117] It has accepted statistical evidence based on published data which are not contested by the defendant institution and which are capable of proving certain facts.[118] Damages will not be awarded for speculative losses, but future losses can be anticipated by a declaratory judgment if they are imminent and the cause is established. Damage also must be quantifiable, capable of being expressed in a specific sum of money.[119]

The Inter-American Court of Human Rights has focused less on proof of causation and more on limiting the remoteness of claims. The Court in the *Aloeboetoe v. Suriname* case first discussed the issue of proximate harm, noting that all human actions cause remote and distant effects. It is not clear why the Court raised the matter, although it may relate to the Court's concern about the Saramaca tribe's claim for moral damages or the claims of the parents of the victims. Whatever the underlying reason, the Court was not helpful in distinguishing between compensable injury and harm that is too remote from the act for the actor to bear responsibility. According to the Court, the responsible party must 'make reparation for the immediate effects of such unlawful acts, but only to the degree that has been *legally* recognized'.[120] This suggests a double limitation: the injury must be 'immediate' (undefined) *and* one that has already been recognized by law. This is an exceedingly difficult test to apply in a new court where there is little precedent.

The Inter-American Court in *Gangaram Panday v. Suriname* [121] discussed causality more directly, in the process creating considerable hurdles for victims seeking a remedy. Gangaram Panday was illegally detained and died while in government custody. The complaint alleged that Suriname violated the victim's rights to life, humane treatment, personal liberty and judicial protection, as well as the general obligation to respect and ensure the Convention rights. The Court unanimously found a violation of the right to personal liberty, but in its first divided opinion, held 4–3 that the government's responsibility for the victim's death had not been proved. It also noted that the finding of responsibility for deprivation of personal liberty was reached 'by inference'. Seemingly *because* of this, it awarded nominal damages not including lost earnings or other indirect damages and it denied costs.[122] The victim's wife and any children were to be paid US$10,000 or its equivalent in Dutch florins within six months of the date

---

[117] A.G. Toth, *supra* n. 25, at 84, n. 22.

[118] Joined Cases T–17/89, T–21/89, and T–25/89, *Brazzelli Lualdi and others v. Commission* [1992] E.C.R. II–293, 312.

[119] The Court has nonetheless awarded damages, albeit usually small in amount, for intangible injury, such as anxiety and suffering caused employees who were wrongfully discharged or otherwise mistreated. See, e.g. Cases 7/56, 3–7/57, *Algera v. Assembly* [1957] E.C.R. 39 and Case 110/63, *Willame v. Commission* [1965] E.C.R. 659. See T.C. Hartley, *The Foundations of European Community Law* (1988), 462–65.

[120] *Aloeboetoe Case*, *supra* n. 29, para. 49 (emphasis added).

[121] *Gangaram Panday Case*, *supra* n. 29.

[122] 'Since Suriname's responsibility has been inferred, the Court decides to set a nominal amount as compensation . . . Also based on the fact that Suriname's responsibility has been inferred, the Court considers that it must dismiss the request for an award of costs': *ibid.*, para. 70, 71.

of the judgment. The judgment wrongly conflates the decision on the merits with the judgment on compensation; the type and quantum of evidence leading to a finding of responsibility has no bearing on whether costs are awarded, nor on the amount of damages. The amount and type of evidence goes to a determination of whether or not the state is responsible. The degree of wrongfulness of a state's conduct may be a variable in awarding moral damages, but in no case does the amount of evidence affect the amount of actual damages suffered by the victims. It is a general principle of tort law that criteria of liability are separated from criteria of damages. Once liability is established, the plaintiff recovers the full amount of her injuries, regardless of how close the judgment might have been.

Apart from theoretical objections to the Court's decision, it undermines respect for the Convention. In the Honduran cases, the Court rightly held that the state cannot rely on failure of proof as a defence if the evidence cannot be obtained without the state's cooperation. In contrast, the Court in the *Gangaram Panday* case failed to shift the burden to the government to explain how the victim died while in custody. By not requiring the government to come forward with evidence on the treatment and fate of the custodial victim, the Court imposed a heavy and undue burden on future litigants. It signals to states accused of violations that they can avoid being held responsible or having to compensate victims if they succeed in withholding or concealing evidence that would prove the allegations.

In recent cases, the Court has continued to appoint experts to assist in the evaluation of damages. In *Loayza Tamayo v. Peru*, the Court requested from the Colegios Medicos of Chile and Peru, as additional evidence, the designation of one or more of its members to report on the physical and psychological health of the victim and the psychological health of her children. In the case of *Neira Alegria et al. v. Peru*,[123] the Court appointed an actuary and instructed him to use the figure of US$125 per month as the probable monthly income of the deceased, who died in a prison uprising.

F. VALUATION AND CALCULATION OF DAMAGES

The problem of calculating damages is complex. A court considering the case of a victim who suffers a permanent disability as a result of official torture[124] can calculate the costs already incurred, such as past medical expenses, therapy charges, damage to property and lost earnings prior to judgment. Justice also demands, however, that the court consider lost future earnings and opportunities, and other losses which require prediction of future events, including loss in

---

[123] *Neira Alegria et al. Case (Reparations)*, (1998) 29 Inter-Am. Ct.H.R. (ser. C).

[124] See M. Brody, 'Inflation, Productivity, and the Total Offset Method of Calculating Damages for Lost Future Earnings', (1982) 49 *U. Chi. L.Rev.* 1003.

enjoyment of life. Reduced life expectancy may be claimed, although national jurisdictions are split on whether this is recoverable.[125]

Loss of life produces several kinds of injury. The victim and her or his successors are deprived of the income the victim would have earned during the remainder of the victim's working life. In addition, each member of a family contributes personal services and emotional support and these are lost at death. Last but not least, the victim also has been deprived of the intangible but most valuable enjoyment of life.

Lost wages frequently are included as an element of compensatory damages where death, injury or any other consequence of the violation limits or precludes future employment. To calculate a future earnings award, the court must predict what the victim would have earned during her or his lifetime, including all prospects for advancement. This requires consideration of the victim's personal characteristics: age, occupation, education and projected lifespan, issues of fact that are case-specific. It is important to consider life cycle variations in income. A maturing worker becomes more proficient, acquires new skills and generally progresses to more responsible jobs. After a certain age, the improvement slows and abilities may diminish, leading to decreased wages. Occupation wage profiles in the relevant country can assist in determining the appropriate amount of earnings using actuarial figures. In death cases, mortality tables published by insurance actuaries are accepted as accurate by many courts in determining life expectancy. If the victim is unemployed or without fixed wage, recovery may be had for impairment of earning capacity. On the other hand, if the victim is in business and his or her efforts are the predominant factor in business earnings, this loss should be claimed as well.

Economic theory offers guidance in quantifying damages for the reduction in a victim's ability to enjoy life, something that may be particularly important in torture and other mistreatment cases that produce lasting mental and emotional consequences. Many jurisdictions now recognize the lost enjoyment of life either as a separate element of damages or as a component of pain and suffering. Several studies support this approach to assessing damages, which values the positive, intangible aspects of living, the 'hedonic' value of life.[126] Hedonic damages are based on the notion that it is possible to value the joy of watching children grow, of sharing dinner with close friends, and other pleasures that amount to more than the economic value of services.[127] The Inter-American Court's recognition of injury to *proyecto de vida* supports this approach.

[125] See J. Fleming, 'The Lost Years: A Problem in the Computation and Distribution of Damages', (1962) 50 *Cal. L. Rev.* 598.

[126] See e.g. *Sherrod v. Berry*, 629 F.Supp. 159, 162–63 (N.D.Ill.1985), aff'd, 827 F.2d 195 (7th Cir. 1987), rev'd on other grounds, 856 F.2d 802 (7th Cir. 1988) (en banc). In a civil rights action on behalf of a deceased killed by a police officer, the trial court ruled that evidence on the 'hedonic' value of life is admissible. The award included US$850,000 specifically for damages for the lost pleasure of living.

[127] Richard A. Palfin and Brent B. Danniger, *Hedonic Damages: Proving Damages for Lost Enjoyment of Living* (1990).

Various economic methods of valuing human life may be used to calculate damages for loss of life.[128] One approach estimates the value of life per year, assuming that a younger person will value his or her life more highly than an elderly person, because of the longer life expectancy. An economist may take the annual value for each year of life expectancy of the victim and arrive at a present estimate of the value of human life and/or the loss of enjoyment of living, which may be adjusted for inflation and interest.[129] The economic model also may infer the value of life and freedom from serious injury from the premiums that people charge to incur very small risks of death or serious injury.[130] Studies have been done on workers in hazardous occupations, and on the prices that consumers are willing to pay for safety devices.[131] Economists measure how much people in society are willing to pay or willing to forego to reduce their chances of dying from three in 10,000 to two in 10,000. If the answer is US$100, then a life is deemed worth 10,000 times US$100 or US$1 million. The measurement does not mean that a person would willingly exchange their life for that amount of money, but it represents the balancing point people use to assess whether a given risk is worth the extra income or benefits. Economists compare wages and risks in different jobs as well as consumer purchasing patterns for safety related items establishing the premium or higher wages that workers demand for engaging in high risk occupations. The results in the USA yield a figure of $1.5 to $3 million for loss of life.[132]

Where a deceased leaves minor children, another kind of loss occurs and should not be overlooked: the pecuniary value of parental nurture as an element of harm separate from loss of parental love and affection.[133] A child gains definite practical and financial value from parental guidance that the court may estimate and award as damages when the parent is lost through the wrongful conduct of another.[134] The intellectual, moral, and physical training provided to minor

[128] See D. Violette and L. Chestnut, *Valuing Reductions in Risks: A Review of the Empirical Estmates* (EPA, 1983); *Valuing Risks: New Information on the Willingness to Pay for Changes in Fatal Risks* (EPA, 1989).

[129] In the USA, values tend to average about US$120,000 per year See, I. Mathur, 'Estimating Value of Life per Life Year', (1990) 3 *J. Forensic Econ.* 95. He estimates the average value per year at US$121,508.

[130] *Ibid.* at 198–200.

[131] See W. Viscusi, *Risk by Choice* (1983), 93–113. Studies suggest that a typical life is worth 1 to 3 million dollars. See Miller, 'Willingness to Pay Comes of Age: Will the System Survive?' (1989) 83 *N.W. U.L.Rev.* 876, 893.

[132] A 1983 study by the United States Environmental Protection Agency, updated in 1989, *supra* n. 128, is based on economic studies of the value of human life.

[133] Wrongful death statutes in virtually every American jurisdiction provide that a child who sues for the wrongful death of a parent can receive compensatory damages for loss of parental nurture. See Stuart M. Speier *et al.*, *Recovery for Wrongful Death and Injury* (1992), s. 3:48, at n. 14 (listing by state major decisions allowing recovery for loss of parental nurture). See also Note, 'Calculating Damages for Loss of Parental Nurture Through Multiple Regression Analysis', (1995) 52 *Wash & Lee L. Rev.* 271. The United States Federal Tort Claims Act also permits recovery for loss to a child of parental care, counsel, training and education. See *Edwards v. United States*, 552 F.Supp. 635, 640 (M.D. Ala. 1982).

[134] *Moore-McCormack Lines v. Richardson*, 295 F.2d 583, 593 n. 9a (2d Cir. 1961), cert. denied,

children by a parent may be calculated,[135] based on the underlying concept of compensating the child for lost opportunities in the future due to the death of a parent.

'Nurtural' damages attempt to determine the economic losses to minor children that will extend beyond the age of majority. Courts have constructed various quantitative tests to determine the accuracy of an award for parental loss.[136] Some take a fixed percentage of the deceased's annual income multiplied by the remaining years of the children's minority.[137] Others have attempted to establish ranges within which damages must fall or constructed tests unrelated to actual loss.[138] A recent test suggests that the value of the loss of a parent can be measured through the reduction in future income the child will suffer. This may be the standard best calculated to redress the pecuniary harm caused by loss of parental nurture.[139] A more restrictive measure that has the benefit of being relatively easy to calculate is the cost of obtaining substitute services[140] including care, counsel, training, and education that the child might reasonably have received from the parent and which can be supplied by the compensated service of another. In general, however, the market value of a replacement parent does not adequately measure the value of parental nurture.[141] Replacing services does not necessarily replace nurture. Courts that award nurtural damages point to the bearing parental nurture has on a child's eventual station in life. Demographic studies confirm this view.[142] Lost future income, based on statistical analysis, appears to most accurately measure the impact of the loss of parental nurture on a child.

Multiple regression analysis is a common method of determining lost or future earnings as determines the relationship between variables, e.g. income and years of education.[143] It does not establish causality, but relationship, although causality is often assumed because of a temporal order of the variables. Thus, if a relationship is established, a researcher may estimate an individual's income range by knowing the number of years of education.[144] Using such methodology, analysts

479 U.S. 989, and cert. denied, 370 U.S. 937 (1962). See also *Law v. Sea Drilling Corp.*, 510 F2d. 242, 250–51 (5th Cir. 1975) (noting distinction between loss of parental love and affection and loss of parental nurture, training, and guidance); *Briscoe v. United States*, 65 F.2d 404, 406 (2d Cir. 1933) (parental nurture has pecuniary value).

[135] *First Nat'l Bank v. National Airlines, Inc.*, 171 F.Supp. 528, 537 (S.D.N.Y. 1958), aff'd, 288 F.2d 261 (2d Cir), cert. denied, 368 U.S. 859 (1961).

[136] *Ibid.* at 276.

[137] See *Hudgins v. Serrano*, 453 A.2d 218 (N.J. Super. Ct.App.Div. 1982).

[138] See cases cited in T. Franklin, 'Calculating Damages for Loss of Parental Nurture Through Multiple Regression Analysis', (1995) 52 *Wash & Lee L.Rev.* 271, 278 nn. 36–39.

[139] *Ibid.* at 275 et seq.

[140] See *Michigan Central Railroad v. Vreeland*, 277 U.S. 59 (1913).

[141] Franklin, *supra* n. 138 at nn. 43–49.

[142] See N. Astone and S. McLanahan, 'Family Structure, Parental Practices and High School Completion', (1991) 56 *Am. Soc.Rev.* 309.

[143] Wayne Curtis, *Statistical Concepts for Attorneys* (1983), 154.

[144] Franklin, *supra* n. 138, at 298–305.

have demonstrated that a child's future income can be based on the characteristics of the parents.[145] The most complete study that has been undertaken showed that a child's future success was influenced by the family's average background characteristics during the time the child grew up, accounting for nearly half the variance in occupational status and 15 to 35 per cent of the variance of income.[146] Such analysis should be part of any claim for loss of parental nurture.[147] There is no doubt some scientific uncertainty in the conclusions, but the basic theory and approach provides a means to compensate for real losses that are often overlooked or viewed as too speculative.

In sum, a lawyer seeking a damage award where physical or mental injury has occurred due to a human rights violation should present to the court at least the following information: the victim's age, state of health, activities, interests and responsibilities; medical reports; occupation with pre-injury gross and net earnings; lost earnings; security of employment; likely future earnings and earning capacity; cost of past and future medical treatment, nursing care and other assistance or special equipment made reasonably necessary by the injury; benefits and other monies paid to the claimant by the state or by others; likely effect of government taxes on income from a lump sum award; pain and suffering.

Where the claim involves interference with or deprivation of property, there are three direct methods of calculating the loss based on the fair market value of the property. Actual sales of the property (e.g. trees or livestock) allows reference to *market price*, that is, the price at which the property is sold at an arm's length transaction at the time of valuation. Market price is actual sale, while market value is a hypothetical price used in the absence of an actual sale. The second direct method uses *comparable sales* where there is an active and free market for comparable assets. This method usually is strictly applied and requires like assets, such as publicly traded shares of the same entity. The third, *work-back* method takes the down-stream sales price and deducts the costs incurred in moving or transforming it from the point of valuation to the actual point of sale.

Property often is unique, making it impossible to utilize direct methods of valuation, so tribunals must have recourse to indirect methods. Here, also, different methods are used. Indirect methods of valuation may or may not include lost

---

[145] See e.g. Peter Blau and Otis Dudley Duncan, *The American Occupational Structure* (1976); Christopher Jencks, *Who Gets Ahead?* (1978); W. Sewell and R. Hauser, *Educational, Occupation, and Earnings* (1975); W. Sewell and V. Shah, 'Social Class, Parental Encouragement, and Educational Aspirations', (1968) 73 *Am. J. Soc.* 559–72. Characteristics that are significant in proof of lost parental nurture are:

(1) parental characteristics including occupation, age, training or education, community or school affiliations, special skills or qualifications, religious affiliation;

(2) family characteristics: contributions of parent to the family, church attendance, participation, encouragement and interest in school activities and problems; participation and encouragement in cultural, athletic and recreational activities; imparting of special skills or training; concern with adolescent problems.

[146] C. Jencks, *supra* n. 145, at 63, 81.

[147] See Franklin, *supra* n. 138.

profits. Accounting methods utilize either (a) *net book value*, which is the value of assets at acquisition cost, as contained in an enterprise's book of accounts, less depreciation; or the value that is derived by deducting the liabilities of the assets of a company in the amounts that these items appear on the company's books of account; or (b) *replacement cost*, which is the cost of replacing physical assets at the time of valuation, less actual depreciation. The 'going concern' method values a profit-generating business or property by measuring earning power, taking into account the loss of future profits. Measurement may be done through a discount cash flow or capitalization of income. *Discount cash flow* (DCF) assesses the amount and timing of the revenue that is expected over the remaining life of the asset, less the costs required to operate and maintain the asset; this is the 'future net cash flow' of the asset and the rate at which the projected cash flow of the asset should be discounted to produce the 'net present value' of the cash flow. The discount rate must account for risk, inflation, and the real rate of interest. Any analysis also must take into account the risk that profits will deviate from the amount projected. *Capitalization of income* estimates future profits by projecting past earnings. Capitalization involves multiplying the projected or average earnings for a single year by a capitalization rate corresponding to a price-earnings ratio on comparable investments. It is accurate only in cases where earnings have been, and are expected to remain, stable over time.

In practice, litigation may centre on the choice of valuation methodology. Tribunals tend to emphasize abstract legal concepts[148] and equity considerations[149] resulting in standards of compensation that are economically invalid or

---

[148] See *Aminoil: American Independent Oil Co Arbitration* (1982) 21 I.L.M. 976 involving Kuwaiti nationalization of a long-term oil concession in the 1970s. Kuwait argued for net book value. Aminoil sought lost profits and looked at the period just before the submission of its memorial, adjusted by the addition of appropriate interest, and at the future until the expiration of the contract, adjusted down for a discount rate. Profits were projected in both cases based on the amount and volume of oil to be produced factoring in remaining crude oil reserves, facility capacity, volume of sales, prices at which the sales would have been made, operating and capital expenditures incurred and taxes and other payments to the government. Aminoil emphasized the high degree of certainty of the figures in the historical segment and argued that the projection forward by its method was more reliable than other methods. The Tribunal said it would apply 'principles of international law' that included assessing the replacement value of the physical assets and a separate appraisal of 'legitimate expectations' plus interest. It accepted in principle the discounted cash method of valuation and rejected net book value. It made an award based on a 'reasonable rate of return' as stipulated in the contract. The tribunal also firmly chose replacement costs, rather than net book value for physical assets.

[149] See *Liamco, Libyan American Oil Company (LIAMCO) v. Government of the LAR*, (1981) 62 I.L.R. 140. Liamco was nationalized and the USA made a claim for lost profits in the sum of US$186,270,000, calculated through DCF for the life of the concession. Alternatively, an 'unjust enrichment' figure of US$56,895,645 was proposed. Libya argued for book value only. The arbitrator found that the award of lost profits in the case of a lawful nationalization was not an established principle in international law. Relying on 'equitable' compensation he awarded US$14 million for lost physical assets and US$66 million as 'equitable' compensation without discussing how these figures were chosen. Nonetheless, the decision indicated that more than book value is due even when the taking is lawful. See Robert von Mehren and Nicholas Kourides, 'International Arbitrations between States and Foreign Private Parties: The Libyan Nationalization Cases', (1981) 75 *Am.J.Int'l L.* 477.

unclear because the tribunal provides no clear explanation of its methodology. In addition, lump sum settlements arrived at through diplomatic negotiation, with figures ranging from 10 to 90 per cent of asset value, have limited precedential value, because the results encompass distortions generated by political and other considerations .[150] While earlier arbitral and court awards relied on the net valuation of a firm's physical assets as the principal valuation criterion, since the 1970s there has been an overall tendency to move towards using the 'going concern' approach, awarding lost profits calculated by the discount cash flow. The cases generally approve of the discounted cash flow method and, importantly, erase the distinction between lawful and unlawful actions for the award of lost profits, although they are not completely consistent.

The following sections review the jurisprudence of international tribunals evaluating claims for compensatory damages. Punitive or exemplary damages and attorneys' fees and costs are discussed in subsequent chapters.

1. Measuring pecuniary losses

Unlike the European Court, the Inter-American Court has addressed issues of measuring damages for personal injury and wrongful death. In the *Velasquez Rodriguez* and *Godinez Cruz* cases, the Court rejected the notion that criteria for accidental death, such as those used in life insurance policies, should be the measure of loss for a death that was 'the result of serious acts imputable to Honduras'. Instead, pecuniary damages must compensate for lost earnings based upon the income the victim would have received up to the time of his possible natural death, adjusted by the fact that the children 'who should be guaranteed the possibility of an education which might extend to the age of twenty-five' could begin work at that time. The starting point was the salary the individuals received at the time of disappearance, adjusted as necessary 'to arrive at a prudent estimate of the damages, given the circumstances in each case'. In *Velasquez Rodriguez*, the amount was set at 500,000 lempiras.[151] The Court used the same approach in the *Godinez Cruz* case.

In *Aloeboetoe v. Suriname*, the Commission argued that the quantum of material damages for each dependant should be based on the total loss to the family members. The Commission invoked the factors cited by the arbitrator Parker in the *Lusitania Cases*,[152] calling on the Court to first estimate net present value of the amounts which the deceased, had he not been killed, would probably have contributed to the claimant. Total net present value thus requires calculating the age at death of each victim and annual earnings at that time, the life expectancy

---

[150] See D. Bowett, 'State Contracts with Aliens', (1988) 59 *BYIL* 49, 65 and Restatement of Foreign Relations Law (Third), s. 712, reporter's note 1.

[151] The family of Godinez Cruz was awarded 650,000 lempiras.

[152] See *Opinion in the Lusitania Cases*, Judgment of 1 November 1923, p. 363, discussed, *supra* Chapter 4.

of each victim determined by actuarial tables, and annual earnings taking into account inflation rates. To this should be added the pecuniary value to such claimant of the deceased's personal services in claimant's care, education, or supervision, and reasonable compensation for mental suffering or shock.

Although it listed the factors applied in the *Lusitania* arbitration, the Commission calculated and demanded only lost revenues; the deceased's personal services and value to the family were not considered.[153] The Commission similarly has failed to include a valuation for personal services in all of the subsequent damage claims. The Court mentions the value of services rendered in its discussion of compensation to non-successors, but has not considered the pecuniary value of lost services to successors, perhaps because it considers it too subjective or difficult to calculate. Whatever the reason, the absence of an award for personal services, plus the admittedly 'extremely conservative'[154] calculation of lost revenues, has led to substantially less being claimed and awarded in material damages than was actually suffered resulting in a consistent undervaluing of life. Both the Commission and the Court appear to equate the pecuniary value of life with the earnings of an individual.

The *Aloeboetoe* case victims and the Commission sought a lump sum of 5,114,484 Surinamese florins (SF), representing the material and moral damages of the deceased and including SF1,114,484 in material damages to the children. They also requested an annual sum representing actual damages of SF84,080 for the adult dependants, to be divided among them.[155] Although the victims were stripped of their personal possessions before being killed, the Commission failed to present a claim for either restitution or reimbursement.[156]

Calculation of compensatory damages in *Aloeboetoe* followed the approach taken in the Honduran cases and the Court generally accepted the Commission's proposals, although it appointed its own experts to acquire information needed to fix the amount of the compensation and costs. In addition, the Court sent its Deputy Secretary to Suriname to gather additional information regarding the economic, financial and banking situation of the country. Compensation for actual damages comprised both indirect damages (*daño emergente*) and loss of earnings (*lucro cesante*). A 'prudent estimate of damages' was defined as the income that the victims would have earned throughout their working lives had

---

[153] Mental suffering and shock are not included in the claim for pecuniary losses, because they are considered a basis for assessing moral damages.

[154] The Commission and the lawyers for the victims underestimated the actual damages, choosing to base their calculations on 'extremely conservative assumptions' about the inflation rate in Suriname. They noted that the actual state of the economy would 'indicate much higher figures' and 'substantially higher' damages: Commission Brief, p. 9. This approach could be the result of concern for the economic situation in Suriname or the fact that the Saramaca are a largely non-cash society, or it could have been a strategic decision connected with the range of innovative claims made in the case.

[155] The names and relationships of the family members and other dependants, as well as information relevant to material and moral damages, were obtained in large part through detailed questionnaires prepared by the Commission and administered to the Saramaca.

[156] *Aloeboetoe Case, supra* n. 29, at para. 96.

they not been killed, based on the income that they would have earned for their economic activities during the month of June 1993.[157] To avoid the problems that arose in the Honduran cases with high inflation in the country, the Court calcu- lated the annual income of each victim in local currency then converted it into US dollars at the free market exchange rate. Wages back to 1988 were computed, along with interest, and the resulting amount was increased by the current net value of the expected income during the rest of the working life of each of the victims. The amounts ranged between US$19,986 and US$55,991.

In computing loss based on a 'prudent estimate of the possible income of the victim', the Court has stated that it does not use 'rigid criteria',[158] an approach that emphasizes the Court's discretion. It can be helpful when the victims lack normal evidence of income such as tax records or receipts. In *Aloeboetoe* the victims and their families were part of a community that was largely a non-cash economy. The Court relied upon sworn affidavits of family members to establish wage earnings.[159] In other cases the Court has calculated damages utilizing the minimum wage in the state at the time of death.[160] The parties have the burden of producing reliable evidence on the minimum wage if evidence of actual earnings cannot be obtained.[161] Lacking any evidence on the lost earnings of a deceased, the Court has said that it will determine an amount on the basis of equity and the actual economic and social situation 'in Latin America'.[162] Expert testimony presented by the parties can be and has been used to establish proof of lost earn- ings or life expectancy. The Court may also appoint its own actuaries or other experts.[163]

In *El Amparo v. Venezuela*, the state did not contest the facts and accepted its international responsibility for the deaths of 14 of 16 fishermen attacked by members of the military and the police. Most of the dispute in the case concerned the calculations of lost earnings. The Government provided notes pertaining to human development indicators in the State of Apure, where the killings occurred. The attorneys for the families asked for a lump sum of US$240,000 to be divided equally among the 14 families and two survivors,[164] because they lacked proof of the exact amount of loss incurred by each family, due to the conditions in which

---

[157] The judgment is dated 10 September 1993. The massacre took place on 31 December 1987. June 1993 was selected because in that month a free exchange market was established in Suriname. This made it possible to avoid the distortions produced by a system of fixed rates of exchange in a highly inflationary economy.

[158] *Velasquez Rodriquez Case (Reparations), supra* n. 29, at paras 26–28.

[159] See D. Padilla, *supra* n. 53, at 546.

[160] *El Amparo Case, supra* n. 29, at para. 28; *Neira Alegria Case, supra* n. 29, at para. 49.

[161] *Neira Alegria Case, supra* n. 29, at para. 50.

[162] *Ibid.* at para. 49.

[163] In both the *Aloeboetoe* and *El Amparo Cases*, the court employed experts and made use of its own staff in gathering evidence: *El Amparo Case, supra* n. 29, para. 34. *Aloeboetoe Case, supra* n. 29, para. 87.

[164] During oral hearings on reparations, Venezuela labelled the sum demanded 'astronomical' and 'disproportionate': *El Amparo Case, supra* n. 29, para. 18.

they lived. The Commission proposed a different approach seeking to have the Court calculate lost earnings for the fishermen on the basis of the rural minimum wage in October 1988, incorporating increases during the subsequent period, and adjusted by the inflation index. Based on a life expectancy of 69 years, this calculation was said to represent a 'prudent estimate of the damages'. The amount claimed for each of the deceased was between US$5508.59 and US$5558.85; on behalf of each of the two survivors US$2773.87 was claimed.[165] The claim for monetary compensation also contained some new elements. Relying on the distinction made in the *Aloeboetoe* case between indirect damages and loss of earnings, the Commission sought to include in the damages claim the costs incurred by the victims and their families as a consequence of the violations.[166]

The Court applied a more generous approach than that proposed by the Commission. It calculated the amount due on the basis of the age and life expectancy of each victim using as the base salary an amount 'not less than the cost of the basic food basket', which was higher than the minimum rural wage at the time of the events. On the other hand, the Court made clear that it would be consistent in deducting 25 per cent of the total as an estimate of the deceased's personal expenses; the Court should balance this deduction with a contribution representing the value of the deceased's personal services to the family. Interest was added accruing from the date of the events up to the present. The total amounts ranged from US$23,139.44 to US$28,641.52. The two survivors were awarded US$4,566.41 for the two years during which they were unable to work.

Neira Alegria v. Peru,[167] concerned the disappearance, during or after suppression of a riot by the military, of two men detained at a Peruvian correctional facility and accused of terrorism. The Court unanimously found Peru responsible for violations of the numerous rights cited and left it to the parties to agree on compensation, retaining jurisdiction over the case whether or not the agreement was reached. The parties failed to reach agreement because, according to the government, the Commission assumed that the individuals would have worked and earned the minimum wage, and this assumption was not substantiated. The government argued that had the individuals lived it was probable that they would have been sentenced to years of imprisonment for terrorism and would not have been able to work. The Court rejected the government's argument because the

---

[165] During the hearings, the victims claimed that the Commission had made an error in calculating the damages based on the minimum wage. After further consultations, the Commission re-calculated the sums and arrived at figures between US$67,000 and US$197,000 for the victims and US$5,000 for the survivors. The government objected to the revision, calling it a radical modification that was procedurally incorrect. The Court allowed the changes to be presented, but did not award the amounts claimed.

[166] The brief listed professional fees for legal and administrative actions, medical costs, photocopies, telephone charges, translation of testimony, notary costs and other costs of legal assistance, plus publication of press communications.

[167] *Neira Alegria (Reparations), supra* n. 29.

victims were not convicted and sentenced, and therefore 'the general legal principle of the right to be presumed innocent must apply'.

The Court found insufficient both the Commission's and the government's submissions regarding the minimum wage in Peru. The Court 'for reasons of equity and in view of the actual economic and social situation of Latin America', fixed the amount at US$125 a month. In setting the lost wages above the minimum wage level, the Court avoided placing high burdens of proof on the applicants that would have the effect of denying a remedy. The Court also rejected the Commission's calculation of lost earnings, which simply took the estimated annual income and multiplied it by their life expectancy without discounting to present value or adding the interest that would have accrued. The Court calculated lost earnings based on life span and monthly salary, discounted to present value. The Commission also failed to deduct the personal expenses of the victim, which the Court has consistently estimated at one-quarter of the income. The amounts awarded in the case were US$31,065.88, US$30,102.38 and US$26,872.48.

The European Court of Human Rights has developed methods of calculation primarily in cases concerning interference with property rights, where compensation is based on the market value of the property, i.e. the price that could have been realized in a sale as of the date of the wrong. If there is no available market, then the Court may resort to the most comparable market. Some cases allow subsequent increases in value to be taken into account where there has been conversion of goods commonly dealt with on exchanges. In rare cases where there is no market value because the property is not saleable or market value would clearly be inadequate compensation, value to the owner may be substituted. Rental value is appropriate for temporary loss while the cost of restoration may be appropriate for damage to property that does not involve full loss.

The Court has held that the Convention does not guarantee a right to 'full' compensation because legitimate objectives of public interest, such as those pursued in measures of economic reform or measures designed to achieve greater social justice, could call for less than reimbursement of the full market value. In *James v. United Kingdom*,[168] the Court accepted the Commission's proposed standard of compensation for a taking, agreeing it should be the payment of an amount 'reasonably related' to the value of the property. Where a state has chosen a method of compensation, the Court has said that its power of review is limited to ascertaining whether the choice of compensation terms falls outside the state's wide margin of appreciation. In some cases, the Court explicitly has denied the applicability of the international standard of 'prompt, adequate and effective compensation' for expropriated property, deciding that it traditionally applied only to the taking of property of non-nationals. 'As such, these principles did not relate to the treatment accorded by States to their own nationals.'[169] There are

---

[168] *James v. United Kingdom, supra* n. 49.
[169] *Ibid.* at para. 60.

strong textual arguments in opposition to the Court's decision, which also seems contrary to the principle of non-discrimination. Nonetheless, the Court generally has adhered to its view that the international standard only applies to taking the property of non-nationals, although recent cases may suggest a shift in its views.[170]

The Court has suggested that it has difficulty assessing property damage due to the nature of real estate and the complexity of the calculations made by experts acting for the applicants and the governments. 'They arise above all from the virtual impossibility of quantifying, even approximately, the loss of opportunities.'[171] 'Hypothetical redevelopment', suggested by the applicants in one case, was called an 'extreme or outside' hypothesis not supported by the facts. Another method, 'actual use', proposed by the government was found equally unacceptable, being called 'inflexible and incomplete'[172] because it disregarded depreciation in value of the properties and the possibilities of improvement had the wrongful measures not existed. While the Court rejected both methods proposed, it decided it did not have to establish another because the circumstances of the case allowed it to make an overall assessment of the factors which it found to be relevant.

In most cases, the Court does not employ experts to assess property valuation. In *Hentrich v. France*[173] the applicant complained of the seizure of land and initially claimed FF800,000 pecuniary loss on property valued at FF1 million. The government objected that the amount was speculative. The Court suggested that restitution of the land would be the best remedy—without making an order to that effect—and that failing restitution the calculation of pecuniary damage must be based on the current market value of the land. In the deferred proceeding on just compensation, Hentrich revised her estimated loss to FF2,875,550. The Court did not employ experts to value the land, but 'on an equitable basis' awarded the FF800,000 she originally claimed as a loss.

Difficult issues of valuation arose in *Papamichalopoulos and others v. Greece*.[174] Land near Marathon, Greece, belonging to private individuals had been occupied in 1967 during the military dictatorship by the Navy Fund in breach of the right to property guaranteed by Article 1 of Protocol I to the Convention. The military used the land to build a coastal vacation resort for military officers. The Court unanimously found that the occupation of the land constituted a clear interference with the applicants' exercise of their right to peaceful enjoyment of their possessions, amounting to a *de facto* expropriation. It was neither a legitimate control of the use of property nor an expropriation. The 14 applicants were unable to use their property, sell it, bequeath it, or mortgage it. In

---

[170] See also *Lithgow et al. v. United Kingdom*, (1986) 102 Eur.Ct.H.R. (ser. A).
[171] *Sporrong and Lönnroth* (Article 50), (1984) 88 Eur.Ct.H.R. (ser. A) at para. 27.
[172] *Ibid.* at para. 30.
[173] *Hentrich v. France*, (1994) 296 Eur.Ct.H.R. (ser. A).
[174] *Papamichalopoulos and others v. Greece*, (1995) 330–B Eur.Ct.H.R. (ser. A) (Article 50).

the absence of restitution, which the government seemed unwilling to do, the land thus had to be valued as of 1967 and 1994, the date of the proceeding.

The Court invited the government and the applicants to agree on experts to value the disputed land. After the experts were appointed, their report was delayed because the Greek Minister of Defence refused permission for them to enter the officers' holiday village 'for imperative administrative reasons which cannot be disclosed' and 'for reasons of national security'. The applicants contested the reasons cited, claiming that the period was the peak holiday period when the experts would have seen the unique natural beauty of the coastline, thus enhancing its value. The experts themselves stated they thought the reasons for their exclusion 'have to do with the end of the naval officers' summer holidays'. The Court wrote to the parties and the experts, expressing concern about the government's apparent reluctance to cooperate. Probably because of the delays, the Court assessed the costs of the experts' opinion on the Greek government. When the report was finally filed the government contested its validity because the government expert on the three member committee did not sign it.

The report first valued the land in 1964, at which time it was partly undeveloped and partly consisted of farms and fallow fields. By 1994 the land and surrounding woods were fully developed with buildings erected and trees and shrubs planted. The physical characteristics and situation of the land and the beauty of the region were found to make it an ideal spot for building a hotel complex. According to the report, 'it was one of the few quiet, unspoilt regions of Attica and was exceptionally valuable in commercial terms because of the current shortage of comparable areas of land'. This was decisive in the valuation. The experts looked at tax records, information supplied by the government and the applicants, and data from the real estate market. They took into account fluctuations in the rate of inflation. According to the experts, the total value of the land had jumped from 29,800,000 drachmas (US$101,288) in 1967 to 5,151,000,000 (US$17,507,903) in 1994. To that had to be added the value of the buildings the government constructed, another 1,713,490,000 drachmas (US$5,824,037).

The Commission argued in favour of accepting the experts' findings, referring to international arbitration tribunals and Court case law on expropriation. It asserted that just satisfaction had to consist in compensation to the amount of the full current value of the land in issue. As of the date of the judgment on the merits, 24 June 1993, an obligation of *restitutio in integrum* under Article 50 arose and because the property had not been returned, the state had to pay its monetary equivalent.

The applicants and the government agreed on the need for compensation, but supplied vastly different valuation figures for the disputed property. The applicants submitted a 1994 valuation of 14,455,740,000 drachmas (US$49,134,089), stressing the natural beauty and geographic situation of the region. They also claimed ownership of the buildings, based on Greek law, and loss of use of their properties for 27 years. For the latter they used a figure of 6 per cent on the current value. Pleading in the alternative they asked either for the land back plus the figure for the loss of use, or for payment of the value of the land and buildings and compensation for the loss of use, for a total of 42,849,811,000 drachmas (US$145,643,630). The government claimed that the land was worth only 520,000 drachmas in 1967 and 312,000,000 in 1994. It also asserted that the buildings which it constructed were worth 82,900,000 (US$281,772) originally and worth 1,525,500,000 (US$5,185,072) in 1994. In arguing for a lower value, the government emphasized the steep, rocky and marshy nature of the terrain and the lack of economic activities in the region.

Recalling that the judgment on the merits referred to the actions of the government as 'de facto expropriation' unlawfully dispossessing the owners of their rights for more than 27 years, the Court held that the unlawfulness of the dispossession 'inevitably affects the criteria to be used for determining the reparation owed by the respondent State, since the pecuniary consequences of a lawful expropriation cannot be assimilated to those of an unlawful dispossession'. In contrast to earlier decisions rejecting reference to international legal precedents, the Court found that 'international case-law, of courts or arbitration tribunals, affords the court a precious source of inspiration; although that case-law concerns more particularly the expropriation of industrial and commercial undertakings, the principles identified in that field are valid for situations such as the one in the instant case'.[175]

The Court held that it should not limit the award to the value of the properties at the date on which the Greek Navy took them, but should consider the developments made on the property. Return of the land would be the preferred remedy, together with the buildings, in that it 'would fully compensate [applicants] for the consequences of the alleged loss of enjoyment'. If the respondent state did not make restitution within six months, the Court ordered payment of the current value of the land, and the appreciation brought about the construction of the buildings. The Court adopted the findings in the expert report and set the value of compensation at 4,200,000,000 drachmas (US$14,275,518) for the land and 1,351,000,000 (US$4,591,958) for the buildings, plus interest at 6 per cent from the end of the six months until the payment was made.

The Court did not speculate about the possible use of the land had the original owners held on to it. They might have retained it for agricultural purposes or sold it to private developers. This is in issue. The improvements made were transferred back with the land to the benefit of the original owners, without an obligation on their part to reimburse the government for the improving expenditures.[176]

---

[175] *Ibid.* at para. 36.
[176] The case might have been different had the property been transferred to an innocent purchaser for value. Although one who wrongfully takes property usually cannot pass good title, a good faith purchaser may be reimbursed the cost of conserving or improving the property for the true owner. This

The Court also faced difficult issues of property valuation in the case of *Selçuk and Akser v. Turkey*, where it found that house burnings violated both Article 3 ('In view of the manner in which the homes were destroyed and their personal circumstances, they must have been caused suffering of sufficient severity for acts of security forces to be categorized as inhuman treatment') and Article 8. The petitioners claimed pecuniary damages for the loss of their houses, cultivated land, household property, livestock and one applicant's mill, as well as the cost of alternative accommodation. The government said the amounts awarded should be limited to take into account economic conditions in Turkey, the minimum monthly wage was said to be FF700 (US$116) and the net maximum senior judge's wage FF7,250 (US$1204). The Court agreed that there should be some pecuniary award, but 'since the applicants have not substantiated their claims as to the quantity and value of their lost property with any documentary or other evidence, the Government have not provided any detailed comments, and the Commission has made no findings of fact in this respect, the Court's assessment of the amounts to be awarded must, by necessity, be speculative and based on principles of equity'.[177] The amounts awarded included loss of the houses, lost income, and rents. The first applicant received UK£17,760.32 (US$28,737) and the second UK£22,408.48 (US$36,258). In the similar case of *Mentes and others v. Turkey*, the government did make a proposal for valuation and the Court accepted the suggested methodology. The applicants' claim for pecuniary damages was based on 'the costs of reconstructing their family life in the environment which had been destroyed' but was unsupported because they applicants asserted they could not obtain records. The Court based its award on the average rate per square metre proposed by the government and 50 per cent of the surface area claimed by the applicants.[178]

The applicants did not include a value for their personal property, agricultural machinery and tools, and livestock and feed. The Court nevertheless considered that compensation should be awarded 'in the light of equitable considerations and the level of comparable awards made in *Akdivar and Others* (Article 50) judgment on the basis of an expert report and in the *Selçuk and Asker* judgment'.[179] In all the Turkish cases, the Court has been less exacting in requiring proof of

---

may become an important issue in restitution of expropriated property in central and Eastern Europe. For cases involving personal property, see e.g. *Autocephalous Greek-Orthodox Church of Cyprus v. Goldberg & Feldman Fine Arts, Inc.*, 717 F.Supp. 1373 (S.D. Ind. 1989), aff'd 917 F.2d 270 (7th Cir. 1990). See also, Robert M. Collin, 'The Law and Stolen Art, Artifacts, and Antiquities', (1993) 36 *How.L.J.* 17; H. Kennon, 'Take a Picture, It May Last Longer if Guggenheim Becomes the Law of the Land: The Repatriation of Fine Art', (1996) 8 *St.Thomas L.Rev.* 373; Karen Burke, 'International Transfer of Stolen Cultural Property: Should Thieves Continue to Benefit from Domestic Laws Favoring Bona Fide Purchasers?', (1990) 13 *Loy. L.A. Int'l & Comp. L.J.* 427.

[177] *Selçuk and Akser v. Turkey, supra* n. 91, para. 106.
[178] *Mentes and others v. Turkey, supra* n. 91. The Court stated that the methodology was based on *Akdivar and others v. Turkey* (Article 50), *supra* n. 91, para. 19.
[179] *Ibid.* at para. 14.

loss, accepting that the destruction of records and the security situation in the area created particular difficulties in adducing evidence.

Different questions of valuation arise when the property has not been expropriated or destroyed, but only subject to interference. The case of *Loizidou v. Turkey*,[180] referred to the Court by Cyprus, concerned deprivation of access to and use of property since 1974. The Court found a violation of Article 1 and Protocol 1(1). The individual applicant did not ask for the property to be valued as if expropriated, but for the loss of use of the land and lost opportunity to develop or lease it based on a Valuation Report that estimated the loss at CYP621,900 (US$1,171,473) from 1990 (the date Turkey accepted the compulsory jurisdiction of the Court). The method used in the Report involved calculating the market price and increasing it by 12 per cent a year, then calculating a return of 6 per cent for each of the years in question. The total was said to represent the aggregate of rents that could have been collected during the period. Cyprus supported the applicant's claim, while Turkey maintained that no damages could be awarded without discussing the amount claimed. The Commission contended that the report was unrealistic and did not take into account the general political situation on the island that might have affected development; it proposed that the Court award CYP100,000 (US$188,370).

The Court held that the applicant was entitled to compensation in respect of losses directly related to the violation of her rights and considered as reasonable the general approach of the Report in assessing the losses with reference to the annual ground rent calculated as a percentage of the market value of the property that could have been earned on the properties during the relevant period. The Court nonetheless found that the method still involved a 'significant' degree of speculation given a volatile property market. Given the uncertainties, the Court determined that CYP300,000 (US$565,110) was an equitable amount.

One of the highest awards the European Court has made to date is the property case of *Stran Greek Refineries and Stratis Andreadis v. Greece*.[181] The case was brought by the Stran company and its sole shareholder who had contracted with the Greek military government in 1972 to build a crude oil refinery at an estimated cost of US$76,000,000. The contract was ratified by legislative decree and land was expropriated for the project. In late November 1973, the government decided to return the land to its previous owner and ordered work on the project to cease. After the restoration of democracy, the government announced that the contract and decree were prejudicial to the national economy, probably because it was concluded under the military regime. It invited the applicants to renegotiate or terminate the contract. When the applicants failed to respond, a ministerial committee on the economy terminated the contract.

Prior to termination of the contract, Stran had filed a court action seeking

---

[180] *Loizidou v. Turkey* (Article 50), Judgment of 28 July 1998.
[181] *Stran Greek Refineries and Stratis Andreadis v. Greece*, (1994) 301–B Eur.Ct.H.R. (ser. A).

reimbursement for expenditures it had made in connection with the contract. The state subsequently filed a competing arbitration petition and sought to have the arbitration court declare that the civil court claims were unfounded. The arbitration proceeding went forward and concluded that the state was 70 per cent responsible for the losses suffered by the company. It awarded 116,273,442 drachmas (US$395,206), US$16,054,165, and FF614,627 (US$102,142), plus interest at 6 per cent from November 1978. It also declared that the state was unlawfully retaining a 240 million drachma cheque (US$815,744) which had been given by the company as security. The state challenged the arbitration award in court but lost at both the first instance and on appeal. While a final appeal to the Court of Cassation was pending, the Greek Parliament passed a law that attempted to change the result in the case, declaring that arbitration awards concerning contracts concluded during the military regime were invalid and unenforceable. The judge-rapporteur of the Court of Cassation originally recommended declaring the provision unconstitutional, but after the death of one of the judges, the court upheld the law. On remand to the court of first instance, the arbitration award was declared void.

The European Court declared Article 6(1) of the Convention applicable because the arbitration award involved a civil right within the meaning of the Article.[182] It held that Greece had deprived the applicants of a fair trial when Parliament intervened to legislate on a pending case. The government argued it was attempting to remove vestiges of the military dictatorship and restoring democratic legality. The Court was not persuaded: 'The principle of the rule of law and the notion of fair trial enshrined in Article 6 preclude any interference by the legislature with the administration of justice designed to influence the judicial determination of the dispute'.[183] It unanimously found a violation of Article 6. It also held that the government interfered with the applicants' property interests in violation of Article 1, Protocol 1.

In regard to redress, the applicants argued that only the full amount awarded by the arbitration decision, plus interest of 6 per cent from 10 November 1978 to the date of the violation, would be just satisfaction. They sought 175,869155.78 drachmas (US$597,767), along with US$24,282,694.28 and FF929,652.81 (US$154,494). In the alternative, they asked for interest until the date of the Court's judgment. The Commission seemed concerned with the amounts, its Delegate stressing that Article 50 requires only just satisfaction and not necessarily complete satisfaction.[184]

The Commission Delegate invited the court to subject the sums to careful scrutiny. The Court referred to the operative part of the arbitration award and held

---

[182] Article 6(1) entitles everyone to a fair and public hearing within a reasonable time 'in the determination of his civil rights and obligations or of any criminal charge against him'. The remainder of the article establishes the minimum conditions for a fair hearing.

[183] *Stran Greek Refineries and Stratis Andreadis*, (1994) 301–B Eur.Ct.H.R. (ser. A) at para. 49.

[184] *Ibid.* at para. 79.

that the applicants were entitled to the entire amount. It made no mention of the cheque for security or of moral damages. While it found that the arbitral tribunal had not determined that an award of interest was necessary, it should be given in part because 'the adequacy of the compensation would be diminished if it were to be paid without reference to various circumstances liable to reduce its value, such as the fact that ten years have elapsed since the arbitration decision was rendered'.[185] It therefore awarded interest from 27 February 1984 to the date of judgment.[186]

The government delayed payment of the award and the Committee of Ministers ultimately took unprecedented action in the case. In 1996, it stated that the mode of payment proposed by the Greek government failed to conform to the obligations imposed by the Court's judgment. It invited the government to immediately pay the damages owed.[187] In May 1996, the Committee noted that the government still had not payed the award and insisted on its obligation to do so and to maintain the value of the award. Finally in September 1996, the President of the Committee of Ministers addressed a letter to the Foreign Minister of Greece insisting on the fact that the credibility and effectiveness of the Convention system rests on respect for the obligations freely undertaken by contracting parties, notably respect for decisions of the supervisory organs. Subsequently, the government informed the Committee that it had transferred to the applicants, on 17 January 1997, US$30,863,828.50 in satisfaction of the judgment and that the applicants could freely enjoy the funds without interference. The Committee found that this amount corresponded to the amount of the judgment augmented to compensate for the loss of value caused by the delay of payment. It then declared the case closed.[188]

2. Calculating non-pecuniary damages

There are few developed principles for calculating awards of non-monetary injuries like pain and suffering, fright, nervousness, grief, anxiety, and indignity.[189] While these injuries constitute recognized elements of damages, they are particularly personal and therefore difficult to measure. There is no objective test to measure the severity of a victim's pain, yet common human experience recognizes the reality of physical and emotional suffering.[190] The inherently subjective reaction to claims of pain and suffering can lead judges to award widely varying amounts for similar injuries. Some argue that intangible injury is so difficult to

---

[185] *Ibid.* at para. 82.
[186] The Court also awarded costs and attorneys' fees of UK£125,000 on a claim of UK£171,041. An additional claim was denied as untimely.
[187] Committee of Ministers, Interim Resolution DH (96) 251 of 15 May 1996.
[188] Committee of Ministers, Final Resolution DH (97) 194.
[189] See M. Plant, 'Damages for Pain and Suffering', (1958) 19 *Ohio State L.J.* 200.
[190] M. Geistfeld, 'Placing a Price on Pain and Suffering: A Method for Helping Juries Determining Tort Damages for Nonmonetary Injuries', (1995) 83 *Cal. L.Rev.* 773.

assess that there should be a conventional, set figure, perhaps calculated by unit of time.[191] Others claim that intangible harms like the loss of enjoyment of life are economic losses that can be consistently calculated from an *ex ante* perspective that asks how much a reasonable person would have paid to eliminate the risk that caused the injury.[192]

The guiding principle in most courts for calculating damages for non-monetary injury as an intangible loss is 'fair compensation' or equitable assessment. The European Court of Justice has awarded damages for non-material injury (*préjudice moral*) for shock, disturbance and uneasiness caused by the prospect of an unlawful dismissal[193] as well as uncertainty, mental and emotional injury,[194] and physical or mental suffering.[195] The amounts are assessed on an equitable basis and the Court has on occasion awarded symbolic damages of one ECU.[196]

The Inter-American Court says that the amount of moral damages should be 'based upon the principles of equity' considering the 'special circumstances of the case'.[197] In its first judgments in the Honduran disappearance cases, the Court awarded moral damages of US$125,000 without discussion of the basis for the award other than its mention of equity. In the *Aloeboetoe* case, the Commission asked SF660,000 (approximately US$330,000) for moral damages to the children; SF1,340,000 (approximately US$670,000) for moral damages to the adult dependants, and a lump sum of SF2 million (approximately US$1 million) for moral damages to the tribe. The basis of the claim was psychological harm resulting from the deaths of loved ones, from being denied information as to the victims' whereabouts, and from being unable to bury the bodies. The Commission also argued that the family members had suffered a loss of position in their culture due to the death of each husband or father, because the traditional standing of each family is based in part on the contributions of working men to their parents and grandparents and their dignity reflects on the family as a whole. The government agreed to compensate for moral damages to the family members, but objected to the request to compensate the tribe.

---

[191]   B.S. Markensinis, *Tort Law* (1994), 708.

[192]   The dollar value of non-pecuniary loss is said to equal the difference between what people are willing to pay to avoid a particular risk or injury or death and the solely financial component—medical expenses, lost earnings—associated with that risk. Even someone fully insured against economic losses will pay for some safety measures and require a wage premium to run risks at work. Such behaviour is said to show the economic value of non-economic losses. See T. Miller, 'The Plausible Range for the Value of Life: Red Herrings Among the Mackerel', (1990) 3 *J. Forensic Econ.* 17.

[193]   Joined Cases 7/56 and 3–7/57, *Algera v. Common Assembly* [1957–1958] E.C.R. 39 at 66–67.

[194]   Case 152/77, *Miss B. v. Commission* [1979] E.C.R. 2819 at 2834–35; Joined Cases 169/83 and 136/84, *Leussink-Brummelhuis v. Commission* [1986] E.C.R. 2801 at 2827–28.

[195]   Case C–308/87, *Grifoni v. EAEC* [1994] E.C.R. I–341, at 366.

[196]   See e.g. Case 18/78, *Mrs. V. v. Commission* [1979] E.C.R. 2093 at 2103.

[197]   *Velasquez Rodriguez Case (Compensatory Damages)*, supra n. 29, at para. 27; *El Amparo Case*, supra n. 29, at para. 37.

The Court found that the victims had suffered moral damages due to abuse by an armed band that deprived them of their liberty and later killed them:

The beatings received, the pain of knowing they were condemned to die for no reason whatsoever, the torture of having to dig their own graves are all part of the moral damages suffered by the victims. In addition, the person who did not die outright had to bear the pain of his wounds being infested by maggots and of seeing the bodies of his companions being devoured by vultures.[198]

As the Court noted, anyone subjected to the aggression and abuse described will experience moral suffering; these claims were survivable. The Court awarded the full amount claimed for the individuals, which came to US$29,070 for each of six families and US$38,155 for the seventh. The Court denied all claims on behalf of the tribe.

In recent cases the Court has awarded an identical amount to each victim rather than individualizing the award,[199] setting the amount at US$20,000 per victim. Given that the average monthly income in one case was estimated at US$125, the sum is significant, although it is considerably less than the moral damages awarded in the *Velasquez Rodriguez* and *Godinez Cruz* cases. This may indicate a focus on governmental wrongdoing, because the Court clearly found that the disappearances in the Honduran cases were part of a systematic government practice. In contrast, incidents in the *El Amparo* and *Neira Alegria* cases were not shown to be part of a pattern or practice of violations. Moreover, the state accepted responsibility in the former case and this was explicitly relied upon by the Court as a factor in assessing moral damages. While an apology or acceptance of responsibility may alleviate the suffering of the survivors, assuming it is sincere, it does nothing for the deceased. In any event, in neither case did the governments offer an apology to the victims. Moreover, the Court made the same US$20,000 award of moral damages in the *Neira Alegria* case even though Peru did not accept responsibility as did the governments in *Aloeboetoe* and *El Amparo*. If the Court seeks to offer an incentive to states to come forward, alleviating possibly difficult issues of proof, it should be consistent in taking into account the government's attitude.

In *El Amparo*, the victims argued that the psychological damage was equal to that in the Honduran cases because the families knew that their relatives were murdered and additional violations were committed; they requested US$125,000 per family of those who died and half that amount for the two survivors.[200] In *Neira Alegira*, the Commission also sought US$125,000 moral damages per victim, a sum which the government called 'exorbitant'. The government invoked

---

[198]   *Aloeboetoe Case*, *supra* n. 29, at para. 51.

[199]   *El Amparo* and *Neira Alegria Cases*, *supra* n. 29.

[200]   According to the brief, all compensatory damages would be paid one-third to the surviving spouse and two-thirds to the children. One-half the moral damages would be given to the children, one-quarter to the spouse and one-quarter to the fathers.

the practice of the European Court, mistakenly asserting that the judgment 'normally' constitutes just reparation for the damage inflicted. The Court rejected the government's submission that the judgment alone should satisfy because of 'the extreme gravity of the violation of the right to life and of the moral suffering inflicted on the victims and their next of kin'. The Court rejected using prior cases as precedent, stating that each case must be looked at on its own facts and that compensation must be awarded on an equitable basis.

In the *Neira Alegria* case, the government asserted that the case should be distinguished from a forced disappearance: 'it is a case of persons who were charged with a crime and unfortunately lost their lives when an organized revolt was being crushed'. According to the government, the moral damages were inflicted on the next of kin by the victims themselves 'when they unlawfully took part in acts connected with terrorism, which was the reason for their arrest and untimely deaths'. The Court rightly rejected the government's approach of blaming the victim for the violation.

The European Court of Human Rights damage awards for non-pecuniary harm are difficult to comprehend other than as subjective judgments about the moral worth of the victim and the wrongdoer. *Ringeisen* was the first case in which the Court made a monetary award and it set the pattern for subsequent decisions. The applicant had complained of the length of his detention on remand in Austria. The Court rejected two of the applicant's complaints, but held that there had been a breach of Article 5(3) in that Ringeisen's detention had continued longer than a reasonable time. The total time involved was slightly less than two years and five months, which the Court found exceeded the reasonable amount by 22 months. Ringeisen claimed moral injury for his 'unjustified detention', damage to his reputation and irremediable damage to his health which reduced his life expectancy and required constant medical care. He did not furnish, however, any expert opinion or medical evidence that his health had declined during his detention. In assessing moral damages, the Court explicitly noted that Ringeisen was found guilty and sentenced to a term in prison for which his time in remand was credited, and the detention was 'less severe' than the regime in prison. Nonetheless, the Court noted that he had protested his innocence and 'certainly felt such excessive detention on remand to be a great injustice'. The detention also interfered with his ability to conclude his bankruptcy. Assessing all the factors, the Court fixed DM20,000 (US$11,147) as the sum to be paid. In a later interpretation of the judgment, the Court held that the amount due must be free from creditors.

In subsequent cases, the Court has failed to award any moral damages in many cases. The factors that appear determinative include reasonable ones, such as the nature and duration of the wrong, which normally will impact on the degree of suffering by the victim, and those that are harder to justify, such as the conduct and seemingly the social status of the applicant. In prison cases, the parties and the Court sometimes discuss the conditions of confinement in assessing damages.

Arguably, even where the issue is the wrongfulness of the detention, the conditions under which the wrongfully detained person is held may impact on the degree of suffering, thus varying the amount of moral damage. On the other hand, unless the conditions of confinement are severe enough to constitute an independent human rights violation, they are probably not relevant to the feelings of frustration and outrage suffered by someone wrongfully detained. Nonetheless, in *Guzzardi v. Italy*, the Court's determination of moral damages was accompanied by the comment that the applicant's 'enforced stay at Cala Reale was markedly different from detention of the classic kind and involved far less serious hardships'.[201] The attitudes of the Commission and the government towards the applicant's claim also influence the Court.

In its early decisions, the Court rarely awarded moral damages for procedural violations (Article 5(1)–(4) and Article 6(1)). More recent cases show a trend in favour of moral damages, at least for psychiatric patients, if not for convicted prisoners. Yet, it remains hard to observe the workings of any principled decision-making.[202] The *Casciaroli*[203] and *Tusa*[204] judgments are illllustrative. Both cases were brought against Italy and concerned the length of civil court proceedings. Both proceedings involved car accidents; in *Casciaroli* the husband of the applicant was killed, but the *Tusa* proceedings lasted two years longer. The applicant in *Casciaroli* was awarded 60 million lira (US$33,779), while the *Tusa* claimant received 10 million lira (US$5,630). The damages seem linked more to the results of the accident and sympathy for the widow than to the length of proceedings that constituted the violation of the Convention.

A few decisions of the European Court have awarded high moral damages and appear to focus extensively on the wrongdoing of the government; indeed the *Bozano*[205] case may be close to an award of exemplary damages. Bozano, an Italian national, was forcibly taken by the French police from Limoges to the Swiss border. The applicant subsequently was extradited from Switzerland to Italy where he began to serve a life imprisonment sentence on the island of Elba. The sentence had been imposed after a trial *in absentia*. Bozano sought a presidential pardon or a reopening of the criminal proceedings against him. He also sought compensation for material and non-material damage for himself and his wife, assessed at more than FF3,300,000 (US$548,409) for the detention. He based his claim in part on a rate of FF2,000 a day for his detention in France, in Switzerland, and in Italy from the night he was taken by the French police until 18 June 2005, the first date when he might be eligible for parole. The Court rejected the first claims as not being linked to the French violation as well as any

---

[201] *Guzzardi v. Italy, supra* n. 23, at 42, para. 114.
[202] *Megyeri v. Germany*, (1992) 237A Eur.Ct.H.R. (ser. A); *Herczegfalvy v. Austria*, (1992) 244 Eur.Ct.H.R. (ser. A).
[203] *Casciaroli v. Italy*, (1992) 229C Eur.Ct.H.R. (ser. A).
[204] *Tusa v. Italy*, (1992) 231–D Eur.Ct.H.R. (ser. A).
[205] *Bozano v. France*, (1987) 124–E, Eur.Ct.H.R. (ser. A) (Article 50).

claims on behalf of Mrs. Bozano who was not a party to the proceeding. The French government countered that he should be given a nominal award of FF1,000.

The Court found that the French sum was 'far from being commensurate with the seriousness of the breach' of the Convention. The Court characterized the violation of the right to liberty and to security of person as 'a disguised form of extradition designed to circumvent a negative ruling by the appropriate French court, and an abuse of deportation procedure for objects and purposes other than its normal ones'.[206] The Court said that the attendant circumstances inevitably must have caused the applicant substantial non-pecuniary damage. Noting that the European Commission had rejected complaints by Mr. Bozano against both Switzerland and Italy, the Court held that the award of just satisfaction could not include compensation for any of the events in those two countries. Nonetheless, the forcible removal of Mr. Bozano from Limoges was held to have caused him real damage, although the amount could not be precisely assessed. The Court decided on an equitable basis to award the applicant FF100,000 which it felt to be commensurate with the scale of the relevant damage, and also awarded the full amount of attorneys' fees claimed, less the sums received in legal aid.

Herrman Bock v. Germany,[207] differs from other Article 6(1) cases concerning the length of civil proceedings because much of the period was spent refuting unfounded allegations about the state of the applicant's mental health. The Court called this a serious encroachment on human dignity and awarded DM10,000 (US$5,573). In *Allenet de Ribemont v. France*[208] the Court awarded a lump sum FF2 million (US$332,369) for pecuniary and non-pecuniary damage when the length of proceedings was coupled with a violation of the presumption of innocence. The latter aspect seems to have played a key role in the decision. Finally, in one of the few Article 3 cases to reach the Court, *Tomasi v. France,*[209] the Court awarded FF700,000 (US$116,329) stating that 'the applicant sustained undeniable non-pecuniary and pecuniary damage'.

In awarding moral damages, the European Court has failed to consider the impact of discrimination in violation of Article 14 of the Convention. The Court declines to consider a claim of discrimination once it has found an independent violation of a right. In *Luedicke, Belkacem and Koç v. Germany,*[210] for example, Turks living in Germany alleged discrimination because they had to pay the costs of interpretation during trial. The Court held that Germany had violated Article 6(3), concerning proper trial procedure, and that this finding made unnecessary a

---

[206] *Bozano v. France,*. at para. 8, citing the judgment on the merits, *Bozano v. France,* (1986) 111 Eur.Ct.H.R. (ser. A), paras 60–61.

[207] *Bock v. Germany,* (1989) 150 Eur.Ct.H.R. (ser. A).

[208] *Allenet de Ribemont v. France,* (1995) 308 Eur.Ct.H.R. (ser. A).

[209] *Tomasi v. France,* (1992) 241–A. Eur.Ct.H.R. (ser. A).

[210] *Luedicke, Belkacem and Koç v. Germany (Merits),* (1978) 29 Eur. Ct.H.R. (ser. A); (Article 50), (1980) 36 Eur.Ct.H.R. (ser. A).

determination that discrimination motivated the government's behaviour. The Court's approach mistakenly ignores the impact of discrimination on the dignity of the individual and provides no deterrence to discrimination. A violation of Article 14 should be considered an aggravating factor in the assessment of moral damages because it normally causes further harm to a victim to know that the violation was motivated by racial, religious or linguistic prejudice. The Court should always make a determination on the Article 14 claim when moral damages are sought and enhance the award if it finds a violation of this guarantee.

The European Court, as previously noted, also seems to give unjustified weight to the character and reputation of the victim. All too frequently the Court's decision to award compensation, and the amount awarded, are explicitly linked to its assessment of the worthiness of the victim. As early as the *Vagrancy* cases the Court indicated that it was not necessary to afford the victims compensation taking into account their social status.[211] In other words, because the applicants were homeless and unemployed they need not be afforded moral damages for the actions of the government.

G. INFLATION, INTEREST, AND TAXATION OF DAMAGES

Monetary awards are affected by economic changes over time and by tax policies in the country where the money is received. Most courts, including the Inter-American Court, discount the total predicted future earnings in recognition of the fact that money held today is worth more than money to be received in the future.[212] In addition, international tribunals make efforts to ensure that awards are protected from loss of value.

1. Discounting and inflation

Where lost future earnings comprise part of an award of pecuniary damages, courts may adjust the amount to account for inflation where persistent inflation would most likely lead to an increase in the victim's wages each year. Predicting future earnings without considering the effects of inflation on wage levels produces an unrealistically low estimate of the victim's total future earnings. It is a growing trend for courts to attempt to account for the effects of inflation either

---

211 The government referred in the '*Vagrancy* cases' to the law on 'social misfits': *De Wilde, Ooms and Versyp v. Belgium, supra* n. 23 at 6, para. 12 and 7, para. 13.

212 The United States Supreme Court ruled in 1916 that awards for lost future earnings in certain federal cases must be discounted: *Chesapeake & O. Ry. v. Kelly*, 241 U.S. 485, 489–91 (1916). The present value of future earnings is the amount of money that a future claim would be worth today. For example, if the interest rate is 10 per cent, the present value of US$100 to be paid one year from now is approximately $91 because $91 could be invested at 10 per cent and increase in value to $100 in one year. See F. Fabozzi and H. Weitz, 'Discounting and the Determination of Economic Damages', *Trial Law Q.*, Spring–Summer 1976, at 39.

by incorporating inflation into the computation of future earnings, then using the market interest rate as the discount rate or by using a discount rate equal to the market interest rate minus the inflation rate. Discounting to present value is more commonly done, because there is less agreement over how future inflation is to be considered.

There are at least three ways to discount future losses to present values and adjust for inflation: exact off-set of inflation against discount rate, yielding a zero rate; partial off-set to achieve one discount rate (a real interest rate) or separate calculation of inflation and discount rates, to be applied jointly. Some analysts have demonstrated that in stable economies the factors that lead to discounting awards are almost totally off-set by factors that lead to increasing the awards. Thus, no adjustment is the most accurate predictor of lost future earnings.[213] The inflating factors are wage increases due to inflation and productivity gains; the discounting factor is the interest rate, which reflects both inflation and the real interest rate. The same inflation rate should be used both to inflate and to discount, making the net effect of inflation zero, leaving only productivity-based wage increases and the discount effect of the real interest rate. According to this view, the traditional method is under-compensatory[214] by failing to increase the award to account for productivity gains and because it discounts the award not only by the real interest rate,[215] but by the inflation rate. If the real interest rate and productivity increases are equivalent, total off-set works by increasing and decreasing the award by the same amount.[216] Although this method may be valid in stable economies, it is questionable whether it would be appropriate in unstable economies with very high inflation rates and interest rates that do not keep pace with them.

In each case, courts should look carefully at the economics of the situation to determine the rate of productivity and real interest rate, rather than using simple discounting and increasing by inflation. The goal of a court awarding damages for lost future earnings is to provide the victim with a sum of money that will replace the money he would have earned had there been no disability or death. Awards

---

[213]　*Trial Law Q.*, Spring–Summer 1976, at 39.

[214]　If a tort victim is given US$91 to invest at 10 per cent for one year to yield $100, but workers in his former occupation are earning $110 because of inflation, the award is under-compensatory.

[215]　The nominal interest rate is the rate observed in the money markets. The real interest rate is the nominal interest rate minus the rate of inflation: Paul Samuelson, *Economics*, 10th edn. (1976), 609.

[216]　In theory, the real interest rate and the rate of change in productivity are said to approach an equilibrium condition in which the two rates are equal. Investors will borrow to invest in productive enterprises until the return from their investment is equal to the cost of borrowing funds. If the real interest rate is less than the economy's productivity, increased investment will take place, driving up the demand for money and increasing the interest rate until it equals the productivity of investment. If the real interest rate is greater than the productive return from investment, investment will slow until the two rates become equal: Irving Fisher, *The Theory of Interest* (1930), 182–83. Empirically, there is some question whether this is always the case. In the USA, the average productivity rate increased by 2.57 per cent from 1950 through 1979, close to the estimates of real interest rates viewed by economists.

that do not account for increases due to inflation and labour productivity gains are likely to be under-compensatory. Conversely, awards that are not discounted to account for the time value of money will be over-compensatory. Total off-set, where appropriate, has the virtue of ease of application if the economic indicators support it.

In the *Akkus v. Turkey*[217] judgment of 9 July 1997, the European Court of Human Rights accepted the applicant's contention that a state must consider the impact of inflation if it delays paying a sum due for expropriation of property. Although statutory interest was paid for the 17-month delay, inflation at the time was running at 70 per cent per annum. The difference was held to be a loss deriving from the expropriation of the applicant's land and therefore an interference with the right to property protected by Article 1 of Protocol No. 1. The applicant was awarded the difference in US dollars, as she had requested, but according to the Court's calculation the difference was not the US$50,000 demanded by the applicant, but US$48. In other Turkish cases, the Court has awarded damages in UK pounds 'in view of the high rate of inflation in Turkey'.[218]

The impact of inflation must be taken into account in cases of procedural delay. In *Estima Jorge v. Portugal*,[219] the applicant complained that it took 13 years to execute a notarial deed providing security for a debt. She asserted that the delay caused her losses of 2,327,516 escudos (US$12,655) due to inflation over the course of the proceedings, because in 1981, when she commenced her action, her claim was for 553,800 escudos and in 1994 she received 772,135 escudos, the amount of the claim plus interest. In fact, she contended, the amount of 553,800 escudos in 1981 was equivalent to 3,049,651 escudos (US$16,582) in 1994, based on the consumer price index. The government argued that she was due interest on the claim only and that she had received the full amount of interest on the debt. The Court awarded 1 million escudos on an equitable basis, pointing to the very small difference between her 1981 claim and the 1994 award. The Court also awarded the entire amount of non-pecuniary damages claimed, on the basis that the hardship of non-repayment caused the applicant anxiety and bouts of depression. The judgment provoked several dissents, one of which found that the full amount of inflation should have been awarded as the applicant requested. At the opposite extreme, another dissent suggested that the contractual interest rate of 12 per cent was due, but that the risk of inflation should have been taken into account when contracting the loan and the state should not be liable for the payment where a bad bargain was made. While the dissent's point may be true in general, the applicant did not bargain for a 13-year delay in enforcement of the contract, a delay that the Court found to be the responsibility of the state. The Court's judgment appears reasonable on the facts.

---

[217] *Akkus v. Turkey*, 43 Reports of Judgments and Decisions 1997–IV 1300.
[218] See e.g. *Mentes and others v. Turkey* (Article 50), *supra* n. 91, para. 16.
[219] *Estima Jorge v. Portugal*, Judgment of 21 April 1998, 69 Reports of Judgments and Decisions 1998–II 762.

In the Inter-American Court, the Honduran judgments on compensatory damages were the subject of further proceedings due to high levels of inflation in Honduras and the need to protect the value of the award. The Commission asked that the amount of the award be indexed, calculated in US dollars as of 20 October 1989 and that it maintain that same value throughout the life of the trust.[220] In agreeing with the Commission, the Court repeated that compensation due victims or their families must attempt to provide *restitutio in integrum* for the damages caused by the measure or situation that constituted a violation of human rights:

> The desired aim is full restitution for the injury suffered. This is something that is unfortunately often impossible to achieve, given the irreversible nature of the damages suffered, which is demonstrated in the instant case. Under such circumstances, it is appropriate to fix the payment of 'fair compensation' in sufficiently broad terms in order to compensate, to the extent possible for the loss suffered.[221]

The Court interpreted its award concerning the establishment of a trust fund 'under the most favorable conditions permitted by Honduran banking practice' to mean that any act or measure by the trustee must ensure that the amount assigned maintains its purchasing power and generates sufficient earnings or dividends to increase it. The trustee has to perform the task 'as would a good head of family' with the power and the duty to select various investments that will achieve the mandate. The decision of the Court to place the award in a trust fund was precisely because it is an institution that 'is designed to maintain and increase the real value of the assets'. The Court therefore rejected the Commission's request that the government be ordered to disburse additional sums periodically to maintain the value of the original award for so long as the trust remains in effect. However, the Court did order the government to pay lost opportunity costs due to the decline in value of the lempira since the date of judgment. This constituted a real loss which must be compensated by the government resulting from its failure to comply with the judgment in the time ordered.

2. Interest

The award of interest is generally based on what the victim probably would have obtained if he invested his money during the time he was deprived of it. It is largely for pecuniary losses and not for bodily injury, emotional distress or injury to reputation. On the other hand, payment of a sum of money is always subject to monetary instability and it is rare that a prompt payment of damages will be made at the moment when the right to compensation arises. Roman law recognized that

---

[220] *Velasquez Rodriguez Case (Interpretation of the Compensatory Damages Judgment)*, *supra* n. 29, at para. 20; *Godinez Cruz (Interpretation of the Compensatory Damages Judgment)*, *supra* n. 29, at para. 20.
[221] *Ibid.* at para. 27.

minus solvit, qui tardius solvit.[222] A delay in payment adversely affects the value of the amount of money due, occasioning a loss for which the creditor must be compensated. Otherwise a further injury occurs. The award of interest should guarantee that the victim's assets are restored as closely as possible to the condition in which they would have been if the harmful act had not taken place. In national legal systems interest is considered an essential part of the damages owed for an injury.[223]

The European Court of Human Rights began as of 1 January 1996 awarding default interest when the respondent state does not pay the judgment within three months. In addition, the Court may award interest on pre-judgment losses under Article 50.

Very different views exist on whether the interest runs from the date of the loss, the date the claim is filed, or the date of judgment.[224] All interest depends upon a principal claim; if it does not exist or disappears, the claim for interest is extinguished. Some legal systems rely on the date of the harmful event or on the date of the occurrence of the loss, if the dates are different. In contrast, in European Community cases under Article 215(2), the European Court of Justice has consistently held that the obligation to pay interest arises on the date of the judgment establishing the obligation to make good the damage.

In the *gritz* and *quellmehl* cases,[225] the ECJ held that, in light of the principles common to the legal systems of the member states, a claim for interest on amounts awarded by way of damages is admissible in general. In those cases the Court ordered that interest at 6 per cent should be paid as from the date of the judgment, since the obligation to pay arose on that date. In more recent cases, the Court has applied a rate of interest of 8 per cent except where the applicant has claimed a lower rate.[226] In one staff case the Court awarded 8 per cent from the date of the administrative complaint lodged by the applicant.[227] In another case the Court took account of inflation which had occurred during the eight years since the act which gave rise to the damage.[228] The ECJ underlined that the principle of integral compensation should comprise the award of interest. Because of the construction of a hypothetical (what would have been the situation in the absence of the wrongful act), the Court will accept realistic approximations such

[222] 'Who pays late, pays less', *Digest* 50.16.12.1.

[223] In many countries the possibility of awarding interest on damages is provided by statute, e.g. France, Code Civil, Article 1153. The Conseil d'Etat has declared this provision applicable in actions before the Administrative Courts. See judgment of 21 March 1973, Conseil d'Etat, Soc. CFI Argenson, Rec. 240.

[224] See A. van Casteren, 'Article 215(2) and the Question of Interest', in Ton Heukels and Alison McDonnell, *The Action for Damages in Community Law* (1997), 199.

[225] Cases 64, 113/76, 167, 239/78 and 27, 28, 45/79, *P. Dumortier Frères SA v. Council* [1979] E.C.R. 3091; Case 238/78, *Ireks-Arkady GmbH v. Council and Com'n* [1979] E.C.R. 2955 at 2975.

[226] See Case C–152/88, *Sofrimport v. Commission*, [1990] E.C.R. I–2477 at 2512; see also *Mulder and others v. Council and Comm'n* [1992] E.C.R. I–3061 at 3135–37.

[227] Case 58/75, *Sergy v. Commission* [1976] E.C.R. 1139 at 1155.

[228] See further A. van Casteren, *supra* n. 224.

as averages and comparisons based on sampling methods customarily used in economic surveys, provided that the basic facts are sufficiently reliable.

3. Taxation

Many states exclude compensatory damages from income taxes because they are viewed as producing no gain; they simply restore the victim to the pre-injury position.[229] It should be noted, however, that if the damages include an amount for lost wages, which would have been taxable, then taxation may be appropriate. Other theories seek to justify non-taxability out of compassion for the victim; it considers only the victim and not the purpose of the recovery.

H. PROCEDURAL DELAY CASES IN THE EUROPEAN COURT OF HUMAN RIGHTS

The European Court has been inundated with procedural delay cases, most of which have been filed against Italy. The Court has selected two areas of law where speed is deemed required: employment matters[230] and civil status and capacity.[231] The Court has not emphasized criminal matters in a similar way, although the Convention itself calls for 'prompt' and 'speedy' determination of deprivations of liberty (Article 5(3), (4)). Both civil and criminal trials are to be held within 'a reasonable time' (Articles 5(4), 6(1)). It can be argued that the uncertainty and loss of reputation attendant to being accused of a crime should place these matters on a priority basis where there is a backlog of cases and that the Court should be sensitive to the potentially far greater moral harm done due to delay when one is accused of a crime.

The Court's decisions on damages in delay cases reflect many of the problems with its lack of analysis or articulation of principles in regard to damages generally, but the deficiencies are more apparent because of the number of cases involved. The Italian delay cases are often assigned to the same chamber for consideration together so differences in the amounts awarded cannot be attributed entirely to different panels. Far more delay cases concern civil matters than crim-

---

[229] See D. Cohen-Whelan, 'From Injury to Income: The Taxation of Punitive Damages "on Account of" United States v. Schleier', (1996) 71 *Notre Dame L. Rev.* 913; C. Cutler, 'Taxation of the Proceeds of Litigation', (1957) 57 *Colum.L.Rev.* 470; M. Cochran, 'Should Personal Injury Damage Awards be Taxed?' (1987–88) 38 *Case W.Res.L.Rev.* 43; E. Yorio, 'The Taxation of Damages: Tax and Non-Tax Policy Considerations', (1977) 62 *Cornell L. Rev.* 701.

[230] *Vocaturo v. Italy*, (1991) 206–C Eur.Ct.H.R. (ser. A) at 32, para. 17. See also *Ruotolo v. Italy*, (1992) 230–D Eur.Ct.H.R. (ser. A) at para. 17 and the disability pension cases: *Nibbio v. Italy*, (1992) 228–A Eur.Ct.H.R. (ser. A); *Borgese v. Italy*, (1992) 228–B Eur.Ct.H.R. (ser. A); *Biondi v. Italy*, (1992) 228–C Eur.Ct.H.R. (ser. A); *Monaro v. Italy*, (1992) 228–D Eur.Ct.H.R. (ser. A); *Lestini v. Italy*, (1992) 228–E Eur.Ct. H.R. (ser. A).

[231] *Bock v. Germany*, (1989) 150 Eur.Ct.H.R. (ser. A) at 23, para. 29 (Regard must be had 'to the particular diligence required in cases concerning civil status and capacity'). See also *Gana v. Italy*, (1992) 230–H Eur.Ct.H.R. (ser. A) at para. 17.

inal ones. The amount of time involved ranges from four years, five months (*Pugliese II*) to more than 18 years (*Tusa, Pannellfelli*) and the damages awarded range from a declaration that the judgment is sufficient satisfaction to an award of 150,000,000 lira (US$84,448) plus 5,200,000 lira in costs and expenses. In considering whether or not there has been a violation, the Court considers the complexity of the case, the conduct of the applicant, and the conduct of the government. On the merits, the Court distinguishes delays in procedure that are attributable to the conduct of the litigants from those due to problems in judicial administration. The simplicity or complexity of the case then becomes a factor in determining whether the length of time involved in resolving the case is a 'reasonable' one or not.

As in all cases, damages must be requested in a timely fashion. In several of the Italian cases no request was made for any award. The Court, as in other kinds of cases, did not take up the issue on its own. In several of the early cases, the Court appeared to presume the existence of some pecuniary as well as non-pecuniary harm, awarding a lump sum for both.[232] In later cases, the Court has taken a stricter approach to the proof of pecuniary losses attributable to the delay and almost never makes an award under this heading.

The assessment of damages seems influenced by additional factors. While it might be assumed, given the nature of the violation, that the amount of time the domestic proceedings exceeded the guarantees of the Convention would be the key factor in assessing moral damages, with a greater amount awarded for a longer delay, this is not the typical result. Cases with identical delays result in very different awards, while shorter delays sometimes are compensated with higher awards than are longer delayed cases. The period of delay is only one of the elements apparently taken into account, and seems decisive only when all other elements in the case are equal, which is rarely the situation. While the Court never discusses the basis for the awards it makes, leaving much to speculation, analysis of the cases shows several factors to be significant.

(i) The type of case   Employment and civil status cases are given priority. The few cases in which the applicants were awarded the full amount of the compensation they claimed include *Salesi* (disability pension), *Caleffi* (employee salary dispute), and *Vocaturo* (employee salary dispute). The amount of delay in the cases was seven years, seven months (*Caleffi*); 12 years, four months (*Vocaturo*); and more than six years (*Salesi*). The amounts claimed and awarded were 10, 10.5 and 11 million lira. Larger claims have been made in other cases, but only in one other matter did the Court award the full amount that the applicant claimed. That case, *Triggiani*, is not an employment matter but a criminal

---

[232] See the following cases: *Capuano v. Italy*, (1987) 119–A Eur.Ct.H.R. (ser. A); *Bagetta v. Italy*, (1987) 119–B Eur.Ct.H.R. (ser. A); *Milasi v. Italy*, (1987) 119–C Eur.Ct.H.R. (ser. A); *Brigand v. Italy*, (1991) 194–B Eur. Ct.H.R. (ser. A).

case and it resulted in the largest amount the Court has awarded for procedural delay.

Triggiani was a bank employee accused of bank fraud, forgery and criminal association. The prosecution lasted 12 years, two months, at the end of which he was found not guilty. In the meantime he lost his job and his family. The Court awarded him 150 million lira (US$84,448) damages plus costs and expenses of 5.2 million lira. *Triggiani* suggests, and other cases appear to confirm, that the nature of the delayed matter seems to influence the Court. Accusations of crimes of moral turpitude can result in higher awards if the applicant is found innocent, as in *Angelucci*,[233] where the applicant was wrongly accused of involvement in drug-trafficking. It required eight years, two months to clear his name and he was awarded 30 million lira. The Court found other violations besides the breach of Article 6(1).

Several procedural delay cases have arisen from Poland. In the case of *Styranowski v. Poland*[234] the Court held that a procedural delay of two years, eight months and 16 days violated Article 6(1) in respect of a proceeding on a pension claim of a retired judge. The Court found that in view of his age, the proceedings were of undeniable importance for him and called for an expeditious decision on his claim. While it made no award on the applicant's claim for pecuniary damage, finding a lack of causal link, the Court awarded PLN15,000 in non-pecuniary damages, being of the view that the applicant could reasonably be considered to have suffered frustration on account of the protracted nature of the proceedings, which contributed to the sense of injustice he felt about the impact of the new pensions regulations on his livelihood. The second case, *Podbielski v. Poland* found an unwarranted delay where the applicant, for six and one-half years, had sought payment on a contract for construction works which his company had carried out for the municipality and pecuniary penalties resulting from the defendant's breach of the terms of the contract. In assessing the reasonableness of the delay, the Court suggested that expeditious handling of claims for money owed is especially required where there is high inflation. It is also significant that the Court refused to excuse the delay despite the government's demonstration that it was caused to a large extent by legislative changes resulting from the requirements of transition from a state-controlled to a free-market system and by the complexity of the procedures that surrounded the litigation and that prevented an expeditious decision on the applicant's claim. The Court recalled that Article 6(1) imposes on contracting states the duty to organize their judicial systems in such a way that their courts can meet each of its requirements, including the obligation to decide cases within a reasonable time. The applicant sought an award of US$17,403,624 to compensate him for the financial loss he suffered on account of the unreasonable length of the proceedings, based on lost business

---

[233] *Angelucci v. Italy*, (1991) 196–C Eur.Ct.H.R. (ser. A).
[234] *Styranowski v. Poland*, Judgment of 30 October 1998.

opportunities. The Court found the claim speculative in nature, stating that it could not inquire into what the outcome would have been if the applicant had obtained a final decision on his action within a reasonable time. The Court accordingly dismissed the claim and granted, on an equitable basis, PLN20,000 in non-pecuniary damages.

Where the applicant in prior domestic proceedings sought a declaratory judgment, such as determination of who has a right of way, and there is little or no money at stake, the Court usually finds its judgment is sufficient for the moral harm, regardless of the delay involved.[235]

(ii) The result of the proceeding   National plaintiffs who eventually won the domestic case do better than national plaintiffs who lost and both do better than national defendants that lost. In criminal cases, the awards will be much lower where the domestic proceeding eventually found the applicant guilty or resulted in an ambiguous outcome (e.g. amnesty before judgment or discharge for insufficient evidence). In civil cases, the Court appears to feel that a plaintiff and especially a defendant who ultimately lost the domestic case did not really suffer from the delay because the judgment against them was deferred. Thus, in *Steffano*, the Court found the judgment alone just satisfaction where the applicant, a lawyer, had lost her fees claim in a domestic court proceeding lasting eight and one-half years. The Court always notes when the applicant received monetary damages at the conclusion of the domestic proceeding, but this does not preclude an award of non-pecuniary damages by the Court. In cases that are still pending at the domestic level when the European Court decides the case, the Court often reduces the damages on the basis that it is possible the applicant may still recover in the domestic proceeding. Thus, the applicant in *Zanghi* was not awarded any damages.

Criminal defendants who are convicted are also treated less well than defendants who are acquitted, especially when the charges are serious. In *Milasi*, the applicant was acquitted after nine years, seven months. He received 7 million lira. The same panel awarded *Bagetta* 15 million for political accusations of which he was found innocent after more than 13 years. In three cases that lasted roughly the same amount of time (between seven and seven and one-half years), the applicant in *Motta*, who was accused of medical fraud and amnestied, received 10 million lira, while the *Manzoni* applicant, convicted of drug offences, received 1 million lira; *Alimena*, acquitted of contempt of court charges, also received 10 million lira. In a case that lasted more than two years longer than these three, the applicant *Ficara*, who was acquitted of malicious prosecution after nine years, seven months, also received 10 million lira. Suspected guilt and the behaviour of the applicant also seemed to influence the Court in its award in the *Girolami* case,

---

[235] Compare *Cifola v. Italy*, (1992) 231–A Eur.Ct.H.R. (ser. A) (more than five years) with *Ridi v. Italy*, (1992) 229–B Eur.Ct.H.R. (ser. A) (13 years).

where the applicant, a butcher accused of fraud in meat sales, ran away when the charges were filed. The case was dismissed due to insufficient evidence. The applicant asked for 3 million lira in non-pecuniary damages, but the Court found that the judgment constituted just satisfaction.

(iii) The social standing or other characteristics of the applicant   In two criminal cases, where the accused were a member of parliament (*Frau*) and a colonel (*Viezzer*), the damages were more than double cases of similar length where the applicants also were acquitted. Frau was accused of extortion and acquitted after proceedings that lasted six years, eight months. Yet, he received 20 million lira, twice the damages awarded for the somewhat longer *Alimena* and *Motta* cases. Colonel Viezzer received 25 million lira for delays in a still-pending (after nine years, six months) accusation that he disclosed sensitive confidential governmental information to which he had access. In *Maj*, where the applicant was suspected of terrorist sympathies and also prosecuted on a weapons charge, the five years, eight months' proceeding came to an inconclusive result. The European Court awarded 5 million lira. The same relatively low award was made in the *Messina* case, where the applicant was accused of drug-trafficking and being a member of the Mafia. He had claimed 3,000 million lira, for a proceeding that lasted seven years, four months and was still pending at the time of the European Court's judgment.

In civil cases, the Court has distinguished between individual applicants and companies, refusing to award moral damages to the latter and even questioning whether legal persons are capable of suffering moral harm.[236] The cases have involved civil proceedings lasting between eight and 11 years. The Court has been very inconsistent in its awards when the affected person died during the pendency of the national proceedings. In *Lombardo*, which challenged the length of time that a case regarding a judge's pension had been pending (eight years, four months), the claim was pursued by the judge's heir, his daughter. The Court found the judgment constituted just satisfaction. In contrast, in *Casciaroli*, the widow of a man who was killed in a traffic accident, was awarded 60 million lira (the Court's second highest judgment in these cases) for a 16-year proceeding in a rather simple case.

(iv) The finding of other violations   In *Angelucci*, the applicant received 30 million lira where findings of other violations were made.

(v) Detailed and convincing pleadings   In many cases, the applicants or their lawyers made no specific claim to monetary compensation, referring generally to the Court's discretion. In others, the sums claimed are clearly excessive (3,000

---

[236] See *Cooperativa Parco Cuma v. Italy*, (1992) 231–F Eur.Ct.H.R. (ser. A); *Idrocalco v. Italy*, (1992) 229–F Eur.Ct.H.R. (ser. A); *Manifatture v. Italy*, (1992) 230B Eur.Ct.H.R. (ser. A); *Caffe Roversi S.p.a. v. Italy*, (1992) 230–G Eur.Ct.H.R. (ser. A).

million lira in *Messina*). Applicants sometimes lump together claims for pecuniary and non-pecuniary damages, providing no evidence of the former. *Triggiani* was a rare case where the applicant gave specific information on how the lengthy proceeding had directly impacted his life. He received a high award.

Delay cases are capable of being resolved on the merits through application of an almost mathematical formula, based on the Court's assessment of what would have been a reasonable length of time for the case subtracted from how long the proceeding actually took and minus any delays due to the conduct of the applicant. The result is the time the proceeding exceeded the requirements of the Convention. From this the Court could assess pecuniary and moral damages based on the type of case and its outcome.

Where pecuniary loss is claimed, delay in a civil case can impact either the plaintiff or defendant and affect the outcome of the proceeding. Witnesses and other evidence may disappear or become less reliable. While the European Court cannot re-try the domestic case, it can put the risk of loss on the state. If a case has been won at the national level, the Court should ask what would have been the value of the amount won if the case had been decided in a timely manner. What are the lost opportunities for investment? Courts routinely make similar calculations in assessing the present value of future earnings. Alternatively, the Court could award interest on the amount won in the national proceeding, dating from the time the verdict should have been rendered. The interest should not be charged to the national defendant who is not responsible for the delays, nor should the plaintiff bear the losses.

If the applicant to the European Court lost the delayed civil proceeding and claims the delay caused the verdict, the issue is more complicated. The question becomes one of who should have to prove that the outcome would have been different. If the applicant has the burden of proof, it will be even less possible to succeed than during the delayed proceeding at the national level. The delay that led to the allegedly wrong verdict in the national court only becomes longer as the case proceeds through the European system. The burden of proof will be impossible to meet in nearly all cases. It would seem fairer to make the state that is responsible for the delay demonstrate that the result would not have been different if the case had been heard in a timely manner.

In criminal cases, the results similarly can be either a conviction or acquittal. Where the applicant has been convicted, the European Court presently holds the view that it cannot order the state to release or re-try the accused. It is possible that the applicant will not claim that the outcome was affected and will only seek compensation for the uncertainty that was present until the verdict was rendered. In other cases, the applicant may challenge the outcome of the delayed proceeding, because the delay allegedly hampered the defence. As in the civil case, if the burden of proof is on the applicant to demonstrate that the outcome would have been different, the applicant will nearly always lose because the further delay makes the evidence even less likely to be available. Putting the burden on the state may be even more justified than in a civil case because delay always increases the possibility of wrong verdict. The longer the delay the greater the possibility that the conviction was erroneous. Damages could be measured in such a case by taking a percentage which increases over time and multiplying it by the years of sentence and the lost (legal) income over that period. The percentage would have to be based on the Court's view of the probability that the verdict was erroneous, but the approach offers some degree of certainty in assessing pecuniary losses in cases of procedural delay. Those who are found innocent after a delayed criminal trial should recover all the lost income and costs involved in defending themselves against the accusations during the excessive time period.

Moral damages in delay cases will also depend upon whether the case is civil or criminal and on the outcome of the proceeding. In criminal cases where the person is detained and ultimately found not guilty, there should be no variation in amounts awarded for loss of liberty for equal times spent in detention. All innocent persons can be deemed to suffer the same moral injury for each day of wrongful detention. The treatment afforded during that time may be considered only if the applicant alleges that it falls below the standards required by the Convention. Similar amounts should also be given for the uncertainty and anxiety resulting from delayed proceedings. For one found guilty, the Court should still consider moral damages, as having the charges pending for years may impact on mental health, which is often precarious from the beginning. Failure to conclude the proceedings in a timely fashion also delays rehabilitation.

In civil cases, delay in concluding proceedings can lead to anxiety and frustration. It is not clear that this should vary with the type of case, although the European Court of Human Rights has found employment cases to be a high priority. It is not clear that an employment dispute over past salary is any more important to resolve quickly than dispute over occupancy of one's home or access to children in state care. In all civil proceedings the applicants are seeking vindication of rights and justice. The maxim applies in all cases that justice delayed is justice denied.

I. CONCLUSIONS

The European Court's damage awards are clearly influenced by its sympathy for the applicant. This bias probably can be overcome with more detailed and better argued submissions by applicants, with clear reasoning about why the Court should protect the rights of convicted criminals as well as civil plaintiffs. Applicants often have failed to present detailed claims or legal arguments to support their demands for compensatory damages. As the burden of cases increases, international tribunals will increasingly need to rely on the pleadings of litigants before them. Attorneys representing victims of human rights abuses must be more attentive to the remedial phase of proceedings to ensure that the outcome affords redress to their clients. They may refer to the deterrent and sanctioning functions of damage awards, particularly in light of some of the increasingly serious violations being considered by the European Court. The Inter-American Court also needs assistance from the Commission and litigants to ensure that full redress is afforded victims of human rights violations.

Compensatory damages should be awarded in many cases, although as seen they are not common in the European system due to the high standard of proof that has been established. In the Inter-American system they are more common and even presumed for the types of violations that have come before the Court, i.e. loss of life. The amount of compensation is determined by the 'American Convention and the applicable principles of international law'.[237] The Court, unlike the European Court of Human Rights, has not stated that it has complete discretion in determining the amount of compensation for actual damages; rather it has stated that it must adhere to international law in determining the award.[238] The Court now consistently repeats that the American Convention provision applicable to remedies 'contain[s] one of the fundamental principles of international law' citing the *Chorzow Factory* case and the ICJ opinion in *Reparation for Injuries Suffered in the Service of the United Nations.*[239]

There are serious problems caused by variability of awards in human rights tribunals. First, fundamental fairness requires that similarly situated parties be treated in a similar fashion by the legal system. The inability to achieve consistency in awards tends to erode general confidence in justice and the integrity of the human rights systems. In addition, highly variable, unpredictable valuations undercut the deterrence function of tort law. For the object and purpose of human rights treaties to be achieved, much more attention should be given to compensatory damages.

---

[237] *Velasquez Rodriguez Case (Compensatory Damages), supra* n. 29, at para. 31.
[238] *Aloeboetoe Case, supra* n. 29, at para. 87.
[239] [1949] I.C.J. 184.

9
Punitive or Exemplary Damages

Remedies have a reparative effect, providing restitution or money substitutes for injury suffered, but they also require that the wrongdoer afford the remedy. The community interest in making whole the injured justifies the remedy, while it is the wrongful nature of the conduct that supplies the reason for making the wrong-doer pay. Apart from risk allocation through strict liability regimes, remedies generally are based on fault, a pre-requisite of liability. Decisions imposing liabil-ity and affording remedies thus represent moral judgment of wrongdoing, a condemnation of the act, and have a retributive as well as a compensatory purpose. Punishment is not anomalous in civil actions, therefore, it is inherent in decisions that the conduct in question breached a relevant norm and requires action to repair resulting injuries.[1] Damage awards and other remedies do not impose an otherwise absent punishment; instead, they increase the severity of punishment already inherent in the judgment. An award of punitive or exemplary damages makes the admonitory function of reparation more important and express than it would be if money judgments were limited to compensatory damages. It also provides an incentive to victims who have suffered little compen-satory loss to pursue wrongdoers who would otherwise go unsanctioned.

In addition to redressing individual injury and sanctioning wrongdoers, reme-dies serve societal needs. Concern for the potential impact of a wrong on a community calls for a response that will deter the wrongdoer from repeating the injurious act and deter others from emulating what was done. A judgment condemning wrongful conduct and affording remedies to the injured is assumed to discourage repetition of the act as well as to warn others who might be simi-larly inclined. The linkage of compensation, sanction and deterrence supplies the reason for taking money from the wrongdoer and for giving it to the injured party.[2] Fulfilling all three functions may require that the nature and scope of the remedies be grounded in the gravity of the offence and the injury it has caused or may cause. Punitive damage awards warn potential wrongdoers that similar judg-ments may follow; this knowledge may serve to discourage similar misconduct.

The compensatory, retributive, and deterrent elements in remedial awards are

---

[1] Some view punishment as an expression of solidarity for victims. The root of 'retribution' is 'retribuere' which conveys the idea of 'paying back'. *Vergeltung* in German conveys the same point of applying to the offender that which he has imposed on the victim. Note that for criminal law, there need not be a victim: running a red light is an offence even if no one is hit. It may be risk avoidance which is served by the deterrent function of punitive damages.

[2] Other reasons include the economic security of the injured who substitute money damages for losses and the general security promoted by discouraging the conduct.

hard to measure together. The sum required to make the victim whole may be too severe or too lenient to deter or admonish the wrongdoer. The allowance of punitive, exemplary or aggravated damages is one way partially to separate compensation from sanction and deterrence. Moral damages can also sanction and deter if they are based on an assumption that the egregiousness of the wrongdoing can be used to measure the moral injury. Even some damages traditionally thought of as compensatory in nature increasingly are recognized as having a large punitive element, such as restitutionary damages measured by the wrongdoer's gain rather than the victim's loss. Rulings on whether damages are proximate or too remote are another means of limiting or stretching compensation to reflect the degree of wrongdoing. Awards of attorneys' fees furnish additional reparation and in some instances are imposed as a sanction. Punitive or exemplary damages thus are only one of many means to vary the size of money judgments in order to sanction and deter.

In many instances, punitive or exemplary damages contain elements of compensation, deterrence and punishment. The existence of a compensatory element is indicated by the fact that the nature and degree of harm suffered is sometimes a measure of punitive damages;[3] however, a serious wrong that happens to cause small pecuniary loss may be under-deterred if the punitive damages are linked to the compensatory award. Similarly, serious punitive damages based on large compensatory awards may over-deter.

The retributive and deterrent functions also may be separated from each other. As discussed *supra* in Chapter 3, national legal systems generally refer to exemplary damages when deterrence is the dominant concern. Awards of punitive damages, as the name indicates, emphasize the sanctioning element rather than the interest in deterrence, looking back at the conduct of the wrongdoer to see if sanctions are deserved and in what measure. The degree of sanction should be proportionate to the gravity of the act deserving of punishment. Deterrence, in contrast, seeks to influence the behaviour of the particular wrongdoer and all others who might be tempted to act in the same way in the future. Rational actors are assumed to weigh the anticipated costs of wrongdoing against the anticipated prospective benefits. The prospect of punishment may affect future conduct. Thus, deterrence looks forward: how much punishment is necessary to reduce or eliminate this harm. Punitive and exemplary damages can be a deterrent in an amount that may be less or more than the retributive measure.[4]

In many instances the wrongdoer achieves an advantage through inflicting the harm. In this type of case, where the actor's gain may be as great or greater than the loss of the injured, the wrongdoer can pay compensatory damages and still be

---

[3] See *Kewin v. Massachusetts Mutual Life Ins. Co.*, 295 N.W. 2d 50,55 (Mich. 1980) (exemplary damages are intended to compensate for injury). See also *Peisner v. Detroit Free Press*, 376 N.W.2d 600 (Mich. 1985).

[4] B. Feldthusen, 'Punitive Damages in Canada: Can the Coffee Ever Be too Hot?', in Symposium on Punitive Damages, (1995) 17 *Loyola LA Int'l & Comp L. J.* 765–861, 793 at 798.

or consider itself to be in a position as good as or better than it was before the commission of the wrong. This is true in many human rights cases where the state may feel it worthwhile to pay compensatory damages to be rid of a political dissident or silence a critical press. An award of compensatory damages alone can amount to an inexpensive sale of the option to continue committing the wrong. Disincentives such as additional awards and non-monetary remedies, may be needed to guarantee non-repetition of the act.

Punitive or exemplary damages clearly are awarded more to punish and deter the wrongful conduct of the defendant than to compensate the plaintiff for loss.[5] In practice, however, punitive and exemplary damages also sometimes compensate for losses that are difficult to prove or impossible to measure or when the rules of damages do not bring sufficient relief. Such awards encourage victims to bring public interest actions as 'private attorneys general'. An incentive may be especially justified when no criminal prosecution is possible and punishment is necessary for retributive purposes.[6] Society as a whole benefits when victims of human rights violations are encouraged to bring actions as private attorneys general. An award of punitive or exemplary damages offers an incentive to the victim who risks bringing the action, allowing cases to go forward that otherwise would not be pursued.

It also has been suggested that large damage awards are necessary to counterbalance the likelihood of wrongdoers escaping without liability[7] or the expectation of wrongdoers that they never will be caught and held liable. If only half the cases of wrongdoing are brought and proven then damages should double to deter adequately. Failure to provide punitive damages where there is a large likelihood of wrongdoers not being held accountable could lead victims denied relief to undertake self-help to avoid future injury, e.g. from armed rebellion to departure and requests for asylum. To deter, the optimal magnitude of damages thus depends upon the wrongdoer's gain, the victim's harm, and the probability of escaping liability. The higher the probability of escaping condemnation, the higher the total award should be and the larger the ratio of the punitive to the compensatory component in the total award.

---

[5] The United States Restatement Second of Torts, s. 908 provides:

'(1) Punitive damages are damages, other than compensatory or nominal damages, awarded against a person to punish him for his outrageous conduct and to deter him and others like him from similar conduct in the future.

(2) Punitive damages may be awarded for conduct that is outrageous, because of the defendant's evil motive or his reckless indifference to the rights of others. In assessing punitive damages, the trier of fact can properly consider the character of the defendant's act, the nature and extent of the harm to the plaintiff that the defendant caused or intended to cause and the wealth of the defendant'.

Punitive damages have also been described as private fines levied by civil juries to punish reprehensible conduct and to deter its future occurrence: *Gertz v. Robert Welch, Inc*, 418 U.S. 323, 350; 94 S.Ct. 2997, 3012, 41 L.Ed.2d 789 (1974).

[6] Friefield, 'The Rationale of Punitive Damages', (1935) 1 *Ohio St.L.J.* 5, 6–9.

[7] Darryl Biggar, 'A Model of Punitive Damages in Tort', (1995) 15 *Int'L Rev. of Law and Economics* 1.

The legitimacy of awarding punitive or exemplary damages in civil cases in order to deter and punish morally reprehensible behaviour is enshrined in many legal systems, as described *supra* in Chapter 3. The general requirement is that the conduct of the defendant be malicious, reckless, oppressive, abusive, evil, wicked or so gross that some type of deterrent or punishment is necessary. As the language used may indicate, punitive damages are not routinely granted; indeed recent studies demonstrate that they are sparingly awarded[8] and they are often reduced on appeal. Strong opposition to punitive damages also exists within states,[9] one judge claiming that punitive damages are awarded in practice only against '(1) really stupid defendants; (2) really mean defendants; (3) really stupid defendants who could have caused a great deal of harm by their actions but who actually caused minimal harm'.[10] They are seen as particularly objectionable in cases of systematic or mass violations where the same defendant could be repeatedly punished for the same course of conduct.[11]

The main objection raised to punitive damages is that they are criminal or quasi-criminal in nature and have no place in a civil action the object of which is to restore the victim to the position he would have been in had the wrong not occurred. In this regard, some argue that punitive damages violate the principle of *nullum crimine sine lege*, by establishing criminal penalties with a lower burden of proof than is required by criminal law.[12] In response, it may be noted that civil fines are common in most legal systems and are not subject to the

---

[8] R.A. Brand, 'Punitive Damages and the Recognition of Judgments', (1996) XLIII *NILR* 143, 156 n. 86. In product liability, where there are nearly 22,000 deaths and 30 million injuries in the USA each year, there have been only 355 punitive damage awards between 1965–1990. In more than one-third of those cases, the compensatory damages were actually larger than the punitive damages. In almost every case where punitive damages were awarded, the plaintiff was seriously injured or killed and there was evidence of knowing misconduct.

[9] The judge in the American case of *Fay v. Parker* spoke of punitive damages as 'a monstrous heresy . . . an unsightly and an unhealthy excrescence, deforming the symmetry of the body of the law': *Fay v. Parker* 53 N.H. 342, 382 (1873).

[10] 187 W.Va. at 474–475, 419 S.E.2d at 887. The United States Uniform Law Commission issued a draft Model Punitive Damages Act on 6 February 1996 in which it discussed the concern that awards often bear no relation to deterrence and merely reflect dissatisfaction with a defendant and a desire to punish without regard to the true harm threatened. The model does not define the types of cases in which the award may be made but provides that a defendant may be liable for punitive damages where the harm was intentional or of high risk or it was certain that harm would result; was malicious or fraudulent or constituted a conscious and flagrant disregard for the rights or interests of others; and an award should be made for the purpose of punishing the defendant for the conduct or deterring the defendant and others from similar conduct in like circumstances (s. 5).

[11] In asbestos litigation in the USA there are at least 9,000 cases. See *Juzwin v. Amtorg Trading Corp.* 705 F.Supp. 1953 (D.N.J. 1989).

[12] B.S. Markensinis, *A Comparative Introduction to the German Law of Torts*, 3rd edn. (1994), 90. Concern that the evidentiary and procedural safeguards of criminal law, designed to protect the accused, are circumvented by civil law imposition of penalties, is said to explain the reluctance of Australian courts to award exemplary damages, even though the law permits them to be awarded in cases where the defendant engaged in conscious wrongdoing in outrageous disregard of another's rights. Further, such awards are deemed to allow the plaintiff to profit from the wrongdoing: Michael Tilbury and Harold Luntz, 'Punitive Damages in Australia', in *Symposium on Punitive Damages*, *supra* n.4, at 771.

requirements of criminal procedure. In addition, because the stigma of a civil damage award is not as serious as that of a criminal conviction, lower standards of proof should not be seen as a serious problem.[13] Critics assert that even if punishment is an appropriate goal of the civil law, that is no reason why the victim should receive the windfall. The injury is the moral outrage of society.[14] Some systems remedy this by removing all or a portion of the award from the injured party.[15]

A. ENTERPRISE LIABILITY

When the state is the defendant, punitive damages may provoke objection because the underlying claim is based on 'enterprise liability', with damages assessed against the state as a whole and enforced against the public treasury, where they are said to fall on the 'innocent' who have had no direct involvement in the misconduct.[16] Punishment is founded in conceptions of fairness or just desserts,[17] demanding that elements of fairness be kept in mind in imposing sanctions. In the case of governmental enterprise liability, some view damages based on vicarious liability as an 'unfair' basis for punishment because no one should be held to account for another's wrongdoing. On the other hand, enterprise liability is often based on fault, on failure to take action to prevent the wrong or the subsequent condoning of the wrongful acts of agents. Where the principal is at fault, enterprise liability is clearly appropriate and punitive damages may be necessary.

The aim of deterrence also suggests that punitive damages may be appropriate in an enterprise context. In the corporate world, courts have stressed that losses to shareholders occasioned by punitive damages may be useful to encourage shareholders to take an active role in overseeing corporate activity and in choosing corporate officers and policy.[18] Similarly, on the basis of deterrence, the law may impose liability for wrongs committed by state agents because the state employer is in a position to control the activities of the employee. The state has the capacity and is likely to punish wrongdoing by agents if the state will have to pay for any damage caused. If states are likely to punish, then punitive damages may have

---

[13] *Symposium on Punitive Damages*, at 760

[14] See J. Ingram, 'Punitive Damages Should be Abolished', (1988) 17 *Capital U.L.Rev.* 205.

[15] B.S. Markensenis, *supra* n. 12, at 691. Nine states in the USA have enacted statutes that designate that a portion of any punitive award goes to the state (from 20 per cent in New York to 75 per cent in Iowa and Georgia). Another recently developed idea is that the punitive element of the award goes to charity.

[16] This is also true of compensatory damages, but as between the public and the victim, justice requires compensating the victim for actual losses.

[17] Gary Schwartz, 'Deterrence and Punishment in the Common Law of Punitive Damages: A Comment' (1982) 56 *S. Cal.L.Rev.*133.

[18] See e.g. *Martin v. Johns-Manville Corp.* 469 A.2d 655, 666–67 (Pa. 1983); *Wangen v. Ford Motor Co.* 294 N.W.2d 437, 453–54 (Wis. 1980).

a role to play, especially when compensatory damages are likely to be inconsequential. Non-punishment could even amount to condoning or ratifying the wrong. More generally, punitive damages may be needed and appropriate to ensure citizen scrutiny of government if, as some argue, imposing such liability will encourage greater care in selecting, training and electing officials.

It is worth recalling that punitive damages originated in cases of outrageous abuses of authority by government officers.[19] In the first case in English common law awarding punitive damages, Woods and the king's messengers ransacked Wilkes' house because of a 'libelous' pamphlet he had published. The instructions to the jury specifically authorized damages that would punish the defendant and deter future misconduct. The judge found the common law allowed the possibility of punitive damages:

I still continue of the same mind, that a jury have it in their power to give damages for more than the injury received. Damages are designed not only as a satisfaction to the injured person, but likewise as a punishment to the guilty, to deter from any such proceeding for the future, and as a proof of the detestation of the jury to the action itself. [20]

Another early judgment, *Huckle v. Money*,[21] awarded exemplary damages in order to fine the Crown for false imprisonment. The award of UK£300 was the equivalent of nearly two year's salary for the journeyman printer taken into custody in the course of a raid on a newspaper. He was held in custody for only about six hours and was treated 'very civilly'. The rationale is worth quoting at length:

[T]the personal injury done to [the plaintiff] was very small, so that if the jury had been confined by their oath to consider the mere personal injury only, perhaps 20 pounds damages would have been thought sufficient; but the small injury done to the plaintiff, or the inconsiderableness of his station and rank in life did not appear to the jury in that striking light in which the great point of law touching the liberty of the subject appeared to them at the trial; they saw a magistrate over all the King's subjects, exercising arbitrary power, violating Magna Charta, and attempting to destroy the liberty of the kingdom, by insisting upon the legality of this general warrant before them; they heard the King's Counsel, and saw the solicitor of the Treasury endeavouring to support and maintain the legality of the warrant in a tyrannical and severe manner. These are the ideas which struck the jury on the trial and I think they have done right in giving exemplary damages.

More recently, in *Rookes v. Barnard*[22] Lord Devlin's opinion concluded that only three categories of cases exist 'in which an award of exemplary damages can serve a useful purpose in vindicating the strength of the law and thus affording a practical justification for admitting into the civil [law] a principle which ought logically to belong to the criminal'.[23] The first of these are cases in which there

---

[19] *Wilkes v. Wood*, 98 Eng.Rep. 489 (C.P. 1763).   [20] *Ibid.*

[21] *Huckle v. Money*, 95 Eng.Rep. 2 Wils. K.B. 206, 95 Eng. Rep. 768 (C.P. 1763).

[22] *Rookes v. Barnard*, [1964] A.C. 1129.   [23] *Ibid.* at 1226.

is 'oppressive, arbitrary or unconstitutional action by servants of the government'. There are general guidelines for such an exceptional award: (1) the plaintiff must be the victim of the punishable behaviour; (2) the amounts of the awards are limited and (3) the means of the parties are relevant in the assessment. The House of Lords confirmed this analysis in *Broome v. Cassell & Co.*[24]

As these decisions reflect, compensatory remedies may not suffice to provide in full the needed redress for human rights violations, because they derive from a private law system that aims only to remedy the wrongdoer's unlawful conduct committed against one victim. Human rights procedures, in contrast, are also compliance mechanisms that aim to fulfil the public policy of upholding the constitutional or treaty regime and the community interest in respect for human rights. Punitive damages allow expression of moral outrage in response to illegal conduct and send a signal that outrageous violations may carry a high price, a valuable mechanism at least until the establishment of the international criminal court where perpetrators can be brought to justice.

It may be particularly important to consider punitive damages in cases of systematic wrongdoing, where a deliberate course of conduct is involved, although these are precisely the cases where public funds may be inadequate to provide even compensatory damages to each victim.[25] Patterns or practices of wrongdoing and the wealth of the wrongdoer are relevant to awards of punitive or exemplary damages because the objective is to make the violation too costly to repeat.[26] In some cases, an enhanced award against the state could encourage a civil indemnification or criminal action against the perpetrators, in order to limit assessment of damages against 'innocent' tax-payers. The state may in fact be obliged to take action against the wrongdoer as part of its reparations obligation.

B. AWARDS OF PUNITIVE DAMAGES IN HUMAN RIGHTS CASES

Neither the European nor the Inter-American Court has to this point awarded punitive damages. In the European Court of Human Rights, applicants first argued for an award of exemplary damages in the case of *Silver v. United Kingdom*, citing *Rookes v. Barnard*.[27] They admitted that the European Court is not bound by precedents in domestic law relating to the award of damages but argued in favour of them when it is a question of government misconduct. The Court denied the request without discussion. More recently, in the series of cases brought against Turkey, the applicants regularly have included requests for puni-

---

[24] *Broome v. Cassell & Co* [1972] App. Cas. 1027.
[25] Contrast Canada (generally cannot punish for course of conduct) and the USA (awards are given for a general course of conduct). See Ontario Law Reform Commission, *Report on Exemplary Damages* (1991), 14–15.
[26] *TXO Production Corp. v. Alliance Resources Corp.* 113 S.Ct. 2711 (1993).
[27] [1964] A.C. 1129 at 1226.

tive and aggravated damages on the basis that the acts complained of were egregious and deliberate violations of the most fundamental rights, including life, freedom from torture and cruel, inhuman and degrading treatment, and home and private life.[28] The Court regularly has rejected the claims without comment.

In the Inter-American system, in the *Velasquez Rodriguez* and *Godinez Cruz* cases, the Commission specifically requested punitive damages in the amount of 2,422,000 Honduran lempiras 'because the case involved extremely serious violations of human rights'.[29] The Court rejected the claim, finding that the expression 'fair compensation' used in Article 63(1) is compensatory in nature and not punitive. More broadly and incorrectly, the Court added, 'this principle is not applicable in international law at this time'.[30]

The European Court has a stronger textual basis to award punitive damages, as there is clear precedent for punitive damages in the arbitral decisions on state responsibility for injury to aliens. The term 'satisfaction' has a broader meaning than is reflected in the judgments of the European Court. The Inter-American Court, for its part, will have more difficulty finding a basis in the language of Article 63 which allows it to (1) rule that the injured party be ensured the enjoyment of his right or freedom that was violated; (2) rule that the consequences of the measure or situation that constituted the breach be remedied; and (3) rule that fair compensation be paid to the injured party. The Court would have to determine it has inherent power to develop the remedies necessary to fulfil the object and purpose of the system. As it has already expanded its powers in various ways, this is not impossible, although it is unlikely. In the Inter-American system, the few sanctions taken for human rights violations have been decided by political organs of the Organization of American States.[31]

---

[28] See, e.g. *Selçuk and Asker v. Turkey*, Judgment of 24 April 1998, 71 Reports of Judgments and Decisions 1988–II, 891 at para. 119. The Court found violations of Article 3 and 8 due to the burning of the applicants' homes. Each applicant sought UK£10,000 in punitive damages and UK£10,000 in aggravated damages. The Court denied each claim without comment. In *Aydin v. Turkey*, 27 September 1997, a case of rape and other mistreatment of a detainee, the applicant asked for UK£30,000 to be paid to a charitable institution in Turkey by way of aggravated damages for the practice of ill-treatment and intimidation as well as UK£30,000 in punitive damages. The Commission argued that the award should be significant in light of the gravity of the violation, without direct comment on the concept of punitive or aggravated damages. In *Mentes and others v. Turkey*, Judgment of 24 July 1998 (Article 50) each applicant claimed UK£30,000 in moral damages, UK£15,000 in punitive damages, and UK£20,000 in aggravated damages because they were the victims of an administrative practice. They submitted that the award should reflect the character of the violations and the need for deterrence. The Court explicitly rejected the claims for punitive and aggravated damages, but agreed with an award for non-pecuniary damage, 'bearing in mind the seriousness of the violations': para. 20. See also, *Akdivar and others v. Turkey,* Judgment of 1 April 1998 (Article 50), Reports 1998–II, para. 38 and *Tekin v. Turkey*, Judgment of 9 June 1998 (treatment in police custody and conditions of confinement a violation of Article 3; claim of UK£25,000 aggravated damages rejected, but UK£10,000 awarded in moral damages).

[29] *Velasquez Rodriguez Case, (Compensatory Damages)*, (1990), 7 Inter-Am.Ct.H.R.(ser. C) para. 37.

[30] *Ibid.* at para. 38.

[31] See, e.g., Resolution II of the XVII Meeting of Consultation of Ministers of Foreign Affairs,

In the EU, while punitive damages may not be required by EU directives, it seems clear that they may be acceptable in some instances, although they have not been awarded by the ECJ. In the *von Colson* and *Harz* cases,[32] the ECJ was called on to consider whether the damages as sanctions laid down in German legislation purporting to implement the 1976 Equal Treatment Directive complied with the requirements of Article 6 of that Directive.[33] The German law confined damages in cases of discriminatory hiring to the loss incurred as a result of reliance on a belief that there would be no discrimination, an amount that was found to be travel expenses of DM7.20 in the *Von Colson* case and DM2.31 in *Harz*. The German courts referred several questions concerning the adequacy of their remedies to the ECJ. The Court replied that Article 6 of the Directive requires member states 'to adopt measures which are sufficiently effective to achieve the objective of the directive and to ensure that those measures may in fact be relied on before the national courts by the persons concerned'.[34] Access to judicial process in the Court's view, required access to 'effective judicial protection' such as provisions requiring adequate financial compensation, backed up where necessary by a system of fines or offering a post to the person subject to discrimination. The choice was left to the state, provided an appropriate system of sanctions was imposed. This system of sanctions had to be sufficient 'to guarantee real and effective judicial protection. Moreover, it must also have a real deterrent effect on the employer. It follows that where a Member State chooses to penalize the breach of a prohibition of discrimination by the award of compensation, that compensation must in any event be adequate in relation to the damage sustained'.[35]

Administrative tribunals have awarded punitive damages in rare cases. In *Bluske v. WIPO*,[36] the International Labor Organization Administrative Tribunal ordered the organization to pay the complainant 10,000 Swiss francs by way of penalty for each month of delay in discharging its obligation to decide on the applicant's reinstatement.

International human rights litigation in United States courts has resulted in

which addressed human rights violations by the Somoza regime of Nicaragua and which called for 'immediate and definitive replacement of the Somoza regime' and urged member states to take steps to 'facilitate an enduring and peaceful solution of the Nicaraguan problem' on that basis: OAS Doc. OEA/Ser.F/II.17, Doc. 40/79, rev. 2 at 1–2 (1979).

[32] Case 14/83, *Von Colson and Kamann v. Land Nordrhein-Westfalen*, [1984] E.C.R. 1891; Case 79/83, *Harz v. Deutsche Tradax GmbH* [1984] E.C.R. 1921. See J. Steiner, 'EEC Directives: A New Route to Enforcement?', (1985) 101 *Law Q.Rev.* 491; A. Arnull, '*Sanctioning Discrimination*', (1984) 9 *Eur.L.Rev.* 267; D. Curtin, 'Effective Sanctions and the Equal Treatment Directive: the von Colson and Harz Cases', (1985), 22 *Common Market L.Rev* 505.

[33] Christopher McCrudden, 'The Effectiveness of European Equality Law: National Mechanisms for Enforcing Gender Equality Law in the Light of European Requirements', (1993) 13 *Oxford J. Legal Studies* 320, 342–44.

[34] Von Colson, *supra* n. 32, at para. 18.

[35] *Ibid.* at para. 23.

[36] *Bluske v. WIPO*, ILOAT judgment No. 1362 of 13 July 1994.

awards of substantial punitive damages. In *Filartiga v. Pena-Irala*,[37] an action brought under the United States Alien Tort Claims Act, the judge awarded punitive damages against a Paraguayan torturer. A magistrate first recommended that such damages be denied on the ground that they are not recoverable under the Paraguayan Civil Code, noting that 'Paraguayan law, in determining the intensity and duration of the suffering, and the consequent "moral" damages, takes into account the heinous nature of the tort. The magistrate found that Paraguayan moral damages are not designed to punish, however, but to compensate for the greater pain caused by the atrocious nature of the act'.[38] The District Court overruled the magistrate, finding that damage awards must be based on international law, not Paraguayan or United States law. It held that because of the non-prosecution of Pena, 'the objective of the international law making torture punishable as a crime can only be vindicated by imposing punitive damages'.[39] In determining the amount of the damages, the court found it appropriate to consider the extent of Pena's assets and held that the burden was on him to show his modest means if he wished that fact to be considered in mitigation. The nature of the acts, characterized as 'the ultimate in human cruelty and brutality'[40] was important. The court pointed out that chief among its considerations was 'the fact that this case concerns not a local tort but a wrong as to which the world has seen fit to speak. Punitive damages are designed not merely to teach a defendant not to repeat his conduct but to deter others from following his example'.[41] The court held that it must make clear 'the depth of the international revulsion against torture and measure the award in accordance with the enormity of the offense'. The court concluded that it was essential and proper to grant the remedy of punitive damages in order to give effect to the manifest objectives of the international prohibition against torture.[42]

In another Alien Tort case involving a Guatemalan military official,[43] the plaintiffs analogized punitive damages to moral damages in civil law. The Declaration of the plaintiff's expert stated:

[M]oral damages under Guatemalan law do partake of a 'punitive dimension', as that concept is applied in the United States. 'Moral' damages take into consideration the heinousness of the crime and whether it was intentional or accidental. The more heinous the tort, the larger the damage award. Further, 'moral' damage awards also consider the relative economic strength of the tortfeasor's liability in order to have a substantial economic impact, if he is a person with extensive resources. Thus, in practice, the determination of the amount of 'moral' damages under [Guatemalan law] does go beyond strict compensation to the victim.

The United States Torture Victim Protection Act (TVPA), passed to implement the United Nations Convention against Torture and Other Cruel, Inhuman or

---

[37] *Filartiga v. Pena-Irala*, 577 F.Supp. 860 (1980).
[39] *Ibid.* [40] *Ibid.* [41] *Ibid.*
[43] *Xuncax v. Gramajo*, 886 F.Supp. 162 (D.Mass.1995).
[38] *Ibid.* at 863.
[42] *Ibid.* at 864.

Degrading Treatment or Punishment, provides that an individual who subjects another to torture or summary execution 'shall, in a civil action, be liable for damages'.[44] No definition of damages is provided either in the statute or the legislative history; however, *Filartiga* is mentioned with approval in the legislative history. In the Guatemalan case, the court considered whether the TVPA permits punitive damages and held that it does.

C. CONCLUSIONS

Many claims of human rights violations brought to international tribunals are based on laws enacted in good faith in error about the obligations imposed by the relevant human rights instruments. Other violations are due to acts of state agents not authorized by law. In such cases a declaration of the wrong together with compensatory and moral damages will likely suffice to serve the compensatory, remedial, and retributive functions of remedies. Deliberate and egregious violations raise other problems. In individual cases, where a single dissident may be arbitrarily arrested or killed or certain members of a particular religious minority may become targets of repression, high awards of moral damages could substitute for an award of punitive damages, particularly if the punitive and deterrent functions of the award are articulated. It may also be appropriate, however, to identify punitive or exemplary damages as such where the conduct clearly warrants a severe response. In particular, where there is clear evidence of a pattern of gross and systematic violations deliberately committed by the government, international tribunals concerned about impunity must consider enhancing awards or looking to non-monetary remedies. It is important that governments not continue to violate human rights after paying nominal or low compensatory damages to victims. The credibility and effectiveness of international human rights protections requires that the more severe violations be treated more severely. This need not result in a windfall to applicants, if other tribunals follow the present practice of the Inter-American Court in establishing trust funds for victims, especially if the funds could be extended to provide redress for those not involved in filing the complaint but who suffered similar violations.

Most human rights tribunals have either a textual or inherent basis for enhancing damage awards to deter and punish wrongdoing. Fundamentally the question of punitive or exemplary damages is one of utility.[45] Several justifications can be given for their use: punishment; deterrence; preservation of the peace; inducement for private law enforcement; compensation for otherwise uncompensated losses and payment of costs and fees. In cases of consistent non-prosecution of

---

[44] §2(a).
[45] S. Daniels and J. Martin, 'Myth and Reality in Punitive Damages', (1990) 75 *Minn. L.Rev.* 1.

individual perpetrators, monetary awards may be indicated in order to express disapproval of the actions of the government, and to repair the full dignitary losses sustained by private individuals. The purpose is to reprove a state for its conduct and deter it from similar actions in the future.

10

Non-Monetary Remedies

Ubi jus, ibi remedium: Where there is a right, there is a remedy.[1] This maxim has long been part of common law legal systems[2] and appears in Roman/Dutch law. The implication is that courts have the inherent power to devise the appropriate remedy to conclude cases that come within their jurisdiction. Among the possible remedies are those that order specific conduct by the wrongdoer, from restitution to negative and mandatory injunctions.[3] These probably should be the preferred remedies, because damages only substitute by giving money in the place of a remedy that would specifically undo the wrong.[4]

Remedial orders developed in common law legal history because the law courts often did not provide effective redress of legal wrongs.[5] The inherent power of the courts to devise remedies became particularly important in cases of wrongdoing by government officials. Nearly 300 years ago, in *Ashby v. White*,[6] the court implied a damages remedy after the plaintiff claimed that an official had improperly denied him the right to vote in a parliamentary election. The majority decided that the offence was a public one and therefore no action should lie, that the case involved a legislative matter that should be left to Parliament to decide. Moreover, the plaintiff could show no actual pecuniary loss. Chief Justice Holt dissented, finding that the plaintiff had the right to vote and that a remedy should be given even though the statute creating the right failed to specify one:

A right that a man has to give his vote at the election of a person to represent him in Parliament . . . is a most transcendent thing, and of a high nature . . . The right of voting [is] so great a privilege, that it is a great injury to deprive the plaintiff of it . . . If the plaintiff has a right, he must of necessity have a means to vindicate and maintain it, and a

---

[1] *Black's Law Dictionary* 6th edn. (1990), 1120.

[2] In England, the chancellor spoke in the name of the king and, on the presentation of a petition or bill, issued a writ in the name of the king to order the party complained of to appear before the court to answer the complaint and abide by the order that might be made: Robert N. Leavell, Jean C. Love, Grant S. Nelson and Candace S. Kovacic-Fleischer, *Equitable Remedies, Restitution and Damages, Cases and Materials*, 5th edn. (West, 1994). The order ran directly in the name of the king, becoming a direct command to do or refrain from doing certain things. Most of the early Chancery cases concerned disputes between wealthy and poor, restraining the power of the former: *Ibid.* at 4. As part of the common law it was incorporated into the law of former English colonies. See Paxton's Case, 1 Quincy 51, 57 (Mass. 1761) ('[T]he Law abhors Right without Remedy').

[3] An injunction is a remedy in the form of an order directing the defendant to act, or to refrain from acting in a specified way: D. Dobbs, *The Law of Remedies*, 2nd edn. (1993), 162–64. Injunctions that forbid future misconduct are frequently coupled with an award of damages for harm already done.

[4] See Dobbs, *ibid.* at 210.

[5] J. Story, *Commentaries on Equity Jurisprudence as Administered in England and America* (1836), 30–32, 53; W. Holdsworth, *A History of English Law* 7th edn. (1956), vol. 1, 398.

[6] *Ashby v. White*, 92 Eng. Rep. 126 (K.B. 1703).

remedy if he is injured in the exercise or enjoyment of it; and indeed it is a vain thing to imagine a right without a remedy.[7]

Holt also indicated the judicial reasoning linking the right and the remedy: '[w]here a man has but one remedy to come at his right, if he loses that he loses his right'.[8] On appeal, Chief Justice Holt's dissenting opinion was accepted by the House of Lords and judgment was entered for the plaintiff.[9]

There are several reasons why remedial orders may be appropriate or necessary in human rights cases. First, the government may not be responsive to less intrusive measures, such as an award of damages.[10] Secondly, it may be impossible to estimate damages because of uncertainty or because what was lost is unique. Damages are especially inadequate when the victim can show no economic loss from the violation of her right[11] and where the violation causes irreparable injury. Also, the violations may be on-going or likely to be repeated and repetition is neither legally nor morally acceptable. With damage awards, the government can continue to violate rights as long as it is willing to pay.

The main policy question is whether to vindicate a substantive interest with money or seek to assure enjoyment of the interest in fact. Orders do not allow the wrongful conduct to continue or be repeated. It may be particularly unjust to allow the violation to continue after compensating a victim. While money is an acceptable substitute for many recognized interests, if the claim is of great importance, it is not adequate to allow the wrongdoer to simply pay for the injury. While some legal systems disfavour orders because of their intrusion on the freedom of action and discretion of the party subject to the order,[12] this reluctance comes at the cost of the victim's rights. Nonetheless, there are disadvantages to non-monetary awards that must be recognized, because many injunctions require continuing and costly supervision by the court, and some injunctions impose costs on third parties.

Opinion is divided on the ability of international courts to issue non-monetary

---

[7]   92 Eng. Rep. at 135–37 (Holt, C.J. dissenting).

[8]   *Ibid.* at 136.

[9]   *Ibid.* at 138. See also *Rowning v. Goodchild*, 96 Eng. Rep. 536 (K.B. 1773); Anonymous, 87 Eng. Rep. 791 (Q.B. 1703); *Turner v. Sterling*, 86 Eng. Rep. 287, 289 (K.B. 1683); *North v. Musgrave*, 82 Eng. Rep. 410 (K.B. 1639).

[10]   National courts that issue remedial orders can go beyond what is required to restore the plaintiff's rightful position if there is a demonstrated risk that the defendant's will not comply with a narrower order. See *Hutto v. Finney*, 437 U.S. 678, 98 S.Ct. 2565, 57 L.Ed.2d 522 (1978) (enjoining punitive isolation of prisoners for longer than 30 days).

[11]   Consider *Bell v. Southwell*, 376 F.2d 659 (5th Cir. 1967) where the black minority was unable to prove that the outcome of the election would have been different if the authorities had conducted a racially-neutral election in conformity with constitutional requirements. The court ordered another election *because such practices infect the processes of the law and diminish the interests of all: ibid.* at 665 (emphasis added).

[12]   The United States Supreme Court has shown concern for the rights of the states in the federal system and the consequent limitations on its equity power. Like international tribunals, it has relied on 'the well-established rule that the Government has traditionally been granted the widest latitude in the dispatch of its own internal affairs'.

remedial orders. Reitzer argues that jurisprudence demonstrates the principle of the complete freedom of the judge or arbitrator, that there are no rules for reparations.[13] Arango-Ruiz[14] posits that satisfaction is 'closely interrelated and frequently confused with the guarantees of non-repetition'[15] and could include in serious cases 'demands of abrogation of discriminatory, racial or segregational legislation, popular consultations such as free elections or plebiscites, restoration of fundamental rights and freedoms, etc'.[16] Personnaz finds that it is impossible for an international tribunal to annul a national act but he sees satisfaction as separate from compensation or punishment, designed to address irreparable injury.[17] It is a question of moral injury, which can be repaired symbolically as well as by money. He also notes that measures of satisfaction in practice include action taken against the wrongdoer.

A. INTERNATIONAL PRACTICE

In practice, there is thus nothing unusual or unprecedented about remedial orders issued by international tribunals. Restitution itself, often cited as the preferred remedy, is a remedial order to restore that which has been taken from the victim. Restitution comes from the Roman law form of redress known as *restituere in integrum* which the *praetor* granted to re-establish a prior situation where, for example, an otherwise valid contract had been procured through fraud or force. Recission of the contract restored the status quo *ante*. The theory of restitution is to restore what the defendant has unlawfully taken, avoiding unjust gains. Restitution is not a punitive remedy, although the measure of damages may be determined by the nature of the act creating the need for restitution. Thus, the wrongdoer may be required to restore or pay for what the victim lost, even if this is more than the wrongdoer gained. The basic purpose of restitution is to take something from the wrongdoer to which the victim is entitled and restore it to the victim.

Human rights bodies sometimes issue specific orders or recommendations to states. The Human Rights Committee, for example, if it finds a violation on the merits of a complaint under the Optional Protocol, adds what in its opinion should follow. Although it lacks the power to issue orders, it will indicate to the state in question, in a separate conclusion, that it has not only a duty to provide individual reparation but one to take preventive measures for the future.[18]

---

[13] Ladislas Reitzer, *La Reparation Comme Consequence De L'Acte Illicite en Droit International* (1938).

[14] Rapporteur, Seventh Report on State Responsibility, U.N. Doc.A/CN.4/469, 9 May 1995.

[15] *Ibid*. at 11, para. 29.

[16] *Ibid*. at 13, para. 32.

[17] Thus, satisfaction appears 'a la suite d'un acte sur lequel il est impossible de revenir, d'une offense irréparable et constitue plutôt une mesure destinée a apaiser le sentiment de l'Etat lésé par ce fait'. Jean Personnaz, *La Reparation du Prejudice en Droit International Public* (1938) 298.

[18] 'This is now a settled interpretation of its role'. T. Opsahl, 'The Human Rights Committee', in P. Alston, *The United Nations and Human Rights: A Critical Appraisal* (1992), 427.

The power to award non-monetary remedies may be an inherent judicial power, but some treaty provisions implicitly or explicitly provide for it. The explanatory notes to the draft Protocol to the African Charter on the Establishment of an African Court on Human and Peoples' Rights[19] make it clear that its Article 25 'ensures the competence of the Court to pronounce upon the violation of human rights and *to order the violation to be remedied*'.[20] It also allows the Court to order the payment of compensation to the victim. Article 27 allows the victim to enforce the compensation part of the judgment in national courts and provides a follow-up mechanism.[21]

The European and Inter-American Courts have both inherent and treaty-based power to award non-monetary remedies. Article 63 of the American Convention gives the Inter-American Court broad remedial authority which it has utilized in some of its cases to issue specific orders. The European Court has interpreted its powers narrowly, but could frame remedial decisions as part of 'just satisfaction'. Satisfaction in international practice has never been restricted to monetary compensation and the drafting history of the European Convention says nothing about the power of the Court to issue remedial decisions; it only indicates that the Court itself lacks power to annul a national act. Moreover, the inherent power of the Court changes with the entry into force of Protocol 11 and its alteration of the juridical status of the applicant. In the *Vagrancy* cases, the lack of standing of the applicant was viewed as a sufficient reason for limiting remedies under Article 50 and distinguishing the authority of the European Court from that of other international tribunals. The Court said:

Although the duty to make good the damage resulting from an injury which has been established by the decision of an international court derives from general international law, it was necessary to confer expressly upon the Court, by a clause in the European Convention on Human Rights, jurisdiction to grant satisfaction to the person injured. Since the applicant is not party to the proceedings before the Court, the object of those proceedings, strictly speaking, is not the damage suffered by him but the violation of the Convention alleged against the respondent state.[22]

Protocol 11 now makes the individual an initiating party to the proceedings and a direct focus or object of the case. The Court therefore could rely upon the inherent powers of international tribunals to afford adequate remedies to the injured party before it. Even without Protocol 11, Article 50 is broader in scope than the Court has accepted.

To date, the European Court has rejected every request for non-monetary relief. In *Le Compte, Van Leuven and De Meyere*,[23] the Court held that it was not

[19] OAU, 6–12 September 1995.

[20] *Ibid.* at 7.

[21] *Ibid.* at 8.

[22] *De Wilde, Ooms and Versyp v. Belgium* (the *Vagrancy* cases) (1972) 14 Eur.Ct.H.R.(ser. A) (Article 50) at 18.

[23] *Le Compte, Van Leuven and De Meyere v. Belgium*, (1982) 54 Eur.Ct.H.R. (ser. A).

empowered under the Convention to direct the Belgian state to annul the disciplinary sanctions imposed on the three applicants and the criminal sentences passed on one of them.[24] In *Campbell and Cosans*, Mrs. Campbell sought an undertaking that her children would not be subjected to any form of corporal punishment at public schools in the United Kingdom. The Court refused the request, stating that its judgments 'leave to the Contracting State concerned the choice of the means to be utilized in its domestic legal system for the performance of its obligation under Article 53'.[25] The Court therefore concluded it lacked the power to make the order.[26] In *Gillow v. United Kingdom*, the applicants sought a judgment directing the government to restore their residence qualifications in Guernsey. The Court refused to issue the order.[27]

In recent cases, particularly those involving human rights violations in Turkey, applicants have sought to obtain various types of non-monetary relief from the Court. In the Turkish cases involving village burnings, applicants have asked for orders re-establishing them in their homes.[28] In *Castillo Algar v. Spain*, the applicant sought not only pecuniary and non-pecuniary damages for harm he had sustained as a result of detention following his conviction by the Central Military Court. He also sought an order quashing his conviction and requiring the state to promote him to the rank of Brigadier General, since that would have been his rank had he not been convicted. In all these cases, the Court has reiterated that it lacks jurisdiction to issue orders.

In some cases, monetary compensation may be able to substitute, at least in part for the losses. In *Vasilescu v. Romania*, Judgment of 22 May 1998, for example, the 101-year-old applicant asked for return of 327 gold coins, property wrongfully taken by the government. The Court agreed that return of the coins would be the most appropriate remedy, but accepted the government's assertion that they could not be found and awarded FF60,000 (US$10,000) in pecuniary damages as well as FF30,000 (US$5,000) in non-pecuniary damages, for a total about one-half what she asked. In other cases, compensation is clearly inadequate and inappropriate to remedy the harm. In *Guerra and Others v. Italy*,[29] the applicants sought and received compensation for environmental damage to their homes. They also sought, however, an order requiring the government to decontaminate the entire industrial estate, carry out an epidemiological study of the area

---

[24] *Le Compte, Van Leuven and De Meyere v. Belgium*, at 7, para. 13. There was also a causality problem, in that the sanctions imposed were not seen as 'caused' by the breach of Article 6(1).

[25] *Campbell and Cosans v. United Kingdom* (Article 50), (1983) 60 Eur.Ct.H.R. (ser. A) at 9, para. 16.

[26] *Ibid.* citing *Marckx v. Belgium*, (1979) 31 Eur.Ct.H.R. (ser. A) at 25, para. 58 and *Dudgeon v. U.K.* (Article 50), (1983) 59 Eur.Ct.H.R. (ser. A) at 8, para. 15.

[27] Requests for orders were also submitted in *Dudgeon v. United Kingdom*, supra n. 26; *X v. United Kingdom* (Article 50), (1982) 55 Eur.Ct.H.R. (ser. A), 4 E.H.R.Rep. 188; *F v. Switzerland*, (1988) 128 Eur.Ct.H.R. (ser. A) and *Democoli v. Malta*, (1991) 210 Eur.Ct.H.R. (ser. A).

[28] See, e.g. *Akdivar v. Turkey*, 1998–II (No. 69), Reports 711, *Mentes v. Turkey*, and *Selçuk v. Turkey*, 1998–II (No. 71), Reports 891.

[29] *Guerra and others v. Italy*, 1998–I (No. 64), Reports 210.

and the local population, and undertake an inquiry to identify the possible serious effects on the residents most exposed to substances believed to be carcinogenic. The Commission agreed and said a thorough and efficient inquiry should be done with a full accurate report published, including the harm actually caused to the environment and people's health. The Court refused, noting 'that the Convention does not empower it to accede to such a request. It reiterates that it is for the State to choose the means to be used in its domestic legal system in order to comply with the provisions of the Convention or to redress the situation that has given rise to the violation of the Convention'.[30] It is notable that in the Turkish cases where the Court found a breach of Article 8 due to deliberate destruction of applicants' homes, the Court declared a duty to investigate, while here it was held beyond the Court's jurisdiction.

In contrast to the practice of the European Court, Inter-American institutions have directed states to take specific action to remedy human rights violations. After an investigation of human rights abuses in El Salvador, the Inter-American Commission recommended that the government prosecute the wrongdoers, admit the wrongdoing, provide treatment for the injured, and prevent future violations by training and teaching. Such a range of remedial orders also can be found in decisions of the Inter-American Court, which has expanded its use of non-monetary orders over time. In the initial Honduran cases, the victims claimed more than monetary compensation. They asked the Court to order Honduras to take various remedial measures, including an end to disappearances in Honduras; an investigation and public disclosure of what had happened to the disappeared in some 150 cases; trial and punishment of those responsible;[31] and:

a public act to honor and dignify the memory of the disappeared. A street, park, elementary school, high school, or hospital could be named for the victims of disappearances; actions against death squads and in favor of humanitarian organizations; an end to all forms of pressure against the families of the disappeared and a public recognition of their honor.[32]

In the same cases, the Commission asked for an order requiring Honduras to investigate, prosecute and punish those responsible for the disappearances. The

---

[30]   *Ibid.* at 230, para. 74, citing *Zanghi v. Italy*, (1991) 194–C Eur.Ct.H.R. (ser. A), *Demicoli v Malta*, (1991) 210 Eur.Ct.H.R. (ser. A), and *Yagçi and Sargin v. Turkey*, (1995) 319–A Eur.Ct.H.R. (ser.A).

[31]   There is a vast literature on the duty to investigate and prosecute, much of it stemming from the impunity and amnesty laws passed in Latin American states after periods of human rights abuses. See: L. Weschler, *A Miracle, A Universe: Settling Accounts with Torturers* (1990); Carlos Nino, 'The Duty to Punish Past Abuses of Human Rights Put into Context: The Case of Argentina', (1991) 100 *Yale L.J.* 2619 (1991); Diane Orentlichter, 'Settling Accounts: The Duty to Prosecute Human Rights Violations of a Prior Regime', (1991) 100 *Yale L.J.* 2537; Jo M. Pasqualucci, 'The Whole Truth and Nothing but the Truth: Truth Commissions, Impunity and the Inter-American Human Rights System', (1994) 12 *Boston U. Int'l L.J.* 321; Naomi Roht-Arriaza, 'Comment, State Responsibility to Investigate and Prosecute Grave Human Rights Violations in International Law', (1990) 78 *Cal.L.Rev.* 449.

[32]   Brief of the Commission.

Court's judgment referred back to its decision on the merits, noting that some of the requested measures would be required as part of the reparation of the consequences of the violation of rights rather than being part of the indemnity. It reiterated that its judgment on the merits required Honduras to investigate the cases, prevent future violations and punish those responsible. The Court also found, like the European Court, that its judgment on the merits is a type of reparation and constitutes moral satisfaction of significance and importance. No requests for non-monetary reparations were granted.

The Court did, however, issue an order regarding the mode of payment of the compensatory damages. In addition to ordering a lump sum payment within 90 days free of taxes or payment in six monthly instalments, the Court ordered establishment of a trust fund for the children, created in the Central Bank of Honduras 'under the most favorable conditions permitted by Honduran banking practice'. The children were entitled to receive monthly payments from the fund until the age of 25 years, when the corpus must be distributed.

In the case of *Aloeboetoe v. Suriname*,[33] the Commission's report, issued prior to the case being lodged at the Court, recommended that Suriname investigate the violations and try and punish those responsible, as well as take necessary measures to avoid a recurrence of the incident. In its memorial to the Court of 1 April 1991, the Commission requested that the government be directed to take measures to restore the good name of the victims, issue a public apology and return the remains of the seven victims to their families.

The victims in *Aloeboetoe* also sought measures other than compensation: an apology from the President of Suriname and the Congress, publication of the Court's decision, return of the bodies of the deceased victims to the families, the naming of a park or square or prominent street after the Saramaca tribe, and investigation and punishment of the responsible persons. The Court ordered specific non-monetary remedies, requiring that the government re-open and staff the school and health dispensary in the area where the victims' families lived. The Court did not discuss the other requests, except to note briefly the continuing obligation of Suriname to inform the families of the location of the bodies of the victims. The last was considerably less than the Commission and victims requested, but the order was nonetheless far-reaching. Although the Court called opening the school part of the compensation awarded to the children of the victims, enabling them to complete their education, the school closure was in no way a consequence of the violation. Had the state not killed the victims there still would have been no school, so the order can only be deemed 'just satisfaction' to the community as a whole.

In the *El Amparo* case, in addition to a declaration of Venezuelan responsibility, the Commission asked for various non-monetary remedies: investigation and

---

[33] *Aloeboetoe et al. Case, Reparations*, (1993) 15 Inter-Am.Ct.H.R. (1993) (ser. C) at paras. 9, 20.

punishment of the actual and 'intellectual' authors of the wrong; a declaration regarding the incompatibility of Article 54(2) and (3) of the Military Code of Justice,[34] and an order for its revision. In its judgment on the preliminary objections to the case, the Court made no specific mention of the non-pecuniary reparations asked by the Commission. Judge Cançado Trindade, concurring, added that the Court was reserving the right to decide on the compatibility of the sections of the Military Code, and should have so stated. On the merits, the Commission argued that *restitutio in integrum* could be accomplished and should be ordered by the Court. Specifically, the Commission repeated its call for government action to reform the Code of Military Justice and to investigate and punish the authors of the harm, as well as monetary compensation. In addition, the representatives of the victims requested that Venezuela call a press conference and inform the public of its responsibility for the *El Amparo* killings, that it issue a 'declaration of no tolerance' of such acts, and create a foundation 'for the purpose of promoting and disseminating international human rights law throughout the region where the events occurred'.[35] Finally, they called for a public admission, published in the principal newspapers of the country and abroad, and a memorial or plaque in memory of the victims.

In its judgment on the merits, the Court decided to refrain from making an 'abstract' pronouncement on the compatibility of the Code of Military Justice with the Convention and thus refused the Commission's request to order a revision of the Code. Investigation and punishment were again referred to as continuing obligations. In the reparations phase in the *El Amparo* case, the Commission emphasized the objectives of reparations, which are to re-establish respect for international norms by restoring the status quo *ante* or paying damages when this is not possible. In this regard, the Commission and the victims viewed it as essential to go beyond the payment of compensation to conform to the requirements of Article 63(1) and the earlier judgment. In fact, only in respect of the right to life and personal integrity was compensation required, because of the irreversible nature of the injury. In regard to the other violations, the Commission again called for government action to reform the Code of Military Justice.

The state responded that nothing in the request concerned redress of the case before the court because the Military Code provision in question was not used in the case. The state's brief also declared that the non-pecuniary reparations were not consistent with 'either international case law in general, or with the case law of the Inter-American court in particular'.[36] It claimed that moral damages cover all satisfaction and that the judgment and recognition by Venezuela of its respon-

---

[34] The Military Code provision in question permits the President of the Republic to order that a military trial not be held when he deems it in the national interest or to order the discontinuance of military trials when he deems it advisable.

[35] *El Amparo Case, Reparations*, (1996) 22 Inter-Am. Ct.H.R.(ser. C) at para. 50.

[36] *Ibid.* at para. 51.

sibility for the violation fully restored the honour and reputation of the victims and their next of kin.

The Court agreed with the government that the Code provision had not been applied in the case. It also, consistent with earlier opinions, found it unnecessary to order the investigation and punishment, finding it a continuing obligation of the state which must be discharged seriously. The Court held Venezuela's acceptance of international responsibility adequate reparation for the remaining demands. Judge Cançado Trindade dissented regarding the Court's refusal to address the compatibility of the provision in the Code of Military Justice. In his view, the non-application of the statutory provision did not affect the Court's competence because 'the very existence of a legal provision may per se create a situation which directly affects the rights protected by the American Convention. A law can certainly violate those rights by virtue of its own existence and, in the absence of a measure of application or execution, by the real threat to the persons(s), represented by the situation created by such law'. In his view, the provision in question was incompatible with the general duties imposed by the Convention of *ensuring* respect for the rights recognized therein (Article 1) and of adopting provisions necessary to give effect to them.[37]

In the *Neira Alegria* case, the Commission asked that the Court order Peru to investigate, identify and punish the perpetrators; and inform the next of kin of the whereabouts of the disappeared. In its judgment, for the first time, the Court agreed that '[a]s a form of moral reparation, the Government has the obligation to do all in its power to locate and identify the remains of the victims and deliver them to their next of kin'.[38] Similarly, in the *Caballero Delgado and Santana* case,[39] when the Court found Colombia responsible for the detention and disappearances of the two named persons, it found that 'reparations should consist of the continuation of the judicial proceedings inquiring into the disappearance of Isidro Caballero-Delgado and Maria del Carmen Santana and punishment of those responsible in conformance with Colombian domestic law'.[40] The Commission also asked the Court for reform of the penal law of Colombia as it regulates habeas corpus and disappearances; investigation and punishment of

---

[37] The proceedings concerning the Military Code did not end with the judgment on the merits or decision on reparations. The Commission requested an interpretation of the last part of the judgment in which the Court affirmed that Article 54 of the Code of Military Justice had not been applied in the case. According to the Commission's filings in the case, the article had been applied '*en terminos generales*'. It involved action taken at the first instance in the domestic case by the President, after which the case proceeded, according to the Court, '*en forma normal*'. The Commission argued that the government itself had acknowledged that the Article had been applied. The government denied this. In a resolution adopted 16 April 1997, the Court declared once more that Article 54 of the Code of Military Justice did not fall within the facts of the case, in spite of its findings that there had been an interruption in the domestic proceedings as a result of presidential actions based on Article 54.

[38] *Neira Alegria et al. Case, Reparations*, (1996) 23 Inter-Am.Ct.H.R. (ser. C) at para. 69.

[39] *Cabellero Delgado and Santana Case*, Judgment of 8 December 1995, Annual Report of the Inter-American Court of Human Rights, OAS/Ser.L/V/III.33, Doc 4, at 125 (1996).

[40] *Ibid.* para. 69.

those responsible; and actions to repair the damage caused to the honour and good name of the victims and their families.

In *Loayza Tamayo v. Peru*,[41] the Inter-American Court issued its strongest orders to date. The Commission alleged violations of Articles 7 (right to personal liberty), 5 (right to personal integrity), 8 (judicial guarantees) and 25 (judicial protection) in relation to Article 1.1 of the Convention, stemming from the illegal deprivation of liberty, torture, cruel, inhuman and degrading treatment, denial of judicial guarantees and double jeopardy of Maria Elena Loayza Tamayo. The victim had been acquitted after being held *incommunicado* and allegedly tortured, but was re-tried, convicted and sentenced to 20 years in prison in violation of the principle *non bis in idem*. The Commission asked the Court to declare that Peru should provide full reparations to the victim for the serious material and moral damage suffered by her and to order Peru to decree her immediate release, and pay an indemnity and the costs of the proceeding. The Court found that during the period of detention there existed in Peru a generalized practice of cruel, inhuman and degrading treatment in criminal investigations of those suspected of treason or terrorism.[42] The Court held that Peru violated Articles 7 and 25 by illegally detaining the victim and depriving her of judicial process. It found cruel, inhuman and degrading treatment in the prison conditions, although it did not find evidence of the rape she had alleged. The Court also found a violation of Article 8.4 because of the double jeopardy imposed. The Court ordered Peru to release her from prison within a reasonable time and pay fair compensation to her and her family, and reimburse the expenses they incurred before the Peruvian authorities.[43] The order of release took immediate effect. For the other remedies, the Court asked for details and proof and continued the process.[44]

In its reparations judgment in the *Loayza Tamayo* case, the Court focused on rehabilitation and reintegration of the victim. As restitution, it ordered Peru to take the necessary measures to reinstate her in her prior teaching position in the public sector, with the salary and other benefits equivalent to the amount of her remuneration for her work in both the public and private sectors at the moment of her detention, based on their present value at the date of the judgment. It also demanded that the state provide full retirement benefits taking into account the period of detention and ensure no adverse consequences from the judgment in the domestic proceeding occurs. The Court further required, as other non-monetary

---

[41] (1997) 33 Inter-Am.Ct.H.R. (ser. C). [42] *Ibid.* para. 46(1).

[43] The Court stated 'Como consecuencia de las violaciones señaladas de los derechos consagrados en la Convencion, y especialmente de la prohibicion de doble enjuiciamiento, en perjuicio de la señora Maria Elena Loayza Tamayo y, por aplicacion del articulo anteriormente transcrito, la Corte considera que el Estado de Peru debe, de acuerdo con law disposiciones de su derecho interno, ordenar la libertad de la señora Maria Elena Loayza Tamayo dentro de un plazo razonable': *ibid.* para. 84.

[44] Judge Montiel dissented on the issue of double jeopardy and also objected to the order of release, viewing it as an annulment of a national judicial decision, something that can only be done by '*un superior competente*': dissent of Judge Alejandreo Montiel Arguello, para. 11.

reparations, that Peru take the necessary internal legal measures to conform its domestic law on terrorism and treason to the Convention and investigate, identify and sanction those responsible.

The Court's awards of symbolic reparations are important in demonstrating a concern with the reputation of the victims. Many applicants have been accused of subversion, terrorism, or other misconduct alleged to justify the actions taken against them. Suspicions that the victims 'deserved' the treatment they received can harm them and their families even in the best of circumstances. In *Suarez Rosero v. Ecuador*, the applicant, the first to testify in person before the Court, emphasized the importance of the restoration of his dignity, reputation and rights through an exculpatory official declaration or judgment. He offered evidence from his therapist of the importance of vindication and recognition of his dignity. The state asserted that its cooperation during the reparations phase was itself the recognition as sought by the applicant. The Court found that the judgment in the case was itself a form of reparation and moral satisfaction of importance to the petitioner. Thus far, however, the Court has rejected claims requesting that the state honour the memory of victims through symbolic actions such as naming a street, park or other public structure.

B. TYPES OF NON-MONETARY REMEDIES

The kind of non-monetary remedies a human rights tribunal might award depends on the nature of the violation. Orders may be reparative, such as restitution or requiring the defendant to restore the plaintiff to a pre-existing entitlement. Preventive injunctions aim to prevent the loss of an entitlement and are used where there is a threat of future commission of a wrong. Repetitive wrongdoing may require preventive orders. Professor Owen Fiss has argued that there is a third type of injunction, the structural injunction that attempts to remodel an existing social or political institution to bring it into conformity with legal requirements: e.g. restructuring a school system to facilitate equality of educational opportunity, or restructuring a prison to eliminate cruel and inhuman punishments. Such on-going violations may involve social conditions, behavioural patterns and organizational dynamics that 'disable' the wrongdoers from complying with a general directive to cease violating the law. In such cases, an international judicial organ may leave it to the individual state concerned, devise a specific affirmative order, or rely on the international political organs to take action.

1. Rehabilitation

All victims of serious abuse and their dependants should be rehabilitated. Rehabilitation, the process of restoring the individual's full health and reputation after the trauma of serious attack on their physical or mental integrity, aims to restore what has been lost and is crucial to prevent further deterioration. It seeks to achieve maximum physical and psychological fitness. Without it, there may be long-term negative consequences to society. Torture, other violence and ill-treatment result in physical injuries and/or disability, as well as emotional and psychological consequences. Victims of these abuses need rehabilitative care that may range from occupational therapy and physiotherapy to surgery and wheelchairs. International tribunals should insist on rehabilitation of victims of serious abuse. The tribunal either can evaluate the costs of existing rehabilitation programmes, and award compensation equal to the costs, or require that rehabilitation be provided and leave the evaluation of the costs to the state.

2. Truth-telling

Another remedy that is often sought is knowledge of and acknowledgment of the truth of events involved in the violation. While some fact-finding occurs naturally in the course of the international proceedings, not all evidence can be or is uncovered during international litigation, especially the identity and motivation of individual perpetrators. Although most human rights treaties do not explicitly state a right to know the truth, such a right has been held to be encompassed in the conventional duty to 'ensure' or 'protect' human rights[45] and thus is an obligation of the state.[46] The Inter-American Commission on Human Rights asserts that 'every society has the inalienable right to know the truth about past events, as well as the motives and the circumstances in which aberrant crimes came to be committed, in order to prevent repetition of such acts in the future'.[47] The failure to investigate and prosecute violations may be tantamount to 'a passive abuse of human rights' if it places those rights in future peril.[48]

Independently of the social goal of deterrence, victims and their families have a particular 'need to know' and this can be considered a right of the family[49] where the victims are deceased or disappeared. The state must use the means at its disposal to inform the relatives of the fate of victims and, if they have been killed, the location of their remains.[50] In addition to resolving lingering uncertainty about the fate of the victim, public dissemination of the truth corrects any negative image

---

[45] Article 1(1) of the American Convention requires State Parties to 'ensure to all persons subject to their jurisdiction the free and full exercise' of the rights provided in the Convention: American Convention on Human Rights, 22 November 1969, 9 I.L.M. 673, OEA/Ser.K/XVI/I.1, doc. 65 rev. 1 corr.1 (1970) (entered into force 18 July 1978).

[46] *Velasquez Rodriguez Case*, (1988) 4 Inter-Am.Ct.H.R. (ser. C), para. 174, OAS/ser.L/V/III.19, doc. 13 (1988).

[47] Inter-American Commission on Human Rights, Annual Report, 1985–86, OEA/Ser.L/V/II.68, doc. 8 rev. 1, 191, 192–93 (1986).

[48] Carlos Nino, *supra* n. 31 at 2639.

[49] J. Pasqualucci, *supra* n. 31 at 331.

[50] *Velasquez Rodriguez Case*, *supra* n. 46, at para. 181.

that may have been created about the victim. The Chilean Truth Commission stated that 'only the knowledge of the truth will restore the dignity of the victims in the public mind, allow their relatives and mourners to honor them fittingly, and in some measure make it possible to make amends for the damage done'.[51]

3. Punishment of perpetrators

A decision calling for prosecution and punishment of the perpetrators is also important and has considerable precedent in the awards of satisfaction issued by arbitral tribunals for injury to aliens. In many cases, international tribunals have indicated that it is not necessary to refer explicitly to prosecution and punishment because this is an on-going obligation of the state where the violations occurred, part of the generic duties imposed by human rights treaties.

The American Convention guarantees a right to recourse to a competent court or tribunal for protection against acts that violate human rights, even though such violation may have been committed by persons acting in the course of their official duties. According to Pasqualucci, it is not clear whether victims could ask the court to require the state to allow them to initiate prosecution in those states that normally permit the victim to make the charge in a criminal proceeding (e.g. Argentina).[52] Claimants before the Inter-American Commission have argued that Article 8 of the Convention (right to fair trial) is violated when they are denied their right to be the party making the charge in a criminal proceeding in which they have been victims of rights violations. Article 8 provides for judicial consideration of 'rights and obligations of a civil, labor, fiscal or any other nature' and it is questionable whether the drafters intended the right of victims to bring criminal charges to be included.

The issue of punishment usually arises in cases of gross and systematic violations, where failure to punish leads to impunity. Van Boven sees a link in such situations between punishment and reparation: '[i]t cannot be ignored that a clear nexus exists between the impunity of perpetrators of gross violations of human rights and the failure to provide just and adequate reparation to the victims and their families or dependents'.[53]

C. ASSESSING THE NEED FOR NON-MONETARY REMEDIES

With non-monetary remedies there is often a controversy about future probabilities rather than evaluation of a completed set of events. Liability becomes in part

---

[51] Comision Nacional De Verdad y Reconciliacion, *Report of the Chilean National Commission on Truth and Reconciliation* (Philip Berryman, trans.), at 5 (quoting Supreme Decree No. 355 of 25 April 1990, which created the Commission).

[52] See J. Pasqualucci, *supra* n. 31, at 356.

[53] Theo van Boven, *Study Concerning the Right to Restitution, Compensation and Rehabilitation for Victims of Gross Violations of Human Rights and Fundamental Freedoms*, U.N. Human Rights. Comm. 45th Sess., U.N. Doc. E/CN.4/Sub.2/1993/8, at 51.

a prediction of what is likely to occur and relief is an effort to devise a programme to contain future consequences.[54] Remedies may order measures specifically designed to prevent or end the abuse, including enjoining particular action or sanctions for repeated abuse. This is particularly appropriate where harm is threatened that is irreparable (e.g. death). Where this is the case, and the harm is one for which money damages cannot adequately compensate, non-monetary relief can be used to prevent permanent injury.

Several factors could be considered by international tribunals in deciding whether non-monetary remedies are warranted:

(1) Is it acceptable to substitute money damages for the invaded interest or are those interests too basic to permit the violator to buy the choice to continue the violation?

(2) Does the court have the administrative capability to supervise compliance or is there a related political organ capable of follow-up and enforcement, if necessary?

(3) Has the victim been deprived of something that only specific restitution will remedy?

(4) Would multiple actions have to be brought to stop the wrongdoing?

(5) Can damages be accurately measured?

As the caseloads of the courts become greater, the fourth element may become an important consideration. In the European system, the Italian government appears to have chosen to pay each litigant for delays in its judicial system rather than reform the system as the Convention requires. If the Court takes its role seriously, it should either impose damages on a level that no longer makes it economical for the government to continue the violation, or it should order the violation to cease. Remedies that fail to bring the violation to an end undermine the integrity of the system and are an example that should not be held up to the new member states of the Council of Europe.

D. CONCLUSIONS

In public law, some interests are so basic that society and the courts think people deserve to enjoy them in fact. Monetary compensation that tolerates the wrong and allows the perpetrator to buy injustice is not appropriate where inalienable rights are concerned. Performance must be the preferred remedy.[55] It contravenes notions of human rights to reduce them to 'a series of propositions assuring the payment of money to the victims'.[56]

---

[54] Abram Chayes, 'The Role of the Judge in Public Law Litigation', (1976) 89 *Harv. L.Rev.* 1281.

[55] D. Louisell and G. Hazard, *Cases and Materials on Pleading and Procedure* 4th edn. (1979), 109.

[56] O. Fiss, *The Civil Rights Injunction* (1978), 75.

Courts that award damages rather than non-monetary relief may do so because orders are seen to create potential procedural and substantive burdens. Non-monetary awards can be difficult to adjudicate, formulate, administer and enforce. When deciding whether to order a political body to act, courts may ask whether it will be difficult or impossible to secure compliance,[57] probably speculating about this more often at the international level where the courts are relatively young and the habit of compliance is not yet ingrained. Disobedience may cause the court to lose prestige, and provide a disincentive to others to accept the court's jurisdiction. The risk of non-compliance may make courts reluctant to issue an order, especially because the wrongdoer has already shown a disregard for the substantive law. When, however a court considers the likelihood of obedience in adjudicating remedies, it improperly places the victim's rights at the mercy of defendant's obduracy.[58]

---

[57] See e.g. *Giles v. Harris*, 189 U.S. 475, 487–88 (1903).

[58] Note that the ability of the applicant in *Dudgeon supra* n. 27, to seek relief was similar to civil rights declaratory judgment cases in national law. See H. Wilkinson, 'Anticipatory Vindication of Federal Constitutional Rights', (1977) 41 *Albany L.Rev.* 459).

11

Costs and Fees

On no issue have international tribunals been as divided as on the awards of costs and attorneys' fees. The European Court of Human Rights nearly always awards all or part of them to successful applicants, while the Inter-American Court of Human Rights until 1998 granted local costs but did not award attorneys' fees for proceedings on the merits before it or the Commission. Human rights organs that recommend measures of relief almost never mention them. Administrative tribunals are also split with some awarding costs and fees while others deny them or hide them in large damage awards.

In national legal systems, fees are often awarded and the amount is usually calculated on the basis of the number of hours reasonably expended during the litigation, multiplied by a reasonable hourly rate. Other factors may be considered, such as the novelty and difficulty of the legal questions; skills required to perform the legal work properly; opportunity costs; customary fees; the fixed or contingent nature of the attorney-client agreement; time limitations imposed by the court or rules; the amount of money or importance of interests involved in the case; the experience, reputation and ability of the attorneys; the undesirability of the case (i.e. whether the attorneys took risks in accepting the case); and awards in similar cases.

Attorneys who bring human rights cases need to be paid because fee awards encourage them to represent victims who are often indigent, social outcasts, or marginalized. Some attorneys put themselves at risk pursuing human rights cases, as has been documented by the Center for the Independence of Lawyers and Judges[1] and the United Nations Special Rapporteur on the Independence of Judges and Lawyers.[2] Without financial recompense, attorneys in repressive states have little incentive to provide services for those most in need. Like all professionals, lawyers are economically motivated actors, at least in part; they will wage socially beneficial 'private attorney general' actions if the costs are not too great.

There is also an argument based in restitution for an award of attorneys' fees.[3]

---

[1] See e.g. Center for the Independence of Judges and Lawyers of the International Commission of Jurists, *Attacks on Justice: the Harassment and Persecution of Judges and Lawyers 1990–1991* (1992).

[2] The United Nations Commission on Human Rights appointed the Special Rapporteur by resolution 1994/41, endorsed by the Economic and Social Council in decision 1994/251. The Special Rapporteur has filed annual reports since 1995. See *Report of the Special Rapporteur on the independence of judges and lawyers*, E/CN.4/1995/39, E/CN.4/1996/37 (1996), E/CN.4/1997/32 (1997), and E/CN.4/1998/39.

[3] Charles Silver, 'A Restitutionary Theory of Attorneys' Fees in Class Actions', (1991) 76 *Cornell L. Rev.* 656.

Restitution encompasses both claims for return of specific items and claims for compensation grounded in notions of unjust enrichment,[4] the latter being particularly applicable when a case has broad remedial impact on a defined group or society as a whole. If legal aid or the amount the petitioner can pay fails to cover the reasonable value of the attorneys' time, then those who benefit from changes in the law or practice resulting from the lawsuit profit at the attorneys' expense, calling for application of the equitable principle that persons who are unjustly enriched must make restitution. When a state violates human rights, everyone within the territory and subject to the jurisdiction of the state is a potential victim and benefits when the law or practice changes. The theory of restitution suggests that all should share in the costs of the litigation. Society generally benefits from assessing human rights awards from the public treasury because the benefits received are usually more valuable than the amount of taxes paid from which the damages are drawn.[5]

It may be countered that the law of restitution disfavours forced exchanges, even exchanges that leave the parties better off.[6] A basic principle of restitution is that a person who receives a benefit voluntarily conferred in the absence of mistake, coercion, request, or emergency is not unjustly enriched and has no obligation to pay. The law of restitution would presume that uncomplaining citizens, who may or may not have been victims of similar human rights violations, have no obligation to pay for the benefits they receive from a decision against the state brought by the victim who does come forward. It is nonetheless possible to assert that attorneys' fees and costs should be awarded according to the law of restitution, when the following conditions are met:[7]

(1) It is impracticable or impossible to bring an action on behalf of all victims or potential victims. Most courts 'start with the premise that one should not be compensated for intervening in the affairs of another without request'.[8] Where possible, therefore, an attorney should contract for services with those who will benefit from the litigation. In human rights litigation, however, there are legal barriers to actions for multiple victims or potential victims; e.g. in the European system only actual victims may file applications and 'class actions' are almost unknown in human rights tribunals. In these cases, a denial of compensation will not encourage attorneys to bargain with potential clients because, by assumption, bargaining cannot occur.

---

[4] Douglas Laycock, 'The Scope and Significance of Restitution', (1989) 67 *Tex. L. Rev.* 1277, 1279.

[5] See, e.g., Richard Epstein, *Takings: Private Property and the Power of Prominent Domain* (1985), ch. 1

[6] See George E. Palmer, *Law of Restitution* (1978), vol. 2, 10.1 (noting 'judicial disapproval of unsolicited intervention . . . where the intervener expects compensation'); Restatement (Second) of Restitution 2, at 34 (Tent Draft No. 1 1983) (hereinafter Restatement (Second)) ('no one should be empowered to thrust a benefit on another and by that means become his creditor').

[7] Adapted from Silver, *supra* n. 3.

[8] G. Palmer, *supra* n. 6, at 360–61.

(2)　As a result of the successful human rights action, other victims and potential victims enjoy benefits they would not otherwise receive. 'There can be no unjust enrichment unless there is enrichment first. The law of restitution generates no obligations to support lost causes. It requires people to pay compensation only when benefits actually are received.'[9]

(3)　Other victims and potential victims either voluntarily accept the benefits of the litigation or have no opportunity to decline them. Lawyers who represent human rights victims confer benefits involuntarily, in that they only seek to assist their clients. They cannot restrict access to the benefits they help produce. All other victims and potential victims as a consequence may enjoy the benefits of the action.

(4)　Other victims and potential victims are better off receiving the benefits of the litigation and paying attorneys' fees and costs than doing without the benefits entirely.

In this context, restitution is based on justice as reciprocity or fair return, imposing a duty on those who benefit from another's efforts to offer something of value in return.[10] Because attorneys help produce the gains, albeit intangible in many cases, that victims and potential victims of human rights violations enjoy, justice obligates the payment of reasonable fees in return. As one commentator explains, '[t]he concept of justice as reciprocity has long informed the law of restitution. It explains why people who confer benefits on others can sometimes secure compensation, even when recipients are themselves innocent of wrongdoing'.[11] There also may be a problem of the 'free-riders' who benefit from the cessation of the violation but are unwilling to take the risk of litigation themselves. Victims who are unwilling to step forward to complain of human rights violations nonetheless enjoy the benefits when the breach is remedied. In addition, lawyers often are discouraged from litigating human rights cases because the victims' claims are small and the costs of identifying, locating, and contacting witnesses and acquiring evidence are prohibitive. Attorneys cannot contract with potential group members who have yet to be victimized, although such individuals may be numerous. Nor is it equitable to insist that non-governmental human rights organizations who represent victims assume the burden of the costs and fees. Such organizations are not-for-profit, must engage in constant fund-raising and are often short of resources.

In the European system, costs and fees fall within the provisions of former Article 50 meaning that they are afforded 'if necessary'. The Court nearly always finds them so at least in part. It dealt with the issue at some length in its plenary

---

[9] Silver, *supra* n. 3, at 676. Note that this view supports a denial of compensation for hours spent on unsuccessful claims, because time spent on unsuccessful claims that are unrelated to a winning claim confer no benefits.

[10] See, e.g., John Rawls, *A Theory of Justice* (1971), 112; H.L.A. Hart, 'Are There Any Natural Rights?', (1955) 64 *Phil. Rev.* 175.

[11] Silver, *supra* n. 3, at 667.

decision in *Sunday Times v. United Kingdom*,[12] after the applicants filed an unquantified claim for costs and expenses incurred in both the domestic litigation and proceedings before the European Commission and Court. In holding that there had been a breach of Article 10 of the European Convention due to an injunction granted against the *Sunday Times* in accordance with the English law of contempt of court,[13] the Court reserved the issue of costs and expenses as a remedy under Article 41 (then Article 50). In the separate proceeding, the applicants referred to English law, where the litigant must bear his own costs unless the court otherwise orders.[14] Although the European Court reviewed the material submitted, it concurred with the Commission's view that the Convention would be the basis of any judgment for a claim in respect of costs. The Court agreed with the government that 'the injured party is not entitled to his costs as of right because "just satisfaction" is to be afforded "if necessary" and the matter falls to be determined by the Court at its discretion, having regard to what is equitable'.[15]

In the *Sunday Times* case, the applicants claimed: UK£15,809.36 for the costs of litigation in England; UK£24,760.53 for proceedings before the Commission and Court; and an additional amount for the Article 50 proceedings. In respect of the entire amount it asked for 10 per cent per annum interest. The Commission supported the applicant's claim. The government argued in the alternative that (1) just satisfaction did not require the award of any costs, citing previous cases where the Court had held that the decision alone amounted to just satisfaction; (2) that the parties had reached an agreement that precluded the award and that in any event the costs were not necessarily incurred; (3) that no amounts should be recovered for claims that were rejected by the Commission and the Court; and (4) that any amounts the Court did decide to award should not exceed the rates payable under the Commission's legal aid programme.

The Court distinguished, as it had previously, between damage caused by a violation of the Convention and costs necessarily incurred by the applicant. It noted that even in those cases where it had found that the decision itself was just satisfaction for the injury suffered, 'the Court's general practice has been to accept claims in respect of the [costs necessarily incurred by the applicant] . . . *In fact, it is difficult to imagine that the finding of a violation could of itself constitute just satisfaction as regards costs*'.[16] The Court does not explain why this is the case, when such a finding is deemed adequate for moral damages, although

---

[12] *Sunday Times v. United Kingdom* (Article 50), (1980) 38 Eur. Ct.H.R. (ser. A), (1981) 3 E.H.R.R. 317.

[13] *Sunday Times v. United Kingdom* (Merits), (1979) 30 Eur.Ct.H.R. (ser. A).

[14] *Sunday Times* (Article 50), *supra* n. 12 at 7. As a general rule, English courts will order the unsuccessful party to pay his opponent the latter's costs, 'although the actual amount recoverable will be assessed by the court and will very rarely cover the full expenditure' *ibid.*

[15] *Ibid.* at 9.

[16] *Ibid.* at 10. Emphasis added.

perhaps it views out-of-pocket expenses as a category of pecuniary loss that is the direct consequence of the violation and must be reimbursed.

The government argued that an award of costs should be denied because in its view the litigation was 'welcomed' by the applicants as a means of testing the law. The Court rejected this contention on the basis that there was no other means of challenging the law, apart from violating it and running the risk of sanctions for contempt of court. The Court explicitly referred to the practice of member states in finding that test cases could be appropriate ones for the award of costs. Significantly, the government's assertion that it was in the process of changing its law was not deemed sufficient to bar an award of attorneys' fees, the Court finding it 'not relevant' to the claim because the contracting states 'are in any event under an obligation to adjust their domestic law to the requirements of the Convention'.

The Court applied the test of necessity in deciding to award costs for the domestic litigation. It found that the costs in England were incurred by the applicants in asserting their freedom of expression, a right guaranteed by the Convention. In addition, the Court pointed out, the domestic proceeding was a pre-condition to any submission of the matter to the European Commission. Nonetheless, the Court denied the costs of the domestic litigation because of an agreement between the government and the applicants that each would bear its own costs of litigation.

As for expenses incurred before the Strasbourg institutions, the Court articulated a test that asks whether the costs (1) were actually incurred, (2) were necessarily incurred and (3) are reasonable as to quantum.[17] It has applied this standard in all subsequent cases.

The government asserted that the applicant's three counsel were unnecessary in view of the Commission's role in the case. The Commission and the Court agreed with the applicants, however, on the need for representation, noting that the applicants were not formal parties to the proceedings and the Commission's role was not to represent them but to assist the court 'in the capacity of defender of the public interest'.[18] This important distinction between the interests of the applicants and the interests of the Commission has been referred to by the Inter-American Court in its decisions, but the latter court has failed to draw the appropriate conclusion about the necessity of compensated applicant representation during most stages of the proceedings.

The European Court did reduce somewhat the amount claimed in *Sunday Times*, from UK£12,000 to UK£10,000, on the basis that not all the applicant's counsel were necessary at the hearings. On the other hand, the Court deferred to the Commission on the necessity of attendance of the advisers and the applicants

---

[17] *Ibid.* at 12 citing *Neumeiser v. Austria*, (1974) 17 Eur. Ct. H.R. (ser. A) (Article 50) at 209, para. 43 and *König v. Germany* (Article 50), (1980) 36 Eur.Ct.H.R. (ser. A) at 18–19, paras 24–26.

[18] *Ibid.* at para. 30 quoting *Lawless v. Ireland*, (1960)1 Eur.Ct.H.R. (ser. A).

at hearings before the Commission, awarding the full amount claimed. It also allowed the travel expenses of the applicants to attend the Court hearings, finding their presence 'of value,' but it rejected their costs for attending the delivery of the Court's judgment, finding it unnecessary.

Other claims included the cost of:

(1) expert opinions on the contempt laws of eight countries. Although these laws were included as part of the applicant's submissions, the Court found the opinions unnecessary;

(2) copies of the book 'Thalidomide: My Fight'. The Court found that the book gave some background information, but was not necessary to the presentation of the case;

(3) fee for applicant's advisor : UK£7500;

(4) translation expenses: UK£26.84;

(5) typing: UK£231.62;

(6) air freighting and shipment of documents: UK£70.02;

(7) telephone calls: UK£250.

The last five were all found necessary. It is worth noting that the government did not contest them. In subsequent cases, the Court has allowed claims for translation expenses, travel to Strasbourg for lawyers and applicants, expert opinions, and subsistence expenses in Strasbourg. The Court has rejected claims for training and education, such as registration in a course on procedures followed by the Strasbourg institutions.[19] Consultancy fees often are denied as well.

A major issue on the 'necessity' of incurring costs and fees relates to unsuccessful pleas. In the *Sunday Times* case, the government contended that the applicants should be denied costs incurred in advancing submissions rejected by the Court. The applicants replied that they had to assert their case to the best of their ability and that evaluation by hindsight was the wrong approach.[20] The Court agreed:

> The Court cannot accept the Government's contention, even on the assumption that there is a satisfactory method of surmounting the difficulties of calculation which it involves. In its above-mentioned Neumeister judgment . . . the Court drew no distinction between costs referable to successful pleas on Article 5 para. 3 and costs referable to unsuccessful pleas on article 5(4) and 6(1). Whilst it is in the interests of a proper and expeditious administration of justice that the Convention institutions be not burdened with pleas unrelated or extraneous to the case in hand, the submissions now in question cannot be so described.[21]

The Court added, importantly and correctly, that 'a lawyer has a duty to present his client's case as fully and ably as he can and it can never be predicted with

---

[19] In *Sporrong & Lönrroth v. Sweden* (Article 50), (1982) 88 Eur. Ct. H. R. (ser. A), the SEK1,000 enrolment fees was objected to by the government as not being attributable to a particular case. The Court agreed and denied the award.

[20] *Sunday Times, supra* n. 12, at 14.   [21] *Ibid.*

certainty what weight a tribunal may attach to this or that plea, provided that it is not manifestly otiose or invalid'.[22] Subsequently, in *Eckle v. Germany*,[23] the government also sought to have the fees reduced because three issues were not won by the applicants. As in the *Sunday Times* case, the Court denied this contention, noting that the three issues were not rejected as manifestly ill-founded, but continued to the admissibility stage where they were rejected after a preliminary inquiry into the merits. The examination called for the lawyer's participation and hence costs could be awarded.

As the Court's caseload has grown, it has failed to adhere to these precedents. Increasingly it has been discounting fees and costs claimed for pleadings that it denies on the merits. The result is likely to create a conservative bar that is unwilling to assert new claims or innovative arguments, leading to a static interpretation of the Convention. *Olsson v. Sweden*[24] indicates the shift in the Court's approach to fees for claims decided against the applicant. In *Olsson II*,[25] the applicants asked SEK1,800 per hour for 625 hours work as well as travel and translation expenses. The government protested that the applicants could have used Swedish legal aid in their domestic proceedings. The government also asserted that 'the way in which the lawyer for the applicants conducted the proceedings before the Commission should be taken into consideration'.[26] It is not clear what this means, although it may be a reference to dilatory tactics. The government further argued the amount of time claimed was unnecessary and the rate of the fee was too high. The Court rejected the first contention, holding that there is no obligation on applicants to apply for legal aid. The domestic amounts were approved, but in regard to the Strasbourg proceedings, the Court effectively reversed its holding in the *Sunday Times* case. In *Olsson II* it limited costs and fees: 'bearing in mind that the applicants have succeeded only on the points mentioned . . . and making an assessment on an equitable basis, the Court considers that the applicants should be awarded under this head 50,000 kroner' from which it deducted legal aid received from the Council of Europe. The SEK50,000 represented less than 5 per cent of the requested fees of SEK1,269,000.

The issue of the reasonableness of the quantum of fees claimed has been repeatedly raised in cases before the European Court. In *Konig v. Germany*,[27] relied on extensively in the *Sunday Times* case, the Court held that the applicant was entitled to reimbursement of sums expended in exercising such national remedies as were intended to expedite the proceedings against him. Concerning expenses at Strasbourg, the government argued that the Court should adopt a uniform European rule and suggested the scale established by the Commission

---

[22] *Ibid.*
[23] *Eckle v. Germany* (Article 50), (1983) 65 Eur.Ct.H.R. (ser. A).
[24] *Olsson v. Sweden (Olsson I)*, (1988) 130–A Eur.Ct.H.R. (ser. A).
[25] *Olsson v. Sweden (Olsson II)*, (1992) 250–A Eur.Ct.H.R. (ser. A).
[26] *Ibid.* at para. 112.
[27] *Konig v. Germany, supra* n. 17, at 15.

for free legal aid. The Commission disagreed, noting that the result would be that those applicants coming from countries where justice is less expensive would thereby obtain full indemnification while others would have to pay sometimes considerable amounts themselves.

In *Konig*, as in *Sunday Times* and *Eckle v. Germany*, the Court stated that it is not bound by domestic scales or standards for lawyers' fees. The government noted that the fees charged by the lawyers for Konig were nearly double normal fees according to the scales in force in Germany. The Court nonetheless found them reasonable. In the *Sunday Times* case the government objected that the costs, especially the lawyers' fees, exceeded those normally awarded in English courts. The Court held it is not bound by domestic scales or standards on quantum and found all the amounts claimed were reasonable.[28] The Court does review amounts and shows some scepticism about high fee claims. In *Eckle*, the Court noted that the attorney-client agreement to pay higher fees than that provided in the German scale was presented to the European Court some five years after the final national decision. While expressing that it had 'no cause to believe that it is confronted with a bogus document drafted solely for the purposes of the proceedings pending before it since the judgment of 15 July 1982', the Court accepted the suggestion of the Commission that only DM1,500 be awarded out of a claimed DM10,866.50.

In *Silver and others*, the applicants' attorneys submitted a bill of UK£17,093.63 for costs and expenses in Strasbourg. They had primary responsibility for the conduct of the seven joined applications before the Commission and Court. The government argued that an excessive number of hours was billed at an excessive rate (UK£40 per hour). The Court expressed its concern over high fees, quoting its opinion from *Young, James and Webster*:[29]

high costs of litigation may themselves constitute a serious impediment to the effective protection of human rights. It would be wrong for the Court to give encouragement to such a situation in its decisions awarding costs under Article 50. It is important that applicants should not encounter undue financial difficulties in bringing complaints under the Convention and the Court considers that it may expect that lawyers in Contracting States will cooperate to this end in the fixing of their fees.

The Court accepted the applicant's figures on the number of hours (294) for the seven cases over seven years, but lowered the fee to UK£35 pounds per hour. Two lawyers who claimed fees for appearance before the Court ('brief fees') in the amount of UK£16,250 saw these reduced to UK£3,000.

The Court's approach raises concern that individuals will be unable to obtain representation if the fees are substantially below those that attorneys can recover by taking other kinds of cases in their domestic legal systems. Of course, individuals

---

[28] *Sunday Times*, *supra* n. 12 (citing *Konig v. Germany*, *supra* n. 17, at 18–19, para. 22–23.)
[29] *Silver v. United Kingdom*, (1983) 67 Eur.Ct.H.R. (ser. A) (Article 50), at 9, para. 18.

who bring cases to the European system can be provided with legal aid; however, 'compared with the amounts offered by way of legal aid in many national systems the money offered in respect of fees are meager, if not derisory, and it may be asked whether this operates to discourage lawyers from bringing cases to Strasbourg'.[30] While some claim that 'in many cases lawyers are not motivated by the prospect of financial gain when they agree to appear in proceedings before the Court',[31] the possibility of recovering fees can be important to the ability of clients to obtain representation. At present, the prestige of appearing in Strasbourg still appears to be an incentive to many advocates to take cases in spite of the limited recovery possible. In the long term, however, failure to compensate attorneys adequately may diminish the quality and quantity of legal services available to applicants by discouraging better lawyers from taking human rights cases.

The applicant must be legally obliged to pay the costs in order to have them awarded.[32] In the case of *X v. United Kingdom*,[33] the Court granted attorneys' fees even though the attorney had not pursued the recovery of his fees from the client because of the client's poverty. The Court rejected the government's argument that the legal fees were not actually incurred, holding that the decision of the attorney not to bill the client did not affect the existence of a civil debt and therefore should not affect the award of fees. In another case, the Court rightly rejected the claim of a non-governmental organization that requested an award of fees for filing a brief *amicus curiae*. In *Dudgeon v. United Kingdom*,[34] on the other hand, fees were awarded to a non-governmental organization that actually represented the applicant. In the spate of cases brought in the 1990s against Turkey, the Turkish government has consistently objected to the involvement of British lawyers because of their higher fees. It has insisted that their appointment had the effect of inflating expenses for travel, communication, interpretation and translation.[35] The Court has rejected this argument, generally awarding the fees in full at a rate of compensation varying from UK£100 per hour for one UK lawyer to UK£25 per hour for Turkish counsel. While the lawyers usually have received the full amount claimed, the Court has not awarded costs or fees in most cases to participating Turkish non-governmental organizations, such as the Kurdish Human Rights Project or Association[36] and the Kurdistan Human Rights Group.[37]

The Inter-American system has not followed the approach of the European

---

[30] D.J. Harris, M. O'Boyle and C. Warbrick, *Law of the European Convention on Human Rights* (1995), 665.   [31] *Ibid.*

[32] *Öztürk v. Germany* (Article 50), (1984) 85 Eur. Ct. H.R. (ser. A).

[33] *X. v. United Kingdom* (Article 50), (1982) 55 Eur.Ct.H.R. (ser. A) at 17–18.

[34] *Dudgeon v. United Kingdom* (Article 50), (1983) 59 Eur.Ct.H.R. (ser. A).

[35] *Mentes v. Turkey*, Judgment of 27 July 1998, para 106 (1997–VIII Reports 2693).

[36] *Aydin v. Turkey*, 27 September 1997, 1997–VI (No. 50) Reports 1866.

[37] *Kurt v. Turkey*, 25 May 1998, 1998–III (No. 74) Reports 1152.

Court despite the greater poverty in most of the Western hemisphere and the fact that one of the consequences of a violation is the need for legal representation. The Inter-American Commission has no programme of legal aid and victims typically rely on non-governmental organizations or private attorneys to bring cases to the Commission. As the case proceeds, the victim has no standing before the Court except during the reparations phase and can only be represented by a lawyer acting as 'advisor' to the Commission with the Commission's permission. For most of its history the Court took the term 'advisor' literally and viewed the victims' attorneys as participating on behalf of the Commission rather than as representing the victim.

In each of its early cases the Court found a basis to deny costs and attorneys' fees. In *Velasquez Rodriguez v. Honduras* and *Godinez Cruz v. Honduras*, the Court refused to award costs and fees because they had not been pleaded.[38] In *Aloeboetoe v. Suriname,* attorneys for the victims pleaded costs and fees to avoid the defect the Court had found in the Honduran cases. They sought amounts for attempting to ascertain the whereabouts of the victims and for pursuing the claim at the local level, before the Commission and before the Court, including attorneys' fees.[39] The requests for legal costs were US$35,785 and US$18,533, while the amount of expenses was US$32,375. The government argued that the Commission was working with outside attorneys, listed as attorneys for the victims, who performed work that the Commission should be doing. The Court agreed and further found that the US$250 per hour fee for services 'bears no relationship to prevailing conditions in the Inter-American system'.[40]

In the *Aloeboetoe* case, the Court misapprehended the function of the Commission and the 'advisor' when it characterized the latter as someone the Commission had 'contracted' to use instead of using its own staff to process the case. According to the Court, the Convention assigns responsibility to the Court and the Commission whose costs are financed out of the budget of the Organization of American States. The Court viewed the Commission as 'preferring' to contract its work elsewhere, and found, in consequence, that 'the Commission cannot demand that expenses incurred as a result of its own internal work structure be reimbursed through the assessment of costs'. The Court failed entirely to see the separate interests of the Commission and the victim.

---

[38] *Velasquez Rodriguez (Compensatory Damages),* (1989) 7 Inter-Am.Ct.H.R. (ser. C) (at para. 193; *Godinez Cruz Case,* (Compensatory Damages), (1989) 8 Inter-Am.Ct.H.R. (ser. C) at para. 202, citing Article. 45(1) of the Court's Rules of Procedure. This decision was repeated during the damages phase of the case. See *Velasquez Rodriguez, (Compensatory Damages), ibid.* at paras. 41–42 where the family sought reimbursement of costs of the investigation to locate the disappeared. The Court notes that the costs were neither pleaded nor proven opportunely.

[39] *Aloeboetoe Case (Reparations),* (1993) 15 Inter-Am.Ct.H.R. (ser. C). These costs included a visit to Suriname by the attorney representing the victim, a visit to the interior of the country by part of the non-governmental organization involved, the appointment of research assistants to prepare the three hearings for the case before the Commission and the initial memorandum to the Court, and the hiring of an associate professor to take over the law course of the victims' attorney.

[40] *Aloeboetoe et al. Case (Merits),* (1991) 11 Inter-Am. Ct. H.R. (ser. C).

In *El Amparo v. Venezuela*, the Court was persuaded by the Venezuelan argument that adequate proof of the costs was lacking and that the sum claimed was disproportionate. Instead of the US$240,000 requested, the Court awarded US$2,000 to each of the families and each of the survivors for the costs incurred regarding actions taken within the country. The Court once more denied costs and attorneys' fees for proceedings before the Commission and the Court, continuing to confuse the representation of the victims with the work of the Commission.

In *Neira Alegria v. Peru*, the Commission asked that the Court order Peru to pay the court costs and attorneys' fees. As in prior cases, the Court held that Peru must pay the expenditures that the victim's next of kin may have incurred during the national proceedings as well as fair compensation, but it again insisted that:

the Commission cannot demand that expenses incurred as a result of its own internal work structure be reimbursed through assessment of costs. The operation of the human rights organs of the American System is funded by the Member States by means of their annual contributions.[41]

As in the *El Amparo* case, the Commission sought costs and expenses of the families in Peru estimated at US$6,300 to be divided equally among the three families. The government asked for proof of actual expenditures. The evidence was conflicting on whether free legal assistance had been given the families. Nonetheless, the Court awarded a 'fair' indemnity of US$2,000, the same as in *El Amparo* in spite of there being 'no documentary evidence of actual expenditures'. No costs were awarded for proceedings before the Commission or the Court. The Court stated that the victims did not appoint anyone to represent them, a mistake of fact. The attorney in question represented two non-governmental organizations and was designated 'legal advisor' to the Commission to facilitate his participation in the case.[42] As these decisions indicate, the Inter-American Court generally has ordered the state to pay the expenses borne by the families in investigating the whereabouts of the victims and in processing the case at the domestic level, and has awarded an amount based on equity in the absence of proof as to the amount.[43]

The Court's approach to costs and attorneys' fees was a major disappointment and justifiably criticized, but both the Commission and representatives of the victims could have presented stronger arguments to the Court. The Court's award of US$2,000 to each claimant for costs resulted in large part from the lack of proof presented by the Commission and the victims.[44] It also seems that the

---

[41] *Neira Alegria et al. Case*, (1996) 22 Inter-Am.Ct. H.R. (ser. C), para. 87, quoting *Aloeboetoe*, *supra* n. 39, para. 114.

[42] David J. Padilla, 'Reparations in Aloeboetoe v. Suriname', (1995) 17 *Hum Rts. Q.* 541, 548–49.

[43] *Caballero Delgado and Santana*, (1996), 22 Inter-Am.Ct.H.R. (ser. C) para. 71–72; *Aloeboetoe*, *supra* n. 39, at 94–95.

[44] No documentary proof was submitted and the amounts claimed were based on estimates. The Court considered it 'fair' nonetheless to award US$2,000 to each as compensation for the expenses they incurred in their various representations to the national authorities.

claims for costs made in the *El Amparo* case were excessive; it is hard to avoid the suspicion that they constituted an effort to receive attorneys' fees for work done at the Commission and the Court, as well as in internal proceedings.

The Court failed to see the difference between the interests of the Commission and those of the victims, although it was recognized in the initial proceeding before the Court. In the *Viviana Gallardo* case,[45] the Court identified the interest of the victims in having the full enjoyment of their rights be protected and assured. The Court also referred to the institutional interests in the integrity of the system and the governmental interest in a speedy judicial process.[46] The Court noted that no person is entitled to submit cases to the Court because individuals do not have standing. The system requires 'that the Convention be interpreted in favor of the individual, who is the object of international protection'.[47] The Commission's role was likened to that of the 'Ministerio Publico' which carries out an initial investigation, attempts a friendly settlement and proposes appropriate recommendations to remedy the violation it has found to exist.

With its 1998 reparations judgment in *Garrido Baigorria v Argentina*,[48] the Court began awarding costs and fees for proceedings before the Inter-American Commission and Court. The awards corresponded to a change in the Rules of Court allowing direct victim representation at the reparations phase, but probably had more to do with the intense criticism of the Court's earlier opinions and to a change in the composition of the Court. In the 1998 and 1999 reparations judgments in *Suarez Rosero v. Ecuador*, *Castillo Paez v. Peru* and *Loayza Tamayo v. Peru*, the Court awarded attorneys' fees and costs for proceedings before the international institutions. *Suarez Rosero* was the first case where the Court awarded the claimed costs and fees in full, amounting to US$6,804.80 for the merits phase and US$3,635.65 for the reparations phase of the case. The Court referred to the jurisprudence of the European Court in deciding that costs should be awarded on an equitable basis and paid if reasonable in quantum and sufficiently linked to the decision.[49] It could have referred as well to judgments of the ILOAT, which awards costs 'to the extent warranted by the circumstances of the case, that is to say its nature, importance and complexity and the actual contribution made by the complainant or his counsel to the proceedings'.[50]

The convergence of the Inter-American and European Courts on awards of fees and costs is welcome. Victims need their own attorneys before international tribunals; indeed, this may be required for due process.[51] Procedures before such bodies have not been created for the sole benefit of the States, but in order to

---

[45] *In the Matter of Viviana Gallardo et al.*, (1984) G 101/81 Inter-Am.Ct.H.R. (ser. A).
[46] *Ibid.*, para. 13.
[47] *Ibid.*, para. 16.
[48] The Court awarded attorney's fees of US$20,000 and costs of US$45,000.
[49] The Court cited *Brincat v. Italy*, (1992) 249A Eur.Ct.H.R. (ser. A).
[50] See, e.g. *Ghaffar v. WHO*, ILOAT Judgment No. 320 of 21 November 1977, Consideration 19; *Lamadie v. IPI*, ILOAT Judgment No. 262 of 27 October 1975, Consideration 5.
[51] See American Convention on Human Rights, Article 8.

allow for the exercise of important individual rights. If the victims and their families are unable to recover costs and fees, the goal of *restitutio in integrum* is defeated because the victims suffer unrecovered losses as a direct consequence of the violation. Those who suffer human rights violations will be vindicated only if they have access to legal assistance and that assistance will only come if it is compensated. To ensure *restitutio in integrum*, international tribunals must liberalize their views on attorneys' fees and costs. The victims deserve and are entitled to their own representation. Where the state has caused the wrong, it should pay for the procedures necessary to achieve a remedy.

It is costly to finance complex litigation and victims of human rights violations can rarely afford to hire attorneys or pay the amounts necessary to prove the wrongdoing. At present, the registry of the Inter-American Court estimates that it costs more than US$80,000 to take a case through the Inter-American system. Lawyers are understandably reluctant to shoulder these burdens and it will become worse if fees and costs are not reimbursed. Similarly, single litigants can rarely if ever spend as much money on lawsuits as all victims or potential victims would if they could act in their collective interest. Without fee shifting, victims will often be unable to sue, undermining the effectiveness of the systems designed to protect human rights.

12

Gross and Systematic Violations

International human rights law, especially as developed within the United Nations, recognizes a category of situations of gross and systematic violations of human rights. Though never exactly defined, it constitutes the jurisdictional threshold for consideration of human rights complaints submitted pursuant to ECOSOC Resolution 1503.[1] The phrase 'gross and systematic' includes both a quantitative and a qualitative element: 'gross' violations are those that are particularly serious in nature because of their cruelty or depravity, while 'systematic' violations suggest an official, widespread pattern or practice.

The quantitative and qualitative differences between gross and systematic violations and individual cases affect the scope and nature of remedies that can and should be afforded. First, gross and systematic violations often accompany internal armed conflicts where the sheer number of victims and perpetrators may overwhelm the best efforts to provide redress.[2] Rwanda and Cambodia illustrate extreme situations where tens of thousands of individuals participated in mass killings and in the process destroyed each state's national judiciary and infrastructure.[3] Secondly, even where such numbers are not present, the transition from repression or conflict may be accompanied by a weak government presiding over a weak economy with few governmental resources.[4] The money that is available usually is needed to restructure and rebuild national institutions, leaving insufficient funds to redress all injuries committed by the prior regime. Thirdly, the overall social context in which the remedies for gross and systematic viola-

---

[1] ECOSOC Resolution 1503 (XLVIII) (1970) authorizes the United Nations Sub-Commission on Prevention of Discrimination and Protection of Minorities to consider communications received from individuals and groups that 'appear to reveal a consistent pattern of gross and reliably attested violations of human rights and fundamental freedoms'.

[2] Rudolf Rummer estimates that internal conflicts and systematic human rights violations this century have caused some 170 million deaths, compared to 33 million persons killed in international military conflicts: Rudolf J. Rummel, *Death by Government* (1994) 9. Jennifer Balint claims that the period from the end of the Second World War to 1996 included at least 220 non-international conflicts that may have resulted in 86 million deaths: Jennifer Balint, 'An Empirical Study of Conflict, Conflict Victimization, and Legal Redress', in Christopher C. Joyner, (ed.), *Reining in Impunity for International Crimes and Serious Violations of Fundamental Human Rights, 14 Nouvelles Etudes Penales 1998* 107 (1998), 101, 107.

[3] More than 100,000 Rwandans were probably involved in the genocidal slaughter that took place in the country. Ninety-five per cent of the country's lawyers and judges were either killed or in exile or prison. With 115,000 Rwandans detained in prisons, the Ministry of Justice had seven attorneys on its staff at the end of the conflict. See 'Symposium, Accountability for International Crimes and Serious Violations of Fundamental Human Rights' (1996) 135, 50 *Law and Contmp. Prob.* 135.

[4] *Right to restitution, compensation and rehabilitation for victims of grave violations of human rights, Report of the Secretary-General prepared pursuant to commission resolution* 1995/34 CN.4/1996/29/Add.1 (4 January 1996).

tions must be afforded differs from the individual case. Where there have been widespread human rights abuses, the entire society often has suffered. It is unlikely that healing can occur without redress of individual victim wrongs, but the reparative function may be impossible to achieve fully because of the former policy of state terror that 'reaches deeply into the fabric of society, affecting large sectors of the population'.[5] Remedies may have to be adjusted to achieve other goals, including cessation of conflict, prevention of future conflict, deterrence of individual wrongdoing, rehabilitation of society and victims, and reconciliation of individuals and groups.

Not surprisingly, responses to gross and systematic violations have varied in practice, following political transitions in countries of Central and Eastern Europe, Asia, Latin America and Africa.[6] Most of the approaches are compromises that allow partial accountability and limited redress; they also necessarily leave many victims without full remedies and perpetrators without complete sanction. Some governments have chosen to prosecute the 'worst' violators, while others have offered reduced sentences or pardons in exchange for full confessions and apologies. Others have chosen not to prosecute at all, but to rely on truth commissions and/or civil remedies.[7] A United Nations study of the administration of justice and rights of detainees divides state responses into three parts, the right to know, the right to justice, and the right to reparation.[8] The right to know encompasses commissions of inquiry, preservation of and access to archives. The right to justice includes the duty of states with regard to the administration of justice, the distribution among courts, and restrictions on impunity such as prescription, amnesty, asylum, extradition, due obedience, and military court jurisdiction. Reparations includes general principles and guarantees of non-repetition.

Whatever the means chosen, policies to respond to gross and systematic human rights abuses generally have two overall objectives: to prevent the recurrence of the violations and to repair the damage that they caused, to the extent possible.[9] Ascertaining and acknowledging the truth is an imperative, a first step that may be followed by a range of options: international prosecutions for international crimes, national prosecution, lustration or purging of individual wrongdoers, civil remedies, international or national compensation mechanisms, partial

---

[5] *Ibid.* at 36.

[6] Stanley Cohen, 'State Crimes of Previous Regimes; Knowledge, Accountability, and the Policing of the Past', (1995) *A.B.A. J. L. & Soc. Pol'y* 7.

[7] See Luc Huyse, 'Justice After Transition: On the Choices Successor Elites Make in Dealing with the Past', (1995) 20 *L & Soc. Inquiry* 51.

[8] See *Question of the Impunity of Perpetrators of Violations of Human Rights (Civil and Political Rights): Final Report prepared by Mr. Joinet pursuant to Sub-Commission Resolution 1995/35*, Sub-Commission on Prevention of Discrimination and Protection of Minorities, ESCOR, 48th Sess., Annex II, Agenda Item 10, U.N. Doc. E/CN.4/Sub.2/1996/18.

[9] J. Zalaquett, 'Confronting Human Rights Violations Committed by Former Governments: Principles Applicable and Political Constraints', 1989 *Aspen Inst., State Crimes: Punishment or Pardon* 29.

or total amnesties, and symbolic or other non-monetary reparations. No single formula can apply to all conflicts. Each response must be seen as an instrument of social policy to achieve the goals of peace and justice, taking into account the need to end conflict and victimization, prevent future wrongs, rehabilitate society as a whole and victims individually, and reconcile different groups and people. Where internal conflict or repression has destroyed the credibility or existence of the judicial or administrative structures, external resources may be necessary to provide technical assistance or staff to assist in the re-building process and national prosecution or civil remedies.

A. PROSECUTIONS

Most, if not all, gross and systematic violations necessitate prosecution of the perpetrators in addition to civil remedies for the victims. Genocide, crimes against humanity, and war crimes are not only human rights violations, they are international crimes. The obligation on states to prosecute or extradite those accused of any such offence exists in several international agreements, including the Genocide Convention,[10] the Geneva Conventions of 1949,[11] and the 1977 Protocol I to the Geneva Conventions.[12] A similar duty is imposed by global and regional conventions against torture.[13] These agreements require states to cooperate with each other in the investigation, prosecution and adjudication of those charged with the included crimes and the punishment of those convicted. In 1971, the United Nations General Assembly affirmed that a state's refusal to cooperate in the arrest, extradition, trial, and punishment of persons accused or convicted of war crimes and crimes against humanity is 'contrary to the United Nations Charter and to generally recognized norms of international law'.[14] The

---

[10] Convention on the Prevention and Punishment of the Crime of Genocide, 9 December 1948, 1 U.N. GAOR Res. 96, 11 December 1946, 78 U.N.T.S. 277.

[11] See the Four Geneva Conventions of 12 August 1949: Convention for the Amelioration of the Condition of the Wounded and the Sick in Armed Forces in the Field, 6 U.S.T. 3114, 75 U.N.T.S. 31; Convention for the Amelioration of the Condition of Wounded, Sick and Shipwrecked Members of Armed Forces as Sea, 6 U.S.T. 3217, 75 U.N.T.S. 85; Convention Relative to the Treatment of Prisoners of War, 6 U.S.T., 75 U.N.T.S. 135; Convention Relative to the Protection of Civilian Persons in Times of War, 6 U.S.T. 3516, 75 U.N.T.S. 28.

[12] Protocol I Additional to the Geneva Conventions of 12 August 1949, and Relating to the Protection of Victims of International Armed Conflicts, 1125 U.N.T.S. 3, reprinted in 16 I.L.M. 1391.

[13] See Convention Against Torture and Other Cruel, Inhuman or Degrading Treatment or Punishment, 10 December 1984, U.N.G.A. Res. 39/46, reprinted in (1984) 23 I.L.M. 1027; European Convention for the Prevention of Torture and Inhuman or Degrading Treatment or Punishment, 26 November 1987, E.T.S. No. 126,(1988) 27 I.L.M. 1152; Inter-American Convention to Prevent and Punish Torture, 9 December 1985, AG/RES.783 (XV–0/85), O.A.S. General Assembly, 15th Sess. IEA/Ser.P. AG/Doc. 22023/85 rev. 1 at 46–54 (1986), O.A.S. T.S. No. 67, reprinted in (1986) 25 I.L.M. 519.

[14] Resolution on War Criminals, G.A. Res. 2840 (XXVI), 26 U.N. GAOR Supp. (No. 29), at 88, U.N. Doc. A/8429 (1971).

Commentary to the Geneva Conventions also confirms that the obligation to prosecute is 'absolute' for grave breaches committed in the context of international armed conflicts.[15]

The absence of a conventional definition of crimes against humanity leaves open the possibility of conflicting judgments about the criminality of particular acts.[16] A rapporteur of the International Law Commission, attempting to distinguish 'internationally wrongful acts' (delicts) from international crimes, has broadly proposed that the latter category include 'a serious breach on a widespread scale of an international obligation of essential importance for safeguarding the human being, such as those prohibiting slavery, genocide, and apartheid'.[17] The Chairman of the United Nations Committee on Crime Prevention and Control also has referred to 'criminal violations of human rights'.[18] The Statute of the International Criminal Tribunal for Rwanda is more specific, granting the Tribunal the power to prosecute violence to the life, health and physical or mental well-being of persons, in particular murder, cruel treatment such as torture, mutilation or any form of corporal punishment; collective punishments; taking of hostages; acts of terrorism; rape, enforced prostitution and other indecent assault; pillage; summary executions; and threats.[19] The Statute also grants jurisdiction in regard to persecutions on political, racial, and religious grounds, and 'other inhumane acts' 'when committed as part of a widespread or systematic attack against any civilian population on national, political, ethnic, racial or religious grounds'.[20]

Human rights conventions are silent about the duty to punish violations, but the obligation to ensure rights is held to encompass such a duty, at least with respect to the most serious violations.[21] The European and Inter-American Courts

---

[15] Virginia Morris and Michael Scharf, *An Insider's Guide to the International Criminal Tribunal for the Former Yugoslavia: A Documentary History and Analysis* (1995), 114, nn. 341, 356.

[16] The Nuremberg Charter defined crimes against humanity as 'murder, extermination, enslavement, deportation, and other inhumane acts committed against any civilian population, before or during the war, or persecutions on political, racial, or religious grounds in execution of or in connection with any crime within the jurisdiction of the Tribunal': Charter of the International Military Tribunal annexed to the Agreement for the Prosecution and Punishment of the Major War Criminals of the European Axis, August 1945, 82 U.N.T.S. 279, 59 Stat. 1544, E.A.S. No. 472.

[17] See Draft Articles on State Responsibility, Article 19 (1976), [1976] *Y.B. Int'l L. Comm'n*, U.N. doc. A/CN.4/Ser.A/1976/Add 1 (pt. 2, ch III; Commentary to art. 19, para. 34).

[18] Manuel Lopez-Rey, 'Crime and Human Rights', 42 *Federal Probation* 10–15, 13 (March 1978).

[19] Statute of the International Criminal Tribunal for Rwanda, adopted at New York, 8 November 1994, S.C. Res. 955, U.N. SCOR, 49th Sess, 3453d mtg., U.N. Doc. S/RES/955 (1994), (1994) 33 I.L.M. 1598, Article 4.

[20] *Ibid*. Article 2.

[21] While there are numerous treaty-based obligations to prosecute, Michael Scharf argues that customary international law does not include a broad-based duty to prosecute, but limits it to international crimes as contained in treaties explicitly establishing the duty. The obligation to ensure respect for human rights can be met without prosecution by establishment of a truth commission, purges of wrongdoers from office and limited prosecutions, together with victim compensation and civil redress: Michael Scharf, 'Swapping Amnesty for Peace: Was There a Duty to Prosecute International

both have interpreted their Conventions in this way.[22] Similarly, the United Nations Human Rights Committee has stated that where acts of torture occur, Article 2(3) of the Covenant places the government 'under a duty to . . . conduct an inquiry into the circumstances of [the victim's] torture, to punish those found guilty of torture and to take steps to ensure that similar violations do not occur in the future'.[23] The Committee also has called for investigation and prosecution in cases involving arbitrary executions and disappearances.[24] In *Bautista de Arellana v. Colombia*,[25] the Committee found that disciplinary and administrative remedies alone were not 'adequate and effective' to redress the violation, suggesting that anything short of criminal prosecution would not comply with the Covenant's requirements. More broadly, in a 1992 General Comment, the Committee stated that amnesties for acts of torture 'are generally incompatible with the duty of States to investigate such acts; to guarantee freedom from such acts within their jurisdiction; and to ensure that they do not occur in the future'.[26] Further, 'States may not deprive individuals of the right to an effective remedy, including compensation and such full rehabilitation as possible'.[27]

In 1996, the Inter-American Commission concluded that the Chilean Truth Commission[28] was an inadequate response to the violations that took place during the Pinochet regime. According to the Commission, the government's recognition of responsibility, its partial investigation of the facts and subsequent payment of compensation were 'not enough, in themselves, to fulfill its obligations under the Convention'. Instead, 'the State has the obligation to investigate all violations that have been committed within its jurisdiction, for the purpose of identifying the persons responsible, imposing appropriate punishment on them, and ensuring adequate reparations for the victims'.[29] The Commission found two serious defects with the Chilean approach. First, it had failed specifically to identify the perpetrators, which made it virtually impossible for the victims to establish

Crimes in Haiti', (1996) 31 *Tex Int'l L.J.* 1, 40. A conference held by the Aspen Institute similarly concluded that there is no general obligation under customary international law to punish the violators: 1989 *Aspen Inst., State Crimes: Punishment or Pardon.*

[22] See *Velasquez Rodriguez Case*, (1988) 4 Inter-Am.Ct.H.R. (ser. C), para. 164.

[23] *Report of the Human Rights Committee*, U.N. GAOR, 39th Sess., Supp. No. 40, Annex XIII, para. 13, at 188, U.N. Doc. A/39/40 (1984).

[24] See *Baboeram v. Suriname*, Comm. Nos. 146/1983 and 148–154/1983, 40 U.N. GAOR Supp. (No. 40), Annex X, para. 13.2, U.N. Doc. A/40/40 (1985) (duty to investigate and bring to justice persons responsible for executions); *Quinteros Almeida v. Uruguay*, Comm. No. 107/1981, 38 U.N. GOAR Supp. (No. 40), Annex XXII, U.N. Doc. A/38/40 (1983) (duty to investigate and bring to justice any persons responsible for disappearances).

[25] Comm. No. 563/1993 (1995).

[26] *General Comment 20 (44)* (Article 7), para. 15 in Official Records of the Human Rights Committee 1991–92, CCPR/11/Add.1 (1995), 370.

[27] *Ibid.*

[28] See *Report of the Chilean National Commission on Truth and Reconciliation* (Philip E. Berryman trans., 1993).

[29] Garay Hermosilla *et al*, Report 36/96, Case 10.843 (Chile), Annual Report of the Inter-Am. Comm'n. H.R. 1996, 156, at para. 77.

responsibility before civil courts. Secondly, the state failed to take any punitive action against the perpetrators.

The question of punishment of wrongdoers is often debated despite the duties imposed under international law.[30] Proponents claim that prosecution, conviction and punishment act to deter the specific wrongdoers from future violations and are also general deterrents to human rights violations. Further, prosecution and punishment serve as retribution and an expression of the moral condemnation of society, which should proclaim and enforce its condemnation of abuses in order to affirm the rule of law and fundamental societal norms. Punishment fosters the advance of constitutional and international legal principles when the government asserts its authority over violators. Accountability also gives significance to the suffering of the victims and serves as partial reparation, preventing private acts of revenge and helping to rehabilitate the victims.[31] On the other hand, the national reconciliation and healing necessary to establish a stable, democratic society may be made more difficult when there are numerous prosecutions and punishment. Jose Zalaquett argues that 'to set standards which are perceived as too rigid and impractical could also end up by undermining international law'.[32]

A key role of prosecution is to establish an authoritative record of abuses that will withstand later revisionist efforts. The emphasis in criminal trials on full and reliable evidence in accordance with due process usually makes the results more credible than those of other, more political proceedings, including truth commissions. The Chief Prosecutor at Nuremberg said that the documentation of Nazi atrocities was one of the most important legacies of the trials. The Nazi actions were documented 'with such authenticity and in such detail that there can be no responsible denial of these crimes in the future and no tradition of martyrdom of the Nazi leaders can arise among informed people'.[33]

The problem of the military is widespread and particularly serious. Often there is no remorse, but, instead, military leaders justify human rights abuses on the basis of national security, perhaps conceding some 'unavoidable excesses'. Governments may lack the power to carry out their obligations of dealing with past human rights abuses in the face of such obduracy, especially where the people who should be prosecuted remain in positions of power. Efforts to prosecute can induce the military to close ranks, to challenge democratic institutions or to attempt to overthrow the democratic government.[34] In Argentina, efforts to

---

[30] *Ibid.*

[31] Mob justice can be seen in cycles in countries where impunity is known. See Scharf, *supra* n. 21, at 14.

[32] J. Zalaquett, *supra* n. 9, at 27.

[33] See *Report to the President* from Justice Robert H. Jackson, Chief of Counsel for the United States in the Prosecution of Axis War Criminals (7 June 1945), (1945) 39 *Am.J. Int'l L.* (Supp.) 178, 184.

[34] Dianne Orentlicher traces the Uruguayan amnesty law to the challenge mounted by the military when summoned to appear to answer charges relating to human rights violations committed in the 1970s. The military defendants refused to respond: D. Orentlicher, 'Settling Accounts: The Duty to Prosecute Human Rights violations of a Prior Regime', (1991) 100 *Yale L.J.* 2537, 2611.

prosecute led to several rebellions during the 1980s against the civilian government.[35]

The problems raised by efforts to prosecute perpetrators of human rights abuses have led some governments to negotiate or declare amnesties, arguing that the need for reconciliation outweighs the interests in accountability and redress.[36] The practice has been challenged by commentators and international tribunals who note the questionable legality of such a measure and that even if an amnesty achieves a short-term restoration of peace and human rights, it still may jeopardize long-term interests.[37] According to Michael Scharf, 'history records that the international amnesty given to the Turkish encouraged Adolf Hitler some twenty years later to conclude that Germany could pursue his genocidal policies with impunity'.[38] Condoning human rights abuses through amnesty may incite other regimes to bargain a restoration of peace for amnesty, breeding contempt for the law and inviting future violations. The United Nations Human Rights Commission and the Sub-Commission have concluded that impunity is one of the main reasons for the continuation of grave violations of human rights throughout the world,[39] increasing abuses in some instances.[40] A report of the Lawyers' Committee for Human Rights notes: 'Government critics and human rights groups charge that the persistence of torture in Argentina is a direct result of President Menem's pardons of police officials and military officers accused of torture during the military dictatorship, many of whom still hold high posts in government'.[41] The United Nations Working Group on Involuntary or Forced Disappearances similarly claims: 'Impunity is perhaps the single most important factor contributing to the phenomenon of disappearance. Perpetrators of human rights violations ... become all the more irresponsible if they are not held to account before a court of law'.[42]

In 1998, a decision of the Inter-American Commission resolved numerous complaints against Chile and condemned the amnesty that exempted those involved in the military regime from any criminal responsibility for acts that they committed.[43] The government argued that it had attempted to repeal the

---

[35] D. Orentlicher, 'Settling Accounts', at 2545.

[36] Examples of such laws include Ley 104 of 30 December 1993, *Regimen Penal Colombiano* envio 36 (februro/abril de 1994) and envio 38 (noviembre de 1994), ss 8122 *et seq* (Colombia); Decree Law 2.191 of 18 April 1978, *Diario oficial* No. 30/042 (19 April 1978) (Chile); Decree Law 22.924 of 22 September 1983, *Legislacion Argentina* (1983–B), at 1681 (Argentina).

[37] Scharf, *supra* n. 21 at 11.

[38] *Ibid.*, citing Morris and Scharf, *supra* n. 15, at 6 n. 1.

[39] *United Nations Commission on Human Rights: Report on the Consequences of Impunity*, U.N. Doc. E/CN.4/1990/13.

[40] See cases cited in Scharf, *supra* n. 21, at 12, n. 81.

[41] Lawyers Committee for Human Rights, *Critique: Review of the Department of State's Country Reports on Human Rights Practices 1992*, (1993), 20.

[42] *Report of the Working Group on Enforced or Involuntary Disappearances*, U.N. ESCOR, Comm'n on Human Rights, 47th Sess., para. 406, U.N. Doc. E/CN.4/1991/20 (1991).

[43] Report No. 25/98, Cases 11.505, 11.532, 11.541, 11.546, 11.549, 11.569, 11.572, 11.573, 11.583, 11.585, 11.595, 11.562, 11.657, 11.675, 11.705 (Chile), Inter-Am.Comm'n H.R., *Annual Report of the Inter-American Commission on Human Rights 1997*, OEA/Ser.L/V/II.98 (1998) 512.

Decree Law granting amnesty, but that a majority of those in the Senate did not favour the law. It also noted that it had called upon the Supreme Court to declare that the amnesty cannot be an obstacle to the investigation and punishment of crimes. It requested that the Commission take into account the historical context surrounding the events and the special situation of the return to a democratic regime. The Commission's decision focused on the fact that the amnesty law emanated from an illegitimate military regime that usurped power and whose actions, therefore, could not be considered legal. According to the Commission:

[t]he Chilean constitutional order must necessarily allow the government to fulfill its fundamental obligations and release it from limitations imposed by the military usurper regime and which are contrary to the law, since it is not juridically acceptable that the constitutional government should be limited in its efforts to consolidate democracy; neither is it acceptable that the actions of the de facto regime be given the attributes of a de jure government.[44]

The Commission agreed with the petitioners who argued that the government has an immutable obligation to make a thorough investigation of the facts, to establish who should be held accountable, and to punish those responsible for the human rights violations which took place, especially considering the seriousness of the violations, which included a systematic strategy of repression resulting in thousands of cases of disappearance, summary execution and torture. The Commission decided that the amnesty decree, by precluding identification and punishment of perpetrators of human rights violations, violated the right to legal protection provided for under Article 25 of the American Convention.

In practice, prosecution can be national or international, although the role of international tribunals is viewed generally as subsidiary to national institutions that should be the primary fora for accountability. Only where national prosecution is absent or highly unlikely does an international tribunal become necessary, as in the cases of the former Yugoslavia and Rwanda. Cherif Bassiouni argues that as a matter of policy, international prosecutions should be limited to leaders, policy-makers and senior executors with national trials taking jurisdiction over the remaining offenders. National prosecution of offenders has taken place in Ethiopia[45] and to some extent in Argentina,[46] but even within states, efforts may be made to distinguish the leadership from other perpetrators of egregious or minor violations.

---

[44] *Ibid.* at para. 21.

[45] See Girma Wkjira, 'National Prosecution: The Ethiopian Experience', in *Reining in Impunity*, *supra* n. 2, at 189.

[46] See Nunca Mas, *Informe de la Comision Sobre la Desaparicion de Personas* (1985); Carlos Santiago Nino, *Radical Evil on Trial* (1996).

B. TRUTH COMMISSIONS AND INTERNATIONAL INVESTIGATIONS

With the restoration of democracy and respect for human rights, governments must investigate reports of human rights violations committed by predecessor regimes. Truth commissions are a common response during transitions and may be international, e.g. El Salvador,[47] or national, e.g. Chile[48] and Argentina.[49] Commissions establish a record of what has happened and disseminate the results. When conducted by the national governments they can include a formal acceptance of responsibility or precede prosecutions by identifying perpetrators.[50] When properly done, the reports of truth commissions contain a comprehensive and integrated historical record of the offences in question and the context in which they occurred. South African Justice Richard Goldstone has noted the importance of establishing the historical record: 'If it were not for the Truth and Reconciliation Commission people who today are saying that they did not know about apartheid would be saying that it didn't happen. This is a fact, and it cannot be underestimated'.[51] The results not only provide knowledge but can and should include an official acknowledgment or statement of regret for human rights abuses.[52]

The United Nations and regional organizations have mounted several international investigations of gross and systematic human rights abuses and have mediated in conflicts where such abuses have occurred. The United Nations Truth Commission Report on El Salvador made extensive findings and issued recommendations for remedying past human rights abuses based on a desire to deter and 'in order to avoid any risk of reverting to the *status quo ante*'.[53] The Report

---

[47] See *From Madness to Hope: The 12-Year war in El Salvador, Report of the United Nations Commission on the Truth For El Salvador*, U.N. Doc. S/25500 (1993).

[48] See *Chile Report, supra* n. 28.

[49] See Nunca Mas, *supra* n. 46. See also Priscilla B. Hayner, 'Fifteen Truth Commissions—1974 to 1994: A Comparative Study', (1994) 16 *Hum. Rts.* 597, 607 (1994).

[50] In some states, however, prosecution is precluded. Argentina investigated and published the truth, passed legislation providing compensation to the victims and families, and judged and imprisoned several of the junta leaders. The victims were unable to pursue criminal prosecutions of individual violators. See, Inter-Am. C.H.R., *Argentina, Report No. 28/92*, reprinted in (1992) 13 *Hum.Rts.L.J.* 336. Uruguay also declared an amnesty, but permitted victims to seek damages in civil court: Inter.-Am. C.H.R., *Uruguay Report, 29/92* reprinted in (1992) 13 *Hum. Rts. L.J.* 340, para. 27. Identification of perpetrators by truth commissions is controversial because if the reporting body has no prosecutorial powers, then individuals may be identified as wrongdoers without the benefit of a proper defence in a fair hearing.

[51] Justice Richard Goldstone, 'Justice or Reconciliation', The University of Chicago Law School, Center for International Studies Conference, The University of Chicago, 26 April 1997. See also Sir Roland Wilson, Bringing Them Home: Report of the National Inquiry into the Separation of Aboriginal and Torres Strait Islander Children from Their Families (1997).

[52] *Report on El Salvador, supra* n. 47; Honduran National Commissioner for the Protection of Human Rights, *The Facts Speak for Themselves* (1994); Nunca Mas, *supra* n. 46; *Report on Chile, supra* n. 28.

[53] *Report on El Salvador, ibid.*, Annex.

outlined basic prerequisites to ensure that the transition concluded with a democratic society where the rule of law prevails and human rights are fully respected and guaranteed. It called for removal from office of perpetrators as well as prosecution, but found that there were insurmountable difficulties 'in view of current conditions in the country and the situation of the administration of justice'.[54] It noted the 'glaring inability' of the judicial system to investigate or punish which was part of the very reason for the truth commission and suggested that the incapability of the courts to fulfil the requirements of justice would make any attempt to punish run the risk of reviving old frustrations. The Commission called instead for reforms in the military and public security, investigation of illegal groups, and various human rights protections, including making the remedies of *amparo* and habeas corpus 'truly effective'[55] and impossible to suspend during times of emergency. It also recommended compensation and non-monetary remedies for victims.

The United Nations also helped conclude the Guatemala-Unidad Revolucionaria Nacional Guatemalteca Agreement[56] which ended a long civil war marked by massive human rights violations. The chapters of the Agreement concerned with rebuilding Guatemalan society and redressing past wrongs, included recommendations on establishment of a truth commission[57] and an agreement on the rights of indigenous peoples. Article III of the Agreement recognized the 'need for firm action against impunity', as part of which the government pledged not to sponsor the adoption of any measure to prevent the prosecution and punishment of persons responsible for human rights violations. The government also agreed to amend the penal code to enhance the measures against involuntary disappearance and summary or extra-judicial executions. Article VIII recognized that 'it is a humanitarian duty to compensate and/or assist victims of human rights violations' and said it should be effected by means of government measures including socio-economic programmes directed at those with the greater need. A specific chapter called for resettlement of uprooted populations while other substantial and generalized reparative measures include greater spending on education and social security. The United Nations agreed to verify compliance with the accord.

Truth telling is heavily emphasized because it protects and deters, de-politicizes and shows solidarity with victims. Most victims seek the truth as part of justice, because it validates the individual experience. Victims may have faced social ostracism or an assumption that what was done to them was warranted, reflecting the usual official explanation that the victim was a criminal, terrorist,

---

[54] *Ibid.* at 177–78.   [55] *Ibid.* at 183.

[56] Agreement between the Government of Guatemala and Unidad Revolucionaria Nacional Guatemalteca (Guatemala City, 29 December 1996), reprinted in (1997) 36 I.L.M. 258.

[57] The Guatemalan Commission for Historical Clarification issued its report 25 February 1999, in which it found the government responsible for the vast majority of human rights abuses that occurred during the internal conflict.

subversive or otherwise deserving of the mistreatment that occurred. Acknowledgment is thus important; it 'is what happens to knowledge when it becomes officially sanctioned and enters the public realm'[58] where it can educate citizens about the nature and extent of prior wrongdoing and become a powerful tool of rehabilitation. Where the report identifies victims, it can establish the predicate for compensation. In any event, truth commissions can make the victims of violations their main concern and enhance the therapeutic benefit of testifying, in contrast to prosecution which necessarily centres on the accused's acts.

C. LUSTRATION LAWS[59]

National lustration is a purging process that removes from positions of authority those individuals who participated in violations of human rights. A lustration law may be broadly drawn to remove or bar classes of people from holding public office or participating in politics, or it may add such a result to the penalties for conviction of certain offences. The social, political and economic consequences can be severe and may be punitive without affording the due process rights guaranteed during criminal prosecution and may lack individualization of liability.

It appears that the use of civil penalties such as lustration, applied to individuals properly identified as perpetrators of human rights abuses, will survive a challenge that they violate the civil and political rights of the persons to whom they apply. Indeed, the United Nations Commission on El Salvador recommended that human rights violators be dismissed from the armed forces, from the civil service and the judiciary. Moreover, 'under no circumstances would it be advisable to allow persons who committed acts of violations . . . to participate in the running of the state'.[60] Thus, those dismissed should be disqualified from holding public posts or offices for a period of not less than 10 years and permanently disqualified from 'any activity related to public security or national defense'.

The Inter-American Commission on Human Rights rejected on the merits a petition from Jose Efrain Rios Montt, who claimed that his political rights were violated when he was barred from being a candidate for the presidency of Guatemala in 1990.[61] Rios Montt had been part of a military coup and *de facto* leader of Guatemala between 1982 and 1983, when he was overthrown by another military coup. The new leadership declared an amnesty in 1985 on the basis of which Rios Montt sought to run in the 1990 elections. The 1986 Constitution

---

[58] *Uruguay Report, supra* n. 50, at 18.
[59] See Herman Schwartz, 'Lustration in Eastern Europe', in 1 (1994) *Parker Sch.J.E. Eur.L.* 141.
[60] See *Report on El Salvador, supra* n. 47, at 174.
[61] IACHR, Report 30/93, Case 10.804 (Guatemala), *Annual Report of the Inter-American Commission on Human Rights 1993*, 206, OEA/Ser.L/V/II.85, doc. 9, rev.(1993).

limited office-holders, stipulating in Article 186 that the following may not hold the office of the presidency: 'the leader and chiefs of any coup d'etat, armed revolution or similar movement that changes the constitutional order, nor those who become head of the government as a result of such actions'.[62] The Commission addressed the question of whether an individual's permanent ineligibility to hold office based on a breach of the constitutional order is consistent with the American Convention on Human Rights. The Commission referred to the importance of constitutional democracy to the American system and the practice of other states in similarly barring from office anyone who has taken power through unconstitutional means, calling it 'a customary constitutional rule with a strong tradition in Central America'. The Commission noted that various kinds of regulations and eligibility were established in different constitutional orders to defend the authenticity of political rights and of elections. Lustration laws have been used most often in central and eastern Europe,[63] but as this case indicates are also common in Latin America.

D. COMPENSATION

Compensation is important and should be awarded where it is possible. It aids victims to manage the material aspects of their losses; it can represent an official acknowledgment of the wrong done; and it imposes a financial cost that may deter future abuses. Compensation and other remedies are part of the rehabilitation process of torture victims and other survivors of gross violations. Dr. Derek Summerfield, a psychiatrist with the Medical Foundation in London asserts: 'Some torture victims seek psychological help but all of them want social justice . . . Allied to this is the vital question of official reparation for human rights crimes. Victims may better become survivors if some part of the legacy of the past is addressed . . . Justice, even if long delayed, is reparative'.[64]

In balancing needs and ability to pay, compromise is probably necessary in many cases because there are insufficient funds to provide full compensation to all victims. A United Nations Victims of Crime report recommended that 'if it is uncertain whether the budgetary means of the State will be sufficient to cover an unknown number of claimants, a fund should be established to limit the financial

---

[62] *Ibid.*, para. 6.

[63] See Neil J. Kritz (ed.), *Transitional Justice: How Emerging Democracies Reckon with Former Regimes*, Vol. III. Law, Rulings and Reports (1995); Maria Lon, 'Lustration and Truth Claims: Unfinished Revolutions in Central Europe', (1995) 20 *L. & Soc. Inquiry* 1, 117; Adrienne M. Quill, 'To Prosecute or Not to Prosecute: Problems Encountered in the Prosecution of Former Communist Officials in Germany, Czechoslovakia, and the Czech Republic', (1996) 7 *Ind. Int'l & Comp.L.Rev.1*, 165; Mark S. Ellis, 'Purging the Past: The Current State of Lustration Laws in the Former Communist Bloc', (1996) 59 *Law & Contemp. Prob.* 181.

[64] D. Summerfield, *Addressing Human Response to War and Atrocity: Major Themes for Health Workers* (1993).

burden. A basic amount should be paid out immediately and the difference paid later, the final amount payable to each claimant being known only at the time when it is clear how many claimants filed claims and the amounts distributable out of the fund'.[65] The United Nations Commission on El Salvador recommended compensation for victims. 'Legislation should be passed granting a simple, swift and accessible remedy to anyone who has been a victim of a human rights violation enabling them to obtain material compensation for the harm suffered'.[66] The Commission recommended that a special fund be established under the control of an autonomous body with the necessary legal and administrative powers, to award appropriate material compensation to the victims of violence in the shortest time possible.[67] It should be funded with contributions from the state and the international community 'especially the wealthier countries and those that showed most interest in the conflict and its settlement'.[68]

Reparations were first developed in the aftermath of international armed conflicts, but now extend to contexts of gross and systematic violations of human rights. While the former usually have been established by international agreement, recent democratic transitions have extended the reach of compensation mechanisms through domestic laws to remedy widespread human rights violations.

1. War reparations

Restitution and compensation for losses suffered in international and internal armed conflict have a long history. The Treaty of Westphalia, ending the Thirty Years War in 1648, provided that all those of the Holy Roman Empire who had suffered prejudice or damage at the hands of one or the other party, should in respect of their territories and freedoms be fully reinstated in the estate and stations which they had enjoyed. A French law of 1825 ordered indemnification of revolutionary emigrées and their heirs for property confiscated or sold by the state in 1792.[69] The Hague law on armed conflict enshrined the obligation to make reparations for violations of humanitarian norms. At the 1907 Peace Conference, a German proposal led to Article 3 of Hague Convention IV of 18 October 1907: 'A Belligerent Party which violated the provisions of the said Regulations shall, if the case demands, be liable to pay compensation. It shall be responsible for all acts committed by persons forming part of its armed forces'.

---

[65] *Victims of Crimes: Working Paper prepared by the Secretariat*, 7th United Nations Congress on the Prevention of Crime and the Treatment of Offenders, A/CONF.121/6 at 39 (1985). See also, United Nations, Declaration of Basic Principles of Justice for Victims of Crime and Abuse of Power, para. 13, G.A. Res. 40/34, 29 Nov. 1985, annex.

[66] *Report on El Salvador, supra* n. 47, at 184.   [67] *Ibid.* at 186.

[68] *Ibid.*

[69] Loi concernant l'indemnité á accorder aux anciens propriétaires des beinsfonds confisqués et vendus au profit de l'Etat, en vertu des lois sur Emigrés, les condamnés et les deportés. Bulletin des Lois du Royaume de France, 8e ser., no. 30 (1825).

The provision is repeated in Article 91 of the 1977 Protocol I Additional to the 1949 Geneva Conventions.

War reparations are usually settled by agreement between the belligerents. The peace treaties concluded after the First World War included clauses on reparations and compensation,[70] establishing a Reparation Commission representing the victorious Allied powers that determined the level of damages to be paid by Germany. A provision of the Treaty of Sevres concluded between the Allies and Turkey in 1920 similarly provided for the restitution of property of the Armenians killed by the Turks. At the conclusion of the Second World War, Article 14 of the 8 September 1951 Peace Treaty between the Allies and Japan 'recognized that Japan should pay reparations to the Allied Powers for damage and suffering caused by it during the war'. Article 16 of the same treaty dealt with indemnification of former prisoners of war in the hands of the Japanese:

As an expression of its desire to indemnify those members of the armed forces of the Allied Powers who suffered undue hardships while prisoners of war of Japan, Japan will transfer its assets and those of its nationals in countries which were neutral during the war, or which were at war with any of the Allied Powers, or, at its option, the equivalent of such assets, to the International Committee of the Red Cross which shall liquidate such assets and distribute the resultant fund to appropriate national agencies, for the benefit of former prisoners of war and their families on such basis as it may determine to be equitable.[71]

The Article thus gave the International Committee of the Red Cross (ICRC) a mandate to distribute funds on an equitable basis. With the accord of the beneficiary states, the ICRC decided that each national quota would be directly shared among beneficiaries according to criteria chosen by the national agencies. Solutions varied from one state to another.

One of the most comprehensive systems of compensation for war-time human rights violations was created by Germany for victims of Nazi persecution. From 1939 onward, those who had escaped from countries overrun by the Germans demanded compensation for property and monies taken from them.[72] Some argued that in addition to individual compensation, a collective claim must be presented for reparation to the Jewish people for the property whose owners were unknown or dead, for institutions and communities that had been destroyed or

---

[70] Treaty of Peace at Versailles, 28 June 1919, Articles 231–247 and the seven annexes that appear between Articles 244 and 245. Annex I mentions compensation due to civilians and prisoners of war: Treaty of Peace at Versailles, 28 June 1919, Ger.-Allies, 225 Consol. T.S. 188, Article 231.

[71] Japanese Peace Conference, San Francisco, California, September 1951, Doc. 3, pp. 13–14.

[72] The first public demand came from Shalom Adler-Rudel, who left Germany and became Director of the Central British Fund to aid Jewish refugees. On 10 October 1939, he drafted a memorandum containing concrete proposals for collecting factual information relating to Jewish demands for compensation from Germany. On 6 March 1941, he wrote a second memorandum estimating the damage inflicted by the Nazis on the Jews of Germany and Austria at DM4 billion. 'He also underscored the *sui generis* character of the situation as being not one of warring states, but of a state's striking at and declaring war on its own citizens'. Nana Sagi, *German Reparations: A History of the Negotiations* (1980), 15.

had vanished, and for damage done to the very fabric of the Jewish people's existence.[73] Collective reparations became a key issue and by 1945, the estimates exceeded 6 billion dollars.[74] On 29 September 1945, Chaim Weizmann presented the four Powers with the first post-war Jewish claims, which became the basis of the claim of the state of Israel, for (1) restitution of property; (2) restoration of heirless property to representatives of the Jewish people to finance the rehabilitation of victims of Nazi persecution; (3) a percentage of all reparation to be paid by Germany to be transferred also for rehabilitation and resettlement in Palestine; and (4) all assets of Germans formerly residing in Palestine should form part of the reparations.

The first Allied statement on restitution and reparation (5 January 1943) announced that the governments reserved all their rights to declare invalid any transfers of property or title of property in territory under Axis control, whether the transfers were effected by force or by quasi-legal means.[75] At the Paris Reparations Conference (November 9–December 21 1945), after the issue of restitution of property was added to the planned agenda, the Conference accepted the principle that individual and group compensation should be paid to the 'victims of Nazi persecution in need of rehabilitation and not in a position to secure assistance from governments in receipt of reparation from Germany'.[76] Receipt of rehabilitation funds would not prejudice a later claim for compensation. Restitution would apply to identifiable property which had been seized during the period of conquest with or without payment. Indemnification was to be paid for objects of an artistic, educational or religious character which had been seized by the Germans but which could no longer be restored to their rightful owners.[77]

The Claims Conference agreed on several points concerning individual claims, including priority to claims of the elderly and indemnification for damage to vocational and professional training. Claimants who could prove they had been held in concentration camps would receive an overall sum as compensation for deprivation of liberty in the amount of DM3,000. An overall cap of DM25,000 was set for damage that occurred before 1 June 1945. Another DM450 million was paid to the Conference on Jewish Material Claims against Germany, a common holding for 23 Jewish organizations, for the settlement of Jewish victims living outside Israel. Finally, a special fund was created for non-practising Jews of DM50 million.

Successive German Compensation Laws and Agreements were enacted and

---

[73] Nana Sagi, *German Reparations*, at 19.   [74] *Ibid.* at 27.
[75] Sir Herbert Emerson, head of the Inter-Governmental Committee for Refugees, submitted a memorandum to the Allied Governments on 3 June 1943 stating his view that the declaration should apply not only to war-time seizures but also to those carried out before the war on grounds of race, religion or political opinion, and to those who were unable to flee as well as those who had escaped; *ibid.* at 9.   [76] *Ibid.*, at 34–5.
[77] *Ibid.* at 11–12.

concluded between 1948 and 1965, including a 1952 Treaty between the Federal Republic of Germany (FRG) and Israel.[78] The Preamble to the 1952 agreement noted that 'unspeakable criminal acts were perpetrated against the Jewish people' and that Germany agreed 'within the limits of their capacity to make good the material damage caused by these acts'.[79] It also mentioned that Israel had assumed the burden of resettling many destitute Jewish refugees. Article I recited that: 'The Federal Republic of Germany shall, in view of the considerations here-inbefore recited, pay to the State of Israel the sum of 3,000 million Deutsche Marks'. It was a negotiator's opinion 'that the payment to Israel should be of such magnitude as to represent a sincere endeavor to display remorse'.[80]

Between 1959 and 1964 the FRG also concluded conventions with 12 member states of the Council of Europe providing for payment of DM876 million for the injury to life, health and liberty of their nationals. Another DM101 million was provided to Austria. Further contributions were agreed to with states in Eastern Europe for the victims of pseudo-medical experiments (DM122 million) and to the United Nations High Commissioner for Refugees (DM57 million). By 1988 the total sums paid, in billions of DM were:

(1)	for general compensation in Germany	63.03
(2)	for compensation in lieu of restitution	3.93
(3)	under the treaty with Israel	3.45
(4)	under the treaties with 12 European states	1.00
(5)	for civil servants	6.80
(6)	according to state law provisions	1.86
(7)	for extraordinary hardships	0.50
	Total in billions of DM	80.57

In its domestic law, the culmination of German reparations can be found in the Federal Law on Reparation (the *Bundesentschaedigungsgesetz*). Under the law, various categories of damage are provided for anyone who was oppressed because of political opposition to National Socialism, or because of race, religion or ideology, or who suffered in consequence loss of life, damage to limb or health, loss of liberty, property or possessions, or harm to professional or economic prospects.[81] The categories of compensable harm include:

(a) Loss of life, interpreted to include homicide, manslaughter and death as a result of damage to health inflicted on the victim, as well as death caused by a deterioration in health resulting from emigration or from living conditions

---

[78] Treaty between the Federal Republic of Germany and Israel, 162 U.N.T.S. 265.
[79] Sagi, *supra* n. 72, at 212.   [80] *Ibid.* at 113.
[81] K. Schwerin, 'German Compensation for Victims of Nazi Persecution', (1972) 67 *NW.U.L. Rev.* 479, 496. In addition to the national law, Germany concluded agreements with Luxembourg, Norway, Denmark, Greece, the Netherlands, France, Belgium, Italy, Switzerland, Austria, the United Kingdom, Sweden and Israel to provide compensation to claimants not covered by the law.

detrimental to health. Compensation has been paid also in cases of suicide provoked by persecution, including suicide caused by economic difficulties which the victim could not overcome in the country to which he or she emigrated.[82]

(b) Damage to limb or health if the damage was more than insignificant, meaning that it entailed or was likely to entail lasting impairment of the victim's mental or physical faculties.[83]

(c) Loss of liberty, including both deprivations and restrictions of liberty: police or military detention, arrest, custodial or penal imprisonment, detention in a concentration camp and forced stay in a ghetto. Deprivation of liberty also included forced labour under conditions resembling detention. Restrictions of liberty allowing a claim for compensation included compelled wearing of the Star of David and living 'underground' in unfit conditions.[84]

(d) Damage to professional and economic prospects if the victim lost use of his or her earning power.[85] One group of victims, former members of the German civil service or the German government, including judges, professors and teachers, were reinstated in the position, salary or pension group which they would have reached had the persecution not taken place.[86] The absence of similar measures for other victims led to criticisms of inequality of treatment. In addition, damage awards for property loss seemed more generous than those for loss of life or health. A set of national compensation guidelines formulated on the basis of the German experience stresses the importance of the principle of equality of rights of all victims.[87]

In 1990 the former GDR, by a unilateral declaration, offered the World Jewish Congress the sum of US$100 million. More recently, banks, museums, art dealers and governments in several countries have faced claims from victims and their heirs for the restitution of money and works of art stolen during the Second World War. Problems of proof and conflicting local laws are making it difficult to resolve the claims.

In the USA, the Congress voted in 1988 to provide compensation to citizens and permanent residents of Japanese descent who were interned during the Second World War; property losses had already been compensated in 1948. With the new law, each surviving individual was entitled to US$20,000; claims did not survive the death of internees. The amount remained the same for each person although they clearly did not suffer the same harm because the length of time and

---

[82] K. Schwerin, 'German Compensation for Victims of Nazi Persecution', at 499.

[83] *Ibid.* at 500–01.   [84] *Ibid.* at 502.   [85] *Ibid.* 506.

[86] *Restitution, rehabilitation and compensation for victims of grave violations of human rights and fundamental freedoms, Report of the Secretary-General prepared pursuant to Sub-Commission Resolution 1993/29*, E/CN.4/Sub.2/1994/7/Add.1, 22 July 1994, p. 2, para. 3.

[87] *Ibid.* See also, *Victims of Crime, Working paper prepared by the United Nations Secretariat for the Seventh United Nations Congress on the Prevention of Crime and the Treatment of Offenders* (Milan, 26 August–6 September 1985), A/CONF.121/6, para. 124.

conditions of incarceration varied. The compensation came with an apology from the President and an admission from Congress that a 'fundamental injustice' had been committed.

2. United Nations Compensation Commission (UNCC)

The 1990 conflict in the Persian Gulf created new law and procedures on reparations for mass violations during armed conflict.[88] On 2 August 1990 Iraq invaded Kuwait, claiming that Kuwait had been 'an integral part of Iraq until the First World War'. In response, between 2 August and 29 November 1990, the United Nations Security Council adopted 12 resolutions concerning the occupation of Kuwait by Iraq. In Resolution 674 (1990) it reminded Iraq that it was responsible under international law for all damages, losses or injuries suffered by Kuwait or third countries as a result of its illegal occupation of Kuwait. In Resolution 687 (1991) adopted on 3 April 1991, the Council reaffirmed that Iraq, 'is liable under international law for any direct loss, damage, including environmental damage and the depletion of natural resources, or injury to foreign Governments, nationals and corporations, as a result of Iraq's unlawful invasion and occupation of Kuwait'. It also affirmed that 'the Fourth Geneva Convention applies to Kuwait and that as a High Contracting Party to the Convention, Iraq . . . in particular is liable under the Convention in respect of the grave breaches committed by it'.[89]

The United Nations Special Rapporteur on the Situation of Human Rights in Kuwait under Iraqi Occupation found Iraq responsible for gross and systematic human rights violations during the conflict, including summary and arbitrary executions, widespread and systematic torture, deportation of large numbers of civilians to Iraq, the use of third-country nationals as hostages (human shields), and the extensive destruction of crucial infrastructure in Kuwait, including health and educational facilities, as well as environmental damage.[90] The Special Rapporteur devoted a substantial section of his conclusions and recommendations

---

[88] David J. Bederman, 'The United Nations Compensation Commission and the Tradition of International Claims Settlement', (1994) 27 *Int'l L. & Pol.* 1.

[89] Resolutions 670/1990 and 674/1990. Article 148 of the Fourth Geneva Convention states that in respect of grave breaches 'no High Contracting Party shall be allowed to absolve itself . . . of any liability incurred by itself'. Grave breaches are defined by Article 147 as 'those involving any of the following acts, if committed against persons or property protected by the Convention: wilful killing, torture or inhuman treatment, including biological experiments, wilfully causing great suffering or serious injury to body or health, unlawful deportation or transfer or unlawful confinement of a protected person, compelling a protected person to serve in the forces of the hostile power, or wilfully depriving a protected person of the rights of fair and regular trial prescribed in th[e] Convention, taking of hostages and extensive destruction and appropriation of property not justified by military necessity and carried out unlawfully and wantonly'.

[90] Walter Kalin, *Report on the Situation of Human rights in Kuwait under Iraqi Occupation,* E/CN.4/1992/18; E/CN.4/1992/26. See also L. Gabriel, 'Victims of Gross Violations of Human Rights and Fundamental Freedoms arising from the Illegal Invasion and Occupation of Kuwait by Iraq' in *Seminar on the Right to Restitution, Compensation and Rehabilitation for Victims of Gross Violations of Human Rights and Fundamental Freedoms* (SIM Special No. 12), 29.

to state and individual responsibility and compensation.[91] He referred to paragraph 18 of Security Council Resolution 687 (1991) by which the Council decided to create a fund to compensate for claims resulting from Iraq's liability under international law for injury caused by the unlawful invasion and occupation of Kuwait. The Special Rapporteur called for a broad interpretation of the fund's coverage that should include compensation for material and non-material damage to victims of human rights violations and grave breaches of humanitarian norms, regardless of the nationality and present status of the victims. The Special Rapporteur argued that such a broad interpretation would conform to recent developments in international law, where the principle of compensation for victims of human rights violations is gaining acceptance.[92]

As the Special Rapporteur noted, the United Nations Security Council decided to create a fund to pay claims against Iraq, excluding damage caused by Iraq to its own nationals, and to establish the United Nations Compensation Commission (UNCC), to administer the fund. The Commission functions under the authority of the Security Council of which it is a subsidiary organ. The principal organ of the Commission is the Governing Council, composed of the representatives of the current members of the Security Council. The Governing Council is assisted by a number of Commissioners who are experts in fields such as finance, law, accountancy, insurance and environmental damage assessment. They are appointed by the Secretary General and act in their personal capacity.

The decision of the Security Council to establish the UNCC has been analogized to 'what is tantamount to a summary judgment holding Iraq responsible for a whole series of breaches of international law'.[93] The funding mechanism is a fixed share of Iraqi oil proceeds, 30 per cent of the annual value of the exports of petroleum and petroleum products from Iraq.[94] Brower called it a 'reparations royalty'. Critics claim that the revenue from the oil sales will generate only enough to pay the interest accruing on the amount of awards, meaning that the UNCC will have to pro-rate claims. According to an experienced litigator, '[t]here will never, by any projection that anyone has seen, be enough money to pay 100 per cent of the claims'.[95]

Between 1991 and 31 July 1998, the Governing Council adopted 54 decisions governing aspects of (1) claims procedures, including expedited processing of certain claims, means to prove business losses, procedures for individuals not in a position to have their claims submitted by a government, and processing cross-category claims; (2) approval of panel reports and recommendations; (3) decisions

[91] E/CN.4/1992/18 *supra* n. 90, at para. 22.

[92] E/CN.4/1992/26, *supra* n. 90, at para. 260.

[93] S. Gold, 'International Claims Arising from Iraq's Invasion of Kuwait', (1991) 25 *Int'l Law.* 713, 715.

[94] SC RES. 705, U.N. SCOR, 46th Sess., para. 2, U.N. Doc S/RES/705 (1991) reprinted in (1991) 30 I.L.M. 1715.

[95] C. Brower, 'Lessons to be Drawn from the Iran-U.S. Claims Tribunal', (1992) 9 *J. Int'l Arb.* 51, 57.

on payment and distribution of compensation.[96] The Governing Council agreed on 1 January 1995 as the cut-off date for the presentation of individual claims and 1 January 1996 for claims of corporations and other entities (E claims) and government and international organization claims (F claims).

In its work, the UNCC has built upon the practice of international tribunals hearing claims of state responsibility for injury to aliens. It also has looked to United States mass tort claims administration as a model for the Iraq claims process. It has used *'some of the techniques and arts of sampling* that were developed in the [U.S.] asbestos and Dalkon Shield cases'.[97] The Commission is limited to awarding monetary compensation, and cannot impose restitution or punitive damages.

The Commission decided to create six categories of claims and to request states to present their claims accordingly. The amounts awarded are given to the governments for distribution to the applicants.[98] For ease of administration all claims had to be presented exclusively on forms distributed by the Secretariat and submitted either in English or with an English translation. Evidence also had to be translated for certain categories of claims.[99]

The first category of claims, 'A' claims, concerned individuals forced to leave Kuwait or Iraq as a result of the invasion. They could claim a fixed sum of US$2,500 with a limit of US$5,000 per family. Higher amounts (US$4,000 and US$8,000) were allowed if all other claims must be waived. Less evidence was required of 'A' claims and they were processed faster than other claims. Compensation in greater amounts is awarded only if supported by 'documentary and other appropriate evidence sufficient to demonstrate the circumstances and the amount of the claimed loss'. The UNCC reviews claims to determine whether they are realistic or inflated,[100] but the vast number of claims almost precludes close scrutiny of individual cases.

'B' claims concerned serious personal injury or death, and claimants could seek between US$2,500 and US$10,000 per family without lengthy process. Category 'B' claims have priority over all other claims, for humanitarian reasons. Other claims of personal injury, death or other loss, with appropriate evidence, can be filed up to US$100,000 as a category 'C' claim. 'C' claims include losses

---

[96] Decision 3 of 23 October 1991, U.N. Doc. S/AC.26/1991/3, governs personal injury and mental pain and anguish. Decision 7 establishes criteria for additional categories of claims (e.g. corporations) and excludes compensation for losses from trade embargo. Decision 8, 1992/8 of 27 January 1992, determined the ceilings of compensation for mental pain and anguish. Decision 9, 1992/9 of 6 March 1992 established types of business losses and their valuation. Decision 16, 1992/16 of 4 January 1993, covers interest. Decision 19/1994 establishes criteria for compensation of costs of allied coalition forces.

[97] N. C. Ulmer, 'The Gulf War Claims Institution', (1993) 10 *J. Int'l Arb.* 85, 88.

[98] UNRWA can present claims for Palestinian refugees and UNDP for those from the occupied territories.

[99] Rules of the UNCC, Article 6.

[100] N. Ulmer, *supra* n. 97, at 90.

of property or other interests, damages arising from personal injury, 'including mental pain and anguish'. 'D' claims are losses over US$100,000 and were paid after A to C claims have been compensated. Category 'E' covers corporate claims, 'F' comprises claims of governments and international organizations. Members of the armed forces are not eligible for compensation unless they were prisoners of war or the loss or injury 'resulted from mistreatment in violation of international humanitarian law'.[101]

One of the first tasks of the UNCC Governing Council was to draw up criteria for the processing of urgent claims.[102] The Governing Council later supplemented the criteria by a series of decisions.[103] According to the Commission's criteria, 'claims must be for death, personal injury or other direct loss to individuals as a result of Iraq's unlawful invasion and occupation of Kuwait', including any loss suffered as a result of:

(a) military operations or threat of military action by either side during the period 2 August 1990 to 2 March 1991;
(b) departure from or inability to leave Iraq or Kuwait or a decision not to return during that period;
(c) actions by officials, employees or agents of the Government of Iraq or its controlled entities during that period in connection with the invasion or occupation;
(d) the breakdown of civil order in Kuwait or Iraq during that period; or
(e) hostage-taking or other illegal detention.[104]

At its second session, held on 18 October 1991, the Governing Council adopted formulations and definitions of various injuries. It defined serious personal injury to mean: 'dismemberment, permanent or temporary significant disfigurement, such as substantial change in one's outward appearance; permanent or temporary significant loss of use or limitation of use of a body organ, member, function or system; any injury which, if left untreated, is unlikely to result in the full recovery of the injured body area, or is likely to prolong such full recovery'. For purposes of recovery the term also included: 'instances of physical or mental injury arising from sexual assault, torture, aggravated physical assault, hostage-taking or illegal detention for more than three days or being forced to hide for more than three days on account of a manifestly well-founded fear for one's life or of being taken hostage or illegally detained'. Serious personal injury did not include bruises, simple strains and sprains, minor burns, cuts and wounds; or other irritations not requiring a course of medical treatment. The assumption seems to be that armed conflict will produce some injuries that must be borne by the victims.

---

[101] *Decision taken by the governing council of the UNCC at its sixth session, 27th meeting held on 26 June 1992: Eligibility for compensation of members of the allied coalition armed forces,* S/AC.26/1992/11, 26 June 1992.

[102] S/AC.26/1991/1.   [103] S/AC.26/1991/2–7.

[104] S/AC.26/1991/1, para. 18.

Pecuniary losses include loss of income and medical expenses, mental pain and anguish due to the death of a spouse, child or parent of the individual, or the individual's serious personal injury or the individual's suffering a sexual assault or aggravated assault or torture. Compensation may be awarded for mental pain and anguish to individuals for dismemberment, disfigurement, loss of use of a body part, being taken hostage, being illegally detained, having a well-founded fear for one's life, and being deprived of all economic resources such as to threaten one's survival.[105] The United Nations has published a scale of mental pain and anguish for most of the situations faced by individuals during the conflict. Victims of aggravated assault, sexual assault, or torture may claim up to $5,000 per incident.[106]

The Commission will award interest on the principal amount of successful claims, to accrue from the date of the loss until the date of payment. In Decision 16, the Commission deferred determining the rate, but indicated it would select a rate 'sufficient to compensate successful claimants for the loss of use of the principal amount'.[107] The decision was delayed after disagreement over whether interest should be awarded at all. Iraq objected that the imposition of interest conflicted with international principles and 'the trend followed in peace treaties after the Second World War and with the principles of justice and fairness'.[108]

Payments go to the governments, but the Governing Council has required governments to establish mechanisms to ensure distribution.[109] Generally, governments must distribute funds within six months and must report to the UNCC on the amounts of payments distributed.[110] The Governing Council may suspend disbursements to governments that fail to comply with the UNCC requirements.[111] Governments are allowed to deduct small processing fees.[112]

In Decision 8, the UNCC established compensation ceilings:

(a) US$15,000 for the death of a spouse, child or parent; US$30,000 per family;
(b) US$15,000 for dismemberment or permanent disfigurement; US$5,000 if it
     is temporary;

---

[105] *Decision taken by the Governing Council of the United Nations Compensation Commission during its second session, at its 15th meeting, held on 18 October 1991, Personal Injury and Mental Pain and Anguish*, Decision 3, U.N. Compensation Commission, 2d sess. para. 2, U.N. Doc S/AC.26/1991/3.   [106] *Ibid.*

[107] *Decision taken by the Governing Council of the United Nations Compensation Commission during its eighth session, at its 31st plenary meeting, held from 14 to 18 November 1992, Award of Interest*, para 1, UN Doc. S/AC.26/1992/16 (1993), reprinted in (1995) 34 I.L.M. 247.

[108] *Iraq-Kuwait Situation*, 1993 U.N.Y.B. 426, U.N. Sales No. E.94.I.1 at 427.

[109] *Decision taken by the Governing Council of the United Nations Compensation Commission at its 41st meeting held on 23 March 1994, Distribution of Payments and Transparency*, para. 1, U.N. Doc.S/AC.26/Dec.18 (1994), reprinted in (1995) 34 I.L.M. 252.

[110] *Ibid.,* para. 1(d).

[111] R. Bettauer, 'The United Nations Compensation Commission—Developments since October 1992', (1995) 89 *Am. J.Int'l L.* 416, 421.

[112] i.e. 1.5 per cent on individual claims and 3 per cent on larger and corporate claims. This involves a shift of fees to those best able to bear the costs.

(c)   US$5,000 for sexual assault or aggravated assault or torture;
(d)   US$2,500 for witnessing gross violations;
(e)   US$1,500 for being a hostage;
(f)   US$100 per day of detention beyond three days, with a ceiling of $10,000;
(g)   US$1,500 for forced hiding for three days; US$50 per day after three days up to a ceiling of US$5,000;
(h)   US$2,500 for deprivation of economic resources.

In cases of cumulated injury, the Governing Council set an overall ceiling of US$30,000 per claimant or US$60,000 per family. Although the individual amounts are not high, the high number of claimants requires limitation or else the funds will soon be exhausted. It should be noted, as well, that the United Nations has its own schedule of payments for death and disability benefits, based on the nature of the injury its employee suffers:[113]

Loss	Payment (US$)
Both arms or both hands, both legs or both feet or sight in both eyes	50,000
Hearing	17,500
Sight in one eye	12,000
Arm (at shoulder)	30,000
Arm (at or below elbow)	28,500
Hand (at or below wrist)	27,000
Thumb	11,000
Index finger	7,000
Middle finger	5,500
Ring finger	2,500
Fourth finger	1,500
Leg (above the knee)	20,000
Leg (at or below knee)	18,000
Foot (at or below ankle)	14,000

While this schedule is indicative, international tribunals have been reluctant to use figures from accidental injury tables to measure the compensation due for deliberate human rights violations.[114] If the amounts in the schedules include pain and suffering, the approach is correct, because pain and suffering, humiliation, and other emotional injury is likely to be greater for victims of deliberate wrongdoing.

For business losses, Decision 9 provided that compensation is due for Iraqi breach of contract for all actual losses suffered, and may include losses related to

---

[113] United Nations, *Financing of the U.N. Peacekeeping Operations: Death and Disability Benefits*, reprinted in 'The Price of Peacekeeping', *Harper's Magazine*, July 1996, p. 16.

[114] See e.g. the discussion of the Inter-American Court of Human Rights in the *Velasquez-Rodriguez Case*, *supra* Chapter 5.

specially manufactured goods and lost profits 'if they can be calculated under the contract with reasonable certainty'. For loss of tangible property 'depending on the type of asset and the circumstances of the case, one of several valuation methods may be used',[115] including book value (its cost minus accumulated depreciation) or replacement value (the amount required to obtain an asset of the same kind and status as the asset damaged or lost). 'Replacement value would not normally allow for replacement of an old item with a new one.'[116]

Loss of income-producing assets is valued differently because the value 'is determined not only by the value of their individual assets but also by the greater value they possess due to their capacity to generate income'.[117] In principle Iraq is deemed liable to compensate for the loss of a business or commercial entity as a whole resulting from the invasion and occupation. Valuation in this context is based on several alternative concepts: book value; market value; discounted cash flow or price/earnings method. In general lost profits that can be ascertained with reasonable certainty are part of the economic value that is lost, based on past performance including prior earnings and profits.

It should be noted that only category C claims explicitly exclude the possibility of recovering attorneys' fees paid for the presentation of a claim. With no similar provision in other parts of the rules, the UNCC could award attorneys' fees and expenses in the other cases. Given that translations are required for presentation of claims and all evidence, it could be considered unjust that applicants should bear their own costs, especially in light of the limited recovery that is possible.

In May 1994, the UNCC decided to allocate the funding available to pay awards to claimants within each category of claims as well as among the various categories. It was decided that payment of an initial amount of US$2,500 would be made to each successful claimant in Categories A, B and C. Subsequent instalments would be transferred to governments for distribution as available.[118]

In December 1994, the Governing Council approved the first decisions on 1,119 individual claims for serious personal injury or death. It approved 670 'B' claims totaling US$2,747,500, approximately half of which were claims of Kuwaiti nationals.[119] Several months later, the Governing Council decided the first departure claims (category 'A') and approved 53,845 claims. In accordance

---

[115] *Decision taken by the Governing Council of the United Nations Compensation Commission during its resumed Fourth Session, at the 23rd meeting, held on 6th March 1992, Propositions and Conclusions on Compensation for Business Losses: Types of Damages and Their Valuation* para. 15, dec. 9, S/AC.26/1992/9 at 4.

[116] *Ibid.*, para. 15.   [117] *Ibid.*, para. 16.

[118] *Decision Concerning Priority of Payment and Payment Mechanism: Guiding Principles, taken by the Governing Council of the United Nations Compensation Commission at its 41st meeting held at Geneva on 23 March 1994*, U.N. Doc. S/AC.26/Dec. 17 (1994).

[119] See *Decision Concerning the First Installment of Claims for Serious Personal Injury or Death (Category 'B' Claims) taken by the Governing Council of the United Nations Compensation Commission at its 43rd meeting, held on 26 May 1994 in Geneva*, S/AC.26/Dec. 20 (1994).

with its provisions on confidentiality in Articles 30(1) and 40(5) of the Rules, no breakdown of individual amounts awarded is made public, but it is provided to each government and international organization. In December 1994, the first category 'C' awards were made, US$51,053,616 for 2,873 individuals.[120] The United States and Kuwaiti claims accounted for nearly half of the awarded money.

The total amounts are staggering. As of 19 August 1997 claims exceeded US$82 billion for the nearly 6,000 companies with war-related losses and Kuwaiti claims alone exceed US$130 billion. During the filing period, the UNCC received approximately 1 million 'A' claims for departure from Iraq or Kuwait. By 1998 it had awarded six instalments in a total amount of approximately US$3.2 billion on claims of approximately US$3.6 billion. Due to the huge number of claims, the UNCC processed them using computer sampling and computer matching. The category B panel received approximately 6,000 claims seeking 21 million dollars for serious personal injury or death. The panel has awarded three instalments for a total amount of US$13.5 million. Although the panel conducted an individual review of each of these claims, all were paid in full by December 1995.

The larger claims in category C number approximately 400,000 and the UNCC issued six instalments to July 1998, awarding US$2.9 billion on claims of US$12 billion. For these claims it uses sampling and regression analysis. The Category D panel, which considers claims of loss over US$100,000, has received approximately 11,000 claims seeking US$10 billion. The first instalment was approved in April 1997, on 69 claims.

The category E panels consider claims by corporations and have received approximately 6,000 claims asking US$80 billion. Among the cases filed, 117 claims have been categorized as large or complex claims. The first E claims were approved on 3 July 1998, awarding US$187,496,511.62 on claims of over US$2 billion.[121] A threshold issue concerned the meaning of 'direct loss' for which claims can be made. The claimants sought compensation for loss of property, lost profits, interest, lost business opportunities, increased expenses, loss of income-producing assets, interest, and miscellaneous losses, including claim preparation costs and evacuation expenses. Claimant Hyundai also sought lost salary

---

[120] *Decision Concerning the First Installment of Individual Claims for Damages up to US$100,000 (Category 'C' Claims) taken by the Governing Council of the United Nations Compensation Commission at its 48th meeting, held on 14 December 1994 in Geneva,* S/AC.26/Dec. 25 (1994). The Governing Council approved a second group of category B claims in December, involving some 2,349 individual recommendations and US$5,265,000 in damages. Again Kuwaiti claims accounted for more than half the total award, with the government receiving US$3,500,000, more than half the total award. A further 1,904 individual claims under category B were decided and approved in March 1995. The Governing Council approved awards concerning 811 claims for a total of $2,912,500. Further documentation was requested on 189 claims. No compensation was awarded on 325 claims, while 126 were transferred to category C; 515 were held for further consideration.

[121] *Report and Recommendations Concerning Category E2 claims (major corporate claims),* 3 July 1998, S/AC.3/1998/7.

payments to workers, repatriation costs of employees, finance charges and insurance premiums, and termination costs. A supplemental claim was filed of US$861,041,396.22 for losses on construction work projects and US$28,077,587.67 for equipment lost or destroyed at project sites. For some of the claims, the panel inspected business sites in Kuwait to evaluate the lost profits claim. In regard to lost profits as 'direct losses' the panel referred to the decision which allows loss of property and lost profits 'if they can be calculated under the contract with reasonable certainty'. Abandoned assets could be claimed, because leaving was a direct consequence of Iraqi actions. While the panel applied 'general contract law' including a duty to mitigate as reasonable under the circumstances, it found that companies were only required to remove equipment and material where departures were voluntary. Evacuation costs could be included and claims could be made for loss in Saudi Arabia but the loss must be tied to an actual military event.

Lost profits were allowed and based on what the company reasonably could have earned. Past profit performances were seen as unreliable indicators however, because Iraq had difficulties making timely payments from the early 1980s onwards. 'Therefore, in evaluating claims for lost profits on Iraqi operations, the Panel will require specific and persuasive evidence of ongoing and expected future profitability; absent such evidence, no compensation will be made for allegations of lost profits on contracts with Iraq'.[122]

Some have indicated 'concerns that [Iraq's] postwar punishment could drag on for generations'.[123] The first round of Iraqi oil sales in late 1996 provided the UNCC about US$600 million, about one-quarter of which was quickly paid out to individual claimants.

3. National compensation schemes

Several countries have enacted laws to compensate victims of human rights abuses committed by prior regimes. The 1988 Brazilian Constitution contains a provision on reparations that was followed, in 1996, by adoption of a law providing compensation to relatives of 136 members of the *'Guerrilha Do Araguaia'* who disappeared after capture by the Army in the 1960s. The law also created a blue-ribbon commission to receive requests from other presumptive victims of the military dictatorship. In Argentina, the government similarly chose to compensate, having paid compensation to more than 8000 persons held in detention without charges, forced into exile under the state of siege, or tried by military courts between 1974 and 1983. In 1980 a group of persons who had been held by the government failed to obtain judicial satisfaction of their complaints

---

[122] *Ibid.*, para. 223. P. 68.
[123] N. King, 'U.N. Panel is Inundated With Vast Claims, but can Iraq Pay the Bill?' *Asian Wall St. J.*, 19 August 1997, at 1.

because the national courts ruled them time-barred. They took their case to the Inter-American Commission on Human Rights which mediated a friendly settlement designed to resolve the situation for the applicants and for all those in the same legal situation.

The Argentine legislature adopted a series of measures to compensate victims of specific human rights violations, focusing especially on disappearances. The compensation included a non-contributory pension granted to the relatives of persons who disappeared before 10 December 1983.[124] A non-monetary form of reparation allowed those who applied to be exempt from military service if their parents, brothers or sisters disappeared prior to 10 December 1983 in circumstances in which their enforced disappearance could be presumed.[125] A general measure expanded the number of those entitled to reparations to include those who had not instituted legal proceedings for damages.[126] This included conscripts placed at the disposal of military courts, persons held in secret detention centres, and children born while their parents were in captivity. The indemnification was based on a *per diem* amount for the time of detention. Finally, a 1994 law extended the government's policy of 'progressive reparation' to compensate those who were subject to forced disappearance or who died as a result of acts by the armed or security forces or any paramilitary group. The law gave victims five years to submit applications for redress. Argentina's law did not demand a full disclosure of the facts relating to disappeared persons. In the absence of such disclosure, it has been difficult to prove state agents were responsible for the abductions. Without knowledge of the truth, many victims have been unwilling to accept financial compensation.

Chile similarly undertook a programme of compensation and rehabilitation for victims of the Pinochet regime, encompassing life-long pensions for the survivors of those who died in prison, compensation for prison time and for lost income, educational benefits, a national network of medical and psychological services for victims and their families, and exemptions from military service. The law provided for a 'reparation pension', a monthly allowance for the benefit of the relatives of the victims identified in the report of the National Commission and those subsequently recognized as victims. The surviving spouse, the mother or father and children under 25 years of age or handicapped children of any age were entitled to request the reparation pension. The mother of the victim's illegitimate children or their father when the victim was the mother were also eligible. The allowance was shared among the beneficiaries in accordance with percentages laid down by law: 40 per cent for the spouse; 30 per cent for the mother or father;15 per cent for the unmarried mother or father; and 15 per cent for each child, even if the total exceeds 100 per cent of the allowance.

---

[124] Act No. 23,466 of 30 October 1986.
[125] Act No. 23,852 of 27 September 1990. The Act no longer has practical import, since compulsory military service has been abolished in Argentina.
[126] Act No. 24.043, promulgated on 23 December 1991.

As of September 1995, the amount of the allowance where there was only one beneficiary was equivalent to US$350 and when more than one beneficiary about US$490. In addition to the monthly allowance, beneficiaries were granted lump sum compensation equivalent to 12 times the monthly allowance. Education benefits were provided, covering the annual registration fee and the monthly tuition fee for students in middle and higher education, in addition to an educational allowance during the months of the school year. The benefits could be applied for up to the age of 35 years and granted without any age restriction. Children of victims also could be excused from compulsory military service. The Chilean Constitution now expressly provides that individuals have the right to compensation in cases where any of their basic human rights are seriously breached by agents of the state.[127]

Hungary's laws indicate the amount of thought and compromise that go into trying to remedy mass violations committed over a long period of time. First, in the interest of settling ownership relations and providing incentives for investment, Hungary enacted a law to remedy the harm unlawfully caused by state seizure of property.[128] A 1991 Act[129] provided lump sum compensation according to a formula set forth in the Act. Smaller property-holders benefited the most, with those whose damage was less than 200,000 forints (approximately US$2,000) entitled to 100 per cent compensation for the loss. Higher values were compensated as follows:

(a) losses over HF200,000: that amount plus 50 per cent of the excess to 300,000;

(b) losses over HF300,000: 250,000 plus 30 per cent of the amount over 300,000; and

(c) losses over HF500,000: 310,000 plus 10 per cent of the amount over 500,000.

The amount of compensation could not exceed HF5 million per property owned and per former owner. Joint owners shared in the compensation. The compensation was paid in interest-bearing coupons which could be used to purchase property sold during the privatization of state property or to obtain ownership of farm-land. At the request of the person entitled to compensation, coupons also could be transferred into a life annuity within the framework of social security. All claimants were required to submit a claim for compensation

---

[127] 'Any person whose rights are infringed by the State Administration, its agencies or the municipal authorities, may lodge a complaint with the courts provided for by the law, without prejudice to the possible responsibility of the public official who caused those rights to be infringed': Article 38(2).

[128] Hungarian Act XXV of 1991, On Partial Compensation For Damages Unlawfully Caused By The State To Properties Owned By Citizens In The Interest Of Settling Ownership Relations. See Neil J. Kritz (ed.), *Transitional Justice: How Emerging Democracies Reckon with Former Regimes* (1995)

[129] Act XXV of 26 June 1991.

within 90 days of the enactment of the Act. Special valuation rules applied to farm-land based on gold crown value (one gold crown corresponds to 1,000 forints). If the value of a piece of land could not be established from the earlier deed, the gold crown value was calculated by taking the average gold crown data of the village or town according to the location of the farm-land in question, based on its net income data. Cooperatives were required to mark out their farm-land area allowing claims to be made by members of the cooperative. All the land marked out for compensation had to be designated outside protected nature conservancy areas. In *Somers v. Hungary*, the United Nations Human Rights Committee found that the Hungarian compensation scheme for previously expropriated or confiscated property did not discriminate in violation of Article 26 of the Covenant on Civil and Political Rights.[130]

Hungary adopted a separate compensation law regarding attacks on life and liberty.[131] It called for redress for 'immeasurable injuries to the citizens of the country, by depriving them of their lives in the gravest cases, or of their liberty'. Compensation was provided only in part, 'with due regard to the financial possibilities of the national economy' to all who were unlawfully deprived of their lives or liberty between 11 March 1939 and 23 October 1989. HF1 million (approximately US$10,000) was due for the loss of life, divided equally between the living widow or widower, and any child and parent still alive. If none, a brother or sister could claim HF500,000 to be shared among siblings. In the case of clerics forbidden to marry, the diocese was entitled to HF500,000 if there was no person within the categories mentioned. The amounts are substantial, given that the average pension in 1989 was US$75 per month.

Annuities or compensation coupons were provided to anyone who suffered serious restrictions on personal liberty for a period of more than 30 days, with larger amounts for longer detention being paid over the expected life-time of the victim. For those deprived of liberty for up to six months, a lump sum was provided with the amount varying according to the length of detention, payable in two instalments. The deprivation of liberty for which compensation was due included political condemnations, preventive detention, forced medical treatment, internment in camps, forced labour, forced resettlement, and deportation. The surviving spouse received 50 per cent of the compensation due a deceased person. The basic amount of compensation for deprivation of liberty was HF11,000, doubling with each two months of detention for terms up to six months. For the rest, the annuity was determined by computing the duration of deprivation of liberty divided by the life expectancy defined in the schedule and multiplied by the basic amount. All compensation was exempted from taxation.

The law specifically provided that no compensation would be accorded to

---

[130] Views of the Human Rights Committee, 23 July 1996, Communication No. 566/1993, reprinted in (1996) 17 *Hum. Rts L.J.* 412.

[131] Act XXXII of 1992 On the Compensation to Persons Unlawfully Deprived of their Lives or Liberty for Political Reasons was enacted 12 May 1992.

anyone responsible for the violation of basic rights recognized in the International Covenant on Civil and Political Rights, 'unless it can be proved that he has suffered serious prejudice in consequence of criminal procedure due to his activity displayed in the interest of democracy after the violation of basic rights'. No compensation could be paid members of the security organs or political police or those who were involved in the repression of the 1956 revolution. A short four-month statute of limitations applied to filing claims.

Albania also established a procedure to compensate political victims of the former regime. Its Law on Former Victims of Persecution[132] provides in Article 7 that material compensation for victims of political persecution will take the form of immediate cash awards, life pensions, compensation for salary, land, business premises and other forms of material benefit that may be irrevocably given to the persecuted person or to his family, if he has died, in compensation for his loss of life and freedom and his unpaid labour and suffering. These latter forms of benefit have as their principal object the creation of conditions and possibilities for integrating the victim and his family into the normal economic and social life of the country.

In Africa, South Africa and Uganda provide two examples of efforts to remedy past human rights violations in part through compensation. In the aftermath of the dictatorship of Idi Amin Dada, the Ugandan Government enacted the President's War Veterans, Widows and Orphans Charity Fund Act (No. 2 of 1982) on behalf of victims and their relatives who participated in liberation efforts against the dictatorship. In addition, the Expropriated Properties Act (No. 9 of 1982) allowed expelled Asians to return to Uganda and reclaim their properties if the action occurred within 12 years of the taking. Less positively, the National Resistance Government in Legal Notice No. 6 of 1986 reaffirmed the statutory immunity of the government against claims involving loss of life, arrest and detention, seizure, use, destruction or damage to property perpetrated by agents of the government prior to the NRM's assumption of power in Uganda in 1986. The Uganda High Court struck down the immunity as unconstitutional, but Decree No. 1 of 1987 reinstated it.[133] In most cases, the immunity is coupled with a narrow interpretation of the common law of vicarious liability for acts of state agents, leaving victims with little recourse against the perpetrators.

In South Africa, the Truth and Reconciliation Commission based its recommendations on international law as well as the Promotion of National Unity and Reconciliation Act, No. 34 of 1995. That Act states that one of its objectives is to provide for the 'taking of measures aimed at the granting of reparation to, and the rehabilitation and the restoration of the human and civil dignity, of victims of violations of human rights'. The Committee established to formulate the policy

---

[132] Law No. 7748 (29 July 1993), reprinted in 3 Kritz, *supra* n. 63, vol. III at 661.

[133] E. Khiddu-Makubuya, 'Uganda' in *Seminar on the Right to Restitution, Compensation and Rehabilitation for Victims of Gross Violations of Human Rights and Fundamental Freedoms* (SIM Special No. 29), 86 at 94–95.

noted that the amnesty that had been granted favoured the perpetrators of human rights violations, in that all criminal and civil liability for their crimes was extinguished. The Reparations Act, then, 'attempts to restore a moral balance to the amnesty process by allowing victims of gross human rights violations an opportunity to articulate their experiences in an affirming environment and by making provision for the granting of reparation to victims'. According to the Committee, 'the right of victims of human rights abuse to fair and adequate compensation, as a result of that human rights abuse, is well-established in international law'.[134] It added that 'it is not sufficient to award "token" or nominal compensation to victims. *It is therefore important that the quantum of reparation awarded to victims is sufficient to make a meaningful and substantial impact on the quality of their lives*'.[135]

The Commission considered five categories of reparations as part of just satisfaction:

(1) redress: the right to fair and adequate compensation;
(2) restitution: the right to re-establishment, as far as possible, of the situation that existed for the beneficiary prior to the violation;
(3) rehabilitation: the right to the provision of medical and psychological care and fulfilment of significant personal and community needs;
(4) restoration of dignity: which could include symbolic forms of reparation; and
(5) reassurance of non-repetition: including the creation of legislative and administrative measures, which contribute to the maintenance of a stable society and the prevention of the re-occurrence of human rights violations.

The Commission recommended not trying to individualize reparations. Each victim:

will receive the same quantum of final reparation regardless of the number of occasions that they have suffered a gross violation of human rights, the severity and nature of each violation and the consequences of the violations. This is because it is impossible to devise a set of criteria which provide for varying amounts of reparation to be paid to victims according to their degree of suffering without producing unfair or arbitrary results. For example, one may wish to provide more reparation in instances where a violation has resulted in death. However, such a policy may prejudice the family of a breadwinner who has been so severely tortured that he/she is unable to work. Those who are debilitated by human rights violation/s, but nevertheless survive, may place a greater burden on those required to care for them than those who die.

Furthermore, how does one assess degrees of suffering in order to provide for different awards of reparation? Certain individuals can withstand horrendous long term torture and remain relatively healthy and functional, while other individuals may be permanently

---

[134] Truth and Reconciliation Commission, *Final Proposal on Reparation and Rehabilitation Policy*, RRFinpolicy005 (1997), at 6, http://www.truth.org.za/policy.htm.
[135] *Ibid.* (emphasis in original).

debilitated as a result of a single act of violence. One cannot devise a set of objective criteria which will allow for different forms of abuse to be differentiated according to severity because the response to different forms and intensities of abuse is so subjective. If one awards more reparation to those who show ill effects after, for example, torture, one might effectively penalize those who cope. It is for this reason that each victim should receive the same award of reparation.[136]

Note that victims are defined as persons who suffered harm in the form of physical or mental injury, emotional suffering, pecuniary loss or substantial impairment of human rights. To treat all victims the same seems unjust, and surely it is possible to distinguish long-term disability resulting from severe torture from less severe violations. Other approaches are possible, as shown by the United Nations Compensation Commission practice discussed above and the *Marcos* litigation, below. Those identified as being in urgent need will be the first recipients of the final entitlement. The first amount paid is 20 per cent of the total, with the rest paid on a monthly basis over three to five years.

The difficulties that arise with large number of claims should not serve as a pretext for denying all relief or targeting particular groups for exclusion from redress. A Joint Memorandum of the Israeli Ministry of Justice, Ministry of Finance and Ministry of Defense, 20 March 1997, provides an example. The Memorandum proposed a law that would deny compensation to Palestinian residents of the Occupied Territories injured by Israeli security forces during the Intifada[137] but would continue to allow damage claims by Israelis and tourists. The proposed law would grant retroactive and complete exemption to the state, and to all those acting on its behalf, from liability for past and future wrongful acts committed by them in the Occupied Territories and which caused or will cause any bodily damage, handicap or death to Palestinian residents of the territories between 1987 and 1993. The Memorandum made clear that the proposal was intended to preclude Israeli courts from awarding compensation to the estimated 1,000 Palestinians killed and 18,000 injured during the specified years,[138] noting that the courts were expected to obligate the state to pay large compensation sums for torts committed by security forces against Palestinians and expressing a consequent desire 'to protect the State from these claims'.[139] At the time the

---

[136] *Ibid.*

[137] State of Israel, Ministry of Justice, *Memorandum of Law Concerning Handling of Suits Arising from Security force Activities in Judea, Samaria and the Gaza Strip (Exemption from Liability and granting of Payment) 1997–5757*, 20 March 1997, File No. 2–1878.   [138] *Ibid.* at 4.

[139] *Ibid.* at 8. Israeli courts have given a narrow reading to the immunity provided to the state in Article 5 of the Civil Tort Law for 'combatant activity by the Israel Defense Forces'. In Civil Appeal 243/83, *Jerusalem Municipality v. Gordon*, (P.D. 39(1) 113), Chief Justice Barak stated: 'The principle of equity before the law requires the imposition of responsibility on the public authority according to the same standards as applicable to the individual ... A public body, as any other causer of damage, must take reasonable steps of caution in order to prevent damage. It often acts as a good 'spreader of damage', a fact which may sometimes justify the imposition of liability upon it. In this way it will also be guaranteed that safety measures will be taken in the future in order to prevent the recurrence of the negligent event which resulted in liability'.

Memorandum was completed, more than 4,000 claims had already been filed against the state, of which 700 were pending before the courts.[140] The Memorandum proposes an alternative system of offering *ex gratia* 'payments due to humanitarian considerations' in order to replace state liability. It is a discretionary scheme, subject to conditions, loopholes, and procedural hurdles that make it unlikely anyone would qualify for the limited one time payment suggested.[141]

In the USA, the *Marcos* litigation exemplifies the problems associated with efforts to afford all victims some remedy. In the class action, the large numbers of victims necessitated innovative procedures that limited the individualized decision-making, taking of evidence, and procedural fairness to both sides that would normally be required in litigation. Rather than hold separate hearings on each of the 10,059 claims, the United States District Court allowed the use of a statistical sample of the claims in determining compensatory damages. After an initial review, 518 claims were ruled facially invalid, leaving a pool of 9,541 of which 137 were randomly selected by computer. The number chosen was based on the testimony of a statistical expert who stated that a random sample of 137 claims would achieve a 95 per cent statistical probability that the same percentage determined to be valid among the examined claims would be applicable to the totality of claims filed.[142]

The 137 in the random sample, which included torture victims, families of those summarily executed, and those who disappeared, were deposed and the expert reviewed the depositions to determine the claims. Five per cent of the claims were determined to be invalid. Based on the sample, the expert recommended that the 64 torture claimants get US$3,310,000, an average of US$52,719 per valid claim. For summary execution the recommendation was US$6,425,767 for 50 valid claims, an average of US$128,515 per valid claim. For the disappearances, he recommended US$1,833,515, an average of US$107,853 per valid claim. The court applied the 5 per cent invalidity rate found in the random samples in making its awards to the entire class of 10,059 remaining claims.

In calculating the amounts due for torture, the expert ranked the claims on a scale from 1 to 5, with 5 representing the worst abuses and suffering.

---

[140] *Supra* n. 137, at 4.

[141] The claimant must prove that the damage was caused by the security forces not during an operational activity of fighting against or preventing terror, and not during another activity carried out in circumstances of risk of death or bodily injury, unless the act was carried out in true deviation, knowingly, from the instructions applying to the security forces during the event. Eligibility is denied for anyone injured while involved in 'a hostile activity' against the military or civilian population. Anyone previously convicted of terrorist activity, 'or regarding whom there is evidence of such activity', is ineligible unless the damage occurs while the individual is in legal custody. Third party corroborating evidence of the circumstances of the injury is important in establishing eligibility. If the claimant meets these criteria, the resulting injury must amount to death or permanent disability of at least 25 per cent: *ibid.* at 10. All claims must be submitted within one year of passage of the law and must be accompanied by a waiver of any other recourse against the state or state agent.

[142] *In re Estate of Marcos*, 103 F.3d 767, 782

Consideration was given to (1) physical torture, including what methods were used and/or abuses were suffered; (2) mental abuse, including fright and anguish; (3) amount of time the torture lasted; (4) length of detention, if any; (5) physical and/or mental injuries; (6) victim's age; and (7) actual losses, including medical bills. 'Although each claim of torture was unique' the expert determined 'that there were sufficient similarities within a rating category to recommend a standard damage amount to each victim within that grouping'. The amount ranged from US$20,000 for category 1 to US$100,000 for category 5.

For summary executions and disappearances, the existence of torture prior to the death or disappearance was weighed in the damages. Loss of earnings was also factored in, using the formula of $2/3 \times (80 - \text{age of death}) \times$ annual income, a formula adopted by the Philippine Supreme Court. A cap of US$120,000 was placed on lost earnings. Where there was no evidence of earnings, the average for the occupation was utilized.

The jury reviewed all the claims, including the testimony from the 137 random sample claimants. For the most part, the jury followed the recommendations of the expert. It awarded more than recommended to six torture claimants and less than recommended to five torture claimants.

On appeal, the Estate of Marcos challenged the methodology used to award the compensatory damages. The Estate objected that the methodology had not been used before and that it was inappropriate to lump claims together. The court agreed that some individualization was lost. 'On the other hand, the time and judicial resources required to try the nearly 10,000 claims in this case would alone make resolution of [the] claims impossible'.[143] Thus, 'while the district court's methodology in determining valid claims is unorthodox, it can be justified by the extraordinarily unusual nature of this case'.[144]

The *Marcos* cases and the national experiences described above demonstrate the unlikelihood of full compensation even where the desire to provide redress is present. Given the limited resources available, the courts and states have sought a fair way of pro-rating the claims based on the severity of injury. Such an approach maximizes the recovery of all of the victims who came forward, but should be coupled with other remedies, from prosecution to rehabilitation. In the absence of full compensation, alternative relief becomes even more important.

E. NON-MONETARY REMEDIES

The psychology of victims requires appropriate mechanisms to confront and process trauma and abuse, facilitating closure rather than repression,[145] recognizing that

---

[143] *Ibid.* at 786.   [144] *Ibid.*
[145] Neil J. Kritz, 'Coming to Terms with Atrocities: A Review of Accountability Mechanisms for Mass Violations of Human Rights', (1996) 59 *Law & Contemp. Probs.* 127.

dealing with grief, anger, and rehabilitation takes time. Victims may harbour deep resentments that if not dealt with could result in vigilante justice and retribution. The long-term mental health of individual victims and society as a whole may be threatened if adequate treatment and rehabilitation is not provided. States and international organizations have introduced a variety of non-monetary measures to respond to these needs in redressing gross and systematic violations.

The United Nations Commission on El Salvador recommended symbolic reparations to redress the violations it investigated: the construction of a national monument bearing the names of all the victims of the conflict; recognition of the good name of the victims and of the serious crimes of which they were victims; and the institution of a national holiday in memory of the victims of the conflict and to serve as a symbol of national reconciliation.

The Chilean Truth Commission similarly recommended several non-monetary forms of redress[146] after it investigated serious violations of human rights during the period of military dictatorship. 'Serious' violations were defined as violations of the right to life: disappearances, summary executions and extra-judicial killings, torture followed by death, and unsolved kidnapping and death inflicted by private persons for political reasons. The law did not extend to other gross and systematic violations such as torture not resulting in death, prolonged arbitrary detention, or involuntary exile. The Commission recommended that three types of remedies follow the partial redress afforded by uncovering the truth: symbolic reparation to vindicate the victims; legal and administrative measures to resolve issues arising from the death (inheritance, family status, situation of minors); and compensation, including social benefits, health care, and education. The report also put forward specific recommendations to guard against human rights violations in the country and consolidate a human rights culture. A 1992 law[147] created the Chilean National Corporation for Reparation and Reconciliation. Its role was to coordinate, implement and promote the actions necessary to comply with the recommendations contained in the report of the National Commission. One important aspect of its work was the effort to determine the whereabouts of the disappeared. Relevant information on criminal responsibility was to be sent to the courts.

In response to a request from the Group of Relatives of Disappeared Detainees and the Group of Relatives of Victims of Political Executions, the government established the 'Memorial Foundation for Disappeared Detainees and Victims of Political Executions'.[148] Presided over by a representative of the Ministry of the Interior and composed of members of the Group of Relatives of Disappeared Detainees, the Group of Relatives of Victims of Political Executions and persons known in the field of human rights, the Foundation was responsible for the

---

[146] Supreme Decree No. 355 of the Ministry of the Interior of 25 April 1990.
[147] Law 19.123 of 31 January 1992, *Diario Oficial*, 8 February 1992.
[148] Supreme Decree 294 of 13 March 1991 of the Ministry of Justice.

construction of a plaza and a mausoleum in the general cemetery of the City of Santiago. The intent is to preserve the historical memory and bury the remains of victims who have been located. Construction of the plaza began in September 1990 and was completed in March 1994. It contains a marble plaque on which are engraved the names of disappeared detainees and victims of political executions included in the report of the National Commission. A number of disappeared detainees are buried there. Finally, the government created a National Office for Return, an autonomous body with its own resources, to develop programmes for the reintegration of exiled Chileans returning to the country.[149] As a result of the programmes, the Office obtained validation of professional qualifications obtained abroad; papers for free medical care; exemption from customs duties for returning exiles; and housing allowances.[150]

In central and eastern Europe, rehabilitation, including restitution of confiscated property, lost jobs and pensions and other lost benefits, has been of particular concern. In the Czech Republic, the government instituted widespread rehabilitation of persons unlawfully sentenced and otherwise persecuted under the Communist regime.[151] Various criminal provisions were declared illegal on the grounds of inconsistency with the principles of a democratic society. All decisions based on these offences, pronounced between 25 February 1948 and 1 January 1990, were annulled directly by virtue of the law. All persons so sentenced could apply for review and rehabilitation.

In Romania, the government passed an amnesty for persons convicted of political offences under the previous regime, notably actions in connection with the expression of opposition to the dictatorship.[152] The amnesty also covered actions committed in connection with respect for human rights and fundamental freedoms, with the demand for civil and political, economic, social and cultural rights, and the abolition of discriminatory practices. In February 1990, it went further in creating a specialized committee 'to inquire into abuses and violations of basic human rights and to rehabilitate the victims of the dictatorship'. The Committee received over 18,000 claims for reparation of human rights violations committed by the previous government, examining and settling between 4,000 and 5,000 cases. A lack of cooperation on the part of former officials was cited in the Committee's report as one of the reasons for the inability to proceed further.

---

[149] Act No. 18.994, *Diario Oficial* of 28 August 1990. For purposes of the Act, those considered to be exiles were: persons sentenced to custodial penalties commuted to banishment; deportees or persons required by administrative decision to leave the national territory; those who, after travelling abroad normally, were prohibited from re-entering Chile; those who sought refuge in foreign embassies and were subsequently transferred abroad; those who acquired the status of refugees as recognized by the United Nations or found refuge on humanitarian grounds in the host countries; and members of the family groups of all those residing or having resided abroad for three years or more.

[150] See Act No. 19.128, *Diario Oficial* of 7 February 1992; Act No. 19.074, *Diario Oficial* of 28 August 1991.

[151] Laws No. 119/1990 on judicial rehabilitations, as amended by Law No. 47/1991 and 633/1992.

[152] Legislative Decree No. 3 of 4 January 1990.

Another 1990 Legislative Decree granted rights to persons persecuted for political reasons and subjected to deprivation of liberty, psychiatric internment, house arrest, forcible transfer from one place to another, and disability arising from any of the former preventing the person from finding work. The reparations provided took into account the duration of the persecution or its consequences in the calculation of seniority of employment, provided financial indemnities proportionate to the duration of the persecution, and gave entitlements in respect of medical care and housing. Other reparation measures pertained to the elimination of certain injustices in higher education, where students were excluded for political or religious reasons. Teachers who had been persecuted were reinstated.

Hungary acted in 1992 to rehabilitate victims,[153] declaring null and void political offences and sentences for them. According to the Act, 'Law cannot cure all kinds of injury, but it is justified that the persons having suffered injury on the basis of criminal procedures be given—in accordance with the principles of the rule of law laid down in the Constitution—political, moral and legal satisfaction'. (Preamble). All convictions based on offences listed in the Act are deemed null and void and special benefits in the framework of national care are given those who suffered disability or serious health injury connected with the deprivation of liberty.

The South African policy proposals for reconciliation also include a section on 'Restoration of Dignity through Symbolic Reparations' including possible local, provincial and national measures such as

(a) the erection of tombstones and cenotaphs;
(b) exhumation and reburial;
(c) visits to the graves of victims;
(d) issuing of death certificates for the unknown dead and disappeared;
(e) culturally appropriate ceremonies for the unknown dead and disappeared;
(f) restoration of the good name of individuals;
(g) monuments, memorials, museums, archives, peace parks, etc.;
(h) a National Day of Remembrance and Reconciliation; and
(i) changes in educational curricula at all levels to teach the true history of South Africa and an awareness of human rights.

Symbolic measures, rehabilitation and restoration of reputation are important aspects of reconciliation and healing when gross and systematic violations have been committed. They help restore the dignity of the victims and tangibly acknowledge their suffering.

---

[153] Act XI of 19 February 1992. The listed political offences were: conviction of conspiracy, revolt, revolt against another socialist state, insult of authority or official personage, unauthorized crossing of the frontier, insult to community, refusal to return, offence against the freedom of peoples, misdemeanour against the press law; propagation of disquieting rumours; failure to denounce law-breaking by another.

F. CONCLUSIONS

Remedies for gross and systematic violations of human rights differ because of the quality and quantity of the violations. When there are thousands of victims needing justice, both the procedures and the substance inevitably alter. Administrative solutions like sampling, or summary procedures can assist in affording swifter resolution of claims for compensation. Compensation can be only a partial remedy, however, because normally there can be only partial compensation. The numbers of victims, usually in economically weak states, necessitate reduced amounts in order to ensure that all receive some redress. In most instances of mass violations, however, compensation is not the primary emphasis. Society as a whole and all of the victims need to be fully informed of the truth so that those who suffered and society itself can be rehabilitated. Loss of reputation can be as costly to the individual in esteem and self-worth as any pecuniary loss. Symbolic reparations, through recognition by the government of the wrongs done, are an important element in restoring human rights and the rule of law. Lastly, there must be an effort to ensure the accountability of those who perpetrated the abuses. In sum, the same purposes that underlay all remedies—redress for the victims and deterrence for potential violators—apply in this context; but the nature and scope of the violations requires that more be done to redress and to deter.

Conclusions

One of the most important legal developments of the modern era—both nationally and internationally—has been the opening of avenues of complaint for private citizens against oppressive action by government agents and agencies and the affording of remedies when violations are found. The right of access to judicial remedies is widely guaranteed in international human rights treaties and can be considered as part of the corpus of the customary international law of human rights. In regional and global institutions, most human rights procedures open to individuals undertake fact-finding, determine whether or not the state has violated a right guaranteed in the relevant instrument and, if a breach is found, recommend that the state remedy the violation. The recommendations may be general or may detail the action required of the state. The regional courts additionally may issue binding decisions that afford compensation for the wrongs that have been committed and direct that the state afford non-monetary remedies.

Remedies not only provide redress for the individual victim, but they serve the community interest in sanctioning the perpetrator and deterring future violations by the same or other wrongdoers. They thus serve the rule of law at all levels of society. While the establishment of an international criminal court may provide an additional forum for sanctioning the most egregious breaches of human rights law, it will not eliminate the need for civil remedies to redress the harm caused to the victims.

The nature and scope of remedies is generally consistent throughout the world. The notion of remedial justice, of wiping out the consequences of the wrong, is a general principle of law on which there is broad consensus. Remedies begin with a declaration that a wrong has been done or is about to be done. The wrongdoer is expected to conform to the interpretation of the law and decision on the facts, adjusting his actions accordingly. More broadly, legal systems require restitution of the victims' legal and material situation to what it was before the wrong was done. Damages for harm that is incapable of restitution include indemnification of material losses such as lost wages and earning capacity; medical, legal, funeral and incidental expenses; and loss of property. Non-pecuniary damages are awarded for pain and suffering, fear, humiliation and other dignitary harms. Where necessary, national and some international courts may order specific conduct be taken to afford non-monetary remedies, especially to guarantee non-repetition of the acts that constituted the wrong. Deterring future violations is thus part of the structure of the law of remedies. Punitive or exemplary damages reinforce the deterrence and enhance the sanctioning element of remedies.

In general, protection of human rights differs from state responsibility for injury to aliens and from private tort actions. Traditional state responsibility involved inter-state claims where the state itself was deemed injured. Diplomacy and the respective interests and power of states sometimes played a role in the outcome of claims. In human rights law, in contrast, individuals directly seek to ensure respect for the rights they are guaranteed, including making whole the harm that has been inflicted on them; the actions they bring are generally retrospective in assessing acts already performed. States parties and/or supervisory organs established by the relevant treaties have a broader interest in upholding the international rule of law and prospectively returning the breaching state to compliance with the international norm. Individual victims are, of course, also interested in future performance, in ensuring that the breach is not repeated, but they more often focus on what has been done rather than on future possibilities.

In general, international human rights tribunals have paid little attention to the remedial aspect of individual complaints. The European Court of Human Rights has read its mandate narrowly and applied even the powers it admittedly has in a restrictive fashion. The Inter-American Court until the *Loayza Tamayo* decision manifested a reluctance to utilize its power to order non-pecuniary reparations, although these can be extremely important in remedying human rights violations. In some cases, applicants are more concerned to know the truth, such as the whereabouts of the disappeared victim, than they are about receiving monetary compensation. In addition, an award of financial compensation without requiring remedial action may signal to a government that it is permitted to violate human rights provided it has sufficient tax revenues to pay for the resulting harm. Non-pecuniary measures serve to reinforce the validity of the obligation breached, forcing the responsible state to acknowledge responsibility. They also provide a measure of satisfaction to persons injured by the state and serve to send a message to society that the violations will not be tolerated or repeated.

The Inter-American system has been criticized for not advancing the international law of reparations by creating a general fund to pay victims of gross and systematic human rights abuses.[1] It is argued that the result creates an inequity between similarly situated victims because not all cases can reach the Court and thus only some victims will receive compensation. Honduran Human Rights Commissioner Leo Valladares, in his official report on disappearances in Honduras, called it patently unfair 'that only those whose cases were before the Inter-American Court received reparations, and that all of the proven cases of disappearances should receive economic reparations'.[2] It is questionable, however, whether any of the human rights tribunals could award damages to parties not before them. The procedures are designed for individual victims to bring cases. Moreover, if the Court decides in one case that compensation must be paid to the victims, it serves notice on the government in regard to similar

---

[1] Jo Pasqualucci, 'The Inter-American Human Rights System: Establishing Precedents, and Procedure in Human Rights Law', (1994–95) 26 *Inter-Am. L.Rev.* 297, 331–2.

[2] The National Commissioner for the Protection of Human Rights in Honduras, *The Facts Speak for Themselves* (Human Rights Watch/Americas Watch, 1994), 234.

cases that reparations are due and it alerts other victims that remedies are available.

In addition, the Inter-American system may allow class actions to be filed on behalf of all victims. The Convention permits petitions to be filed with the Commission not only by the victim or relative of the victim, but by 'any non-governmental entity legally recognized in one or more member states of the OAS'.[3] The Commission must still decide whether to refer the case to the Court, but should it do so, this type of 'mass tort action' would allow the Court to establish a fund as it did in the *Aloeboetoe* case. United Nations Special Rapporteur Theodoor van Boven calls for such a procedure, stating it is 'necessary that, in addition to individual means of reparation, adequate provision be made to entitle groups of victims or victimized communities to present collective claims for damages and to receive collective reparation accordingly'.[4]

The European and Inter-American Courts' approaches to compensatory damages have been influenced by arguments presented by their respective Commissions. From the beginning, neither has served well the interests of the victims in Court proceedings on remedies. The European Commission rarely commented on compensation claims. The Inter-American Commission for its part has articulated a standard of compensation which it has failed to apply in omitting claims for damages resulting from the loss of personal services of the victim. It also has underestimated the impact of inflation. The Commission in general has failed to develop a coherent and consistent theory and practice of damages.

In large part, the representatives of litigants are responsible for the lack of attention to remedies. In many cases, no claim has been presented or the applicant had requested only that the tribunal afford remedies 'in its discretion'. Claims are often made without supporting legal argument or evidence. In some cases clearly excessive claims have been filed. In future cases, litigants must be as prepared on the issue of remedies as they are on the merits of claims that are made.

Compensatory damages should repair all the proximate direct and indirect consequences of the harm caused by the violaiton. Moreover, with a dual focus on suffering of the victim and wrongfulness of government conduct, it seems that moral damages may partially substitute for punitive damages. Presumed damages for violations of intangible interests, which so often happens in human rights cases, must be awarded. The object must be to undo what has been done; to halt the wrongful conduct and prevent its reoccurrence.

During 1998, the world community marked the fiftieth anniversary of the adoption of the Inter-American Declaration of the Rights and Duties of Man, the

---

[3] American Convention on Human Rights, 22 November 1969, 36 O.A.S.T.S. 1, Article 44(1).

[4] *Study Concerning the Right to Restitution, Compensation and Rehabilitation for Victims of Gross Violations of Human Rights and Fundamental Freedoms, final report submitted by Mr. Theo van Boven, Special rapporteur to the Sub-Commission on Prevention of Discrimination and Protection of Minorities*, U.N. Hum.Rts.Comm'n., 45th Sess., U.N. Doc. E/CN.4/Sub.2/1993, s. VII.

Genocide Convention, and the Universal Declaration of Human Rights. The development of human rights law during the past half-century has been remarkable. It is a reflection of how far the law has progressed that the issue of remedies for international human rights violations is now current. At the outset, there were no complaint mechanisms, no procedures, and little law to restrain a state from abusing those within its power. The law has developed, procedures have proliferated, and individuals may now seek to hold accountable those who commit human rights violations. The development of a consistent and coherent law of remedies can be a part of the process of enhancing the effectiveness of human rights law as we look to the future.

Bibliography

1. General

Anand, R.P., *New States and International Law* (1972).

Anand, R.P., 'Role of the "New" Asian-African Countries in the Present International Legal Order', (1962) 55 *Am. J. Int'l . L.* 383.

Anand, R.P., 'Attitude of the Asian-African States Toward Certain Problems of International Law', (1968) 15 *Int'l. L. & Comp. L.Q.* 55

Aristotle, *The Ethics* (J.A.K. Thompson trans., 1955).

Basdevant, J., *Dictionnaire de la Terminologie du Droit International* (1960).

Baxter, Q., 'Treaties and Custom', (1970) 129–I *Recueil des Cours* 25.

Bourquin, M., 'Règles générales du droit de la paix', (1931) 35–I *Recueil des Cours* 1.

Brierly, J.L., *The Law of Nations* (1965).

Briggs, H.W., *The Law of Nations: Cases, Documents and Notes* (1952).

Brownlie, I., *Principles of International Law* (1966).

Buriette-Maurau, P., *La Participation du Tiers-Monde a L'Elaboration du Droit International: Essai de Qualification* (1983).

Bustamante, A.S., *Derecho International Publico* (1986).

Cavaglieri, A., *Corso di Diritto Internationale*, 3rd edn. (1934).

Cavare, L., *Le Droit International Public Positif*, 3rd edn. (1967) (Tome 1), (1969) (Tome 2).

Chapman, J. (ed.), *Compensatory Justice* (1991).

Charpentier, J., 'L'affaire de la Barcelona Traction', A.F.D.I. 1970.

Cheng, B., *General Principles of Law as Applied by International Courts and Tribunals* (1953).

Dabin, J., *Le Droit Subjectif* (1952).

Darby, W.E., *International Tribunals* (1904).

Delbes, L., *Les Principes Generaux du Contentieux International* (1962).

De Visscher, P., *Theories et Realites en Droit International Public* (1970).

De Vuyst, B.M., *Statutes and Rules of Procedure of International Administrative Tribunals* (1981).

Encyclopedia of Public International Law (Bernhardt, R. (ed.), 1981).

Fauchille, 4 *Traite de Droit International Public* (1921–6).

Friedman, W., *The Changing Structure of International Law* (1964).

Ginsberg, M. *On Justice in Society* (1965).

Grotius, H., *De Jure Belli Ac Pacis* (Kelsey trans., 1925).

Guggenheim, P., 2 *Traite de Droit International Public* (1954).

Haasdjk, S., 'The Lack of Uniformity in the Terminology of the International Law of Remedies', (1992) 5 *Leiden J. Int'l L.* 254.

Hackworth, G.H., *Digest of International Law* (1943).

Hohfeld, W., *Fundamental Legal Conceptions* (W. Cook, (ed.), 1919).

Hyde, C.C., *International Law: Chiefly as Interpreted and Applied by the U.S.* (1947).

Jenkins, I., *Social Order and the Limits of Law* (1980).

Jenks, W., 'The Law of Nature in International Law', *Netherlands Int'l L. Rev.* 1959.

Jenks, W., *The Prospect of International Adjudication* (1964).

Jessup, Ph. C., *A Modern Law of Nations* (1948).

Jimenz de Arechaga, E., 'International Law in the Past Third of a Century', 159–I *Recueil des Cours* 279 (1978).

Kelsen, H., *Principles of International Law* (1952).

Kiss, A., *L'Abus de Droit en Droit International* (1953).

Lauterpacht, H., *The Function of Law in the International Community* (1966).

Lomasky, L., *Persons, Rights and the Moral Community* (1967).

Mosler, H., 'General Principles of Law' in (1984) 7 *Encyclopedia of Public International Law* 89.

Posner, R., *Economic Analysis of Law*, 2nd edn. (1977).

Posner, R., *The Economic of Justice* (1983).

Ralston, J. *The Law and Procedure of International Tribunals* (1926).

Rousseau, C., *Droit International Public* (1965).

Scelle, G., *Précis du Droit des Gens* (1932).

Scerni, M., *L'Abuso di Diritto Nei Rapporti Internazionali* (1930).

Schwarzenberger, G., *International Law*, 3rd edn. (1957).

Scott, J.B., *La Travaux de la Cour Permanente d'Arbitrage de la Haye* (1921).

Sørensen, M., *Manual of Public Law* (1968).

Tunkin, G., *Droit International Public* (1965).

Vattel, E., *Le Droit des Gens* (1758).

Verdross, A., *Volkerrecht*, 5th edn. (1964).

2. State responsibility

Accioly, Hildebrando, 'Principes généraux de la responsabilite internationale d'après la doctrine et la jurisprudence', 96–I *Recueil des Cours 350* (1959).

Actes de la Conference pour la Codification du droit international (c. 3511 (a) M. 145 (2) 1930 V).

Afaki, B.G., 'La Commission d'indemnisation des Nations Unies: Trois ans d'épreuve au service du règlement des differends internationaux', 20 *Droit et pratique du commerce international* 471 (1994).

Ago, Roberto, 'Le délit international', 68–II *Recueil des Cours* 415 (1939).

Aldrich, *The Jurisprudence on the Iran-United States Claims Tribunal: An Analysis of the Decisions of the Tribunal* (1996).

Amerasinghe, C.F., 'Imputability in the Law of State Responsibility for Injuries to Aliens', 22 *Rev. Egyptienne de Droit Inter.* (1966).

Amerasinghe, C.F., 'Issues of Compensation for the Taking of Alien Property in the Light of Recent Cases and Practice', 41 *I.C.L.Q.* 22 (1992).

Anzilotti, D., 'La responsabilité internationale des Etats à raison des dommages soufferts', *R.G.D.I.P.* 1906.

Anzilotti, D., *Theoria Generale Della Responsabilita Dello Stato Nel Diritto Internationale* (1902).

Bederman, D., 'The United Nations Compensation Commission and the Transition to International Claims Settlement', 27 *N.Y.U.J. Int'l L. & Pol.* 1 (1994).

Berlia, G., 'De la responsabilité internationale de l'Etat' in *La technique et les principes du droit public, études en l'honneur de Georges Scelle*, (1950).

Bissonette, P.A., *La satisfaction comme mode de réparation en droit international* (1952).

Bollecker-Stern, B., *Le préjudice dans la théories de la responsabilité internationale* (1973).

Borchard, E.M., 'Important Decisions of the Mixed Claims Commission, United States and Mexico', 21 *Am.J.Int'l.L.* 518 (1927).

Borchard, E.M., *Pecuniary Claims* (1937).

Borchard, E.M. *The Diplomatic Protection of Citizens Abroad* (1916).

Bouvé, L.C., 'Quelques observations sur la réparation due dans certains cas par l'Etat responsable', 11 *R.D.I.L.C.* (1930).

Brierly, J.L., 'The Theory of Implied State Complicity in International Claims', 9 *Brit. Y.B. Int'l L.* 42 (1928).

Briggs, H.W., 'The Punitive Nature of Damage in International Law and Failure to Apprehend, Prosecute or Punish', in *Essays in Political Science in Honor of W.W. Willoughby* (1937).

Brownlie, I., 1 *System of the Law of Nations: State Responsibility* (1983).

Bueres, A.J. and Bustamante, A., *Responsabilidad por dans* (1990).

Canfado Trinidade, A.A., 'Denial of Justice and its Relationship to the Exhaustion of Local Remedies in International Law', 53 *Philippine L. J.* 404 (1978).

Carella, G., 'I punitive damages e la riparazione del danno morale in diritto internazionale', 7 *Rivista di Diritto Internazionale* 67 (1984).

Carlebach, A., *Le problème de la faute et sa place dans la norme du droit international* (1962).

Cannone, A., 'Il diritto alla riparazione previsto dagli accordi internazionali sui diritti dell'uomo e l'ordinament italiano', 9 *Rivista di Diritto Internazionale* 38 (1986).

Castañeda, J., 'Les principes de la protection diplomatique des nationaux a l'étranger, 3 *Bibliotheca Visseriana* 1 (1924).

Cavaré, L., 'Les transformations de la protection diplomatique', 1958 *Zeitschrift fur Auslandissches Recht und Volkerrecht.*

Chapus, René, 'Responsibilité publique et responsabilité privée', Thèse Paris, *L.G.D.J.* (1957).

Christenson, G., *International Claims: Their Preparation and Presentation* (1962).

Clagett, B.M., 'The Expropriation Issue Before the Iran-United States Claims Tribunal: Is "Just Compensation" Required by International Law or Not?', 16 *Law & Pol'y Int'l Bus.* 813 (1984).

Clark, G., 'The English Practice with Regard to Reprisals by Private Persons', 27 *Am. J. Int'l L.* 694 (1933).

Cohn, G., 'La théorie de la responsabilité internationale', 68–II *Recueil des Cours* 207 (1939).

Commission franco-mexicaine des réclamations, 'La réparation des dommages causés aux étrangers par des mouvements révolutionnaires: jurisprudence de la Commission franco-mexicaine des réclamations', 1924–1932 (1933).

Crooke, J.R., 'Applicable Law in International Arbitration: The Iran-U.S. Claims Tribunal Experience', 83 *Am. J. Int'l L.* 278 (1989).

De Beus, J.G., *The Jurisprudence of the General Claims Commission, United States and Mexico under the Convention of September 8, 1923* (1938).

De Visscher, C., 'Le déni de justice en droit international', 52–II *Recueil des Cours.* 366 (1935).

De Visscher, C. 'La responsabilité des États, 2 *Bibliotheca Visseriana* 87 (1924).

De Visscher, P. 'La protection des personnes morales', 102–1 *Recueil des Cours* 394 (1961).

Decenciere-Ferrandiere, *La responsabilité internationale des Etats à raison des dommages subis par des etrangers* (1925).

Delbez, 'Responsabilité internationale des Etats pour des crimes commis sur le territoire d'un Etat', *R.G.D.I.P.* (1930).

Dumas, J., *De la responsabilité internationale des Etats* (1930).

Dumas, J., 'Du déni de justice consideré comme condition de la responsabilité internationale des Etats en matière criminelle', *Rev. Dro. Inter. Leg. Comp.* 277 (1929).

Dunn, F.S., *The Protection of Nationals: A Study in the Application of International Law* (1932).

Dunn, F.S., *The Diplomatic Protection of Americans in Mexico* (1933).

Dupuis, Ch., 'La Responsabilidad de los Estados', 10 *Revista de Der. Inter.* 5 (1926).

Durand, C., 'La responsabilité internationale des Etats pour déni de justice', 5 *Rev. Gene. Dro. Inter. Publ.* (1931).

Eagleton, C., *The Responsibility of States in International Law* (1928).

Eagleton, C., 'International Organization and the Law of Responsibility', 76–I *Recueil des Cours* 819 (1951).

Eagleton, C., 'Denial of Justice in International Law', 22 *Am. J. Int'l L.* 538 (1928).

Eagleton, C., 'Measure of Damages in International Law', 34 *Yale L. J.* 52 (1929–30).

Eibe, R., 'Damages', in 10 *Encyclopedia of International Law* (Bernhardt, R. (ed.), 1987).

Eustathiadés, C. Th., 'Les sujets du droit international et la responsabilité internationale: nouvelles tendences', 84 *Recueil des Cours.* 401 (1953).

Eustathiadés, C. Th., 'Principes généraux de la responsabilité internationale' (1959).

Eustathiadés, C. Th., *La responsabilité international de l'Etat pour les actes des organes judiciares et le probleme du déni de justice en droit international* (1936).

Feller, A.H., *The Mexican Claims Commission* (1935).

Fitzmaurice, G.G., 'The Meaning of the Term "Denial of Justice",' 13 *Brit. Y.B. Int'l L.* 93 (1932).

Fitzmaurice, G.G., 'The Case of *I'm Alone*', *Brit. Y.B. Int'l L.* (1936).

Foighel, I., *Nationalization and Compensation* (1964).

Freeman , A.V., *The International Responsibility of States for Denial of Justice* (1938).

Garcia-Amador, F.V., *The Changing Law of International Claims* (1984).

Garcia-Amador, F.V., *Principios de Derecho Internacional que Rigen la Responsabilidad* (1963).

Garcia-Amador, F.V. *et al.*, *Recent Codification of the Law of State Responsibility for Injuries to Aliens* (1974).

Garde Castillo, J., 'El acto ilícito internacional', 3 *Revista espanola de Der. Inter.* 121 (1950).

Graefrath, B., 'Responsibility and Damages Caused: Relationship Between Responsibility and Damages', 185–II *Recueil des Cours* 9 (1984).

Gray, C.D., 'Is There an International Law of Remedies', 65 *Brit. YB Int'l L.* 25 (1985).

Gray, C.D., *Judicial Remedies in International Law* (1987).

Gros, A., *Observations sur les méthodes de protection des intérêts privés a l'étranger* (1964).

Guerreo, G., 'La responsabilité internationale des États', 3 *Académie Diplomatique Internationale* 18 (1928).

Hauriou, A., 'Les dommages indirects dans les arbitrages internationaux', 31 *Rev. Gene. Dro. Inter. Publ.* 157 (1925).

Hille, W. Van, 'Étude sur la responsabilité internationale de l'État', 10 *Rev. Dro. Inter. Leg. Comp.* (3rd ser., 1929).

Hoijer, O., *La responsabilité internationale des Etats* (1930).

Hoijer, O., 'La responsabilité internationale des Etats en matière d'actes judiciaires', 5 *Rev. Dro. Inter.* 115 (1930).

Hyde, C.C., 'Concerning Damages Arising from Neglect to Prosecute', 22 *Am. J. Int'l L.* 140 (1928).

Iovane, M., *La Riparazione Nella Teoria e Nella Prassi dell'Illecito Internazionale* (1990).

Irizarry, I.P., 'The Concept of "Denial of Justice" in Latin America', 43 *Mich. L. Rev.* 383 (1944).

Jessup, Ph.C., 'Responsibility of States for Injuries to Individuals', 46 *Colum. L. Rev.* 903 (1946).

Jèze, G., 'Le déni de justice en droit international (Note on the *Martini* case)', 47 *Rev. de Dro. Publ.* 542 (1930).

Jimenez de Arechaga, E., 'International Responsibility' in *Manual of Public International Law* (Sorensen, M. (ed.), 1968).

Kelsen, H. 'Collective and Individual Responsibility for Acts of State in International Law', *Jewish Y.B. Int'l L.* 226 (1948).

Kiss, A., 'La protection diplomatique des actionnaires dans la jurisprudence et la pratique internationales', in *La personnalité morale et ses limites* (1960).

Lapradelle, A. de and Politis, N., *Recueil des arbitrages internationaux*, (Bd. I, 1905, Bd. II, 1932; Bd. III, 1959).

Lillich, R.B., *International Claims: Post-War British Practice* (1967).

Lillich, R.B., *The International Law of State Responsibility for Injuries to Aliens* (1983).

Lillich, R.B. and Christenson, G., *International Claims: Their Preparation and Presentation* (1962).

Lillich, R.B. and Weston, B., *International Claims: Their Settlement by Lump Sum Agreements* (1975).

Lissitzyn, O., 'The Meaning of Denial of Justice in International Law', 30 *Am. J. Int'l L.* 632 (1936).

Mann, F.A., 'The Consequences of an International Wrong in International and National Law', 48 *Brit. Y.B. Int'l L.* 65 (1976–77).

Maurtua, V.M. and Scott, J.B., *Responsibility of States for Damage caused in Their Territory to the Person or Property of Foreigners* (1930).

Moore, J.B., *International Adjudications, Ancient and Modern; History and Documents, together with Mediatorial Reports, Advisory Opinions, and the Decisions of Domestic Commissions, on International Claims* (1929).

Moore, J.B., *History and Digests of the International Arbitrations to which the United States has been a Party, together with Appendices containing the Treaties relating to such Arbitrations, and Historial and Legal Notes* (1898).

Mouri, A., *The International Law of Expropriation as Reflected in the Work of the Iran-U.S. Claims Tribunal* (1994).

Murphy, C.F., 'State Responsibility for Injuries to Aliens', 41 *N.Y.U.L. Rev.* 1125 (1966).

Nagy, K., 'The Problem of Reparation in International Law', 3 *Questions Int'l L.* 173 (1986).

Olivart, M., 'Responsabilidad de los Estados por los actos de notoria injusticia de sus tribunales', 4 *Revista Juridica de Cataluna* 64 (1898).

Penfield, W.S., 'The Place of Denial of Justice in the Matter of Protection', *Proc. Am. Soc'y Int'l L.* 137 (1910).

Personnaz, J., *La réparation du préjudice en droit international public* (1939).

Podestá Costa, L.A., 'La responsabilidad internacional del Estado', 2 *Cursos Monograficos Academia Inter-Americana de Derecho Comparado e Internacional* 157 (1952).

Przetacznik, F., 'La responsabilité internationale de l'Etat à raison des préjudices de caractère moral et politique causés à un autre Etat', 78 *RGDIP* 919 (1974).

Rabasa, O., *Responsabilidad Internacional del Estado con Referencia Especial a la Responsabilidad pro Denegacion de Justicia* (1933).

Ralston, J., *International Law, National Tribunals and the Rights of Aliens* (1971).

Ramcharan, B.G., 'State Responsibility for Violations of Human Rights Treaties', in *Contemporary Problems of International Law: Essays in Honour of Georg Schwarzenberger on his Eightieth Birthday* 242 (Cheng, B. and Brown, E.D. (eds.), 1988).

Reitzer, L., *La réparation comme conséquence de l'acte illicite en droit international* (1938).

Riedel, R., 'Satisfaction', in 10 *Encyclopedia of Public International Law* (Bernhardt, R. (ed.), 1987).

Ripert, L., *La réparation du préjudice dans la responsabilité délictuelle* (1933).

Riphagen, W., 'State Responsibility: New Theories of Obligations in Interstate Relations', in *The Structure and Process of International Law: Essays in Legal Philosophy, Doctrine and Theory* (MacDonald, R. St. J. and Johnston, D.M. (eds.), 1983).

Root, E., 'The Basis of Protection to Citizens Residing Abroad', 4 *Am. J. Int'l L.* 517 (1910).

Roy, S.N.G. 'Is the Law of Responsibility of States for Injuries to Aliens a Part of Universal International Law?' 55 *Am. J. Int'l L.* 863 (1961).

Salmon, J., 'La place de la faute de la victime dans le droit de la responsabilité internationale, in *Le droit international à l'heure de sa codificataion: études en l'honneur de Roberto Ago* (1987).

Salvioli, G., 'La responsibilité des Etats et la fixation des dommages et intérêts par les tribunaux internationaux', 28-III *Recueil des Cours* 231 (1929).

Sasi, N., *German Reparations: A History of the Negotiations* (1980).

Seidl-Hohenveldern, 'Evaluation of Damages in Transnational Arbitrations', 33 *A.F.D.I.* 7 (1987).

Sibert, M., 'Contribution à l'étude des réparations pour les dommages causés aux étrangers en conséquence d'une législation contraire au droit des gens', 48 *Rev. Géne. Dro. Intr. Publ.* (1941–1945).

Sohn, L.B. and Baxter, R.R., 'Responsibility of States for Injuries to the Economic Interests of Aliens', 55 *Am. J. Int'l L.* 545 (1961).

Soldati, A., *La responsabilite des Etats dans le droit international* (1934).

Spiegel, H.W., 'Origin and Development of Denial of Justice', 32 *Am. J. Int'l L.* 63 (1938).

Stuyt, A.M., *A Survey of International Arbitrations 1794–1970* (1972).

Ténékides, G., 'Responsibilité internationale', 2 *Répertoire Dro. Inter* (1969).

Thomsen, S.D., 'Restitution', in 10 *Encyclopedia of Public International Law* (Bernhardt, R. (ed.), 1987).

Vasarhelyi, I., *Restitution in International Law* (1964).

Verdross, A., 'Les régles internationales concernant le traitement des étrangers', 37 *Receuil des Cours* 327 (1931).

Vitanyi, B., 'International Responsibility of States for their Administration of Justice', 22 *NILR* 131 (1975).

Vitta, E., 'Responsabilità degli Stati', *Estratto del Novissimo Digesto Itliano* (1967).

Weston, B., 'International Law and the Deprivation of Foreign Wealth: A Framework for Future Inquiry', in 2 *The Future of the International Legal Order* 36 (R. Falk and C. Black, (eds.), 1970).

Whiteman, M.M., *Damages in International Law* (1937, 1943).

Yates, G., 'Postwar Belgian International Claims: Their Settlement by Lump Sum Agreements', 13 *VA.J. Int'l. L.* 554 (1973).

Yntema, H.E., 'The Treaties with Germany and Compensation for War Damages', 24 *Colum. L. Rev.* 135 (1924).

3. National law and remedies

Amin, S.H., *Middle East Legal Systems* (1985).

Anderson, J.N.D., *Islamic Law in Africa* (1970).

An'Na'im, A.A., 'The Right to Reparation for Human Rights Violations and Islamic Culture(s)' in *Seminar on the Right to Restitution, Compensation and Rehabilitation for Victims of Gross Violations of Human Rights and Fundamental Freedoms* 174 (SIM Special Pub. No. 12).

Bandes, S., 'Reinventing Bivens: The Self-Executing Constitution', 68 *S. Cal. L. Rev.* 289 (1995).

Barrot, R., *Le dommage corporel et sa compensation: pratique médico-légale et judiciare* (1988).

Baxi, U., 'Taking Suffering Seriously: Social Action Litigation in the Supreme Court of India', *Law and Poverty* 387 (1988).

Belli, M.M., 'Punitive Damages: Their History, Their Use and Their Worth in Present-Day Society', 49 *U.M.K.C.L. Rev.* 1 (1980).

Berger, R., *Government by Judiciary: The Transformation of the Fourteenth Amendment* (1977).

Bin-Nun, A., *The Law of the State of Israel: An Introduction* (1990).

Bocchiola, M., 'Perdita di una chance et certezza del danno', 30 *Riv. Dir. Proc. Civ.* 55 (1976).

Bochenek, M.G., 'Compensation for Human Rights Abuses in Zimbabwe', 26 *Colum. Hum. RTS. L. Rev.* 483 (1985).

Borchard, E.M., 'Challenging "Penal" Statutes by Declaratory Action', 52 *Yale L.J.* 445 (1943).

Braveman, D., *Protecting Constitutional Freedoms: A Role for Federal Courts* (1989).

Bussani, M. and Mattei, U., 'Making the Other Path Efficient. Economic Analysis and Tort

Law in Less Developed Countries' in E. Buscaglia and R. Cooter (eds.), *Law and Economics of Development* (1997).

Butler, W.E., 'Comparative Law and International Law', in 10 *Encyclopedia of Public International Law* 495 (Bernhardt, R. (ed.), 1987).

Bydlinski, F., *Probleme der Schadensverursachung nach Deutchem und Osterreichischem Recht* (1964).

Castañeda, J., 'The Underdeveloped Nations and the Development of International Law', 15 *Int'l Org.* 38 (1961).

Chapman, S., 'Appointment of Liability between Tortfeasors', 64 *L. Q. Rev.* 26 (1948).

Chayes, A., 'The Role of the Judge in Public Law Litigation', 89 *Harv.L.Rev.* 1281 (1976).

Chinese Civil Code (trans. H.R. Zheng), 34 *Am.J.Comp.L.* 669 (1986).

Cian, G. and Trabucchi, A. (eds.), *Commentario Breve al Codice Civile* (1984).

Coffin, F.M., 'The Frontier of Remedies: A Call for Exploration', 67 *Cal.L.Rev.* 983 (1979).

Cohen, F., *Handbook of Federal Indian Law* (1942).

Coke, *Second Institute*, 4th edn. (1671).

Comparative Law of Israel and the Middle East (Kittrie, N. *et al.*, (eds.), 1971).

Compensation for Damages: An International Perspective (McLean, S. *et al.*, (eds.), 1993).

Constantinesco, Leontin Jean, *Les problèmes résultant de la responsibilité extra-contractuelle concomitante de la communaute et d'un Etat Membre*, (1980).

Cotran, E. and Rubin, N.N. (eds.), *Readings in African Law* (1969).

Dahl, B., Melchior, T. and Rehof, L., (eds.) *Danish Law in a European Perspective*.

Dalcq, R.O., 'L'obligation de minimiser le dommage dans la responsabilité quasi-délictuelle', *R.D.A.I.* 363 (1987).

Dalcq, Roger O. and Glansdorff, F., 'La responsabilité délictuelle et quasi-délictuelle', *Revue Critique de Jurisprudence Belge* (1987).

Daube, D., *Studies in Biblical Law* (1948).

David, R. and Jauffret-Spinosi, C., *Les grands systèmes de droit contemporains* (1988).

Diez-Picazo, L. and Gullon, A., 2 *Sistema de Derecho Civil* (1988).

Dobbs, D.R., *Law of Remedies: Damages, Equity, Restitution* (1993).

Duboc, G., *La compensation et les droits des tiers* (1989).

Duquaire, C., *Etude sur l'obligation civile de réparer et son fondement juridique en droit romain et en droit canonique* (1940).

Durry, G., 'Compensation for Personal Injury in France', in *Compensation for Personal Injury in Sweden and other Countries* (1988).

Easterbrook, F. 'Civil Rights and Remedies', 14 *Harv. J.L. & Pub. Pol'y* 193 (1991).

Ebendorf, T.A., *Damages for Embarrassment and Humiliation in Discrimination Cases: The Right to Compensation for Psychic Injury Resulting from Housing Discrimination* (1982).

El-Hakim, J., *Le dommage de source délictuelle en droit musulman: sur vivance en droit syrien et libanais* (1964).

Elias, T.O., *The Nigerian Legal System*, 2nd edn. rev. (1963).

Englard, I., *The Philosophy of Tort Law* (1993).

Eorsi, G., *Private and Government Liability for the Torts of Employees and Organs* (1972, Supp.1980).

Fanichi, L., *La justice administrative* (1980).

Feinberg, P.C., 'Federal Income Taxation of Punitive Damages Awarded in Personal Injury Actions', 42 *Case W. Res. Rev.* 339 (1992).

Feldthusen, B., 'Recent Developments in the Canadian Law of Punitive Damages', 16 *Can. Bus. L. J.* 241, 1990.

Fernandes Martin-Granizo, M., *Los danos y la responsabilitad oblevita en el derecho positivo espanol* (1972).

Fiss, O., *The Civil Rights Injunction* (1978).

Fleming, J.G., *The Law of Torts* (1957).

Fleming, J.G., *Collateral Benefits* (1970).

Friedman, G., *The Law of Torts in Canada* (1989).

Galanter, M. and Luban, D., 'Poetic Justice: Punitive Damages and Legal Pluralism', 42 *Am. U. L. Rev.* 1393 (1993).

Gaskins, R., 'Tort Reform in the Welfare State: the New Zealand Accident Compensation Act', 18 *Osgoode Hall L. J.* 238, 1980.

Geraint, G.H., *Comparative Product Liability* (1993).

Gewirtz, P., 'Remedies and Resistance', 92 *Yale L. J.* 585 (1983).

Ghersi, C.A., *Reparacion de danos: accion del hombre, autoria, relacion de causalidad, imputabilidad, ijuridicidad, culpabilidad, factores objectivos, equidad, formas de reparacion* (1989).

Glansdorff, F., 'Les conséquences de la dépréciation monétaire entre accident et le moment du jugement', 10130 *R.G.A.R.* (1980).

Great Qing Code (W.C. Jones trans., 1994).

Gregory, C., Kalven, H. and R. Epstein, *Cases and Materials on Torts* 3rd edn. (1977).

Haddock, D.D. *et al.*, 'An Ordinary Economic Rationale for Extraordinary Legal Sanctions', 78 *Cal. L. Rev.* 1 (1990).

Hanotiau, B., 'Régime juridique et portée de l'obligation de modérer le dommage dans les ordres juridiques nationaux et le droit du commerce international', *RDAI* 393 (1987).

Hellner, J., 'Social Insurance and Tort Liability in Sweden', 16 *Scan . Stud. L.* 187 (1972).

Hilf, M. 'Comparative Law and European Law', in *Encyclopedia of Public International Law* (Bernhardt, R. (ed.), 1987).

Honoré, A.M., *Causation and Remoteness of Damage* (1969).

Ingber, S., 'Rethinking Intangible Injuries: A Focus on Remedy', 73 *Cal. L. Rev.* 772 (1985).

Ingram, J.D., 'Punitive Damages Should be Abolished', 17 *Cap. U. L. Rev.* 205 (1988).

Tunc. A., (ed.) *International Encyclopedia of Comparative Law, vol. XI, Torts* (1986).

Jackson, T., *The Law of Kenya—An Introduction* (1970).

Johns, C.H.W., *The Oldest Code of Laws in the World* (1903).

Katz, A., 'The Jurisprudence of Remedies: Constitutional Legality and the Law of Torts', 117 *U. Pa. L. Rev.* 1 (1968).

Kaye, P., *Private International Law of Tort and Product Liability* (1990).

Kocourek, A. and Wigmore, *Sources of Ancient and Primitive Law* (1915).

Kojima, T. and Taniguchi, Y., 1 *Access to Justice* (1978).

Kossow, T.M., '*Fein v. Permanente Medical Group*: Future Trends in Damage Limitation Adjuducation', 80 *NW. U. L. Rev.* 1643 (1986).

Krzecznowiccz, G., *The Ethiopian Law of Compensation for Damage* (1977).

Lambert-Faivre, Y., *Le droit du dommage corporel: systemes d'indemnisation*, 2nd edn. (1993).

Lange, H., *Schadenseratz. Handbuch des Schuldrechts in Einzeldarstellungen*, 1990.

Lawson, F.H. and Markensis, B.S., 1 and 2 *Tortious Liability for Unintentional Harm in the Common Law and Civil Law* (1982).

Laycock, D., *Modern American Remedies: Cases and Materials*, 2nd edn. (1994).

Leage, R.W., *Roman Private Law* (1937).

Le Torneau, P., *La responsabilité civile* (1982).

Liebesny, H., (ed.), *The Law of the Near and Middle East* (1975).

Lippman, M., McConville, S., and Yerushalmi, M., *Islamic Criminal Law and Procedure* (1988).

Lookofsky, J.M., *Consequential Damages in Comparative Context* (1989).

MacCormack, G., 'Revenge and Compensation in Early Law', 21 *Am.J.Comp.L.* 69 (1973).

Malloy, R.P. *Law and Economics: A Comparative Approach to Theory and Practice* (1990).

Markensinis, B.S., *A Comparative Introduction to the German Law of Torts*, 3rd edn. (1994).

Martin, A. and Psacharapoulos, G., 'The Reward for Risk in the Labor Market: Evidence from the United Kingdom and a Reconciliation with Other Studies', 90(4) *J. Pol. Econ* 827 (1982).

Martin, J., 'Myth and Reality in Punitive Damages', 75 *Minn. L. Rev.* 1 (1990).

Mazeaud, H., Leon and J., 'Traité théorique et pratique de la responsabilité civile délictuelle et contractuelle (I–1958, II–1970).

McChesney, F.S., 'Problems in Calculating and Awarding Compensatory Damages for Wrongful Death Under the Federal Tort Claims Act', 36 *Emory L. J.* 149 (1987).

McGregor, H., *McGregor on Damages* (1988).

McGregor, H., *Personal Injury and Death* (1969).

D. McIntosh and Holmes, D., *Personal Injury Awards in EU and EFTA Countries: An Industry Report*, 2nd edn., (1994).

McMahon, B.M.E. and Binchy, W., *A Casebook on the Irish Law of Torts*, 2nd edn. (1990).

Meltzer, 'Deterring Constitutional Violations by Law Enforcement Officials: Plaintiffs and Defendants as Private Attorneys General', 88 *Colum.L.Rev.* 247 (1988).

Mommsen, W.J. and Demoor, J.A., (eds.), *European Expansion and the Law* (1992).

Morris, C., 'Punitive Damages in Tort Cases', 44 *Harv. L. Rev.* 1173 (1931).

National Committee of Inquiry into Compensation and Rehabilitation in Australia (1975).

Nagel, R.F. 'Controlling the Structural Injunction', 7 *Harv.J.L. & Pub.Pol'y* 395 (1974).

Nichol, G.R., '*Bivens, Chilicky*, and Constitutional Damage Claims', 75 *Va.L.Rev.* 1117 (1989).

Note, 'Constitutional Guarantees of a Certain Remedy', 40 *Iowa L.Rev.* 1202 (1964).

Oda, H., *Japanese Law* (1993).

Ogus, A.I., *The Law of Damages* (1973).

Philippson, C., *The International Law and Custom of Ancient Greece and Rome* (1911).

Plant, M.L., 'Damages for Pain and Suffering', 19 *Ohio St. L.J.* 200 (1958).

Posner, R., 'The Concept of Corrective Justice in Recent Theories of Tort Law', 10 *J.Leg.Studies* 187 (1981).

Prosser, W., *Handbook of the Law of Torts*, 4th edn. (1971).

Redden, K.R. and Schlueter, L.L., (eds.), *Modern Legal Systems Encyclopedia* (1996).

Rendleman, D., 'The Inadequate Remedy at Law Prerequisite for an Injunction', 33 *U. Fla. L. Rev.* 346 (1981).

Rendleman, D., 'Prospective Remedies in Constitutional Adjudication', 78 *W.Va.L.Rev.* 155 (1976).

Rosen, P., 'The *Bivens* Constitutional Tort: An Unfulfilled Promise', 67 *N.C.L.Rev.* 337 (1989).

Rotenberg, D., 'Private Remedies for Constitutional Wrongs–A Matter of Perspective, Priority and Process', 14 *Hastings Const.L.Q.* 77 (1986).

Roth, A., *Schadenersatz fur Verletzungen Privater Bei Völkerrechtlichen Delikten* (1934).

Rustad, M. and Koenig, T., 'The Historical Continuity of Punitive Damage Awards: Reforming the Tort Reformers, 42 *Am. U. L. Rev.* 1269 (1993).

Ruxton, F.H., *Maliki Law* (1916).

Saks, M.J., 'Do We Really Know Anything About the Behavior of the Tort Litigation System—And Why Not?', 140 *U. Pa. L. Rev.* 1147 (1992).

Salvi, Cesare, 'Risarcimento del danno', in *XL Enciclopedia del Diritto* 1084 (1989).

Salvi, Cesare, 'Responsibilità extracontrattuale (diritto vigente)', in *XXXIX Enciclopedia del Diritto* 1186 (1988).

Schuck, P. *Suing Government: Citizen Remedies for Official Wrongs* (1983).

Schwartz, G.D., 'Deterrence and Punishment in the Common Law of Punitive Damages: A Comment', 56 *S. Cal. L. Rev.* 133 (1982).

Seltzer, R.A., 'Punitive Damages in Mass Tort Litigation: Addressing the Problems of Fairness, Efficiency and Control', 52 *Fordham L. Rev.* 37 (1983).

Speiser, S.M. *et al.*, *Recovery for Wrongful Death and Injury*, 3rd edn. (1992).

Spier, J. (ed.), *Limits of Liability: Keeping the Floodgates Shut* (1996).

Stoll, H., 'Consequences of Liability: Remedies' in 8 *International Encyclopedia of Comparative Law* (1971); Supplement (1981).

Street, H. *Government Liability: A Comparative Study* (1953).

Street, H. and Brazier, M., *The Law of Torts* (1988).

Strossen, N., 'Recent U.S. and International Judicial Protection of Individual Rights', 41 *Hastings L. J.* 805 (1990).

Sturm, S., 'A Normative Theory of Public Law Remedies', 79 *Geo.L.J.* 1357 (1991).

Sutherland, J.G., *A Treatise on the Law of Damages* (1916).

Symposium, 'Punitive Damages', 17 *Loy. L.A. Int'l & Comp. L.J.* 765 (1995).

Symposium, 'Corrective Justice and Formalism: The Care One Owes One's Neighbors', 77 *Iowa L. Rev.* 403 (1992).

Szollosy, P., *L'evaluation du dommage résultant de l'invalidité dans divers pays européens: etude comparative du droit de responsibilité civile notamment de Suisse, d'Allemagne, d'Autriche, De France et de Norvège* (1974).

Tang Code (W.C. Johnson, trans., 1979).

Todd, S. *et al.*, *The Law of Torts in New Zealand* (1991).

Trotabas, L., 'Liability in Damages under French Administrative Law', 12 *J.Comp.L.* 44 (1930).

Veitch, E., *East African Cases on the Law of Tort* (1972).

Viney, G., *La réparation du dommage corporel: essai de comparaison des droits anglais et français* (1985).

Walker, D.M., *The Law of Damages in Scotland* (1955).

White, J.P.M., 'Irish Law of Damages for Personal Injuries and Death', in 1 *Law and Practice* (1989).

Whiteman, C., 'Constitutional Torts', 79 *Mich.L.Rev.* 5 (1980).

Williamson, J.A., 'Hedonic Damages in Section 1983 Actions: A Remedy for the Unconstitutional Deprivation of Life', 44 *Wash. & Lee L. Rev.* 321 (1987).

Xamir, I. and Colombo, S., (eds.), *The Law of Israel: General Surveys* (1995).

Yudof, M., 'Liability for Constitutional Torts and the Risk-Averse Public School Official', 49 *S.Cal.L.Rev.* 1322 (1976).

Zeigler, D.H., 'Rights Require Remedies: A New Approach to the Enforcement of Rights in the Federal Courts', 38 *Hastings L.J.* 665 (1987).

Zimmerman, R. and Visser, D., (eds.), *Southern Cross: Civil Law and Common Law in South Africa* (1996).

4. Human rights law and institutions

Alston, P., 'UNESCO Procedure for Dealing with Human Rights Violations', 20 *Santa Clara L.Rev.* 665 (1980).

Bernhardt, R., 'Thoughts on the Interpretation of Human-Rights Treaties', in *Human Rights: The European Dimension, Studies in Honour of Gerard J. Wirda* 65–71 (F. Matscher and H. Petzold, (eds.), 1988).

Buergenthal, T. and Shelton, D., *Protecting Human Rights in the Americas*, 4th edn. (1966).

Castberg, F., *The European Convention on Human Rights* (1974).

Castro-Rial Garonne, F. *La protección en el convenio europeo de derechos humanos* (1985).

Cohen, S., 'State Crimes of Previous Regimes: Knowledge, Accountability and the Policing of the Past, 20 *L. & Soc. Inquiry* 7 (1955).

Cohen-Jonathan, G., *La convention européenne des droits de l'homme* (1989).

Council of Europe, *Collected Edition of the Travaux Préparatories of the European Convention on Human Rights, Council of Europe* (1975–1985).

Council of Europe, *La réparation du dommage tant materiel que moral dans la jurisprudence de la cour* (1989).

Council of Europe, *European Court of Human Rights, Survey of Activities* 1959–1989 (1900).

Davidson, S., *The Inter-American Court of Human Rights* (1992).

Dawson, F.G. and Head, I. *International Law, National Tribunals and The Rights of Aliens* (1971).

De Gasquet, Pierre, *Portée et efficacité de la protection juridictionnelle des droits de l'homme par la cour de Strasbourg: vices publics et vertus cachées* (1986).

De Hoogh, A., *Obligations Erga Omnes and International Crimes* (1996).

Drzemczewski, A.Z., *The European Human Rights Convention in Domestic Law: A Comparative Study* (1983).

Fawcett, J.E.S., *The Application of the European Convention on Human Rights* (1987).

Flauss, Jean-François, 'La pratique de Comité des Ministres du Conseil de l'Europe au titre de l'article 54 de la Convention européenne des droits de l'homme (1985–1988), 34 *A.F.D.I.* 408 (1989).

Frowein, J., 'Entschädigung für Verletzungen von Grundrechten', in *Des Menschen Recht Zwischen Freiheit und Verantwortung*. Festschfirt für Karl Josef Partsch 317–326 (Jürgen Jekewitz *et al.*, (eds.) 1989).

Gainen, L.F., 'The Application of Article 50 of the European Convention for the Protection of Human Rights and Fundamental Freedoms: the Vagrancy Cases and the Ringeisen Case', 7 *N.Y.U.J.Int'l L. & Pol.* 177 (1974).

Gearty, C.A., (ed.), *European Civil Liberties and the European Convention on Human Rights: A Comparative Study* (1997).

Ghebali, V.-Y., *The International Labor Organization: A Case Study on the Evolution of U.N. Specialized Agencies* (1989).

Golsong, H., *et al.* (eds.), *International Kommentar zur Europäischen Menschenrechtskonvention* (1986).

Golsong, H., *Das Rechtsschultzsystem der Europaischen Menschenrechtskonventinon* (1958).

Golsong, H., 'Quelques réflexions à propos du pouvoir de la Cour européenne des droits de l'homme d'accorder une satisfaction équitable', I René Cassin Amicorum Discipulorumque Liber 89 (1969).

Grabitz, Eberhard, *ed. Kommentar zum Ewg-Vertrag* 1990.

Grossman, C., 'Disappearances in Honduras: The Need for Direct Victim Representation in Human Rights Litigation', 15 *Hastings Int'l L & Comp.L.Rev.* 363 (1992).

Guradze, H., *Die Europäische Menschenrechtskonvention* (1968).

Harris, D., O'Boyle, M. and Warbrick, A., *Law of the European Convention on Human Rights* (1995).

Heukels, T. and McDonnell, A., (eds.), *The Action for Damages in Community Law* (1997).

Higgins, R., 'Damages for Violation of One's Human Rights', in *Explorations in Ethics and International Relations, Essays in Honour of Sydney D. Bailey* (Sims, N. (ed.), 1981).

Hondius, F.W., 'The Other Forum', in *Protecting Human Rights: The European Dimension, Studies in Honour of Gerard J. Wirda* (Matscher, F. and Petzhold, H. (eds.), 1988).

Imbert, P.-H., 'La réforme de la procédure devant les organes de contrôle de la Convention européenne des Droits de l'Homme: quelques observations prospectives', 1 *Eur. J. Int'l L.* 292 (1990).

Jacobs, F.G., *The European Convention on Human Rights* (1975).

Klaffenböck, Sylvia, *Die Spruchpraxis des Europäischen Gerichtshofs für Menschenrechte zu Art. 50 EMRK, Untersucht Anhand der für Verletzungen des Art. 6 EMRK Gewährten Entschädigung* (1990).

Kruger, H.C., 'Selecting Judges for the New European Court of Human Rights', 17 *HRLJ* 401 (1996).

Kruger, H.C. 'Some Reflections on Some Aspects of Just Satisfaction under the European Convention on Human Rights' in *Liber Amicorum Marc-Andre Eissen* (1995).

Lallah, R., 'The Domestic Application of International Human Rights Norms, 17 *Commonwealth L. Bull.* 665 (1991).

Lutz, E., 'After the Elections: Compensating Victims of Human Rights Abuses', in *New Directions in Human Rights* 195 (Lutz, E., Hannum, H. and Burke, K. (eds.) 1989).

Luzzatto, Riccardo, 'La Corte europea dei diritti dell'uomo e la riparazione delle violazioni della convenzione', in *Studi in Honore de Manlio Udina* 423 (Facoltá di giurisprudenza della Università di Trieste, (ed.), 1975).

Marks, S., 'The Complaint Procedure of the United Nations Educational, Scientific and

Cultural Organization' in *Guide to International Human Rights Practice*, 2nd edn. (H. Hannum, (ed.), 1992).

McBridge, J., 'Redress for Human Rights Violations', in *Droit sans Frontières. Essays in Honour of L. Neville Brown* 161 (Hand. G. and McBride, J. (eds.), 1991).

Mendelson, M.H., 'The European Court of Justice and Human Rights', 1981 *Y.B.Eur.Law* 125 (1982).

Merrills, J.G., *The Development of International Law by the European Court of Human Rights* (1988).

Miele, Mario, 'L'art. 50 della Convenzione europea sui diritti dell'uomo e le sue prime applicazioni giurisprudenziali', in *Studi in Honore di Manlio Udina* 537 (Facoltá di giurisprudenza della Università di Trieste, 1975).

Nedjati, Z.M. *Human Rights under the European Convention* (1978).

Neuwal, N. and Rosas, A., (eds.), *The European Union and Human Rights* (1995).

Panzera, Antonio Filippo, 'Le pouvoir de la Cour européenne des droits de l'homme d'accorder une satisfaction équitable à la partie lésée' in *Les clauses facultatives de la Convention Européenne des Droits de l'Homme. actes de la table ronde organisée par la faculté de droit de l'Université de Bari en liaison avec le Conseil de l'Europe et l'Institut International des Droits de l'Homme* 255 (1974).

Parry, C., 'Some Considerations upon the Protection of Individuals in International Law', 90 *Recueil des Cours* 658 (1956).

Pasqualucci, J.M., 'The Inter-American Human Rights System: Establishing Precedents and Procedure in Human Rights Law', 26 *Inter-Am.L.Rev.* 297 (1995-1995).

Pasqualucci, J.M., 'The Whole Truth and Nothing But the Truth: Truth Commissions, Impunity and the Inter-American Human Rights System', 12 *B.U. Int'l L.J.* 321 (1944).

Pettiti, L.-E., Decaux, E., and Imbert, P.-H., *La Convention Europeene des Droits de l'Homme: commentaire article par article* (1995).

Polakiewicz, J. and Jacob-Foltzer, V., 'The European Human Rights Convention in Domestic Law: The Impact of Strasbourg Case Law in States Where Direct Effect is Given to the Convention', 12 *H.R.L.J.* 66 (1991).

Roht-Arriaza, N., 'State Responsibility to Investigate and Prosecute Grave Human Rights Violations in International Law', 78 *Cal. L. Rev.* 451 (1990).

Seminar on the Right to Restitution, Compensation and Rehabilitation for Victims of Gross Violations of Human Rights and Fundamental Freedoms (SIM Special No. 12).

Sharpe, J.L., 'Awards of Costs and Expenses under Article 50 of the European Convention on Human Rights', *The Law Society's Gazette* 905 (1984).

Shelton, D., 'The Participation of Nongovernmental Organizations in International Judicial Proceedings', 88 *Am.J.Int'l L.* 622 (1994).

Shelton, D., 'Private Violence, Public Wrongs, and the Responsibility of States', 13 *Fordham Int'l L.J.* (1989-90).

Sohn, L. 'The New International Law: Protection of the Rights of Individuals Rather than States', 32 *Am.U.L.Rev.* 1 (1982).

Sohn, L. and Buergenthal, T., *International Protection of Human Rights* (1973).

Stephens, B. and Ratner, M., *International Human Rights Litigation in U.S. Courts* (1996).

Thune, G.H., 'The Right to an Effective Remedy in Domestic Law: Article 13 of the European Convention on Human Rights', in *Broadening the Frontiers of Human Rights, Essays in Honor of Asbjorn Eide* (D. Gomien, (ed.), 1993) 79.

Vallée, C., 'Une application de l'article 50 de la Convention européenne des Droits de l'Homme', *RGDIP* 1105 (1972).

Valticos, N., 'The International Labor Organization', in *The Effectiveness of International Decisions* 134 (S. Schwebel (ed.), 1971).

Van Dijk, P. and Van Hoof, G.J.H., *Theory and Practice of the European Convention of Human Rights* (1990).

Vegleris, P., *Modes de rédressement des violations de la Convention Européenne des Droits de l'Homme* (1968).

Vis, W., 'La réparation des violations de la Convention européenne des Droits de l'Homme', in *La protection internationale des droits de l'homme dans le cadre européen*. Travaux du colloque organisé par la Faculté de Droit et des Sciences Politiques et Economiques de Strasbourg en liaison avec la Direction des Droits de l'homme du Conseil de l'Europe 279 (1961).

Weil, G.L., *The European Convention on Human Rights. Background, Development and Prospects* (1963).

Weschler, L., *A Miracle, A Universe: Settling accounts with Torturers* (1990).

Western Rights? Post Communist Application (Sajo, A. (ed.), 1989).

Zalaquett, J., 'Balancing Ethical Imperatives and Political Constraints: The Dilemma of New Democracies Confronting Past Human Rights Violations', 43 *Hastings L.J.* 1425 (1922).

5. Valuation and calculation

Action, J.P., 'Measuring the Monetary Value of Lifesaving Programs', *Law and Contemp. Prob.* 40 (1976).

Albrecht, G., 'Issues Affecting the Calculated Value of Life', 5 *J. Forensic Econ.* (1992).

Anderson, R.R., 'Incidental and Consequential Damages', 7 *J. L. & Com.* 327 (1987).

Arlen, J.H., 'An Economic Analysis of Tort Damages for Wrongful Death', 60 *N.Y.U.L.Rev.* 1113 (1985).

Arnould, J.R. and Nichols. L.M., 'Wage-Risk Premiums and Worker's Compensation: A Refinement of Estimates of Compensating Wage Differential', 91 *J. Pol. Econ.* 332 (1983).

Bailey, M.J., *Am. Enterprise Inst., Measuring the Benefits of Life Saving* (1979).

Bailey, M.J., *Am. Enterprise Inst., Reducing Risks to Life* (1980).

Barrett, P.A., 'Price of Pleasure', *Wall St. J.*, Dec. 12, 1988, at 1.

Becker, W. and Stoud, R., 'The Utility of Death and Wrongful Death Compensation', 5 *J. Forensic Econ.* (1992).

Beggs, Steven D., 'Diverse Risks and the Relative Worth of Government Health and Safety Programs: An Experimental Survey', *U.S. Environmental Protection Agency*, EPA-230-04-85-005, June 1984, NTIS no. PB85-212389.

Blomquist, G., 'The Value of Human Life: An Empirical Perspective', 19 *Econ. Inquiry* 1557 (1981).

Blomquist, G., 'Estimating the Value of Life and Safety: Recent Developments', in *The Value of Life and Safety* (M.W. Jones-Lee, (ed.), 1982).

Blomquist, G., 'Value of Life Savings: Implications of Consumption Activity', 87 *J. Pol. Econ.* 540 (1979).

Blum, A., 'More Suing Over Lost Joy of Life, *Nat'l L. J.*, April 17, 1989, at 1.

Bodily, S.E., 'Analysis of Risks to Life and Limb', 28 *Operations Research* 156 (1980).

Bovbjerg, R.R. *et al.*, 'Valuing Life and Limb in Tort: Scheduling "Pain and Suffering",' 83 *NW. U. L. Rev.* 908 (1989).

Brookshire, D.S. *et al.*, 'Valuing Public Goods: A Comparison of Survey and Hedonic Approaches', 72 *Am. Econ. Rev.* 165 (1982).

Brookshire, M. and Smith, S., *Economic/Hedonic Damages—A Practice Manual for Plaintiff and Defense Attorneys* (1990).

Broome, J., 'Trying to Value a Life', 9 *J. Pub. Econ.* 91 (1978).

Butcher, A., *A Review of Methodologies to Estimate the Value of Life Saving* (1981).

Chestnut, L. and Violette, D., 'The Relevance of Willingness-to-Pay Estimates of The Value of a Statistical Life in Determining Wrongful Death Awards', 3 *J. Forensic Econ.* (1990).

Cohen, L., 'Toward an Economic Theory of the Measurement of Damages in a Wrongful Death Action', 34 *Emory L. J.* 295 (1985).

Conley, B.C., 'The Value of Life in the Demand for Safety', 66 *Am. Econ. Rev.* 45 (1976).

Cook, R., 'Hedonic Damages', 62 *Okla. B. J.* 2358 (1991).

Cooke, P.J. and Graham, D.A., 'The Demand for Insurance and Protection: The Case of the Irreplaceable Commodity', 91 *Q. J. Econ.* 141 (1977).

Cramer, C.R., 'Loss of Enjoyment of Life as a Separate Element of Damages', 12 *Pac. L. J.* 965 (1981).

Cropper, M.L., 'Measuring the Benefits from Reduced Morbidity', 71 *Am. Econ. Ass'n Papers & Proceedings* 235 (1981).

Cropper, M.L. and Sussman, F.G., 'Families and the Economics of Risks to Life', 78 *Am. Econ. Rev.* 255 (1988).

Dardis, R., 'The Value of Life: New Evidence from the Marketplace', 70 *Am. Econ. Rev.* 1077 (1980).

Dawson, F.G. and Weston, B.H., ' "Prompt, Adequate and Effective": A Universal Standard of Compensation?' 30 *Fordham L. Rev.* 727 (1962).

Dickens, W., 'Assuming the Can Opener: Hedonic Wage Estimates and the Value of Life', 3 *J. Forensic Econ.* 51 (1990).

Gillette, C.P. and Hopkins, T.D., *Federal Agency Evaluation of Human Life: A Report to the Administrative Conference of the United States* (1988).

Hapgood, F., 'Risk-Benefit Analysis: Putting a Price on Life', 243 *Atlantic* 33 (1979).

Harrington, L., 'The Valuation of Life Shortening Aspects of Risk', *U.S. Environmental Protection Agency*, EPA-230-07-85-007, (1984).

Havrilesky, T., 'The Misapplication of the Hedonic Damages Concept to Wrongful Death and Personal Injury Litigation,' 6 *J. Forensic Econ.* (1993).

Havrilesky, T., 'Valuing Life in the Courts: An Overview', 3 *F. Forensic Econ* 71 (1990).

Hermes, P.J., 'Loss of Enjoyment of Life—Duplication of Damages Versus Full Compensation', 63 *N. D. L. Rev.* 561 (1987).

Hilton, K. and Goldstein, C., 'Damages for the Loss of Enjoyment of Life in Personal Injury Cases', *For the Defense* 2 (November 1988).

Jones-Lee, M.W., 'The Value of Human Life in the Demand for Safety: Comment', 68 *Am. Econ. Rev.* 712 (1978).

Jones-Lee, M.W., *The Value of Life: An Economic Analysis* (1976).

Kaplow, L. and Shavell, S., 'Accuracy in the assessment of Damages', 39 *J.Law & Econ.* 191 (1996).

Leebron, D.W., 'Final Moments: Damages for Pain and Suffering Prior to Death', 64 *N.Y.U. L. Rev.* 256 (1989).

Lillich, R.B., *The Valuation of Nationalized Property in Interntional Law* (1972).

Linnerooth, J., 'The Value of Human Life: A Review of the Models', 17 *Econ. Inquiry* 52 (1979).

Luntz, H., *Assessment of Damages for Personal Injury and Death*, 3rd edn. (1990).

Mathur, I., 'Estimating Value of Life per Life Year', 3 *J. Forensic Econ.* 95 (1990).

McClurg, A.J., 'It's a Wonderful Life: The Case for Hedonic Damages in Wrongful Death Cases', 66 *Notre Dame L. J.* 57 (1990).

Miller, T., 'The Plausible Range for the Value of Life: Red Herrings Among the Mackerel', 3 *J. Forensic Econ.* 17 (1990).

Mishan, E.J., 'Evaluation of Life and Limb: A Theoretical Approach', 79 *J. Pol. Econ.* 687 (1971).

O'Hara, E.A., 'Hedonic Damages for Wrongful Death: Are Tortfeasors Getting Away With Murder?', 78 *Geo. L. J.* 1687 (1990).

Persson, U., 'The Value of Risk Reduction: Results of a Swedish Sample Survey', *The Swedish Institute for Health Economics* (1989).

Riley, S., 'The Economics of Hedonic Damages', 23 *CTLA Forum* 13 (July/August 1993).

Staller, J. and Sullivan, B., 'Comment: On the Accuracy and Usefulness of Hedonic Loss Estimates, 5 *J. Forensic Econ.* 75 (1991).

Stern, B., 'Loss of Enjoyment of Life: A Quantitative Approach', *Nat'l Trial Law.* 52 (1992).

Violette, D.M. and Chestnut, L.G., 'Valuing Reductions in Risks: A Review of the Empirical Estimates' (1983).

Violette, D.M. and Chestnut, L.G., 'Valuing Risks: New Information on the Willingness to Pay for Changes in Fatal Risks' (1986).

Viscusi, W.K., 'Labor Market Valuations of Life and Limb: Empirical Evidence and Policy Implications', 26 *Pub. Pol'y* 359 (1978).

Index